Virtual Worlds and E-Commerce:
Technologies and Applications for Building Customer Relationships

Barbara Ciaramitaro
Ferris State University, USA

BUSINESS SCIENCE Reference

BUSINESS SCIENCE REFERENCE
Hershey · New York

Director of Editorial Content: Kristin Klinger
Director of Book Publications: Julia Mosemann
Acquisitions Editor: Lindsay Johnston
Development Editor: Joel Gamon
Publishing Assistant: Casey Conapitski
Typesetter: Casey Conapitski
Production Editor: Jamie Snavely
Cover Design: Lisa Tosheff

Published in the United States of America by
Business Science Reference (an imprint of IGI Global)
701 E. Chocolate Avenue
Hershey PA 17033
Tel: 717-533-8845
Fax: 717-533-8661
E-mail: cust@igi-global.com
Web site: http://www.igi-global.com/reference

Library of Congress Cataloging-in-Publication Data

Virtual worlds and e-commerce : technologies and applications for building customer relationships / Barbara Ciaramitaro, editor.
p. cm.
Includes bibliographical references and index.
Summary: "This book presents various opinions, judgments, and ideas on how the use of digitally created worlds is changing the face of e-commerce and extending the use of Internet technologies to create a more immersive experience for customers"--Provided by publisher.
ISBN 978-1-61692-808-7 (hardcover) -- ISBN 978-1-61692-810-0 (ebook) 1. Electronic commerce. 2. Virtual reality. 3. Consumers. I. Ciaramitaro, Barbara L. II. Title.

HF5548.32.V567 2011
658.8'72--dc22

British Cataloguing in Publication Data
A Cataloguing in Publication record for this book is available from the British Library.

Table of Contents

Detailed Table of Contents

This chapter provides an overview of e-commerce marketing focused on history, trends and future predictions for the field – leading into the development and application of virtual worlds and v-commerce. It includes a survey of developments in marketing convergence, as businesses integrate their customer-centric online/offline marketing efforts and databases. The chapter continues with an overview of business-to-business Internet marketing, including the profit strategies businesses employ in the online world. To set the stage for the chapters to come, the chapter concludes with a preview of what is on the horizon for "v-commerce" – with opportunities and applications that are capturing the imagination of consumers and marketers alike.

This chapter explores the characteristics and features of online games and their potential for e-commercial exploitation via the communities of interest that have evolved within and around the gaming environments. The author discusses their evolution to date and how they have intertwined with the evolution of commercial interests in the internet for online business (e-business). Beginning with a review of the emergence and transformation of games and commercial contexts, the first two sections of the chapter subsequently review relevant industry reports, research and theoretical underpinnings to the contemporary online gaming, virtual and mirror world context for e-commercial activities. This is then drawn together in the final section, which discusses the emergence and convergence of online economies and the issues arising from their increasing integration with the real world.

This chapter will examine the evolution of some of the most remarkable projects taking place within this virtual world, featuring the passion of early adopters, the role of the media, current examples of virtual work, the evolution of the virtual workforce, the shift in the role of managers toward a collaborative virtual model, the relationship between education and virtual work, and virtual goods and services.

This chapter examines how Virtual Worlds are being used in business today. It examines the first wave of companies who have used virtual worlds and presents evidence to its next phase. By defining the spectrum of different uses of Virtual Worlds, this chapter will cover key lessons learned and guidelines, current barriers to adoption, and the business value of using Virtual Worlds for business purposes.

The use of virtual worlds by the military, intelligence and homeland security agencies is the topic of Chapter 7 by Drs. Ciaramitaro and Jones of the Unites States. The combined military forces of the United States are over 3 million strong; currently command a defense budget of $540 billion with an additional allocation of $306 billion for the Global War on Terror; and has spending power of nearly $14 billion. In addition to the impact this strong military presence has on our country and the world, these numbers underscore the influence the military has on technology trends, tools, and vendor offerings through its acquisition of various technology software and hardware components. This chapter focuses on the use of virtual worlds by the U.S. military, intelligence, and homeland security sectors for their internal training and education, and recruitment.

Virtual education is a multi-billion dollar business and maintains a firm place in the world of E-Commerce. It is a mode used by educational institutions, the military, professional organizations, commercial companies, and others to inform, educate and interact with students, consumers, and participants. This chapter discusses the varying ways that virtual worlds have been incorporated into education. It examines several virtual worlds to see what they offer in terms of content and user experience. The authors also discuss how virtual education how it compares with traditional forms of teaching and learning. It concludes with an examination of what the future holds for virtual education.

This chapter takes a look at the economies of virtual worlds with respect to the business of operating them. Against logic, virtual economies are closer to true market economies than any real world economy. They are also rapidly growing in size and value. With increasing attention from real world governments and tax authorities, virtual economies are stimulating changes in the business of virtual worlds. Virtual world operators have an opportunity to, through their responses, either preserve their investments and their businesses by ensuring a secure role for the market economies they have created, or face serious threats to their business as the real world interferes with virtual fun.

Section 2
Human Factors, Legal and Security Issues of Virtual Worlds

This chapter presents a detailed survey and summary of the laws and regulations affecting virtual worlds. Cyberspace is such an enormous concept that trying to briefly explain the "rules" for E-Commerce or "cyberlaw" is next to impossible. For an E-Commerce, it is important to understand that there are business-to-business transactions and those involving consumers. In addition to requiring a mastery of many legal specialties, E-Commerce presents legal issues in a virtual environment. Many business practices in a cyberspace are untested in the courts. New and innovative methods of competition, as well as the effects of an international playing field change the playfield constantly. The legalities of this great new frontier pose an impressive and intellectually stimulating challenge.

Web 2.0 has demonstrated how new technologies can change the structure of the customer-provider relationship. This is evident in the many new business opportunities that have arisen including the growth of 3D environments and virtual worlds. The development of more specialized services and consumer integration creates new marketplaces with new rules of the game. As these new opportunities come to the scene, they will change the face of the world into 3D environments and a multi-agent collaboration. The adoption of virtual worlds depends a great deal on the user experience. The challenges of providing the user with virtual realism is a challenge as many supporting technologies are still in the early development phase. This chapter will discuss several of the issues and tradeoffs involved in developing accurate and realistic virtual worlds.

This chapter discusses the environmental and individual user differences that influence the training time required to ensure effective virtual environment spatial knowledge acquisition. Individual factors discussed include: the importance of knowledge and experience; the importance of gender; the importance of aptitude and spatial orientation skills; and the importance of cognitive styles. Environmental factors discussed include: Size, Spatial layout complexity and landmark distribution. Since people are different, a one-size fits all approach to training time does not seem logical. The impact of this research domain is important to virtual world training in general, however within service and military domains ensuring appropriate spatial training is critical in order to ensure that disorientation does not occur in a life / death scenario

Although participants in virtual worlds are generally considered by law to be the owner of any Intellectual Property (IP) they create, content creators and owners of OpenSim-based virtual worlds struggle with issues surrounding licensing, content delivery, and usage in these immersive spaces. The Fashion Research Institute (FRI) is specifically exploring these issues in a case study involving the licensing its Shengri La virtual world creations to external users. This case study is the basis of ongoing legal research by FRI's legal steering committee of attorneys from the American Bar Association's Virtual Worlds and Online Gaming committee who are working on a pro bono (volunteer) basis. This chapter presents the result of the ongoing case study. It offers a practitioner's view of issues related to licensing and distribution of content in OpenSim-based virtual worlds.

This chapter looks at security and privacy concerns of virtual worlds by investigating the use and capabilities of current and emerging technologies such as gaming, blogging, podcasting, virtual meetings, and virtual worlds. Security and privacy concerns will be investigated in the context of exploits and IT-related security risks, access management and confidentiality, reputation and product risk management, resource management, financial considerations and accountability, and safety. Several technologies and personal practices are reviewed, as well as ways to mitigate or eliminate their associated risks. The core principles of information security -confidentiality, integrity, and availability - provide an overall framework for the chapter.

Virtual e-commerce can deliver product information that is similar to the information obtained from direct product examination. Both interactivity and customer involvement can enhance the entertainment value of the online shopping experience. However, if virtual e-commerce aim to become a truly global platform for collaboration, then it is vital to keep in mind that consumers' behavior is bound by their cultures. This chapter provides a diagnosis of the six dimensions of the socio-cultural factors that influence the design of virtual e-commerce targeting the Saudi Arabian female market using the foundations of organizational semiotics. An organization – centered analysis and design tools that bridge the gap between the notions of 'culture' and 'IT'

Section 3
The Future of Virtual Worlds and E-Commerce

This chapter discusses the topic of standards for Virtual Worlds with emphasis on their usability as a stable and reliable basis for long-term investments into 3D-E-Commerce. The author explains why standards are important for the success of Virtual Worlds as well as the business in these shared online 3D environments, and what the relevant criteria are to decide for the right technology and/or provider. Although sometimes in the shadow of popular proprietary platforms there are already many different candidates for a Virtual World standard, currently in different states of development. By choosing a 3D platform, E-Commerce providers will decide about their business potential and at the same time strengthen one or another standard in the current technical competition phase. This chapter provides an overview about the current approaches, their advantages and disadvantages as well as the tendencies for the future developments.

The future of the evolving, collaborative communications structure will be impacted to an ever increasing degree by the merging of e-commerce and virtual worlds. Such media outlets will bring new and innovative methods by which companies can interact with clients and customers, as well as business to business. As these technologies continue to evolve, bringing higher definition, realism, and the power to manipulate potential customer experiences, increasing numbers of people will come to the realization that virtual worlds and similar environments are an essential part of an online communications experience.

This chapter examines the many aspects of virtual worlds and the solutions they offer in terms of the concept of good enough replacements. A number of solutions currently provided by virtual worlds will be described and evaluated in their present state in comparison to real world equivalents. Dimensions such as cost, usability and functionality are all subject to an initial analysis, followed by thoughts on what trajectories could be followed for virtual world solutions to evolve further and provide more advantages.

Foreword

Should I be interested in virtual worlds? That is a question I am often asked. It is one that the authors of this book are also asked, as experts in the field. It is an unusual question once you start to consider it. Virtual worlds, metaverses, are an extension of how we are able to communicate with one another across distance. Virtual worlds have evolved using the technology of the web and of video games. They exist amongst a growing social acceptance that there are digitally mediated forms of communication for business and pleasure. Telephone, email, blogs, social media status updates, fax, videos, photos, podcasts, websites, games and text messages all form part of this spectrum. People use some, or all, of these methods everyday in both business and social contexts. Each one has its own benefits and drawbacks. However, I would suggest, this is not the end of our evolution in communicating at distance, we have not solved everything yet. There is room for enhancement. Ideally we need things that work better for us and not just to fit in with the technology. We need something that does not overly filter or restrict how we need to communicate as humans.

So the question is should I be interested in people and how they choose to work, play, communicate and transact with one another?

If you are a technology or communication business this would seem an obvious answer. If you are part of a different industry then how your colleagues, customers, partners and competitors communicate needs to be looked at. If you are customer, friend, enthusiast or relative then you need to consider how to stay in touch with your peer group. If you have knowledge to share, people to educate or inform and you cannot all get your carbon atoms in the same place at the same time, then virtual worlds need consideration.

Virtual worlds are not the only solution; they do not replace all of the other ways of interacting. They do not replace physical human interaction, evolved over millions of years, either. They are not one thing tightly defined, it is not a binary decision, virtual world or not. When you drive your car with satellite navigation device and a needle telling you how much fuel you have in the tank you are already using elements of recreated spacial representation to assist you. Virtual worlds are already here, are already used in a multitude of ways to immerse people with one another at events and in data. Essentially people have been put back in the technology. That unleashes a great deal of creative and business generation talent. There is more potential to be unlocked in enterprise, education, art, entertainment and cross cultural understanding. The authors of this book have gathered together a large body of knowledge and experience with many types of virtual world interaction and applications. The authors also explore the path for the future. Hence this book forms a strong and well researched foundation on which to build or verify your knowledge. It can help you discover new business models and enhance existing ones of your own.

In technology and social adoption of ideas many people will go through the cycle of first considering it a joke, then worrying about it as a threat before moving onto understanding it is obvious. For those who understand the inevitability of the use of these forms of interaction the authors are here to help build on what you know. Those who are concerned about the threats and risks will find those honestly addressed too, "Nothing will ever be attempted if all possible objections must first be overcome." - Samuel Johnson. Anyone still considering this a joke is welcome to find the punchline for us.

For me the bonds and interactions in the metaverse has had a massive impact on the way I work and who I work with. It has also changed how I interact socially with many more people, including the authors and editors of this book. You will see, I hope, this is all very real.

Ian Hughes / epredator
Metaverse Evangelist and Founder of Feeding Edge Ltd

Ian Hughes a.k.a. epredator *when online is a Metaverse Evangelist. He set about leading a band of like minded individuals and subsequently many thousands of colleagues in IBM into virtual worlds like Second Life in 2006, and beyond. A Consulting IT Specialist in IBM for 19 years and who has worked on leading edge emerging technologies his entire career is now an independent consultant and director of Feeding Edge Ltd, Taking a bite out of technology so you don't have to. He has been a programmer since he was 14. As a gamer he has seen a massive increase in the capability and design ethics within games and the rise of online gaming. In 1997 Ian started working on all things web, changing his perspective on the technology and the business due the much richer mix of people involved in the web revolution. Graphic Designers, Producers and Programmers all having to work together. As a digital native his epredator persona spans many Web 2.0 places, blogs, PSN, WoW, Xbox Live, Twitter, Flickr, Linkedin, Second Life etc. Understanding how to use that presence, still representing himself but with elements of theatre brought about by more creative expression online leads him to no longer be the programmer he grew up as.*

Preface

With the rise of the collaborative Web 2.0 technologies, the face of E-Commerce has evolved from a static presentation of products and services to an interactive participatory relationship with customers. The use of Web 2.0 tools such as blogs, podcasts, discussion forums, Twitter, YouTube, and other technologies have brought businesses closer to their customers. However, these relationships are still asynchronous in nature and cannot parallel the real-time face-to-face communication that the brick and mortar world provides. This constraint is now being lifted through the use of virtual worlds in E-Commerce where customers and visitors are immersed in a world that provides real-time communication and the opportunity to establish relationships with other customers and companies.

E-Commerce is commonly associated with transactions conducted over the Internet. These transactions focus on business conducted between consumers, businesses, government agencies, and other organizations. E-Commerce is also associated with the term E-Business which has a broader focus of transforming business processes through the use of Internet tools and technologies.

Virtual worlds are digital worlds. They are created using computer technologies and often model elements of the real world such as buildings, roads, trees, etc. Participants in virtual worlds use avatars to represent themselves. Avatars are graphic characters that can resemble humans, animals, or mythical creatures. Virtual worlds allow multiple users to share a common space that is represented in visual formats employing a variety of two and three dimensional designs. Immersion is an important aspect of virtual worlds. The more participants feel that they are a part of the digitally created world, the more they will interact and participate in the virtual world activities. E-Commerce providers can use virtual worlds to interact in real-time with their customers and develop personal relationships with each of them. This can result in stronger loyalty to the company which translates into sales and revenue. It is for this reason, that the newest face of E-Commerce is the face of virtual worlds.

My personal experience with virtual worlds has influenced me a great deal. Recently, I attended a security conference. It was an all day event that included speakers from a variety of business, government and industry sectors. The conference activities were located in three buildings: an auditorium for the speaker presentations; an exhibition hall where a number of companies in the security industry presented their products and gave away gifts to visitors for which conferences are so well known; and a lounge where attendees could mingle and talk with speakers and company representatives. In attendance was a monkey typing away on a typewriter, a ballerina, an alligator, a unicorn, and a large number of blue heads. This was a virtual conference held in a virtual world. The participants had created avatars, graphical representations of themselves, to participate in the virtual commerce. Welcome to the newest face of E-Commerce: virtual worlds. As an educator, I have become very familiar with the use of virtual education offered by a growing number of educational institutions and other agencies and organizations in Second Life®. I can attend lectures, visit exhibits, interact with hands-on displays, and interact with other residents – all virtually. As an amateur online game enthusiast, I am constantly in awe of complexity of virtual worlds created by companies such as Blizzard in their World of Warcraft game. I have become totally immersed in that world for hours at a time. As we will see in this book, this type of immersive experience is forming the basis for a new way of communicating with consumers, students, and military recruits.

The goal of this book is to present current research and thoughts from virtual world experts from around the world. They will present various opinions, judgments, and ideas on how the use of digitally created worlds is changing the face of E-Commerce and extending the use of Internet technologies to create a more immersive experience for customers. This book will present current research on various aspects of the use of virtual worlds including a discussion of the elements of virtual worlds; the evolution of Electronic Commerce (E-Commerce) to Virtual Commerce (V-Commerce); the convergence of online games and virtual worlds; current examples of virtual worlds in use by various businesses, the military, and educational institutions; the economics of virtual worlds: discussions on legal, security and technological issues facing virtual worlds; a review of some human factor issues in virtual worlds; and the future of virtual worlds and E-Commerce. This book has three sections focused on different aspects of virtual worlds.

Section 1: The Changing Face of E-Commerce

This section begins Chapter 1 by authors David Oyarzun, María del Puy Carretero, Amalia Ortiz and Alex García-Alonso of Spain. They establish the foundation for the remainder of the book by providing a definition of what constitutes a virtual world: history, main features and elements.

Chapter 2 is authored by Dr. Yesha Sivan of Israel in which he sets forth his model for the use of virtual worlds in E-Commerce. He proposes a paradigm referred to as 3D3C definition. In it, he defines virtual worlds as an integration of four factors: 3D – the ability to present virtual world contents in 3D format; Community – the ability to act and communicate with others in groups; Creation – the ability to allow users to create content and value; and Commerce – the ability to earn real money from actions in virtual worlds.

In Chapter 3, Professor Jones of the United States presents a historical analysis of the evolving nature of E-Commerce to V-Commerce. She presents an overview of E-Commerce focused on its history, trends and future predictions for the field – leading into the development and application of virtual worlds and V-Commerce.

Chapter 4 follows with a discussion by Dr. Tracy Harwood of the United Kingdom of the convergence of online gaming and E-Commerce. This chapter explores the characteristics and features of online games and their potential for e-commercial exploitation via the communities of interest that have evolved within and around the gaming environments.

In Chapter 5, Rita King, CEO and Creative Director of Dancing Ink Productions of the United States follows with an examination of some of the most remarkable projects taking place within virtual worlds, featuring the passion of early adopters, the role of the media, current examples of virtual work, the evolution of the virtual workforce, the shift in the role of managers toward a collaborative virtual model, the relationship between education and virtual work, and virtual goods and services.

Chapter 6 focuses on real world applications of virtual worlds by businesses. Paul Blowers of the United States examines the first wave of companies who have used virtual worlds and presents evidence to its next phase. By defining the spectrum of different uses of Virtual Worlds, this chapter covers key lessons learned and guidelines, current barriers to adoption, and the business value of using Virtual Worlds for business purposes.

The use of virtual worlds by the military, intelligence and homeland security agencies is the topic of Chapter 7 by Drs. Ciaramitaro and Jones of the Unites States. The combined military forces of the United States are over 3 million strong; currently command a defense budget of $540 billion with an additional allocation of $306 billion for the Global War on Terror; and has spending power of nearly $14 billion. In addition to the impact this strong military presence has on our country and the world, these numbers underscore the influence the military has on technology trends, tools, and vendor offerings through its acquisition of various technology software and hardware components. This chapter focuses on the use of virtual worlds by the U.S. military, intelligence, and homeland security sectors for their internal training and education, and recruitment.

In Chapter 8, the multi-billion dollar business of virtual education is examined by Dr. Ciaramitaro. Virtual education is a mode used by educational institutions, the military, professional organizations, commercial companies, and others to inform, educate and interact with students, consumers, and participants. This chapter discusses discuss the varying ways that virtual worlds have been incorporated into education. It examines several virtual worlds to see what they offer in terms of content and user experience and how virtual education compares with traditional forms of teaching and learning. It concludes with an examination of what the future holds for virtual education.

The economics of virtual worlds is the last chapter of Section 1. In Chapter 9, Lee Hwang of the United States takes a look at the economies of virtual worlds with respect to the business of operating them. Against logic, virtual economies are closer to true market economies than any real world economy. They are also rapidly growing in size and value. With increasing attention from real world governments and tax authorities, virtual economies are stimulating changes in the business of virtual worlds. Virtual world operators have an opportunity to, through their responses, either preserve their investments and their businesses by ensuring a secure role for the market economies they have created, or face serious threats to their business as the real world interferes with virtual fun.

Section 2: Human Factors, Legal and Security Issues of Virtual Worlds

Section 2 begins with a chapter by Professor Dan Hoops who is also a practicing attorney in the United States. Chapter 10 presents a detailed survey and summary of the laws and regulations affecting virtual worlds. Cyberspace is such an enormous concept that trying to briefly explain the "rules" for E-Commerce or "cyberlaw" is next to impossible. For E-Commerce, it is important to understand that there are business-to-business transactions and those involving consumers. In addition to requiring a mastery of many legal specialties, E-Commerce presents legal issues in a virtual environment. Many business practices in a cyberspace are untested in the courts. New and innovative methods of competition, as well as the effects of an international playing field change the playfield constantly. The legalities of this great new frontier pose an impressive and intellectually stimulating challenge.

In Chapter 11, authors Arman Gukasyan, Nadezhda Ilyina, and Alexander Lavrov of Russia discuss several issues and tradeoffs involved in developing accurate and realistic virtual worlds. Web 2.0 has demonstrated how new technologies can change the structure of the customer-provider relationship. The development of more specialized services and consumer integration creates new marketplaces with new rules of the game. As these new opportunities come to the scene, they will change the face of the world into 3D environments and a multi-agent collaboration. The authors maintain that the adoption of virtual worlds depends a great deal on the user experience. The challenges of providing the user with virtual realism is a challenge as many supporting technologies are still in the early development phase.

Chapter 12, authored by M. Kyritsis, S.R. Gulliver, and S. Morar of the United Kingdom This chapter discusses the environmental and individual user differences that influence the training time required to ensure effective virtual environment spatial knowledge acquisition. Individual factors discussed include: the importance of knowledge and experience; the importance of gender; the importance of aptitude and spatial orientation skills; and the importance of cognitive styles. Environmental factors discussed include: Size, Spatial layout complexity and landmark distribution. Since people are different, a one-size fits all approach to training time does not seem logical. The impact of this research domain is important to virtual world training in general; however within service and military domains ensuring appropriate spatial training is critical in order to ensure that disorientation does not occur in a life / death scenario.

In Chapter 13, Shenlai Winkler of the Fashion Research Institute located in the United States reports on a current case study involving her organization. Although participants in virtual worlds are generally considered by law to be the owner of any Intellectual Property (IP) they create, content creators and owners of OpenSim-based virtual worlds struggle with issues surrounding licensing, content delivery, and usage in these immersive spaces. The Fashion Research Institute (FRI) is specifically exploring these issues in a case study involving the licensing its Shengri La virtual world creations to external users. This case study is the basis of ongoing legal research by FRI's legal steering committee of attorneys from the American Bar Association's Virtual Worlds and Online Gaming committee who are working on a pro bono (volunteer) basis. This chapter presents the result of the ongoing case study. It offers a practitioner's view of issues related to licensing and distribution of content in OpenSim-based virtual worlds.

Chapter 14 by Dr. Greg Gogolin closes out Section 2. In this chapter, Dr. Gogolin looks at security and privacy concerns of virtual worlds by investigating the use and capabilities of current and emerging technologies such as gaming, blogging, podcasting, virtual meetings, and virtual worlds. Security and privacy concerns will be investigated in the context of exploits and IT-related security risks, access management and confidentiality, reputation and product risk management, resource management, financial considerations and accountability, and safety. Several technologies and personal practices are reviewed, as well as ways to mitigate or eliminate their associated risks. The core principles of information security -confidentiality, integrity, and availability - provide an overall framework for the chapter.

In Chapter 15, authors Khulood Ramboo and Kecheng Liu from the United Kingdom discuss the impact of socio-cultural factors on female participation in e-commerce and virtual worlds. Virtual e-commerce can deliver product information that is similar to the information obtained from direct product examination. Both interactivity and customer involvement can enhance the entertainment value of the online shopping experience. However, if virtual e-commerce aim to become a truly global platform for collaboration, then it is vital to keep in mind that consumers' behavior is bound by their cultures. This chapter provides a diagnosis of the six dimensions of the socio-cultural factors that influence the design of virtual e-commerce targeting the Saudi Arabian female market using the foundations of organizational semiotics. An organization – centered analysis and design tools that bridge the gap between the notions of 'culture' and 'IT'.

Section 3: The Future of Virtual Worlds and E-Commerce

Section 3 begins with Chapter 16 which is a discussion on the topic of standards for virtual worlds with emphasis on their usability as a stable and reliable basis for long-term investments into 3D-E-Commerce. Jorg Kloss of Germany explains why standards are important for the success of Virtual Worlds as well as the business in these shared online 3D environments, and what the relevant criteria are to decide for the right technology and/or provider. Although sometimes in the shadow of popular proprietary platforms there are already many different candidates for a Virtual World standard, currently in different states of development. By choosing a 3D platform, E-Commerce providers will decide about their business potential and at the same time strengthen one or another standard in the current technical competition phase. This chapter provides an overview about the current approaches, their advantages and disadvantages as well as the tendencies for the future developments.

In Chapter 17 William G. Burns III of the United States discusses the future of V-commerce. He maintains that the future of the evolving, collaborative communications structure will be impacted to an ever increasing degree by the merging of e-commerce and virtual worlds. Such media outlets will bring new and innovative methods by which companies can interact with clients and customers, as well as business to business. As these technologies continue to evolve, bringing higher definition, realism, and the power to manipulate potential customer experiences, increasing numbers of people will come to the realization that virtual worlds and similar environments are an essential part of an online communications experience.

Chapter 18 is the final Chapter of Part 3 and the book. Charles P Schultz of the United States examines the many aspects of virtual worlds and the solutions they offer in terms of the concept of good enough replacements. A number of solutions currently provided by virtual worlds will be described and evaluated in their present state in comparison to real world equivalents. Dimensions such as cost, usability and functionality are all subject to an initial analysis, followed by thoughts on what trajectories could be followed for virtual world solutions to evolve further and provide more advantages.

This book presents a comprehensive discussion of the current state of virtual worlds presented by virtual world experts from around the world. The breadth of topics covered by the authors is remarkable and results in a thorough and thoughtful compendium of the current state of Virtual Worlds and E-Commerce. I hope you enjoy reading it and find the information valuable.

Barbara L. Ciaramitaro, Ph.D
Ferris State University, USA

Acknowledgment

This book could not happen without the efforts of a remarkable group of virtual world experts from around the world who made up our Editorial Advisory Board and Contributing Authors. I would first like to thank the members of the Editorial Advisory Board who volunteered their time to ensure that the content of this book was worthwhile and reflected the current state of virtual worlds and e-commerce.

Barbara L. Ciaramitaro
Editor

Section 1
The Changing Face of E-Commerce

Chapter 1
Virtual Worlds:
Definition, History and the Elements that Compose Them

David Oyarzun
Vicomtech, Spain

María del Puy Carretero
Vicomtech, Spain

Amalia Ortiz
Enne, Spain

Alex García-Alonso
University of the Basque Country, Spain

ABSTRACT

This chapter presents an introductory overview of virtual worlds. Its purpose is to give the reader a basic knowledge about what a virtual world is. It also discusses some open issues that, from the author's point of view, should be taken into account when new virtual worlds, or new applications running over existing virtual worlds, are designed. The chapter provides a general definition of a virtual world, presents a historic review of these systems and describes the main features and elements that they are composed of. The chapter aims to be useful to the non-technical readers in that it shall provide a clearer concept of virtual worlds. In the case of technical readers, it attempts to be a reference for further research.

BUT, WHAT IS A VIRTUAL WORLD?

Nowadays, most people when ask what is a Virtual World is can give a more or less clear answer. This question prompts most to think about general purpose virtual worlds such as *Second Life*® or There, or perhaps game-oriented worlds like World of Warcraft.

In this manner, we think of concepts related to them, such as multiuser capabilities, sense of presence, etc.

But, the truth is that an universally accepted definition of Virtual World does not exist. That is, there is no existing agreement about the concrete features that compose a virtual world and, and therefore the characteristics that distinguish it from other applications. Instead of this, there are

DOI: 10.4018/978-1-61692-808-7.ch001

several existing definitions that maintain basic concepts but present little differences. In each of these definitions the group of systems that can be understood as virtual worlds changes.

Therefore, the first step in this chapter will be the review and study of different definitions of virtual words. Then, a definition that compiles the terms and concepts that specify a virtual world, as considered by this book, will be proposed.

Definitions of virtual world have evolved through the years, much in the same way that virtual worlds have also evolved. Perhaps, one of the first definitions that is closed to the modern concept of virtual worlds is the definition which was established by Klastrup in 2003 (Klastrup, 2003). From Klastrup's point of view, a virtual world is a persistent on-line representation that offers the possibility of synchronous interaction between users, and between the users and the world, in the frame of a space designed as navigable universe.

In the same year, Bartle (Bartle, 2003) defined a virtual world as an environment where their inhabitants are auto-contented.

Both definitions although the evolution of virtual worlds from 2003 should be highlighted do not take into account important aspects of current virtual worlds.

In the case of Klastrup, the representation of users in a virtual world is not specified. That is, presence and co-presence features in the virtual world are not reflected the fact that the user has the illusion of being immerse in the virtual world and sees the rest of the users immersed too. It could perhaps be deduced from the term 'navigable universe', but it is not clear. In the case of Bartle, the definition is quite general. According to this definition, a literal interpretation would class a videoconferencing system as a virtual world also.

More recently, other authors such as Castronova (Castronova, 2006) have defined virtual worlds as artistic spaces in the computer that have been designed to contain containing a large number of people. On the other hand, Spence (Spence, 2008) defines them as persistent, tridimensional and not game-oriented spaces, and he further contends that they are mainly social spaces.

Another case is the work of Schroeder. He distinguishes between virtual reality, collaborative features and virtual worlds (R. Schroeder, 2008). In Schroeder's point of view, virtual reality is a computer generated viewer that allows users to have the illusion of being in an environment different to the environment where they are and to allow them interact with it; collaborative features are the virtual environments, that he defines as environments where users experiment with other users as present in the same environment and interact with them; and virtual worlds as online persistent spaces.

These definitions establish some common characteristics such as presence, persistence in the world, synchronous interaction, etc. but keep a social focus about virtual worlds.

The vision in the framework of this chapter is somewhat different. It is true that these environments have had a strong social focus until recent years and in many cases it remains so. However, there is a current trend foreseen by different European technological platforms that study the Future Internet. With this trend, virtual worlds will grow in functionality and services (Eiffel, 2009). That is, they will not be only social or leisure places, but they will become portals for accessing general purpose services.

Following this trend, there are recent definitions that are more specific and are not only focused on the virtual world's social features. This is the case of the definition established by Bell (Bell, 2008). He defines a virtual world as a synchronous and persistent network of people represented by avatars and supported by networks of computers. Moreover, Bell explains the terms that compose the definition. These terms are those that characterize a virtual world from his point of view:

1. **Synchronous.** Refers to the concept of common time that allows people to perform

coordinated and collaborative activities. Moreover, virtual worlds offer spatial sensation, distance and coexistence with other participants.

2. **Persistence.** In the sense that the virtual world does not pause. It continues to exist existing when a participant leaves the virtual world.
3. **Network of people.** People are the focus of the virtual world. They participate in it, communicate between themselves and interact with other people and the environment.
4. **Avatar representation.** An avatar is a digital representation (graphical or textual) with ability to take action and is controlled by a user in real-time.
5. **Supported by computer networks.** Without this characteristic, a table game, for example, could be understood as a virtual world.

In this article, this definition has been taken as basis of the final definition. It is complete and contains a set of terms that characterize a virtual world in a form coherent with the understanding of modern virtual worlds.

However, nowadays the concept of entities that are represented in a virtual world should be extended. They not only should be persons but also intelligent software agents. An intelligent software agent tries to faithfully simulate the interactions and intelligent behavior of a human being. This feature turns it into a component that inhabits the virtual world in the same way as the users. In this manner, we propose a new definition based on Bell's one:

A virtual world is a synchronous and persistent network of inhabitants, being users or autonomous software agents, represented by avatars and supported by computer networks.

Consequently the meaning of the terms should be extended to the concept of inhabitant.

We therefore should speak of a network of *inhabitants* as participative elements, and the synchronous collaboration, persistence and representation by means of avatars should be extended to users and intelligent software agents.

The following section gives an overview of virtual worlds from a historical point of view, starting from their birth until modern virtual worlds. Then, current functionalities of virtual worlds are explained. Taking into account these functionalities, a list of current virtual world is presented. Finally, the elements that they are composed of are explained.

ONE STORY ABOUT VIRTUAL WORLDS

From a technological point of view, virtual worlds are provided by evolutions in different fields such robotics, artificial intelligence or computer graphics. Perhaps due to this situation, an agreement for considering a concrete prototype as the first virtual world does not exist. Instead of this, there exists a set of milestones that have given shape to this concept throughout the last 30 years.

The usual association made between virtual worlds and virtual reality is another factor that can contribute to the confusion. Both are research and development fields that have many features in common. In fact, virtual worlds feed from the advances in the field of virtual reality.

However the term '*virtual reality*' refers to virtual simulation of real world aspects. Its objective is that user has the illusion of being immersed in a virtual environment. The term 'virtual world', as it is understood today, is based on the presence and co-presence concepts (Slater, Steed, McCarthy, & Maringelli, 1998). That is, the user feels immersed in the world, but, at the same time, the user also feels immersed with the rest of users. Thus, one of the main differences with virtual reality is the multiuser feature.

While virtual reality has been studied since the birth of modern computers prototypes can be found from the 1960's, the milestones that have marked the advent of virtual worlds were passed some years later.

At the very beginning, virtual worlds, like many other technological developments, grew with the evolution of the video game. It is difficult to make a comprehensive study about the events that have guided the evolution of these applications. However due to the features they introduced, some of them cannot be omitted from any study.

In 1974, a game called *Maze War* appeared (Musseum, 2009). This is considered the first multiuser 3D shooter game. In this game, users were represented by spheres and they chased each other in a maze. The game was developed for a specific computer: the Imacs PDS-1.

Some years later, the predecessor of current MMORPGs (Massive Multiplayer Online Role Playing Game) appeared: the MUD.

Although in this type of game the user had no graphical representation – they were based on a text interface- they possessed some similarities to current virtual worlds: capacity for a large number of users and work over general purpose networks MUD was accessed via *telnet*. Afterwards, applications closer to the modern concept of virtual world began to be developed.

For example, in 1986 *Habitat* was born (Morningstar & Farmer, 1991). It was created by Lucasfilm Games and Quantum Link. This virtual world can be considered as the basis of current virtual worlds. Its interface made use of 2D graphics and the user was represented by means of a configurable avatar. The world consisted of 20,000 connected regions a region was a screen in the world, and the users could interact with objects and communicate amongst themselves.

Perhaps one of the more surprising aspects of Habitat is the fact that it created a virtual currency for purchasing things in the world. This currency had no real value, but each time the world was accessed the user was given a new amount of currency. However, the similarities with current virtual worlds are surprising.

Later the evolution of virtual world's sped up. The Internet was no longer just a scientific or academic environment, but a core element in global communications. Thus, many virtual worlds started to appear. Each of them brought an added value over the previous one, and they presented a constant evolution in functionalities, user capacities and graphic quality.

For example, in 1993 Ericsson developed its first prototype of CyberTown as a proof of concept of a 3D online E-Commerce system (E-Spaces, 2009).

In 1994, the use of 3D avatars started to proliferate with the appearance of virtual communities such as *WorldsChat* developed by World Inc. and AlphaWorld (Inc., 2009). In the latter, the user could select among 12 possible avatars.

In 1995, ID Software launched Quake. This game changed the concept of online game playing, and became a massive phenomenon. In the same year, Fujitsu acquired the Habitat technology and developed a more advanced version of Habitat called WorldsAway (Damer, 1997). On the other hand, in the same year, Time Warner developed *The Palace* (Bumgardner, 2009), the first virtual community that was run on distributed servers rather than a single server. This way it was able to reduce the problems of an increasing number of users.

In the following years there was an exponential evolution and, in 2003, Second Life® was born (Life, 2009b). This virtual world has been able to change the concept of a virtual world. It has created not only a virtual environment where thousands of users can collaborate without looking for a common goal (because it integrates multiple applications), but moreover, it has generated a business model without precedent in this sector. However, the evolution of virtual worlds does not end with Second Life. In fact, its appearance has prompted the appearance of a many more virtual worlds. Some of the most relevant are described in following sections.

More information about the history and evolution of virtual worlds can be found at (Koster, 2009; Tampere, 2009).

MAIN FEATURES OF A MODERN VIRTUAL WORLD

These are some of the main features that distinguish modern virtual worlds from other kind of applications:

- **Presence.** Refers to the ability of the virtual world to represent users or virtual software agents.
- **Communication.** Refers to the channels that a virtual world enables for users to enable communicating and interaction amongst themselves.
- **Collaborative capacity.** The ability to manage and allow interaction either more or less users simultaneously. One of the keys for allowing a high collaborative capacity will be the correct design of the network architecture that supports to the virtual world.

Presence

The ability to configure avatars that represent users and distinguish them from other users is an important factor in current virtual worlds. In fact, several studies demonstrate that when users access a virtual world, they spend a lot of time configuring their avatar (Anderson, Ashraf, Douther, & Jack, 2001; Cheng, Farnham, & Stone, 2002).

Virtually all current virtual worlds allow the physical appearance of the avatar to be configured. For example, in the case of Second Life®, the user can specify features as granular as eye color or the size of the nose. Additionally, the avatar can be further personalized by means of models and accessories developed by third parties, either commercial or free.

The current negative aspects, -that research centres and companies are working on through different initiatives-, are the lack of definition of the avatar identity and interoperability.

Regarding identity, current virtual worlds do not allow, for example, the configuration of features such as personality. In any case, the necessity or advantage of creating a virtual identity is already an open discussion.

The other aspect is more important. Until now, there has been a lack of interoperability between virtual worlds. The clearest example is that if the user customizes an avatar for a specific virtual world, they must configure another from scratch to use in another world. There are several initiatives, such as the new MPEG-V standard that tries to address this lack of standardization (Consortium, retrieved in January 2009.).

Communication

Instead of other computer-mediated communication systems, like traditional text-based chats, virtual worlds allow the simulation of the principal human-human communication channels, that is, the natural channels at least, potentially.

The representation by means of an avatar can allow the simulation of both verbal and gestural communication and through the use of certain peripherals, e.g. haptics, senses such as touch can also be stimulated.

As Schroeder points out (Ralph Schroeder, 2002), to allow a total sensory simulation, there exists peripherals that stimulate the senses of taste and smell. But these systems are in a prototype stage and have yet to show satisfactory results. It is unlikely that this situation will be improved in the medium-term. Following Schroeder's thinking, the loss of these two senses causes an absence of multimedia richness and cues in interpersonal relations. However, it is currently not possible solve this problem with technology.

On the other hand and although opinions may differ, several studies such as Robertson *et al.* (Robertson, Card, & MacKinlay, 1993) conclude that people are more accustomed to using desktop computers than complex immersive systems and for this reason first ones decrease the physical and psychological stress.

Almost all virtual worlds that present multimodal communication capabilities are focused on exploiting typical communication channels that are enabled by means of the sense of sight and hearing. That is, sight, gesticulation, speech and hearing. The application of these channels does not require costly specialized hardware as is the case with haptics, but the use of standard peripherals as a monitor, headphones, etc. are sufficient.

For example, regarding channels that are perceptible by the ear, a pioneering and representative case is that developed in 2002 by DiPaola and Collins (DiPaola & Collins, 2002): OnLive Traveller, a 3D environment for chatting by voice.

In this environment, users are represented by 3D talking head avatars. In order to give a better illusion of immersion, the audio corresponding to the speech of each user is synchronized with the Avatar's lips.

The objective of this project was the use of the natural communication channels so that users have experience a more satisfactory interaction with other users. As they can use voice for chatting, they are free to move about in the environment simultaneously, instead of typing comments.

Regarding sight, almost all commercial virtual worlds that use avatars for representing users allow the user to gesture with the avatar. More advanced studies are focused on the automatization of these gestures and their emotional coherence. That is, not to launch a set of movements explicitly during the course of a conversation, but to generate the gestures that composes the non-verbal language. For example, the Miralab centre has conducted several studies for generating non-verbal language with emotional traits (Egges & Magnenat-Thalmann, 2005).

Collaborative Capacity

One of the main functional features of a virtual world is that it allows simultaneous access to a large number of users from different locations. Therefore, one of the key factors in a virtual world will be the network structure that supports it. Joslin et al. (Joslin, Giacomo, & Magnenat-Thalmann, 2004) have defined five basic aspects that should be taken into account for the design of a network structure that supports both virtual world and collaborative environments:

- **Network Topology.** There are three basic topologies:
    - *Peer-to-peer.* The information transmission is between clients.
    - *Client/Server.* Clients send the information to a central server. This server is responsible for distributing the information to the other clients.
    - *Multicast.* Each client sends the information to a specific IP address that implies all of the other connected clients receive it.

Current topologies should be based on one of these topologies or a combination of them.

- **Dead Reckoning.** It is a technique for reducing the message flow among clients or between client and server. The client sends changes of state in the avatar instead of continuous movements.
- **Area of Interest Management.** This technique defines a visibility area around the client avatar that is shown with higher detail. The rest of the virtual world is optimized.
- **Scene Segmentation.** It is the same idea as that of the Area of Interest, but each area is managed by a different server.
- **Compression.** It implies the compression of the messages between clients and server. Nowadays, almost all worlds use this kind of technique.

A special case is Second Life® which has been overloaded due to its success. The developers have started to implement a new network architecture that divides its client/server architecture in two domains: agents and regions. The first will be responsible for managing all information about avatars and users (profile, personal data, inventory, access data…) and the second will be responsible for the virtual world regions management (Life, 2009a).

CURRENT VIRTUAL WORLDS: APPLICATION ENVIRONMENTS

As has been previously mentioned, in recent years, and above all, after the success of Second Life®, many more virtual worlds has appeared. The most significant worlds are shown in this chapter. For achieve this, and due to large number of virtual worlds that have reached certain level of popularity, these worlds have been categorized by their objectives.

It is true that many virtual worlds maintain a strong social character, but more and more worlds are appearing with different objectives other than social.

These are the most significant virtual worlds classified by their application environment:

- **Developers.** Due to the popularity of virtual worlds, there are companies that are focused on the creation of virtual worlds for other companies. Some well known examples are Muse, OpenSim or Open Cobalt.
- **Leisure.** Almost all virtual worlds –although not necessarily the most popular-, are focused only on leisure. Leisure refers to social relations they are basically 3D chats or games. Examples of these worlds are CyberTown, Dreamville, The Manor, Moove, Playdo, The Sims Online, TowerChat, Traveler, Virtual Ibiza or VPChat. A technologically eye-catching development is Sora, which accesses by mobile phone.
- **General Purpose.** In general, this field is where most popular virtual worlds lay. They do not present a particular focus, but they simulate different aspects of real life. They may even have an economic and monetary system based on a virtual currency that can be purchased with real money. The most popular examples are Active Worlds, Second Life®, Habbo Hotel or There.
- **Promotional.** Some companies, seeing the popularity of virtual worlds, have created environments whose goals are to promote their products or events. Examples of these worlds are Coke Studios, created by the Coca Cola Company, Disney's Toontown Online and Virtual Magic Kingdom, created by Disney, and Dubit, a world with a big commercial focus where several companies are represented.
- **Educational.** Apart from the case of general purpose worlds such as Second Life®, where a large number of educational institutes are represented in the case of Second Life®, Harvard University and Imperial College London, to centers for medical or astronomy (Educational, 2009)-, virtual worlds with a complete educational focus also exist. Some examples are Mokitown (Mokitown, 2009) for child road traffic education or Whyville (Whyville, 2009), a virtual world focused on teaching the sciences to children.

More information about existing virtual worlds can be found in (Review, 2009).

MAIN ELEMENTS THAT COMPOSES A VIRTUAL WORLD

There is no existing common and universal agreement of the main elements that compose a virtual world. Therefore we present a description, as valid or invalid as any other, with the objective of obtaining a better understanding of the common elements that may appear in a virtual world.

From our point of view there are four main elements that play the role functionality containers in the virtual world. They are the user, the avatar, the intelligent software agent and the virtual world itself. They can be schematized as shown in Figure 1.

The following sections detail each element and their function in the virtual world environment.

The User

The user is the main element in the virtual world system. Virtual worlds, like most other computer applications are focused on offering services to users either directly or indirectly. In this schema, services can be both part of the virtual world –as its own content- or offered to the user through software agents.

The user is an intelligent element that interacts through their avatar. The communication between user and avatar is made by means of input/output devices.

The definition of all the aspects that characterizes a human being is beyond the scope of this work. However, the basic aspects that are necessary for representing a person in a virtual world have been compiled. That is, a minimum set of traits that make two persons different and can be represented in a virtual world.

A Human being is composed of body and mind (Carolis, Carofiglio, Bilvi, & Pelachaud, 2002). Body features are related by appearance and movements. The aspects of the mind related by emotions, mood and personality (Gebhard, 2005).

In general, personality affects the way a person perceives the world; emotions are precise personality modifiers that depend on the environmental conditions; while mood is a mid-point between emotions and personality. They are personality modifiers with longer duration than emotions and they are usually caused by the addition of several emotions (Gebhard, 2005; Kasap & Magnenat-Thalmann, 2007).

These factors should be taken into account for representing a user in a virtual world. This will faithfully represent the user in a virtual world from the rest of the users' points of view.

Another factor to be taken into account will be the user communication features. A user could have the ability for some specific way of communicating (for example, via text or via voice). The importance of this factor is increased when it is transformed into a necessity. A user with some type of disability would not to be able to use a particular channel and thus depends on other means of communication.

In fact, according to a press report written by Gartner, an important ICT consultancy, in 2011

Figure 1. Elements that composes a virtual world

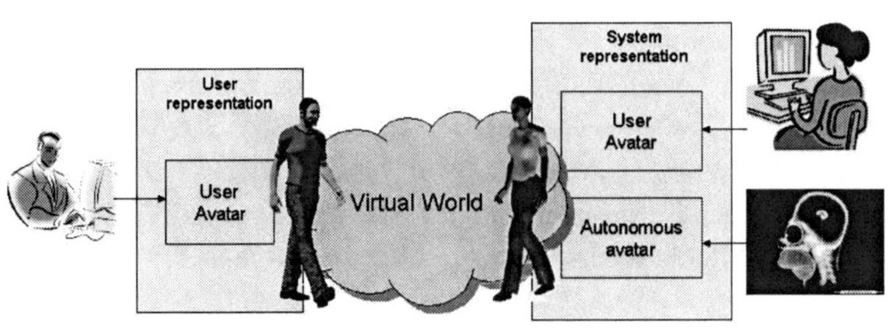

80% of Internet users will have a Second Life® in virtual worlds. Such forecasted growth that does not consider accessibility would create a new digital gap. Users with disabilities who cannot access virtual worlds in their current conception, will exclude from using these future virtual worlds.

There have been some recent initiatives for increasing the accessibility of current virtual worlds by means of external devices and plug-ins. Hansen has compiled most significant of these tools in (Hansen, 2008).

On the other hand Trewin et al. (S. Trewin, Hanson, Laff, & Cavender, 2008; S. M. Trewin, Laff, Cavender, & Hanson, 2008) have studied the possibility of developing accessible virtual worlds. They have tested their efficiency using a multiuser game due to its technological similarity to a virtual world.

They present two types of existing applications for users with disabilities: Developments that are for the disabled exclusively and developments for the general public that take accessibility into consideration. In their study, they highlight the need for research into the second type of application to avoid the growth of a new digital gap.

There is currently some directives and recommendations for the management of each type of disability in a 3D virtual world. However, they have yet to be implemented in real scenarios.

The Agent

Agents are software applications that are mainly related to the field of Artificial Intelligence. Their base characteristics are autonomy and sociability. The autonomy refers to their ability to decide on tasks to do to obtain their objectives. Sociability is related to the need to collaborate with other agents to carry out their goals (Morales, 2008).

Although, different classifications of agents exist, one of the classic and extended divisions depends on their form of reasoning. That is deliberative, reactive and hybrid agents (Morales, 2008; Moya & Tolk, 2007; Nwana, 1996):

- **Deliberative Agents.** They have a symbolic representation of the world, including objects and intentions. Based on this world knowledge, they take decisions through inference mechanisms.
- **Reactive Agents.** They contain an internal representation of the virtual world where they are that is very simplistic. The intelligence of the agents comes from interaction between them.
- **Hybrid Agents.** Are agents that are not pure reactive or hybrid, but they have subsystems of both kinds.

This system of classification is appropriate for any kind of agent, that is, any kind of application that works autonomously.

In the case of virtual worlds, we define an agent as a subset of these systems whose objective is the simulation of human behavior in a virtual world in an autonomous manner. That is, systems that are part of the artificial life field –or *ALife*- (Bedau, 2003). In a virtual world other kinds of agents could exist that act as content search robots, for example. However, they will be dependent on the content of each particular virtual world.

The definition of agent as a main virtual world element is closer to that of AVA –Autonomous Virtual Agent-, defined by Luengo (González, 2005). Luengo defines these three features as characteristics of an AVA:

- Its natural place is a 3D graphically simulated world.
- It has a graphic representation of the world that it inhabits, and it is able to perceive, adapt and react to the environment, exhibits a human-like graphical behavior.
- It is an independent software entity that is conscious of environmental changes and is able to response to them autonomously, that is without need of external instructions or control.

Some examples of these kinds of agents can be found, usually represented by means of avatars. As an example, as early as 1995, Maes et al. (Maes, Darrell, Blumberg, & Pentland, 1995) developed an agents system using mixed reality with some validation scenarios called ALIVE. One of the scenarios was an agent represented by a puppet-like avatar.

The Avatar

Nowadays the use of avatars for representing users or intelligent software agents in virtual worlds is very common. Their advantages or disadvantages are a topic of open field of discussion. However, there is a set of studies who have concluded that they have more advantages than disadvantages. Some of these, compiled in the work of Ortiz (Ortiz, 2008) are:

- **It Facilitates Social Interaction with the Machine.** Prendinger et al. in (Prendinger, Ma, Yingzi, Nakasone, & Ishizuka, 2005) stated that the individual interactions of computer users are fundamentally social. Also they included that the user hopes to obtain the same type of social behavior. Therefore, they proposed to give the interface personality aspects and voice synthesis to improve the human machine interaction.
- **The User then Considers the System to be more Reliable and Credible.** A user needs to believe in an agent's reliability in order to have the confidence to delegate certain tasks to it. There are evaluations that demonstrate that confidence and credibility increase with the personification of the agent, in other words, by giving it a face, eyes, body or voice. If the aspect of the character is also realistic, the agent is seen to be more intelligent and friendly (Koda & Maes, 1996).
- **The Commitment of the User Increases.** Personifying the agents increases the user's commitment to the application (Kim, 2004).
- **It Catches the Attention of the User.** Hongpaisanwiwat et al. (Hongpaisanwiwat & Lewis, 2003) concluded that the avatar is capable of catching the user's attention and this increases if the avatar is credible, as it generates the illusion of life in the system.
- **It Focuses the User's Attention.** An avatar can be used to focus the user's attention on points of interest (Prendinger et al., 2005).

Moreover, Casanueva (Casanueva, 2000) states that a virtual collaborative environment that is seen as being satisfactory and usable to users, should create a grand illusion of presence and interaction with other users.

Slater et al. (Slater et al., 1998; Slater et al., 1996) divided this illusion of presence into two components: the personal presence and the shared presence, or co-presence. The first refers to the subjective feeling of being in the virtual world, and the second, to the feeling that the rest of the users are in the virtual world. The better these factors are fulfilled, the more effective and satisfactory the virtual world will be.

The user representation elements improve this feeling of presence. In fact, numerous studies (Benford, Bowers, Fahlén, Greenhalgh, & Snowdon, 1995; Slater & Usoh, 1994; Snowdon & Jaa-Aro, 1996; Vilhjalmsson, 1997) conclude that having a visual representation of users improves the feeling of presence and especially the feeling of co-presence. More specifically, evaluations in the work of Casanueva (Casanueva, 2000) state that the use of a realistic avatar, both in appearance and in movement, improves this feeling even more.

Therefore, we define an avatar as an important element of the virtual world that represents intelligent entities (Figure 2) and enables, at least potentially, these communication channels:

- **Verbal.** The avatar enables the possibility of verbal communication in a similar way to human-human communication. This means of communication is possible without the need for an avatar. But the avatar provides the possibility of synchronizing verbal communication with lip animation, creating the illusion of seeing and hearing a person speaking.
- **Gestural.** On the other hand, the avatar allows the transmission of gestural information, information that is part of non-verbal communication.

Authors as Mehrabian (Mehrabian, 1968), and Bickmore and Cassells (Bickmore & Cassell, 2001) highlight the importance of this kind of communication for transmitting a message. More exactly, Mehrabian states that the acceptance of a message transmitted face-to-face depends on the acceptance of words used at 7%, acceptance on the way the voice is used at 38% and acceptance of gestures at 55%. This kind of gesturing is divided in four types depending on the purpose of the gestures (Cassell et al., 1994):

- *Iconics.* Represent something concrete about the conversation.
- *Metaphorics.* Represent an abstract feature about the conversation
- *Deitics.* Indicate a point in space (people, places…)
- *Beats.* Soft movements that emphasizes parts of the dialog.

Moreover, although voice and gestures do not express the same idea, they always express complementary information. The avatar gives the potential to reproduce these four types of gestures.

Until this point, in case of user representation, the features that the avatar enables, do not give an overall added value, for example, a video conferencing system. However, to take advantage of the virtual world potential it is important to exploit the illusion of presence. That is, users consider that both they and the rest of users are contained in the virtual worlds. Regarding this, the avatar provides two additional functionalities that would be barely applicable with other kind of representation:

- **Navigation in the Environment.** The avatar provides the entity that it represents movement in the environment. This is an

Figure 2. Representation by means an avatar

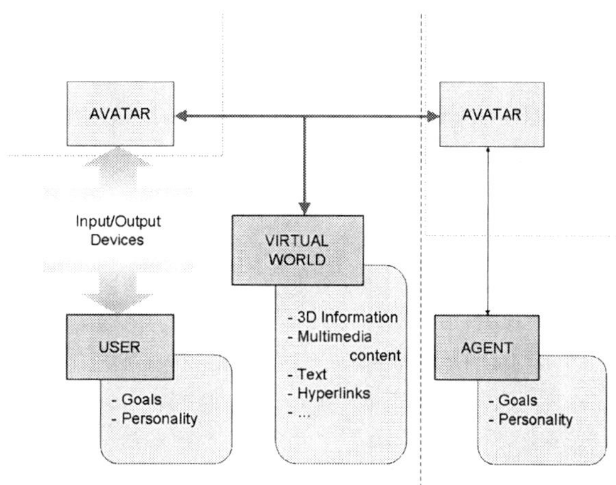

important point because this way the rest of the entities can see this entity as contained within the virtual world, as in the real world.

- **Interaction with Other Elements.** The avatar allows object manipulation and interaction with other avatars in a similar way as happens in the real world.

In summary, the avatar is an interactive element of the virtual world system that provides verbal and non-verbal communication channels, and enables functionalities for navigation and interaction with objects.

The Virtual World

The concept of the virtual world, as contemplated in this scheme, involves the interaction issues not directly related to users, agents or avatars. It includes the terms content and medium that Straaten defines in his categorization of virtual worlds (Straaten, 2000).

The virtual world in this schema is the medium that channels the interactions that takes place, including content and rules that drive the application. Its specific features are:

- **Functionalities**
  - *Interactions channeling.* The virtual world is the element that allows interactions amongst avatars to take place. Although an avatar is the element that allows interaction amongst users, and between users and agents, this interaction cannot take place without a medium that allows it. This is one of the main functionalities of the 'virtual world' element in the schema
  - *Physical rules.* These are the rules that drive the avatar interactions. They can be realistic rules such as 'an avatar cannot go through a wall', or not as is the case with the Second Life® avatars that can fly. Each virtual world will establish its own rules and physical laws that condition the interactions.
  - *Logical rules.* Refer to the objectives or goals of a virtual world and they are dependent on each specific virtual world.
- **Additional Features: Content**
  - *3D objects.* Dynamic or static 3D objects, in the sense they have an associated behavior or not. They include those from the models that compose the environment and those that the user or agent can interact with. The behavior the object has –let suppose a virtual pen that an avatar can use for writing- will be defined by the same object or by virtual world rules. Actions are usually defined in the object itself and the avatar and the virtual world does not need to know all the possible actions with all possible objects. The object 'tells' the avatar or the virtual world which the possible actions are. This technique was developed at the end of 90s and is known as Smart Objects (Goncalves, Kallmann, & Thalmann, 2001).
  - *Information.* This is general information. It can be static or dynamic. Static information can be text, videos, images, etc. Dynamic information might be for example, a mapping of Google search engien in the virtual world. This dynamism is driven by virtual world rules or by an agent not represented by an avatar.

In summary, the virtual world allows the interactions among avatars to take place and offers users services and information.

CONCLUSION AND FUTURE TRENDS

The objective of this article has been to provide an overview of what virtual worlds are, what their functionalities are, and what elements they are composed of.

Future trends in virtual worlds are principally focused on obtaining interoperability between them. In the same way, Web portals for E-Commerce can be accessed by means of different Web browsers maintaining a unique client account; virtual worlds should also allow the same. From the author's point of view, this is a key factor in order to create a tool that establishes a new evolution in Internet and E-Commerce tools.

REFERENCES

Anderson, J., Ashraf, N., Douther, C., & Jack, M. (2001). Presence and Usability in Shared Space Virtual Conferencing. *Cyberpsychology & Behavior*, *4*(2), 287–305. doi:10.1089/109493101300117965

Bartle, R. (2003). *Designing Virtual Worlds*. New Riders Games.

Bedau, M. A. (2003). Artificial life: organization, adaptation and complexity from the bottom up. *Trends in Cognitive Sciences*, *7*(11), 505–512. doi:10.1016/j.tics.2003.09.012

Bell, M. (2008). Toward a Definition of Virtual Worlds. *Journal of Virtual Worlds Research*, *1*(1).

Benford, S., Bowers, J., Fahlén, L. E., Greenhalgh, C., & Snowdon, D. (1995). User embodiment in collaborative virtual environments. *CHI '95: Proceedings of the SIGCHI conference on Human factors in computing systems*, 242-249.

Bickmore, T., & Cassell, J. (2001). Relational agents: a model and implementation of building user trust. *CHI '01: Proceedings of the SIGCHI conference on Human factors in computing systems*, 396-403.

Bumgardner, J. (2009, Retrieved in January 2009). The Palace history web: http://www.jbum.com/history/index.html.

Carolis, B., Carofiglio, V., Bilvi, M., & Pelachaud, C. (2002). APML: A markup language for believable behavior generation. *Embodied conversational agents - let's specify and evaluate them! held in conjunction with AAMAS02*.

Casanueva, J. S. (2000). *Presence and co-presence in collaborative virtual environments*. University of Cape Town, Department of Computer Science.

Cassell, J., Pelachaud, C., Badler, N., Steedman, M., Achorn, B., Becket, T., et al. (1994). Animated conversation: rule-based generation of facial expression, gesture & spoken intonation for multiple conversational agents. *SIGGRAPH '94: Proceedings of the 21st annual conference on Computer graphics and interactive techniques*, 413-420.

Castronova, E. (2006). *Synthetic Worlds: The Business and Culture of Online Games*. University Of Chicago Press.

Cheng, L., Farnham, S., & Stone, L. (2002). Lessons Learned: Building and Deploying Shared Virtual Environments. *The Social Life of Avatars: Presence and Interaction in Shared Virtual Environments and Scientific Visualisation,* pp. 90-111.

Consortium, M. (retrieved in January 2009.). MPEGV, 2009: http://www.chiariglione.org/mpeg/working documents.htm#MPEGV

Damer, B. (1997). *Avatars! Exploring and Building Virtual Worlds on the Internet*. Berkeley, CA: Peachpit Press.

DiPaola, S., & Collins, D. (2002). A 3D Virtual Environment for Social Telepresence. *in Proc. Western Computer Graphics Symp.*

E-Spaces. (2009). *CyberTown first prototype.* Retrieved in January, 2009, from http://www.e-spaces.com/lbw/portfolio/projects/port_cyber-town.htm.

Educational, S. L. (2009). *Simteach.* Retrieved in August, 2009, from http://www.simteach.com/wiki/index.php?title=Top_20_Educational_Locations_in_Second_Life

Egges, A., & Magnenat-Thalmann, N. (2005). Emotional Communicative Body Animation for Multiple Characters. In *Proc. First International Workshop on Crowd Simulation (V-Crowds'05)*, 31-40.

Eiffel. (2009). *European Future Internet Portal.* Retrieved in January 2009, from http://www.future-internet.eu/

Gebhard, P. (2005). ALMA: a layered model of affect. *AAMAS '05: Proceedings of the fourth international joint conference on Autonomous agents and multiagent systems*, 29-36.

Goncalves, L., Kallmann, M., & Thalmann, D. (2001). Programming Behaviors with Local Perception and Smart Objects: An Approach to Solve Autonomous Agent Tasks. *SIGGRAPH 2001.*

González, F. A. L. (2005). *Nuevas Técnicas para la Animación del Comportamiento de Agentes Virtuales Autónomos.* (Phd Thesis). Departamento de Matemática Aplicada y Ciencias de la Computación de la Universidad de Cantabria.

Hansen, S. (2008). Virtual Worlds: Synopsis of User Interfaces and Accessibility Initiatives. In *Proc. of 14th Australasian World Wide Web Conference, AusWeb.*

Hongpaisanwiwat, C., & Lewis, M. (2003). *Attentional Effect of Animated Character.* INTERACT.

Inc., W. (2009). Worlds Inc. Retrieved in January 2009, from http://www.worlds.com/

Joslin, C., Giacomo, T. D., & Magnenat-Thalmann, N. (2004). Collaborative Virtual Environments, from Birth to Standardization. *IEEE Communications Magazine. Special Issue on Networked Virtual Environments*, *42*(4), 65–74.

Kasap, Z., & Magnenat-Thalmann, N. (2007). Intelligent virtual humans with autonomy and personality: State of the Art. *Intelligent Decision Technologies*, *1*(1-2), 3–15.

Kim, Y. (2004). *Pedagogical agents as learning companions: the effects of agent affect and gender on student learning, interest, self-efficacy, and agent persona.* Department of Educational Psychology and Learning Systems.

Klastrup, L. (2003). A Poetics of Virtual Worlds. *Proceedings of the Fifth International Digital Arts and Culture Conference, RMIT.*

Koda, T., & Maes, P. (1996). Agents with faces: the effect of personification. In *Proc. of the IEEE International Workshop on Robot and Human Communication*, 189-194.

Koster, R. (2009). *Online World Timeline.* Retrieved in January 2009, from http://www.raphkoster.com/gaming/mudtimeline.shtml

Life, S. (2009a). *Second Life® Architecture.* Retrieved in January 2009, from http://wiki.secondlife.com/wiki/Structural_Design_Overview

Life, S. (2009b). *Second Life®.* Retrieved in January 2009, from http://www.secondlife.com

Maes, P., Darrell, T., Blumberg, B., & Pentland, A. (1995). The ALIVE system: full-body interaction with autonomous agents. In *Proceedings of Computer Animation '95.* 11-18, 209.

Mehrabian, A. (1968). Communication without words. *Psychology Today*, *2*(4), 53–56.

Mokitown. (2009). *Mokitown*. Retrieved in January 2009, from http://www.mokitown.com/mokitown_prehome/home_en.jsp.

Morales, J. T. P. M. R. M. (2008). *Inteligencia Artificial: Técnicas, métodos y aplicaciones*. New York: McGraw-Hill.

Morningstar, C., & Farmer, F. R. (1991). The lessons of Lucasfilm's habitat. 273-302.

Moya, L. J., & Tolk, A. (2007). *Towards a taxonomy of agents and multi-agent systems*. Paper presented at the SpringSim '07: Proceedings of the 2007 spring simulation multiconference.

Musseum, D. C. (2009). Maze War 30th anniversary. Retrieved in January 2009, from http://www.digibarn.com/history/04-VCF7-MazeWar/index.html.

Nwana, H. S. (1996). Software Agents: An Overview. *The Knowledge Engineering Review*, *11*(3), 205–244. doi:10.1017/S026988890000789X

Ortiz, A. (2008). *Avatars for emotional interaction*. University of the Basque Country.

Prendinger, H., Ma, C., Yingzi, J., Nakasone, A., & Ishizuka, M. (2005). Understanding the effect of life-like interface agents through users' eye movements. *ICMI '05: Proceedings of the 7th international conference on Multimodal interfaces*, 108-115.

Robertson, G. G., Card, S. K., & MacKinlay, J. D. (1993). Nonimmersive Virtual Reality. *Computer*, *26*(2), 81–83. doi:10.1109/2.192002

Schroeder, R. (2002). Copresence and Interaction in Virtual Environments: An Overview of the Range of Issues. In *Proceedings of the 5th Annual International Workshop: Presence*, 274-295.

Schroeder, R. (2008). Defining Virtual Worlds and Virtual Environments. *Journal of Virtual Worlds Research*, *1*(1).

Slater, M., Steed, A., McCarthy, J., & Maringelli, F. (1998). The influence of body movement on subjective presence in virtual environments. *Human Factors*, *40*(3), 469–477. doi:10.1518/001872098779591368

Slater, M., & Usoh, M. (1994). Body centered interaction in immersive virtual environments. *Artificial life and virtual reality*, 125-148.

Slater, M., Usoh, M., Benford, S., Snowdon, D., Brown, C., Rodden, T., et al. (1996). Distributed Extensible Virtual Reality Laboratory (DEVRL). *Virtual Environments and Scientific Visualisation*, 137-148.

Snowdon, D., & Jaa-Aro, K. (1996). Body-Centred Configuration in Collaborative Virtual Environments. In *Proceedings of the 2nd FIVE International Conference*, 48-54.

Spence, J. (2008). Demographics of Virtual Worlds. *Journal of Virtual Worlds Research*, *1*(2).

Straaten, P. V. D. (2000). *Interaction Affecting the Sense of Presence in Virtual Reality*. Research Task Final Report, Delft University of Technology, Faculty of Information Technology and Systems.

Tampere, U. o. (2009). *Review of Virtual Communities*. Retrieved in January 2009, from http://www.cs.uta.fi/~kjr/ACHCI/tang.html.

Trewin, S., Hanson, V. L., Laff, M., & Cavender, A. (2008). PowerUp: an accessible virtual world. *ASSETS*, 177-184.

Trewin, S. M., Laff, M. R., Cavender, A., & Hanson, V. L. (2008). Accessibility in Virtual Worlds. *CHI '08 extended abstracts on Human factors in computing systems*.

Vilhjalmsson, H. H. (1997). *Autonomous Communicative Behaviours in Avatars*. Media Laboratory, Massachusetts Institute of Technology.

Whyville. (2009). *Whyville*. Retrieved in January 2009, from http://www.whyville.net/smmk/nice

Chapter 2
3D3C Real Virtual Worlds Defined:
The Commerce Challenge

Yesha Sivan
The Academic College of Tel aviv-Yaffo, Israel

ABSTRACT

The goal of this chapter is to two fold: first to define and expose the domain of "Real Virtual Worlds" and secondly to define the critically of Commerce within this domain. It is the assumption of this chapter that this new field of virtual worlds is destined to become a major force in 5-10 years. Much like the internet, Real Virtual Worlds, will change, enhance, and sometimes hamper how we learn, have fun, work, and perform human action. Virtual worlds are defined as an integration of 3D, Community, Creation and Commerce (3D3C). Building on this definition, we develop the "commerce" factor. My goal is to establish commerce in a critical integral part of virtual worlds. Even more, without commerce, we will probably miss the larger potential of real virtual worlds.

"Commerce changes the fate and genius of nations" - Thomas Gray

INTRODUCTION: MESHING WORLD OF WARCRAFT, FACEBOOK, YOUTUBE, AND AMAZON

In this chapter, I wish to share my perspective about Commerce in Real Virtual Worlds. This perspective stems from over four years of extensive research, practice, and "being in" virtual worlds. I have also conducted many discussions with users of virtual worlds, players of games, developers, merchants, other new people wishing to learn about virtual worlds. These discussions, led to the "commerce" emphasizes of this work.

To explain "virtual worlds," I have proposed the 3D3C definition. In it, we define virtual worlds as an integration of four factors (Sivan, 2008).

- **3D:** the ability to present objects, people, and land in three dimensions, including

DOI: 10.4018/978-1-61692-808-7.ch002

movement, and perspective (similar to the game World of Warcraft visual 3D display)

- **Community:** the ability to act in groups, to facilitate communication and action (similar to Facebook or Ning).
- **Creation:** the ability to allow users to create content and value (much like people create videos in YouTube, or create content in Wikipedia).
- **Commerce:** the ability to gain real money from actions in virtual worlds. The ability to work, sell, and conduct business (similar to what Amazon is doing with selling books, or their experimentation with Mechanical Turk, a seminal example whereby work is distributed digitally).

I have noticed that the most difficult part of this virtual worlds definition is "commerce." Apparently, "commerce" is difficult in a different way for at least three kinds of people.

- **Lay people** find commerce hard to accept because, as I often hear, why would one "pay for a virtual shirt that you do not get the shirt."
- **Developers**, often from the gaming worlds, do not sense the urgency of commerce, therefore commerce is often "slapped" on top of the design of the system, creating a cumbersome feel to the user, and hard to maintain worlds.
- Even **for leaders of advanced worlds** like Second Life®, or IMVU, which practice real commerce with real money, the nature of commerce is not clear. Lack of "commerce" knowhow cause such leaders to change the "rules" of commerce without enough reflection causing merchants to loose their investment and their trust in the respective world.

Thus the goal is this chapter is first to offer a general detailed definition of virtual worlds, and in parallel emphasize, explicate, argue for, and demonstrate the meaning and importance of commerce within this definition.

The parts of the chapters include:

- The background first part will present what I call the parents of the virtual worlds: "virtual reality" and "gaming worlds."
- Then, Real Virtual Worlds will be defined using (a) the detailed example of Second Life®, (b) a formal definition of 3D3C (3 dimensions, Community, Creation and Commerce) and (c) a short comparative analysis of several worlds as a method to explicate the 3D3C definition.
- The next three parts will further expose and present Community, Creation and Commerce. These three parts will use Second Life® as a background for the discussion.
- The conclusion part will connect the supply (of powerful technology) and demand (from both young and adult users) with the sustained innovation that stem from 3D3C and specifically commerce – to create a reinforcing cycle that will propel Real Virtual Worlds forward.

BACKGROUND: THE PARENTS OF REAL VIRTUAL WORLDS

The young field of Real Virtual Worlds can be seen as the offspring of a marriage of two fields plus additions from other "related" fields. The father field is "Virtual Reality," the mother field is "Gaming Worlds." Other related fields are also affecting the virtual worlds range from economy (for example, of virtual goods), sociology (nature of communities), and law (copyrights and ownership), to biology (new brain based human-computer interfaces), computer science (performance, reliability and scalability), and mathematics (algorithms for 3D rendering and animation).

The keen reader should immediately notice the omission of business (or commerce) from the above fields. This is what I strive to "correct" in this chapter. As we will see later, both parents have almost no commerce background in them.

Father: Virtual Reality

Virtual reality is the first parent of Real Virtual Worlds. Burdea and Coiffet (2003), in there seminal book define "Virtual Reality" as "a simulation in which computer graphics is used to create a realistic-looking world. Moreover, the synthetic world is not static, but responds to the users' inputs [such as] gestures verbal commands, etc.)." Later in their formal definition, they state:

Virtual reality is a high-end user computer interface that involves real time simulation and interactions through multiple sensorial channels [including these...] modalities: visual, auditory, tactile, smell and taste.

Later in the discussion, Burdea and Coiffet point the 3-Is as the gist of virtual reality as the ability to "feel" the reality ("immersion") and to change and modify it ("interaction"). They further, and humbly, add "imagination" stating that "the extend to which these application solve a problem depends very much on the human "imagination." They depict the 3-Is in the following diagram which demonstrate a triangle that exist mainly because of our imagination.

The field of virtual reality has a long history, with patents starting in 1962 (the Sensorama simulator). It was pushed and developed mainly in the defense industry where high-end systems where used to save costly training. A tipping point came around 2000, when the cost of high-end graphics processors (often called GPU – Graphical Processor unit) dropped. Instead of paying $100,000 for a high-end computer from a company like Silicon Graphics, you could pay $5000 for a PC grade machine. More advancement and cost reduction will soon bring us augmented reality – the ability to connect the virtual and the real in one view (example: you sit near a desk with few people in real and view on the table a virtual model of a planned future car (Bimber & Raskar, 2005.

For these pioneers, virtual reality was first and foremost a technical project. The actual line-of work engineers, in these seminal efforts, which were often funded by big defense contracts, never had to bother with basic commerce issues like how to protect an asset from being duplicated

Figure 1. The 3-I's of Virtual Reality: Immersion, Interaction, Imagination

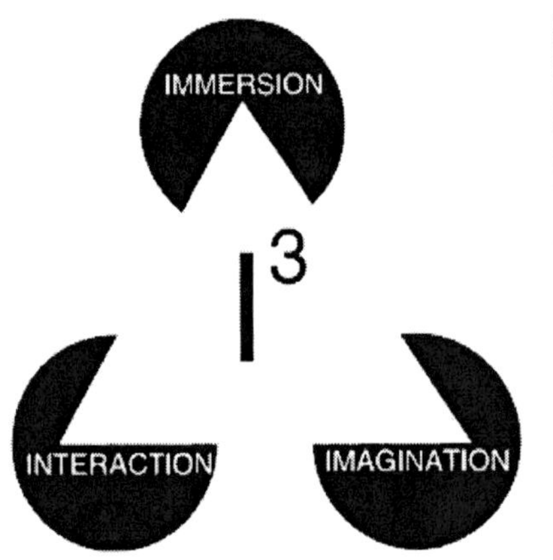

maliciously, what to do with the money left in the account of an avatar that died or how to "sell" property in virtual worlds.

Mother: Gaming Worlds

If "virtual reality" is the father of Real Virtual Worlds, "Gaming Worlds" is the mother. In "gaming worlds," I include anything from the first MUD (1978) to World of Warcraft (WOW), and to some extent Second Life® (picked interest in 2007, and still a major force today in 2008). (a major source for this table is the summative work on designing virtual worlds Bartle, 2004).

This is a very compact presentation of a much larger effort that included many more games and innovation in games (See for example Morningstar & Farmer, 1991, Taylor, 2006; Alexander, 2003; Alexander, 2005). Yet for the purpose of this work, it will have to suffice. Since the border between gaming worlds and Real Virtual Worlds is located between World of Warcraft and Second Life®, it is important to highlight what is so unique about WOW.

The attraction WOW was demonstrated with the release of an extension called The Burning Crusade (Jan 16, 2007). Blizzard, the producer of WOW, sold 2.4 million copies of this extension in North America and in Europe during the first 24 hours of distribution. Priced at $40 per box, that's about 100 million dollars in one day! (The latest record for a game: in May, 2008 Grand Theft Auto 4 raked in more than $500 million in its first week in stores, selling more than 6 million units worldwide).

Not only these are huge figures, they also indicate a significant distance from their competitors. WOW's meticulous design made it into a successful game. Every aspect of the game – from the design of the monsters and the land to the parent control of time limits for users – is crafted artfully and skillfully. Blizzard, makers of WOW, was

Table 1. Using 3D3C to view sample worlds

Year	World	Uniqueness & Commerce Take
1978	MUD (Multi-User Dungeon)	The first text based multi-user world. While it had no graphics, it included a rich imaginary "world." MUD released a flurry of text based worlds and is considered the granddaddy of all the following. Some MUD-like systems introduced the idea of GOLD (local in-game money)
1997	Ultima on-line.	3D graphical world. Got to then the amazing number of 100,000 users by the end of year 1. Introduced monthly pay per use ($9.95). This was the first time, a 3D game made money to its makers albeit as a service.
1999	EverQuest	Key point: People power. It allowed the camera to roam around instead of fixing it to the avatar eyes. EverQuest was unique because it demonstrated the power of community. You started the game for some reason, but you continued to play because of your friends. EverQuest supported small groups and allow them to play together. EverQuest was called by some players EverCrack to hint at its strong pull.
2002	Sims on-line	Took the idea of "user created content" to the next level with tools that allow creatively in 3D creation – albeit mostly moving and arranging items. Sims was really an game of economy. Again, money was not real, although embedded in the world.
2004	World of Warcraft ("WOW")	Massively parallel world. With millions of users, each paying about $10 a month. An amazing success from both the gaming and business points of view. WOW was also one of the first to create a secondary market for items. People would pay real $ to get virtual Gold. "gold framing" in China became a major problem.
2006	Second Life® ("SL"")	While starting earlier (in 2003) and operating on the sidelines of the hard core gaming worlds, SL gained a lot of exposure in 2006 and 2007. The first world to combine 3D, community, creation, and commerce – which I will later define. Exposed the idea of real money into the game. Second Life® position on real money is duel. On one hand, Linden dollar is real money, touted as exchange-able currency, on the other hand Terms of Service state that (See later box: convertible currency or funny money?)

able to pack a lot of wisdom into their creation (Fawcett, 2006).

We can take few lessons from WOW: first, it is technically feasible to run a world with millions of users. Second, virtual worlds can enormously attractive. In addition, we should remember that WOW caters to a limited audience: those who like the WOW style (monsters, quests, battles, etc.) the Hard Core Gamers. SL, on the other hand, while technologically immature, caters to a much larger audience. After all, in Second Life® you can do much, much more than killing monsters.

3D3C: 3D, COMMUNITY, CREATION AND COMMERCE

I will use three methods to define Real Virtual Worlds:

a. **By example** in which I will explore what makes Second Life® a real virtual world.
b. **By formal** definition that define Real Virtual Worlds as a combination of 3D, Community, Creation and Commerce.
c. **By analysis** where I will use the 3D3C definition to examine some of the current worlds, to further clarify and discuss the definition

An Example: Second Life®

Second Life® (SL) was conceived in 1999 by Linden Labs as an implementation of the Metaverse. The term "Metaverse" first appeared in 1992 in a science-fiction book named Snow Crash by Neal Stephenson. The Metaverse was described as a three-dimensional world in which human characters spent their time, played, worked and lived. In Stephenson's words, "the Metaverse [is] my invention, which I came up with when I decided that existing words (such as 'virtual reality') were simply too awkward to use." (Snow Crash, 2007).

In Linden version of the Metaverse, which I consider the prime example to a real 3D3C virtual world, any user may install the software and create a three-dimensional character for him/herself (AKA "Avatar"), adjusting properties such as the shape of his body, skin, hair and lips. (Note: "he" and "she" may both be used hereafter to denote both genders). He may select to wear a hat, shirt, or skirt, and add rings, earrings or nose rings. After the body is constructed, the user may purchase a car, a plane or a yacht; he may build a room, an apartment or a castle. He can meet people, robots, or dragons.

At first glance, many view SL as a game – a direct descendant of games such as Sims, World of Warcraft, and Doom. Veteran users will probably recall the worlds of Dungeons and Dragons and other paper-based fantasy games. Indeed, many of the action patterns and techniques of SL resemble these games. This is a good starting point. But the rest is far more profound and meaningful, exciting and scary. The interaction of avatars, the believability of what you see, and the money involved, all create a new level of experience, a kind of parallel world, a different world – a real virtual world. A world where anyone can choose their own life-style and actions: from a life of hedonistic leisure and entertainment to a life of lucrative work and creativity (in the real world).

Pepe is one of these avatars. Her figure, her blonde hair, and her fluent speech (with a Spanish accent) make her very popular among visitors to the club where she works. Pepe hired a fashion consultant, who matched her looks and clothing to her career. Thus, her blonde hair was matched with her police shirt, which bears the letters "SLPD" an internal joke that means Second Life® Police Department.

Pepe is a dancer at a nightclub. Every evening she mounts the stage, holds on to the pole and moves to the music while smiling at the club's customers. Many of them show their appreciation by tipping some money in the Tip Jar. The tip could be a few cents or a few dollars worth, using

Figure 2. Pepe policewoman or dancer? (sample avatar)

the local currency: the Linden Dollar (more on that later).

Pepe is in the center of a human, social, and commercial undertaking, which also includes dancers of both sexes, DJs, club owners (who rent out private rooms to visitors), land owners, landscape designers, building contractors, architects, lighting experts and musicians. I chose Pepe as an example because most new users of Second Life® will be amazed when they meet her at the club. The nightclub scene in Second Life® appeals to most newcomers (and to their purses). Newbies visit various clubs to meet people; to see and to be seen. The exhilarating dances (bolero, waltz, slow) are the first encounter a newbie has with the power of Real Virtual Worlds.

Let us leave Pepe dancing on the stage and look outside. What, in fact, makes SL a real virtual world? Let's analyze Pepe's story:

- Pepe and the club she is working in has a three dimensional representation (3D), the users can zoom in and out, pan and explore everything from the texture of her shirt to the coil in the lamp that is located 10 meters above her. While Pepe is moving herself, other users can roam around the room.
- Pepe can dance on the stage, because she belongs to a group of dancers of the club (**Community**). Groups allow several users to act together in the Real Virtual Worlds, to buy land, to work, to get certain permissions etc. While at work she is using the group of the club; when she is shopping at Canimal fashion store, she is using the group of the Canimal; while she studies English, she is part of a small group of English as a Second Language (ESL) for Spanish speaking people.
- Pepe is both a creator and a beneficiary of other creations (**Creation**). She creates by mixing and matching her outfit, the color of her skin and her hair, the jewelry, and her shoes. All of which were created by others. She can also buy furniture for her small county house and arrange them. With the right permissions, she can also create a garden for herself. With the programming skill, she can program the flowers in the garden to grow or just buy the growing flowers from someone with the programming skill.
- All of her actions, for work, fun, learning, or relations relay upon an economy that connect the virtual world to the real world (**Commerce**). She can make money by working at the club, she can pay for her house, she can make money by selling flowers, and she can pay her English teacher.

The claim of this example is two staged: first, the combination of 3D, and 3C (Community, Creation, and Commerce) define a new medium. Second, as Real Virtual Worlds become more 3D and more 3C, we will fulfill the immense potential of the medium.Convertible currency or funny money (Sivan, 2009)

While many consider the Linden Dollar real money, Linden Lab's Terms of Service tell another story:

1.4 Second Life® "currency" is a limited license right available for purchase or free distribution at Linden Lab's discretion, and is not redeemable for monetary value from Linden Lab. You acknowledge that the Service presently includes a component of in-world fictional currency ("Currency" or "Linden Dollars" or "L$"), which constitutes a limited license right to use a feature of our product when, as, and if allowed by Linden Lab. Linden Lab may charge fees for the right to use Linden Dollars, or may distribute Linden Dollars without charge, in its sole discretion. Regardless of terminology used, Linden Dollars represent a limited license right governed solely under the terms of this Agreement, and are not redeemable for any sum of money or monetary value from Linden Lab at any time. You agree that Linden Lab has the absolute right to manage, regulate, control, modify and/or eliminate such Currency as it sees fit in its sole discretion, in any general or specific case, and that Linden Lab will have no liability to you based on its exercise of such right [emphasis added].

So far, Linden has treated the Linden Dollar as a fully exchangeable currency, and I see no sign that it won't continue to do so. Nevertheless, caveat emptor.

3D3C: A Formal Definition

Let's now formally define Real Virtual Worlds as an aggregate of four factors: a 3D World, Community, Creation, and Commerce (See original definition Sivan, 2007)

3D World: A dynamic world where viewers see objects like avatars, houses, and cars. The world has land, a sky, a sun (or maybe more than one sun), wind, gravity, water and fire. Avatars move around freely (for example, in SL you may fly up to a height of 200 meters). The user can further examine the world from different points of points (roaming camera).

Community: Man is a social animal. Unfortunately, during the past century we gradually distanced ourselves from socializing – mainly through the advent of television. We sat alone in front of the screen, watching passively and without much interaction. We did not react, we didn't create and we couldn't see how others felt or reacted. The Web actually enhanced this feeling of "solitude" (in a manner of speaking). Then emails emerged, followed by the "chat," the cellular phone, SMS and multi-player worlds. So we are now actually returning to the Community, to friends, to people. Amazon began this trend by allowing readers to review and recommend books. Later, companies like YouTube allowed users to upload video contents. Moreover, of course, blogs (which include comments), social sites such as FaceBook and MySpace the ultimate in this genre where anyone may create a personal site to communicate with his friends. (Please note all avatars in SL represent real users. There are no computerized avatars as in regular computer games such as World Of Warcraft).

Creation: Second Life®'s greatest invention and technological achievement was in giving users the capability to develop their own "things" (or in SL jargon: objects). In fact, the entire contents of SL (barring a few sample and demo objects) were created by users. Constructing objects may be done at a couple of levels – first, by moving pre-constructed objects from one place to another (i.e., rearranging furniture in a home, or setting up a nightclub). Second, an object (i.e., a house) may be assembled from basic components such as walls and ceilings, and "painting" them with various textures. These basic components, called primitives, allow the construction of complex objects at a very high level of precision (see the SL example of Susan Vega's guitar, which is made out of more than a hundred primitives). Linden hit the nail on the head when they built a programming language (LSL - Linden Script Language) into the world. LSL allow users with programming abilities to endow their objects with behavioral attributes. As a result, we can see fish swimming in schools, a game of golf, pistols that shoot, and even Pepe's dancing. Largely, these are expansions of the capabilities found in worlds such as Sims, combined with industrial CAD software packages.

Commerce: This is *the* Linden innovation. Linden has created a new currency the Linden Dollar (or L$, for short). There is a defined exchange rate between the Linden Dollar and the US Dollar in 2008 one US$ was worth about L$265. The entire economics of the SL world is based on this currency. The credibility of this economy is built on two levels one conceptual and the other technical. At the conceptual level, Linden established and runs its own exchange. Within it, Linden guarantees the exchanging of L$ to US$ immediately and at any time. For instance, if Pepe earned L$000 from tips, she could access the Linden website and exchanged them for about US$10 which would be immediately transferred to her real account. Going the other way, if Pepe needed L$6,000 for a new hairdo, she could buy them for about US$20 immediately. At the technical level, Linden has currency and commerce integrated into the game. For example, every object can have purchase-ability and price.

Ultimately Real Virtual Worlds stem from the integration of the 3D, Community, Creation and Commerce. Second Life® reveals the emergence of this integration. In SL you'll find a price for objects, permissions (i.e., an object may be restricted from being sold), and ownerships. The commerce is structured into the world itself. For example, let us assume that we enjoyed Pepe's dancing (and her Spanish accent) and wish to tip her. We point to her and transfer money to her by clicking a button. If Pepe wants to buy a new blouse, she goes to the shop, points to the blouse of her choice and buys it for L$2,000. The blouse is defined as a unique object in this world, and Pepe will not be able to copy it. The shopkeeper will receive L$500 for the blouse, and the blouse manufacturer will receive L$1,500 (in accordance with a previously defined business agreement between them). At the end of the month the shopkeeper will pay rent to the land owners, also by predetermined agreement.

This integration of a 3D world, organized and managed communities, immediate creation capabilities of objects and services, and a virtual commerce which actually becomes real – is the basic allure of SL in particular and of Real Virtual Worlds in general.

Typical Worlds via the 3D3C Prism

After the definition by example where we looked at Real Virtual Worlds via Second Life®, and the formal definition of the 3D3C, let us turn into using the definition to highlight some of the differences between specific worlds. The purpose of the following table is to highlight the different levels of each factor. The worlds represent a spectrum of worlds; they were selected to highlight various aspects of the 3D3C definition and not because of their impact on the field. (An earlier version of this table was first presented in Metanomics, a virtual broadcast, hosted by Bloomfield (Ed.), 2007).

- WOW (World of Warcraft) is the #1 multi-user game with more than 10 million users (described in more details earlier in section 0). WOW has relatively good 3D graphics. Since it is centrally created the graphics delivery can be optimized. Creation, is relatively limited, (you can select your avatar and dress it, but you can not change to the environment). Real commerce is limited. I noted one star ('*') because you can buy money on the net).
- IMVU is a chat world merged with MySpace-like home page. It does not allow your avatar to walk around, you move from one scene to another. In many ways it is a limited world compared to WOW or SL. Still it has 3D (only 3 stars); a strong

community infrastructure (with groups, group chat, friends, and who visited my page capacity albeit without permissions), and real money commerce – where you can buy and sell money.

- Penguin Club, now part of Disney (it was purchased for US$700m in 2007) is a kids world. It does not have 3D representation but rather 2D approach. It has no ability to use money. Penguin Club is presented here to show that you do not have to be a 3D3C real world in-order to be successful.
- Second Life® is the prime example to a full 3D3C world. It now has "full" (more than 3) stars in all the factors. Graphically it is less powerful then WOW, although the addition of reflective water and amazing skies in mid 2008 bring it one step closer to four stars. (Note: new Graphical Processor Units emerge from the likes of Nvidia and AMD-ATI, coupled with better 3D algorithms, we should expect the graphics to become better and better. The number of stars should be adjusted to relative market conditions).
- Activeworlds is a platform for worlds and not a special world. It supports 3D and some of the features needed for community, creation, and commerce. It is really for the world owner to make a decision as to how to use the various factors in their world.
- Sony Home for the Sony PlayStation 3 is a new addition to the realm of virtual worlds. While at this point we do not know how it will exactly behave, early demos present a superb graphics as well as ability to create items. I'm unclear about the ability to program objects and commerce. Note that if Sony Home turn into merely an arena to playing games (as some of the previews suggest) it will loose its ability to "play" in the area of virtual worlds.
- Google Earth is here because in theory it can become a virtual world or an infrastructure to build and run worlds. With Sketchup, Google's simple and free editing tool, one could create 3D objects easily. We are still missing structured community and commerce but 3rd party tools, as well as Google tools like "Open Social" (for community) or Checkout (for commerce) or may close that gap.

In this initial and cursory analysis, I have outlined some of the intended qualities of the 3D3C factors. The factors are designed to be *comparative* (how is the 3D of WOW compared to the one of IMVU), *relative* (IMVU did not have many social features when it started, as it developed it gained

Table 2. Different worlds viewed by the 3D3C prism

Sample Worlds	3D	Community	Creation	Commerce
1. WOW	*****	***	*	*
2. IMVU	***	***	**	***
3. Penguin	*	*	*	*
4. Second Life®	***	*****	*****	*****
5. ActiveWorlds	***	*	***	(per case)
6. Sony Home	*****	**?	**?	**?
7. Google Earth	***	*?	*** (Sketchup)	?

Key: "*" = Relative Low. "*****" = Relative High.

more stars), and *explorative* (Google Sketchup is an option for creation).

This analysis also reveals some of the limits of the 3D3C factors, as they do not fully uncover the intricate nature of field. We did not cover physics (yes for SL, no for Activeworlds); voice; real devices and so much more. The 3D3C definition is designed to be a top level starting point. As such, these factors alone are complex and deep as their nature often goes beyond their usual usage – and that is the focus on the next three sections that will cover Community, Creation and Commerce in greater length (assuming the 3D was well covered in the previous sections).

COMMUNITY IN DEPTH

We now turn into a deeper exploration of the 3Cs: *Community, Creation, and Commerce*. In fact, these three factors are integrated together in a tight manner. The value of Real Virtual Worlds will stem from this integration.

Background

Since the 1970s the term CMC (computer mediated communication or community) have been used sporadically (Harasim, 1989; Rice, 1992). While Rice (1992) says that "there is little theoretical or empirical research in this area" he, with others, published a few hundred papers about the topic.

Such pre-1995 research dealt mostly with text-based systems that were used by computer users. The "texiti-ness" and the "computer-ness" have changed dramatically with the emergence of the internet. As of 1996, with the rise of HTML, even novice users can use CMC with relatively easy-to-use Graphical User Interfaces (GUIs). (For a good summary of this age, see Rheingold, 2000)

The emergence of virtual worlds gave the term virtual community a completely new meaning. For the first time, you could DO things together (mostly fight monsters, but also fish and visit places). Community became a key factor in virtual worlds.

Then in 2003, My Space changed the picture of communities. MySpace re-created the landscape of virtual communities because it used new web technology (like DHTML and CSS) to support user-generated content (UGC). Other sites like LinkedIn and FaceBook re-packaged and enhanced the model. The Social web was re-born (yet another word for "community").

Yet, when we look at Real Virtual Worlds, and we take Second Life® as an example, we find many community structures and facets. Most users start as loners. Their anonymity detaches them from their usual friends, and allows them to roam the new world and to meet new aspects of community. Let us examine some of these aspects.

The Individual

In SL, the profile is the main communication instrument by which you greet new people and old friends from the past. It has a number of tabs.

The 2nd Life tab includes a picture, your SL date of birth and the groups you belong to (if you click on one of the groups you'll get its profile). Further information: whether or not the avatar has a Partner, and a general description area called About. You will notice that the SL profile is akin to the MySpace or FaceBook page.

Then you have the Web tab, with a reference to a detailed description (if you have a personal page or a site); the Interests tab, where the avatar describes its topics of interest and its aims; the Picks tab, displaying the places best liked; the Classified tab where notices may be posted (for a fee) and they will be entered into the world's built-in search engines. The next tab, the 1st Life tab, is the place for the avatar to describe its real life user. Many write in the style of "Keep SL and

Figure 3. Example of a Second Life® profile

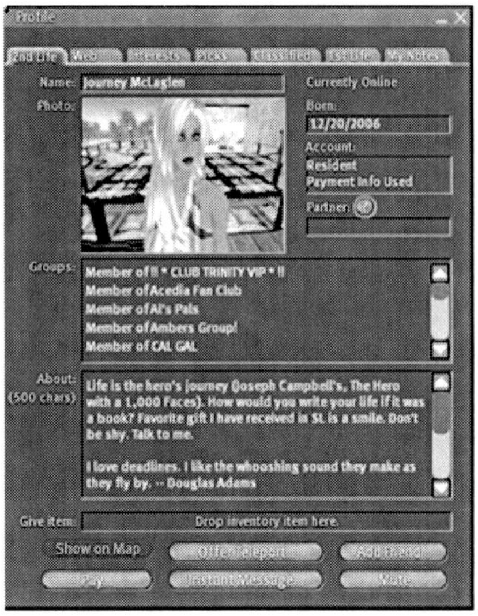

Figure 4. Roberto in his typical Gor outfit

RL separate" or "Only for Friends." Others spell out where they live, gender, age and additional basic details. Finally, there's the My Notes tab where you can record any comment such as when you met a certain avatar, what you know about her, what she thinks is important, etc. This tab is visible to the composer of the notes only – no other avatar may view it.

A common course for the individual usually is to emulate real life: renting a room, renting a house, building a house and furnishing it. During this time the character amasses assets, gains new friends, and learns the secrets of getting around in the new world. This could eventually lead to a mansion, a yacht or a plane all with just a few dollars. Anyone could become rich.

Another direction is role playing. Here, too, there are multiple opportunities. In the following exhibit, we see Roberto in the role of a typical Gor warrior. As such, he is part of a world taken out of the John Norman books. This is an entire culture with laws, costumes, and behavior patterns, akin in scope to the Hobbit civilization or the Star Wars saga.

Partnership and Family

The next social structure is the Partnership (in SL jargon). This feature supports a public declaration of relationship with a partner. Avatars (usually veterans) frequently join up as pairs. They live together, do things together - all very cozy. I once saw two avatars, both dressed in bunny outfits, lying embraced in a wooden hut. These two people were AWAY (meaning, not at their computers at the time), and a caption read: "We're so in love that we're always together here."

Virtual relations are not new. For example, "Love online: Emotions on the Internet" is a 352-page book and one of the important academic works on the subject (Ben-Zeev, 2004). Its author, the current President of the University of Haifa in Israel, provides a good starting point for the understanding of the basic concepts of **love** on the Internet. He proposes a number of ways to distinguish between various types of relationships in the Internet. In particular, there is a distinction between net-sex and net-romance. Net-sex concerns sex taking place between two people in different locations, and net-romance deals with romantic relationships between two people. Of course, there are variations and combinations of sex and romance, a flirt and a fling, remote sex and visual sex, with one partner or two – the only limit is imagination.

Another enhancement, which could be even more far reaching, is the Family. People may create their own virtual families. Not only mom, dad and kids, but also grandparents, cousins, neighbors, etc. Some detailed family descriptions are hilarious. By the way, due to the name-allocation methods of Second Life®, family members usually have different surnames – quite an amusing situation.

Groups

The social dimension now extends to the **Group**. There are various thematic groups and communities. For example, the Fur culture is a large and amazing culture; it flourishes in and outside SL. The Fur people have their own locations where they spend their leisure time, party, live or just meet with other Fur people. Their outfits, which are of the most elaborate in Second Life®, include ears, tails, whiskers, and other essentials for Fur people.

A group could include thousands of members or just few. They could all share a life-style and an economical infrastructure. Linden has made great investments in group-managing tools, and they allow role creations, permissions and various other features within the group. Groups may purchase real estate with common funding. There are thousands of groups in SL, at various stages of maturity. In fact, anyone can create a group for L$100 - such as the "Yesha's Friends" group. Most groups are used for messages and communication. Thus, I could notify all my friends in my group of an event.

One interesting example to a community is a group called LifeChurch. LifeChurch is the virtual group of one of the modern USA churches. The real LifeChurch is centered in Oklahoma and is led by a charismatic priest. It has about ten branches all over the USA and in all of them sermons are screened alongside a rock group. They definitely speak the language of today's youngsters.

The church decided to open another branch this time in Second Life®. They employed the services of a Anshe Chung Studio build a full-size church, with video screens, stages and lighting. The following pictures were taken at a sermon I attended. The sermon was named "Experience," and indeed, that's what it was. Please pay attention to one of the participants at the sermon – in particular, her shirt exhibits a novel way to worship the Lord.

Another community activity, more of an ad-hoc nature, occurred in 2007 Holocaust Memorial Day. A virtual ceremony was led by a young American named Carter Giacobini. It included the lighting of memorial candles and the reading

Figure 5. The world of the Fur group

Figure 6. A Religious experience in the virtual world

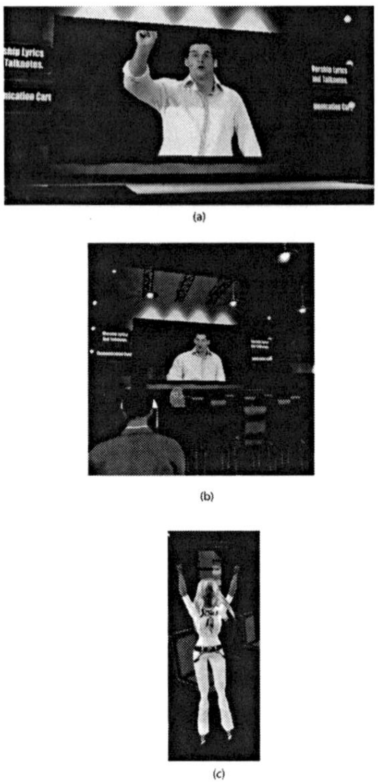

of the Kaddish in Hebrew and in English. The ceremony lasted for about a quarter of an hour and was one of the most moving I had ever attended. People from all over the world assembled for a unifying event together. The ceremony was repeated several times that day for the benefit of users worldwide in various time zones. Please note the text in the pictures.

The last two examples demonstrate cross-global communities. These ceremonies became meaningful because of their linkage to the real world. For the participating avatars this is a singular medium for their respective spiritual experience.

Conclusion

The word "community" means different things to different communities. We have only touched about the main features of the term when it comes to virtual community. We did not cover crime, law, avatar rights, griefing and many more aspects of communities in Real Virtual Worlds. Much of what we know regarding internet-based communities (from the early mailing lists, to the latest 2008 FaceBook craze) is exacerbated in virtual worlds.

What is interesting about Real Virtual Worlds is the ability to define the different terms of the community in a technical manner. For example, "leadership" has concrete set of permissions. A leader can also appoint sub-leaders and give them certain permissions. In that sense, Second Life® has a done a good job in defining a set of tools to define permissions. While more can and should be done to further facilitate communities, already SL's pre-defined "switches" allow community leaders to shape and build their communities. Of course, the Community takes a new level of meaning when you add the Creation factor.

CREATION IN DEPTH

Background

The Sims (2000) focuses on the lives of virtual people called Sims, placing the player in control of their virtual "world" and their daily activities, such as sleeping, eating, reading, and bathing. Will Wright, the game's designer, calls it a "digital dollhouse." Many choices lead a player's sim to a large family or a lonely life.

Sims was the first game that enabled and encouraged users to build their own content (still for themselves with no multi-user effect). An earlier version of creation in games allowed users to design their own levels.

But the dawn of web 2.0 and user generated content really expose the various motivations for creation. What lead people to edit Wikipedia, to write Amazon comments on books, and to publish videos in YouTube? Can we harness this energy of creation? A platform that enables and facilitates

Figure 7. Holocaust day ceremony in the virtual world

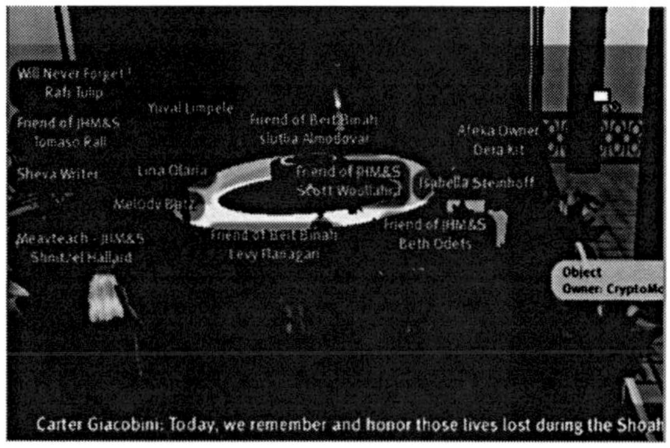

(a)

(b)

individual and communal creation is destined to blossom. Let's examine some of the facets of creation in virtual worlds.

My Avatar

The word Avatar originated in Hindu philosophy. It means incarnation on a different level. In the Real Virtual Worlds, the avatar becomes the visual representation of the user or player.

In SL, the avatar has a face, body, limbs, etc. Many of the body parts may be modified by changing their size, shape and color. You can also add on various accessories such as jewelry. Here Journey models as an avatar. Note her flowing hair, her dark skin, her blue eyes, the lace blouse, the sparkling necklace, the spectacles and the earrings.

Any relationship with an avatar begins with the outward image followed by the profile. The avatar is the first place of creation when you can modify your looks in various ways. As you advance in your skills, you will further shape your avatar using skins, clothing and accessories – you will enjoy the fruits of the SL fashion industry.

Objects

The object is a three-dimensional shape: cube, tetrahedron, cone, sphere, etc. Complex objects are those containing holes or predefined shapes (for instance, shrubbery or trees). The objects have properties such as position, color and. An object with "Texture=Wood" could look like a block of wood. An object with the property "Z=1" would

Figure 8. Journey models an avatar

be positioned a meter above the ground. An object with the property "Behavior=Physical" would follow gravitational laws.

The entire world of SL is built up from these primary objects, or, as they're called in Second Life® jargon, the Primitives (or Prims, for short). Furthermore, objects may be merged and joined. For example, a simple car may be assembled from ten objects: body, four wheels, four yellow lights and a windshield. A more complex car would have dozens of component objects.

In addition to properties such as position and appearance there are properties such as **Lock**: can the object be easily shifted or modified (similar

Figure 9. Simple and complex objects in Second Life®

(a)

(b)

to file locking), **Physical**: does the object obey the laws of physics – like falling, being pushed, etc., as opposed to being immovable in space, **Phantom**: the object does not occupy physical space in the world so people and objects can pass through it. Phantom objects are usually used for curtains, swimming pools and lighting in clubs.

From the visibility point of view an object may possess properties such as Shininess, Color, Hollow and Transparency. We also find Flexible objects, which give the sense of realism to hair, curtains, armchairs, or a scarf and other clothing. It should be noted that flexibility is processed on your personal computer and is not dependent on the servers and, therefore, does not degrade performance. The type of Material determines the sound made by the object when it collides with another (wood, metal, glass, etc.)

Figure 10. A Simple car with 10 objects

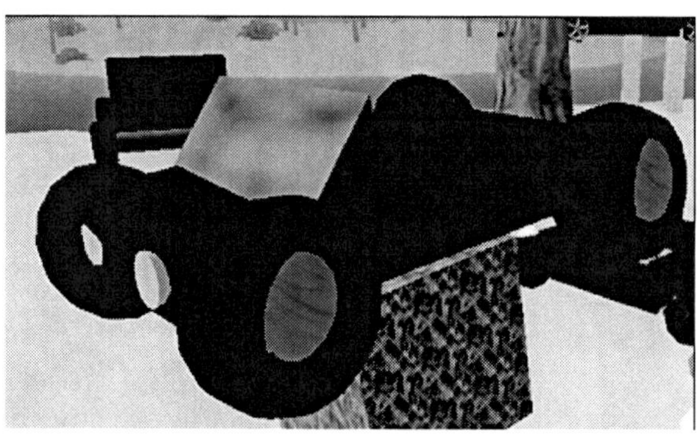

Figure 11. A Complex car (Ferrari) with 30 objects

One of the unique properties of objects in SL is that they are programmable. A special programming language LSL (Linden Script Language) allows the objects to act and activate. Thus, planes fly, cars go, doors open, wheels revolve, robots walk, trees grow, etc. Programming is not for intended for every user, but it is a vital component for the experts to create unique products, services, and environments.

In the example above the object will say "Hello, Avatar!" when it (the object) is activated. When touched, it will say: "Touched." More complex scripts could run into tens and hundreds of lines and could handle characteristics of the object such as changing its shape, moving it, rotating it, or making it a component of a larger object, etc. Naturally, when you can create scripts (which are actually pieces of code) you permit the creation of bugs, viruses and other glitches common to computer environments.

To sum up, the objects in Second Life® are the atoms of which this world is made. The integration of physical and shape properties, together with the capability of programming, result in almost unlimited flexibility. Add to that intellectual ownership and creator's rights, and we get a full and fertile infrastructure for commerce and social activities.

Land

Just as in real life, land is the basis for all activities in SL. Linden elected to use land as the focus of their business model. Each and every room, apartment, club, mall, factory, gallery or any other type of edifice anywhere in the virtual world must be located on a given piece of land. This is one choice, other Real Virtual Worlds may choose

Figure 12. An example of simple Linden Script Language (LSL)

```
default
{
    state_entry()
    {
        llSay(0, "Hello, Avatar!");
    }

    touch_start(integer total_number)
    {
        llSay(0, "Touched.");
    }
}
```

a different model. In the current architecture, it makes sense to charge for land since land is translated directly into a computer that needs to have resources (electricity, network, maintenance, etc).

In SL, The basic unit of land is called a SIM (short for Simulator). Every SIM is a square of 256 by 256 meters, or 65,536 square meters. Each SIM is managed by a computer with one CPU (actually, there are cases wherein a computer with several processors could manage multiple SIMS but we won't go into these technical details here). It is important, however, to note that each SIM contains all the land attributes and data, the buildings, roads, cars, etc. When the avatar is on the SIM all these elements are activated by the simulator.

In this next exhibit (upper left) nine SIMs are displayed. The blue house indicates where my own house is located. The yellow dot is the representation of the current location of the avatar.

There are two types of land – land on the main continent (Mainland) and private land. The Mainland is managed by Linden that sells off small parcels. Private land is managed by private entities who may own just one island (a single SIM) or tens or hundreds of islands (like the area owned by Anshe Chung). Cities may be built along a specific theme – most of our real cities are represented in SL (recently, Amsterdam was sold for US$50,000). Location *does* have some importance, especially when you are trying to attract user traffic, but due to the fact that getting from one place to another is very rapid (teleporting) location is not that critical. By the way – if you're interested in purchasing your own island you'll need to shell out about US$1,000 (prices dropped in April 2008 and created a minor turmoil in the real estate business in SL) and an additional US$300 per month for storage on the servers.

Land is defined not only by its physical shape, size and location, but also by the rights it possesses and the attributes associated with it. You can look up the land attributes under World → About Land. Several tabs allow you define the properties of the entire region. The General tab contains the name and description of the land, as well as the

Figure 13. Various land representations (global map, local map, and actual)

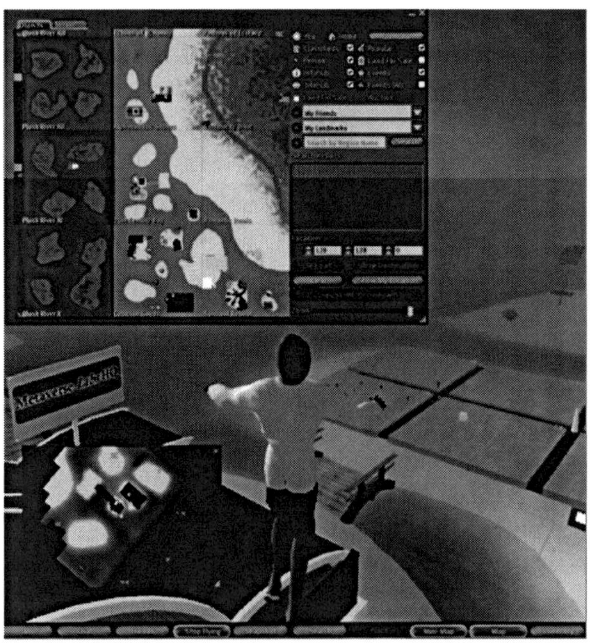

owner and group rights in the area. Here, too, is the place where you prepare the land for sale and determine its price.

The Covenant tab defines the basic rules of the area. The owner of the SIM usually writes it. The covenant could define, for example, that no high-rise building will be permitted on the land or that only family-style homes are allowed, etc. Here the landowner defines what a good neighbor really means. Some areas have empty covenants, with nothing defined – these regions typically become islands of chaos, unruliness and a motley of building styles. On the other hand, areas may be defined as have no commerce on them at all. These are usually intended for private homes. Perhaps this is the time to clarify that dedicated residents invest a great deal in their homes. This is one of the most popular pastimes players. The covenant permits – in a typical Linden fashion – inherited definitions. The continent owner defines the continent's attributes. The SIMS (the actual islands) inherits these attributes as their own rules. These, in turn, are passed on to the land lots. Some of these rules are enforced by technological means (i.e., who may enter the area). Others require human management – supervisors could, for example, measure the heights of buildings or the usage of advertising billboards, which are prohibited in residential areas.

Editing

Linden has faith in the citizens of the SL world. They see themselves as providers of an infrastructure that permits residents to build, live and experience the world. Many objects may be created, from the very simple to the very complex from a chair or a bed to a plane, a watch or a magic carpet that brings you to 15 different places.

I distinguish between two levels of editing:

- **Arranging:** which is mainly positioning, relocating and organizing.

Figure 14. About land main features

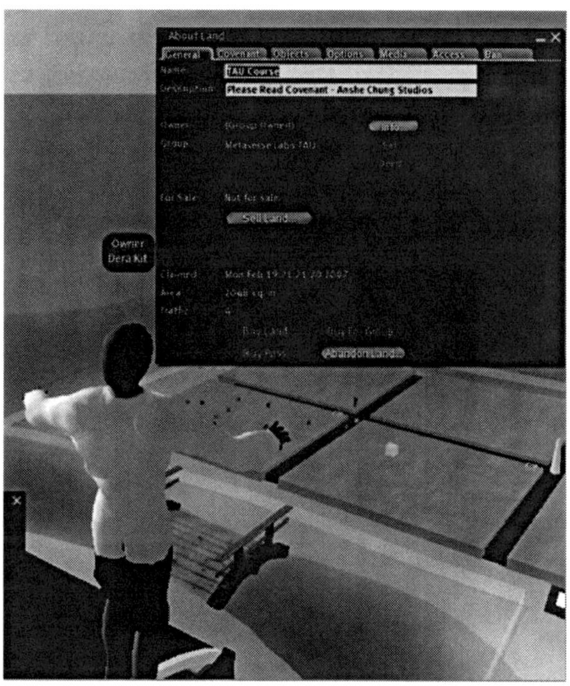

- **Making**: which is mainly the building of new objects, combining them, adding textures, sounds, integrating objects and composing blocks of code.

The next example shows a line of domino tiles. A panel appears with several functional options. You can Move, Rotate or Stretch the tile. If the owner of the item has permitted it, additional functions will be available and you may change the Texture, Unlink, set a price, etc. If you wish to advance from simple arranging (such as shifting furniture around the house or organizing the pool) to complex and flexible making you'll need several hours to get acquainted with the various options.

Conclusion

The Creation factor of the 3D3C is a combination in the middle between the forces of Wikipedia, YouTube and FaceBook, and the forces of the Open Source movement of Linux, Firefox, and MySQL. I claim that the unified nature of 3D3C Real Virtual Worlds has tremendous wealth. (For an initial discussion on the field see for example, Benkler, 2006).

Creation is the human trait that drives many of us individually, and more importantly advance us as small and global groups. 3D3C Real Virtual Worlds offer creators a space that include managed audience (community) as well as optional monetary pay.

COMMERCE IN DEPTH

Background

Amazon was the first player that convinced us that it is OK to buy on-line. It is ok to give some website our credit card number and "hope" to get the book in a few days. Then, eBay convinced us to buy from different people, not only we are giving our credit card number over the net, we are giving it to someone based on how they were rated on a web page. Then, PayPal, allowed us to transfer money in the internet via every site.

While this is major progress it is still difficult today to start a web site that sell things. You have to connect with credit card companies or connect with larger shop makers, you have to develop a user authentication scheme and you have to develop a way to connect with your clients. Not a simple task. In contrast, for example, if you are an artist in SL that wants to sell paintings virtually, you assign a price and that is it. (If you want to also send your customers a real painting, you will need

Figure 15. Editing for everyone: editing, shifting, rotating and stretching

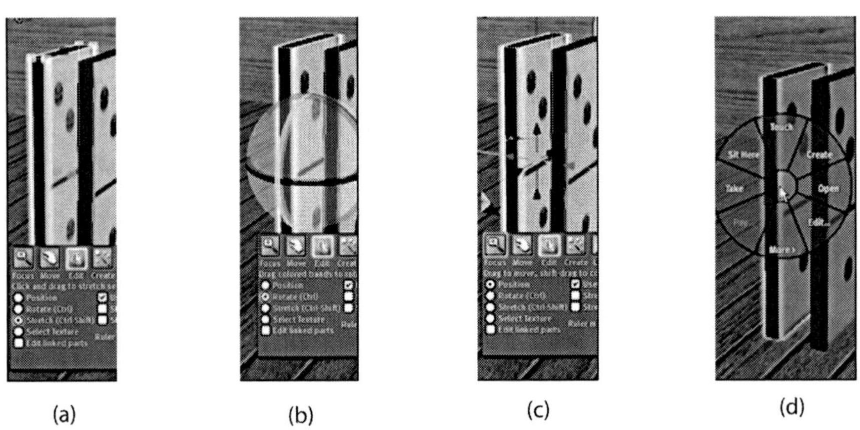

to get their address and ship them the item directly money can still be received via SL).

It is often hard to digest that "yes, people do pay for virtual shirts." A common response "do you mean to tell me people pay $2 for a shirt they will not own." In talks, I often have to repeat the fact that "yes, this is real money that you can buy milk with."

Real money in online games is not new. eBay allowed you to buy items in WOW, Ultima Online and other games (Dibbell, 2006, Castronova, 2005). What is unique is the embedded nature of commerce and the real/virtual exchange of L$ that is supported by Linden.

Linden Dollars

Many games, particularly role-playing games, have a monetary component. Money is the human standard for evaluating worth, for exchange for products and services, and for any economical transaction. Linden's innovation was the support for exchanging virtual money to real money, in addition to the common exchange of real to virtual money. Linden was one of the first companies that authorized people to sell the virtual money for real money, officially and legally.

The SL local currency is called the Linden Dollar (or L$ for short). At the top right of the panel we can see how much money we have available. In this case we have L$1,811. The adjacent button has the logo "L$" on it. Clicking this button will bring up the panel for acquiring L$ cash.

We enter in the amount of Linden Dollars we require and we get it on the spot (and naturally, our payment method to the Linden company is duly charged). That's it easy, simple, and immediate. Henceforth, we may use this cash to buy products (such as attire, body parts, cars, land) or services (such as entrance to a club, builders costs or dancers fees). Commerce with the Linden Dollar at its core is integrated into the basic operation of Second Life®. You can pay any avatar by clicking on it and clicking the "Pay" button. Or you could buy any product by using the "Buy" function.

Every object in SL is owned by someone. The Owner has some rights to the object, but not all. Every object also has a Creator who is fixed and immutable. A part of SL's philosophy is the recognition of the rights of the contents creators. The creator and the owner may decide whether a certain object may have the properties of Modify, Copy or Transfer, which allow other users to change, duplicate or pass the object to others.

Figure 16. Cash acquiring panel

Moreover, every object has a Price, which is an integral property determined by its owner. Please note: as this is a virtual world an object may be copied numerous times, thereby proliferating objects (such as trees, cars, houses, etc.).

The sales mechanism is integrated within the object. For example, let us assume that I have created a red car, priced it at L$100, and positioned it on the ground. Anyone who sees it may buy it by clicking a button. Actually, he'd be buying a copy of the car. If I, as the creator of the car, had enabled the appropriate properties, the buyer could subsequently sell it or change it color. Perhaps I'd give him the permission to change the price. On the other, if I did not give him the permission to transfer it, he could never transfer the ownership of the car to anyone else. Please note that the right to copy is not the same as the right to transfer. Copying means creating duplicates for self usage and not for transfer. Transferring refers to the changing of ownership of objects.

Services

If you wish to make money in virtual worlds be prepared to invest time, money, and a lot of thinking and energy. Today only a few actually make money in SL. Very few. But many make the attempt – they open a club or a shop and try their luck. But only a few persevere, and find a stable business niche that provides a steady income. In fact, there are two ways to make money: *inside the world* and *outside of it.*

Outside the world you can profit from providing services to those who would like to learn, use, experiment, and just experience. There are a number of companies who provide consultation, construction and other services such as Electric Sheep, Anshe Chung, Millions Of Us, Virtual Italian Parks, and Rivers Run Red. This is a burgeoning area which will grow even more with the development of virtual worlds – but we shall not cover this issue here.

Inside the world are a number of different business types, each requiring its own level of investment in terms of time and money.

Camping – you may actually can make money in SL by doing nothing. Some places pay just to have a character in the world. In general, this is called "camping." It began with special chairs that paid avatars just for sitting in them. These chairs create green dots on the map, which attracts other avatars looking for people (often called "replacing expensive electricity for cheap lindens").

There are many camping stations today in the form of street cleaners, window cleaners and guards. You can usually see the paying price of a chair in the title in the case above: L$4 for every 12 minutes.

Escorts a popular "occupation" in SL. Many women (and men) try out the oldest profession in the world. Ms. Sireen Toll works for two to three hours a day, and earns only US$10 (including tips). When she was interviewed, she said: "It's nice I like to help others. Besides, I welcome the break from being an Australian 19-year-old first year law student. LOL. [Laughing Out Laud] With what I save, I hope to open a clothing shop. I work at the Sins Club."

The process is usually simple: you post an advertisement on the notice board, you rendezvous at the club, you present your escort card with the price per unit of time, various activities, preferences and limits – and off to work. There is an entire industry dealing in brokerage, accessories, and interest groups that form a robust community regarding this topic. Having said that, it must be remembered that after two or three weeks, escorting becomes somewhat boring, and many drop out in favor of other activities.

Host, dancer, guard, companion, etc. are other kinds of occupations. All of them require the character to invest time and be paid by the hour – including hosts at a club, restaurant, counselors, dancers (not too complex), guards (requires equipment such as a gun), companions and Personal Shoppers (who assist advanced avatars with their shopping). These jobs also involve being nice to customers, but there is no sexual aspect (which is characteristic of the escorting profession). Salaries are a few tens of Linden Dollars an hour.

Owning a shop, club or recreation place – avatars in Second Life® love to buy and have a good time. There is an abundance of malls and shops selling clothes, hair, furniture, clocks, robots, diving equipment, etc. If you wish to own a shop you'll need products, and you'll need to make contact with the producers in order to sell the goods. Another option is opening a club. Here you'll need to invest more in the place, equipment and supplies, dances, hiring staff (hosts, dancers) and DJs. Clubs pop up and disappear all the time. Managing a successful club is quite a complicated and demanding job, and most clubs do not make a profit.

Products

Product developers there is a large demand for products in SL as many users spend their time buying, visiting malls, etc. You can manufacture cars, games, houses, furniture, clothes, clocks, sleds, hovercrafts, flowers, dances, expressions, television in fact, if you can imagine it you can create it.

Figure 17. A paying chair

Maya Hofner is a full time fashion designer in SL. She quit her job as a graphics team leader at an advertising company, for a virtual occupation under the name of Canimal Zephyr. Her creations for women (and for men) are considered highly prestigious in SL. She owns an island where she sells her products from her own shop. One fashion critic says "I don't like begging… but please, Canimal… give us more and more."

Real estate brokers – buying, developing, leasing, and selling land is a profitable business, albeit somewhat intricate. Land areas acquired from Linden are empty and arid. The new owners redesign them, parcel them into lots, erect houses and then sell or lease them. Leasing houses and residential areas is lucrative – but it demands constant handling and a critical mass. In addition, there is a lot of competition.

Conclusion

To sum up, there is a certain aura regarding "SL work" and making money in the new world. Many

Figure 18. Ms. Sireen Toll in her place of work

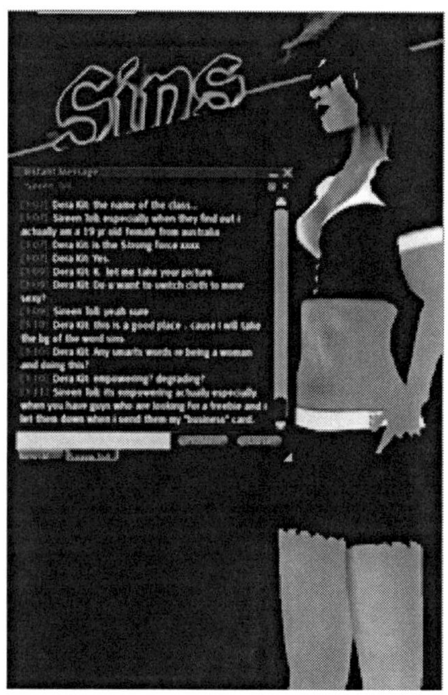

Figure 19. Maya's Canimal shop

recommend (as do I): at start it is better to work in the real world. In the virtual world it's far more fun to water-ski, dance in a club, scuba dive, or listen to a concert rather than taking care of customer service, handling Griefers, paying for the land, etc. Just whip out your credit card, invest a few tens of dollars, and have a good time.

Yet the inclusion of commerce into the fabric of the world, together with the realistic look of 3D, the access to the managed community, will drive creation. The four factors reinforce themselves and create a closed sustained loop of innovation.

CONCLUSION: TOWARDS REAL VIRTUAL WORLDS

In the first part of this work, we have exposed the parents of Real Virtual Worlds "virtual reality and "gaming worlds". In the second part, we defined Real Virtual Worlds, using the Second Life® example, a formal definition of 3D3C, and a sample comparative analysis of different worlds. Then the next three parts, I delved into a deeper discussion regarding the different aspect of Community, Creation, and Commerce.

I chose to conclude this work depicting the driving forces that will continue to push virtual world forward, and the special role of Commerce in this forces.

Figure 20. Supply, demand and sustained innovation for Real Virtual Worlds

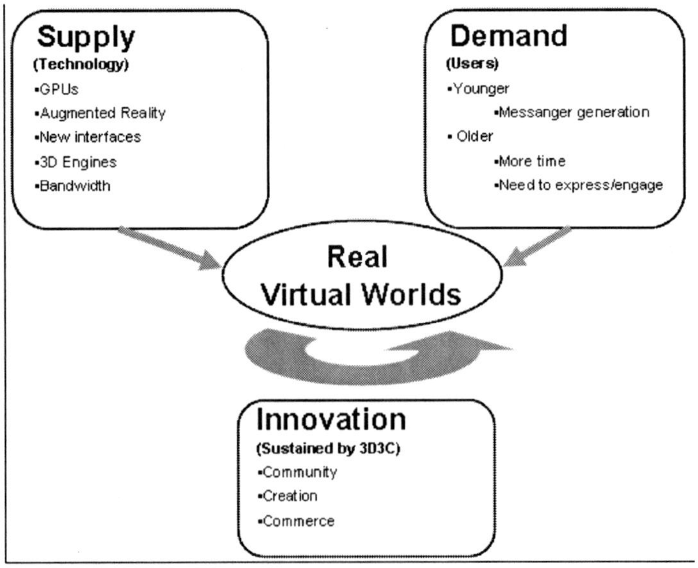

Real Virtual Worlds enjoy both a healthy *supply* and a growing *demand.* The supply side stems from a more affordable and powerful technology. New advances in Graphics Processor Units (GPUs) coupled with new interfaces like the Nintendo Wii, 3D engines like Havok Physics, and abundant bandwidth are bringing Real Virtual Worlds closer to the personal and enterprise user. At the same time, the demand is growing from both the young and the old. On one hand, we have a younger, messenger crazed users, that crave the interaction and on the other hand perhaps more importantly we have the older folks that have more time, more money and a need to express themselves.

I am the first to note that we have not yet crossed the infliction point when it comes to supply and demand of virtual worlds. Apparently, we do not have enough supply and demand to move virtual worlds forward in a rapid pace. We still lack bandwidth, 3D server power, client speed, and user awareness. But we are making solid progress in the last 3 years, and I'm positive we will reach the infliction point. Then, I claim, we will see rapid growth.

I claim that the long lasting booster of Real Virtual Worlds is the combination of 3D, Community, Creation and Commerce. When combined into one system these factors create something that is bigger than the simple addition of 3D3C. The immersion of the 3D world, the engagement of the community, the ability to express, and innovate that stem from creation and most critically the ability to gain from it economically (read: money) is what will propel Real Virtual Worlds.

Within the 3D3C factors, the importance of commence, commercial principles and commercial infrastructure to virtual worlds is immense. In many ways, with the Internet, we have failed to build a universal platform for commerce. While individual sites and solutions do allow commerce (Amazon, eBay, PayPal, and numerous other systems and tools), overall commerce is relatively complicated (compared starting to see vs. loading a video to YouTube). In the internet, Commerce was an afterthought, an added layer to a very technical apparently good internet design. In virtual worlds, we have the chance to embed commerce into the system.

With commerce built into real virtual worlds, we will enjoy a constant stream of creations, services, and products. Things like art, medicine, learning, and shopping will be enhance by virtual galleries, home treatment clinics, learning kiosks and family owned stores. Going full circle, I believe the positive impact on our lives, the enablement of creation and value that allow people to make a living using their creations will ultimately enhance the sense of community we all need.

REFERENCES

Active Worlds. (2008). *Active Worlds*. Retrieved June 8, 2008, from http://www.activeworlds.com/

Alexander, R. (2003). *Massively Multiplayer Game Development*. Hingham, MA: Charles River Media, Inc.

Amazon (2009). *mturk*. Retrieved September 21, 2009, from https://www.mturk.com/mturk/welcome

Avatar. (2008). In *Wikipedia, The Free Encyclopedia*. Retrieved June 6, 2008, from http://en.wikipedia.org/w/index.php?title=Avatar&oldid=216339962

Bartle, A. R. (2004). *Designing Virtual Worlds*. Berkeley, CA: New Riders Publishing.

Ben-Zeev, A. (2004). *Love Online: emotions on the internet*. Cambridge, UK: Cambridge University Press. doi:10.1017/CBO9780511489785

Benkler, Y. (2006). *The wealth of networks: How social production transforms markets and freedom*. New Haven: Yale University Press.

Bimber, O., & Raskar, R. (2005). *Spatial augmented reality: Merging real and virtual worlds*. Wellesley, MA: AK Peters.

Bloomfield (Ed.) (2007). *Metanomics*. Retrieved 17:49, June 8, 2008, from http://www.dryesha.com/2007/12/video-of-3d3c-metaverse-metanomics-talk.html and http://www.metanomics.net/

Brainyquote (2009). *Brainyquote*. Retrieved 14:52, December 05, 2009, from http://www.brainyquote.com/quotes/keywords/commerce.html

Burdea, G. C., & Coiffet, P. (2003). *Virtual reality technology*. Hoboken, NJ: John Wiley & Sons.

Castronova, E. (2005). *Synthetic worlds: The business and culture of online game*. Chicago: University of Chicago Press.

Clubpenguin (2008). *Clubpenguin*. Retrieved 17:49, June 8, 2008, from http://corporate.disney.go.com/news/corporate/2007/2007_0801_clubpenguin.html and http://venturebeat.com/2007/08/01/disney-buys-club-penguin-in-700-million-deal/

Dibbell, J. (2006). *Play money: or, How I quit my day job and made millions trading virtual loot*. New York: Basic Books.

Fawcett, B. (Ed.). (2006). *The battle for Azeroth: Adventure, alliance and addiction: insights into the World of Warcraft*. Dallas, TX: BenBella Books, Inc.: Distributed by Independent Publishers Group.

Fur Culture. (2008). *Fur Culture*. Retrieved June 8, 2008, from http://furry.wikia.com

Gos. (2008, April 13). In *Wikipedia, The Free Encyclopedia*. Retrieved June 6, 2008, from http://en.wikipedia.org/w/index.php?title=Gur&oldid=205242560

Harasim, L. (1989). On-line education: A new domain. In Mason, R., & Kaye, A. (Eds.), *Mindweave: Communication, Computers and Distance Education* (pp. 50–62). Oxford, UK: Pergamon Press.

IMVU. (2008). *IMVU*. Retrieved 17:49, June 8, 2008, from http://imvu.anshechung.com/index.php

Inflection Point. (2009). *In Wikipedia, The Free Encyclopedia*. Retrieved 07:03, September 1, 2009, from http://en.wikipedia.org/w/index.php?title=Inflection_point&oldid=311230495

Level design. (2008). In *Wikipedia, The Free Encyclopedia*. Retrieved June 9, 2008, from http://en.wikipedia.org/w/index.php?title=Level_design&oldid=209252053

Morningstar, C., & Farmer, F. R. (1991). The Lessons of Lucasfilm's Habitat. In Benedikt (Ed.), *Cyberspace: First Steps*. Cambridge, MA: MIT Press. (also Retrieved June 9, 200 from http://www.fudco.com/chip/lessons.html

Power Level. (2008). Retrieved June 8, 2008, from http://www.power-level.net/

Reuters, E. (reporter) (2007). *Second Life*. Retrieved June 8, 2008, from http://secondlife.reuters.com/stories/2007/03/27/amsterdam-sold-for-us50000/

Rheingold, H. (2000). *The virtual community: Homesteading on the electronic frontier.* Cambridge, MA: MIT Press (Earlier version of this book appeared in 1993, and 1994).

Rice, R. E. (1992). Contexts of research on organizational computer-mediated communication: a recursive review. In Lea, M. (Ed.), *Contexts of computer-mediated communication* (pp. 113–144). New York: Harvester Wheatsheaf.

Sensorama. (2008, February 26). In *Wikipedia, The Free Encyclopedia*. Retrieved June 6, 2008, from http://en.wikipedia.org/w/index.php?title=Sensorama&oldid=194083017

Sivan, Y. (2008). The 3D3C Metaverse: A new medium is born. In Samuel-Asran, T., & Caspi, D. (Eds.), *New Media and Innovative Technology* (pp. 133–159). Beer-Sheva, Israel: Ben-Gurion University Press.

Sivan, Y. (2008). 3D3C real virtual worlds defined: The immense potential of merging 3D, community, creation, and commerce. *Journal of Virtual Worlds Research*, *1*(1).

Sivan, Y. (2009). Identity 3D3C: Confronting the Security and Privacy Challenges in virtual Worlds. *Cutter IT journal, 22*(4), 35-42.

Snow Crash. (2007). *In Wikipedia, The Free Encyclopedia*. Retrieved February 23, 2007, from http://en.wikipedia.org/w/index.php?title=Snow_Crash&oldid=108444297

Stephen, T. (2008). *'Grand Theft Auto IV' posts record first-week sales*. Retrieved June 8, 2008 from http://www.mtv.com/news/articles/1586971/20080507/id_0.jhtml

Susan Vega Second Life® Show (2006). *The making of.* Retrieved June 8, 2008, from http://www.youtube.com/watch?v=bQL8_HB1HtQ

Taylor, T. L. (2006). *Play between worlds: Exploring online game culture*. Cambridge, MA: MIT Press.

The Sims. (2008). In *Wikipedia, The Free Encyclopedia*. Retrieved June 7, 2008, from http://en.wikipedia.org/w/index.php?title=The_Sims&oldid=217644539

Virtualeconomies (2007). *Virtualeconomies.* Retrieved June 8, 2008, from http://www.virtualeconomies.net/2007/01/23/50-of-wow-users-bought-crusade-in-first-24-hours/

Chapter 3
From E-Commerce to V-Commerce

Susan Jones
Ferris State University, USA

ABSTRACT

This introductory chapter provides an overview of e-commerce marketing focused on history, trends and future predictions for the field leading into the development and application of virtual worlds and v-commerce. It begins with a discussion of the transition from Web 1.0 to Web 2.0 and Web 3.0. Next is a survey of developments in marketing convergence, as businesses integrate their customer-centric online/offline marketing efforts and databases. The chapter continues with an overview of business-to-business Internet marketing, including the profit strategies businesses employ in the online world. A commentary on the evolution of browsers, portals and search engines is followed by a discussion of social networking's movement toward a money-making model. To set the stage for the chapters to come, the piece concludes with a preview of what is on the horizon for "v-commerce" – with opportunities and applications that are capturing the imagination of consumers and marketers alike.

INTRODUCTION AND BACKGROUND

In the mid-1990s, novice visitors to the World Wide Web were excited at the opportunity to visit simple sites with intuitive URLs and colorful pictures. Compared to their experience with the text-only Internet, this vibrant new Web offered more opportunities than many had ever dreamed possible. Dialing up on a regular phone line, using their newly acquired 28.8K or 56K modems, Web users waited patiently for pages to load and could only imagine being able to watching short videos let alone see entire movies or participate in 3D interactive adventures on their trusty computers.

Back then, e-commerce enhancements were sorely limited by what the average well-heeled online consumer could view in a timely manner. Many Web sites were little more than Internet brochures with a rudimentary web response form for lead generation. This was Web 1.0 a mere

DOI: 10.4018/978-1-61692-808-7.ch003

conduit for text and images with "static sites, and initial efforts at dynamic content and interactivity" (Hoffman, 2008).

In little more than 10 years' time, the average American web surfer advanced from a dial-up modem to a broadband connection obtained through the phone company or local cable television provider. According to an April 2009 survey, even amid a severe recession and rising costs for Internet access, 63% of adult Americans had broadband Internet connections at home, representing a 15% increase over April 2008 (Horrigan, 2009).

Broadband patrons reveled in their newfound ability to view real-time video, and to download and use robust software applications. Meanwhile, firms were developing increasingly sophisticated databases that allowed them to fulfill the long-awaited promise of true one-to-one marketing. Many of these same companies focused their attention on integrating their traditional offline efforts with their online e-commerce and customer service functions. The business-to-business e-commerce marketing model evolved right along with the consumer model, and indeed firms selling B2B far outstripped consumer marketing in terms of sales volume, even while investing about half as much in online and offline promotions (Jones, Creative Strategy in Direct and Interactive Marketing, 2006).

While AOL made an initial splash as the lead partner in the AOL/Time-Warner merger in early 2000, it soon found its relevancy as an Internet service provider (ISP) challenged by broadband ISPs and sophisticated browsers such as Internet Explorer and Mozilla Firefox, not to mention big-money portal/search engines like Yahoo and Google. Burgeoning social networks including MySpace, Facebook, and LinkedIn amassed audiences in the millions yet struggled to match Yahoo and Google in terms of "monetization," or profit potential.

All of these developments took place in conjunction with the unfolding and maturation of Web 2.0. This is Web as operating system, in which "the Web facilitates sharing and participation with a seamless connection of applications" such geographic mapping and photo-sharing (Hoffman, 2008). In Web 2.0, individuals take charge of their Web experience by doing "mash-ups" that combine text, graphics, audio, video and animation from various sources. They might then post the results on YouTube, which allows most anyone with a Web connection, some creativity, and some time to become a published video maker.

Against the backdrop of Web 2.0 and with the promise of the artificial intelligence of Web 3.0 on the horizon marketers took their first toe dips into "personal virtuality" and online virtual commerce and gaming. Here are some examples.

- Lands' End (http://www.landsend.com) invites customers to enter their own virtual dressing room by creating a model of their exact height, weight, build, skin/eye/hair color, face shape, eye shape, and nuances of fit. Then patrons can try on clothing items to see how they will look before ordering. Lands' End is one of a number of e-commerce marketers using My Virtual Model™ for this application.
- Jellyvision (http://www.jellyvision.com), creator of "You Don't Know Jack" and the "Who Wants to be a Millionaire" home game, provides e-commerce marketing firms with what Jellyvision calls "interactive conversations" that seem as customized and personal as a chat with a live person. As their web site explains, " Because of the massive branching structure of an Interactive Conversation, you are able to instantly engage every visitor to your site with a unique experience that is tailor-made to their individual wants, needs and desires. This visitor-specific content focuses in on exactly what it is they are seeking, and dynamically charts the most relevant path for them, toward your ultimate goal of conversion." Jellyvision clients have in-

cluded Netflix, Disney Interactive, BMW, Microsoft, Oracle, and many others.

- In February 2007, the social media site Facebook (http://www.facebook.com) started embedding the e-commerce feature of virtual gifts. The manager for the virtual gifts product, Jared Morgenstern, blogged on February 8, 2007 to announce the new product and to suggest that Facebook users give their friends charity-related virtual gifts, or purchase a series of presents that become more meaningful in sequence. For an irreverent example, he showed a bare-bottomed troll doll gift followed by a toilet paper gift, and then a bar of soap (Morgenstern, 2007). Then as now, most gifts on Facebook cost $1.00, and could be paid for by purchasing "gift credits" by credit card.
- Zynga (http://www.zynga.com) allows Facebook and MySpace members to play social games ranging from Texas Hold 'Em to Fashion Wars to FarmVille. With 16 million daily users and 60 million monthly users as of July 2009 (O'Neill, 2009), Zynga reigns as the number-one social gaming site on the web. Zynga reportedly had revenues of $50 million in 2008 through the sales of virtual goods and "game add-ons." (Carlson, 2009).

Meanwhile, entire virtual worlds such as Cybertown (launched 1995), Second Life® (launched 2003), and There (launched 2003) started surfacing and taking advantage of broadband connection, instant personalization features, and increasing success with the appearance of 3D virtuality.

While the promise of true artificial intelligence (Web 3.0) is still on the horizon for most applications, advancements in e-commerce marketing, database management, gaming technology and 3D imagery are paving the way for the maturation of virtual worlds as platforms for consumer engagement and profitable e-commerce.

This chapter will:

- Chart the evolution of Web 1.0 to 2.0 and 3.0 and explain the significance of these advancements as they relate to e-commerce and virtual worlds
- Survey the developments in marketing convergence, as businesses integrate their customer-centric online and offline marketing efforts and databases.
- Offer an overview of business-to-business Internet marketing, including the profit strategies businesses employ in the online world.
- Comment on the evolution of browsers, portals and search engines and discuss social networking's movement from a focus on sheer numbers toward a money-making model.
- Set the stage for the chapters to come with a preview of what is on the horizon for "v-commerce" – including Second Life® and other virtual worlds that are capturing the imagination of consumers and marketers alike.

WEB 3.0: ARE WE THERE YET?

"The appearance of new means of information does not destroy earlier ones; it frees them from one kind of constraint or another. " -Umberto Eco

A survey of the history of art and communications media reveals that new methods of communicating words and pictures tend to begin with the figurative training wheels on. Over time they advance as creativity and technology allow. Crude artwork on cave walls paved the way for a centuries-long maturation to Old Master paintings. Matthew Brady's stiff daguerreotype portraits of the mid-1800s evolved over generations to the artistic fashion photography of Richard Avedon. Early motion pictures were little more than filmed stage plays, and the first television programs were shot with only one camera until Desi Arnaz broke new ground with a three-camera shoot for "I Love Lucy" in the early 1950s.

Thus it makes perfect sense that the World Wide Web should evolve over time from a rather one-dimensional medium (Web 1.0) into a more dynamic, customer-centered, personalized experience for individuals (Web 2.0). While most agree that we are currently immersed in Web 2.0 as evidenced by the growing empowerment of the online consumer we are on our way to yet another level of development called Web 3.0, in which the web becomes an intelligent agent for consumers. In Web 2.0, participation in virtual worlds like Second Life® becomes possible. In Web 3.0, it will be optimized and personalized.

One of the most authoritative academics focusing her work on the movement toward Web 3.0 is Professor Donna L. Hoffman, Chancellor's Chair and Co-Director, Sloan Center for Internet Retailing at University of California, Riverside (http://sloan.ucr.edu/).

Professor Hoffman sets the stage for our future advancement to Web 3.0 by defining it, along with Web 1.0 and Web 2.0.

- **Web 1.0:** The Web is conduit for text and image. The basic Web offers static sites, and initial efforts at dynamic content and interactivity.
- **Web 2.0:** The Web is an operating system. The Web facilitates sharing and participation with a seamless connection of applications like geographic mapping and services such as photo-sharing.
- **Web 3.0:** The Semantic Web. The Web can "understand itself." It's less a catalog and more a guide, offering a world wide database and harnessing the power of artificial intelligence to provide customized recommendations (Hoffmann 2008).

Writing in *AdWeek*, Greg Smith, COO of Neo@Ogilvy, North America, a digital and direct media agency based in New York, says that to understand how Web 3.0 will work, we can look at the "intelligent agent" activities of the TiVo digital video recorder. Smith explains, "Express interest in, say, George Clooney, and TiVo's 'agent' searches for and records any of his movies airing on TV. But it also finds and records content related to Clooney, such as films he directed or produced, reruns of 'ER', 'The Facts of Life' and other credited work, interviews and gossip items about him, even the 'Tears of a Clooney' episode of 'American Dad' that mocked his persona. Now substitute your brand for 'Clooney' and 'the entire Web' for 'TV,' and you get some idea of Web 3.0's potential reach" (Smith, 2009).

Tim O'Reilly of O'Reilly Media coined the term Web 2.0 in 2004, and offered a valuable set of reference points to distinguish Web 1.0 from Web 2.0 (O'Reilly 2005). In Web 1.0, we see one-way communications between marketer or content provider and the consumer. In Web 2.0, collaboration and community become part of the mix along with consumer empowerment in the evolution of a web site.

Since 2004, there have been tremendous advancements in the application of Web 2.0, considering the possibilities presented by this dynamic Web platform. Web 2.0 is characterized by consumer empowerment, community building, and sharing. More examples of Web 2.0 in action include social networks like Facebook and LinkedIn, the mini-blog site Twitter, Google maps and many other mapping sites, wikis like Wikipedia, and the Flickr photo sharing site.

Web 2.0 consumer recommendations and community appear on all manner of travel sites and online retailers, especially those that serve as third parties to offer goods and services from many sources. Hotels.com (http://www.hotels.com) invites visitors to customize their search by moving an online meter for the choice of 1 to 5 stars on hotel ratings, another meter from 1 to 5 rankings on customer feedback, and still another for nightly price ranges from $0 to $500-plus. Eye Buy Direct (http://www.eyebuydirect.com/ allows consumers looking for new eyeglasses to upload their own picture, try on frames virtually, and then get feedback on how they look from other site users. Zappos (http://www.zappos.com) lets visitors sort shoes, boots and other clothing items by popularity as well as by price, available sizes, and other factors, and then offers a chance for buyers of these products to leave comments about comfort and fit.

When will sites like these advance to Web 3.0? When the consumer can provide a set of parameters and have the site itself use its intelligent agents to provide answers. For example, a parent might visit a travel site and tell the virtual agent there, "I would like a warm-weather vacation near water. There are three of us in the family – my husband, myself, and our 11-year-old daughter. We live in Chicago, we have a week for the vacation, and we have $3500 to spend." (Hoffmann, 2008). Using its combination of consumer recommendations, information about appropriate destinations, what it's been told about this visitor, and what it can discern about her from databases and other sources, the virtual agent will make helpful recommendations for the customer.

Table 1.

Web 1.0		Web 2.0
DoubleClick	-->	Google AdSense
Ofoto	-->	Flickr
Akamai	-->	BitTorrent
mp3.com	-->	Napster
Britannica Online	-->	Wikipedia
personal websites	-->	blogging
evite	-->	upcoming.org and EVDB
domain name speculation	-->	search engine optimization
page views	-->	cost per click
screen scraping	-->	web services
publishing	-->	participation
content management systems	-->	wikis
directories (taxonomy)	-->	tagging ("folksonomy")
stickiness	-->	syndication

While much of what e-commerce marketers offer today stays squarely in the realm of Web 2.0, many virtual worlds have led the way into experimentation with bold Web 3.0 applications. According to virtual worlds expert and research analyst Vahid Dejwakh, "Within the context of the evolution of the Internet from Web 1.0 to Web 3.0, virtual worlds especially the 3D kinds are classified under the Web 3.0 category because of their profound ability to integrate multiple types of content, information sources, and feeds into one highly engaging and interactive format" (Dejwakh, 2008).

Indeed, as early as 2006, Second Life® invited its members to experiment with this type of integration. They could tie together del.icio.us with Second Life® to bookmark locations inside Second Life®. Around that same time, Second Life® allowed for Flickr photos to be fed into Second Life®, and Snapzilla let Second Life® visitors take screenshots in Second Life® and post them on Snapzilla. Regarding these developments, blogger Pete Cashmore noted, "Clearly, SL is becoming a web service. This will inevitably blur the lines between the virtual world and the web, creating endless possibilities events mashups, online calendar integration, even commercial mashups with Lindens as a payment option. This is the tip of a very big iceberg" (Cashmore, 2006).

MARKETING CONVERGENCE

In the early 1990s, marketers spoke hopefully about the forthcoming *convergence* of television, computer and telephone as later described in an article from the November 2000 issue of *Scientific American* magazine. "Creating Convergence" examined what it would take to "achieve the union of audio, video, and data communications into a single source, received on a single device, delivered by a single connection" (Forman, 2000).

This idealistic concept met with defeat after agonizing defeat as cable television, telephone and computer firms failed to come to terms for their planned mergers and acquisitions. But finally after decades of promises that convergence would be right around the corner the "Triple Play" of broadband Internet, phone and television is available to a good percentage of Americans from their cable company, their phone company, and perhaps in the near future from their power company as well.

The Meaning of Marketing Convergence

Just as this union of TV, phone and computer has been achieved in recent years, a number of sophisticated companies have already scored significant successes with *marketing convergence.* This term refers to the orchestration of Information Technology, Marketing and Design required to ensure that companies present an integrated, consistent, clear and interactive message across all the media they use. Today's efforts at marketing convergence are fueled by the growth of the Internet and the World Wide Web, but marketing convergence is complicated by the fact that the Internet represents so much more than "just another medium to add to the mix." For example:

- The Internet allows for targeting very specific groups and individuals, making one-to-one marketing a reality.
- The Internet allows marketers to cultivate true, real-time conversations with their customers rather than one-way messages or delayed communications.
- The Internet allows for unprecedented depth of information, product assortment, and personalization -- even modification "on the fly" to deal with a customer's wishes.
- The Internet represents a new challenge in that instead of merely "pushing" media messages to customers and prospects, it requires that customers be attracted to the Web site. Once there, they are not confined by a linear message but must be attracted to "dig deeper."

Indeed, marketers long have recognized the incredible potential for Internet marketing efforts. Not the least of these is the fact that the Internet provides a ready research resource for buyers, sellers and learners alike. Buyers can compare and contrast products, prices and even nuances like shipping charges without leaving the comfort of their homes. Sellers can track the movements of visitors to their sites and offer pop-up surveys both before and after the purchase process. With the caveat that information on the Web is not always completely credible (Wikipedia for example), students and other learners can take advantage of a wealth of well-organized, easily accessed information online.

Here are some other plusses for established marketers who have migrated significant resources to the Web:

- Strong brands have an edge online as their customers and admirers seek them out
- Technology allows customers to serve themselves on their own time and at their own speed, both for initial purchases and easy repeat buys.
- Online testing helps marketers to get fast answers about the relative merits of new products and offers, and then move the "winners" to media with longer lead times.
- Personalization opportunities abound online, especially for firms like Second Life®, There and other virtual communities that are able to customize responses "on the fly" as visitors make more selections, visit new parts of the site, and supply more and more information.

- Unlimited real estate online allows firms to provide deeper and deeper information for visitors who want it, and to expand their product offerings exponentially yet cost-effectively (compared to the cost of a traditional paper catalog or direct mail package).
- Strategic alliances and affiliations abound in the online world, with powerful back-end software allowing for accurate yet inexpensive reporting and payments to appropriate parties.

Caveats for Convergence Marketers

With a few notable exceptions like Amazon.com and eBay, it's become clear that pure-play e-commerce retailers (at least those selling physical rather than virtual merchandise) are generally not as successful as firms that integrate their databases and promotions across all media. Virtual worlds have an edge in this regard since clothing, hairstyles, living quarters and much more can be tried on virtually and purchased with a mouse click, so there is no need for physical retail environments or catalogs.

Back in the physical world, though, smart companies facilitate customers to buy when they want and where they want – whether that's online, via catalog, other media, telephone, or face-to-face retail. Firms like Lands' End and Amway/Quixtar learned very quickly that doing without or even cutting back on print communications is not an option – the "in your face" nature of print puts Web sites at the top of the customer's mind. What's more, many customers prefer to shop via print and then go online to finalize the transaction.

Many pundits predicted that online marketing would save money for firms that could automate most of their functions and cut down on the depth of print materials. For instance, a postcard might replace a full-fledged direct mail package, driving traffic to the web for the in-depth information. Indeed, customers have shown they prefer some Web functions that save time for them and save money for the seller. These include self-directed research, buying and customer service as well as those robust Extranets in the business-to-business world.

On the other hand, some of the predicted online savings have not materialized. For instance, conversion rates to online promotions are relatively low, and Web site maintenance plus continuous improvement have proven both costly and time-consuming. What's more, customer service conducted via e-mail is more expensive than originally anticipated, considering all the back-and-forth communications involved, and the fact that e-mail communicators need more costly skills the phone communicators.

The Warmth of the Web

While some people contend that the Internet is "cold and robot-like," this medium actually offers great potential for meaningful human interaction often much more satisfying than in today's typically anonymous retail store environment. The smartest companies are "humanizing" the online experience with real-time conversations between buyers and sellers as well as between people with the same affinities and interests and then picking up that conversation in offline media and retail interactions as well.

For firms like the online grocery seller Peapod, online ordering plus friendly home delivery brings a nostalgic touch to buyers' Internet experience. Vendors like LivePerson (http://www.liveperson.com) add virtuality by providing live chat functions that put customers in touch with a real person. This friendly guide can help them make purchase decisions, help head off shopping cart abandonment, or "co-browse" the site to help the customer find what they are looking for.

Numerous vendors help Web sellers add the humanizing warmth of a "virtual real person" video spokesperson to show visitors around their site, point out important features, and activate a call to action. Ideally this site host would be integrated into all media as a spokesperson for the company or brand. For example, while Nutrisystem's Web site features a video of spokesman Dan Marino, and Jenny Craig's site has a video of spokeswoman Valerie Bertinelli, these celebrity endorsers could just as easily appear as "virtual real people" on the site as illustrated on http://www.liveactor.com/, http://websitetalkingheads.com and similar sites. Still other sites like http://www.sitepal.com/ and http://www.codebaby.com/ offer functionality for "interactive digital characters" that are business-like versions of the avatars in Second Life® and other virtual worlds.

BUSINESS-TO-BUSINESS INTERNET MARKETING

Business-to-business (B2B) buyers and sellers were among the first to discover the benefits of e-commerce, both for saving money and making money. Business customers are more likely than consumers to enjoy swift broadband connections. They embrace the efficiency of online customer service options, and the money-saving possibilities inherent in both forward and reverse auctions. With the rising cost of personal sales calls, B2B marketers appreciate the opportunity to pave the way for face-to-face selling with online comparison tools, white papers and in-depth information. What's more, in some cases they have been able to overcome potential channel conflict to sell direct to the end buyer thus eliminating costly steps in the supply chain.

The recessionary economic challenges that manifested themselves in 2008 actually boded well for the growth of cost-effective online B2B marketing. For example, e-mail offers an incredibly efficient way to communicate with business customers and prospects. Indeed, the Direct Marketing Association has branded e-mail the most cost-effective medium ever invented, with ROI in the $45.00 range for every dollar invested (Direct Marketing Association, 2008-2009). What's more, online marketing is measurable – an extremely positive attribute when money is tight. With proper preparation and tracking mechanisms in place, leads, orders, and long-term value of customers can all be calculated to the penny.

Frugal marketers are discovering that B2B Social Networking generally costs time rather than money. Basic functions on LinkedIn, Plaxo and other B2B networking sites are free, and corporate upgrades are quite inexpensive. Sponsored Search (on Google and more focused sites like business.com) is measurable, cost-effective, adjustable on the fly, and affordable for even the smallest businesses. Search Engine Optimization helps ensure that visitors find B2B sites, and basic SEO functions can be done right on the desktop by marketers themselves.

The recession also hastened what was probably an inevitable move to the Web for many narrow-niche B2B trade publications. In general, B2B print advertising pages are down a trend that started after 9/11/2001 and has continued to the present with a brief, small upturn circa 2003-2005. For the first five months of 2009 alone, B2B magazine revenues declined 26.3%, and ad pages were down by 30.3% (American Business Media, 2009). Month by month, more and more trade publications are announcing that they will now be offered less often and/or in online forms only. As an example, in the direct and interactive marketing field, *DM News* now publishes biweekly instead of 50 times per year. *Direct* and *Promo* no longer exist as print publications, but now have been folded into a print publication called *Chief Marketer,* that is also available in a web version. All these publications offer a host of online newsletters and downloadable resources on a daily, weekly or monthly basis.

Following the lead of B2B publications, savvy B2B marketers are increasing their use of online strategies for lead generation via the Web, e-mail and online advertising, Internet events, e-fulfillment, community building, partnerships, and e-commerce marketing.

Online Lead Generation

According to B2B marketing expert John Coe, the cost of an average sales call "has soared over $500" (Coe, 2003). What's more, an industrial sale (based on consultative selling rather than "selling off the shelf") may well require an average of four to five calls to complete. If online marketing can open the door to a salesperson more efficiently, that cost can be controlled. What's more, many straightforward, "product off the shelf" sales that were previously closed face-to-face now can be completed via online lead generation, cultivation and sales using "call me" technology or the type of "live person" customer service described earlier.

Online lead generation is both cost-effective and accountable. B2B marketers can use special URLs in both print and online advertising leading to customized landing pages. These Web pages then can provide prospects with information to meet their specific needs and usher them to an easy-to-complete Web response form. The burgeoning field of variable data printing allows B2B marketers to send personalized direct mail pieces to prospects, inviting each of them to an individual, customized, value-added web site that recognizes them by name and captures information that helps build the marketer's database. B2B marketers also have the opportunity to collect prospects' and customers' e-mail addresses and ask them to opt in to receive valuable information via newsletter or white paper.

Many B2B marketers now question the effectiveness of traditional banner advertising, although some do use banners on their own sites to promote upcoming events, new products or white paper offers. There is much more excitement around sponsored search and pay-per-click advertising on Google and other sites (including the B2B specialist business.com). Marketers can control their own sponsored search and pay-per-click budgets, investing just a few dollars at a time if they wish, and testing as many different keywords and ads as they choose either for lead generation, actual selling of products, or both. Many marketing firms offer their services to ensure that sponsored search and pay-per-click programs are monitored and adjusted effectively, but it's also quite possible for businesses to assign in-house experts to handle the budgeting, testing and implementation of their own programs. Google offers extensive self-study tools and videos online, and the certification test to become a Google Advertising Professional costs just $50.00. Google Analytics and other online monitoring systems are available free or at reasonable cost to help marketers evaluate the effectiveness of their campaigns and make changes that show up online almost instantly.

Internet Events

While face-to-face conventions, trade shows and seminars show no signs of disappearing from the B2B marketing horizon, buyers and sellers alike have long complained about the costly and frustrating problems inherent in such events. Logistics of travel, hotels and venues, arranging for reliable and inspiring speakers, fears of bad weather and tied-up traffic often have meeting planners losing sleep for weeks before the big event. Face-to-face meetings represent a substantial investment for promoters and attendees This is a high-stakes game in which a beautifully planned seminar or convention can nonetheless be sabotaged by freakish weather that cancels flights and ties up traffic, illness/lateness/poor performance on the part of the main speaker, or since the recent recession began last-minute belt-tightening on the part of exhibitors and attendees. What's more, even when all goes well, no-show rates of 50-60% are common for free promotional seminars offered at a specific time and place (Jones, Business-to-Business Internet Marketing, 2009).

To supplement or in some cases even to replace face-to-face events, many marketers have now embraced Internet events of many kinds. Rather than expecting busy prospects to travel to a venue, everyone can "meet" at a URL hosted by proven companies like Cisco's WebEx, Go to Meeting or Cvent. These Internet events represent a much smaller investment of time, talent and money than a face-to-face meeting. They offer much better quality control with the help of a trusted vendor like WebEx or its competitors. For seminars and speeches, attendees only have to invest an hour or so, and then can even multi-task while monitoring the event off their desktop. Alternately, employees can gather together in a conference room to watch and discuss a meeting as a group. Senior executives who are unlikely to take the time to travel to such a seminar in person may log on individually or with their employees, as well.

While videos of in-person seminars often leave much to be desired unless they are produced by expensive professionals, online seminars can be recorded for later use and they offer the same production values and functionality of the actual live event. This means that prospects who are unavailable at the set time for the online event may watch it at their leisure.

It is possible to set up an entire trade show that takes place online either as a replacement for the face-to-face event, or as an option for those who choose not to attend. According to Dr. Allen Konapacki, President of the INCOMM Center for Trade Show Research in Chicago, "Only about one-third of interested people actually attend a show, so virtual shows [can potentially] reach 66-70% of the people who don't actually attend" (Valente, 2009). The ultimate online trade show event is an experience that takes place in a virtual world, as offered via 6connex (http://www.6connex.com) for clients including Cisco, WebEx, Procter& Gamble, and Intel.

E-Fulfillment

Traditional fulfillment of B2B leads usually consists of a mailing package or fax. The mailing package can be expensive and difficult to customize, while the fax is sorely limited in design possibilities and limited to black and white. What's more, there is a delayed gratification factor in these media. With online fulfillment, the prospect often can click on the relevant material and download it immediately.

Adobe Acrobat's universal PDF format can be used to capture anything from a one-page document to a book-length piece. These pieces can be offered for free download at no obligation, or "unlocked" only after the site visitor fills out a form and discloses information to the marketer.

Updating a PDF is easy and fast, so companies are no longer burdened with boxes of outdated brochures. What's more, the Web facilitates individualization of online fulfillment based on previous requests, or adaptation on the fly as the customer fills out a Web response form. Online demos and trials can offer a taste of a software package that will time out at a certain point if the user decides not to pay.

Community Building and Partnerships

The traditional model for buyer and seller relationships saw the seller having an individual relationship with each buyer. (Visualize the seller at the hub of a wheel with each customer as an individual spoke). Today the ideal – as espoused by Victor Hunter in his book, *Business-to-Business Marketing: Creating a Community of Customers* is to develop a network of customers all of whom can be in touch with each other for mentoring, partnering or idea sharing if they opt to do so (Hunter, 1997). The selling company or vendor earns both loyalty and credibility as the convener of the network. (Visualize a spider web of individual and multiple connections).

An example of a highly successful community builder is Cisco, which offers small business communities including an Innovators Forum, a Small Business Support Community, and a Small Business Partner Community for Cisco partners. Cisco also offers Virtual Roundtables and collaboration tools on its site at http://www.cisco.com to facilitate conversations and real-time teamwork without geographic barriers.

Dell offers a "My Way" portal that allows customers and prospects to enjoy a highly customizable web home page that offers easy access to "all things Dell" as well as news, weather, entertainment, and an organization method for collaborative and social networking groups. Recognizing that community groups and forums can only thrive with active and enthusiastic participation, in April, 2009, Dell announced a plan to offer virtual goods as a reward for participation in its official forums. Eligible activities would include asking and answering questions or posting information (Dell Considering Virtual Goods System on Official Forums, 2009).

In addition to communities sponsored by individual companies, there are also a number of business communities and exchanges. Many of these are presented in the form of a vortal, or vertical portal. For example, Plastics Net (http://www.plasticsnet.com) offers a community, news and information source for the plastics industry, and Business.com (http://www.business.com) provides directories and resources for business-people in a wide range of industries.

B2B partnerships thrive online thanks to collaboration software that allows all participants to view the same real-time reporting of leads and sales, and to enhance their databases with information gained through the partnership. The simplest form of online partnership is affiliate marketing, where a business rewards its online partners a certain amount of money for each new visitor or customer earned through the affiliate's marketing efforts.

Masters of B2B E-Commerce and V-Commerce Marketing

Each year, *B2B Magazine* publishes its list of "10 Great Web Sites," as selected by a panel of five top industry leaders. The magazine and its web site provide a narrative from the experts explaining why these sites are so remarkable. For 2008, the industry leaders were: Hoa Loranger, user experience specialist, Nielsen Norman Group; William Rice, president, Web Marketing Association; Alan Webber, senior analyst, Forrester Research; Aaron Kahlow, chairman and founder of the Online Marketing Summit and managing partner of search and usability firm BusinessOnLine; and Dana Todd, CMO of Newsforce Inc. and chairwoman of Search Engine Marketing Professional Organization's (SEMPO's) education committee.

The 10 web sites they selected can be used as an online learning lab for excellence in B2B E-Commerce…and increasingly for B2B V-Commerce as well. The 2008 "great web site" companies and examples of their virtual world involvement and applications are:

- Adobe (http://www.adobe.com) has an eLearning space inside Second Life®
- Cisco Systems (http://www.cisco.com) parent of Web Ex (http://www.webex.com) and its GeoConnect Virtual Classroom Solutions
- Formway Furniture (http://www.formway.com) Maker of chairs that are designed to facilitate participation in the virtual world
- InFocus Corp. http://www.infocus.com) Makes projectors that can be used with 3D glasses to create three-dimensional virtual reality spaces
- IT Toolbox (http://it.toolbox.com/) A knowledge sharing community that presents numerous white papers on the application of virtuality in business
- Johns Manville (http://www.johnsmanville.com) Has used a virtual document repository for access by employees worldwide since 2000
- Tech Smith Corp (http://www.techsmith.com) Creators of Camstasia Studio, a video production software that is used frequently in Second Life®

- Suni Imaging (http://www.suni.com) Offers products for 3D panoramic medical imaging
- Thomas Net (http://www.thomasnet.com) Connects potential customers with makers of software and equipment for virtual reality applications
- USPS (http://www.usps.com) Offers Automated Postal Centers (APCs) which are virtual stand-alone Post Offices, an online virtual library of postal information, and virtual passport stamps based on its "Greetings from America" stamp series.

Virtual Worlds in B2B

According to a Forrester Research report released in mid-2009, to date only 11 percent of businesses have adopted virtual worlds at work. Report author TJ Keitt notes, "From the point of view of most business leaders, the utility of virtual worlds in business is not apparent. Heretofore, virtual world vendors have not done a particularly good job articulating the value because many are wrongly trying to set up their solution as an alternative to flawed but good enough Enterprise 2.0, collaboration, and conferencing solutions. This strategy obscures what should be the central message of virtual world providers: They allow for groupings that can be augmented or reduced on the fly while also allowing users to consider information from multiple applications simultaneously."

In other words, businesses have opted for simpler and more straightforward collaboration tools (Cisco's WebEx, for example) rather than get bogged down in the time-consuming process of creating virtual campfires, islands and egocentric avatars for collaboration purposes. Keitt predicts that when vendors of virtual world solutions adapt their messages to the "grouping application opportunity," they will "have a storyline that can appeal to a broader customer base as well as unified communication providers with whom they can partner." Keitt suggests that virtual world vendors trying to sell into the B2B space are too focused on nifty avatars and fun-type applications. Instead they should work with vendors who provide collaboration tools to integrate virtual world elements (TJ Keitt, 2009).

THE EVOLUTION OF BROWSERS, PORTALS AND SEARCH ENGINES

Browsers Make the Web Accessible

In the early 1990s, when the World Wide Web was young, a group of scientists at the University of Illinois' National Center for Supercomputing Applications (NCSA) developed a web browser simply put, a program used to read HTML documents called Mosaic. While Mosaic also worked with earlier, all-text Internet applications such as file transfer protocol (FTP), Usenet and Gopher, its reputation rests on the fact that it was the browser that first popularized the World Wide Web. Unlike previous browsers, Mosaic displayed images in sync with related text instead of showing images in a separate window.

Netscape Navigator, created by many of the same individuals who developed Mosaic, debuted in late 1994 as a commercial venture. Its claim to fame was that its interface was identical on any computer. Sensing the potential power of Netscape, Microsoft approached the young company and proposed a partnership, which Netscape refused. Not long after that, Microsoft released its own browser, Internet Explorer 1.0, as part of Windows 95. Thus began the so-called "browser wars," in which Microsoft flexed its muscles as an overall operating system while Netscape attempted to add attractive features that would keep users loyal.

In a move to counter Internet Explorer's growing domination, Netscape launched its open-source Mozilla browser project in 1998. American Online (AOL) acquired Netscape in 1998, and by the early 2000s the once-dominant browser had virtually disappeared within AOL. Meanwhile Mozilla's Firefox browser has evolved into a viable competitor for Internet Explorer, with Google recently introducing a new browser called Chrome, and Apple supporting its own browser called Safari.

Each browser has its own rabid adherents (including some who still prefer Netscape), and there are hundreds of lesser-known browsers in existence as well. The Web contains numerous comparisons of the various browsers on criteria of specific importance to everyone from online gamers to IT professionals, but perhaps the acid test is percentage of users for each major browser. According to Market Share by Net Applications, in July 2009, Internet Explorer commanded 67.68% of browser users, while Firefox had 22.47%, Safari had 4.07%, and upstart Chrome's number was at 2.59%. Other browsers reported to have significant numbers of users were Opera at 1.97%, Netscape at 0.67%, and "other" at 0.55% (Net Applications, 2009).

Portals and Search Engines

A web portal organizes and presents information from a wide range of sources. Horizontal portals like Google and Yahoo offer news, sports, weather, entertainment, maps, shopping sources and much more. Google presents itself originally as a clean page, ready for individual customization and searches. Yahoo fills every pixel of its generic home page with suggestions and enticements, all of which can be customized to the user's preference.

While Google and Yahoo are the largest and most widely used portals, there are many other horizontal portals including AOL, Ask, and Microsoft's recent entry called Bing. There are also specialized portals such as YouTube (videos), MySpace and Facebook (social networking), Blogger (a free blog site) and Wikipedia (open source encyclopedic information).

There are a number of vertical portals that focus their subject matter on virtual learning, virtual research, and virtual games. Many universities and schools maintain their own virtual learning portals as centers for their online teaching and research activities. In addition, the Multiplayer Game and Virtual World Research Portal resides at http://mgvw.lcc.gatech.edu/.

A search engine is a tool that allows searchers to locate information on the World Wide Web. Just as they reign as number-one and number-two in the United States web portal department, Google (72.07%) and Yahoo (17.00%) hold the first and second-place spots in the search engine category. Microsoft's Bing (7.31%) was gaining share as of July 2009, and was beginning to put a small dent in the larger engines' dominance (Top Ten Search Engines – Top 10 SEs, 2009). While Microsoft's once-anticipated takeover of Yahoo fizzled, the two companies now have joined forces to take on Google. If their arrangement passes muster with the antitrust forces in Washington, Yahoo's search engine will feature Microsoft's Bing. In terms of V-commerce, there is a specialized search engine called Meta-Mole (http://www.meta-mole.com) that provides a database of virtual world environments for use by individuals, business and government.

Portals and search engines are defined differently in theory, but in practice they are usually combined. What's more, since their original functions have evolved as services that Web visitors expect to get for free, sites like Google, Yahoo and Bing have had to find other ways to make money. Under pressure from shareholders and in an attempt to grow and monetize their businesses, both Google and Yahoo have evolved from simple portals and search engines into Internet companies. The most visible manifestation of this development is the growth of sponsored search advertising, where Google has emerged as the clear winner with about 75% market share (Efficient Frontier, 2009).

SOCIAL NETWORKING MOVING TOWARD MONETIZATION

A social network is an online community structure that allows for communication and sharing among individuals and/or organizations. Social networks can be general in nature or they can be focused on specific topics of interest like business (LinkedIn, Plaxo), or specific demographic groups such as children and teens (YourSphere) college students (the original Facebook), baby boomers (Eons), Asians in the U.S. (Asian Social Network), or African-Americans (BlackInAmerica). They can allow for full-blown profiles, robust interaction and scores of pictures to be posted (like Facebook), or they can provide for as little as 140 characters per post (the mini-blogging site Twitter, where posts are known as "tweets").

Precursors to today's social networks all of which are still in use online today include listservs, news groups, forums, bulletin boards, discussion boards, and instant message systems. One of the first true social networks was SixDegrees, which launched in 1997. It is acknowledged as the first site to combine user profiles, friends lists, and potential for sharing of friend information (Boyd 2007).

The status and make-up of social network users has remained in flux in recent years. MySpace attracted tens of millions of users in the mid-2000s but lost its number-one status later in the decade with the ascendancy of Facebook. Facebook's announcement that it would open to everyone – not just high school and college students – swelled its user ranks but earned a skeptical reception from some young users who were appalled when their parents and grandparents attempted to "friend" them on "their" site.

As of early 2009, 65% of American teenagers between 12 and 17 years of age had profiles on social networking sites, while only about 35% of American adults (18 and over) had such profiles. That said, adult participation is rising rapidly: in 2005 just 8% of adult Internet users had participated in social networking, and in 2006 that number was 16%. The younger the adult, the more likely it is that he or she is a social networker. African-Americans (43%) and Hispanics (48%) are more likely to have social networking profiles than whites (31%), but male and female social networkers appear in approximately equal numbers. Twitter users are overwhelmingly young (median age 31) but they are older than MySpace users (median age 27), Facebook users (median age 26) and LinkedIn users (median age 40) (Lefebvre, 2009).

Can V-Commerce Help Monetize U.S. Social Networks?

Early efforts at social networking seemed to be aimed at getting tens of millions of participants signed up, and in that aspect, the largest networks have been very successful. Facebook, for example, boasted 68.5 million unique visitors as of early 2009, while MySpace came in second with 58.5 million unique visitors (Top Social Networks Re-Rank, 2009). Now that big money from Rupert Murdoch, Microsoft and other deep-pockets investors is part of the mix however, the focus has moved toward improvement of monetization–with mixed results.

According to Bill Gurley, a venture capitalist who blogs at http:///www.abovethecrowd.com, "the consensus seems to be that social networks have a monetization problem. On this topic, both the leading technology industry blogs and the world's top news organizations agree. The problem is not that these sites have no revenue. I 'guesstimate' that MySpace and Facebook have annual revenue run-rates of approximately $650 million and $450 million respectively – highly reputable numbers. The perceived problem relates directly to revenue per user or page view, as these are two of the most heavily trafficked sites on the Internet. As a comparison, other companies with similar usage, like Yahoo, are doing $7.2 billion in annual revenues. When reporting earnings from the fourth quarter of 2007, Google also opined on the difficulty in monetizing social networking sites. Sergey Brin noted, 'I don't think we have the killer best way to monetize social networks yet'" (Gurley, 2009).

Gurley goes on to comment that historically, some of the most-visited sites on the Web have suffered from relatively low revenues. Examples include instant messaging sites like AIM, and free e-mail sites including Hotmail and Yahoo Mail. These sites involve their visitors in non-buying activities such as chatting with friends or sending and receiving e-mail. By contrast, sites with much lower traffic but that are visited with "purchase intention" book-selling sites and travel sites for example have very high Effective Costs Per Thousand Impressions, or eCPMs.

Another barrier to monetization is the fact that most social networks launched their sites with little or no advertising to distract visitors. What's more, these sites traditionally have offered their main services for free. This has created a culture of entitlement, in which American social networkers have expressed outrage when the sites that serve them reveal plans to collect and capitalize on information about their visitors for targeted ads or database building and sharing, or even to redesign their sites to make them more advertising-friendly.

Bill Gurley proposes a "monetization solution" to MySpace, Facebook and their competitors: he suggests that they embrace the model exemplified by a Chinese Web portal called TenCent, which also provides QQ, the leading instant messaging service in China. Rather than focus on advertising, which produces just 12% of its revenues, TenCent makes most of its money through the sale of digital items and games.

Waxing rhapsodic about the brilliance of the TenCent model, Gurley reports on his first conversation with the firm's founder, Pony Ma. "He was selling virtual clothes and accessories for digital avatars that represented his users online. Think about it; this is a beautifully high gross margin business with very low marginal costs. He even told me he thought digital shirts should deteriorate over time like real ones. Pure genius" (Gurley, 2009).

FROM E-COMMERCE TO V-COMMERCE

A host of technological and social forces need to converge in order for v-commerce to flourish. As this chapter recounts, those necessary elements are now developing and maturing. The robust "web as operating system" known as Web 2.0 is in full swing, with the artificial intelligence of Web 3.0 seemingly just around the corner. Traditional businesses have mastered the art of marketing convergence, in which they integrate their customer-centric online and offline marketing efforts and databases. Many firms in the business-to-business space are now engaging in sophisticated e-commerce and v-commerce operations, side-by-side with their consumer marketer colleagues. Advanced versions of browsers, portals and search engines allow for the integration of robust databases, customized applications and lightning-fast, one-to-one personalization.

Traditional social networking site managers are experimenting with virtual gifts and avatars that may enhance their efforts toward monetization moving these sites closer to the Second Life® model. Indeed, a relatively new world called Twinity (http://www.twinity.com) is attempting to bridge the gap between social networking sites like Facebook and MySpace and virtual worlds like Second Life®. Calling itself "a 3D mirror world based on real cities and real people," Twinity began by replicating cities including Berlin and Singapore, and provides for avatars that can be made to look much more true-to-life than those of most virtual worlds. Unlike the fantasy profiles that many users create in other virtual worlds, Twinity members use real profiles.

While some virtual worlds and participants remain firmly entrenched in fantasy with users creating sometimes outrageous avatars and profiles and indulging their imaginations to the utmost there is a growing focus on serious virtual business and educational uses as well as monetization of virtual worlds and social games. Online publications like *Virtual Worlds News* (www.virtualworldsnews.com) and *Virtual Goods News* (http://www.virtualgoodsnews.com), and conferences like the Social Gaming Summit, the Virtual Worlds Expo and the Virtual Good Conference illustrate the fact that virtual worlds and v-commerce are now established business disciplines. Educational events including Blackboard BbWorld and the Lilly Conferences on College & University Teaching regularly feature academic speakers who share their innovative uses for Second Life® and other virtual worlds in their classrooms and online teaching.

For years, individual participants in Second Life® and its competitors have made part-time or full-time incomes creating and selling clothing and other accoutrements for participants' avatars. As early as 2007, residents of Second Life® were participating in sales of more than $1 million a day (in U.S. dollars). At that time more than 800 residents were making greater than $1,000 a month selling virtual clothing alone (Farber, 2007).

Similar to the early days of Web sites when firms went online "just to have a presence," corporations ranging from Herman Miller to Coca-Cola jumped on the virtual world bandwagon in the mid-2000s. That said, many companies that did not immerse themselves fully in the virtual games and protocols that take place in these worlds found themselves struggling for significance and credibility there.

CONCLUSION

What does the future hold for virtual worlds and v-commerce? Linden Labs founder Philip Rosedale seems to wonder the same thing, considering that the theme of Second Life®'s sixth birthday party in the summer of 2009 was "The Future of Virtual Worlds." Rosedale did predict that virtual worlds will grow by virtue of the same forces that fed the World Wide Web. "Just like the Web, a network effect business is driven by creativity and economic success," he has said (Farber, 2007). Rita J. King, who is CEO of the creative content development and research company Dancing Ink Productions, predicts that virtual worlds will augment what she calls "the Digital Culture". She explains, "I envision virtual worlds evolving for business and cultural development as the medium becomes more ubiquitous" (Yahia, 2009).

Perhaps the most vivid future is painted by journalist Michael Parsons, commenting on what he envisions happening with virtual worlds by 2017. "Over that period, I see a great alignment between what businesses want a controlled environment which is one click away from a transaction and what virtual worlds can provide. I see convergence between the virtual 2D world of the web and 3D spaces and very successful commercial environments in the style of Second Life®. I also see great convergence between other forms of entertainment and virtual spaces it seems to me that books, movies, and games will increasingly gain another life around shared worlds, so that you will be able to experience the world of say, *Star Wars*, in all forms of media, including virtual ones. It's simply another way to enter into the imaginative live of a world you like" (Parsons, 2007).

REFERENCES

American Business Media. (2009, July 21). *Business-to-Business Magazines Continue to Decline*. Retrieved August 23, 2009, from American Business Media: http://www.americanbusinessmedia.com/abm/NewsBot.asp?MODE=VIEW&ID=2093

Applications, N. (n.d.). *Market Share by Net Applications*. Retrieved August 25, 2009, from Market Share: http://marketshare.hitslink.com/browser-market-share.aspx?qprid=1

Carlson, N. (2009, January 8). *Time To Stop Laughing: Selling Virtual Goods, Zynga Profits On Revenues Close To $50 Million.* Retrieved August 23, 2009, from www.businessinsider.com: http://www.businessinsider.com/2009/1/time-to-stop-laughing-selling-virutal-goods-zynga-profits-on-50-million-revenues

Cashmore, P. (2006, May 30). *Second Life® + Web 2.0 = Virtual World Mashups!* Retrieved August 23, 2009, from mashable.com: http://mashable.com/2006/05/30/second-life-web-20-virtual-world-mashups/

Coe, J. M. (2003, October 1). *The New B-to-B Fundamentals.* Retrieved August 23, 2009, from Target Online: http://www.targetmarketingmag.com/article/the-new-b-to-b-fundamentals-1-907-words-27824_1.html

Dejwakh, V. (2008). *Virtual Worlds and Web 3.0: Examined, Compared, Analyzed.* In-Stat.

Dell Considering Virtual Goods System on Official Forums. (2009, January 9). Retrieved from Virtual Goods News: http://www.virtualgoodsnews.com/2009/01/dell-considering-virtual-goods-system-on-official-forums.html

Direct Marketing Association. (2008-2009). *The Power of Direct Marketing.* New York: Direct Marketing Association.

Ellison, D. M. (2007). Social network sites: Definition, history, and scholarship. *Journal of Computer-Mediated Communication*, *13*(1), 11.

Farber, D. (2007, August 1). *The Future of Virtual Worlds.* Retrieved August 29, 2009, from blogs.zdnet.com: http://blogs.zdnet.com/BTL/?p=5825

Forman, R. W. (2000, November). Creating Convergence, *Scientific American.*

Frontier, E. (2009, January 20). U.S. [Sunnyvale, CA: Efficient Frontier]. *Search Engine Performance Report, Q4*, 2008.

Gurley, B. (2009, March 2). *How to Monetize a Social Network: MySpace and Facebook Should Follow TenCent.* Retrieved August 29, 2009, from AbovetheCrowd.com: http://abovethecrowd.com/2009/how-to-monetize-a-social-network-myspace-and-facebook-should-follow-tencent/

Hoffman, D. L. (2008). *Generating Customer Insights from the "Social Web": Are Marketers Ready to Give Up Control? Direct Marketing Educational Foundation Research Summit.* Las Vegas: Direct Marketing Educational Foundation.

Horrigan, J. (2009, June 17). *Home Broadband Adoption 2009.* Retrieved August 23, 2009, from www.pewinternet.org: http://www.pewinternet.org/Reports/2009/10-Home-Broadband-Adoption-2009.aspx

Hunter, V. (1997). *Business-to-Business Marketing: Creating a Community of Customers.* Lincolnwood, IL: NTC Business Books.

Jones, S. K. (2006). *Creative Strategy in Direct and Interactive Marketing.* Chicago: RACOM Books.

Jones, S. K. (2009). *Business-to-Business Internet Marketing* (5th Edition ed.). New York: Maximum Press.

TJ Keitt, E. D. (2009). *The Real Value of Virtual Worlds: A Guide for Hooking Business Customers and Partners With This New Technology.* Forrester Research.

Lefebvre, R. C. (2009, February). *Demographics of Social Network Users.* Retrieved August 29, 2009, from http://socialmarketing.blogs.com/r_craiig_lefebvres_social//2009/02/demographics-of-social-network-users.html

Morgenstern, J. (2007, February 18). *Gift gifts on Facebook!* Retrieved August 23, 2009, from www.facebook.com: http://blog.facebook.com/blog.php?post=2234372130

O'Neill, N. (2009, July 16). *Zynga Expands The Gap, Surpassing 60 Million Monthly Active Users.* Retrieved August 23, 2009, from All Facebook: http://www.allfacebook.com/2009/07/zynga-expands-the-gap-surpassing-60-million-monthly-active-users/

O'Reilly, T. (2005, September 30). *What Is Web 2.0: Design Patterns and Business Models for the Next Generation of Software.* Retrieved August 23, 2009, from Oreilly: http://oreilly.com/web2/archive/what-is-web-20.htm

Parsons, M. (2007, October 26). *The Future of Virtual Worlds: The Passionate Fans of Online Worlds Such as Second Life® are Looking Forward to a Bright and Intriguing Future.* Retrieved August 29, 2009, from technology.timesoneline.co.uk: http://www.islamonline.net/servlet/Satellite?c=Article_C&cid=1248078566632&pagename=Zone-English-HealthScience%2FHSELayout

Smith, G. (2009, June 15). Why marketers will approach the semantic Web with different language and tools. *AdWeek*.

Top Social Networks Re-Rank. (2009, January). Retrieved August 29, 2009, from Compete.com: http://www.compete.com

Top Ten Search Engines - Top 10 SEs. (n.d.). Retrieved August 25, 2009, from SEO Consultants: http://www.seoconsultants.com/search-engines/

Valente, A. (2009). *Trade Shows -- Going Virtual.* Retrieved August 25, 2009, from http://www.fitcommerce.com: http://www.fitcommerce.com/Blueprint/Page.aspx?pageId=517&portalId=2&tabindex=5

Yahia, M. (2009, July 21). *The Future of Virtual Worlds: At the Crossroads Between Real and Sci-Fi.* Retrieved August 29, 2009, from islamonline.net: http://www.islamonline.net/servlet/Satellite?c=Article_C&cid=1248078566632&pagename=Zone-English-HealthScience%2FHSELayout

ADDITIONAL READING

Bannan, K. (2009). *The mandate to integrate.* Retrieved February 2, 2009, from: http://www.btobonline.com/apps/pbcs.dll/article?AID=/20090119/FREE/301199973

Bartle, R. A. (2004). *Designing Virtual Worlds.* Indianapolis, IN: New Riders Publishing.

Bell, L., & Trueman, R. (2008). *Virtual Worlds, Real Libraries.* Toronto, ON: International Press Publication Inc.

Boyd, D. M., & Ellison, N. B. (2007). Social network sites: Definition, history, and scholarship. *Journal of Computer-Mediated Communication, 13*(1), 11. http://jcmc.indiana.edu/vol13/issue1/boyd.ellison.html.

Cassell, J., & Thórisson, K. R. (1999). The power of a nod and a glance: Envelope *vs.* emotional feedback in animated conversational agents. *Applied Artificial Intelligence, 13*, 519–538. doi:10.1080/088395199117360

Hughes, A. M. (2003). *Bonding click-by-click.* Retrieved January 31, 2009 from http://directmag.com/disciplines/email/marketing_bonding_click_click/index.html

Jones, S. K., & Spiegel, E. J. (2003). *Marketing Convergence.* Chicago: RACOM Books.

Nass, C., Moon, Y., Fogg, B. J., Reeves, B. J., & Dryer, D. C. (1995). Can computer personalities be human personalities? *International Journal of Human-Computer Studies*, 43.

Reeves, B. (2000). Social Issues and the Effects of High-Bandwidth Interactions. *Proceedings of the Internet2 Socio-Technical Summit*, 81-89.

Rickel, J., & Johnson, W. L. (1999). Animated agents for procedural training in virtual reality: Perception, cognition, and motor control. *Applied Artificial Intelligence*, *13*(4-5), 343–382. doi:10.1080/088395199117315

Stone, B., & Jacobs, R. (2008). *Successful Direct Marketing Methods* (8th Edition ed.). New York: McGraw-Hill.

Virtual Worlds Comparison Chart. (2007). Retrieved August 29, 2009, from virtualenvironments.info: http://www.virtualenvironments.info/virtual-worlds-comparison-chart

Wilson, N. (2009, February 13). *Virtual Worlds for Business*. Retrieved August 29, 2009, from Clever Zebra: http://cleverzebra.com/book

WorldAccounts, V. *Q22009: 25+*. (2009, July 13). Retrieved August 29, 2009, from Kzero.com.uk: http://www.kzero.co.uk/blog/?p=2787

KEY TERMS AND DEFINITIONS

E-Commerce: The buying and selling of goods and services on the Internet

Virtual World: A computer-based, simulated environment in which avatars interact

Virtual Commerce: E-Commerce conducted in a virtual world and/or selling virtual products and services

Web 2.0: The World Wide Web as an operating system

Web 3.0: The World Wide Web encompassing artificial intelligence

Marketing Convergence: The customer-centric integration of online and offline marketing activities

Business-to-Business Marketing: Marketing aimed at producing commerce transactions between businesses

Browser: A program used to read HTML documents

Portal: A web site that organizes and presents information from a wide range of sources

Search Engine: A tool that allows searchers to locate information on the World Wide Web

Chapter 4
Convergence of Online Gaming and E-Commerce

Tracy Harwood
De Montfort University, UK

ABSTRACT

This chapter firstly explores the characteristics and features of online games and their potential for e-commercial exploitation via the communities of interest that have evolved within and around the gaming environments. The chapter then considers the most common models of e-commercialization applied in online games, virtual and mirror worlds by developers, outlining the types of relationships that exist between organizations and consumers, and the issues of co-creation and co-production that exist within each of the relational contexts identified. Finally, the chapter will review the emergence and convergence of online gaming economies and the issues presented at the boundary between real and fictional worlds, such as managing currencies, social identities and relational networks.

INTRODUCTION

The chapter explores the nature of online games, their evolution to date and how they have intertwined with the evolution of commercial interests in the internet for online business (e-business). Beginning with a review of the emergence and transformation of games and commercial contexts, the first two sections of the chapter subsequently review relevant industry reports, research and theoretical underpinnings to the contemporary online gaming, virtual and mirror world context for e-commercial activities. This is then drawn together in the final section, which discusses the emergence and convergence of online economies and the issues arising from their increasing integration with the real world.

Objectives of the chapter are to:

- Review the emergence of massively multiplayer online role-playing games (MMORPGs) and virtual worlds;

DOI: 10.4018/978-1-61692-808-7.ch004

- Examine the nature of contemporary online games, their characteristics, differences and similarities;
- Discuss the roles of identity and social identity within gaming contexts;
- Identify the influence of technology developments for online gaming participation;
- Review the role and behavior of online gaming communities and tribes;
- Identify the range of commercial models applied to online gaming contexts;
- Discuss the forms, nature and evolution of relationships between players and game developers;
- Evaluate the role of co-creation and co-production within virtual world experience environments;
- Examine the emergence of online gaming economies;
- Discuss the issues arising from convergence of online gaming economies with real world activities; and
- Highlight gaps in research and application of relevant theories.

CHARACTERISTICS AND FEATURES OF ONLINE GAMES

Online gaming has had a varied path to its current metamorphosis into an influential sector that is now being used for much more than purely entertainment. The games sector's rise has, however, been tied to the development of commercial networks and the internet. Table 1 identifies the origins of online gaming which can be traced back to the 1960s (for a detailed history of the emergence of online role playing games in particular see also Barton, 2008).

In 1989 networks used for business purposes were becoming more widespread and a number of games making use of UNIX based systems emerged, played typically at universities by students with access to the systems. With the release of a second so-called 'first person shooter' game called Doom, game developer ID Software had set the scene for a phenomenon known as LAN parties. LAN parties are defined as a temporary gathering of people who network their computers together to play multiplayer games, and are an acronym for 'Local Area Network' (Bedford, 1998). Whilst Doom enabled up to four players to play against one another, the physical locality of players was also enabled by the internet. The internet had been created by linking various networks together back in 1983 but it was not until 1988 that real-time text messaging (internet relay chat) to facilitate group communication became commonplace. The World Wide Web (www) as we know it today was switched on in 1992.

ID Software's subsequent release of Quake in 1996 added additional functionality and immersiveness for games players it was 3D and enabled up to 16 players to play one game simultaneously and was, therefore, created for networked play. Quake was also a 'client-server' game that enabled players to access their games at different times, and in turn resulted in an evolved type of LAN party. Quake could be played on a number of different systems, including Macintosh and PC (Linux, DOS and Windows).

By allowing the source code for games to modifiable, game developers have enabled players to create new games by adapting existing game resources and adding new game resources as well as fixing problems. The mods as they are known (modifications) are subsequently distributed over the internet and have themselves led to popular spin-off games such as Counter-Strike, developed by its community of users. Other interesting phenomena have also emerged through game play. Quake has, for example, been influential in the development of the artistic and cultural movement that since 2000 has become known as machinima. Machinima is the making of original films using computer games play, recorded and edited in real-time (Academy of Machinima Arts and Sciences, 2009). This will be discussed further later in this chapter.

Whilst other games emerged during this period, it was Quake that led to the first large scale, tournament style LAN party, QuakeCon, held in 1996 in Texas USA, hosting around 100 players many of whom had heard about the event through internet chat rooms. Organized by fans, QuakeCon took place just a couple of months after the game was first released and close to ID Software's offices, whose development team took the opportunity to visit the event to talk to participants. The following year, around 650 players gathered for the second tournament and similar LAN parties remain commonplace at gaming events around the World today. QuakeCon, for example, in 2009 had an estimated total attendance of 7000 people with participants from the USA, Western and Eastern Europe and Scandinavia and is backed by the game developer and various sponsor organizations.

Networked games and LAN parties are the forerunners of massively multiplayer online role-playing games (MMORPGs) and virtual worlds. LAN parties are also 'anchoring events', that is, they are meet ups in the real world that help to reinforce the values of the community that otherwise remains virtual.

The first 'massive' game was NeverWinter Nights (Stormfront Studios) whilst Ultima Online (Electronic Arts) has been credited with drawing attention to the MMORPG genre. Released 1997, Ultima Online was the first game to reach 100,000 subscribers. Subsequently, MMORPGs have themselves become popularized as 'cultural' phenomena and many have distinctive communities that have developed and evolved around the games and their related technologies. Currently, the Western World's most popular MMORPG is World of Warcraft (Blizzard Entertainment). This game was released in 2004 and in 2009 had grown a subscriber base of more than 11 million players. By Comparison, MapleStory (Wizet), a game based on Eastern folklore, was stated as having in game participation levels of 14 million

Table 1. Early timeline of selected online games

Date	*Game*	*Comments*
1960s	Spacewar	2 player, by early 1970s up to 1000 players simultaneously on PLATO service (time sharing system)
1970-77	Star Trek, Avatar (became Wizardry), Airfight	Multiplayer on PLATO service and first PC game
1979-83	Multi-User Dungeon (MUD)	University hosted by mainframe (DEC-10) which, through hacking and illegal copying of code, was distributed globally and eventually found its way to the internet
1982	Islands of Kesmai (became Legends of Kesmai in 1984)	ASCII text role-playing game for CompuServe; Legends still available
1982-98	MegaWars I (another Kesmai game)	Longest running paid-for online game on CompuServe
1985		QuantumLink (became America Online) graphics based online service for Commodore 64/128 users, first serious competition to CompuServe
1986	Stellar Warrior (renamed from MegaWars 1)	Released through GEnie online service (developed in 1985) – the first multiplayer online game
1987	Air Warrior (Kesmai) Rabbit Jack's Casino	First massively multiplayer game released on GEnie Released on QuantumLink (first online casino)
1988-1996	Advanced Dungeons & Dragons: NeverWinter Nights	Quantum Computer Services launches AppleLink for Apple II but it was not until 1996 that Apple signed Gemstone III and Dragon's Gate Quantum Computer Services buy license and run as a paid for game until 1996
1989		Online gaming industry takes off

Source: based on Mulligan (1999)

Figure 1. At QuakeCon 2009

Korean, 9 million Japanese, 25 Million Chinese and 3.5 million Taiwanese subscribers in 2006 (Huhh, 2006). These figures, however, may reflect multiple characters owned by players in game so actual subscriber numbers may be lower.

Role playing games have characteristics and features that are embedded within the game context. In 1998, for example, Jarok, stated in his Guide to Roleplaying that *"if you are not in character, you are not role playing... of course to be in character one first needs to have an understanding of who your character is"* (online). Thus, role playing requires the player to identify personal characteristics and goals for their character which are not necessarily related to their own character (e.g. love, power, money, success) and also to identify game role playing goals, i.e., aims and objectives in playing with others. Examples include to see how many people will help you to find something you have lost; returning a lost object to its owner; convincing others to join a quest. Games such as World of Warcraft engage players in long-term play through complex plots and numerous levels in which characters created may be migrated to new scenarios; guilds of groups of players may be formed to achieve quests; players may play against other players as well as the game environment and extensive communication between players within guilds may take place. Guilds, defined loosely within games as groups of players who share a common space and resources with similar goals, have developed their own characteristics and economies which has led to an online market for games players, game resources and related artifacts.

Many communities have the active and full support of the original games developers; others have emerged without this endorsement. The MMORPG game context, with the emergence of distinctive communities at both game and guild levels, has enabled researchers to investigate various psychological and sociological aspects of game play. Many games are based on fantasy, violence and other forms of extreme escapism yet research findings often suggest it is difficult to separate real-life and real-world experiences from in-character and in-game experiences (e.g., Salen & Zimmerman, 2004; Juul, 2005; Castronova, 2005; Taylor, 2005; Pargman & Jakobsson, 2006) and the emergence of out-of-game fora where communities discuss in-game issues are not uncommon. This has resulted in a range of services offered to game players and an economy related to game play but not acted out or contained within the game context. It is this augmentation of gaming initially through support of community fora and subsequently through in-game content that has enabled established commercial organizations to enter virtual worlds as themselves by way of advertising and branded assets. This has led, for example, to authors such as Newman (2004) to suggest that video games are engaged with by players through an 'intertextual' web of implicit and explicit references to other media that necessitates them to be considered alongside tie-in media such as movies, cartoons, advertising and marketing materials that exist alongside the game. This will be discussed further in the section on commercial contexts whereas the next section focuses upon the community aspect of online gaming.

Socio-Technical Evolution of Online Gaming

The socio-technological evolution of online gaming is an interesting aspect to consider. Apperley (2006) suggests that MMORPGs in particular are an example of a convergence between computing, telecommunications, media and information sectors that "blur the boundary between game and community completely" (p. 18), where players play the game and communicate simultaneously. This is, of course not restricted to role-playing games and other genres of games identified (Apperley, 2006) include the most popular forms of simulation (e.g., flight and driving sims), strategy where the player gradually learns to think like the game (Friedman, 1999) and action which is often performance based (Atkins, 2003). Indeed, Wolf (2001) has identified 42 categories of game genre using iconography (from film studies), thematics, structure and interactivity, based on the work of the Library of Congress Moving Imagery Genre-Form Guide many of which have communities within and without the game. Although subsequently much criticized not least because it fails to recognize some hybrid forms of game, Wolf's categorization does illustrate the incredible array of different games now available and hints at the fragmentation, convergence, transformation and emergence of the online gaming sector that makes the study of online gaming and its communities especially challenging.

Indeed, Apperley (2006) argues that games genres are better understood when considering their interactive forms, referring to 'ergodic' activity i.e., the navigation through non-trivial texts to play the game (Aarseth, 1997). Thus, interactivity (or 'ergodic understanding') and the extent to which communication takes place within the context of the game are central to appreciating game evolution but this form of game categorization is not well developed in theory or practice. Furthermore, Apperley argues that the experience a player has of playing the same game will change depending on the hardware platform used e.g., PC, console, hand held device and mobile. This is not surprising given the methods of interacting with the range of technologies, their accessibility, ease of use and cultural acceptance varies considerably depending on user sophistication (see e.g., Grimes & Feenberg, 2009).

User sophistication has been found to influence enjoyment and motivation for gaming. Ryan et al (2006) research identified that game enjoyment was a function of feelings of competence and immersion within the game. The study of motivation remains, however, a relatively little researched area despite online gaming and virtual worlds being one of the fastest growing areas of entertainment for particularly the teen to 40 years old demographic groups. Indeed research has tended to centre on the negative impacts of online games and behavior such as addiction, violence and social problems (see, e.g., Ng & Wiemer-Hastings, 2005; King et al, 2009) with comparatively few investigations and more recent emergence of research on positive aspects such as learning, self-efficacy and development of transliteracy skills (see, e.g., Schrader & McCreery, 2008). More positive perspectives have arisen from the growth and diversity of games and hardware technology solutions to game controllers and which appeal to a broader and more mass market (e.g., sport and fitness related, brain training, etc.) than the 'geek male teen' as was the stereotypical description in the early days of online gaming. Interestingly, in both positive and negative scenarios, discussion focuses upon the social, manipulation-control, narrative-identity, reward-punishment and aesthetic-representational features of the games as influencing how they are played (see, e.g., Claro's 2007 background paper on video games and education at www.oecd.org/dataoecd/14/60/39548100.pdf).

Self and social identity theories are at this juncture worthy of further comment given their relevance to understanding how and why people participate in online communities and gaming. Self-identity combines the 'threads' of one's life such as age, class, ethnicity, gender, etc. (Burr, 1995) with personal roles fulfilled (Stryker & Burke, 2000). Self-identify also comprises the attachment between an individual and an object (Hunt & Bashaw, 1999) that may include perceptions, beliefs and expectations associated with the object that enables the prediction of some behavior, known as the theory of reasoned action (Ajzen & Fishbein, 1980). Identity of self is also said to depend upon how well these roles are fulfilled (Stryker & Burke, 2000) and are, thusly, linked to social identity. Social identity theory is about an individual's association with group(s) of people which may differ in intensity or importance, for example, with family members and in roles such as those between supervisors and subordinates (Deaux et al., 1995). Individuals may, therefore, categorize and identify themselves according to their social environment (Ashforth & Mael, 1989). Belonging to social groups also promotes 'camaraderie', a sense of 'community' and 'solidarity' (Zillman et al., 1989) which concepts underpin the formation, development and maintenance of online gaming communities.

Online communities have for some time been considered by organizations as being important to commercial success by adding significant value (e.g., McKinsey-Jupiter Media Metrix) and this is now gaining in momentum (see e.g., Li & Bernoff, 2008; Leadbeater, 2009). From the organizational perspective, communities are often referred to as brand communities and consumption communities formed around branded products and services. Value is derived from the information the organization may generate from the community; by recognizing the community as a unique segment with specific characteristics at which the organization may target specific products and services; and by the community's reach it may enhance brand loyalty, encourage sales and generally act to promote its products via word-of-mouth marketing (Kozinets, 1999).

Another community type has, however, evolved around marketspaces i.e., shared interests, where individual brands may not be the focus of the group, such as societies. In online communities, social interaction and general information exchange takes place that may result in strong levels of commitment to the group (Williams & Cotherell, 2000). Rheingold (1993) referred to these groups as virtual communities where distinctive patterns of behavior and 'social norms' emerge which potentially result in long-term relationships between community members. Kim et al (2008) have also considered the potential impact virtual communities have on brand commitment, finding a link between organizations and consumer repurchase behavior, word-of-mouth marketing, involvement in marketing practices and participation in organization-sponsored activities. These authors also identify that commitment to online communities is determined by community values, support for member communication, frequency of member contributions and freedom of expression. Despite geographical and spatial dispersion, these communities are able to connect synchronistically with each other in real time (Grassian & Trueman, 2007) although, similar to off-line communities, participation reflects differing levels of personal commitment. Blanchard and Markus (2004) summarize Nielsen's 'inequality of participation' 90-9-1 rule, suggesting participants in online communities may be classified as 'leaders' (the 1% of those who participate often and are recognized within the community), 'posters' (the 9% who post less frequently) and 'lurkers' (the remainder who do not post but read the information within the community) (see http://www.useit.com/jakob/). Communities, therefore, are a place of friendship, ideology, power, protocols and sense of place (Clark Vance, 2008).

Where levels of commitment are emotionally bound, a subculture may emerge which some have referred to as tribes (e.g., Godin, 2008; Cova et al 2007). The term tribe has been defined as representing temporary collective identities, the result of the modern consumer society wherein individuals constantly move between social groups in order to reflect their changing interests but which fundamentally seek to 'bypass hierarchical domination' (O'Neil, 2009). Tribes self-regulate and prefer a democratic style which directly addresses the needs of its membership. This was apparent in Dibbell's (1993) A Rape in Cyberspace, the infamous tale of a virtual crime and attempts by the community within an early role-playing game to address it by creating rules and resolving social conflict. Whilst comparison of online communities to archaic [human] tribes has been criticized for a lack of rigor in the approaches taken, the term appears to have been used primarily as a descriptive analogy of primitive behaviors encouraged within the game context, being applied to MMORPGs in particular. For example, Naughton (2008) states: "[3D virtual worlds such as Everquest, Second Life®, Ultima Online] are viewed as inviting visitors to indulge in retribalization" (p. 191).

Within online games, and the complex web of subcultures, guilds and tribes that exist, game developers have an enormous challenge on their hands to police against criminal activity and promote positive behavior (see for example Figure 2). At what point do they intervene in game play? Within non-game online consumption communities intervention by brand owners often results in negative publicity by community members. Clearly games have rules that guide decision-making and these are stated explicitly to games players as part of their subscription to the game or are written implicitly within the game to guide play through narrative texts and stories. Yet within the gaming culture, hacking and modding (modifying game code) to cheat, acquire resources and assets, create machinima films, engage in non-game defined quests and potentially criminal activity is prevalent. Indeed, some of this is encouraged by game developers implicitly through beta releases that encourage participation in developing fixes for problems and creating content and explicitly by providing tools and resources that enable players to produce and share films (see e.g., Lowood, 2005; 2006; Abrams and Grun, 2008).

Thus, moderating tribes within virtual worlds is challenging. Nonetheless, there have been attempts by some games developers to intervene to normalize behavior albeit this is often reliant on members reporting members and in so doing these behaviors and actions reflect real-world values that blur the boundary between real-life and in-game contexts.

MMORPGs, Virtual and Mirror Worlds

As already discussed, role-playing games (MMORPGs) have emerged as particular social constructions that have generated an enormous public following. World of Warcraft (Blizzard Entertainment), for example, has shown year-on-year exponential growth since its launch. There is a genre of MMORPG, however, that some have suggested are not games but are social virtual worlds (Sanchez, 2009). Worlds such as Second Life® (Linden Labs), which currently has a residency of 16M users, are similar in their virtual context and characteristics to MMORPGs and may contain games but they are not considered to be game-based per se. Not all authors agree, and virtual social worlds have also been described as 'open-ended games' (Green and Hannon, 2007).

Figure 2. Howgego's map of World of Warcraft online communities (Source Howgego (2008))

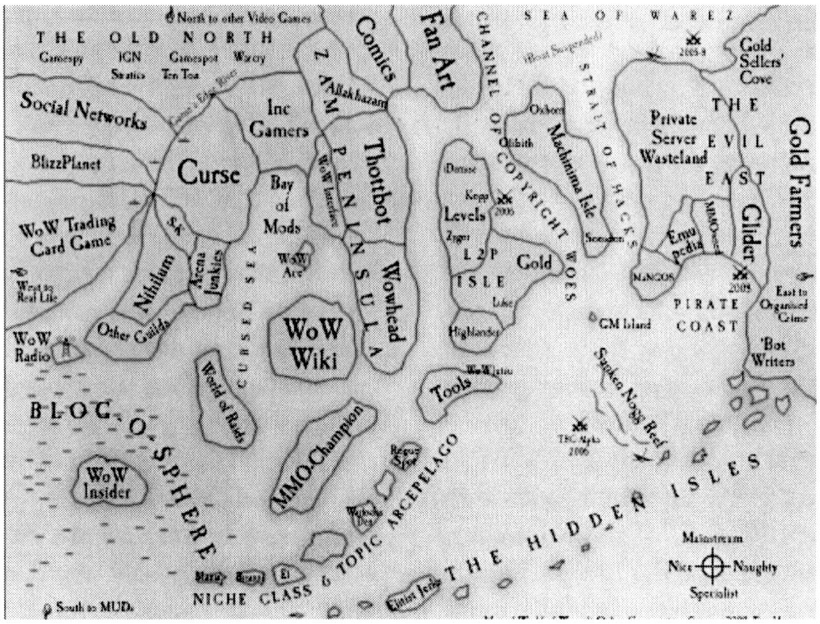

It is helpful to review common characteristics of MMORPGs and social virtual worlds. These have been identified as (Book, 2004):

- **Shared Spaces**: the worlds are used by many players simultaneously;
- **Graphical User Interface:** the world is seen visually;
- **Immediacy:** interaction in world occurs in real time;
- **Interactivity:** the world can be altered by the users; and
- **Persistent:** the world continues after the player logs out.

Sanchez (2009) suggests that differences are in the nature of role-play and the extent to which it mimics activities in the real world. For example, Second Life® (Linden Labs) in-world residents build, socialize, collaborate, design and may be entrepreneurial by selling clothing, vehicles, homes and furniture to other residents, as opposed to participate in quests or fights. Others argue that role-play within virtual worlds is distilled events that simulate real life, much like a flight simulator, in order to practice for real life experiences (Howard, 2008), where avatars may be viewed by players as extensions of their real world self (Kelly, 2004). Whilst the separation between real and virtual is evidently close for some, Boellstorff's (2008) comments help to maintain a distinction between the two: he defines a virtual world as a place where human culture is realized through computer software and the internet, stating the difference between the virtual and real worlds is about "approaching the actual *without arriving there" (p.19)*. He also suggests the gap between the two is particularly important: without it there would be no virtual world and no real world either.

Whereas, however, the boundary between virtual and real may be blurring, it is perhaps helpful to reflect on the definition of a game. Wittgenstein, the Austrian-British philosopher, identified characteristics of a game as being play, rules and competition, whilst others have suggested it is about participative storytelling (Callois, 1957). It is evident that virtual worlds do have clear rules that guide how players participate and interact but the notions of competition and play need further explication. Competition is about challenge to achieve goals. Albeit the goals may be player defined, they do nonetheless exist within virtual worlds at numerous levels from navigating spaces to trading online which may be described as 'player versus environment' in a similar way to role-playing games. Play according to Garvey (1990) involves simulation, imagination and socialization and may be structured (as in a game bounded by rules) or unstructured (for further discussion see http://nifplay.org/). Furthermore, many see games as promoting learning, imagination and creativity with simulation being an integral component. Thus, social virtual worlds may be argued as a genre of online game with differing levels of simulated reality apparent. Whilst a game developer's perspective may be biased to promote market positioning, it is nonetheless evident that Linden Labs (Rymaszewski et al, 2007) description of Second Life® as a 3D online digital world that is "imagined, created, and owned by its residents" (p. 4), for example, appears to be consistent with the notion of an online game.

Another term used in the context of social virtual worlds is that of 'metaverse', where meta means 'beyond' and verse is a shortening of the word 'universe'. The term was first used by science fiction novelist Stephenson (1992) to describe a successor to the internet based on virtual reality technologies. These are a range of software and hardware that enable immersive user experiences that are now increasingly used as controllers for gaming, including haptic, eye gaze and biometric devices. Metaverse is, therefore, used to describe an immersive fictional virtual world albeit that it is now being used more widely than purely a gaming and fictional context (see e.g., Smart et al, 2009). Indeed, the scalability of the underpinning technologies has enabled the development of many different metaverses that may increasingly are able to support players simultaneously within multiple metaverses, the 'multiverse' (Kametsu, 2007).

The extent of simulation versus reality also gives rise to a term where game elements may be less obvious. The term 'mirror world' has been used to describe a microcosm of the real world (Gelernter, 1992) that is an informationally enhanced reflection of the real (physical) world (Smart et al, 2009). Mirror worlds may contain information from geospatial mapping, such as Google Earth, be augmented with historical blogging and used with location aware technologies such as the Apple iPhone. These types of worlds tend to have been developed at Government levels or by large corporations, typically to virtually map terrain on a large scale such as cities and towns (see for example Twinity.com). They are now beginning to be integrated with gaming technologies, albeit that neither software nor hardware technologies are currently sophisticated enough to realize the visions of immersion that the merger of gaming and real worlds suggests. The realities presented by these worlds, however, are currently perceived as having the richest potential for development of e-commerce, which is discussed further in the next section.

One of the key aspects of MMORPG evolution that has enabled the development and emergence of social virtual worlds is the accessibility of high speed internet access and home computers, gaming technologies, virtual reality and mirror worlds which all aid immersive user experiences. Collectively, these developments lower barriers to entry for non-traditional gamers and, insofar as they have been realized to date, have facilitated the growth of online gaming and participation in virtual world activities. Other key aspects that have proven influential are the interdependencies among players in their collaborations to maximize benefits from game play. In turn, this has lead to development of strong social systems both within and outside the gaming and virtual world environments.

The next section discusses the emergence of e-commercialization in online gaming and virtual world contexts whilst the final section expands further upon the economies introduced in this section.

COMMERCIAL CONTEXT OF ONLINE GAMING

The first general commercial interest in the internet began in 1992 and grew rapidly, the result of combining information services with communication services which enabled commercial organizations to reach consumers in new ways, where space and time became less relevant for transacting business (Lynch & Rose, 1993). E-Commerce is the focus on transactions in e-business, which is about attracting and retaining over time the right customers. E-business can include the complete supply chain effort, from procurement of materials to sales of goods and services to end users and incorporates communication and online research. E-business has for some time become "just business" (Strauss et al., 2003) and similarly, e-commerce is now just another mode of transacting between organizations and their customers – it is an embedded component of service delivery, driven by consumer demand. This has emerged because technologies have enabled a power shift from the organization to consumer, and has also resulted in diminishing roles for proximity and time in the delivery of services, approaches to knowledge management and the increasingly important context of digital culture and living, including online entertainment and gaming.

Early e-commerce was, however, primarily an extension of existing business practice merely conducted in an electronic format. Early online corporate information was, for example, printed promotional materials made available via web pages (Farhoomand & Lovelock, 2001). With email, bulletin boards and newsgroups, it became easier for businesses to transact online whilst web sites remained relatively static but the potential to reach an international market resulted in competitive activity to increase traffic to sites. With the development of html coding (the World Wide Web), web pages became more interactive and services on- and offline began to integrate albeit apparent that there were significant differences between the traditional commercial marketplace and the online 'marketspace' (Rayport & Sviokla, 1994). Trading online focused on business-to-consumer (B2C) home shopping and banking, business-to-business (B2B) transacting using electronic data interchange (EDI), information gathering (research) and information distribution (Lawrence et al, 2003). Aspects of e-commerce that quickly came to the fore as presenting challenges to organizations included legal, logistical, financial and cultural differences resulting from the global reach which made it difficult to determine jurisdiction, supply chain structure, payment methods and serve local practices. Security issues arose from the diversity of open platforms and array of personal information retrievable. These issues remain current and are the subject of ongoing collaborative international exchange, research and development.

Commercial interests in online gaming were underpinned by the formation of America Online (AOL), a global internet services and media company that its owners, Time Warner, announced would be spun out as a public liability company by the end of 2009. AOL began life in the early 1980s as Control Video Corporation serving the Atari 2600 console with a service called Gameline. For a fee of $49.95, customers bought a modem that along with a $15 one-off fee and monthly $1 subscription enabled them to download games and track high scores. After struggling to remain commercially viable, the company was rebranded as Quantum Computer Services in 1985 and following a major reorganization released a dedicated service for Commodore 64 and 128 computers. This was offered in 1988 on Apple II and Macintosh computers via collaboration between Quantum and Apple and, working with Tandy Corporation, a PC version of the service was also offered. Quantum changed its name to America Online in 1989 after it split with Apple. Although late to take advantage of the internet, the company quickly grew and surpassed its CompuServe and GEnie competitors with a range of novel online gaming services (see previous section), chatroom and usenet (user-network) facilities and by the mid 1990s had over 10M subscribers.

By 2000 the number of US based consumers playing games online was 9.5M - a 77% year-on-year growth. A similar pattern of growth was observed in other countries across Europe and Scandinavia. More than 85% of use was PC based (Datamonitor, 2002). With developments in broadband technologies, market penetration increased rapidly and it is currently estimated that more than 250M of the world's estimated 1B PCs are being used for online gaming (BBC, 2009). The console market has grown rapidly with 7th generation additions such as PlayStation (Sony), Xbox (Microsoft), Game Cube and Wii (Nintendo) (for a history of game consoles see www.thegameconsole.com) and in 2007 the Guiness Book of World Records (Video Game Edition) stated the Nintendo DS was the World's fastest selling console with 40M units sold in 28 months (Polsson, 2009). Overall market penetration of consoles, however, remains lower than PCs at present.

E-Commerce for online gaming companies was originally, therefore, derived from subscriptions to internet services, revenue from calls (play time) and paid-for games. A relatively small proportion of around 2-7% of games offered online were free, these primarily being augmented services by internet service providers. Many smaller organizations offering online gaming struggled to generate sufficient revenues to compete and whilst advertising was another revenue source that had been identified, this was unpredictable in the early days. Costs for game development increased as consumers demanded more immersive play experiences and e-commercial models adapted accordingly. Pay-for-play, event-based play (tournaments for prizes), sponsorship, add-ons and expansion packs became popular business models for organizations, including market leaders Electronic Arts (EA), Infogames, Microsoft, Sony and Vivendi (Datamonitor, 2002). Game developers also began to license their game brands to third parties to generate wider audiences and revenues. See Table 2 Models of e-Commercialization for a summary of approaches to revenue generation from different forms of online gameplay.

Global sales of video games (software) are expected to exceed that of box office movies for the first time in 2009, reaching a value of more than \$26.7B (Ernst, 2009; Brightman, 2008). In 2008, US consumers spent over \$21B on video game hardware, software and accessories, a year-on-year increase of 30%. In September 2009, Linden Labs, developer of Second Life®, claimed their residents had spent more than \$1B in transactions within the game and more than 1B hours online (around 115,000 years!), their in-world economy growing more than 94% year-on-year (IndustryGamers, 2009). Other statistics released by Linden state that more than 250,000 new virtual goods are created every day, now accounting for more than 270 terabytes of content in Second Life® (a year-on-year increase of approximately 100%); 18B minutes of voice chat have been used since it was introduced in 2007; approximately 1,250 text messages are sent every second; more than 600M words are typed in a day; 60% of residents are non-US representing more than 200 countries communicating in 10 languages. Linden also state that approximately 2B square meters of virtual land is now occupied in-world, an area equivalent to the state of Rhode Island. These figures illustrate not only the economic impact of games, but also the enormous growth in both social and economic transactions within online games and virtual worlds. Indeed, some game developers see social networking as one of the main drivers for growth on the internet (e.g., Electronic Arts) and are predicting the emergence of new models based on these platforms where

Table 2. Models of e-commercialization

Model	*Description*	*Selected examples*
Game distribution models		
Selling the Game	Selling physical, boxed product via stores. Online retail is a fast-growing area as well. Long-term future of the games industry is all about online distribution. This model includes PC direct-to-consumer services such as SteamPowered.com from Valve Software and Direct2Drive from IGN. Digital distribution also means unlocking access to a game already on a service.	Microsoft, Nintendo and Sony
Subscription	Games are paid for monthly, usually by credit card or automatic debit payment. Sometimes this service is aligned with a retail purchase to get access to the install files and user manual, maps, etc. Commonly, players set up direct payments to keep the game 'available'	World of Warcraft
Pay Per Play Pay As You Go Pay for Time	Players pay per turn, usually for a pre-set number of lives, or as long as they can last. This is also used in Internet cafes and game arcades where computer time is sold. This model is also used for game time online.	
Try Before You Buy	Trialware / Shareware / Demoware / Timedware - partial, shortened, or restricted-time free versions of the game.	Xbox Live use this to encourage consumers "Buy the full version to continue!"
Freeware	This model does not make money but has been a way for some to generate acquisitions of software, organization, or technology.	
Rental	Rental stores can drive early sales of boxed products since they stock new titles when they are first released.	GameFly
Host Private Game Server	Aimed at hard-core players where fast network-response times are important for gameplay. Dedicated servers are rented with the gameplay server software pre-installed, meaning players have access to a "ready to go" dedicated server. They share this access with their group of close friends (who may help pay the fee)	Counterstrike
Third party / promotional models		
In-Game Advertising	An in-game world can include paid-for billboards or clearly branded resources, including product placement (clothing, sunglasses, or vehicles). Paid advertising can be built into a game as a story element.	Double Fusion Inc's fusion.sdk enables ad placements to be tracked and reported GA Worldwide Inc's Radial enables advertisers, developers, and publishers to target various consumers across a range of platforms and genres while they play
Around-Game Advertising	Banner and skyscraper ads around the gameplay window. The revenue comes from CPM (cost per thousand views), CPC (cost per click), CPA (cost per acquisition of a player—who plays the game), or CPP (cost per paying player—who buys something). Clicks are generally only worth a few cents, but paying players can earn a company many dollars.	Flash game aggregator sites such as Kongregate.com, Google or Commission Junction
Advert-Games Advergaming Re-Dress	Commonly used with movie tie-ins, the game is an advertisement. The advertiser helps fund the game which tends to be a function of the reputation of the game developer. A variation is to re-dress a game for an advertiser to build a custom version.	US Army recruitment campaign and Burger King for Xbox 360. Re-dressed game Bejeweled.
Finder's Fee from First Dollar	Where other websites are offered either a percentage of net revenue or a 'Finder's Fee from First Dollar'. Money is made from a player who has been directed to you from another site, that finder takes all the money until an agreed fee is reached (e.g., $1.50 per player). Whilst other sites accept the risk they are often good at promoting the game.	
Sponsored Games Donationware	Also known as Serious Games (usually games played to learn things, or improve the world), these are the games that in some way help society. They could be paid for by a philanthropist, state or government grants, a charity, or by a nonprofit. No money is made from the game itself as it is often given away.	Onebiggame

continued on following page

Table 2. continued

Model	*Description*	*Selected examples*
Virtual Item Sponsorship	Advertisers pay reduced fees to buy large quantities of virtual items that they then offer for free to gamers. Revenue is made from the advertisers, and the gamers are happy to receive an item from a sponsor. Then the game shows a pop-up where a product offer is made to players.	Coca-Cola magic potions that boost a character's energy at a low cost
Loss Leader	The game is sold below value alongside a focal product where real income is generated. This technique is often used for building brands by generating awareness, say, for characters.	KiddieCastle.com is using this approach to generate awareness of its vending machines at airports and theme parks
Distribution Deals	Often used to expand foreign distribution, here the developer signs a third party to help with distribution of the product to a new market.	
Sell Player Access Co-Registration Offers	Special offers or personal profile questions are included in the registration process which may be in return for virtual points. The data owner may then sell the leads.	PrimeQ.com
Game augmentation – hardware and software add-ons		
Episodic Entertainment Expansion Packs	Players buy episodes of games as they become available, or pay to unlock new content for a period of time, or pay for certain parts of the game. Delayed episodes are often called 'expansion packs'. These introduce more content, characters or places.	World of Warcraft
Velvet Rope or Members Club	Players pay for VIP access to receive special privileges and access. They sometimes get access to new products before anyone else. This can be in-game, such as a game character who may charge a player a fee, e.g., paying the ferry man to visit an island where the player pays the ferry man real money to gain access to this exclusive area.	
Feed Me or I Die!	Players spend a lot of time making characters they care dearly about. There are two techniques to keep virtual characters 'alive': pay to feed them (by buying virtual food) or, less creatively, pay to get access to them. Designers are now adding more and more things a player needs to do to keep a character alive.	
Micro-Transactions	Small, impulse-driven purchases bought for reasons of vanity, saving time, better communications, or even moving up a level more quickly. They are often paid for using virtual points, either earned in game play or bought for real money. A new trend is offering virtual items in exchange for access to a player's real-world friends. So for example, 'You can have this magic sword, if you invite a friend to play.'	
Consumables	Another trend in free-to-play games, consumable items such as virtual bullets to fire guns, virtual birthday cards for other players, or even the virtual gas you need to drive a car, may be sold separately.	
Peripheral Enticement	A game (software) cannot function without a piece of hardware equipment.	Nintendo Wii Fit game with the Wii Balance Board or gym equipment (such as virtual bikes or rowing machines) and Rock Band (Electronic Arts)
Download Insurance	Insurance for a small additional fee paid by the gamer with their subscription to secure gameplay in the event of, say, a hard drive failure	
Consumer-based models		
Pay Players to Meet a Challenge	The developer plays players to play elements of the game. The game generates revenue elsewhere to cover payments. The bigger the game gets, the bigger the reward gets.	
Skill-Based Progressive Jackpots	Players buy a ticket to enter a virtual tournament that produces a virtual jackpot. The player who reaches a certain status wins. The developer retains a percentage of the jackpot. The game is skill-based to align with international gambling laws.	King.com and Prize.com

continued on following page

Table 2. continued

Player-to-Player Trading Auctions	Players trade land, property, characters, and items directly with each other and also through auctions. The service provider (developer) keeps a percentage of all money exchanged in return for providing a safe transacting environment. Some games let players cash earned money out of the game, and managing the transactions can become a full-time job but this has also been a major area of criminal activity where fraudsters use fake credit cards to trade	Live Gamer is a service that is attempting to overcome some of the criminal activity issues
Model	*Description*	*Selected examples*
Peripheral Enticement	A game (software) cannot function without a piece of hardware equipment.	Nintendo Wii Fit game with the Wii Balance Board or gym equipment (such as virtual bikes or rowing machines) and Rock Band (Electronic Arts)
Download Insurance	Insurance for a small additional fee paid by the gamer with their subscription to secure gameplay in the event of, say, a hard drive failure	
Consumer-based models		
Pay Players to Meet a Challenge	The developer plays players to play elements of the game. The game generates revenue elsewhere to cover payments. The bigger the game gets, the bigger the reward gets.	
Skill-Based Progressive Jackpots	Players buy a ticket to enter a virtual tournament that produces a virtual jackpot. The player who reaches a certain status wins. The developer retains a percentage of the jackpot. The game is skill-based to align with international gambling laws.	King.com and Prize.com
Player-to-Player Trading Auctions	Players trade land, property, characters, and items directly with each other and also through auctions. The service provider (developer) keeps a percentage of all money exchanged in return for providing a safe transacting environment. Some games let players cash earned money out of the game, and managing the transactions can become a full-time job but this has also been a major area of criminal activity where fraudsters use fake credit cards to trade	Live Gamer is a service that is attempting to overcome some of the criminal activity issues
Player-to-Player Wagering	Players place wagers before playing. The winner keeps the pot and the developer keeps a percentage of every pot. As with the jackpot business model, these games must be skill-based. Gambling virtual items is another model that enables players to buy, earn or trade virtual items, then bet them.	
User-Generated Content (including Machinima)	Players make new content (such as virtual buildings, clothing, music, etc.), and then they sell or exchange it with each other. The design of the game may include user stores, where the game developer takes a commission	

Derived from Perry (2009); IndustryGamers; et al

research has indicated that motivations include social, hedonic and functional factors (e.g., Lehdonvirta, 2009).

Research, however, suggests there may be high skill-based barriers to entry of online gaming and virtual world environments that must be considered. Davis et al (2009) identify in their comprehensive review of metaverse research that where virtual worlds are intended for collaborative outputs, then one of the key challenges is in managing variances in the virtual team's proficient use of the technologies synchronistic performance being a particular problem. Other issues relate to the close association the technologies have with entertainment and play, which may be a psychological barrier to some organizations in participating although their potential to augment communication via more traditional methods is clearly an attractor. Virtual worlds, unlike mirror worlds which are constrained by real life models, may for example offer the potential to create enhanced, customized and unique experiences which in turn may positively stimulate and influence team performance in creative solution building for real-world business problems.

Another important aspect is that of managing online relationships. Trust is fundamental to all interpersonal and commercial relationships (Golembiewski & McConkie, 1975; Morgan & Hunt, 1994) without which it is difficult to transact, share information and cooperate (Harrison McKnight & Chervany, 2002). There are, of course, different relational contexts that may be considered, based on the table of commercial models above:

- Business-to-Business (B2B) where the transactions are between organizations (organizational members);
- Business-to-Consumer (B2C), evident in the typical game distribution models;
- Consumer-to-Consumer (C2C) where players transact directly in trading auctions;
- Consumer-to-Business (C2B) such as the paid-for play model; and
- Where consumers may also become providers to organizations (C2B2C), for example, content that is then sold for a commission by the organization to other consumers.

In this context, trust among collaborators within online gaming contexts is an area of ongoing investigation, there currently being some debate as to how and when trust-based systems such as those used to rank individuals on internet trading sites such as eBay and Amazon may be incorporated.

Online Relationships

In B2B relationships, trust is a function of cultural understanding, where the culture of the organization is historically free from corruption and misdemeanor and is therefore related to minimizing risk. This is not straight forward, however, since these aspects are themselves related to a number of factors that may be outside organizational control and part of the macro-environment. For example, Berthon et al (2008) lists factors such as connectivity and technology infrastructure, the general business environment, consumer and business adoption of e-commercial tactics, the legal and policy environment, the range of supporting e-services and social and economic factors, all of which effectively support the organization's e-commercial trading activities. Trust is also derived from the extent of familiarity and similarity between the trading partners. For example, the World Value Survey (see www.worldvaluessurvey.org/) identifies that trust is greater between those cultures that enable greater freedom of expression and has grouped together trading partners that are similar in their approaches (e.g., economies based on English traditions; Scandinavian countries; etc). These are, of course, not simply limited to business relationships but will also influence the B2C trading environment. The main difference between B2B and B2C being the complexity, formality and size of the transactions between the parties.

Research suggests the most important factor enabling B2C e-commerce is that of technology acceptance (for a summary see Holsapple & Sasidharan, 2005). Figure 3 shows a model that has proven consistent in a range of studies. Based on the Theory of Reasoned Action (Ajzen & Fishbein, 1980, mentioned in the previous section) the model describes how ease of accessibility of the technology to the user influences actual use. Whilst online games and virtual worlds do have high barriers to entry, associated with the ease of use of the systems, this is likely to diminish over time as users become familiar with these environments (the learning curve effect), and research published over the last ten years on technology adoption would seem to indicate this is generally a truism. With the emergence and rapid growth of online gaming and virtual worlds, an interesting aspect that is not well understood, however, is the impact that challenges, play and rules (as the key features of online games) have on user experiences where e-commerce takes place within the game context and the barriers to entry are intentionally high to maximize user enjoyment (such as in a MMORPG, virtual or mirror world). It may be expected that the range of technologies in this context needs to be further investigated, say for example, by differentiating between hardware, software, including interface and avatar control, appearance, use of telepresence, etc.

The internet has facilitated development and growth of networks of consumers engaging in direct communication, transactions and relationships with each other, as evidenced in the discussion about communities and tribes in the previous section, however, the purposeful trading exchanges identified in the Table above are not well researched at present. Kardaras and Karakostas (2007) have identified four different types of virtual community:

- **Transaction-Based:** trading focus;
- **Interest-Based:** common focus;
- **Fantasy-Based:** social exchange and experimentation in fictional environments (e.g., MMORPGs); and
- **Relationship-Based:** focus on mutual support among groups of collaborators.

With evolution of online gaming, virtual worlds and social virtual communities and e-commerce within these environments, however, this typology becomes less apparent. There is nonetheless some consistency with the supposition that cultures do engage with other similar cultures, assuming that each community is distinctive, shares interests and other characteristics.

In C2C relationships, as is also evident in B2C relationships discussed, trust is related to interpersonal factors such as integrity, competence and benevolence integrity that the individual will prove reliable and adhere to the agreement; competent in the ability to deliver what is agreed; and, benevolent in the sense that individuals will not act opportunistically (see Sutanonpaiboon & Abuhamdieh, 2008, for a literature review). Research into C2C online trust by Sutanonpaiboon & Abuhamdieh (2008) found five factors influence its existence:

- The individuals' general propensity to trust others;
- Knowledge and expertise;
- Risk propensity;
- The extent of their personal acquaintances and relationships; and
- Prior transaction experience.

To an extent, relationships and levels of trust are mediated by the forum in which the relationships develop and, in some instances, the forum will itself rank individuals according to their trustworthiness based, for example, on numbers of transactions, user feedback ratings, etc. Thus, how and by whom these fora are moderated will also influence C2C relationships. Whilst virtual com-

Figure 3. Technology Acceptance Model (Source Davis (1989, 1993); Davis et al (1989) in Holsapple & Sasidharan (2005))

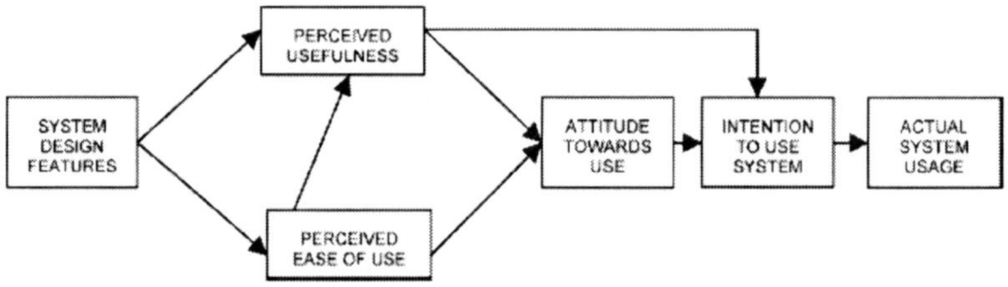

munities may be self-evolving (Rheingold, 1993), some are built by the organization as a means of deriving business benefits (Hagel & Armstrong, 1996; 1997) such as generating product and brand loyalty; increasing purchase intention; research; product development; direct income; indirect income from lower cost of servicing consumers (Shan et al, 2007). Such communities may have considerable benefits but are also subject to risks associated with negative customer feedback – an unhappy customer, it has often been suggested, will tell far more people about their experience than a happy one, thus virtual communities mediated by an organization carry the risk of mass distribution of undesirable messages.

In virtual fora other factors influencing trust arise including the authenticity of identities and personas that individuals may portray. Hine (2000), for example, suggests that a combination of factors must be considered for authenticity to be apparent: personal testimony, objective statement, external validation of sources and choice of image (and text) whereas Ridings (2006) suggests that trust within virtual communities may be a function of the social capital (relationships) created and managed by community members themselves where the defining features of social capital are (Ridings, 2006):

- Created through exchanges by community members;
- Owned jointly, because it is about exchange neither party has complete control;
- Built by generalized reciprocity - encourages cooperation among members;
- Benefits the collective group through cooperative behaviours; and
- Exhibited by generalised trust that is a necessary condition for exchange.(Blau, 1964; Coleman 1988; Kramer, 1999)

C2B and C2B2C are types of relationships that reflect the power of the community and their potential to add value and bring revenue to the organization. Although such models may well result in a form of 'strategic lock-in' to the organization for those consumers who invest considerable time and effort in contributing to the business, open business models are fundamentally about working collaboratively with consumers to develop products and services by utilizing their skills and competences. Long used in software development domains, open source makes use of virtual communities, which have been defined as communities of developers who voluntarily collaborate with commercial organizations to develop software they need (see Hemphill, 2006; Carillo and Okoli, 2007; Agerfalk & Fitzgerald, 2008). The Open Source Initiative (www.opensource.org) identifies a number of aspects that extend beyond the principle of merely sharing of software, distinct from freeware that is available free of charge:

- Free redistribution of source code and compiled programmes
- Derived works must be permitted
- Integrity of the author's source code
- No discrimination against persons, groups or fields applied to
- Mandatory distribution of open source license, which is not specific to a product and does not restrict other software licenses or redistribution

Trust in this context is deeply embedded in the relationship between the virtual community and the organization since without it open source projects would fail. From the organization's perspective, the challenge is to encourage participation by developing and fostering a sustainable community by, for example, inviting core community members to contribute non-trivial solutions. It does this by making considerable information available to the community. Evidently, the organization is placing its valuable assets e.g., intellectual property, in the hands of consumers but it does this knowing the results of any participation will exceed those the organization alone could achieve greater knowledge and advanced technology (von Hippel & von Krogh, 2003). In turn, the consumer contributes to something it values a bug free, extended use/ improved performance technology but also gains credibility and other personal benefits from having participated. From both perspectives, trust in the relationship acts to minimize the risk of opportunistic behavior (see, e.g., Fleming & Waguespack, 2007; Sutanonpaiboon & Abuhamdieh, 2008). Such relationships have been called 'bi-directional' (Sawhney & Prandelli, 2000).

The range of e-commercial models in online gaming and virtual world contexts is therefore extensive and evidently evolving to reflect community involvement. In this sense key features are that of co-creation and co-production.

These two themes have recently emerged in the relationship marketing literature and provide important insight into understanding the interactions between consumers and organizations. Prahalad and Ramaswamy (2000) suggested that consumers need to become involved in creating value for organizations and in turn these organizations need to learn how to use consumer competences to add value to the business in ways, for example, that have been identified above. Co-creation is unique to an individual consumer in terms of the value derived from use of a product or service ('value-in-use') that takes place in an experience environment comprising the organization's product ('value proposition') and the consumer's specific skills and competences. Co-production, however, is about "*participation in the development of the core offering itself. It can occur through inventiveness, co-design, or shared production of related goods*", such as the co-production of software in an open source project (Lusch and Vargo, 2006:284).

One of the key themes to emerge in the literature is that of providing 'experience environments' that are unique to and determined by individual consumers (Vargo & Lusch, 2008). Individual consumers create value in their use of the products or services through, for example, their play, mental effort, and social processes when participating in an online game where the developer has merely provided computer coding. In this sense, the organization (developer) has offered a 'value proposition' and acts as a 'value facilitator' to the consumer who plays the game to generate value for themselves (Grönroos, 2008). This has also been described as the concept of 'prosumption' (Toffler, 1980) consumers *pro*duce a product (game experience) for their own con*sumption*. Of course, one of the main challenges for an organization is being able to 'capture' the value created by consumers to add further value to their business and, increasingly, open models of innovation are being incorporated that seek to directly involve end users (consumers) in creating organizational offers, as outlined above in the overview of C2C relationships.

The next section extends these ideas and those introduced in the first section of the chapter into the evolving online economies developing within MMORPGs, virtual and mirror worlds.

EMERGENT AND CONVERGENT ECONOMIES

Discussion thus far has highlighted the emergence of economies within games, such as MMORPGs, social virtual worlds and mirror worlds where virtual trade has a real world value and beneficiaries are now both individuals and organizations. Indeed, trade of virtual property has grown significantly since the evolution of online games into MMORPGs and virtual worlds such that virtual property been defined as having five specific indications of existence (Blazer, 2006):

- Rivalry – the property is owned by one or a small number of people;
- Persistence – the property is maintained even when not being used, such as when players are offline or between games;

- Interconnectivity – the property may influence or be influenced by other players and their property, where value may vary according to the skills of the player in manipulating the game environment
- Secondary markets – the property may be created, traded, bought and sold and real world assets (such as money) may be exchanged; and
- Value added by players – value of the property may be developed or improved by the player through customization.

In 2005, however, the Economist newspaper published an article about whether virtual economies should be encouraged or banned. The article argued that online games were principally a medium for fun and escapism rather than efficiency but highlighted that moderating against trade, suggested at the time to have reached a value of $100M, had become an unmanageable task for games owners such as Blizzard Entertainment (World of Warcraft), despite its discouragement of in-game trading through game design techniques (for a discussion, see Alves & Roque, 2007). In 2009, the Virtual Economy Research Network (Hamari, 2009) also reported on China's attempts to restrict the exchange of real goods or money for virtual currencies with new legislation, although exchange for virtual goods is acceptable. Hamari identifies the reasons for this as being:

- Prevents illegalities;
- Prevents gambling;
- Prevents money laundering; and
- Preempts a negative impact on the Chinese financial system.

This highlights some of the macro-environmental issues that online gaming economies are bringing to the fore – they impact on social, economic, political and technological environments and are seen by some countries as a potential threat to their economic stability. This is primarily because the virtual worlds exist below a visible trading line across international boundaries making it especially difficult to apply taxation and evaluate the contribution of virtual exchange to national trade balances (see, e.g., Camp, 2007; Seto, 2008; Mack, 2008).

Convergence with the real world at this level is therefore a painful process but not all agree. An investigation by Castronova et al (2009) suggests that virtual world economies are different to the real world in a number of ways: they do not comprise banking or financial sectors, governments and taxation are not present per se (for example, Governments do not contribute to in-world activities with funding) and trade is immediately international; they are also subject to management rules set by the game developer and this influences the ways in which people trade. They do not, therefore, map to the real world, at least, to those large economies of stable countries. Their conclusions suggest, however, there may be some similarities to the emergent economies of volatile countries (frontier, black market and developing economies). That said, these are areas in which little research has been conducted to date and much more needs to be understood, for example, about the influence of game developers' management on in-world economies. With this proviso, the following discussion examines the emergent economies.

Online gaming economies are best discussed with reference to the divergent examples of World of Warcraft and Second Life. World of Warcraft (Blizzard Entertainment), as previously identified, is a fantasy world, classified as a MMORPG (role-playing game). Second Life® (Linden Labs) is a social virtual world, a game comprising varying degrees of simulated real life characteristics. Both worlds have in-world economies that are described as being 'synthetic' i.e., virtual (Castronova, 2005).

World of Warcraft's (WOW) economy is derived from the trade of weapons and gold and 'alternate' currencies in a form of barter trade (goods and services for goods and services) (see http://

us.blizzard.com/support/index.xml?locale=en_US&gameId=11&rootCategoryId=2318). These constitute game assets and are used by players to enhance their in-game experiences. Specific weapons are used to slaughter powerful opponents (monsters) and gold is 'earned' as a reward and is accumulated as a goal of gameplay that may be used to enhance status, traded for in-game resources and to participate in quests. Gold may be purchased with real world currency, and is often traded within guilds (communities of players). Currencies are also traded on different servers where the game is played. Hence there are multiple markets equating to the online servers and guilds within them. However, the assets are often tied to a specific character that means there is a secondary trading market for characters with powerful armories that may have progressed to high levels of gameplay. Thus, two aspects of secondary trade (out-of-game) and markets exist for the gold and the characters. There are numerous internet sites trading in WOW gold. As at September 2009, average gold prices for US Dollars were approximately US$0.002-4 (see e.g., http://www.mmofly.com) and characters such as trolls, gnomes and elves were selling for between US$110 and US$200 (see e.g., http://www.wowtrades.com/wow-buy-accounts/World-Of-Warcraft-US). The latter asset has been the subject of considerable controversy recently. 'Farmers' are employed by game players as cheap labor to acquire in-game resources that enable character development in exchange for real world money.

Second Life's (SL) economy is derived from the trade of in-world assets for the game currency, called Linden Dollars. The assets are created by players (residents), including the buildings, furniture, vehicles, avatar, clothing, body art and adornments, pets and numerous other objects (see Figure 4) that remain the intellectual property of its creator whether or not the asset remains in-world (see item 3 at http://secondlife.com/corporate/tos.php). The intellectual property to individual objects is traded using the virtual currency at prices

Figure 4. SL in-world image (Dileoo Kirax) (The virtual sculpture above has a L$ price tag of 6999 a real world equivalent value of approximately $26 (as of September 2009))

that are determined between the buyer and seller in the context of the broader market ecosystem (Castronova et al, 2009). Linden Labs have created the Linden Dollar (L$) as a 'floating currency' which means the exchange rate is determined relative to the real world currency of the US Dollar – for example, as at September 29, 2009, the exchange rate for Lindens was reported as being L$262.02 per US$1 (see http://secondlife.com/statistics/economy-market.php). The exchange rates are monitored on the LindeX, a currency market. The existence of this feature adds to the realism of the in-world context.

These two economies illustrate the creativity in online trading through gameplay. The activity of trading clearly has significant implications for the game developer, the economy as a whole and also for the players (Papagiannidis et al, 2008). For example, Lehdonvirta (2009) identifies different ways that users think of real-money and its influence on the worlds in which it operates include:

- **Competition:** in MMORPGs, for example, trading in real money is often considered to be tantamount to cheating where the net result is some competitive advantage;
- **Socializing:** trade using real money is a way that players may express themselves through buying behavior, personal and social identity;
- **Customization:** using real money to trade facilitates players to modify their experiences to their personal taste.

Indeed, Papagiannidis et al (2008) summarize a number of important considerations for the future of online gaming within MMORPGs and virtual worlds (see Figure 5) where the fine line between game and real world presents issues for policy makers and organizations.

The figure identifies that whilst entrepreneurism and innovation are key benefits of the emergent online gaming economies, the challenges yet to be resolved lay in the development at Government and organizational levels of policies related to economic, governance, technology and organizational ethics given their potential impact upon social issues, including but not limited to, health / wellbeing (e.g., addiction) and self-fulfillment, employment / work, wealth, democracy and freedom, knowledge, access, privacy and security; trade related issues of taxation, fair trade, sustainability and corporate reporting; and technological

Figure 5. The fine line between real and virtual world trade (Reprinted from Technological Forecasting and Social Change, 75, pp. 610–622, Papagiannidis, S., Bourlakis, M. and Li, F. Copyright (2008), with permission from Elsevier.)

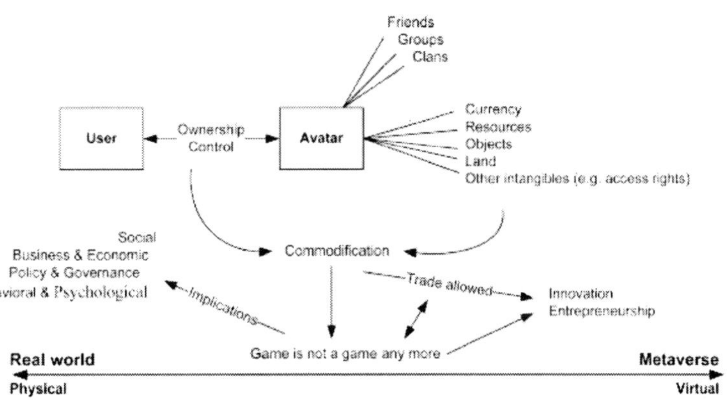

developments including internet infrastructure, digitization and education.

In essence, these issues relate to convergence of virtual and real life worlds, where financial considerations are fundamental components of sustainable economies. Thus, an important consideration for convergence is the portability of currencies and activity between online worlds. Steps have already been made in this direction by the development and release of services that enable portability (Nuttall, 2008; Castranova et al, 2009). Other aspects relate to the values of players in the various gaming environments – issues of identity and social identity, communication, relationships and networks and environmentally mediated trust (technology performance, etc.) as well as technological compatibility and an assumed inter-organizational infrastructure that supports a range of social activities including dispute resolution will also need consideration (see Noane, 2008). These are likely to prove difficult to realize in practice because implementation will undoubtedly require organizations to work together to develop initiatives, however, in so doing they will also need to share profits to maximize the interests of all. Further aspects will relate to the ways in which organizations integrate marketing activities with consumer behavior – how brands appear, how co-creation and co-production takes place and how third party owners engage with these. The complexity of this is exacerbated by the nature of internet trade and the dynamics of its ongoing rapid evolution.

CONCLUSION

This chapter has presented a review of topics and discussion pertaining to the convergence of online gaming with e-commerce. MMORPGs and virtual worlds have a relatively recent history but industry figures reveal staggering popularity and growth rates, where within one game environment alone has now seen in-game trades of more than $1B since its launch just six years previously. Their popularity has been tied to evolution of the internet which is widely considered to be an enabler of online trade and this chapter has identified a range of different commercial business models that are used within contemporary gaming environments. The models of commercialization relate to game distribution, third party involvement, game augmentation and player consumption. These constitute different types of trust-based relationship between organizations and players, including business-to-business, business-to-consumer, consumer-to-consumer and consumer-to-business. Issues arise of personal and social identity and how socialization in online communities of interest is mediated and moderated by the games developers and related technologies. The online game and virtual world 'experience environment' highlights the intertwined nature of co-creation and co-production between the game player and developer that has the potential to evolve games. Despite the early identification of pertinent issues around economic transactions and associated legalities, these remain unresolved in the research literature and under-developed by games organizations and governments.

REFERENCES

Aarseth, E. J. (1997). *Cybertext: Perspectives on Ergodic Literature*. Baltimore, MD: John Hopkins University Press.

Abrams, S., & Grun, S. (2008). Mundanes at the Gate… and Perverts Within: Managing Internal and External Threats to Communities Online. In Adams, T. L., & Smith, S. A. (Eds.), *Electronic Tribes*. Austin, TX: University of Texas Press.

Ågerfalk, P. J., & Fitzgerald, B. (2008). Outsourcing to an unknown workforce: exploring opensourcing as a global sourcing strategy. *Management Information Systems Quarterly*, *32*(2), 385–409.

Ajzen, I., & Fishbein, M. (1980). *Understanding attitudes and predicting social behavior*. Upper Saddle River, NJ: Prentice Hall.

Alves, T. R., & Roque, L. (2007) Because Players Pay: The Business Model Influence on MMOG Design. *Proceedings of DiGRA 2007: Situated Play*, September, Tokyo, Japan, (pp. 658-663).

Anon. (2002). Online Gaming Industry Reports, *Datamonitor*, Retrieved September 10, 2009, from www.datamonitor.com.

Anon. (2005). A model economy. *Economist*, January 22, p. 73

Anon. (2009). *About QuakeCon*, Retrieved September 14, 2009, from http://web.archive.org/web/20000816025343/www.quakecon.org/about.html

Anon. (2009). Second Life® transactions reach $1B. *GamingIndustry*, Retrieved September 23, 2009, from http://www.gamedaily.com/articles/news/second-life-transactions-reach-1-billion/

Apperley, T. H. (2006). Genre and game studies: Toward a critical approach to video game genres. *Simulation & Gaming*, *37*(1), 6–23. doi:10.1177/1046878105282278

Ashforth, B., & Mael, F. (1989). Social Identity Theory and the Organization. *Academy of Management Review*, *14*(1), 20–30. doi:10.2307/258189

Atkins, G. (2003). *More than a Game: the Computer Game as a Fictional Form*. Manchester, UK: Manchester University Press.

Barton, M. (2008). *Dungeons and desktops: the history of computer role-playing games*. Wellesley: A K Peters

Bedford, C. (1998). LAN Parties: It's a Scene Baby! *Looneygames*, Retrieved September 14, 2009, from http://www.loonygames.com/content/1.8/feat/index2.php

Berthon, P., Pitt, L., Cyr, D., & Campbell, C. (2008). E-readiness and trust: macro and micro dualities for e-commerce in a global environment. *International Marketing Review*, *25*(6), 700–714. doi:10.1108/02651330810915592

Blanchard, A., & Markus, M. (2004). The Experienced 'Sense' of a Virtual Community: Characteristics and Processes. *The Data Base for Advances in Information Systems*, *35*(1), 65–79.

Blau, P. M. (1964). *Exchange and power in social life*. New York: John Wiley & Sons.

Blazer, C. (2006). The Five Indicia of Virtual Property. *Pierce Law Review*, *5*, 137.

Boellstorff, T. (2008). *Coming of Age in Second Life: An Anthropologist Explores the Virtually Human*. Princeton, NJ: Princeton University Press.

Book, B. (2004). In Moving Beyond the Game: Social Virtual Worlds. Paper presented on the panel The Culture of Play at the conference *State of Play 2: Reloaded*. New York Law School, October 28-30.

Brightman, J. (2008). Video Games Explode: Global Revenues Now on Par with Box Office, *Game Daily*, retrieved September 21, 2009, from http://www.gamedaily.com/articles/news/video-games-explode-global-revenues-now-on-par-with-box-office/?biz=1

Burr, V. (1995). *An introduction to social constructionism*. London: Routledge. doi:10.4324/9780203299968

Caillois, R. (1957). *Les jeux et les hommes*. Gallimard.

Camp, B. T. (2007). The Play's the Thing: A Theory of Taxing Virtual Worlds. *The Hastings Law Journal*, *59*, 1.

Castronova, E. (2005). *Synthetic Worlds: The Business and Culture of Online Games*. Chicago: University of Chicago Press.

Castronova, E., Williams, D., Shen, C., Ratan, R., Xiong, L., Huang, Y., & Keegan, G. (2009). As real as real? Macroeconomic behavior in a large-scale virtual world. *New Media & Society*, *11*(5), 685–707. doi:10.1177/1461444809105346

Clark Vance, D. (2008). Like a Neighbourhood of Sisters: Can Culture be Formed Electronically. In *Adams, T.L. & Smith, S.A. (2008). Electronic Tribes*. Austin, TX: University of Texas Press.

Claro, M. (2007). Video games and education, Retrieved September 14, 2009, from www.oecd.org/dataoecd/14/60/39548100.pdf

Coleman, J. S. (1988). Social capital in the creation of human capital. *American Journal of Sociology*, *94*, 95–120. doi:10.1086/228943

Cova, B., Kozinets, R. V., & Shankar, A. (2007). *Consumer Tribes*. Oxford: Butterworth-Heinemann.

Davis, A., Murphy, J., Owens, D., Kazanchi, D., & Zigurs, I. (2009). Avatars, People, and Virtual Worlds: Foundations for Research in Metaverses. *Journal of the Association for Information Systems*, *10*(20), 90–117.

Davis, F. D. (1989). Perceived usefulness, perceived ease of use, and user acceptance of information technology. *Management Information Systems Quarterly*, *13*(3), 319–339. doi:10.2307/249008

Davis, F. D. (1993). User acceptance of information technology: system characteristics, user perceptions and behavioral impacts. *International Journal of Man-Machine Studies*, *38*(3), 475–487. doi:10.1006/imms.1993.1022

Davis, F. D., Bagozzi, R. P., & Warshaw, P. R. (1989). User acceptance of computer technology: a comparison of two theoretical models. *Management Science*, *35*(8), 982–1003. doi:10.1287/mnsc.35.8.982

Deaux, K., Reid, A., Mizraha, K., & Ethier, K. A. (1995). Parameters of Social Identity. *Journal of Personality and Social Psychology*, *68*(2), 280–291. doi:10.1037/0022-3514.68.2.280

Dibbell, J. (1993). *A Rape in Cyberspace*, Retrieved September 10, 2009, from http://www.juliandibbell.com/texts/bungle.html.

Farhoomand, A., & Lovelock, P. (2001). *Global E-Commerce*. Singapore: Prentice Hall.

Fleming, L., & Waguespack, D. M. (2007). Brokerage, Boundary Spanning, and Leadership in Open Innovation Communities. *Organization Science*, *18*(2), 165–180. doi:10.1287/orsc.1060.0242

Friedman, T. (1999). Civilization and its discontents: Simulation, Subjectivity and Space. In Smith, G. M. (Ed.), *On a Silver Platter* (p. 137). New York: New York University Press.

Garvey, C. (1990). *Play*. Boston: Harvard University Press.

Gelernter, D. (1992). *Mirror Worlds: or the Day Software Puts the Universe in a Shoebox...How It Will Happen and What It Will Mean*. New York: Oxford University Press.

Godin, S. (2008). *Tribes*. London: Piatkus.

Golembiewski, R. T., & McConkie, M. (1975). The centrality of interpersonal trust in group processes. In Cooper, G. L. (Ed.), *Theories of Group Processes* (pp. 131–185). London: John Wiley.

Grassian, E., & Trueman, R. (2007). Stumbling, Bumbling, Teleporting and Flying... Librarian Avatars in Second Life®. *RSR. Reference Services Review*, *35*(1), 84–89. doi:10.1108/00907320710729373

Green, J., & Hannon, C. (2007). *Their Space: Education for a digital generation*. London: Demos.

Grimes, S., & Feenberg, A. (2009). Rationalizing Play: A Critical Theory of Digital Gaming. *The Information Society*, *25*(2), 105–118. doi:10.1080/01972240802701643

Grönroos, C. (2008). Service Logic Revisited: Who Creates Value? And Who Co-creates? *European Business Review*, *20*(4), 298–314. doi:10.1108/09555340810886585

Hagel, J. * Armstrong, A.G. (1997). *Net gain: Expanding markets through virtual communities*. Boston: Harvard Business School Press.

Hagel, J., & Armstrong, A. G. (1996). The real value of on-line communities. *Harvard Business Review*, *74*(3), 134–141.

Harrison McKnight, D., & Chervany, N. L. (2002). What Trust Means in E-Commerce Customer Relationships: An Interdisciplinary Conceptual Typology. *International Journal of Electronic Commerce*, *6*(2), 35–59.

Hemphill, T. A. (2006). A Taxonomy of closed and open source software industry business models. *International Journal of Innovation and Technology Management*, *3*(1), 61–82. doi:10.1142/S0219877006000661

Hine, C. (2000). *Virtual Ethnography*. Thousand Oaks, CA: Sage Publications.

Holsapple, C. W., & Sasidharan, S. (2005). The dynamics of trust in B2C e-commerce: a research model and agenda. *Information Systems and e-Business Management*, 3, pp. 377–403.

Howard, J. (2008). *Quests: Design, Theory and History in Games and Narratives*. Wellesley: A.K. Peters.

Howgego, T. (2009). *Map of World of Warcraft online communities,* Retrieved September 18, 2009, from http://timhowgego.com/map-of-world-of-warcraft-online-communities.html

Jarok (1998). Guide to Roleplaying, *Tharsis Gate: Imaginary Realities*, Retrieved September 12, 2009, from http://www.tharsis-gate.org/articles/imaginary/GUIDET~1.HTM.

Juul, J. (2005). *Half-Real: Video Games between Real Rules and Fictional Worlds*. Cambridge, MA: MIT Press.

Kametsu, A. (2007). Virtual worlds moving towards the 'multiverse' era, *Nomura Research Institute Papers*, October 1, 122

Kardaras, D., & Karakostas, B. (2007). Virtual Communities in Banking Customer Retention. In *Dasgupta, S. Encyclopedia of Virtual Communities and Technologies*. Hershey, PA: Idea Group Reference.

Kelly, R.V. (2004). *Massively Mutiplayer Online Role-Playing Games: The People, the Addiction and the Playing Experienc*e. Jefferson: McFarland & Co.

Kim, J. W., Choi, J., Qualls, W., & Han, K. (2008). It takes a marketplace community to raise brand commitment: the role of online communities. *Journal of Marketing Management*, *24*(3-4), 409–431. doi:10.1362/026725708X306167

King, D., Delfabbro, P., & Griffiths, M. (2009 in press). Video game structural characteristics: A new psychological taxonomy. *International Journal of Mental Health and Addiction.*

Kozinets, R. (1999). E-Tribalised Marketing?: The Strategic Implications of Virtual Communities of Consumption. *The Journal of Consumer Research*, *29*(3), 20–38.

Kramer, R. (1999). Trust and distrust in organizations: Emerging perspectives, enduring questions. *Annual Review of Psychology*, *50*, 569–598. doi:10.1146/annurev.psych.50.1.569

Lawrence, E., Lawrence, J., Newton, S., Dann, S., Corbitt, B., & Thanasankit, T. (2003). *Internet Commerce: Digital Models for Business* (3rd ed.). Milton: John Wiley & Sons.

Leadbeater, C. (2009). *We-Think*. London: Profile Books.

Lehdonvirta, V. (2009). Virtual item sales as a revenue model: identifying attributes that drive purchase decisions. *Electronic Commerce Research*, *9*(1/2), 97–113. doi:10.1007/s10660-009-9028-2

Li, C., & Bernoff, J. (2008). *Groundswell: Winning in a World Transformed by Social Technologies*. Boston: Harvard Business Press.

Lowood, H. (2005). Real-Time Performance: Machinima and Games Studies. *International Digital Media and Arts Journal*, *2*(1), 10–17.

Lowood, H. (2006). High Performance Play: The Making of Machinima. *Journal of Media Practice*, *7*(1), 25–42. doi:10.1386/jmpr.7.1.25/1

Lusch, R. F., & Vargo, S. L. (2006). Service-dominant logic: reactions, reflections and refinements. *Marketing Theory*, *6*(3), 281–288. doi:10.1177/1470593106066781

Lynch, D. C., & Rose, M. T. (Eds.). (1993). *Internet System Handbook*. Reading, MA: Addison-Wesley.

Mack, D.J. (2008). iTax: An analysis of the laws and policies behind the taxation of property transactions in a virtual world, *Administrative Law Review*, Summer, 60, 3

Morgan, R. M., & Hunt, S. D. (1994). The commitment-trust theory of relationship marketing. *Journal of Marketing*, *58*(3), 20–38. doi:10.2307/1252308

Mulligan, J. (1999). History of Online Games, *Tharsis Gate: Imaginary Realities*, Retrieved September 14, 2009, from http://www.tharsis-gate.org/articles/imaginary/HISTOR~1.HTM

Naughton, L. (2008). Magic, Myth and Mayhem: Tribalization in the Digital Age. In *Adams, T.L. & Smith, S.A. (2008). Electronic Tribes*. Austin, TX: University of Texas Press.

Newman, J. (2004). *Videogames*. London: Routledge.

Ng, B. D., & Wiemer-Hastings, P. (2005). Addiction to the Internet and Online Gaming. *Cyberpsychology & Behavior*, *8*(2), 110–113. doi:10.1089/cpb.2005.8.110

Noane, E. (2008). One Avatar, Many Worlds: Companies want to let users carry their avatar identities online. *MIT Technology Review*, Retrieved September 25, 2009, from http://www.technologyreview.com/web/20529/page1/

Nuttall, C. (2008). Second Life's maiden voyage across the metaverse, *Financial Times*, Retrieved July, 8, 2008, from http://blogs.ft.com/techblog/2008/07/second-lifes-maiden-voyage-across-the-metaverse/

O'Neil, M. (2009). *Cyber Chiefs: Autonomy and Authority in Online Tribes*. London: Pluto Press.

Papagiannidis, S., Bourlakis, M., & Li, F. (2008). Making real money in virtual worlds: MMORPGs and emerging business opportunities, challenges and ethical implications in metaverses. *Technological Forecasting and Social Change*, *75*, 610–622. doi:10.1016/j.techfore.2007.04.007

Pargman, D., & Jakobsson, P. (2006). The Magic is Gone: A Critical Examination of the Gaming Situation." In *Proceedings of Mediaterra: Gaming Realities*, October 4-8, Athens.

Perry, D. (2009). How video games can sweep in the cash. *Business Week*, Retrieved September 22, 2009, from http://images.businessweek.com/ss/08/08/0815_make_money_from_games/1.htm

Polsson, K. (2009). *Chronology of Video Game Systems*, Retrieved September 20, 2009, from http://www.islandnet.com/~kpolsson/vidgame/vid2007.htm

Prahalad, C. K., & Ramaswamy, V. (2003). The new frontier of experience innovation. *MIT Sloan Management Review*, *44*(4), 12–18.

Rayport, J. F., & Sviokla, J. J. (1994). Managing in the market-space. *Harvard Business Review*, *72*(6), 141–150.

Rheingold, H. (1993). *The Virtual Community: Homesteading in the Electronic Frontier*. New York: Harper Collins.

Ridings, C. M. (2006). Virtual communities and social capital theory. In *Dasgupta, S. Encyclopedia of Virtual Communities and Technologies*. Hershey, PA: Idea Group Reference.

Ryan, R. M., Rigby, C., & Przybylski, A. (2006). The Motivational Pull of Video Games: A Self-Determination Theory Approach. *Motivation and Emotion*, *30*(4), 347–363. doi:10.1007/s11031-006-9051-8

Rymaszewski, M., Au, W. J., Wallace, M., Winters, C., Ondrejka, C., & Batsone-Cunningham, B. (2007). *Second Life: the official guide*. New Jersey: Wiley Publishing.

Salen, K., & Zimmerman, E. (2004). *Rules of Play: Game Design Fundamentals*. Cambridge, MA: MIT Press.

Sanchez, J. (2009). A social history of virtual worlds. *Library Technology Reports*, *45*(2), 9–12.

Sawhney, M., & Prandelli, E. (2000). Communities of Creation: Managing Distributed Innovation in Turbulent Markets. *California Management Review*, *42*(4), 24–54.

Schrader, P., & McCreery, M. (2008). The acquisition of skill and expertise in massively multiplayer online games. *Educational Technology Research and Development*, *56*(5/6), 557–574. doi:10.1007/s11423-007-9055-4

Seto, T.P. (2008). *When is a Game Only a Game?: The Taxation of Virtual Worlds* (August, 12 2008). Loyola-LA Legal Studies Paper No. 2008-24

Shan, L. M., Sutanto, J., Kankanhalli, A., & Tan, B. C. Y. (2007). Virtual community models in relation to e-business models. In *Dasgupta, S. Encyclopedia of Virtual Communities and Technologies*. Hershey, PA: Idea Group Reference.

Smart, J., Cascio, J., & Paffendorf, J. (2007). *Metaverse Roadmap: Pathways to the 3D Web*. Retrieved September 19, 2009, from http://www.metaverseroadmap.org.

Sok Huhh, J. (2006). Some Facts on MapleStory, *GameStudy.org*, Retrieved September 12, 2009, from http://www.gamestudy.org/eblog/?p=32

Stephenson, N. (1992). *Snow Crash*. New York: Bantam Books.

Strauss, J., El-Ansary, A., & Frost, R. (2003). *E-Marketing* (3rd ed.). Upper Saddle River, New Jersey: Prentice Hall.

Sutanonpaiboon, J., & Abuhamdieh, A. (2008). Factors Influencing Trust in Online Consumer-to-Consumer (C2C) Transactions. *Journal of Internet Commerce*, *7*(2), 203–219. doi:10.1080/15332860802067706

Taylor, T. L. (2005). *Play between Worlds: Exploring Online Game Culture*. Cambridge, MA: MIT Press.

Toffler, A. (1980). *The Third Wave*. New York: William Collins Sons and Co. Ltd.

Vargo, S. L., & Lusch, R. F. (2008). Service-dominant Logic: Continuing the Evolution. *Journal of the Academy of Marketing Science*, *36*, 1–10. doi:10.1007/s11747-007-0069-6

von Hippel, E., & von Krogh, G. (2003). Open source software and the "private-collective" model: Issues for organization science. *Organization Science*, *14*(2), 209–223. doi:10.1287/orsc.14.2.209.14992

Williams, R. L., & Cothrell, J. (2000). Four Smart Ways to Run Online Communities. *Sloan Management Review*, *41*(4), 81–91.

Wolf, M. (Ed.). (2001). *The Medium of the Video Game*. Austin, TX: University of Texas Press.

Zillman, D., Byrant, J., & Sapolsky, N. (1989). Enjoyment from Sports Spectatorship. In Goldstein, J. (Ed.), *Sports, Games and Play* (pp. 241–278). Hillsdale: Laurence Erlbaum.

ADDITIONAL READING

Abrams, S., & Grun, S. (2008). Mundanes at the Gate… and Perverts Within: Managing Internal and External Threats to Communities Online. In *Adams, T.L. & Smith, S.A. (2008). Electronic Tribes*. Austin, TX: University of Texas Press.

Ajzen, I., & Fishbein, M. (1980). *Understanding attitudes and predicting social behavior*. Upper Saddle River, New Jersey: Prentice Hall.

Any introductory standard economics textbook on the macro-environment and GDP (gross domestic product)

Berthon, P., Pitt, L., Cyr, D., & Campbell, C. (2008). E-readiness and trust: macro and micro dualities for e-commerce in a global environment. *International Marketing Review*, *25*(6), 700–714. doi:10.1108/02651330810915592

Castronova, E., Williams, D., Shen, C., Ratan, R., Xiong, L., Huang, Y., & Keegan, G. (2009). As real as real? Macroeconomic behavior in a large-scale virtual world. *New Media & Society*, *11*(5), 685–707. doi:10.1177/1461444809105346

Cooper, R., Dibbell, J., & Spaight, T. (2007). *Alter Ego: Avatars and their creators*. London: Chris Boot Ltd.

Cova, B., Kozinets, R. V., & Shankar, A. (2007). *Consumer Tribes*. Oxford, UK: Butterworth-Heinemann.

Davis, A., Murphy, J., Owens, D., Kazanchi, D., & Zigurs, I. (2009). Avatars, People, and Virtual Worlds: Foundations for Research in Metaverses. *Journal of the Association for Information Systems*, *10*(20), 90–117.

Dibbell, J. (1993). *A Rape in Cyberspace*, available online at http://www.juliandibbell.com/texts/bungle.html.

Fleming, L., & Waguespack, D. M. (2007). Brokerage, Boundary Spanning, and Leadership. *Organization Science*, *18*(2), 165–180. doi:10.1287/orsc.1060.0242

Hagel, J., & Armstrong, A. G. (1996). The real value of on-line communities. *Harvard Business Review*, *74*(3), 134–141.

Hemphill, T. A. (2006). A Taxonomy of closed and open source software industry business models. *International Journal of Innovation and Technology Management*, *3*(1), 61–82. doi:10.1142/S0219877006000661

Leadbeater, C. (2009). *We-Think*. London: Profile Books.

Mack, D.J. (2008). iTax: An analysis of the laws and policies behind the taxation of property transactions in a virtual world, *Administrative Law Review*, Summer, 60, 3

Noane, E. (2008). One Avatar, many worlds: Companies want to let users carry their avatar identities online. *MIT Technology Review*, Retrieved September 25, 2009, from http://www.technologyreview.com/web/20529/page1/

Papagiannidis, S., Bourlakis, M., & Li, F. (2008). Making real money in virtual worlds: MMORPGs and emerging business opportunities, challenges and ethical implications in metaverses. *Technological Forecasting and Social Change*, *75*, 610–622. doi:10.1016/j.techfore.2007.04.007

Rayport, J. F., & Sviokla, J. J. (1994). Managing in the market-space. *Harvard Business Review*, *72*(6), 141–150.

Smart, J., Cascio, J., & Paffendorf, J. (2007). *Metaverse Roadmap: Pathways to the 3D Web*. Retrieved September 19, 2009, from http://www.metaverseroadmap.org.

KEY TERMS AND DEFINITIONS

Machinima: Concatenation of 'machine' and 'cinema' (misspelt), it is a term applied to original short films created from edited play of 3D computer games.

Marketspace: Coined by Rayport and Sviokla (1994), it is a virtual (online) market where social interaction and general information exchange takes place around brands.

Metaverse: Meta means 'beyond' and verse is a shortening of the word 'universe'. Originally coined by Stephenson (1992) to describe a successor to the internet based on virtual reality technologies, the term is used to describe an immersive fictional virtual world.

Mirror World: A microcosm of the real world that may be informationally enhanced e.g., Google Earth.

MMORPG: acronym for massively multiplayer online role-playing game.

Prosumption: Concatenation of 'production' and 'consumption', eg., a gaming experience requires the gamer to produce an episode of game play which they simultaneously consume (Toffler, 1980).

WOW: Acronym for World of Warcraft (Blizzard Entertainment), currently the world's most popular MMORPG.

Chapter 5
Evolution of Business in Virtual Environments

Rita King
Dancing Ink Productions, USA

ABSTRACT

Virtual business as defined in this chapter is any business interaction that takes place in an immersive digital space in which individuals are represented by "avatars" in three-dimensional, user-created environments. While there are hundreds of virtual worlds and hundreds of millions of people globally participating in them, this chapter focuses on Second Life®, owned by Linden Lab. At the time of this writing, eighteen million Second Life® accounts have been registered and participants have spent a billion hours in-world. US $1 billion has changed hands in Second Life® between people in more than 100 countries representing hundreds of cultures. Thousands of universities, companies, institutions and organizations have Second Life® bureaus. This chapter will examine the evolution of some of the most remarkable projects taking place within this virtual world, featuring the passion of early adopters, the role of the media, current examples of virtual work, the evolution of the virtual workforce, the shift in the role of managers toward a collaborative virtual model, the relationship between education and virtual work, and virtual goods and services.

INTRODUCTION

The most important fact about virtual business is that it's real. The contents of this chapter are based largely on my own experiences as the CEO and Creative Director of Dancing Ink Productions (DIP), a company that works toward the evolution of a new global culture and economy in the Imagination Age. DIP works globally to maximize the real-world benefits of digital culture in all its forms, and many of our clients, including Fortune 500 companies, universities and think tanks, have created a significant presence in Second Life®. Linden Lab, the company that owns Second Life®, is also now a client.

DOI: 10.4018/978-1-61692-808-7.ch005

Virtual work offers a geographically dispersed global workforce an opportunity to gather, work and learn in real time without the cost of time and resources spent on unnecessary travel. Virtual work enhances vital face-to-face meetings by facilitating gatherings between teams, partners, potential clients and collaborators between real-world meetings. Second Life® is also an extremely useful platform for mixed-media broadcasting to the internet, where a live participatory audience can experience speakers sharing ideas and contribute their own in live, real-time chat, without having to be in Second Life®.

With its focus on user-created content, Second Life® is an ideal venue for collaboration. It allows people to imagine, create and inhabit shared environments that can be infused with multiple streams of mixed media and other business tools. Communication can take place in private or group voice and text chat, enabling multiple simultaneous conversations to unfold. User-created content permits developers to create and sell virtual items, goods and services. This chapter will begin with the earliest pioneers.

EARLY ADOPTERS

When cars were first introduced to the cultural and economic scenes, many people considered them horseless carriages. The idea of traveling 60 miles in an hour's time held little allure for people who had no interest in going that far from home when communities, families and friends were all nearby. Moving pictures seemed similarly absurd at their advent. Why look at moving pictures when life moves right in front of you with no special arrangement required?

Virtual worlds fit into this same category of mainstream reception, but like their predecessors, the novelty will give way to a major cultural and economic transformation. The shift will be tumultuous for those who don't refresh their skills in time, and lucrative for many who have long waited for technology to catch up with the sheer force of the human imagination.

Early adopters of virtual worlds were creative pioneers, learning how to inhabit and collaborate on one another's ideas in three dimensions. This is particularly attractive for sophisticated, tech-savvy employees of companies such as IBM, often working in remote locations without colleagues on site.

I first became aware of IBM's presence in virtual worlds on November 10, 2006, after I completed six months of work on an investigative report, "Big, Easy Money: Disaster Profiteering on the American Gulf Coast." The field of journalism was at the beginning of its own massive, technology-driven shift, creating as many dilemmas as opportunities. Innovation doesn't happen just by peeking over the edge of a competitor's cubicle to see sketches on the drawing board, and the saturation of industry-wide confusion and panic began to far outstrip progress.

I was married not to the idea of print, but rather the profession of storytelling. Instead of documenting what had already gone wrong, I wanted to contribute to finding solutions to economic and cultural crises and document those stories. As I mulled my options, I had no idea that I would soon discover a virtual world in which it would be possible to create a new reality.

Over lunch that fateful day, Clifford Pickover, a friend who works at IBM, asked me if I'd ever heard of Second Life®.

"Second Life®? What's that?"

"In Second Life®, you can be anything or do anything," he said. "You can live in a massive beach house, or in a tree house in the woods with beautiful stained glass windows, and you can create your own appearance, right down to the shape of your nose and the color of your eyes."

He wrote a name down on a napkin and slid it my way. It contained the avatar name of IBM's

Chief Virtual Architect. By now, everybody at the table was listening intently. There was a chorus of questions: "What is this? There's a place where you can do what?"

"Get in touch once you get in Second Life®," he said as I looked down at the napkin.

Amazed, I raced home to check out Second Life®. The website came up instantly, and I found myself choosing a new name, Eureka Dejavu, for my avatar, the generic figure that would represent me digitally until I figured out how to get her a new skin, shape, hair, eyes, fingernails, shoes, clothes—even a new walk and roster of postures.

After a brief struggle with the unfamiliar interface, I attempted to contact IBM's Chief Virtual Architect, known in the physical world as Craig Becker. He responded immediately, much to my initial shock, and became my shaman in this whole new world in those initial weeks and months. He told me how to buy a building and gave me a little plot of land on his private island so I could set up the windmill that I acquired for a few hundred Linden dollars purchased with my credit card. The U.S. dollar cost of the building was a couple of bucks.

Craig gave me the names of several other IBMers and suggested that I talk to them about the remarkable work they were accomplishing within Second Life®. Before long, I'd amassed several thick binders full of interviews. The activities of IBM employees in Second Life® and across numerous virtual worlds, I would soon learn, were mind-boggling. Scientists from multiple continents were at work in virtual labs on very real problems, like protein folding, a process that leads to progress toward treating diseases such as Alzheimer's. They showed me a massive three-dimensional molecule of protein folding in the air above their heads.

Late one night, a guest appeared in my windmill and identified herself as Sandra Kearney. At the time, she directed IBM's exploration of virtual worlds. She wanted to know what I was planning to do with the information I was stockpiling, and I told her that I honestly didn't know. It turned out that her real-world office was a stone's throw from mine, and she asked me to visit her the following week. By the time I left that meeting I had agreed to start a company and take IBM on as my first client.

One of the main reasons why IBM embraced immersion in virtual worlds was because of its capacity to connect a geographically dispersed workforce. In fact, it was the IBMers themselves who chose to direct the company toward an investment in virtual world exploration in 2006, when 37,000 of the company's employees participated in an InnovationJam to determine how $100 million would be spent on 10 key issues.

Every virtual interaction involves real people in the real world. Second Life®'s early adopters understood that intuitively but faced a battle against public perception and skeptical executives who wrongly perceived virtual worlds as productivity-sapping games instead of greatly beneficial environments in which significant interactions and wild innovations routinely take place across geographical and other boundaries.

While working on this chapter, I posted a question to Twitter asking how many people work virtually. The first person who responded was Rob Muhlestein of Mooresville, North Carolina, who identifies himself in his Twitter profile as an "eclectic goof, story teller, Second Life® educator, software engineer, consultant, 3D developer, endorphin addict, linguist, novice designer and machinimist."

In Twitter's 140-character limit he responded, "Programming and such for IBM for nearly 10 years from home office (closet), team scattered. VWs are my water cooler, chat, Skype."

THE MEDIA NARRATIVE

It is much easier to spot and document stellar failures than it is to detect at the onset that sophisticated, visionary business enterprise groups are changing the global economy by collaborating in new and spectacular ways. It doesn't help when those interactions are taking place in cartoonish avatar bodies. It isn't surprising that the media initially latched onto salacious avatars instead of seeking out executives, engineers, designers and visionaries of all stripes at work.

Marketing campaigns with a distinctively real-world style didn't work in a virtual environment that's far more experiential than a billboard or banner ad. This was taken as evidence that the hype around the novelty of Second Life® far outweighed the possibility of substance. Many companies, afraid to miss out on the next big thing, rushed in without a firm understanding of the local culture and overspent on construction of virtual infrastructure without a plan for attracting and providing value for a community of participants.

The advent of virtual platforms represented a new beat for journalists. Just as a reporter can't show up in an unfamiliar region of the physical world and immediately understand the language, customs, rituals, and rhythm of the place, journalists covering Second Life® needed to immerse themselves in the space, and some did. CNN has a bureau in Second Life® that routinely meets and relies on avatars in Second Life® to report on the stories that they encounter. Wagner James Au is Second Life®'s most dedicated independent journalist, publishing the New World Notes blog and writing a book, "The Making of Second Life®," that was published by HarperCollins.

Some social media platforms, such as Facebook, MySpace and Twitter, are easy to understand at face value. Almost any journalist can understand how the platforms are used and the basic etiquette of each environment. This isn't to say that the nuanced applications and motivations arising from each aren't complex, but participating in a three-dimensional immersive space such as Second Life® requires a greater time commitment to learn how to merely navigate and communicate. Public awareness of the global economic collapse triggered a more serious look at three-dimensional platforms that permit real-time interaction without the cost of travel, however, and in 2009 the media narrative around Second Life® began to mature.

Linden Lab also publishes case studies that document the best business enterprise projects that take place within Second Life®. I have collaborated with Linden Lab on the creation of the case studies that are documented in the next section of this chapter.

A VIRTUAL OCEAN OF OPPORTUNITIES

The National Oceanic and Atmospheric Administration, founded in 1970, guides stewardship of oceanic and atmospheric resources. NOAA's work has expanded along with growing awareness of the gravity of climate change. The agency provided a vibrant boost to its innovative approach by developing a presence in Second Life®.

"You can read about a tsunami in a textbook, or you can experience one in a virtual world," says Eric Hackathorn, NOAA's Virtual Worlds Program Manager. "I believe that experience has a greater impact."

The case study published by Linden Lab explains the power of NOAA's build in Second Life®:

"NOAA's Second Life® space includes a variety of dynamic simulations that visitors can experience, such as a glacier that melts before visitors' eyes and demonstrates some of the consequences of climate change. Unlike glaciers in the physical world that freeze and melt in geologic time, this virtual glacier melts and reforms in moments. Visitors to NOAA's "Okeanos" can, with a click, turn up the heat and watch the magnificent reds and pastels of the coral reef go gray, then a ghostly sterile white."

Data overlay maps are rapidly becoming an important business tool. Virtual maps that allow avatars to move through a three-dimensional representation of the data offer significantly increased decision-making capacity compared to viewing it on a flat screen. In Second Life®, NOAA has created a visualization system that combines maps with overlays of thousands of different weather-pattern maps to produce three-dimensional models of weather patterns with real-time data and topographical detail.

Northrop Grumman Corporation (NGC) is a $32 billion global security company with 120,000 employees. The company has a sophisticated five-sim presence in Second Life® for inexpensive prototyping of products and conducting simulations and meetings that would be prohibitively dangerous or expensive or even impossible in the physical world.

Matt Furman, a key member of the Netcentric International Operations Division at NGC, championed an extensive internal communication campaign to help the NGC recognize the power of virtual worlds and the potential of Second Life® initiatives. This led to the company shifting its perception of virtual worlds, viewing them as an innovative new tool that could safely bridge the collaboration and communications gaps between NGC business development teams and potential clients.

"It didn't take long to identify a myriad of effective uses that could either save corporate monies or generate them," Matt Furman said in the case study. "I've been able to collaborate with people I would never have been able to collaborate with before. I can't begin to tell you how important this is. We're now doing development work for clients where 100% of the product and the client relationship is virtual."

NGC uses Second Life® in a variety of ways for employee learning and training, particularly in situations where effectiveness is greatly amplified by virtual immersion because of expense, danger or distance. For example, the Cutlass Bomb Disposal Robot, an armored all-weather six-wheel vehicle equipped with a complete 360° pivot manipulator arm and state of the art gripper, is a very expensive machine. Few of the robots exist in the physical world, and those that do cost thousands to transport and implement for training. The Second Life® version is completely true to the original and can be copied without limits and placed into a variety of simulations at a trivial cost, giving NGC a valuable training opportunity.

But Second Life® isn't just a sophisticated environment for immersive spaces—it's also an ideal platform from which to broadcast to the rest of the world, for a participatory audience that can remain on the outside looking in, yet still meaningfully take part in the conversation at the same time.

THE EVOLUTION OF THE VIRTUAL WORKFORCE

On September 1, 2009, Dancing Ink Productions produced an event, "The Evolution of the Virtual Workforce," for Manpower, Inc. The event was broadcast live from Second Life® to the web, where hundreds of people participated in live real time chat while executives shared insights. The chat stream was monitored by my collaborator and DIP's Chief Global Strategist, Joshua S. Fouts. I moderated the event in Second Life®.

Joshua and I were both in New York the day of the event. The stream was broadcast by the Australia-based TREET.tv. Guests were in multiple countries and across the United States, and yet we assembled around one table in Second Life®. Our builder in Scotland changed the size of the table to accommodate the exact number of guests featured in the broadcast. The walls of the space are transparent so the camera crews can remain outside the venue, which is opaque from the inside and renders their avatars invisible to guests, and get multiple angles of each speaker and the group.

Every aspect of the event was produced with the same exacting standards of a tight television broadcast, though the digital format presents unique challenges and opportunities. The skin, shape, hair, clothes and posture of each avatar is deliberately created in a collaborative process. Professionals handle avatar development, lightning, construction of the space, audio and video production, content, scripting, pre-production interviews and post-production white papers, interviews, strategic business development with current and potential collaborators, and assessment of success metrics.

I routinely direct collaborative groups of up to 15 people, most of whom have never met each other, for events broadcast live from Second Life®. One of our collaborative broadcasts—co-directed by Lawrence Pintak, the former CBS Middle East Bureau Chief and current Dean of the Edward R. Murrow College of Communications and Journalism at Washington State University—featured the Centers for Disease Control and Prevention sharing information about the H1N1 virus with hundreds of journalists and bloggers across 22 countries as Egypt prepared to slaughter all of the nation's pigs in an effort to stave off an epidemic.

The "Evolution of the Virtual Workforce" event sponsored by Manpower featured Don Tapscott, Chairman of nGenera and bestselling author of Wikinomics and Grown Up Digital; Manpower Chairman and CEO Jeff Joerres; Manpower Senior Vice President of Global Workforce Strategy, Tammy Johns; Executive Director of Enterprise Marketing for Linden Lab, Amanda Van Nuys; President of 3D Squared Inc., Spencer Zuzolo; and Virtual Learning Strategy Leader for the IBM Center for Advanced Learning, Chuck Hamilton.

Manpower, a $22 billion company founded in 1948, is a world leader in the employment services industry, "creating and delivering services that enable its clients to win in the changing world of work. The company offers employers a range of services for the entire employment and business cycle including permanent, temporary and contract recruitment; employee assessment and selection; training; outplacement; outsourcing and consulting."

Manpower serves 400,000 clients per year, from small enterprises to the world's largest multinational corporations and across all industry sectors, through a worldwide network of 4,100 offices in 82 countries and territories. Manpower started to look at virtual worlds as emerging global labor markets in 2007, with all the earnestness with which they approached physical markets. A Second Life® team led by Manpower Virtual World Liaison Dan Darrow started by interviewing thousands of people in Second Life® from more than 50 countries and who reported speaking 40 languages.

During "The Evolution of the Virtual Workforce," Tapscott described what he calls the Net Generation, which he's been documenting for years since his own children, now adults in their twenties, were growing up. This generation, he notes, is characterized by creativity, the ability to collaborate, and comfort with multitasking across digital media and even simultaneous multiple realities. He believes that their culture will come to dominate the world of work. Grown Up Digital offers actionable insight into maximizing the transformation for a more productive, meaningful, challenging and fun work environment, whether those desks are in cubicles, bedrooms, or via BlackBerries on the beach.

"What we have is a paradigm shift, and a paradigm is a mental model," Tapscott said. "There's a new paradigm emerging in the workforce, and leaders of the old have great difficulty embracing the new. Vested interests fight against change. And this is compounded by another fact that we have entering the workforce the largest generation ever and the first to come of age in the digital age. They're digital natives. As they come into the workforce they're bringing a whole new modus operandi and culture. At their fingertips are better tools than exist in many of our most sophisticated corporations, and this is the first time in history when young people are an authority about something really important. I was an authority on model trains when I was 11. Today's 11-year-old at the breakfast table is an authority on this digital revolution that's changing business, commerce, marketing work, entertainment, publishing, government, and every institution in society."

Manpower is focusing on solutions for the "skills mismatch" plaguing workforce development. "What we mean by a skills mismatch," Manpower's Johns explained, "is simply that there isn't a shortage of people to do work in the world. It's a shortage of the right skills needed at that time to do the work."

The U.S. Bureau of Labor Statistics reveals that there are 2.6 million open jobs at a time when people are looking for work. The skills mismatch, Johns said, can be overcome by keeping skills fresh. The benefit of virtual work, she said, is that people can work together across physical boundaries on a more flexible basis.

"Practice being flexible," said Manpower CEO Joerres. "Practice breaking down the command and control environment in becoming a contemporary environment." While he doesn't want to be "too melodramatic in talking about a serious state of peril," he is stern about warning that a brand risks being rendered irrelevant if it fails to change quickly enough as the workforce transforms.

"It's kind of the frog in the water not realizing it's getting hotter and hotter," Joerres said. "And they end up floating on top of the water if they're not careful."

Technology, Johns offered, is changing not only how work can be done but also where it can be done.

"Virtual work offers a huge opportunity to both include people in the workforce," she said, "but also it requires a mindset change, and it requires new skills. And one of the key reasons that two years ago we went to Second Life® was about trying to understand how virtual work was going to change as technology evolves. When we went to Second Life®, the idea was to really go in there with an approach to research and development to understand what skills will be required. But also, what will the culture be?"

The digital culture she refers to is one of collaborative creativity. In Second Life®, hospitals can conduct evacuation drills in sims that look exactly like the real-world buildings filled with patients who can't be moved except during physical emergencies. This kind of collaborative environment offers obvious intrinsic benefits; individuals from various departments both within a hospital setting (nurses, physicians, parents with sick children) and those who must communicate with the hospital in case of a real emergency (first responders) become familiar with one another before being faced with an actual calamity, giving both sides an opportunity to spot potentially fatal flaws in evacuation plans.

Extrinsically, however, collaborative immersive environments have significant value that is in the infancy of development. As nurses practice evacuations with dummy patient avatars, developers discover that the mannequins can be scripted with additional information and behaviors that can help a nurse rehearse life-saving skills on a personal level in the absence of pressure from a physical emergency. Groups from all over the world can meet in real-time to practice handling catastrophes in tandem. These skills, gained in a virtual environment, translate back into the physical world.

"Collaboration is much more than just a tool," Johns said. "Skill sets and behaviors need to change, so at Manpower we try to predict not only what skills individuals will need to perform in the workforce but how clients will need to change their work practices. When we came to Second Life®, the average age in Second Life® was 35, and that was really important to us because it sent a message that these skills could be learned. So we're going to continue to look at technology and understand how work practices will change as a result of it."

Tapscott echoed the idea that collaboration itself is changing through technology, enabling peers to work together "within organizations, between organizations and even outside organizations."

"This is very different from the way that workplaces functioned in the past, and where everyone was either a superior or a subordinate in relationships that occurred," he added. "This can be extended to the point where collaboration can occur on an astronomical scale. These norms of the new generation coming into the workforce are very powerful."

Linden Lab's Amanda Van Nuys said that after 15 years of technology marketing experience, she believes "we're at the precipice of the next big technology wave, and it's the three-dimensional internet." I collaborate regularly with Van Nuys, who spearheads her share of the transformation that has taken place within Linden Lab as the profitable, growing company expands and shifts into one of the world's most creative and serious business development opportunities.

"Today's economic, environmental, and business climate is putting tremendous pressure on companies and governments to cut costs, innovate faster, and be greener," Van Nuys said. "It's forcing us all to look for better collaboration and communication tools that enable global distributed teams to work more effectively than we ever have before. We're just seeing the tip of the iceberg when it comes to the real-world benefits that companies are realizing."

THE VIRTUAL ROLE OF MANAGERS

While the event continued and I moderated it live, I kept my eye on the chat stream, in which hundreds of internet participants were able to communicate with each other and the guests. During events, Joshua Fouts sends me messages with some of the most intriguing questions posed in the chat stream, but I also try to stay current with the chat while the event unfolds. A question from Pathfinder Linden about multitasking arises in response to Tapscott's comments about how digital natives have simply learned to operate differently.

"How does this jibe with Stanford's recent research that shows seriously negative effects from heavy multitasking?" Pathfinder Linden asked, and I verbally forwarded the question to Tapscott. "Are you familiar with this?"

The complex answer is integral to the functioning of multiple generations in the workplace. A student writing an essay that requires deep thought, for example, should eliminate as many other activities as possible. On the other hand, Tapscott noted, while engaged in less intensive activities such as reading e-mail or doing light homework, younger people have "better switching abilities and a better active working memory."

Managers, Joerres added, are now translators in a sense, tasked with the responsibility of making sense of larger projects so individuals and teams can contextualize their respective roles within it.

"Today's manager is a leader and coach," Joerres said. "People need to step up to the hard stuff, which is to every day try to change the mindset of the individual and change your own mindset as a middle manager. Middle managers are the ones that get the bad reputations on being the stopping place for ideas and they need to change that. And you do when you say that your job is to lead and to lead and coach and channel all that energy that's going on."

This process also requires leveraging four generations of people in the workplace, Johns pointed out.

One dilemma, as Chuck Hamilton mentioned, is that managers are "increasingly more virtual." At IBM, he said, two out of every five workers do not have a traditional office space. This frequently means that workers are a functioning part of a team of people they've never met in the physical world, and that managers are managing a geographically dispersed team.

"I think there's a lot of pressure on these managers to be able to perform in that kind of environment and so you're on a constant learning curve for the whole time you're in that management role," Hamilton said. "In (IBM's) case, we're having to react quickly and apply every possible connection medium at our disposal to make things work across the world."

3D Squared's Zuzolo is a master at managing the needs of the next generation of digital workers and catalyzing their growth.

CONNECTING IN THE METAVERSE

Zuzolo, of Austin, Texas, is an eloquent speaker who is passionate about the futures of the students with whom he connects and works. I first met him in person in Lafayette, Louisiana, during a Digital Workforce Initiative sponsored by 3D Squared Inc. at Louisiana Immersive Technologies Enterprise (LITE), a $27 million, 70,000-square-foot facility located at the Research Park of the University of Louisiana in Lafayette.

LITE, a snappy, ethereal structure, is an anomaly in the Lafayette landscape with a massive egg-shaped architectural element that glows in the night. It's the only visualization facility of its kind accessible to private industry in North America, and if it seems misplaced in the heart of the Acadian region--Cajun country--that's only because most people haven't heard one of the great untold American stories that sheds light on why it makes perfect sense.

The history of the Cajun culture and the act of genocide that landed French-Canadian settlers in Louisiana is beyond the scope of this chapter, but it must be noted that this culture has explored technology and creativity to revamp the local economy in the past. Leveraging the global fame of Henry Wadsworth Longfellow's epic poem "Evangeline," a retelling of a popular Cajun tale, the locals enticed motor travelers to the region not just with Evangeline tourism opportunities but also with music, tantalizing cuisine, irrepressible storytelling and Southern charm so thick that no pecan pie comes close. LITE is only a modern incarnation of that same creative spirit infused with the benefits of new technology.

LITE includes various technologies to showcase the capabilities of combining supercomputing with sophisticated immersions in which one's own body, in a harness or free-standing, becomes the avatar within the virtual space. In this way, designers and architects are creating hospitals of the future, industries are significantly changing their processes, and new skill sets are being developed to begin to close the "skills mismatch" described by Joerres and Johns.

3D Squared, however, was not there for the full immersion but rather for the ample office, group meeting and auditorium space to facilitate a week-long digital workforce initiative and showcase the work of the teams assembled there to develop new skills in an intensive environment. Forty students from middle school to college spent their spring break at the Digital Workforce Intensive, working 12 hours per day on games and virtual worlds where the focus was on Louisiana's core social problems. The students came from 16 schools across the state to attend lectures, work in group labs, and be mentored by faculty and industry participants.

Each group collaborated on researching issues of social importance, such as coastal erosion, unemployment, and obesity. They started early in the morning and often worked into the evening, stopping only to play short, well-earned bursts of video games. After the students learned about their topic, they chose roles on the team and produced a template for a game in the 2D virtual environment Metaplace, which is accessible via a Flash-enabled web browser and does not require software downloads. Watching the students transform from one day to the next as they became confident that it would be possible for them find gainful, meaningful and fun employment during a time of local and national economic tumult was stunning.

At first, many of them were fearful of public speaking. Others wondered what role he or she might play in their assigned group. This anxiety was overcome largely by Zuzolo's managerial style, which embodies the technique described by Joerris, Johns, Hamilton and Tapscott. Along with his collaborator Joe Castille, he drifted between the rooms to provide a constant stream of feedback on every aspect of the process. He kept the students constantly focused on their individual performances and the overall functioning of the group, what at the same time eliminating impediments, such as the desire to remain too long in gaming breaks or failures to take creative risks with the material.

Finally, the day came when the participants presented their games and processes to industry experts assembled in LITE's state-of-the-art auditorium. Community members, policy makers, parents, friends, educators, executives and Louisiana state Rep. Nancy Landry observed intently as the participants took the stage. They wore business attire, which served to remind that they would soon become the faces of the workforce.

The students dazzled the industry professionals and the audience with their professionalism and confidence, but it was the sheer creative power of their games that blew the high ceiling off the snazzy auditorium. A 14-year-old boy explained his team's game about coastal erosion, which included a segment about problems related to giant river rats called Whack-A-Nutria. When asked by a professional game designer if he fears that the creators of Whack-A-Mole might come after him for copyright infringement, he calmly rolled out a six-point argument defending his team's view that the project was not in violation of the law. Similarly, a girl later explained why the background music of her team's game, Beethoven's "Moonlight Sonata," was legally permissible to use.

While 3D Squared Inc. works nationally and plans to branch out to an international market to meet demand, hosting a series of Digital Workforce Initiatives in Louisiana was a wise decision. The state has unique problems, ranking dead last in key categories such as health and education, with the nation's highest rate of high-school dropouts. The state also faces a skilled labor shortage of nearly 100,000 jobs and leads the nation in out-migration, particularly of young professionals. It is a perfect illustration in many ways of the "skills mismatch" in action. 3D Squared's goal in the state, with a state-funded grant of $750,000, was to contribute to a solution.

"I was getting e-mails every day from young people who wanted to work in the game industry," Zuzolo said. "At first I realized that there was a great need to educate young people about realistic career paths into the game industry. A little later, I realized that young people's enthusiasm for games could revolutionize education. Finally, I realized that the technologies and creative processes that drive the game industry are already transforming whole industries. Ultimately, the global social and economic fabric will be transformed by these next-generation social, learning and collaboration systems. That's when I started 3D Squared."

Zuzolo hopes his new venture can help Louisiana retain its best and brightest young people while providing them with access to globally competitive jobs. The program's inexpensive implementation could also serve as a template for similarly depressed communities from coast to coast and around the world.

Local teacher Helen Connelly sent her son Cole to participate in the program. "What the kids accomplished and learned at the 3D Squared intensive is one of the finest examples of learning that I have ever seen in the 10 years that I have been teaching," she said. "The kids' ability to work together to create a product in such a short period of time is something that many adults might not be able to accomplish."

This approach could be revolutionary for Louisiana because the top reason students drop out is a lack of engagement with the educational system—they simply aren't interested. This confirms what the Gates Foundation has warned: boredom leads to dropping out. Students are interested in games and motivated to learn when lessons are framed by games. In learning how to collaborate on the creation of games, students are being prepared for related collaborative opportunities, such as participation in the state's increasingly robust mixed-media and film production industries and the creation of simulated virtual training environments.

"What makes our program a success is that we put students in a position of responsibility," Zuzolo explained. "Game development is a really powerful tool to get them to learn the things that we want them to learn without feeling like it's crammed in their face. So they become critical thinkers, they become collaborative, they get a chance to experiment, obviously they are very creative and they're also getting to learn some tools and technologies that they may not have been offered in a regular school setting," Zuzolo explained.

Other benefits of the program include the way it opens a dialogue between parents, teachers, students, policy stakeholders and industry professionals about what is important in relation to education and the evolution of virtual work. It helps students articulate their interests, commit to their own futures and mentor each other with blatant disregard for differences in age, gender, race and socio-economic status, all of which are prominent divisions in traditional settings. Above all, while the Digital Workforce Intensive model asks students to make a significant commitment to their own futures, it also promises the creation of a generation of workers who know how to play.

"We have an obligation to keep people learning and growing and finding the next thing and the next area," IBM's Hamilton said. "Essentially the role that business has to play in this is that we have to lead. We have to say that learning is critical. We have to pull it to the front and say that everybody is going to be learning all the time and that it is that informal network, that informal life that we have that is actually our best teacher."

Failure to adapt, Hamilton said, could be disastrous.

"And you might want to think about this as the next digital divide," he said. "If we don't turn this channel on we may be creating a digital divide that we have not ever seen on this scale before."

"When I was a kid and you graduated, you were set for life," Tapscott added. "Now you're set for, I dunno, 15 minutes. And half of what you learn in the first year is obsolete by the time you get to the fourth year if you're taking a technical course. So we each need to invent our knowledge base multiple times. My view is that work and learning are the same activity. And companies would be wise to strengthen the learning component of work. I mean, what is everyone doing today? Are you working or are you learning participating in this Second Life® event?"

Online tools, Tapscott said, are critical for the development of knowledge work. This means that learning can be as fun for people on the job as it is for the participants in the Digital Workforce Initiative. And it is, especially when virtual environments are involved. It isn't the novelty of Second Life® that makes it fun, but rather the potential to create absolutely anything a group can envision, and then accomplish work in the co-created space embedded with mixed-media tools. This represents a new kind of fun for a new breed of worker.

"Fun is defined as a certain amount of freedom," Joerres said. "I think it's now taken to a whole new level. It's taken to a whole new level now because the individual wants to feel that they are contributing. That contribution, and how they collaborate during that contribution, is really the fun factor. It's not the beer party on Friday afternoon. That's hollow if it's not followed up by 'my work is engaging on a daily basis.' Engaging is defined very differently now."

A MARKET FOR VIRTUAL GOODS AND SERVICES

On September 22, 2009, Linden Lab announced that Second Life® residents have spent 1 billion hours in-world, and that $1 billion—real U.S. dollars have changed hands between people from nearly every country and hundreds of cultures.

While there's some debate about what constitutes a full-fledged immersive environment, virtual world consultancy KZero estimates that 600 million people globally are participants in some form of a virtual world, which means that those people are often purchasing virtual goods. Such purchases are generally made for fractions of pennies on the dollar. A virtual house only needs to be aesthetically reflective of its owner's taste, for example, but it doesn't require a plumbing system that's up to code, or a new roof after a major storm. There are no storms in a virtual world unless someone creates one, like the NOAA does in Second Life® to train workers to fly through hurricane conditions and gather weather data prior to facing such a potentially terrifying professional ordeal in real life, when reason needs to beat adrenaline.

Avatars are buying all kinds of goods and services. At the time this chapter was being written at the end of London's fashion week, a show featuring virtual versions of the actress Sienna Miller's dresses and gowns was about to launch in Second Life®, with the idea being that even in a virtual world, if an ensemble is rare and exclusive enough, participants will be willing to shell out real money for the luxury of the appearance of one's dreams, or a fabulous beach house on prime virtual real estate, or a swanky office and all the accoutrements one can dream up.

On Facebook, when participants want to wish someone a happy birthday, they can buy digital images of cakes or balloons for a fee. In Second Life®, user-created content is three-dimensional, which facilitates entrepreneurialism. Entire stores exist that sell cakes, balloons and other holiday gear. The concept is the same regardless of the platform, whether you're buying a special sword for your wizard, a cake for an acquaintance, or an entire office with mixed-media screens and other perks for use by business groups. Real people are sharing experiences in the digital culture, and the texture of those experiences are created in large part by the sale of virtual goods and services. The potential opened up by the creation of an imagination-based market is significant.

"Increasingly, Second Life® is a place that enhances real life personally and professionally," said Linden Lab's Van Nuys. "People are finding real jobs, accessing real therapy, getting real diplomas, and making real business decisions. Second Life® is about real life. And increasingly, sometimes it's even better than real life."

She gave an example from a few weeks earlier, when she attended the Second Life® Community Convention (SLCC) and met one of Second Life®'s most prominent residents, Gentle Heron. Alice Krueger, as Heron's known in the physical world, leads an organization called Virtual Ability. She lives with multiple sclerosis and leads a community of people who equalized in a virtual world because they are mobile, who can more fully express themselves, and also find meaningful work.

"In SLCC, she was featured on a community building panel because she has successfully built a diverse and global community in Second Life®, which is no small task," Van Nuys said. "In Second Life®, she's on equal footing with everyone else. But, in the physical world, it took a five-star hotel nearly 30 minutes to build a ramp so that she could rightfully sit on the dais with the rest of her panelists. But I think that in her grace and patience, she helped us all learn an important lesson on personal growth and the power and freedom, and some of the real benefits of Second Life®."

The potential of virtual business, still so new, represents a valuable opportunity for all industries to explore aspects of their own business development that would otherwise be hindered by physical limitations. As the economy shifts to create greater opportunity for more people, virtual worlds will play an integral role in the evolution of multinational and hyper-local efforts alike, while granting access not only to creative, inexpensive space but also new ways to think and interact in a truly global marketplace. With increased capability for all areas discussed within this chapter as well as analytics, forecasting, extended simulations and data mapping, the benefits of virtual business are only just beginning to emerge.

Chapter 6
Company-Specific Virtual Worlds

Paul Blowers
Kelly Services, USA

ABSTRACT

The rapid rise of Virtual World technology poses exciting opportunities and complex challenges for businesses. Virtual World technology, for the purpose of business usage, can be defined as any 3D immersive and persistent environment that can be accessed concurrently by multiple people for the purposes of conducting E-Commerce. The purpose of this chapter will be to examine how Virtual Worlds are being used in business today. The authors will reflect on the first wave of companies entering Virtual Worlds, which has yielded some key lessons learned, as well as, evidence to its next phase. By defining the spectrum of different uses of Virtual Worlds, this chapter will cover key lessons learned and guidelines, current barriers to adoption, and the business value of using Virtual Worlds for business purposes. Lastly, the authors will examine future trends in Virtual World technology that relate to future Virtual World E-Commerce growth.

INTRODUCTION

The rapid rise of Virtual World technology poses exciting opportunities and complex challenges for businesses. This chapter will look at how Virtual World technology is used by companies focused on conducting E-Commerce within the Virtual World environment. We will examine common use cases, key lessons learned, barriers to adoption, and what the future may hold.

Virtual World technology, for the purpose of business usage, can be defined as any 3D immersive and persistent environment that can be accessed concurrently by multiple people for the purposes of conducting business. At the present time, we have been through the first wave of companies entering Virtual Worlds (2003 – 2008) and have some evidence as to its next phase. As with many new technologies, this first wave of

DOI: 10.4018/978-1-61692-808-7.ch006

Virtual World adoption has been experimental and has generally ended with a lackluster finish. Some important questions will include: Will Virtual Worlds become a broadly accepted platform for E-Commerce? Will Virtual Worlds become the preferred mechanism for engaging and building customer relationships? Will the early adopters of Virtual Worlds create competitive advantage and be able to challenge traditional business models? This chapter will provide some background and evidence to help answer these questions. Let's start by examining how some companies are using Virtual Worlds today.

COMPANIES IN VIRTUAL WORLDS TODAY

It is not uncommon today for a large business, of any industry, to have already experimented with presence in a Virtual World platform. With hundreds of Virtual World platforms available and an estimated 579 Million Virtual World consumer accounts created, it is no surprise that businesses have taken a keen interest in Virtual Worlds (Keegan, 2009). Forecasts predict that by 2012, this user number could rise to a staggering 1 Billion users (Dejwakh, 2008). On top of that, Gartner estimates that 70% of businesses will have established Virtual World presence by 2012 (Gartner, 2008). If that doesn't have a company standing up and paying attention by now, Gartner also projects that by year-end 2011 that 80% of active Internet users will have a presence in a Virtual World (Gartner, 2007). The Second Life® virtual economy transacted $360 MM in 2008, which for any E-Commerce platform is a compelling number.

The analyst firm ThinkBalm states that, in interviews with 66 companies using Virtual World technology for business, 40% expect to see positive return on investment (Driver & Driver, 2009). It should be noted, however, that these companies were heavily weighted towards using Virtual Worlds for meetings to reduce travel expenses. For example, IBM recently stated they saved $320,000 in travel expenses by hosting a 300 person private conference in Second Life® (Linden Lab, 2009). This use of Virtual Worlds for professional and industry conferences is likely to continue to develop as big business. While these are impressive numbers, the first wave of company specific usage of Virtual Worlds ended with an estimated 9 out of 10 failures (Gartner, 2008). Failures in this context are Virtual World investments that are not returning value or discontinued all together. Despite the mixed statistics from the first wave, the future of Virtual Worlds for businesses is still vibrant with potential.

Before diving into business specific use cases for Virtual World technology, it is helpful to first comprehend the entire landscape of Virtual World platforms and how they are used. The research firm KZero provides continued research and coverage of Virtual Worlds technology usage globally. The diagrams below from KZero provide an excellent overview of Virtual Worlds today, both in their current categories and the specific Virtual World platforms deployed. The first diagram (Figure 1) represents the number of accounts registered by age group for all major Virtual World platforms. It also shows the growth in user numbers from when each Virtual World platform started until present time.

The next diagram (Figure 2) from KZero represents the groupings of Virtual Worlds by types or sectors, again with an overlay of age group categories.

The range of Virtual World platforms presented in these diagrams demonstrate the diversity in usage and median age. The diversity presents a significant challenge for businesses looking to determine how to leverage Virtual Worlds. It is important for businesses to closely examine the different types of Virtual World platforms for the target content and resident demographic in order to find those that best align to their market focus. It is not sufficient to de-

Figure 1. Virtual worlds registered accounts Q2 2009. (KZero. Used with permission).

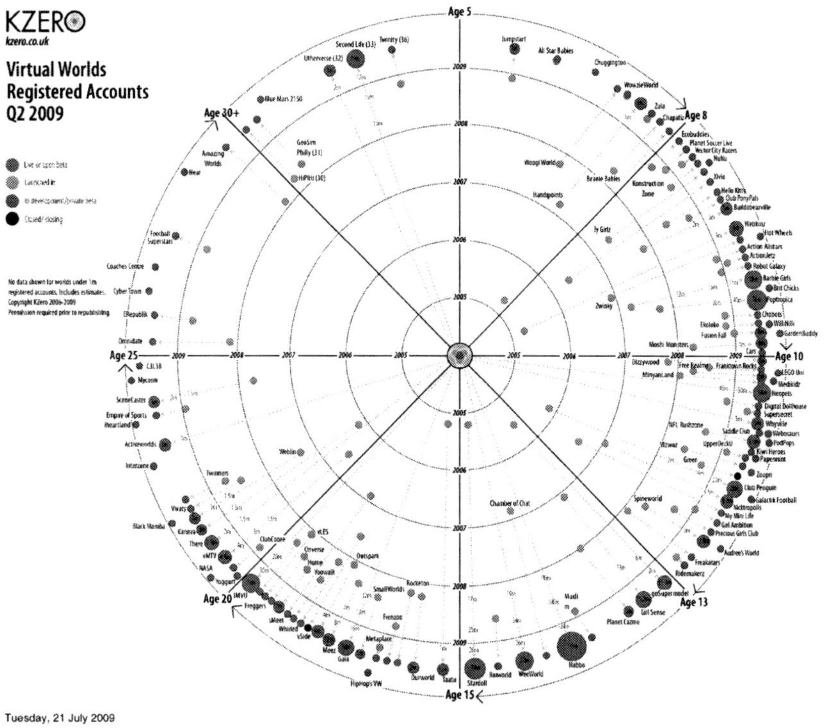

Figure 2. Virtual worlds by Sector Q2 2009. (KZero. Used with permission).

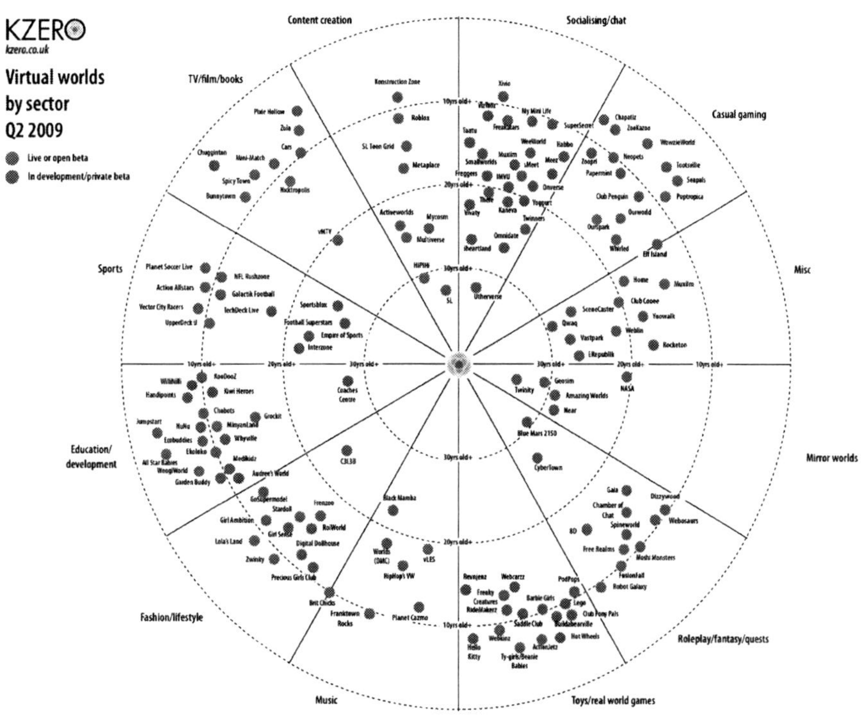

velop content in Second Life®, for example, hoping to reach the youth consumer market. Similarly, companies should not be looking to promote brand awareness for high end automobiles or consumables in the Webkinz Virtual World. With the diversity of Virtual World technology and massive change ahead, it is a necessity that companies make a choice driven by well defined business objectives and outcomes.

Two important data clusters worth noting for business are the heavier concentration of Virtual Worlds targeted at pure Social Networking, and the high concentration of Virtual Worlds dedicated towards a younger generation of our population. These are significant trends that businesses simply can't ignore when leveraging Virtual Worlds. Business must begin to address the blistering growth of social networking and the fact that younger generations are exposed from an early age to technology. Future consumers born in the last few years will experience Virtual Worlds and E-Commerce from a very young age (i.e., a "Webkinz like" childhood). They will grow up demanding digital channels for interaction and rich E-Commerce, and expect to collaborate and interact in the same way. This generation will strongly identify themselves with a digital identity such as an avatar persona, as well as see their friends and family as an electronic social network. These trends point very strongly to Virtual Worlds increasingly playing a role as a platform for E-Commerce as this generation of the population ages.

With that overview in mind, let's examine the various ways that companies use Virtual Worlds today. This basic framework will not only help in understanding current usage and benefits, but also help in providing a way to think about how Virtual Worlds can be leveraged to create new goods and services in the future. Accordingly, a matrix has been developed to illustrate these business use cases (Table 1).

Selling Real World Goods and Services

Just like the early days of the Web, traditional companies have been experimenting in Virtual Worlds with the hope their presence will drive awareness and community back to their real world brand. With this focus, companies hope to leverage the power of immersive 3D environments to create new sales channels, strengthen customer relationships, and create a richer community around real world products and services. Given the tremendous hype and promise around business in Virtual Worlds, most large companies today feel competitively compelled to participate or risk

Table 1. Business use cases of virtual worlds

Business Use Cases of Virtual Worlds	Case Study Examples	Business Value
Selling Real World Goods and Services	Cisco, Lenovo, American Apparel	• Create a powerful new sales channel leveraging the immersive 3D experience • Strengthening existing customer relationships • Create immersive community around real world products in order to support and innovate
Selling Virtual Goods and Services	Xstreet SL, WeeWorld, Twinity	• Market and sell new and innovative virtual goods, services, and new business models • Provide marketing and content development services to companies wanting to setup in Virtual Worlds
Collaboration and Simulation	OLIVE, Unisfair	• Increase employee and customer engagement • Increase collaboration and learning • Reduce travel costs • Conduct immersive business simulations

missing the wave. However, many don't seem to have a clear set of objectives and comprehension of potential outcomes. Let's look at some examples of early entrants in this category.

Cisco has created a tremendous amount of content in Second Life. Not only can you virtually explore their real world product catalog, but you can attend training and conferences at the Cisco Island while standing shoulder to shoulder with fellow Cisco product enthusiasts. Their commitment to create content and meaningful Virtual World experiences around their real life catalog of goods and services is evident. In 2009, Cisco's real world annual user conference was hosted physically in San Francisco, and in parallel, streamed to their Second Life® Island. "In world" participants could view keynote presentations, conduct hands-on learning activities on Cisco products, and socialize with other virtual conference attendees during and after conference hours. While this doesn't directly translate into E-Commerce in the transactional sense, the Virtual World content and experience that Cisco has created allows them to continue to present themselves as an innovated company and engage their customers through additional channels in which technology enthusiasts relate. This Virtual World community also allows Cisco customers to engage with rich interactive product content in a way that their competitors do not provide. In addition, it allows Cisco to start to build expertise in a future platform where they are investing heavily, which is unified communications technology. It is too early to tell if Virtual Worlds will become a platform for unified communications, but companies like Cisco will be able to leverage their Virtual World experience if and when the opportunity emerges.

Lenovo is one of the largest PC and laptop computer makers in the world. Lenovo has setup an innovative Virtual World showroom, called the eLounge, which is supported by the Nortel Virtual World platform called Web.Alive. Nortel describes the Web.Alive platform as Virtual World software that provides a secured platform for collaboration, assisted E-Commerce, and virtual learning and training. The interesting aspect about the Nortel approach is that it is a Virtual World embedded into a traditional web page, so the user can access it on the web with a standard web browser. Consumers can access this Virtual World from the Lenovo web site, which launches them into the Virtual World where they walk around a showroom to see and "touch" various laptop models in 3D, as well as chat with other buyers and Lenovo sales and support representatives.

The Lenovo Web.Alive solution is a good example of using Virtual Worlds to enhance the customer buying experience in ways a traditional E-Commerce site could not. The Lenovo site encourages users to bring friends and family along to assist with the buying decision. In other words, you can ask a friend to come with you to the store virtually, as they don't have to be physically with you as with a traditional shopping experience. This also underscores the opportunity for a Virtual World platform to deliver a community experience that traditional web buying simply cannot do. Using another traditional E-Commerce example, how would a family member "meet you" on Amazon today and interact regarding a potential purchase? It is not possible, and this illustrates the potential of rich and immersive E-Commerce scenarios facilitated by Virtual Worlds.

American Apparel is another example of a business that entered Virtual Worlds during the first wave. The American Apparel approach was highly progressive; aimed at connecting with a Virtual World customer base by entering Second Life® in June of 2006 to market and sell virtual clothes. American Apparel opened a storefront to sell avatar outfits that were modeled after their real-world products. For merchandise purchased in the Virtual World, discounts were issued in the real world. This was a truly innovative way of selling real world goods through a Virtual World storefront. Unfortunately, after approximately one year, American Apparel decided to shut down their "in world" store. They published on their website that they have connected with people, learned a lot, and their time is done for now.

The specific reasons for American Apparel leaving are not abundantly clear, however, there are key lessons learned to point out. As reported in *TIME Magazine*, some Second Life® residents were becoming upset by the increased commercialization of their Virtual World community. Accordingly a group called the Second Life® Liberation Army held a demonstration by gunning down virtual shoppers at American Apparel in Second Life® (Dell, 2007). This type of business disruption has become common by Second Life® residents, also called "griefers" that feel that outside business is looking to disrupt the unique non-commercial culture of the Second Life® community. The lesson learned here not only to make sure that your business objectives and outcomes are connected to a real world business case, but to also make sure that the business is able to understand, communicate, and engage with the current Virtual World resident culture. This is not different than what would be done upon opening up a large factory in a new city, where a company would typically conduct a PR campaign to build community support. This has often been overlooked, and it can lead not only lead to "griefing" events as described above, it can also lead to a spiraling of negative branding and perception of the overall Virtual World endeavor (Rufer-Bach, 2009). While this was likely not the sole reason American Apparel left Second Life® (Figure 3), it certainly underscores the experimental intent of companies entering Virtual Worlds during this initial wave, and a key lesson learned.

In summary, wave one of Virtual World adoption by traditional businesses has ended with mixed results and some key lessons learned. This, of course, is not atypical of new technology waves. Many traditional companies looking to leverage Virtual Worlds to drive real world E-Commerce have not seen results past initial experimentation. In fact, at present it is quite common that companies have stopped actively managing their Virtual World sites. Even if they are still present, they are what can be considered Virtual World ghost towns with little consumer visitation. Dave Fenech, VP of Interactive Marketing at Kelly Services, calls this the "empty shell problem". This is when, after initial content is created and launched in a Virtual World location, residents don't find compelling reasons to continue to visit the site or be engaged. Companies, therefore, struggle with whether or not to update content, provide staff for the site to interact with residents, or remove the site entirely. This author recently

Figure 3. American apparel virtual store front chained and closed

logged into several Virtual Worlds and visited the sites for Coke, Dell, Wells Fargo, and Lenovo and found nobody there. There were no residents, no greeters, and not even automated bots to echo back a hello. These sites are truly ghost towns.

It is no coincidence that we saw a similar pattern in the early Web 1.0 days where companies struggled to find value in keeping their content up-to-date and engaging. Early web sites often sat neglected and static. In the next wave of company specific Virtual Worlds, businesses need to figure out how to maintain customer engagement through, not only creating but, sustaining a vibrant community. The lessons learned here in the first wave is that conducting business in Virtual Worlds has everything to do with keeping customers engaged through compelling content and interaction. For example, Cisco continues to conduct "in world" conferences to promote and attract residents to their content. While the increase in Virtual World consumer accounts and E-Commerce transaction growth will itself increase the probability of business success in Virtual Worlds, the differentiator is sustaining community through compelling content and engagement.

Selling Virtual Goods and Services

While using Virtual Worlds to brand and promote real world products is hardly novel, the growing commerce of goods, content, and services "in world" most certainly is. These goods and services sold in online games, social networking sites, and Virtual Worlds are known as virtual goods. The virtual goods industry is growing rapidly. Some estimate the size of the industry to reach $5.5 Billion USD globally in 2009 (Balfour, 2009). In a recent study by Frank N. Magid Associates, Inc., it is estimated that 12% of all Americans have purchased virtual goods of some type (Wagner, 2009). Although many of these purchases are through social networking sites like Facebook, or online games like World of Warcraft, this is still a striking figure that has applicability for businesses in Virtual Worlds. It is important to note that, in open-ended Virtual Worlds, most of this E-Commerce is of the peer to peer variety. This means that thousands of individuals create and sell content directly, or through virtual storefronts, to other residents. Before we get into examples of this, it is important to provide some background on the E-Commerce engine of virtual goods, called the "microtransaction".

Microtransactions or micropayments are the millions of very small E-Commerce transactions that get executed on the Web. A large proportion of these transactions are in exchange for virtual goods. In normal commerce, these transactions that would be so small they are not worth bothering with, but in aggregate they have to potential to really add up. One key example of this is on Facebook, where social networkers can buy virtual "gifts" and send them to their friends and family. Similarly, the Facebook delivered game Mafia Wars, by Zynga, allows social networkers to buy points in the game with which they can make their mafia team better and stronger. For companies looking to embrace E-Commerce in Virtual Worlds, microtransactions are likely remain a key underpinning for setting up a foundation to do it.

So why are individuals, in a more peer capacity, seemingly successful in Virtual World E-Commerce when companies are not? Some would argue that very few individuals make significant money based on the data. The current data suggests that E-Commerce in Virtual Worlds are still mostly peer to peer and the only business entities to benefit are the platforms, or virtual goods exchanges themselves, that are able to take a cut of the overall aggregate of microtransactions. For example in Second Life®, out of the 28 Million transactions conducted in July 2009, 48% of these were for less than 1 dollar USD. 64% were less than 20 dollars USD (calculated from the published Second Life® Economy Statistics 2009). The guidance for businesses as they enter this type of E-Commerce environment is to target the platform, or be able to differentiate on a unique "in world" good or service that is not easily replicable for peer to peer transactions. Let's look at some examples of Virtual World markets created specifically for virtual goods revenue.

A classic example of virtual goods E-Commerce is the Linden Labs owned Xstreet. XStreet is an online marketplace for buying and selling Second Life® virtual goods and services. Similar to an "eBay" of Second Life®, the marketplace is now selling virtual goods at the rate of 1.25 Million USD per quarter (Linden, 2009). XStreet goods and services range from avatar clothing, animals, land, buildings, vehicles, art, and all types of animations and scripting.

In other domains, the virtual goods market for children and teens is the fast growing. For example, WeeWorld is a Virtual World platform that capitalizes on this trend and boasts 26 Million user accounts. It is targeted at "tweens" with a strong social networking based environment. It creatively overlays the social networking based world with goal oriented objectives to level up your WeeMee (the WeeWorld avatar) and get points with which Virtual Goods can be purchased. The business model for companies engaged with WeeWorld is two-fold. First, generate real world brand awareness through selling advertising space "in world". Second, create and sell virtual goods. WeeWorld accomplishes the former by having organizations such as the NBA present with the "NBA Store", a virtual storefront selling virtual NBA sporting apparel. Secondly, WeeWorld is considered to have a thriving virtual goods market place consisting most of virtual clothing and accessories for your WeeMee avatar, and gifts that one can send to friends and family. Lastly, WeeWorld keeps content and engagement levels high, not to mention generating advertising revenue, by bringing in real world celebrity branding such as Jay-Z, The Jonas Brothers, and Justin Timberlake. This tactic illustrates a key point for companies considering virtual goods for a business model. That is, the content must be compelling and it must continue to connect target users and their real world consumer behavior in innovative and immersive ways. This blending of real world content to sell virtual goods brings us to our last example of "in world" E-Commerce, and involves the concept of Mirror Worlds.

A Mirror World is a Virtual World that attempts to completely replicate the real world in physical structure and the resulting human experience. These platforms often do this by using satellite imagery, geo-tagging, and GPS to accurately model a physical location. Google Earth is perhaps the best known example of a Mirror World. It has used aerial imagery to provide a digital map of the earth, and offers this as a software service. However, Google Earth is not necessarily a Virtual World, as it does not have persistent user avatars with interactivity much the way a full Virtual World platform does.

Twinity is a fully functioning 3D Mirror World that adds the persistent online avatar based community and content creation of an open-ended Virtual World platform. This Virtual World is overlaid on the mirror replicas of real life cities. Twinity started with the development of a 3D mirror city of Berlin. Avatars participate as normal real world residents would, exploring the city, socializing at bars and restaurants, and obtaining and furnishing personal dwellings. At present, Twinity has recently been awarded funding by the government of Singapore to create a replica of this South East Asian business capitol. By establishing a Mirror World in Twinity, Singapore hopes to build credibility as the E-Commerce hub of Asia by making pioneering investments in Virtual Worlds and electronic currency. Mirror Worlds, such as these, provide companies with a more tangible platform with which to offer virtual goods and services that can be linked to their real world business.

In summary, businesses need to consider the many use cases for the E-Commerce of virtual goods and services, and the key differences between the types of commerce and the types of Virtual Worlds that shape the nature of virtual goods. When there is no clear business case for open-ended Virtual Worlds, there could in fact be opportunities for simply mirroring successful real world business models in a Mirror World. Real world entities like the Singapore government are leveraging this technology to engage citizens and a global tourism audience. This lends significant credibility to the potential of Virtual Worlds for real world business.

Collaboration and Simulation

The prior two use cases focused on companies within Virtual Worlds attempting to drive E-Commerce "in world' and out. This section will provide an overview of the third major use case: using Virtual Worlds for collaboration, training, and business simulation. As noted in the *ThinkBalm Immersive Internet Value Study Q2 2009*, "the top motivations for investment in immersive technology in 2008 / 1Q2009 were enabling people in disparate locations to spend time together, increased innovation, and cost savings or avoidance" (Driver & Driver, 2009). This category of business usage of Virtual Worlds is well outlined in Figure 4.

For collaboration purposes, the use cases span from opening up a virtual office space to keep remote individuals connected and engaged, to complex use cases where companies like the Cisco and IBM examples above have hosted large events and conferences in a Virtual World. These large collaboration events not only make for a uniquely engaging experience, but they also eliminate all travel and facility costs. For conferences and meetings, not only can presentation data be displayed in traditional ways (i.e. Power Point upload), it can also be presented in 3D formats so that participants can actually interact with it. ThinkBalm illustrates this concept quite well in their "Think Balm Data Garden" presentation in Second Life® where residents are able to touch and interact with a presentation in 3D. A particularly unique example is the roadblock exhibit where participants actually walk through a corridor only to fall off ledges and hit walls which, in this research case, represent roadblocks to Virtual World adoption by business. Participants get the physical sensation of barriers while being presented the findings of the study data. Among other things, this adds rich mnemonic triggers not available to traditional 2D collaboration. This

Figure 4. Common business use cases in collaboration. (ThinkBalm. Used with permission).

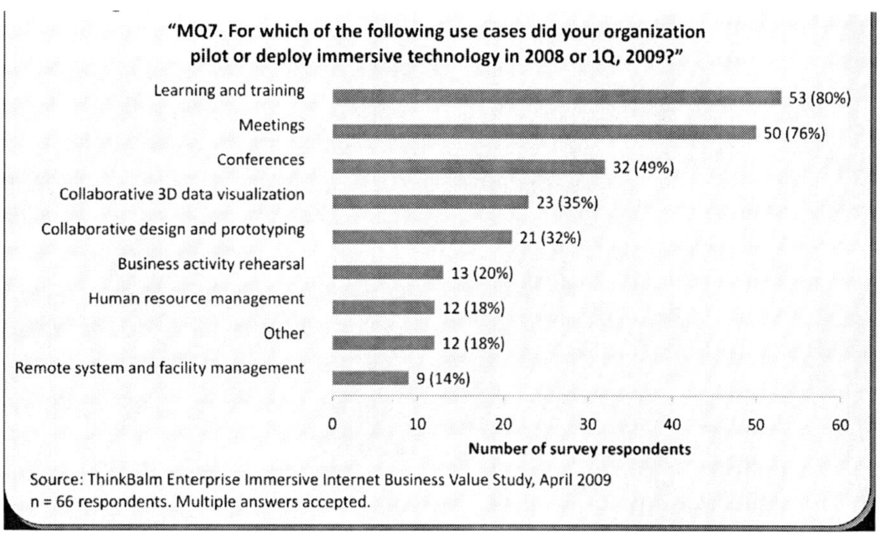

illustrates the power of immersive 3D environments to present and interact with data in new ways. The study finds and exhibit can be found at the Second Life® site: http://slurl.com/secondlife/ThinkBalm%20Island/178/143/31/?title=ThinkBalm%20Island&msg=ThinkBalm%20Data%20Garden

Companies have also found that Virtual Worlds are able to uniquely model business scenarios for training and simulation that are simply not possible in the real world. Forterra's OLIVE platform (On-Line Interactive Virtual Environment) is a key Virtual World product to watch in this space. Forterra positions the OLIVE platform as a private, enterprise grade Virtual World platform to be used for collaborative meetings, training and learning, and events. The OLIVE product takes a unique approach as a private Virtual World that is completely company specific. This alleviates pressing concerns about security and privacy that exist in open-ended public worlds, which will be discussed in detail later in the chapter.

OLIVE and similar enterprise simulation platforms target industries that benefit from business simulation activity that require large scale collaborative activities between employees. Examples are healthcare, education, manufacturing, and government. The experience is 3D with spatial audio, gestures, and the ability to share 2D desktop applications, presentations, and to stream video. Avatars are designed and created from digital photographs of the real world person so that collaboration can be as real life as possible. Further supporting business simulation goals, a full set of record/replay features are also available. Recently, IBM and OLIVE have worked together to integrate the IBM Lotus Sametime instant messaging capability, which provides companies the ability to integrate their current instant messaging client with "in world" communication. OLIVE is also extending avatar profile integration to popular social networking (i.e. Facebook) and corporate HR systems so that an avatar can be linked to your real life social networking attributes. While this is not directly tied to consumer driven E-Commerce, it does have potential to power unique business to business (B2B) E-Commerce scenarios. Companies looking to engage in Virtual Worlds should consider this use for simulating and collaborating across organizational boundaries, or for providing more immersive services (i.e. 3D training as a service).

Unisfair is a virtual events and conference Virtual World platform that companies are leveraging to conduct large meetings, trade shows, and conferences with the hopes of increasing collaboration and participation, and reducing the need for complex travel logistics and expenses. Unisfair boasts over 600 successful virtual events and counting. Not only is it marketed as a "green" solution by eliminating the need for people to travel, it also dramatically reduces the planning latency involved with organizing large events in a physical space. Other benefits that companies are finding from events in Virtual Worlds are increased metrics capability such as overall attendance, booth visits, participation in Q&A, and side bar discussions. Interactions are all easily captured for both evaluating the success of the event and playback for those not able to attend.

Internally focused, the business case for companies to embrace Virtual World technology for increased collaboration and low cost business simulation, while reducing travel costs and becoming more "green" has certainly become one of the key success stories out of the first wave of company specific Virtual World adoption. Externally focused, it is important to note that E-Commerce in general is becoming more collaborative in nature, and that the younger generation now expects more integrated collaboration around their E-Commerce experience. It is reasonable to expect that the internal use of Virtual Worlds for collaboration and simulation will serve as valuable experimental foundation for future E-Commerce scenarios.

VIRTUAL WORLDS E-COMMERCE: RISKS AND ROADBLOCKS

As we look back at the first wave of companies that entered Virtual Worlds, some clear obstacles to success have emerged. Some of the obstacles are related to the specific use case of Virtual Worlds, and some of them span all use cases as a function of the current maturity of Virtual World technology. Let's look at some of the major risks and roadblocks that exist for companies considering the use of Virtual Worlds.

Too Many Platforms and Lack of Standards

Although the number of Virtual World platforms that exist and the projected user base is impressive, the landscape is simply too diverse for mainstream business to approach at present. For companies thinking about capturing a market or reaching a customer base, this fragmentation greatly dilutes the return on investment for creating content and presence specific to just one platform. Content created in one Virtual World is likely not portable to another platform, and with limited standards on the horizon, this problem is likely to persist. Also, the lack of a multi-world avatar or a single avatar identity that consumers can develop and re-use across disparate Virtual World platforms hinders businesses hoping to reach a diverse customer base.

At present, there is little to no integration between Virtual World platforms and internal business application and communication systems. Although we mentioned the IBM Sametime 3D example above, there is little else mainstream to promote a blending of Virtual World platform integration to the business systems that companies use to drive E-Commerce and manage customer relationships today.

Businesses should take note of this roadblock when investing in significant proprietary Virtual World content. One standard to consider would be COLLADA for 3D data exchange that OLIVE and other platforms are supporting. COLLADA is a royalty-free XML schema that enables digital asset exchange within the 3D industry. The importance of COLLADA and similar standards is that it provides a way for 3D content to be shareable across Virtual World platforms and development toolsets.

Law and Regulation is in Early Stages

Laws and regulations that govern E-Commerce in Virtual Worlds are in the early stages of existence. Intellectual property, contracts, taxation, and trademark protection are all likely to be derived from traditional web E-Commerce standards as a precedent. However thorny issues are still to be encountered around things like digital rights management, intermediaries, and content ownership. In Second Life®, for example, many unsanctioned company trademarks can be observed in user created content, even some for profitable sale (Rufer-Bach, 2009). The current Digital Millennium Copyright Act largely applies and can be invoked if companies wish to pursue legal action.

One interesting twist to Virtual Worlds, just as with the Internet more broadly, is that residents live in different parts of the world, governed by different laws and regulation but access the Virtual World in a single location (for example, Asia-Pacific users accessing the Second Life® platform running on servers in California). Interpreting and applying legal protection in advance of these scenarios is non-trivial. A recent example in Australia illustrates this point. A select group of Australian government officials would like to see a more strict enforcement of Internet filtering of content. This has caused a major stir in the Virtual World populations of Second Life® and World of Warcraft. As they are both hosted out of the United States, their "in world" content is only regulated by US laws. If the Australian Government passes a more strict set of content filtering regulation, they need to work with their intermediary Internet Service Providers in Australia to apply filters or ban the Virtual Worlds all together. This example is not dissimilar to what we see with traditional web content filtering today. This issue is expertly covered in the book, *Who Controls the Internet*, by Jack Goldsmith and Tim Wu, and is a must read for companies looking at making major investments in Virtual World capability with objectives of reaching a multi-national audience.

Poor Performance and Usability

Performance and usability problems have plagued the initial wave of company specific Virtual World usage. Virtual Worlds with rich 3D graphics require significant processing power on the end user device as well as the server platform. One of the biggest issues is that companies typically don't deploy high end 3D graphics cards required to render an acceptable Virtual World experience. Most corporate desktops are deployed without any needs for high end graphics cards. Even most home users find that their computers, especially laptops, may be under-powered if they are not setup for 3D gaming.

Similarly, Virtual Worlds like Second Life® have significant recurring performance issues when the number of avatars and/or "prims" (3D objects) that need to be rendered is too high. This causes what is known as "lag" in the Virtual World and can seriously impact the user experience. In addition, companies with many remote sites often struggle to provide broadband equivalent network access to end users. Not only is it expensive, it is largely dependent on the broadband availability in certain geographies. These issues directly impact attempts to make Virtual Worlds a business platform, as the customer experience would only lead to frustration and abandonment.

Lastly, it is not uncommon for the user interface of Virtual Worlds to have a steep learning curve for those not familiar with online gaming. Second Life® is an example of both a richly customizable world, but also one that is complex to initially learn. Virtual Worlds are now coming out to address this problem for users than want quick and easy usability, and don't mind giving up some of the richness in content creation and configurability. WeeWorld is an example of an ultra-simple 2.5D, browser based Virtual World experience that addresses many of the challenges described in this section. At present, however, the general performance and usability of Virtual Worlds for a broad user base is a major hurdle and must be a prominent consideration for businesses.

Skepticism of Virtual Worlds as a Game

Looking back, a curious thing happened with traditional multi-player online gaming. Participants started to value the social interaction as much, or more than, the game itself. The classic example was of course the real life marriages that happened out of games like Everquest and World of Warcraft. From this sprung the concept of more open-ended Virtual Worlds. There was a desire for an online community platform that blends online gaming aspects with the content creation and social interactions possible in real life. Naturally, more and more E-Commerce gradually emerged. This commerce started with basic "gold farming" seen in traditional Massively Multiplayer Online Role Playing Games (MMORPG) and has evolved into more open-ended E-Commerce platforms with services as diverse as selling virtual clothing to virtual psychology counseling services. Because the gaming industry is still a driving force in the advancement of 3D online platforms and the immersive Internet experience, businesses will routinely downcast Virtual Worlds as lacking business credibility.

After all, isn't it just a game? Businesses want to rethink and challenge this inherent cynicism. The *Virtual World News* has recently announced that Mafia Wars by Zynga, a Facebook linked application, has grown past 4 Million daily active users. What business today would not want access to this type of viewership? Although this is "just a game", the richness in social networking interaction and links out to business services illustrates a powerful convergence of the gaming world and real business.

We are also seeing the blending of traditional console games with social networking and E-Commerce market places. Console games are slowly adding feature rich avatar creation and more open-ended 3D interactions between gaming players outside of the game itself. Microsoft XBOX 360 and Sony Playstation 3 are the leading examples. "In world" players can socialize, link their accounts through friendship invitations, buy online content and services (typically gaming content), and document and share gaming achievements. The console gaming market boasts some of the richest 3D graphics processing capability out there for immersive online experiences, and studies have shown that young adults are spending a rapidly growing proportion of their time on online games. The blending of console gaming and with non-gaming Virtual Worlds and social networking is a powerful trend that businesses must openly consider.

General Lack of Security Controls

Enterprise grade security controls must be achieved in virtual worlds if companies are to feel comfortable making significant E-Commerce investments. Little exists in the way of enterprise authentication, identity management and reputation for trusted interactions, non-repudiation, and secure communications. Many gray areas exist for data privacy and the security of the hosted sites that serve up the Virtual World environments. Virtual World providers have dramatically improved in this area, and we expect to see progression in line with continued business investment in Virtual World platforms. For example, Second Life® has added a Registration API, which allows organizations to extend custom web based registration and first log-in process control. By using this toolset, account naming conventions and restrictions to company specific Virtual World locations can be controlled.

Other Virtual World platforms like OLIVE are designed with enterprise grade controls in mind, and can reside internal to a company in order to eliminate the security and privacy issues noted above. It should be noted, however, that this is a completely different use case in that privately or internally based Virtual Worlds do not have access to the public customer and marketplace and are largely geared towards internal collaboration and business process.

Due to the nature of anonymity with avatars in Virtual Worlds, and the lack of any credible identity and reputation services, corporate users are also exposed to people in the Virtual Worlds that may not be whom they say or appear to be. They could be competitors, hackers, or just about anyone trying to disrupt business activities – be it for fun or nefarious intent. This section barely scratches the surface of security challenges for companies entering Virtual Worlds. Let's examine the emerging trend of going "behind the firewall" to add back control.

PUTTING VIRTUAL WORLDS BEHIND THE CORPORATE FIREWALL

One common stumbling block that companies have encountered with Virtual Worlds is the challenge of meeting internal security policies and minding corporate data protection, while also leveraging the power to be fully engaged in open-ended and globally accessible Virtual World platforms. There is the simple issue of allowing internal company desktops to access public Virtual World services on the Internet by opening up the firewall. There are also the more advanced issues of how to ensure users represent the company appropriately in and around other uncontrolled, unsavory, or counter-corporate Virtual World activity. This has raised a fundamental deployment debate for companies in Virtual Worlds. Either deploy publically and accept a rich, yet uncontrolled public social network, or deploy privately and remove the capability to interact with an open community of potential customers and business partners.

Staying Public

In order to support Virtual Worlds today, companies should review and adjust their acceptable use policies and create new policies in order to adequately manage open-ended Virtual World usage within the corporate environment. These policies have to deal with avatar creation, "in world" communication and activities, and ensuring that users are always representing the company brand and image appropriately. Some of the Virtual World architectures, such as Second Life®, have a fairly open client software model. Because of the nature of how Second Life® works, the client is not only technically interacting with the remotely hosted Second Life® servers over the Internet; the client also interacts on a peer to peer basis with other online users. This causes major issues for corporate firewalls that have to open up a gaping range of ports versus specific ranges of IP addresses.

Public Virtual Worlds are generally open for public registration and access, either fee based or free. The Virtual World land and content is then shareable and traversable by the general public. Second Life® is an example of a public Virtual World that has gradually applied a fairly robust access control structure to allow for controlling movement and access to objects and locations. Although Second Life® boasts the largest and most diverse Virtual World platform, it has also historically garnered the bulk of the negative press regarding adult content and "griefers" (people who aim to cause trouble for entertainment). This puts the security burden on the end user or company to properly secure their content according to their requirements. It also makes for a user driven world that is highly configurable and makes for a more realistic and open-ended Virtual World experience. Many companies within Second Life® benefit from purchasing their own island or region upon which they have full control to secure and exclude from other residents when and where they see fit. This, however, would not stop a Linden Labs administrator from seeing and accessing content in that private space should they need to for any reason.

Going Private

When companies leverage Virtual Worlds for online meetings and events, most of the time they need the content and interactions of these events to be private and secure, just as if they were being hosted in the real world within company walls. Similarly, large companies tightly control Internet related activity that poses a threat to employee productivity, company image, or could be offending to customers and employees. To those involved with securing corporate Internet activity with firewalls, web content filtering, and messaging hygiene services, this may at first seem like problems controlled by applying traditional solutions. However, due to the nature of a Virtual World like Second Life®, companies are only able to secure traffic coming in and out of the Virtual World hosting facility (i.e. the Second Life® data center). The network traffic that does traverse the company's border is typically related to remote client rendering of the Virtual World which makes it almost impossible to filter and control content.

When the user is "in world", they are free to roam the Virtual World servers and interact with any content and people in that world. This now exposes the corporate user to web content, activities, and communications with people that would normally be filtered, if not logged and alerted on in normal web surfing type activity. Virtual World providers like Second Life® have rapidly matured their product offerings to address the issue of partitioning content by age appropriate sub-regions of the Virtual World, removing gambling, and partitioning adult content to a separate region requiring age verification to access. However, this still does not solve some of the core problems for corporate users with policies restricting information systems for business only purposes. To address these concerns, Private Virtual Worlds are increasingly being considered.

Private Virtual Worlds are platforms that are only accessible to a specific company and typically on an isolated physical network. Many educational and government organizations have a strict need to control their Virtual World environments, for the reasons aforementioned in this chapter pertaining to data security policy and regulation. Thus, Private worlds are designed to be walled off from the public and operated with hardware and software dedicated only for that directly connected user group. They are deployed to run behind the firewall. In Second Life®, the notion of a Private Virtual World is also referred to a "stand alone grid". This highly anticipated stand-alone version of Second Life®, code named "Nebraska", is currently out in beta testing. This allows companies to host their own private instance of Second Life® on servers behind their own firewall. Linden Lab, in a partnership with IBM, developed this extension to allow for companies an option to stay completely private, but also allow their internal users to traverse out to the public Second Life® Grid seamlessly. A company's avatars could freely travel to the public grid, however only the company issued avatars can be inside the firewall on the private instance, thus securing any data content and internal company communications internally. This is the best of both worlds for companies wishing to both secure internal communications but allow access to the public community for customer engagement.

Recognize the Trade Offs

Companies that choose to isolate and make their Virtual World completely private may be losing out on significant opportunities to participate and interact with public Virtual World consumers. After all, one of the fundamental opportunities of immersive social networking is to be able to organically create a community around company products and services. The choice to contain corporate users and content to a box behind the firewall could end up being short sighted, and severely limit future benefits. This is especially relevant in this early experimental stage of Virtual Worlds where openness and innovation are going to be critically important to test new business models and get collaborative feedback. This brings us back to a recurring theme for business looking to get engaged in Virtual Worlds. This choice, like many others, needs to clearly evolve around an articulated set of objectives and strategy for the company in the Virtual World. Companies will have to evaluate the pros and cons of using public versus private aspects of Virtual Worlds to achieve these objectives. The next section will talk about some considerations for thinking about how to define value in those objectives.

FINDING BUSINESS VALUE IN VIRTUAL WORLDS

In order to describe and comprehend technology trends, we tend to compartmentalize them in neat little boxes. The challenge with this is that business models and objectives don't fit neatly into these boxes. Web 1.0, Web 2.0, and now the 3D Web are examples of defining these technology trends. The current Virtual World trend line evolved from the static World Wide Web, then layered on transactional E-Commerce capabilities, and now has broadened out to engage consumers in rich social communities and Virtual Worlds 3D immersive environments. Companies should consider a strategy that uses a blend of these technologies to engage customers in a holistic and integrated E-Commerce approach, without over-reaching. This section will discuss how to think about using a blend of these technologies, including the use of traditional media to drive customers to new Virtual World channels where it makes sense.

Traditional Measures Still Apply

To begin, the fundamental question a company should ask before pursuing Virtual Worlds is: what are the business outcomes we are trying to accomplish? It sounds simplistic, but it is amazing how often the allure of new technology shrouds this basic question. Review the major use cases for Virtual worlds outlined in the above section to brainstorm on potential opportunities and outcomes. In establishing these outcomes, as the following questions:

- Is the company looking to use Virtual Worlds to extend brand awareness and build community to drive real world products and services?
- Is the company looking to establish a market around virtual goods and services "in world"?
- Does the company have a business process that could be executed more effectively in a Virtual World?
- Which business processes could be recreated in a Virtual World to create new products and services?
- Are new business models or supply chain partnerships opened up by operating in a Virtual World?

After answering these core questions, it is imperative to then define potential benefits. Beyond experimentation purposes, it is not surprising that classic E-Commerce and Customer Relationship Management (CRM) value measurements all still apply here! We have seen that companies found they were able to generate a cool marketing buzz in the first wave of Second Life® simply by getting in on the wave and generating headlines. This was great free media attention, but hardly a sustainable business model. That wave is over. Now is the time to ask how Virtual Worlds are lowering your costs, increasing your profits, and making your customers more engaged and your employees more productive. If we apply common E-Commerce approaches, are Virtual Worlds really lowering your costs per customer interaction, driving up customer loyalty, increasing sales and profit, driving innovative new business models, or improving supplier relationships? Without going into a lengthy discussion on E-Commerce business models, the point is that the criteria for measuring E-Commerce business model success still apply to Virtual Worlds. As a practical starting point, we learned above that companies are already getting value from Virtual Worlds by using them for low cost, immersive collaboration and training environments. Is this an opportunity to start building internal support, experience, and credibility for Virtual Worlds? In summary, achieving success in Virtual Worlds will take a strict dosage of practical and traditional business cases, mixed with a willingness to openly embrace and experiment with new technology.

The Value is Social

It is important that companies analyze the aspects of Web 2.0 social networking that apply to their business. Success with existing social networking communities can be directly leveraged into successful E-Commerce in Virtual Worlds. Just like in the 2D web, successful E-Commerce depends on attracting new customers and retaining existing ones through an enhanced online experience. If you have conquered this for your existing web presence, and have explored social web tools like Facebook, you have already defined the potential for your business. More importantly, you may have already defined the user demographics that you are targeting and their online tendencies for participating in these communities. If you have already created successful communities around your products and customers online, then you are ready to leverage this into Virtual Worlds. You might already understand that creating a robust online community requires substantial investment in content and time to maintain. The Virtual World communities are not different. Is a Virtual World community something that your company can sustain and is prepared to invest the required time in order to do? These are the key questions to consider.

If your company is not fluent in the art of building social web communities, the book *Groundswell – Winning in a World Transformed by Social Technologies*, by Charlene Li and Josh Bernoff is an excellent guide to approaching Web 2.0 social technologies and leveraging them for business. All the same concepts expertly laid out in the *Groundswell* apply very well to considerations for entering Virtual Worlds. *Groundswell* is a metaphor for what it takes to successfully build and sustain successful communities online and, in this case, Virtual Worlds. In *Groundswell*, we learn that building community requires a focus on a series of objectives from being able to listen to your customers, talk and participate in the community, and energize the community. It requires constant support to enable customers to support themselves, as well as, the willingness to foster and embrace customer driven innovation. It is vitally important that companies looking to engage in Virtual World E-Commerce follow the same prescription for successful community building. Build on this foundation by asking about the key properties and attributes of Virtual Worlds that lend themselves to building a more immersive community experience. Whether selling real world or "in world" goods and services, *Groundswell* effectively lays out techniques for extending traditional business functions into value-added communities. Again, these apply to Virtual World presence as much, if not more, than the current buzz around 2D social web communities.

To reiterate a key point, consider blending Web 1.0, 2.0, and Web 3D capabilities to specifically meet objectives. Don't over-reach with Virtual Worlds to meet business objectives that can be simply taken care of with traditional proven technology like standard web sites, targeted email marketing, and standard audio and web conferencing toolsets. Let's look at a case study with Kelly Services to review how one company got in early with Virtual Worlds and how they are finding value.

Kelly Services Case Study

Kelly Services, a global leader in workforce management services and human resources solutions, founded the temporary staffing industry in 1946. This is of importance to note because some companies with rich tradition of working in a high touch industry may find it culturally awkward to evaluate and embrace Virtual Worlds. Kelly did not view it this way.

Dave Fenech, VP, Interactive Marketing at Kelly Services, states that, "Second Life® offers Kelly a unique opportunity to leverage its 60 years of staffing expertise by engaging new audiences in an interactive way." He goes on to say that, "this ground-breaking channel offers endless possibilities for us to provide Second Life® residents with entertaining and innovative ways to explore career opportunities".

Following this strategy, Kelly entered Second Life® in April of 2007. Their Virtual Headquarters launch was timed with media releases to market the event. The Kelly Island also provided a set of richly engaging "in world" activities such as a live concert, free giveaways, a Second Life® money tree for residents to obtain Linden dollars, and a fully staffed team of Kelly avatars ready and willing to engage with customers and employees. The initial objective was not only the branding and media coverage value, but also to provide "in world" residents with an on-line, interactive gaming experience where avatars are able to participate in a range of job seeker scenarios. This strategy has clearly been about connecting with customers, in this case the job seeker. This is a key example of how Virtual Worlds allows for simulation and experiences not readily possible in the real world. For example, a job seeker can virtually find out what it's like to work for Kelly by seeing what Kelly is all about as a company. The unique "in world" scenarios permit Kelly to showcase some of Kelly's career opportunities, as well as, Kelly's ability to engage and care for its employees.

It is important to note that Kelly decided to link this initiative to their core business model, which is engaging and staffing talent across the globe. In Second Life®, residents can explore job opportunities that exist in the real world. Conversely, Kelly created a traditional web site which includes tips for getting started in Second Life®, a teleport link, and snapshot pictures of Kelly's virtual island (http://www.kellysecondlife.com). This was a focal point to drive traditional web traffic into Second Life. The Kelly Services Second Life® site can be found here: http://slurl.com/secondlife/Kelly%20Services%20HQ/50/52/0. The fact that these two mutually supporting customer channels were established illustrates the importance of blending traditional web and Virtual World technologies to achieve a common business objective.

Later that year, Kelly continued to add compelling content in order to keep community engagement level high. One of these features was a job search widget, developed by The Wishfarmers, a leader content provider, called the Jobbit. The Jobbit and other "in word" kiosks allow Kelly to stream job opportunities to Second Life® residents. By leveraging the strengths of their existing global staffing capabilities, Kelly later launched a new business model initiative in which they specifically targeted the staffing of virtual jobs in Second Life. This was a rather groundbreaking move for a Fortune 500 company actually selling "in world" services to generate both "in world" presence, engagement, and most importantly experiment with a Virtual World revenue stream.

Kelly continued to break new ground it made the first staffing placement in Second Life® in June of 2007. Rev. Brenda Monroe (Hildeguard Psaltery as she's known in Second Life) was visiting Kelly Services Island when she met an "in world" representative from Kelly Services. While engaged in the Kelly Services community, she inquired about job opportunities, was connected with one of Kelly's Atlanta branches, and then was placed at a leading U.S. distributor of industrial, medical, and specialty gases in Atlanta.

So has Kelly Services been successful? Dave Fenech puts it this way, "Qualitatively, we have been successful. But we have not yet put the back-end measurement tools in place to prove it quantitatively." He goes on to reiterate the key theme of this chapter, which is companies should "use the same measuring stick" as you do in real life. Engage and set expectations, and connect with people. Kelly Services is now considering the next set of initiatives to continue to build and engage their Virtual World community of job seekers.

FUTURE RESEARCH DIRECTIONS

In this chapter, we have discussed businesses that have got in early and experimented with Virtual Worlds during the first wave. As we look to the future, there are many intriguing questions, such as:

- Where will company specific use of Virtual Worlds be in the future?
- Will Virtual Worlds grow into preferred tools for E-Commerce channels and customer relationship management platforms?
- Are Virtual World platforms the future of our communication and collaboration toolsets?

These are not only important academic questions, but also important to companies considering initially investing in, or sustaining their current investment in Virtual Worlds. This section will explore these questions in a bit more detail.

The Metaverse Continuum: Blending of the Virtual and Real World

In 2008, Stanford University hosted a conference on Virtual Worlds called Metaverse U. It was a mixed reality event (participants in a lecture hall physically, as well as streamed to a Second Life® group of participants). At the event, Mike Liebhold lectured participants to think about real life as people and objects that are becoming draped in data. That is, with GPS and geo-tagging we are seeing more and more a combination of people creating meta-data about the physical world and accessing that in context with various mobile devices (M. Liebhold, Metaverse U Lecture, May 29, 2009). This is giving rise to a new medium called Augmented Reality, which can be conceptualized as a mash-up of the physical world and the virtual world. Augmented Reality uses a "viewer", which could be a video enabled mobile phone for example, to overlay data and images on the physical world.

Building on that point, M. Scott Boone (Appalachian School of Law) points out that we are seeing an interesting convergence between ubiquitous computing in the real world, and the attempt to re-create our physical lives within a Virtual World (M.S. Boone, State of Play Conference, 2007). In the real world, people are increasingly using computers to digitize our real world experience with computer instrumentation in nearly all our day-to-day activities. That is we tag geographical sites with photos and geo-tags, we put cameras and sensors up on every street corner, we attribute our lives with social networking software and Virtual World avatars, and nearly every person is outfitted with a mobile phone that typically has all of these capabilities, in addition to being our personal area networking device. Conversely, in Virtual Worlds, we continue to make them as "real world" as possible with advanced 3D graphics that mirror real world objects, life-like sound and spatial experiences, and integration into both real world communication mediums and traditional web sites. As computing devices become more ubiquitous and Virtual Worlds become more life-like and immersive, there is a fascinating convergence that looms ahead.

This paints a future scenario for businesses to strongly consider, potentially using Virtual Worlds for much more than we saw in the first wave. Seeing it through this lense, we could see E-Commerce developments like a virtual storefront replacing the ubiquitous E-Commerce shopping cart. The shopping cart is the epitome of traditional E-Commerce, but it does not allow you to try on clothes or simulate a buying experience in 3D. Could a traditional E-Commerce leader, like the well trafficked 2D Amazon web site, fall to a competitor who has a virtual storefront of similar proportion? As it turns out, there is a roadmap for this.

The Metaverse Roadmap (Figure 5) is a public research project which aims to project the 10 year forecast of how 3D Web technologies will impact business and society. It has produced a useful model for thinking about the dimensions of virtual and physical worlds, and how these platforms can be viewed on a blended continuum. This is an excellent planning framework for businesses to leverage when considering Virtual World investments and future business models enabled by the blending of geo-tagging based data, lifelogging through social networking, telematics and sensors, and Virtual World platforms.

The Future of the Web and E-Commerce

It is likely that we will see a future blending of online gaming, open-ended Virtual Worlds, and social networks. It is natural that what follows a

Figure 5. The Metaverse Continuum. (The Metaverse Roadmap. Used with permission).

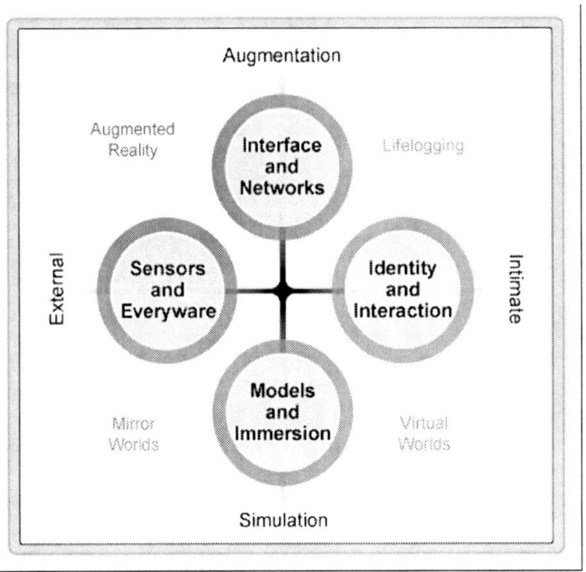

Web 2.0 and 3D Web is an Augmented Reality and Mirror World based World Wide Web. One particular example of this is in the Second Life® Grid. The term "grid" refers to their platform capability of interconnecting Virtual World instances, and following this paradigm, one can think of the future of the World Wide Web as not just a federation of interconnected HTTP (web) servers, but rather a federation of interconnected Virtual World servers, all participating on the Internet grid. For this to be a realistic possibility, however, standards for the creation and exchange of 3D and social networking information would have to dramatically improve, as would the processing power of computers and networks.

If Virtual Worlds are to continue to grow and become the next generation of E-Commerce, it is hard to imagine a scenario where successful companies are not intimately engaged in both business to consumer (B2C) and business to business (B2B) E-Commerce within the Virtual World environment. As in the Web 1.0 and 2.0 waves, we have seen E-Commerce start to blur the distinction between internal and external business processes. Put another way, if companies start to develop value chains that require a combination of B2B integration points spanning both Virtual World and real world based systems, the notion of Private Virtual Worlds behind the corporate firewall are going to become fuzzy. We can naturally expect that the ability to securely and effectively integrate data between business partner systems and internal company systems will also become a competitive differentiator to be able to deliver value through Virtual World E-Commerce. As we see the growth of open API's for Virtual World platforms that facilitate the integration of real world business data into those environments, it is not a stretch to envision a company's CRM or ERP systems and core operations heavily wired into a Virtual World based business process. Whether this is a Mirror World that completely replicates a company's internal physical environment, or a completely new virtual environment, the potential for employees to be virtually immersed in daily operations of a company while inside the Virtual World is extremely powerful. In summary, these are just some of the trends that companies need to keep in mind for potential business model consideration.

CONCLUSION

This chapter has clearly positioned that companies must approach Virtual Worlds like any other successful E-Commerce business venture, by defining business outcomes and having a well structured plan. It is also important to note, that during this experimental phase with Virtual Worlds, it is not all about finding hard value. Virtual Worlds are still in the experimental phase for business E-Commerce, but the future is bright and poised for massive change and growth in the coming years. For innovation, some experimentation and risk is going to have to be taken. Whether or not you have a clear business model defined like Kelly Services, or just want to make a splash and learn from experimentation like American Apparel, both seem warranted if the risks and roadblocks of Virtual Worlds today are carefully taken into account.

It is important to reiterate that the power of social networks and communities to drive innovation and customer engagement has already inspired companies to invest and participate in the Web 2.0 social networking wave. Virtual World technology clearly evolves this trend by offering a new channel for immersive community building. This applies to companies using Virtual Worlds to market and sell real world goods and services, or companies that are looking to experiment with the E-Commerce of virtual good and services, or simply using Virtual Worlds as an effective medium for collaboration and training.

This author would like to close by providing one last caveat emptor. Throughout the chapter, we have referred to historical patterns of web technology waves and how by looking at these we can project the cycle in which Virtual Worlds will behave. This analogy has been played and overplayed. We should point out that it could be risky to assume the same patterns will persist. The rules of the road can change. Things that worked for businesses in a Web 1.0 and 2.0 medium have and will change in a Virtual World. As Linden Lab's Ginsu Yoon puts it: "Virtual Worlds will increasingly trend towards the emotional impact, user demands and human scale of real world interactions" (G. Yoon, Metaverse U Lecture, May 29, 2009). If this holds true, we are in for quite a dynamic and exciting future as businesses continue to leverage and grow Virtual World technology.

REFERENCES

Balfour, B. (2009). Top 3 Reasons People Buy Virtual Goods. *Viximo, Virtual Goods Made Easy Web Site*. Retrieved August 16, 2009, from http://blog.viximo.com/corporate/2009/07/15/top-3-reasons-people-buy-virtual-goods/

Bigelow, L. (2009). How Your Brand Can Click With a Tough Audience. *WeeWorld Web Site*. Retrieved August 16, 2009, from http://www.weeworld.com/about/news_item.aspx?home=yes&NewsID=281

Dejwakh, V. (2008). Virtual Worlds and Web 3.0 Examined, Compared, Analyzed. *In-stat*, IN0804326CM. Retrieved August 16, 2009, from http://www.instat.com/abstract.asp?id=212&SKU=IN0804326CM

Dell, K. (2007). Second Life's Real World Problems. *Time Magazine Web Site*. Retrieved August 16, 2009, from http://www.time.com/time/magazine/article/0,9171,1651500,00.html

Driver, E., & Driver, S. (2009). ThinkBalm Immersive Internet Business Value Study, Q2 2009. *Immersive Internet Analyst Report Series, Issue #2*. Retrieved August 16, 2009, from http://www.thinkbalm.com/2009/05/26/thinkbalm-publishes-business-value-study/

Gartner (2007). Gartner Says 80 Percent of Active Internet Users Will Have A "Second Life" in the Virtual World by the End of 2011. *Gartner Newsroom*. Retrieved August 16, 2009, from http://www.gartner.com/it/page.jsp?id=503861

Gartner (2008). Gartner Says 90 Percent of Corporate Virtual World Projects Fail Within 18 Months. *Gartner Newsroom*. Retrieved August 16, 2009, from http://www.gartner.com/it/page.jsp?id=670507

Keegan, V. (2009). Virtual Worlds are Getting a Second Life. *Guardian.co.uk,* 1. Retrieved August 16, 2009, from http://www.guardian.co.uk/technology/2009/jul/29/virtual-worlds

Lab, L. (2009). How Meeting In Second Life® Transformed IBM's Technology Elite Into Virtual World Believers. *Second Life® Grid Web Site*. Retrieved August 16, 2009, from http://secondlifegrid.net.s3.amazonaws.com/docs/Second_Life_Case_IBM_EN.pdf

Li, C., & Bernoff, J. (2008). *Groundswell - Winning in a World Transformed by Social Technologies*. Boston, Massachusetts: Harvard Business School Publishing.

Linden, T. (2009). The Second Life® Economy - First Quarter 2009 in Detail. *Second Life® Web Site*. Retrieved August 16, 2009, from https://blogs.secondlife.com/community/features/blog/2009/04/16/the-second-life-economy--first-quarter-2009-in-detail

Metaverse, U. (2009). *Metaverse U 1.0*. Retrieved August 16, 2009, from http://metaverse.stanford.edu/metaverse-u-1-0-archive/conference-videos/conference-videos

Roadmap, M. (2009). *Metaverse Roadmap Web Site*. Retrieved August 16, 2009, from http://www.metaverseroadmap.org/

Rufer-Bach, K. (2009). *The Second Life® Grid - The Official Guide to Communication, Collaboration, and Community Engagement*. Indianapolis, Indiana: Wiley.

State of Play Conference (2007). *New York Law School / State of Play Conference*. Retrieved August 16, 2009, from http://www.nyls.edu/centers/harlan_scholar_centers/institute_for_information_law_and_policy/events?lightwindow_url=%2Findex.php%3FcID%3D1721

Virtual World News. (2009). Quickstat – Mafia Wars Hits 4 Million Users Milestone. *Virtual World News Web Site*. Retrieved August 16, 2009, from http://www.virtualworldsnews.com/2009/07/quickstat-mafia-wars-hits-4m-user-milestone.html

Wagner, A. (2009). 12% Of Americans Bought Virtual Goods In Past 12 Months: Survey. *Frank N. Magid Associates, Inc. Web Site*. Retrieved August 16, 2009, from http://www.magid.com/company_info/news_article.asp?articleID=3199

ADDITIONAL READING

An exploratory investigation. *Electronic Commerce Research, 1*(1-2), 77-86. Accessed online at http://www.springerlink.com/content/g8nu8061844glp44/.

Association of Virtual Worlds et al. (2008). The Blue Book: A Consumer Guide to Virtual Worlds. A whitepaper by the Association of Virtual Worlds. Retrieved August 16, 2009 from

Association of Virtual Worlds et al. (2008). The Green Book: A Business Guide to Virtual Worlds. A whitepaper by the Association of Virtual Worlds. Retrieved August 16, 2009 from

Driver, E., & Driver, S. (2008). The Immersive Internet Make Tactical Moves Today For Strategic Advantage Tomorrow. *Immersive Internet Analyst Report Series, Issue #1*. Retrieved August 16, 2009, from http://www.thinkbalm.com/wp-content/uploads/2008/11/thinkbalm-immersive-internet-report-nov-20084.pdf

Driver, E., & Driver, S. (2009). ThinkBalm Immersive Internet Business Value Study, Q2 2009. *Immersive Internet Analyst Report Series, Issue #2*. Retrieved August 16, 2009, from http://www.thinkbalm.com/2009/05/26/thinkbalm-publishes-business-value-study/

Goldsmith, J., & Wu, T. (2008). *Who Controls the Internet – Illusions of a Borderless World*. New York: Oxford University Press.

Guo, Y. & Barnes, S. (2009). Virtual item purchase behavior in virtual worlds:

http://metaverse.stanford.edu/metaverse-u-1-0-archive/conference-videos/conference-videos

http://virtual-economy.org/

http://www.associationofvirtualworlds.com/pdf/Blue%20Book%204th%20Edition%20August%202008.pdf

http://www.associationofvirtualworlds.com/pdf/Green%20Book%204th%20Edition%20August%202008.pdf

Kzero. (n.d.). Retrieved August 16, 2009 from http://www.kzero.co.uk/blog/

Li, C., & Bernoff, J. (2008). *Groundswell - Winning in a World Transformed by Social Technologies*. Boston, Massachusetts: Harvard Business School Publishing.

Metanomics. (n.d.). Retrieved August 16, 2009 from http://www.metanomics.net/

Metaverse U (2009). *Metaverse U 1.0*. Retrieved August 16, 2009, from

Roadmap, M. (2009). *Metaverse Roadmap Web Site*. Retrieved August 16, 2009, from http://www.metaverseroadmap.org/

Rufer-Bach, K. (2009). *The Second Life® Grid - The Official Guide to Communication, Collaboration, and Community Engagement*. Indianapolis, Indiana: Wiley.

State of Play Conference (2007). *New York Law School / State of Play Conference*. Retrieved August 16, 2009, from http://www.nyls.edu/centers/harlan_scholar_centers/institute_for_information_law_and_policy/events?lightwindow_url=%2Findex.php%3FcID%3D1721

The Metaverse Journal. (n.d.). Retrieved August 16, 2009 from http://www.metaversejournal.com/

3DTraining, Learning and Collaboration. (n.d.). Retrieved August 16, 2009 from http://www.3dtlc.net/

Virtual Economy Research Network. (n.d.). Retrieved August 16, 2009 from

Virtual World News. (n.d.). Retrieved August 16, 2009 from http://www.virtualworldsnews.com/

KEY TERMS AND DEFINITIONS

In World: Refers to activity taking place within the Virtual World platform, as opposed to real world activity.

Web 1.0: Refers to the first generation of web technology that largely consisted of static HTML based web sites with little to no rich user experience or collaboration. This platform focused on information publishing and basic E-Commerce transactions.

Web 2.0: Refers to the generation of web technology that offers rich internet applications focused on social networking and collaboration. This is typically thought of as blogs, wikis, social networking sites, and collaboration. Also includes the rise of Web Services and mash-up capabilities between rich web applications.

3D Web: Refers to the generation of web technology that adds 3D graphical experiences to the online user experience. This comes in the form of 3D gaming and Virtual Worlds, as well as, advanced digital media streaming.

2.5D Web: Refers to web technology that uses enhanced two dimensional interactivity in order to simulate a 3D experience without the need for heavy 3D graphical processing engines. Typically refers to using a 2D plane with added depth in user experience and interactivity.

B2B: Short for Business to Business, and refers to E-Commerce transactions that happen between business entities. Makes the distinction from B2C, or Business to Consumer based E-Commerce.

B2C: Short for Business to Consumer, and refers to E-Commerce transactions that happen between an end user consumer and a business entity. Makes the distinction from B2B, or Business to Business based E-Commerce.

Chapter 7
Virtual Worlds and the Military

Barbara L. Ciaramitaro
Ferris State University, USA

James Jones
Ferris State University, USA

ABSTRACT

The combined military forces of the United States are over 3 million strong; currently command a defense budget of $540 billion with an additional allocation of $306 billion for the Global War on Terror; and has spending power of nearly $14 billion. In addition to the impact this strong military presence has on our country and the world, these numbers underscore the influence the military has on technology trends, tools, and vendor offerings through its acquisition of various technology software and hardware components. One particular area of interest to this publication is the $8 billion that the military spends on virtual training. Additionally, the military spends $4 billion on recruitment efforts which include an increased emphasis on the use of virtual worlds to interest potential new recruits to join one of the military forces. Team Orlando, a joint military branch project that collaborates on training and development efforts, is also focused on finding new and better ways to train its soldiers through virtual worlds and simulation. An idea of Team Orlando's influence on the virtual world industry is reflected in the $17.5 billion in contracts awarded to vendors in 2009 alone. Intelligence agencies and Homeland Security have also demonstrated an increased interest in, and use of, virtual worlds evident through various requests for research and development proposals issued recently requesting ideas on ways to use virtual worlds for internal training and collaboration. The Intelligence community is also interested in exploring behavior of virtual world inhabitants and relating them to their real world counterparts. Even the CIA has a presence on Second Life®, albeit not for general public use. In total, the influence that the military, intelligence and homeland security agencies have on the virtual world industry is significant and extends the reach of virtual worlds beyond its commercial uses.

DOI: 10.4018/978-1-61692-808-7.ch007

INTRODUCTION

The combined military forces of the United States are over three million strong; currently command a defense budget of $540 billion with an additional allocation of $306 billion for the Global War on Terror; and has spending power of nearly $14 billion (Globalfirepower, 2009). In addition to the impact this strong military presence has on our country and the world, these numbers underscore the influence the military has on technology trends, tools, and vendor offerings through its acquisition of various technology software and hardware components. One particular area of interest to this publication is the $8 billion that the military spends on virtual training (Encyclopedia.com, 2009). Also of interest, is the $4 billion spent annually by the military on recruitment efforts which have recently included an increased emphasis on the use of virtual worlds to interest potential new recruits to join the military forces (National Priorities Project, 2007). These recruitment efforts have the added benefit of educating the public on the life of soldiers in the military while garnering respect and admiration for their efforts.

Evidence of the military's recent focus on the use of virtual worlds was apparent in the fall of 2008 with the release of an Request for Proposal (RFP) by the U.S. Air Force for the development of *MyBase*, a three dimensional online training software (FedBizOps, 2008a). The following year, several U.S. defense agencies released RFPs for virtual world development efforts including the U.S. Army's Federal Virtual World Challenge; the Department of Homeland Security Request for Information (RFI) for input on virtual world technology and web based systems; and NATO's RFP for the development of virtual worlds to augment or replace existing technologies in use for the education and training of NATO staff (Betterverse.org, 2009).

The Intelligence Advanced Research Projects Activity (IARPA) agency is also involved in researching the use of virtual worlds in the intelligence community. Its *A-Space* virtual site was released in 2008, and is described as a social-networking site for analysts to collaborate and share information among the 16 U.S. intelligence agencies (Conway, 2008). IARPA also released a request for White Papers in 2008 requesting analysis of Cyber-Behavior Research. And in 2009, we saw IARPA approach participation in virtual worlds from a different angle. A new request from IARPA was issued for research on ways to identify behavioral indicators in virtual worlds and multi-user online games that are related to the user's real world characteristics (Mountjoy, 2008).

The federal government is also utilizing the combined influence of its various agencies in the pursuit of virtual world technology. In 2007, the *Federal Consortium for Virtual Worlds* was formed. This consortium is made up of U.S. federal government agencies and contractors including the U.S. Department of Defense and the CIA, who, consisting of a group of U.S. federal government agencies and contractors interested in "exploring the use of virtual worlds in government, sharing best practices and policies, creating shared repositories, and networking. In the past year the Federal Consortium for Virtual Worlds has grown from a handful of agencies to more than 100."(Harris, 2008, p. 1) The Federal Consortium for Virtual Worlds has held conferences each year since its inception drawing presenters and attendees from every aspect of the virtual world domain. The conferences were held in both a live environment and in multiple virtual worlds including Second Life®. In total, the influence that the military, intelligence and homeland security agencies have on the virtual world industry as evident by these Requests and activities is significant and extends the reach of virtual worlds beyond its commercial uses.

This chapter will focus on the use of virtual worlds by the U.S. military, intelligence, and homeland security sectors, although other government entities are using virtual worlds as well. For example, the US Centers for Disease Control and

Prevention has a presence in both Second Life® and Whyville (CDC, 2009), the US National Aeronautics and Space Administration has a Second Life® presence (NASA, 2009), and the National Oceanic and Atmospheric Administration has a Second Life® presence (NOAA, 2009).

VIRTUAL WORLDS IN THE MILITARY

The adoption of virtual worlds by the military has several major impacts. The first impact is on the virtual world industry. The military's spending power acts as a financial inducement to various technology vendors to provide virtual world solutions for diverse concerns including virtual military training and education, remote control of military devices, and the use of virtual worlds to improve cooperation, collaboration and communication among the various military and intelligence sectors. The second impact of virtual worlds in the military is on recruitment efforts to interest potential new recruits to join the military through their participation in virtual world based games and simulations. The third impact, the value of which should not be underestimated, results from the public's exposure to military life through virtual world simulations, and the resulting respect and admiration for the life of soldiers. This respect and understanding of military life by the public can directly translate into congressional support for military activities and spending.

The military's use of virtual worlds to conduct training of its personnel has a long history beginning in the 1930's with simulators to teach pilots instrument control. In the 1950's, simulation training was expanded to include views of terrains which were fed into the simulator through visual feedback from cameras placed outside the simulator. The next adaptations were to simulate an entire field of vision, up to 180 degrees horizontal and vertical, through the use of several monitors and cameras, and lastly to link several simulators together in a distributed environment (Baumann, 1993). More recently, the use of virtual worlds by the military has become strongly associated with the concept of *serious games,* which are virtual training worlds developed for specific training purposes in non-entertainment fields such as military, education, and health care (Wyld, 2008). In fact, the U.S. military maintains that it originally developed the term *serious game* as a more suitable way to describe the use of gaming technology to train its soldiers as the term *war games* had negative connotations among members of Congress (Derryberry, 2008).

One of the first entries into the virtual world of serious games by the military was the release of *America's Army* which was inspired by the video game *Counterstrike.* The idea for America's Army came from Lt. Col. Casey Wardynski, director of the Office of Economic and Manpower Analysis at West Point. His inspiration for *America's Army* was his two video game playing sons and the belief that a video game would be a good way to attract computer savvy young adults to join the Army (Kennedy, 2002). From the start, the Army wanted to ensure a broad audience for *America's Army* and made it free to use. Although *America's Army* was first released in 2002 to improve recruitment efforts by the U.S. Army, its reach and use has grown a great deal since them.

When the Army launched its PC-based video game, America's Army...the service's intention was to connect with young people, encourage teamwork and promote its core values. But now the action game is morphing beyond its original mission, becoming the platform for numerous other military and government training simulation. (Jean, 2006, p 1)

One interesting distinction from commercial first-person shooter video games is *America's Army* emphasis on values, consequences and proper behavior. Players' actions are bound by the U. S. Army Rules of Engagement which describe the degree of force to be used in encounters with the enemy, teamwork and adherence to the seven Army core values of loyalty, duty, respect, selfless service, honor, integrity and personal courage(Military.com, 2008; Corps of Discovery, 2003). Players who do not follow these rules suffer consequences such as imprisonment in a virtual Army prison or failure to achieve higher status and levels in the game. The Army has also used *America's Army* as a way to recognize its *Real Heroes* by incorporating the actions of real Army personnel into its game. These heroes are soldiers "who embody the Army's warrior ethos" (Barnes, 2005). Whether or not the players of *America's Army* decide to join the military, the public relations benefits are significant. Players become strongly connected with the soldier's life through their immersive game play and feel increased support and understanding of the goals of the military and its soldiers.

Beyond meeting its initial recruiting goal, America's Army now acts as the enterprise virtual training platform for its military personnel, weapons systems prototyping, and assisting veterans readjust to life outside a war zone (Testa, 2008). Although America's Army is used to train individual soldiers, the multi-user training platform allows several Army personnel to train together, which more accurately reflects the real world battleground environment. The virtual platform is also used for prototype development such as the rapid response missile (RRM) whose purpose was to more accurately reach targets even in a dense urban environment. Once the prototype evolves to a released weapon, then the same training platform is used to train its military on weapon use. The virtual training platform is also used by the Army to help injured soldiers adjust to civilian life. For example, wounded soldiers use a virtual simulator to learn to drive again in non-combat situations. Beyond merely learning the new driving skills, the virtual world allows the soldier to regain attention and energy control before re-entering civilian life (Ibid).

In 2008, the Army issued an RFP to the general public for its Federal Virtual Worlds Challenge. This Challenge was created by the U.S. Army Research Development and Engineering Command, Simulation and Training Technology Challenge to "explore the possibilities for using virtual worlds that have not...been considered by the government."(Federal Worlds Challenge, 2009). The Challenge required that all training or analysis be conducted within the virtual environment. The Army used Second Life® as their platform to promote the Challenge. Although the Challenge was not limited to Second Life®, it provided a working sandbox environment in Second Life® in which developers could build their submissions. Three Second Life® avatars, *Tami Nightfire*, *Jefferson Supermarine*, and *SirFency Blackheart*, answered questions and provided guidance to interested participants. The Challenge did not restrict entries and its rules were wide open, accepting simple to complex virtual games and simulations.

As mentioned earlier, the Army's use of virtual worlds began as a recruitment tool. It was believed that immersing potential recruits in the life of soldiers would encourage higher levels of recruitment. And this belief has proved to be true.

With 6 million registered users, the PC game (America's Army) has attracted new soldiers to the ranks; 20 percent of the starting class at West Point had played America's Army prior to matriculating, and 20 to 40 percent of recruited soldiers had as well, said Col. Casey Wardynski, director of America's Army...America's Army.com gets 60,000 hits per day. (Jean, p. 1)

The Army has gone beyond the use of online games and virtual worlds to draw new recruits and educate the public. It has established an Army Experience Center at a shopping mall in Philadelphia where it brings the virtual world of the military to the public. The Experience Center is made up of 14,500 feet of various simulators, video gaming stations, and other interactive exhibits. For example, "In the Black Hawk simulator, participants sit in a model chopper and virtually fly through a mountain village, shooting at enemies as they protect a U.S. convoy headed to a medical facility" (Matheson, 2008).

The U.S. Army is not alone in the military's use of virtual worlds to connect with the civilian community through recruitment and public education efforts. The U.S. Navy has developed and released *SOCOM*, a video game with versions available both free online and as a commercial video game. The game scenario requires that the player lead a four-man team of U.S. Navy SEALs through 12 missions in four regions: Alaska, Thailand, Congo, and Turkmenistan on scenarios such as defeating terrorists, rescuing hostages, retrieving intelligence, or destroying terrorist bases. One significant difference between *SOCOM* and America's Army is that the player can choose to be either on the side of the Navy Seals or terrorists. Similar to *America's Army*, *SOCOM* was also first released in 2002 although only as a commercial video game. Later versions of *SOCOM* became available online and on new gaming platforms including handheld devices. *SOCOM's* successful public reach is demonstrated through its high ranking by users of on-line games. Similar to *America's Army*, this game allows non-military personnel to become immersed in the life of Navy Seals. The excitement and challenge of the virtual world immersion in *SOCOM* game play results in increased recruitment interest and public respect for the life and efforts of Navy Seals.

However, the Navy's use of virtual worlds is not limited to the *SOCOM* game. The *Naval Undersea Warfare Center (NUWC)* is currently exploring five types of virtual world applications: training and education, rapid prototyping, general collaboration and conferencing, public outreach, and data visualization (Jackson, 2009). One current project of the *NUWC* environment is testing submarine design.

The Naval Undersea Warfare Center ... has created a Second Life®-like virtual replica of a proposed design of a submarine's control hub using architectural renderings of the new design. By being immersed in a new environment, submarine commanders will have a better idea of the proposed changes to the hub and can offer more constructive feedback. (Ibid, p. 1)

The *NUWC* has established a presence on Second Life® through its *Virtual NUWC*. Its main avatar representative is Maccus McCullough who describes himself as, "the technical point of contact for the US Navy's Virtual Naval Undersea Warfare Center. Our group is engaged in the exploration and investigation of metaverse technologies (including SL) as a cost effective simulation framework" (Second Life®, 2009).

The U.S. Marines also developed a virtual world for recruitment and public education efforts titled *Close Combat*. Similar to *SOCOM*, *Close Combat* resembles a first person shooter game in which the player leaders a team of three Marines through a fictional battle scenario. In order to ensure the accuracy of the game, *Close Combat* was developed with the help of 40 combat experienced marines. Although sold commercially, *Close Combat* is similar to the America's Army in its emphasis in game play on the values of the Marine Corps: honor, courage and commitment (McCullough, 2009).

In January of 2008, the U.S. Air Force released a white paper titled, *On Learning: The Future of Air Force Education and Training*. The White Paper reports that the Air Force educates and trains over 700,000 military and civilian personnel and maintains that it must transform how it educates and trains their workforce. It detailed plans for revamping the Air Force's education system from 2008 to 2030. The core of their vision is a learning organization called *Air Force 2* which is focused on three areas of effort: knowledge management that discusses how the Air Force operates; continuous learning that covers how the Air Force develops people; and precision learning that explains how the Air Force delivers learning (Air Education and Training Command, 2008). At the cornerstone of the new learning organization is a virtual delivery platform known as "MyBase." At the center of the new system is the virtual world *MyBase*, which is a virtual learning environment designed to enhance Air Force recruiting, training education and operations."(Ibid, p. 15) *MyBase* is a virtual education system aimed at potential new recruits, existing Air Force Airmen, and the public. The White Paper acknowledges the impact that concentrated exposure to technology has had on the current generation of potential recruits, described as members of the Millennial generation, born between 1980 and 2001, and wants to use that technology expertise to the benefit of the Air Force.

The young men and women who will lead our Air Force in the future have been living in a digital world their entire lives and are better prepared than any other generation to operate in this environment...It is imperative that we understand their needs and expectations, and develop an enterprise-wide system that fosters learning and captures their most critical asset -- knowledge. (Ibid, p. 2)

The Air Force maintains that the use of virtual worlds in its education programs will provide significant benefits in attracting high quality recruits and training them in the most effective manner. Virtual worlds are able to go beyond the simple education protocols offered by traditional distance learning and allow online exploration and collaboration taught by real world and virtual instructors in areas such as pilot training, plane maintenance, and medicine. *MyBase*, "a virtual learning environment designed to enhance Air Force recruiting, training, education and operations", is the center of the plan (Ibid, p. 2). The proposed new educational platform is described as, "a virtual, exploratory and interactive environment and architecture that supports both continuous and precision learning." (Virtual World News, 2008a). Through the use of virtual interactive scenarios, the *MyBase* immersive training environment will support training in decision-making, communication and negotiation, all of which are considered essential for training new Air Force leaders. The White Paper also highlights a specific type of education called *Precision Learning* which delivers the right training, at the right time and place, in the right medium, to produce the right effect. Precision Training relies on a customized learning environment which entails increased use of virtual technology and visualization techniques. "Learning will be tailored in format, time, media, and frequency for each individual Airman" (Air Education and Training Command, p.14). The *MyBase* learning environment will go beyond visual immersion and use haptic technology to integrate the sense of touch with visual cues that are particularly valuable in training for fire fighting, medical treatment, and flying.

In 2009, the Air Force released *MyBase* to the public, which is a virtual air force base in Second Life®.

There's a visitors center where avatars can read informational posters, link to websites or watch videos about Air Force programs. There's a club with a dance floor where they can mingle. They can test their mettle on an obstacle course and shooting range, or take the virtual P-51 Mustang for a spin...At an area called MyBase Zeta, she (sic) shows me a simulated Afghan compound, which can be used to stage training exercises. It wouldn't be hard to change the scenario from Afghanistan to North Korea...(Air Space Smithsonian, 2009, p. 1)

The Air Force continues to expand its use of MyBase including additional training centers in Second Life® for the training of active Airmen in accordance with their long term plans detailed in the White Paper. An RFI was issued in 2008 requesting proposals from vendors to develop courses for Airmen, "using real-time interactive avatars and streaming audio/video presented in an online 3D virtual learning environment" (FedBizOpps, 2008b).

The various military branches also collaborate on ways to use virtual worlds to enhance training and education of its members, and coordination among the various commands. *Team Orlando* is an alliance formed by US leading military simulation commands. The goal of *Team Orlando* is to research and develop training systems for all branches of the Department of Defense (DOD) and other government agencies. "Team Orlando is all about improving human performance through simulation."(Team Orlando, 2009a, p. 9) The military members of Team Orlando are supported by academic and industry leaders in the fields of modeling and simulation, human performance, and training. *Team Orlando* offers both a physical center located in Orlando, Florida, and more recently, a virtual presence in Second Life®. An idea of Team Orlando's influence on the virtual world and simulation industry is reflected in the $17.5 billion in contracts awarded to vendors in 2009 alone (Team Orlando, 2009b). A few of *Team Orlando* recent projects include:

- Army's *Virtual Battle Space 2 Army* gaming system, which was designed to provide units realistic, integrated training based on lessons learned from the field in Iraq and Afghanistan (King, 2009).
- US Navy's *Surviving the USS Trayer*, a disaster simulation training experience described as the most realistic and ambitious in the world.

"Five days a week, it bears the brunt of multiple enemy missile attacks that result in simulated deaths, injuries and damage. But while the scenario is fictional, the stakes are real. For recruits toward the end of their eight-week basic training course, the Trayer is their baptism by fire and final exam. It's all that stands between them and the right to be called 'sailor.'(Wise, 2008, p. 1)

Second Life® appears to be the virtual world of choice for the military. The Federal Consortium for Virtual Worlds holds all of their conferences live and through a Second Life® island. The Department of Defense has created its *Military Lands*, which is a conglomerate of 20 islands representing the Army, Navy, Air Force. Coalition Island serves as the entry point to *Military Lands*. The purpose of *Military Islands* is to allow Second Life® residents to learn more about the various armed forces. The various islands are used to conduct outreach and family counseling, training and simulation, and prototype development (Second Life®, 2009b). As mentioned above, the Air Force is relying on its *MyBase* Island in Second Life® to be the core of its new training program, and the Navy has established their *Naval Undersea War Center* within Second Life® as well. The Military are also using Second Life® to service its veterans with islands established by the U.S. Veterans Affairs and Disabled American Veterans. These sites were established as a means to communicate information and provide assistance to the growing number of young veterans (Jordan, 2009). A more detailed list of military islands on Second Life® is included in Table 1.

VIRTUAL WORLDS IN INTELLIGENCE

A significant criticism of the Intelligence community that emerged after the September 11, 2001 terrorist attacks was the lack of coordination and communication among the various intelligence agencies. Several reports indicated that the required information about the imminent attack was there, but the lack of sharing of information primarily among the CIA and FBI prevented any action being taken to thwart the attacks (Chalk and Roseau, 2003). As a result the Department

Table 1. Listing of some virtual worlds used by the military, intelligence and homeland security agencies

Agency	Description	Type of Virtual World	Location
U.S. Army	America's Army	Online Game	www.americasarmy.com
		Second Life®	http://world.secondlife.com/group/704afd98-2129-79b9-b815-e146a66e2d3b
U.S. Navy	Naval Undersea War Command (NUWAC)	Second Life®	http://world.secondlife.com/place/c20b7f99-f16b-ac52-1442-7a9ecf1d042b
	SOCOM	Video Game	Play Station
	SOCOM	Online Game	http://www.socom.com/
U.S. Marines	Training and Doctrine Command (TRADOC)	Second Life®	http://world.secondlife.com/group/42321864-5988-e821-fa14-f8302f4039c3
	US Marine Corps Families	Second Life®	http://world.secondlife.com/group/f993c3c9-946d-c41d-8be0-5d67d7cda0f7
	Semper Fidelis: Marine Corps	Computer Game	
U.S. Air Force	MyBase	Second Life®	http://world.secondlife.com/place/a8cf4624-c6af-61fb-b754-9a7f4b525b2a
	US Air Force NCOs (Non-Commissioned Officers)	Second Life®	http://world.secondlife.com/group/d3461e30-bcb4-8f82-b451-1f72118e777e
	Echo Zulu	Online Game	http://www.airforce.com/echo-zulu/
Team Orlando	Team Orlando	Second Life®	http://world.secondlife.com/place/855e3a88-a8ee-e349-138e-38e5f355e333
Department of Defense	Coalition Island	Virtual World in Second Life®	http://slurl.com/secondlife/Coalition%20Island/180/193/25
U.S. Veterans Affairs	VA Island	Virtual World in Second Life®	http://slurl.com/secondlife/US%20Veterans%20Affairs/63/206/22
US Military Veterans' Center	Patriot Island	Second Life®	http://world.secondlife.com/place/b37c08a6-158a-548a-ff28-cfab1432df57
Disabled American Veterans	DAV Island	Virtual World in Second Life®	http://slurl.com/secondlife/DAV/136/12/29
Department of Homeland Security	Department of Homeland Security	Virtual World in Second Life®	http://world.secondlife.com/group/bb931bcb-d7b2-f06c-270e-87b0157d8c0b
Catastrophic Planning and Management Institute	Disaster Zone	Virtual World in Second Life®	http://world.secondlife.com/group/f3b192aa-b5c2-dd34-8aac-acec11c7b64b

of Homeland Security was created to coordinate future responses to security threats. But the criticism also sparked action within the Intelligence community itself. One result is that the intelligence community is actively examining ways in which virtual worlds can be used to enhance their intelligence gathering and decision making. The Office of the Director of National Intelligence (ODNI) is pursuing ways to use virtual worlds as tools for intelligence analysis. ODNI's Intelligence Advanced Research Projects Activity (IARPA) initiated a project in 2007 called the Analysis WorkSpace for Exploitation (A-SpaceX) to examine how virtual worlds can be used for collaboration and decision-making by intelligence analysts (Bain, 2008). The goals of A-SpaceX were to expand the use of serious games to the intelligence community that would enhance collaboration among intelligence analysts. An illustration of A-SpaceX objectives and structure was presented by IARPA as illustrated below. A-Space was released in 2008 and was described as a social-networking site for analysts within the 16 U.S. intelligence agencies. "It's a place where not only spies can meet but share data they've never been able to share before."(Shaughnessey, 2008, p 1) Of course, all of the material is highly classified and available only to those with the proper authorization.

Interestingly, IARPA is also concerned with the impact of virtual world participation by its current or potential employees. IARPA released a request for White Papers in 2008 requesting analysis of Cyber-Behavior Research. This request was based on the assumption by IARPA that an individual's conduct in cyberspace should be a factor in their security clearance process (Conway, 2008). Contracts for the research were awarded to two companies in late 2008. And in 2009, we saw IARPA approach participation in virtual worlds from a different angle. A new Request, referred to as the *Reynard* project was issued for research on ways to identify behavioral indicators in virtual worlds and multi-user online games that are related to the user's real world characteristics with the goal of being able to automatically detect "suspicious behavior" in the virtual world (Mountjoy, 2008).

Starting from the premise that Real World (RW) characteristics are reflected in Virtual World (VW) behavior, the IARPA Reynard program seeks to identify behavioral indicators in VWs and Multi-User Online Games (MMOGs) that are related to the RW characteristics of the users... Attributes of interest include the following: gender, approximate age, economic status, educational level, occupation, ideology or "world view", degree of influence, "digital native" vs "digital immigrant," approximate physical geographic location, native language, and culture. (IARPA, 2009, p. 1)

Other virtual tools recently developed by IARPA include *VideoQuest*, *GeoTime*, and *Paint,* all of which combine visualization software with geographic information systems (GIS) to provide analysts with integrated information from a variety of sources. Even the CIA has joined the virtual world. It has established a virtual presence in Second Life® using a few private islands as means for its employees to communicate and collaborate. These sites are being used to hold unclassified meetings and to conduct training sessions (Wyld, 2008). Not much more is publicly available at this time. Some intelligence agencies believe that virtual worlds could also become an actual intelligence battlefield with terrorists using the environment to plan or conduct cyber attacks. "The intelligence community has begun contemplating how to use Second Life® and other such communities as platforms for cyber weapons that could be used against terrorists or enemies..." (O'Harrow, 2008, p. 1) As mentioned above, there is also current research by IARPA being conducting on identifying specific behavioral characteristics of virtual world inhabitants that could be viewed as suspicious. The U.S. Intelligence Community also drives external virtual world development and innovation through its venture capital organization (In-Q-Tel), providing funding to companies like Forterra Systems (In-Q-Tel, 2009).

VIRTUAL WORLDS AND HOMELAND SECURITY

As mentioned previously, the Department of Homeland Security (DHS) was established in response to the lack of coordination among the various federal agencies in preventing the September 11, 2001 terrorist attacks. Its mission is to protect the nation from various security threats. In implementing its mission, DHS has demonstrated significant interest in virtual worlds since its inception. In 2005, DHS partnered with the Response Research Center at Dartmouth College and created a private island in Second Life® named *Response* to simulate emergency response behavior to threats (Aitoro, 2007). In 2003, control of the Federal Law Enforcement Agency Training

Center (FLETC) was formally transferred from the Treasury Department to DHS. FLETC is the training center for the federal officers of 80 federal agencies serving approximately 48,000 students a year. It also provides training to state, local and internal students (Homeland Security, 2008). The FLETC facility is made up of 40,000 square feet of various physical and virtual simulations. The law enforcement driving simulation is made up of 28 virtual reality vehicles, each of which can provide the officers with hundreds of different scenarios to train and test them in making the best split second decision. The driving simulation is linked to a virtual house from which the officers can enter from their vehicles with guns drawn once again rehearsing the kinds of real world split-second decisions that are part of the daily life of law enforcement officers. Another simulation involves the ambush of a convoy of vehicles appropriate for secret service or military protection agents. "Ambush trains federal agents and military folks to think about their decisions and just like the driving simulator, a replay of their decisions shows what was done right and what needs to happen during the real thing." (Barnard, 2007, p. 1)

In 2008, DHS contracted with a vendor to develop a virtual classroom using avatar-based instructional delivery for on-line virtual world training and education. This virtual classroom will be integrated with a virtual world used by the National Guard (Virtual World News, 2008b). The National Guard will use the site to hold large-scale training exercises, in which people are represented by avatars and locations are modeled as generic town squares. The site will accommodate "so-called massive multi-user events, in which thousands of people worldwide – in this case 5,000 to 10,000 users – can simultaneously interact with one another in a virtual world." (Laurent, 2008, p. 1)

In 2009, DHS issued a Request for Information (RFI) that seeks input on virtual world technologies and web based training systems. The goal of the RFI is to gain a better understanding of how virtual world technologies can be used to enhance training (FedBizOpps, 2009).

This RFI seeks to gain a better understanding of virtual world technologies as well as web based training systems that may be used either independently or can be used in combination with many kinds of models and simulations to enhance simulation based exercise and training activities. (Ibid, p. 1)

The Catastrophic Planning and Management Institute (CPMI) is an advisory group to the federal government that specializes in developing processes and training related to the handling of catastrophic situations (CP-MI.org, 2008). CPMI has launched a project in Second Life® called *The Disaster Zone*, which is described as a disaster awareness project. Its goal is to assist in planning for disasters with virtual worlds. The project involves 14 collaborative islands and "one overarching goal: limiting deaths related to natural disasters (Homeland Security NTARC News, 2009).

ISSUES AND CHALLENGES

Military, Intelligence and Homeland Security Agencies are investing heavily in virtual worlds as a means to improve training, recruitment, research, collaboration, and communication among its members. Unfortunately, this path is not without its very real issues and challenges, and each of these topics could easily warrant a complete discussion on their own. However, this chapter will only touch the surface of these concerns leaving a more in depth discussion to fellow authors of this publication (Hoops, Schultz, and Gogolin).

The Air Force White Paper, *On Learning: The Future of Air Force Education and Training,* places emphasis on the need to attract members of the Millennial Generation, born between 1980 and 2001, as new recruits. They are described *digital natives*, who have grown up surrounded by technology and are fluent in the language of computers, video games and the Internet. Digital natives are in contrast to *digital immigrants* who have adopted many technology tools and have learned the "second language" of technology. The difference is the comfort level with communicating in the digital world including membership in virtual worlds (Wyld, 2008). The last group are the *digitally disenfranchised* who have not learned how to maneuver through the world of technology and consider participation in digital mediums such as virtual worlds to be "unnatural". The military is clearly aiming their recruiting efforts at digital natives as with 62% of new recruits younger than 22, and 90% younger than 28 (National Priorities Project, 2007b). However, their current workforce will be a combination of all three cultures as the demographics a few years ago found that 46% of military personnel were under the age of 25; 18% under the age of 30; 15% under the age of 40; and 21% over the age of 40 (United States General Accounting Office, 2002). The inability of these three cultures to effectively communicate is a significant challenge that must be met.

One important area of concern is finding experienced military educators who can speak the digital language, "because the single biggest problem facing education today is that our Digital Immigrant instructors, who speak an outdated language (that of the pre-digital age), are struggling to teach a population that speaks an entirely new language."(Prensky, 2002, p. 1) Although they may have the necessary military experience and knowledge, if they are unable to speak the language of the digital natives, they will not be successful teachers. This cultural difference is also reflected in the working relationship between new recruits and their leaders. In the past, new recruits were taught and led by seasoned and respected military natives. However, the new digital native recruits are entering an environment that is dominated by digital immigrants and the digitally disenfranchised who feel less comfortable with technology than they do. With the visible emphasis that the military is placing on new virtual modes of learning, research, and collaboration, it is clear that the need to adapt will fall on the shoulders of the older digital immigrants. The digitally disenfranchised will most probably be unable to survive in the new technology-intensive culture as the learning curve to be comfortable in virtual worlds is quite steep for those unfamiliar with the new digital landscape (Editor, 2009).

Security issues plague the Internet, virtual worlds and online games. Some of the security issues of concern to the military are: transmission of malicious code through online games and virtual worlds; an inability to verify identity and the risk of impersonation of virtual avatars; unauthorized access to the content of non-public virtual worlds; and malicious defacement of virtual world sites. Second Life®, a virtual world used by many federal defense agencies training and collaboration has suffered its share of security breaches. In 2006, Second Life® had to shut down due to the ravages of malicious code. Malicious code planted gold rings around the Second Life® site. When Second Life® inhabitants would interact with the gold rings they would replicate slowing down the Second Life® servers to the point that they had to be shut down. (BBC News, 2006). Again in 2006, a hacker was able to access the Second Life® data base and retrieve customer information including account names and passwords, payment information and real life names (Second Life® Blogs, 2006). To their credit, Second Life® has responded to these security threats with improved safeguards in the way it provides access and streams the virtual world presence to its users.

Hacking and malicious code are not the only security risks in virtual worlds. The Gartner Group places the lack of identity management at the top of their list.

The lack of verifiable identity control or access management is a major deficiency in public virtual worlds... Individuals interact in virtual worlds via avatars, which are computer-generated representations of themselves. However, because new accounts can be opened with ease (and at no cost), many individuals have multiple avatars. Thus, it's difficult (if not impossible) to ensure that any specific avatar actually represents the person with whom it's associated. (Beer, 2007, p. 1)

Gartner maintains that public virtual worlds are not the place for private or classified discussions due to their security issues. For those defense agencies that require high security, an internal private virtual world established behind the organization's defenses, such as firewalls and intrusion detection devices, may be the best solution. The public facing virtual worlds will always remain susceptible to security threats (Ibid). Second Life® has responded to this concern by offering an internal version of their virtual world called Second Life® Enterprise. "Companies which had previously shied away from the virtual world because of concerns about proprietary data or 3D models living on Second Life®'s public-facing servers can now host the world within their own security perimeter." (Lamont, 2009, p.1).

Many of the information sharing challenges in the real world, like interoperability, authentication, and content concerns, extend to the virtual world. The goal of inter and intra agency collaboration is put at risk with the lack of interoperability among various virtual worlds. The main cause for this lack of interoperability is that there are no established and agreed upon virtual world standards and policies. IBM has worked closely with Second Life® to develop a common virtual identify that could be transported to various virtual worlds (Terdiman, 2009). Dr. Yesha Sivan, a co-author in this book, has recently published an in depth discussion of virtual world standards (Sivan, 2009). He explains that current competing standards include X3D, a proposed standard by the Web3D Consortium; Project Wonderland, a java based virtual world toolkit; Open Metaverse promoted by the Open Metaverse Foundation; MEPG-V which was developed under the direction of ISO; and Collada, an XML based standard. It is unclear at this time which of the current competing standards, if any, will prevail. As in the real world, separate bits of information can be aggregated to expose more information than the information originator(s) intended. In the intelligence community, sources and methods are considered highly sensitive, and balancing the benefit of sharing information with the risk of exposure is a challenge. Determining what information to share, at what level of detail, with whom, and how to control second-hand sharing are all problems that the intelligence community faces in real and virtual worlds.

THE FUTURE

Given the current state of virtual worlds, near term developments, and possible future developments, we forecast how virtual worlds might be used in the future for job assignments, cyber warfare, and espionage. The military currently uses virtual worlds to inform potential recruits about military life, and it seems an obvious extension to use virtual worlds to evaluate potential or actual recruits for various military roles. The military has a long history of standardized testing to aid in assignments, and the use of virtual worlds for this purpose is imminent. The U.S. military and intelligence communities have publicly acknowledged their offensive information warfare activities, and virtual worlds provide a fertile ground for these activities. The international and dispersed nature of virtual world client applications provides a global reach into the computer systems of both allies and enemies. In the case of U.S. enemies, such access could be leveraged into remote system compromise via the installation of monitoring or malicious software via virtual world client applications. Conversely, it is natural to assume that U.S. enemies are actively working on the same capabilities. Finally, the intelligence community has an established history of propagating disinformation for various purposes (e.g., see (Montagu, 1955)). Virtual worlds provide yet another information dissemination vector. While the U.S. government use of virtual worlds currently emphasizes the dissemination of valid information (presumably), the use of virtual worlds to distribute disinformation is inevitable.

CONCLUSION

Virtual worlds are used broadly by the military, intelligence and homeland security agencies. Their uses span the most common training and development efforts used by all of the military branches, to the more singular purposes of avatar behavior being investigated by the intelligence community. The commitment to build their new training, collaboration, and research efforts around virtual worlds is evident by the immense sums of money currently being spent by the various agencies in their exploration and development of virtual worlds. This commitment is causing not only an overhaul of the various training and collaboration systems currently in use, but is having a direct impact on the culture of these agencies as well. It is clear that the future of these agencies lie with the young, technology savvy individuals they are trying to recruit through their use of virtual world. Table 1 provides a summation of many of the virtual worlds currently in use by the military, intelligence community and homeland security. The listing includes only the public sites but we know that equal effort is being spent on developing virtual worlds for internal only use. Due to its enormous buying power, the influence of these agencies on the virtual world industry has been huge with technology developments continually flowing between the military and commercial worlds. It is expected that this influence on virtual world technologies will only continue to grow.

REFERENCES

Air Education and Training Command. (2008), *AETC White Paper*. Retrieved on 11/29/09 from http://www.aetc.af.mil/library/whitepaper.asp

AirSpace Smithsonian. (2009), Wild New Yonder. *The Daily Planet*. Retrieved on 11/29/09 from http://blogs.airspacemag.com/daily-planet/2009/08/17/wild-new-yonder/

Aitoro, J. (2007). *Uncle Sam Get a (Second) Life*. Channel Web. Retrieved on 11/30/09 from http://www.crn.com/government/199400068;jsessionid=2X20YIPJOUFODQE1GHRSKH4ATMY32JVN

Bain, Ben. (2008). Taking Intelligence Analysis to the Virtual World. Federal Computer Week. Retrieved on 11/28/09 from http://fcw.com/Articles/2008/09/04/Taking-intelligence-analysis-to-the-virtual-world.aspx

Barnard, J. (2007). Homeland Security Goes Virtual with Training. First Coast News. Retrieved on 11/30/09 from http://www.firstcoastnews.com/news/topstories/news-article.aspx?storyid=81724

Barnes, J. (2005). The New Action Heroes. *U.S. News and World Report*. Retrieved on 11/28/09 from http://www.usnews.com/usnews/news/articles/051121/21heroes.htm

Baumann, J. (1993). Military Applications of Virtual Reality. *The Encyclopedia of Virtual Environments*. Retrieved on 11/28/09 from http://www.hitl.washington.edu/scivw/EVE/II.G.Military.html

Beer, S. (2007). *Second Life® a Security Risk for Business: Gartner*. ITWire. Retrieved on 11/30/09 from http://www.itwire.com/content/view/13912/53/

Betterverse.org. (2009). Flood of new government tenders for virtual world projects from DHS, US Army, Canada, and NATO. Retrieved on 11/27/09 from http://www.betterverse.org/2009/09/flood-of-new-government-tenders-for-virtual-world-projects-from-dhs-us-army-canada-and-nato.html

Centers for Disease Control and Prevention. (2009). *Social Media at CDC*. Retrieved on 12.8.09 from http://www.cdc.gov/SocialMedia/Tools/VirtualWorlds.html

Chalf, P., & Rosenau, D. (2003). *Intelligence, Police and Counterterrorism: Assessing Post-911 Initiatives*. Rand Corporation. Retrieved on 11/30/09 from http://www.rand.org/nsrd/ter-rpanel/additional/intelinputv2.pdf

Conway, D. (2008). *ODNI Asks: Which MMOG Make You a Spy? Zero Intelligence Agents*. Retrieved on 11/28/09 from http://www.drewconway.com/zia/?p=197

Corps of Discovery. (2003). *The Seven Army Values*. Retrieved on 11.28.09 from http://www.history.army.mil/lc/the%20mission/the_seven_army_values.htm

CP-MI.org. (2009). Welcome. Retrieved on 11/29/09 from http://www.cp-mi.org/14701.html

Derryberry, A. (2008). *Serious Games: Online Games for Learning*. Retrieved on 11/28/09 from http://www.adobe.com/resources/elearning/pdfs/serious_games_wp.pdf

(Ed.). (2009). *Making the Virtual World Learning Experience Better. ELearning Future*. Retrieved on 12/1/09 from http://www.elearningfuture.com/making-the-virtual-world-learning-experience-better/

Encyclopedia.com. (2009). United States: Worldwide Military Spending on Virtual Training totaled $7.9bn in 2008. Retrieved on 11/27/09 from http://www.encyclopedia.com/doc/1g1-206025778.html

FedBizOpps. (2008a). *MyBase, 3D On-Line Training Environment Software*. Retrieved on 11/27/09 from https://www.fbo.gov/index?s=opportunity&mode=form&id=807445bf1dab0abd47b4829a72a8691c&tab=core&_cview=0

FedBizOpps.gov. (2008b). *MyBase (Prototype) 3D Virtual Learning Environment*. Solicitation Number: FA3002-08-RFI001. Retrieved on 11/29/09 from https://www.fbo.gov/index?s=opportunity&mode=form&tab=core&id=5dfd2502b6ebd48d2493bdf78c807899&_cview=0

FedBizOps. Gov. (2009). *This RFI seeks input on virtual world technologies and web based training systems*. Retrieved on 11/29/09 from https://www.fbo.gov/index?s=opportunity&mode=form&tab=core&id=e2ccbe350033dd333f17f9458695b8e3&_cview=1&cck=1&au=&ck=

Federal, V. W. C. (2009). Challenge. Retrieved on 11/28/09 from http://fvwc.army.mil/FVWC-Main.html

Globalfirepower. (2008). United States of America Military Strength. Retrieved on 11/27/09 from http://www.globalfirepower.com/country-military-strength-detail.asp?country_id=United-States-of-America

Harris, C. (2008). Government Consortium to Investigate Virtual World Best Practices. *Digital Communities*. Retrieved on 11/30/09 from http://www.govtech.com/dc/articles/420596

Homeland Security NTARC News. (2009). Second Life® Raises Awareness with Disaster Zone Project. *National Terror Alert*. Retrieved on 11/29/09 from http://www.nationalterroralert.com/updates/2009/10/26/second-life-raises-awareness-with-disaster-zone-project/

IARPA. (2009). *Reynard Proposer's Day Conference*. Retrieved on 11/28/09 from http://conference.brtrc.com/reynard/Overview.aspx

In-Q-Tel. (2009). *Forterra Systems*. Retrieved on 12/8/09 from http://www.iqt.org/technology-portfolio/forterra_systems.html.

Jackson, J. (2009). Navy Creates a Virtual World to Test Submarine Design. *Government Computer News*. Retrieved on 11/28/09 from http://www.gcn.com/Articles/2009/08/24/Data-visualization-sidebar-2-Navy-sub.aspx

Jean, G. (2006). Game Branches Out into Real Combat Training. *National Defense NDIA Business and Technology Magazine*. Retrieved on 11/28/09 from http://www.nationaldefensemagazine.org/archive/2006/February/Pages/games_brance3042.aspx

Jordan, B. (2009). Island Getaways for Vets a 'Click' Away. Military.com. Retrieved on 12/1/09 from http://www.military.com/news/article/island-gataways-for-vets-a-click-away.html

Kennedy, B. (2002). Uncle Same Wants You (To Play this Game). New York Times. Retrieved on 11/28/09 from http://www.nytimes.com/2002/07/11/technology/uncle-sam-wants-you-to-play-this-game.html?sec=&spon=&&scp=1&sq=wardynski&st=cse

King, W. (2009). Virtual Battle Space 2 Army Gaming system Debuts. Retrieved on 11/29/09 from http://www.army.mil/-news/2009/02/26/17502-virtual-battle-space-2-army-gaming-system-debuts/

Lamont, I. (2009). Second Life® Enterprise to bring security, enterprise apps to virtual meetings. The Industry Standard. Retrieved on 12/1/09 from http://www.thestandard.com/news/2009/11/05/second-life-enterprise-bring-security-enterprise-apps-world-activities.

Laurent, A. (2008). DSHS Joins the Virtual World. Next.Gov. Retrieved on 11/30/09 from http://www.nextgov.com/nextgov/ng_20080514_8611.php

Life, S. ®. (2009a). Resident: Maccus McCullough. Retrieved on 11/28/09 from http://world.secondlife.com/resident/f365f959-24e9-46cc-a2ed-43208a4fbf7b

Life, S. ® (2009b). *Military Lands. Second Life® Wiki*. Retrieved on 12/1/09 from http://wiki.secondlife.com/wiki/Military_Lands

Matheson, K. (2008). Army Experience Center offers simulations at Mall. USA Today. Retrieved on 11/28/09 from http://www.usatoday.com/news/military/2008-08-30-army-experience-center_N.htm?csp=34

McCullough, A. (2009), Wii Combat Game Features Marines. Marine Times. Retrieved on 11/28/09 from http://www.marinecorpstimes.com/news/2009/10/marine_wii_101809w/

Military.com. (2008). Magazine focuses on Army Gaming. Retrieved on 11/28/09 from http://www.military.com/entertainment/games/game-news/magazine-focuses-on-army-gaming

Montagu, E. (1955). *The Man Who Never Was*. Penguin Books.

Mountjoy, B. (2008). When Virtual Meets Reality: WoW, Second Life® May Become Targets of Terrorists, CIA. Firefox News. Retrieved on 11/29/09 from http://firefox.org/news/articles/1580/1/When-Virtual-Meets-Reality-WoW-Second-Life-May-Become-Targets-of-Terrorists-CIA/Page1.html

National Aeronautics and Space Administration. (2009). CoLab Virtual Overview. Retrieved on 12/8/09 from http://colab.arc.nasa.gov/virtual

National Oceanic and Atmospheric Administration. (2009). NOAA Virtual World. Retrieved on 12/8/09 from http://www.esrl.noaa.gov/outreach/#sl

National Priorities Project. (2007a). Spending on Military Recruiting. Retrieved on 11/27/09 from http://www.nationalpriorities.org/charts/Spending-on-Military-Recruiting-2.html

National Priorities Project. (2007b). *Military Recruiting 2007: Army Misses Benchmarks by Greater Margin*. Retrieved on 11/30/09 from http://www.nationalpriorities.org/militaryrecruiting2007

News, B. B. C. (2006). 'Worm" Attack Second Life® World. BBC News. Retrieved on 11/30/09 from http://news.bbc.co.uk/2/hi/technology/6164806.stm

O'Harrow, J. Robert. (2008). Spies Battleground Turns Virtual. The Washington Post. Retrieved on 11/29/09 from http://www.washingtonpost.com/wp-dyn/content/article/2008/02/05/AR2008020503144.html?wpisrc=newsletter&wpisrc=newsletter&wpisrc=newsletter

Prensky, M. (2002). Digital Natives. Digital Immigrants. Learners Together. Retrieved on 11/30/09 from http://www.learnerstogether.net/digital-natives-digital-immigrants/53

Richeson, R. (2008). AETC opens virtual doors to MyBase. U.S. Air Force. Retrieved on 11/29/09 from http://www.af.mil/news/story.asp?id=123126243

Second Life® Blogs. (2006). *Urgent Security Announcement. Second Life®*. Retrieved on 11/30/09 from https://blogs.secondlife.com/community/features/blog/2006/09/08/urgent-security-announcement

Security, H. (2008). *Director, Federal Law Enforcement Training Center: Connie L. Patrick*. Retrieved on 11/20/09 from http://www.dhs.gov/xabout/structure/biography_0125.shtm

Shaughnessy, L. (2008). *CIA, FBI push 'Facebook for Spies'*. CNN. Retrieved on 11/28/09 from http://www.cnn.com/2008/TECH/ptech/09/05/facebook.spies/index.html

Sivan, Y. (2009). Overview: State of Virtual World Standards in 2009. *Virtual Worlds Research*. Retrieved on 12/1/09 from https://journals.tdl.org/jvwr/article/view/671/539

Takashi, P. (2008). Why do we spend so much on National Security? *The Huffington Post*. Retrieved on 11/27/09 from http://www.huffingtonpost.com/patrick-takahashi/why-do-we-spend-so-much-o_b_116535.html

Team Orlando. (2009a). *Team Orlando Capabilities*. Retrieved on 11/29/09 from http://www.teamorlando.org/capabilities/index.shtml

Team Orlando. (2009b). News. Retrieved on 11/29/09 from http://www.teamorlando.org/news/2009/05-21-09.shtml

Terdiman, D. (2007). *Tech Titans Seek Virtual World Interoperability*. CNet News. Retrieved on 12/109 from http://news.cnet.com/Tech-titans-seek-virtual-world-interoperability/2100-1043_3-6213148.html

Testa, B. M. (2008). *Much More than a Game. Defense Systems*. Retrieved on 11/28/09 from http://defensesystems.com/articles/2008/05/much-more-than-a-game.aspx

United States General Accounting Office. (2002). MILITARY PERSONNEL: Active Duty Benefits Reflect Changing Demographics, but Opportunities Exist to Improve. Report to the Subcommittee on Armed Services, US Senate. Retrieved on 11/30/09 from http://www.gao.gov/new.items/d02935.pdf

Virtual World News. (2008a). Air Force Unveils Potential Plans for MyBase Virtual World. *Virtual World News*. Retrieved on 11/29/09 from http://www.virtualworldsnews.com/2008/02/air-force-unvei.html

Virtual World News. (2008b). *Homeland Security Building Virtual Classroom for a Virtual World.* Retrieved on 11/29/09 from http://www.virtualworldsnews.com/2008/05/homeland-securi.html

Wise, J. (2008). Surviving on the USS Trayer, the Navy's Disaster Simulator. *Popular Mechanics*. Retrieved on 11/29/09 from http://www.popularmechanics.com/technology/military_law/4288185.html

Wyld, D. (2008). *Government in 3D: How Public Leaders can Draw on Virtual Worlds*. IBM Center for the Business of Government.

Chapter 8
Virtual Education

Barbara L. Ciaramitaro
Ferris State University, USA

ABSTRACT

Virtual education is a multi-billion dollar business and maintains a firm place in the world of E-Commerce. It is a mode used by educational institutions, the military, professional organizations, commercial companies, and others to inform, educate and interact with students, consumers, and participants. Second Life® is the most well-known forum for virtual education for many colleges and universities, but it is not the only virtual environment used for educational purposes. Many organizations such as the military have developed their own virtual training and education frameworks (See Ciaramitaro and Jones, Chapter 7). Conferences and seminars offered by professional organizations and business consortiums are increasingly using the virtual environment to attract its participants. Even virtual worlds embraced by children provide many educational aspects such as the "working" experience in the Webkinz world. This chapter will discuss the varying ways that virtual worlds have been incorporated into education. The authors will examine several virtual worlds to see what they offer in terms of content and user experience. They will also examine virtual education from the faculty and student perspective, and investigate how it compares with traditional forms of teaching and learning. As is true in all virtual worlds, within the education domain there are issues and challenges that must be addressed before full-scale adoption is achieved and we will discuss several of these. The authors will conclude with an examination of what the future holds for virtual education.

DOI: 10.4018/978-1-61692-808-7.ch008

INTRODUCTION

This chapter takes the position that the purpose of education is to "is to enable individuals to reach their full potential as human beings, individually and as members of a society; this means that these individuals will receive an education which will enable them to think and act intelligently and purposefully" (21st Century Schools, 2009, p.1.) With that goal in mind, we will examine how well virtual worlds are able to meet these objectives. However education is not just an altruistic goal: it is a business and virtual education is big business.

Online education is a multi-billion dollar global industry that has experienced a dramatic increase in the rate of adoption by educational institutions, the military and private organizations (White, 2009). Today, much of online education continues to be delivered in an asynchronous (one way) and somewhat static form using posted lectures, discussion forums, videos, podcasts and other forms of information. But in the past few years we have seen an impressive shift in the mode of online learning toward the use of virtual worlds. The use of virtual worlds in education is distinguished from asynchronous learning environments by the immersive interactive experience they offer their students. Students in virtual worlds adopt a graphical persona or avatar with which they travel walking or flying through the virtual world interacting with other student and teacher avatars. Through their avatars, they learn by listening, observing, talking, and doing.

Virtual education is a relatively new phenomenon in the world of online learning. It goes beyond asynchronous online learning modes in that it offers a three-dimensional (3D) virtual reality environment along with a real-time chat feature. Although there are many 3D virtual education worlds, they all share three characteristics: a virtual world presented in three dimensions; avatars to visually represent users; and an interactive chat (text or voice) through which users can talk with each other (Dickey, 2003).

Virtual worlds are better able to emulate real world experiences than the passive exchange of asynchronous environments. Students are represented by avatars that can travel through the virtual world observing virtual exhibits or presentations, attending lectures, and communicating with other avatars on a real-time basis. Rather than talking about it or merely looking at images, students can enter a virtual representation like the Sistine Chapel or a coral reef and experience the learning on a more personal basis. The students are immersed in the experience rather than simply observing it from a distance.

Student avatars in a virtual Spanish class can float down the Amazon River while listening to a Spanish-speaking guide teach them about the culture of the area, and actually practice their Spanish with natives also using the virtual world (Pechar, 2008, p. 2)

There are several virtual worlds that house educational activities. These worlds can generally be divided into two categories: proprietary and open source. The first group is best represented by *Second Life®* which was developed by Linden Labs. Second Life® offers a proprietary foundation for the development of virtual worlds. It has become the most commonly used hub of virtual education. The second category includes various virtual worlds built on open source foundations. Open source is an open platform that is developed through the concerted voluntary efforts of many developers. Open source virtual education offerings include *Wonderland* by Sun Microsystems (Sun Microsystems, 2009), *Active Worlds*, and *Small Worlds*.

Virtual worlds for education have been adopted by K-12 school systems, colleges and universities, and for internal training and education efforts. As of 2008, 42 states have established virtual schools for K-12, and 18 of them had developed full virtual charter schools. Second Life® had over 100 dedicated islands for educational purposes representing over 120 colleges and universities. However, not all virtual education is offered by academic institutions. There are currently over 150 virtual worlds for kids that supplement their traditional learning (Pechar). Virtual worlds have opened up educational opportunities beyond what could be imagined a few years ago and our youth are ready to take advantage of it. It is estimated that 34% of American teens participate in a virtual worlds at least once a month (Pechar). This is a world that our youth are comfortable with and as a result, we can only expect that virtual education offerings will continue to grow at a rapid pace to meet this demand.

ACADEMIC VIRTUAL EDUCATION

Currently, virtual worlds are most often used in education as a way to expand traditional education rather than replace it. The immersive experience offered by virtual worlds allows students to engage in learning on a different level and to have experiences that would otherwise be impossible to offer in a classroom environment. Some of the benefits to students offered by virtual education include the following (Behar, p.2):

- Virtual participation forces students to think differently. The learning is more inquiry-based rather than fact-based.
- Students are able to interact with other students from around the world without any of the traditional geographic limitations.
- Students in rural or underprivileged communities are able to have experiences that would be unavailable to them in their traditional schools albeit bandwidth and other technological limitation.
- Virtual education is based on communication and collaboration: skills that are considered critical for students to learn to compete effectively in today's environment.

Second Life® is home to hundreds of K-12 and higher educational institutions. Harvard, Texas State, and Stanford are just a few of the universities that have opened their doors to avatar students who can attend classes in the virtual world. Although the most well-known, Second Life® is not the only 3D world that provides virtual education. There are several independent companies that provide virtual world platforms on which to develop custom 3D worlds. *Reaction Grid* describes itself as a 3D Virtual World for business, education, collaboration, and learning. It offers a learning platform that can be customized for individual educational needs as well as many predesigned educational islands. *Caspian Learning* builds virtual learning environments for a variety of educational purposes and also offers a virtual world development platform that allows learning institutions to customize and build their own virtual experience. Intel introduced *ScienceSim* in early 2009 with a goal of creating an environment for experimentation in virtual worlds. *ScienceSim* provides a platform that serves as a testbed for data visualization and science experiments like fusion reactions, biomedical applications, geophysical, intelligence analysis. There are also virtual worlds that provide specific learning experiences. *The Forbidden City* offers a 3-dimensional virtual world experience that explores aspects of Chinese culture and history.

Over 120 universities have a presence on Second Life® and offer complete courses presented by faculty avatars. Some institutions such as Harvard Law School allow the public to sit in their classes demonstrating an open approach to knowledge sharing (Pechar). There are also several virtual worlds that support K-12 education. *Quest Atlantis*, developed by Indiana University, is described as a virtual world where children learn skills to solve the world's problems with an emphasis on social responsibility and compassion. There is even a virtual world that supports homeschooling. *Wilstar3d* supports homeschooling education from grade 6 through high school and offers several predesigned virtual world educational experiences. These virtual worlds represent just a snapshot of the growing emphasis on virtual education (Second Life® in Education, 2009). We will discuss them in more detail in the following sections.

Elementary to High School

Second Life® is a virtual world developed by Linden Labs that has become a central gathering point for virtual educators. Although the presence of virtual colleges and universities in Second Life®, such as Harvard and Stanford, has received media attention, it is less well known that Second Life® has also become home to many K-12 educators. This adoption is in spite of some limitations placed on these worlds by Linden Labs. Second Life® offers two virtual worlds: an adult only Main Grid, and a Teen Grid for users aged 13 to 17. Academic Institutions who build their presence on the Main Grid can take advantage of all of the resources on the Main Grid such as recreations of historic and other useful sites such a virtual Sistine Chapel, Alamo, or coral reef. But the educational resources on the Main Grid are not available on the Teen Grid which limits its values in the eyes of some educators. However, in spite of these limitations, "K-12 educations are flocking to Second Life® in growing numbers." (Waters, 2009, p. 1)

Suffern Middle School has established a virtual presence on the Teen Grid of Second Life®, called *Ramapo Central School District*. One of the blog entries describing their virtual world experience indicated that they were studying the Middle East in their virtual world. As part of the student experience they placed discussion pods in close proximity to the fence that divides *ToMorrow Island* from *Ramapo* in hopes to begin a discussion about barriers (Suffern Middle School, 2009).

Hatters Island was established in the Teen Grid of Second Life® by the Hatboro-Horsham High School. Chris Baker, the creator of Hatters Island, posted an interesting saga of the development of this island from the initial idea stage through its final implementation (Baker, 2008). He accurately describes one of the greatest challenges to widespread adoption of virtual education – the learning curve. Becoming familiar with navigating through Second Life® was only the beginning. Baker learned firsthand that understanding how to purchase the right land and create its content

Table 1. Listing of some virtual education providers

Name	Audience	Site
Active Worlds (AWEDU)	All Ages	www.activeworlds.com
Atlantis	Developed by Indiana University; Children	http://atlantis.crlt.indiana.edu/
Caspian Learning	All ages	www.caspianlearning.com
Forbidden City	History and Culture of Chine	www.beyondspaceandtime.com
Kidz Connect	Youth	www.kidzconnect.com
MetaPlace	All ages	www.metaplace.com
Reaction Grid	All ages	www.reactiongrid.com
Second Life	Teen Grid for ages under 18; Main Grid for ages over 18	www.secondlife.com
ScienceSim	Focused on science	www.sciencesim.com
Small Worlds	K-12	www.smallworlds.com
Wilostar3D	Homeschooling	www.wilostar3d.com
Wonderland	Sun Microsystems	https://wonderland.dev.java.net/

can be an extensive process. His detailed record of activities services as a great guide to new educators looking to explore virtual education.

Kidz Connect is a virtual world whose goal is to connect young people in different countries through art, performance and collaborative creation. The project began in 2006 with students from New York and Amsterdam.

Guided by artists and educators from theatre and digital arts, students learned skills like VJ-ing, Playback Theatre, digital storytelling, and 3D modeling. In Teen Second Life, they met and collaborated to build a hybrid virtual city combining aspects of both New York and Amsterdam. Within that common space, they created a performance that occurred both live and online simultaneously (Kidz Connect, 2009, p. 1).

The *Pacific Rim Exchange* began as a virtual world involving high school students from California and Japan with four islands in Second Life® for its students to meet and collaborate. After a year or so, it merged with the Australian based *Skoolaborate* project, which is considered the single largest 'school based' global cultural exchange. Interestingly, the virtual world experience is supplemented with real world exchange visits with the students traveling to other countries to meet their fellow virtual students (Pacific Rim Exchange, 2009).

East Carolina University launched a virtual world in early 2009 for high school students to earn college credits by attending virtual classes in Second Life. The classes offered include Anthropology, Introduction to Computers, Web Site Design, and English. The virtual site includes classrooms and labs for the students as well as a library and resources center (NMC, 2009). McKinley Tech has offered an opportunity for students to participate in the virtual Holocaust Museum in Second Life® meeting other students from around the world during their visits (Vanegas, 2007). Global Kids also offered high school students an immersive experience studying the Holocaust. The student visitors "traveled virtual Berlin streets designed with scanned materials and documents from the museum's archives and artifacts. They walked past a burned-down synagogue modeled on an actual place of worship. At the end of the exhibit, visitors entered a reflection room—a quiet, uncluttered area, where they could post notes for all to read." (Global Kids, 2009, p. 1)

Homeschooling is even supported by virtual worlds. Wilstar3d offers a comprehensive site providing 3D virtual world education for homeschooled children. They provide virtual education in a number of topics including Math, History, English and Science for middle school and high school students. Some of the advantages of this approach to traditional homeschooling are the shift from passive to active learning; the immersive interactive experience and role playing offered by 3D virtual worlds, and the collaboration required as the students work with others to develop 3D virtual projects (Wilostar3D, 2009).

Colleges and Universities

Wharton School at the University of Pennsylvania is a prestigious business school whose primary purpose is to educate future leaders through their renowned MBA program. They consider that the growing use of virtual education is inevitable and their Dean has stated, "I think that the next big teaching innovation will come from the area of virtual worlds." (Cole, 2006, p. 1) The accuracy of this prediction is evident in the number of colleges and universities who have established a virtual education presence.

As mentioned earlier, over 120 colleges and universities have established a virtual education presence on Second Life. East Carolina University (ECU), mentioned earlier as a provider of classes for high school students, is one of them. Virtual college classes offered include Networking, Hospitality Management, Interior Design, Computer Science, and Law. Some of their classes are offered purely in the virtual environment and others supplement traditional classes on their physical campus. They also use Second Life® to offer additional support to their students with a presence by the career services and library departments. ECU has successful created 3D learning environments to support their curricula. Their hospitality management course occurs in Second Life® in a virtual hotel that has all of the markings of a real world hotel including a lobby, reception desk, dining area, corridor and rooms. The students learn within this virtual world how to manage the hotel through immersive interactive experiences. Computer science students create 3D replicas of a local area network topology within Second Life. The interior design students use Second Life® to obtain feedback from other students on their room layout designs. (Harrison, 2009)

San Jose University has created a virtual university in Second Life® that spans 16 digital acres on which stands replicas of the school buildings. The library science department offers classes for its students in this virtual environment. One interesting focus of these classes is that they emphasize both an understanding of the course content but also of the virtual world itself. Students learn about the underlying application and structure of Second Life® and are encouraged to explore its many islands and locales. They are also using Second Life® as a way to desensitize students who are fearful of public speaking. Through their avatars, they learn to speak in front of the class as a warm-up for real world presentations. (Sherr, 2008)

As a strong runner-up to *Second Life®, Active Worlds* (www.activeworlds.com) claims to host a collection of 1,000 virtual worlds in their "universe". Similar to Second Life®, Active Worlds participants can use the tools provided by the application to design and structure their customized virtual world. Active Worlds supports virtual education through is *Active Worlds Educational Universe (AWEDU)* which has participation from over 100 educational institutions around the world including Cornell University, University of Hong Kong, University of Michigan, and Brown University to name a few (Active Worlds, 2009). Within Active Worlds you can find *SciCentr* created by Cornell University. It is designed to provide hands on exhibits, tours, science fairs, and guest lectures. There is also a world called *Vetinimi,* which is a virtual veterinary clinic designed to provide interactive rooms for study and virtual experience in small animal care. There are several worlds that support a more general education focus such as *Ares*, which is a re-creation of the planet Mars, created from images provided by the Pathfinder Mission and *Luna,* a digital re-creation of the moon. (AWEDU, 2009)

The medical field has also adopted the use of virtual education. The Indiana University School of Medicine has established a virtual clinic in Second Life® for the training of their first and second year medical students. They provide virtual training in diagnosis, laboratory medicine and problem solving. Their students work with virtual patients in the clinic and collaborate with other students to correctly examine them and determine a diagnosis and treatment plan. During their examination with a virtual stethoscope, heart, lung and bowel sounds are transmitted to the student using streaming audio. Laboratory results and x-ray images are also available for the student to review. Indiana University considers virtual education to be advantageous as it provides interactive, hands on, yet safe, learning environment for their students. (Johnson, 2008)

The Ann Meyers Medical Center (AMMC) is also located in Second Life. It was founded by Dr. Ann Buchanan with a goal of providing students with an opportunity to be proficiency in initial examination, patient history taking and analysis of lab and x-ray results. Each student is provided with a volunteer mentor who guides them in their activities. AMMC is also focused on bringing together the global medical community. One activity involved collaboration among medical students from the United States, Canada, Brazil,

Germany and Hungary. The students worked together to review a patient's history and lab results to determine the correct diagnosis. After formulation their diagnosis, the students met in a virtual discussion room to discuss their results with a mentor. (Meska, 2007)

Dr. Peter Yellowlees, author of "Your Health in the Information Age", talks about his use of virtual education in his online blog. He reports that Second Life® is the home to health organizations such as the American Cancer Society, Center for Disease Control and the National Institute of Health, who use the virtual world to hold meetings, conferences, and training sessions. He describes the virtual class he holds in Second Life® that allows students to experience sensations of psychosis to better understand their patients' experience. (Yellowlees, 2009)

Continuing education is critical in the medical field, and it has gone virtual as well. The Aligned Management Institute (AMAInc) describes themselves as a biomedical communication company. Their goal is to provide opportunities for medical professionals to share their experience and research through conferences, seminars and workshops. They sponsor the Medicine Meets Virtual Reality (MMVR) conference which has been meeting for 18 years. They describe their conference as an opportunity to bring together "a multi-disciplinary community of computer scientists and engineers, physicians and surgeons, medical educators and students, military medicine specialists, and biomedical visionaries. Their shared goal is the creation and adoption of data-enabled tools and methods for better patient care and medical education." (NextMed, 2009, p. 1) Topics discussed at the conference include biomedical modeling and simulation; virtual and augmented reality; and serious games.

Of course no one is ready to substitute medical training in Second Life® for traditional medical school. However, there are some advantages to using virtual education as a supplement to traditional medical training. Virtual worlds allow very detailed environments to be created in which students can hone their skills without concern for patient harm. They can practice hands on patient care as well as develop patient doctor communication skills through role playing and simulation. Virtual worlds are always available and a medical student can spend as much time as needed in practicing their skills. Students can be in contact with experts from around the world without being limited by geographic barriers. Challenges include the expertise required to develop accurate scenarios and the learning curve required to adapt to virtual education, not only for the students, but the teachers as well. (Shock, 2008)

The military has also invested millions of dollars in virtual training and education which is discussed in detail in Chapter 8 of this book, Virtual Worlds and the Military by Ciaramitaro and Jones.

OTHER TYPES OF VIRTUAL EDUCATION

Conferences and Seminars

Many organizations are now holding their conferences and seminars in a virtual environment, due in part to budget, time, and geographic constraints. Dell created a presence in Second Life® in 2006 where they established a conference center in which to conduct virtual meetings with its employees who were located around the world. The participating employees reported that they felt much more engaged in the virtual world meetings when compared to participation in conference calls. Dell hopes to use this platform to encourage more employees to work from home but still have the opportunity to interact with their co-workers (Wilson, 2009).

The Generali Group, a large European insurer, also built an island in Second Life® that is used to host meeting for all of their trainees located throughout Europe. During these meetings, the trainees are able to meet virtually with managers from their various departments. Generali maintains that due to time and cost constraints, these meetings would not have been held in the physical world (Ibid).

The Gronstedt Group provides consulting on Web 2.0 media use. They hold weekly meetings in Second Life® where people in the industry could interact and discuss the use of virtual worlds and other technologies. These sessions transformed into highly attended speaker presentations with visits from experts across the industry. Gronstedt also uses Second Life® for all of its internal meetings and many of its meetings with clients.

Kelly Services is a recruitment company who also use Second Life® for internal meetings with its employees. Many of Kelly Services' employees are remote workers who have never visited the physical office and the virtual meetings allow them an opportunity to interact with managers and other employees. Kelly Services has also used Second Life® to host virtual job fairs (Ibid).

Sun Microsystems was well known for its annual Customer Engineering Conference (CEC) regularly held in Las Vegas. Due to budget limitations this conference was only available to senior engineers. In order to expand its participation to junior engineers while cutting costs, Sun determine to take their CEC conference virtual. They held their regular CEC but also held a parallel conference in Second Life® which opened attendance and participation to a much larger group. When they acquired MySQL, Sun felt it was necessary to welcome their new employees and did so through a virtual meeting in Second Life. Sun welcomed 300 attendees to a huge virtual theater and ran a 14 hour Leadership Conference event that included top executive presentations. Sun maintains that this even would not have been possible if they had limited to the physical world (Ibid).

A discussion of virtual world adoption would not be complete with including IBM. IBM has made a significant investment in the use of virtual worlds and claims to have thousands of their employees using virtual world technologies on a regular basis. They have partnered closely with Linden Lab to develop and offer companies an internal version of Second Life. They maintain that placing virtual worlds behind a corporate firewall prevents many of the security issues that

Table 2. A sampling of academic institutions in Second Life® (Wyld)

Academic Institution	Second Life® Location
Bowling Green State University	http://slurl.com/secondlife/Bowling%20Green%20State/117/179/26/
East Carolina University	http://slurl.com/secondlife/ECU%20II/218/204/31
Georgia State University	http://slurl.com/secondlife/Five%20Points/115/144/26
Harvard University	http://slurl.com/secondlife/Berkman/105/74/35
Massachusetts Institute of Technology	http://slurl.com/secondlife/MIT/51/35/23/?title=Massachusetts%20Institute&20of%20Technology
Ohio University	http://slurl.com/secondlife/ohio%20unifersity/20/36/24
Penn State University	Http://slurl.com/secondlife/Penn%20State%20Isle/120/131/41
Princeton University	http://slurl.com/secondlife/Princeton%20University/143/148/24
San Jose University	http://slurl.com/secondlife/SJSU%20SLIS/128/128
Tufts University	http://slurl.com/secondlife/UEPP%20Tufts/130/135/29
University of Notre Dame	http://slurl.com/secondlife/sophia/136/121/23
University of Southern California	http://slurl.com/secondlife/IML/128/129/123

plague virtual worlds. IBM promotes the use of Second Life® virtual worlds through its IBM Business Center that offers virtual tours, speakers, and conferences on a regular basis (IBM, 2009).

Educating Children through Virtual Games

Formal education is not the only form of learning. This is particularly evident in the virtual worlds that provide children an opportunity to plan and learn at the same time. Recent research has indicated that the largest growing population of online gamers is children between the ages of 6 and 11. Additionally it is children oriented virtual worlds that actually dominate the market led by *Webkinz*, *Club Penguin*, *Zwinky*, and *Neopets* (Wyld, 2008). Each of these virtual worlds allows children to play with their online characters and pets, interact with other children, and learn new skills. Webkinz for example offers children the opportunity to perform jobs in order to earn money to purchase items for their pets and rooms. Several of these virtual worlds are linked to products such as stuffed animals that parents purchase for their children. Once the toy is purchased, it is registered in the real world where the child can care for their virtual pet. Some of these virtual worlds are targeted to specific markets such as Zwinky and *BarbieGirls* that focuses on young girls and fashion. *Habbo Hotel* is geared to teenagers and provides a social environment for teens from around the world to meet. Similar to other games aimed at the youth, Habbo Hotel offers the ability to customize rooms to meet individual preferences. Of course, purchasing the Habbo Coins requires real world money.

Each of these virtual worlds serves dual purposes. They offer an interactive fun environment for children and teens to meet and interact with a far larger group than would be possible in their physical world. But is also teaches them how to manage money, communicate effectively with others, acceptance of diversity, and problem solving.

VIRTUAL AND TRADITIONAL EDUCATION

There has been a significant amount of discussion over the years in the academic community on the value of an online learning environment compared to traditional classroom. Most conclude online learning is a viable and effective form of education that offers students a convenient opportunity to learn at their own pace (Cavanaugh,

Table 3. A sampling of companies in Second Life® (Wyld)

Company	Location in Second Life
Accenture	http://slurl.com/secondlife/Accenture%20Careers/121/146/29
Ben & Jerry's	http://slurl.com/secondlife/Ben%20and%20Jerrys/109/160/27
Best Buy	http://slurl.com/secondlif/Geek%20Squad&20Island/185/162/72
Cisco	http://slurl.com/secondlife/Cisco%20systems/17/6/22
Comcast	http://slurl.com/secondlife/Comcast/16/231/22
IBM	http://slurl.com/secondlife/IBM%20Business%20Center
Intel	http://slurl.com/secondlife/Thompson/18/93/23
Kelly Services	http:/slurl.com/secondlife/Kelly%20Services/128/128/0
Microsoft	http://slurl.com/secondlife/microsoft/128/128/0
Sun Microsystems	http://slurl.com/secondlife/Sun%20Pavillion/180/140
Xerox	http://slurl.com/secondlife/xerox/128/128/0

2008;Toles, 2008). However, there has been very little research to date specifically discussing education in virtual worlds (Brown, 2009; Brown and Green, 2009). Brown examined the value of virtual world education as it relates to three concepts: presence, positioning, and community. *Presence* is described as the feeling of social engagement or involvement that a participant experiences. *Positioning* refers to the role of the teacher in facilitating the learning experience. *Community* is the general sense of "social connectedness" felt by the participants. She found that the virtual world of Second Life® provided a strong sense of presence and community with one caveat. As Second Life® is an open environment that puts very little limits on participants' behavior, some students found this openness to be disturbing. She did not find that Second Life® impacted her perception by students to be the facilitator of the course. (Ibid)

Her study does raise another issue related to the concept of positioning. If an instructor is not skilled or adept at teaching in a virtual world environment, their perception as an expert could be negatively impacted. "In addition to being qualified in content knowledge and pedagogical skill, online teachers must be qualified in methods of teaching the content online and have experience in online teaching." (Cavanaugh, p. 11). Cavanaugh presents a developmental continuum for new online teachers in which they acquire experience and are closely mentored by more experience virtual instructors. The National Education Association has issued a set of best practices to guide teachers in the online environment emphasizing the need for teachers to compensate for lack of verbal and visual cues available in asynchronous online learning environments (Ash, 2009). However, the presence offered by virtual worlds eliminates most of these issues. Educators are able to receive both visual and verbal cues from their student avatars.

It is important to note that at this time virtual worlds are most often used in education as a way to expand the classroom or distance learning experience rather than replace it. In fact some educators believe that virtual education should only be used as an enhancement to traditional education (Toles). When considered as an extension rather than a replacement, most of the current research reports that 3D virtual worlds offer effective learning environments particularly in the area of problem solving. The interactive style of learning promotes greater learning for students who rely on a more tactile learning experience (Dickey; Brown). Through their avatars, students experience a greater sense of presence and participation than that offered by traditional asynchronous online learning modes. Additionally

Table 4. A listing of some virtual worlds for children and teenagers

Virtual World	Location
BarbieGirls world	www.barbiegirls.com
Club Penguin	www.clubpenguin.come
Habbo Hotel	www.habbohotel.com
Lego Universe	http://universe.lego.com/en-US
Neopets	www.neopets.com
Nicktropolis	www.nick.com/nictropoplis
Teen Second Life	www.teen.secondlife.com
Webkinz	www.webkinz.com
Whyville	www.whyville.com
Zwinky	www.zwinky.com

virtual worlds are general in that they can be used to educate in almost all disciplines. Customized locations, artifacts, and hands on experiments can be crafted to meet the criteria of the majority of topics. Virtual worlds provide students with the additional benefit of a safe place for role playing and experimentation. Students can assume the responsibilities of experts such as scientists or engineers without worrying about suffering real world consequences.

One advantage of virtual worlds over traditional online learning is that it eliminates much of the isolation students often feel in an asynchronous learning environment. Virtual worlds can offer a sense of camaraderie and interaction similar to that provided in a classroom environment: they feel a sense of presence and can see and interact with other students and their teachers. One recent study found several positive aspects to using virtual worlds to educate children (Jackson and Gauntlett, 2009; Thomas, 2009). Virtual worlds offer an engaging and interactive alternative to the more passive experience of watching television. Children are able to experiment and role play without fear of embarrassment or other real world consequences. Creativity was one attribute that appeared to be fostered by the virtual environment. The students enjoyed the opportunity to create content as a means of self expression. Also there was evidence of significant social skill development as the children explored the virtual worlds. They became accustomed to interacting with a wide variety of other children in a collaborative manner.

Much of the discussion concerning education in virtual worlds has centered on the difference of views between digital natives and digital immigrants. *Digital natives* describe the youth and young adults that have been born in the last 20 or so years and are extremely comfortable and fluent in the language of technology. *Digital immigrants* describe those individuals who have come to adopt technology as a part of their life but did not grow up immersed in it. And lastly there are the *digital laggards* who have not yet adapted to the technological changes that have revolutionized businesses and education. Digital natives and digital immigrants appear to agree that the virtual education experience can offer educators innovative and unique opportunities for expanding their classroom or distance learning education offerings. (Dickey; Brown, 2009). The Air Force has recognized the changing face of its potential recruits and has based its future education and training program on this awareness. They issued a White Paper that acknowledges the impact that concentrated exposure to technology has had on the current generation of potential recruits (Air Education and Training Command, 2008). The Air Force maintains that the use of virtual worlds in its education programs will provide significant benefits in attracting high quality recruits and training them in the most effective manner. Virtual worlds are able to go beyond the simple education protocols offered by traditional distance learning and allow online exploration and collaboration taught by real world and virtual instructors in areas such as pilot training, plane maintenance, and medicine.

The general conclusion among educators is that although virtual worlds offer tremendous potential for teaching and learning, they are still in the very early stages and much more work needs to be done before there is widespread adoption of virtual education (Brown)

ISSUES AND CHALLENGES FACING VIRTUAL EDUCATION

The greatest challenge facing widespread adoption is the learning curve associated with adapting to virtual education as both teachers and students need to feel comfortable in the environment. "There is a distinct awkwardness involved in learning to control one's avatar. It took me a bit of practice to walk and communicate with gestures. It took me even more time to control flying and landing." (Brown, 20090, p. 8). As a result of this common experience, most virtual world providers offer extensive help and guidance. *Second Life®* provides assistance to educational institutions who want to start building their virtual presence. The International Society for Technology in Education (ISTE) has a strong presence in Second Life® and will guide new educators through the various education islands and options (Second Life® Grid, 2009).

An interesting aspect of virtual education is the extensive collaboration among educators who provide support to each other: sharing tips on building virtual environments and providing guidance for building the learning experience. As there can be a significant learning curve associated with adapting to virtual education, *Second Life®* provides assistance to educational institutions who want to start building their virtual presence. The Second Life® Educators (SLED) community is an e-mail distribution list with more than 4,700 participants. It was created to help new educators joining Second Life® on best practices and available resources. Real Life Education is a group located within Second Life® has over 3,500 members focused on sharing information and receiving notice on Second Life® education activities and events (Harrison, 2009b). The International Society for Technology in Education (ISTE) also has a strong presence in Second Life® and will guide new educators through the various education islands and options (Second Life® Grid, 2009).

Lighthouse Learning Island on Second Life® describes itself as a collaborative learning community for K-12 educators that has the involvement of several school districts and state agencies. Lighthouse Learning was the brainchild of Kathy Schrock, a Massachusetts K-12 educator. It was launched in 2007 with the involvement of 4 state school districts. It has since added both additional school districts and state agencies. The main purpose of Lighthouse Learning is to provide guidance and support for teachers and educators who are entering the world of virtual education. The Island offers seminars, conferences, and casual meeting opportunities (Schrock, 2007). Jo Kay, a virtual world's educator, has created an extensive resource on virtual education through her *Islands of JoyKaydei* website (http://jokaydia.com/). The Islands site was launched in September 2007 with a goal to provide a collaborative environment where educators could explore the uses of virtual worlds in education. The Islands of JoyKadei currently have a presence on several education-focused virtual worlds including *Second Life®*, *ReactionGrid* and *MetaPlace*.

Another concern is the degree of technological expertise required in developing accurate virtual world experience. Each virtual world provider offers their own set of tools to develop locations and components within the virtual world. Becoming adept at developing high quality content requires significant technology know how. However, rather than developing the content themselves, all virtual world providers offer a variety of support options to assist in developing their world and content.

There is also a serious question as to how future employers will react to a degree earned in a virtual environment. Already students involved in online programs often received questions and concerns about the validity of their degree from potential employers (McGuire, 2009). It is important that virtual education is able to provide a guarantee of quality in the education provided. This will require the development of virtual education standards and reliable assessment techniques that do not yet exist.

Lastly, there are security and privacy issues that must be resolved. These are discussed in detail in Chapter 12 of this book by Dr. Greg Gogolin.

THE FUTURE OF VIRTUAL EDUCATION

But is it just a passing fad? Gartner Group has predicted that by the year 2011, 80% of active

Internet users will have a virtual world presence. They predict that "the collaborative and community-related aspects of these environments will dominate in the future" (Gartner, 2007, p. 1). However, Gartner recommends that organizations move slowly in adopting virtual worlds. According to their "hype cycle" prediction, virtual worlds reached their height in the hype cycle in 2006 (Gary, 2009). We are now in the process of learning from earlier mistakes and developing reliable and valuable virtual worlds. This assessment certainly applies to the virtual education domain.

One aspect of virtual education that will undoubtedly experience growth in the next few years is the use of intelligent agents to help mentor and tutor students. Intelligent agents are computer based systems represented in many cases as avatars that are able to sense, learn and act autonomously in a dynamic changing environment. They are focused on achieving the goals they have been programmed to accomplish. In a virtual education world we are looking at teaching agents that possess a number of "skills". They are able to communicate effectively with the student, have a thorough understanding of the subject matter and can adjust to the learning pace of the student. "Agent based education opens up whole new and exciting areas of possibility because the agent does not simply teach. The intelligent agent is more than just the teacher, it is also the learner. It adapts to the changing needs of the student, their environment and learning style. The agent builds up a character map of the learner in the same way that classroom teacher does." (Sherson, 1999, p3). One example of a teacher agent currently in use is the *Cognitive Tutor* from Carnegie Learning, a company that began at Carnegie Mellon University. This agent program is designed to help students with math and students who use the agents report that their skills have improved. (Sánchez-Guzmán, César Mora, and R. García-Salcedo, 2009). uMind is a company that offers agent based education in a virtual world environment utilizing simulation-based training to guide the student through complex learning experiences. The student is able to practice the skill repeatedly until mastered guided by intelligent agent technology. (uMind, 2009)

There is no doubt that virtual education offers tremendous opportunities for unique and innovative learning experiences. They offer an ability to be available at all hours and in a variety of delivery modes as is demonstrated by Second Life's availability on mobile phones (Collins, 2008). They offer an ability to interact with students from other cultures and countries. Their adoption rate is increasing at a fast pace among educational institutions, the military and private organizations.

However, the success of virtual education depends upon its acceptance by the academic community as an effective teaching forum. Although there is a lot of discussion among educators about their use, only a very small percentage of educators have actually experimented with virtual worlds (Brown). The barriers to entry including the learning curve and technological expertise must be resolved before the majority of teachers will be comfortable with the environment. This will probably take a few more years of pioneering efforts on the part of virtual world education advocates to work through these issues.

REFERENCES

Air Education and Training Command. (2008), AETC White Paper. Retrieved on 11/29/09 from http://www.aetc.af.mil/library/whitepaper.asp

Ash, K. (2009). Characteristics of 'Highly Qualified' Online Teachers. *Digital Directions*. Retrieved on 12/8/09 from http://www.edweek.org/dd/article/2009/06/17/04characteristics

AWEDU. (2009). *Self Guided Tour*. Retrieved on 12/12/09 from http://edu.activeworlds.com/tour/worlds.html

Baker, C. (2008). *Hatters Island*. Retrieved on 12/8/09 from http://hattersisland.blogspot.com/

Brown, A. (2009). *A Second Look at Second Life: Virtual Worlds and Education*. East Carolina University.

Brown, A., & Green, T. (2009). Issues and Trends in Instructional Technology: Wb 2.0, Second Life® and STEM Share the Spotlight. In Orey, McClendon, V.J. & Branch, R.M. (Eds.) Educational Media and Technology Yearbook, 34, 7-23.

Cavanaugh, Cathy. (2008). Real Learning Happens in Virtual Schools. Threshold. 10; Fall 2008.

Cole, V. 2006). Wharton Dean: Virtual Worlds are the Future of MBA Education. Retrieved on 12/8/09 from http://www.joystiq.com/2006/03/16/wharton-dean-virtual-worlds-are-the-future

Collins, S. (2008). *Virtual Worlds in Education*. EDUCAUSE Evolving Technologies Committee.

Connect, K. (2009). About. Retrieved on 12/11/09 from http://www.kidzconnect.org/about

Dickey, M. (2003). 3D Virtual worlds: An Emerging Technology for Tradition and Distance Leerning. Ohio Learning Network Conference 2003. Retrieved on 12/8/09 from http://www.oln.org/conferences/OLN2003/papers/Dickey3DVirtualWorlds.pdf

Exchange, P. R. (2009). Front Page. Retrieved on 12/1/09 from http://pacificrimx.wordpress.com/2009/10/

Gartner. (2007). Gartner Says 80 Percent of Active Internet Users Will Have A "Second Life" in the Virtual World by the End of 2011. Retrieved on 12/13/09 from http://www.gartner.com/it/page.jsp?id=503861

Gary. (2009). The Virtual Worlds Hype cycle for 2009. Retrieved on 12/8/09 from http://222.muvedesign.com/the-virtual-worlds-hype-cycle-for-2009

Harrison, D. (2009a). Engaging Students in Virtual learning. Campus Technology. Retrieved on 12/8/09 from http://campustechnology.com/Articles/2009/04/22/Engaging-students-in-virtual-learning

Harrison, D. (2009b). Real-Life Teaching in a Virtual World. Campus Technology. Retrieved on 12/8/09 from http://campustechnology.com/articles/2009/02/12/Real-Life-Teaching-in-a-virtual-world

IBM. (2009). IBM Business Center. Retrieved on 12/13/09 from http://www.ibm.com/3dworlds/businesscenter/us/en/

Jackson, L., & Gauntlett, D. (2009). University of Westminister. Retreieved on 12/13/09 from http://www.childreninvirtualworlds.org.uk/pdfs/Gauntlett_and_Jackson_May_2008.pdf

Johnson, M. (2009). A Second Life® Virtual Clinic for Medical Student Training. Retrieved on 12/13/09 from http://www.slideshare.net/magistra12/a-second-life-virtual-clinic-for-medical-student-training-presentation

Kids, G. (2009). The Power of Virtual Civics Education. Retrieved on 12/11/09 from http://www.holymeatballs.org/2009/12/sl_the_power_of_virtual_civics.html#more

McGuire, C. (2009). Online Degrees versus Traditional Degrees. Retrieved on 12/8/09 from http://ezinarticles.com/?online-degrees-versus-traditional-degrees

Meska, B. (2007). *Virtual Doctors: Medical Training in Second Life*. Retrieved on 12/13/09 from http://juniordr.com/world/index.php/20071219160/Life/Virtual-doctors-medical-training-in-Second-Life.html

Microsystems, S. (2009). MPK20: Sun's Virtual Workplace. Retrieved on 12/12/09 from http://research.sun.com/projects/mc/mpk20.html

NextMed. (2009). *MMVR18*. Retrieved on 12/13/09 from http://www.nextmed.com/index.html

NMC. (2009). *Second Life® Virtual Early High School Program at East Carolina University*. Retrieved on 12/11/09 from http://222.nmc.org/spotlight/member/7320

Pechar, E. (2008). *Virtual Worlds and Education*. Office of Policy Analysis and Research. Georgia Tech Research Institute.

D. Sánchez-Guzmán, César Mora, R. García-Salcedo. (2009). Intelligent Agents: A Physics Education Opportunity in Latin-America. Lat. Am. J. Phys. Educ. Vol. 3, No. 2, May 2009.

Schock. (2008). Strengths and Challenges of Medication Education in Virtual Worlds. Retrieved on 12/13/09 from http://www.shockmd.com/2008/10/25/strengths-and-challenges-of-medical-education-in-virtual-worlds/

Schrock, K. (2007). Lighthouse Learning Island. Retrieved on 12/11/09 from http://kathyschrock.net/blog/2007/06/lighthouse-learning-island.html

Second Life® Grid. (2009). *Virtual Environment Enable New Models of Learning*. Retrieved on 12/11/09 from http://secondlifegrid.net/slfe/educaton-use-virtual-world

Second Life® in Education. (2009). *Virtual World Resources*. Retrieved on 12/8/09 from http://sleducation.wikispaces.com/virtualworlds

Sherr, I. (2008). Virtual Campuses: The Education of the Future? Retrieved on 12/8/09 from http://www.mg.co.za/article/2008-06-06-virtual-campuses-the-education-of-the-future

Sherson, G. (1999). Intelligent Agents: An Education System For The Year 2003. Victoria University of Wellington. Retrieved on 12/14/09 from http://www.shersonmedia.com/grant/cv/items/papers/Intelligent_Agents_Education_2003.pdf

21st Century Schools. (2009). The Purpose of Education - Critical Pedagogy for the Democratic Society. Retrieved on 11/14/09 from http://www.21stcenturyschools.com/Purpose_of_Education.htm

Suffern Middle School. (2009). Barriers, Fences and Conflicts. Retrieved on 12/11/09 from http://ramapoislands.edublogs.org/

Thomas. (2009). Virtual Worlds Offer Meaningful Educational Opportunities for Children. Open Education. Retrieved on 2/8/09 from http://www.openeducation.net/2008/06/29-virtual-worlds-offer-meanngful-educational-opportunities-for-children

Toles, J. (2008). The Virtual Classroom: An Enhancement or Replacement to Traditional Education. Georgia State University. Retrieved on 12/8/09 from http://digitalarchive.gsu.edu/univ_lib_ura/3

uMind. (2009).Simulation Based Training. Retrieved on 12/14/09 from http://www.umindsoft.com/En/simulations.html

Vanegas, K. (2007). Second Life® Virtual World. The Washington Post. Retrieved on 12/11/09 from http://blog.washingtonpost.com/hs/mckinley/2007/05/second_life_virtual_world.html

Waters, J. (2009). A 'Second Life' for Educators. The Journal. Retrieved on 12/11/09 from http://thejournal.com/Articles/2009/01/01/A-Second-Life-For-Educators

White, K. (2009). Benefits of Higher Education. Retrieved on 12/9/09 from http://www.street-directory.com/travel_guide/14429/education/benefits_of_online_education.html

Wilostar3D. (2009). Overview. Retrieved on 12/12/09 from http://www.wilostar3d.com/overview.htm

Wilson, N. (2009). Virtual Worlds for Business. Clever Zebra. Retrieved 12/13/09 from http://cleverzebra.com/book

Worlds, A. (2009). Participants. Retrieved on 12/12/09 from http://www.activeworlds.com/edu/awedu_participants.asp

Wyld, D. (2008). *Government in 3D: How Public Leaders Can Draw on Virtual Worlds*. IBM Center for The Business of Government.

Yellowlees, P. (2009). Virtual Reality Meets Health Education. Information Age Health. Retrieved on 12/13/09 from http://informationagehealth.blogspot.com/2009/09/virtual-reality-medical-education-in.html

Chapter 9
Virtual Market Economies and the Business of Virtual Worlds

Lee Hwang
There, Inc., USA

ABSTRACT

Virtual worlds have long been a gleam in the visionary's eye: the essential concept of a virtual world may have originated with Pliny (Biocca & Levy, 1995). Much has been written about the impact of virtual worlds, both socially and economically, on their users. This chapter offers an overview of the economies of virtual worlds and the business impact of managing them. Against logic, virtual economies are closer to true market economies than any real world economy. They are also rapidly growing in size and value. With increasing attention from real world governments and tax authorities, virtual economies are stimulating changes in the business of virtual worlds. Virtual world operators have an opportunity to, through their responses, either preserve their investments and their businesses by ensuring a secure role for the market economies they have created, or face serious threats to their business as the real world interferes with virtual fun.

INTRODUCTION

Trade is almost as old as the human species itself; the history of long-distance commerce between prehistoric peoples has been traced as far back as 150,000 years (Watson, 2005). As long as human beings want things they do not have, trade and markets will inevitably emerge in any social group (Smith, 1994). This is just as true of a social group in a virtual world as it is of a social group in the real world. For virtual world operators and businesses hoping to be virtual world operators, decisions about a virtual economy both shape and are shaped by the real world business of a virtual world operator. Even when the virtual economy is considered secondary to the virtual world – as in, for example, a Massively Multiplayer Online Game ("MMOG"), where the principal activity is game play – the issues for the virtual world operator are many. For example: how can revenue

DOI: 10.4018/978-1-61692-808-7.ch009

be generated by a virtual economy? Is real money trading ("RMT") anathema or a goal in the design of the economy? Can users of the virtual world create and market their own original content? If so, who owns it? Who is responsible if the content is offensive or violates copyright or trademark? How can the operator make money off a market for user content? Is buying and selling virtual goods considered cheating, fun, or employment? This chapter will provide an introductory overview to the economies of virtual worlds and a look at some of their challenges for virtual world operators.

VIRTUAL MARKET ECONOMIES AND THE BUSINESS OF VIRTUAL WORLDS

Virtual worlds are an attractive business. The amount of money spent by users of virtual worlds is substantial; the amount of money spent on virtual goods, in and out of virtual worlds, especially in Asia, is even higher. Investment in virtual worlds indicates that, in fact, a number of entrepreneurs and venture capitalists, as well as established companies, are going after their own slice. In 2009, VentureBeat updated its list of game and virtual world fundings for 2008 to total an estimated \$936.8 million, nearly half the amount invested in the global media and entertainment sector, as opposed to \$613 million in 2007 (Takahashi, 2009). KZero's estimate for the total registered accounts for virtual worlds with at least 1 million accounts, excluding MMOG, is 579 million. The top ten MMOG in terms of revenue earned an estimated \$3.25 billion. Adding in asynchronous games like Zynga's YoVille, and mobile virtual worlds like Bobba and Motropolis, the numbers become near impossible to estimate.

Entrepreneurs, venture capitalists, and investors are not the only ones with a stake in the future of virtual worlds. In his book, *Exodus to the Virtual World*, Edward Castronova offers his predictions for the migration of people from the real world to the virtual and discusses the economic impact of this migration in the form of an increasing investment in dollars in the virtual world (Castronova, 2007). New data appears to be bearing out Dr. Castronova's predictions. Market research firm Strategy Analytics released a report on June 1, 2009, forecasting growth in the global population of virtual world users from approximately 186 million in 2009 to nearly 640 million in 2015, almost 100 million new users a year (Report: Virtual Worlds Growth to Skyrocket, 2009). On July 30, 2009, PlaySpan, a company providing monetization and payment solutions for games and virtual worlds, and the consulting firm Frank N. Magid Associates, announced results from a study of consumer attitudes and behaviors with regard to virtual goods. 12 percent of the population surveyed in the study said that they had purchased a virtual good within the past 12 months, and within those respondents who were virtual world users, the survey revealed that 46 percent had purchased virtual goods.

The vast majority (51 percent) of virtual goods buyers could not recall the amount they spent on virtual goods in the previous year. Of those who could recall, 27 percent said they spent less than \$50 while 15 percent said they spent over \$100. The survey was conducted on April 20-25, 2009. The online survey used a nationally representative sample group of 1,927 people. (12% Of Consumers Have Purchased Virtual Goods, 2009)

In another study from video game market research firm VGMarket, also sponsored by Playspan, the average respondent played three online games. 34 percent of respondents reported making purchases in MMOGs. 80 percent of all respondents reported purchasing virtual goods for their own use and 20 percent purchasing virtual goods as gifts (Rosenberg, 2009).

The Rise of Virtual Economies

Linden Research, Inc. ("Linden Lab") in San Francisco, California, the company that operates the 3D virtual world Second Life®, with a reported 13.2 million user accounts (Nino, 2008), regularly publishes data on user-to-user transactions expressed in U.S. dollars. In January 2009, Linden Lab published data showing a 54 percent increase in user-to-user transactions from Q4 2007 to Q4 2008. The total amount spent on virtual goods and services in Second Life® was reported as $101 million in Q4 2008 (Linden Research, Inc., 2009).

The evolution of virtual goods and virtual economies has had consequences; real world agencies have taken notice. In September of 2007, Linden Lab informed all European Union users of Second Life® that Linden Lab would be collecting Value-Added Tax (VAT) on purchases from Linden Lab in accordance with European Union law (European Commission Taxation and Customs Union, 2009). The VAT is levied on all transactions with Linden Lab, including premium account registration; purchases from the land store; land use fees; private region fees; and land auctions (Linden Research, Inc., 2009): EU purchasers of virtual land in Second Life® must pay VAT on their land transactions. In January of 2009, the National Taxpayer Advocate 2008 Annual Report to the United States Congress was released and included as one of its "Most Serious Problems" an item designated as MSP #13: "The IRS Should Proactively Address Emerging Issues Such as Those Arising from 'Virtual Worlds.'" Linden Lab's Second Life®, along with Blizzard Entertainment's World of Warcraft a MMOG with approximately 10.9 million subscribers – are both named to exemplify the two main categories of virtual worlds acknowledged by the Internal Revenue Service (Olson, 2008). In June of 2009, the Chinese government stepped into the fray: a joint release issued by China's Ministries of Culture and Commerce, claiming that the virtual money trade had exceeded "several billion yuan" in 2008 one billion yuan is worth approximately $146 million with an annual rise of 20 percent annually, declared that "virtual currency, which is converted into real money at a certain exchange rate, will only be allowed to trade in virtual goods and services provided by its issuer, not real goods and services." (Ministry of Commerce, The People's Republic of China, 2009) Plus Eight Star, an Asian consultancy firm, offered their own estimate for the virtual goods market in China, Korea, and Japan combined: $5 billion (Plus Eight Star, 2009). The economic impact of virtual worlds is clearly being felt across the globe.

While virtual economies can be quantified in value to rival many real world economies (Castronova, 2001), they exist in worlds with no governments, no physical property or boundaries, no political existence at all. This makes them a new and unique kind of beast, one whose impact is only now being recognized by authorities like the United States Treasury, the European Commission Taxation and Customs Union, and Ministry of Commerce of the People's Republic of China. The steps that these authorities have taken to date in order to address the economic impact of virtual worlds are only the beginning in an effort to understand virtual worlds and the scope and effect of the market economies operating within and around them. A great deal of adaptation and change is certainly yet to come.

So Just What is a Virtual World?

The two types of virtual worlds described for Congress by the National Taxpayer Advocate are as follows:

One category of virtual world, exemplified by the World of Warcraft (WoW), is game-like, has defined objectives, and a significant amount of operator-developed content ... Another category of virtual world, exemplified by Second Life®, is unstructured, utilizes more user-created content, and is more geared toward commercial and social interaction. (Olson, 2008)

The National Taxpayer Advocate may be slightly behind the times with these two categories. With the rapid rise of social networking sites like Facebook and MySpace and the growing popularity of smartphones and other sophisticated mobile devices, a broader and equally significant division has emerged between *synchronous* virtual worlds, which include the two categories described by the National Taxpayer Advocate for the benefit of Congress, and *asynchronous* virtual worlds, a type of virtual world commonly developed for social networking sites and mobile devices.

Asynchronous and *synchronous*, as distinctions between different types of virtual environments, refer to the nature of multi-user interaction. In a synchronous virtual world, user-to-user interactions are supported in real time. Users see and interact with each other as avatars the same way that they would in the real world; users that are not online and logged in are simply not there, so to speak, and do not participate. In an asynchronous world, however, user-to-user interactions take place indirectly. Because they are developed as game applications accessed through web-based social networks – in the game industry, these fall into the category of *social games* – or as game applications for mobile devices, they are designed to suit the essentially asynchronous nature of their delivery systems and the networked nature of their audience. Whereas users of synchronous worlds log in and interact with whoever happens to be present at the same time, users of asynchronous social games and worlds interact with other users they already know. A social network like Facebook may have 350 million users (Kincaid, 2009), but those 350 million users are not likely to be looking at a Facebook page at the same time as their friends. They are even less likely to be playing the same social game at the same time as their friends. Similarly, mobile device users are not likely to be using their devices at the same time as their friends. Consequently, user-to-user interactions are of necessity designed to be independent of concurrence or simply turn-based. Representations of other users as avatars are partially or entirely simulated, or are completely absent. Examples of asynchronous virtual worlds are FarmVille and YoVille, owned by Zynga, Inc. in San Francisco, California, and Restaurant City and Crazy Planets, owned by Playfish, Ltd. in London, UK, acquired by Electronic Arts in 2009.

Whether an asynchronous environment like YoVille should be defined as a virtual world is at this time a matter for some discussion (Virtual Worlds 2008, 2008). Virtual worlds as a vehicle for social interaction and e-commerce are relatively new, and there is certainly no definitive authority to rule on what is a virtual world and what is not. What is indisputable, however, is the reach and impact of asynchronous virtual worlds. Zynga, for example, reports 200 million monthly active users across all of their games, with 100 million unique monthly users and one million purchasing virtual goods per month. The company says that direct user purchases account for approximately 90 percent of Zynga's revenue (Zynga, 2009). The data that emerged in the study conducted by PlaySpan and Frank N. Magid Associates certainly include virtual goods from asynchronous worlds (12% Of Consumers Have Purchased Virtual Goods, 2009), as do the data from the VGMarket report, also sponsored by PlaySpan (Rosenberg, 2009); in fact, social network games accounted for 23 percent of virtual goods purchases.

Regardless of the categories, there are as many types of virtual worlds as there are visionaries to design them. Some classify themselves as games; in the World of Warcraft Guide, World of Warcraft is described as follows: "As a massively multiplayer online game, World of Warcraft enables thousands of players from across the globe to come together online - undertaking grand quests and heroic exploits in a land of fantastic adventure." (Blizzard Entertainment, Inc., 2009) Other types of virtual worlds are known simply and more generally as virtual worlds. All virtual worlds host a multitude of settings and themes, both licensed and original: sword and sorcery;

superhero; science fiction; steampunk. In some cases, a virtual world Second Life®, for example may host all of the above. Virtual worlds are designed for children, for tweens or teens, for adults over 18 only, or sometimes in the U.S. for a COPA-compliant audience of 13 and up. Users can enter a virtual world as almost any type of player character or avatar, human or non-human, with superpowers, magic, or extraordinary physical prowess. They can quickly acquire an exotic wardrobe; slay legions of digital enemies; establish a new group of exciting and interesting friends; buy and decorate a mansion; drive a sleek red racecar or fly a silver airship. Virtual worlds are the kingdoms of dreams. The real world, as lovely and fascinating and enthralling as it may be, can never fulfill the promise of a fantasy existence as easily and seductively as a virtual world. Even when the virtual world fantasy requires real world money, the amount is never as much as the amount required for the same fantasy if it is even possible in the real world.

While virtual worlds may come in a limitless diversity of flavors, they do have some important elements in common.

One thing that all virtual worlds have is human beings. Whether they are represented in the virtual world by pink space bunnies with green toenails and purple radar dishes for ears, svelte blonde supermodels in black leather, or eight-foot horned warriors in plate armor, human beings populate every virtual world and give it life. Their real-world ages, locations, and even genders might be concealed, but they are human. They bring with them to their new environment human drives, human urges, and human behavior, which translate directly to the virtual world (Eastwick & Gardner, 2009). This includes consumer behavior: in the virtual world, the digital kingdom of dreams, there is nothing that human beings need, but there is clearly a great deal that they want (Martin, 2008).

To help people in the virtual world get what they want, another component that nearly all virtual worlds have a notable exception being some private virtual worlds designed primarily for communications or training, for example those built on the open-source virtual world platform OpenSim, or developed by a serious games company for simulations – is their own currency. Virtual currency takes many forms and may have any name, but it is clearly money: it is accepted in-world, and in some cases outside of it, as a medium of exchange for goods or services.

As in the real world, currency greatly facilitates the virtual world user's goal of getting what he wants; it is a vast improvement on barter in that it eliminates the problem of the coincidence of wants (Jevons, 1876). If one user wants a virtual sheep and has virtual cheese, for example, and the only method of trade is barter, it is necessary to find another user that has a sheep and wants cheese at the same approximate point time in order for everyone to be satisfied. Even in a virtual world, this could potentially be problematic and frustrating. Since the purpose of a virtual world is to provide diversion and entertainment, it is contrary to the purpose of a virtual world and certainly to the purpose of its operator, that hopes to be paid for the entertainment service it provides to create a situation where a virtual world user with cheese, in want of a sheep, is unable to quickly identify a suitable trading counterpart and arrange an exchange. With currency, the cheese and sheep situation becomes an entertaining virtual adventure in the ancient human activity of trade: how much can I get for my cheese? And is it enough to get a sheep? The best part, for the user, is that he needs neither the cheese nor the sheep nor the currency to continue in the virtual world: lack of one or all is a temporary and possibly depressing obstacle in the pursuit of entertainment, but it is not a matter of life or death.

Even in MMOGs where the End User License Agreement ("EULA") states with no debate that the operator owns all the content in the game and no commercial gain in or out of the game is sanctioned, a market economy in goods and currency emerges outside and around the game.

Human beings have repeatedly demonstrated that they will create an economy with little to no help from the virtual world operator, and even in spite of it, wherever possible and profitable. In the absence of control or regulations from any government and relatively little restriction from virtual world operators, virtual economies – including those that function illicitly in defiance of an EULA or Terms of Service ("TOS") – more closely resemble the ideal free market economy than any real world economy (Seiler, 2008). If there is a demand for virtual unicorns, someone will arrive to fill it. If there is a demand for virtual gold, someone will find a way to earn and trade it. Despite cultural skepticism and resistance from many parties, including virtual world operators (Reimer, 2006), these virtual market economies continue to blossom and flourish to astonishing proportions, with millions of participants in World of Warcraft and Second Life® alone: the purest market economies on Earth.

Virtual Economies, Real World Taxes

The opportunity thus arises for virtual world operators to understand the growing economies of their virtual worlds and take steps to shape to their advantage the entrance of virtual economies into the global economy of the real world. In some ways, this is already happening. The question is how changed virtual world operators will be when they emerge from the process, and what the business of virtual worlds will have become as a result. The precedents are about to be set; *are* being set.

What are the possibilities? Imagine that virtual worlds could be treated, economically if not politically, as independent countries. Tax authorities in the real world already have law and regulations in place to treat income from other countries; for a U.S citizen, for example, income earned from EverQuest II could be treated the same as income earned from, say, the United Kingdom. A real world government could refuse to trade with a virtual world the same way it might choose to embargo another real world country, and outlaw income from that virtual world. This type of action against an economic entity with no physical borders, with members that might live anywhere in the real world, and with no particular barrier to migration either in or out, could cause catastrophic effects for a virtual world. Imagine, for example, that the United States chose to treat World of Warcraft's Azeroth like Cuba, but then chose to open official trade relations with EverQuest II's Norrath. It is not hard to imagine that American players might migrate to EverQuest II and take their money with them. Blizzard would end up with a database full of abandoned gold accounts that have effectively dropped out of the World of Warcraft economy. Management at Blizzard would understandably find this alarming. Management at Sony Online Entertainment, on the other hand, the company that owns and operates EverQuest II, might find it thrilling.

This scenario the recognition by real world governments of apolitical trade entities – is unlikely, but speculation on such a scenario highlights the unique market economies that thrive in and through virtual worlds, and the growing awareness of their economic impact in the real world. It seems reasonable to assume that virtual world operators and their customers, virtual world users, would prefer to avoid the attention of real world governments and tax authorities and govern themselves (Johnson & Post, 1996), but that may be impossible as data continues to emerge on virtual economies. Real world governments and tax authorities are actively struggling to adjust to this new reality and determine how to handle the unique market economies of virtual worlds. Julian Dibbell, in the final chapter of his book, *Play Money*, describes his own highly entertaining encounter with agents of the Internal Revenue Service of the United States Department of the Treasury (Dibbell, 2006). Virtual world operators and virtual world users like Dibbell are struggling to manage liability and preserve their business and/or their pursuit of entertainment, in the case of the users in the face of the social and economic changes being wrought by the worlds they have created.

Going forward, there are many questions. Will virtual worlds still be good business? Will people still want to play in virtual worlds once the tax man shows up? Will virtual worlds become work and not entertainment? Most importantly, what can virtual world operators do to influence the answers to these questions? Can they study and understand the burgeoning market economies under their noses and make decisions to preserve their investment in their worlds, the value of their virtual economies, and engender a new model for economic interaction? Or will a new paradigm for virtual worlds be crushed by the real world before it fully emerges?

Virtual Market Freedom

The simple definition of a market economy is an economy where prices and allocation of goods and resources are determined by market forces, without planning or control by any central authority (Unknown, 2009). This would seem to be the one type of economy that a virtual world would logically never have, simply because every virtual world is under the absolute control of a "coding authority" (Castronova, 2006): the virtual world operator. The virtual world operator is in some ways more capable of tracking and acting upon the users of its virtual world than any real world government can with its citizens. An operator could, for example, search for any transactions in the virtual world involving any avatar, and decide to block the owner of that avatar from logging in, based on its findings. An operator could write code to prohibit a set of users from engaging in monetary transactions in world more than once a week. An operator could be truly drastic and simply shut the entire world down.

In light of these powers, it would be a relative simple thing for the virtual world operator to also exercise its considerable control to influence market forces in the virtual world. As Edward Castronova put it:

The coding authority who owns and controls a synthetic world could pave the streets with diamonds if it desired. The coding authority could also order the world to make gems that are more beautiful than diamonds. Or, the coding authority could make diamonds much rarer than they are on Earth, and then also purge the world of rubies, sapphires, and every other type of gem. (Castronova, 2006)

In practice, virtual worlds are remarkably free of economic restrictions, aside from those implicit in their design. Asynchronous worlds entered through social networks, like FarmVille and Restaurant City, for example, have no Terms of Service or End User License Agreement, but they also permit no user-to-user exchange of goods or currency. Blizzard sets some boundaries for World of Warcraft players in the first provision of the World of Warcraft End User License Agreement:

1. Grant of a Limited Use License. If you agree to this License Agreement ... you hereby accept, a limited, non-exclusive license to ... use the Game Client in conjunction with the Service for your non-commercial entertainment purposes only. (Blizzard Entertainment, Inc., 2009)

Note that the language specifies that the Game Client is specifically licensed for "non-commercial entertainment purposes only." The same language is repeated in the World of Warcraft Terms of Use Agreement (Blizzard Entertainment, Inc., 2008). This could have more than one interpretation, but one of the possibilities is certainly a prohibition against trading in virtual World of Warcraft goods and currency for profit in real world currency outside the game. Blizzard is more specific in a later provision of the EULA.

2. Additional License Limitations. You agree that you will not, under any circumstances: ... C. exploit the Game or any of its parts, including without limitation the Game Client, for any commercial purpose, including without limitation (a) use at a cyber cafe, computer gaming center or any other location-based site without the express written consent of Blizzard; (b) for gathering in-game currency, items or resources for sale outside the Game; or (c) performing in-game services in exchange for payment outside the Game, e.g., power-leveling ... (Blizzard Entertainment, Inc., 2009)

Provision 2.C(a) covers the case of operations commonly known as gold farms (Unknown, 2009), where unskilled workers are paid to play the game for the sole purpose of gathering virtual goods for sale. Provision 2.C(b) covers the sale of virtual goods and currency outside the game – i.e., the real world – even if the goods and currency were legitimately earned or acquired by the user. Provision 2.C(c) covers the case of individuals selling in-game services outside the game, even if the activities performed within the game are legitimate. A first-hand exploration of these activities in the MMOG Ultima Online – where they are similarly, though less specifically, prohibited (Electronic Arts Inc., 2009) – is the topic of Julian Dibbell's book, *Play Money* (Dibbell, 2006).

Despite the explicit language in the World of Warcraft EULA, however, a market economy in World of Warcraft gold and goods is clearly flourishing outside the game. One need only enter the terms "wow gold" into an internet search engine like Google to receive not only millions of results, but sponsored links for vendors offering World of Warcraft currency for sale – including advertising slogans like "500+ farmers work for you!" – in clear violation of the World of Warcraft End User License Agreement. Similar internet searches also return results for other MMOG.

The obvious flouting of the World of Warcraft EULA, exposed by a simple search engine query, may seem brazen, but flouters have no reason to fear the knock of law enforcement on their doors. Blizzard has the right to ban World of Warcraft accounts and do their best to block access to violators of the EULA and Terms of Use that are attempting to return to the game and resume their illicit activities, but activities that are prohibited in the EULA, such as gold farming and power leveling, are not yet prosecutable crimes in any legal jurisdiction. In 2007, the government of South Korea passed a law making it a crime to use software designed to hack an online game, and a crime to engage in bulk trade of game items. Either offense can result in a fine of up to $50,000 and imprisonment for up to five years (American Public Media, 2007). Gold farming per se, however, is still not a crime in South Korea or anywhere else as of 2009.

In comparison to Blizzard, Linden Lab does not mention use of their service for commercial purposes in the Second Life® Terms of Service. Second Life® is described as follows: "Second Life® is an online 3D virtual world imagined and designed by you. From the moment you enter Second Life®, you'll discover a universe brimming with people and possibilities." (Linden Research, Inc., 2009) Linden Lab is clear in the Second Life® Terms of Service that the currency used in Second Life®, Linden dollars, is not redeemable for monetary value from Linden Lab, and that Linden Lab has the "absolute right to manage, regulate, control, modify and/or eliminate such Currency ... and that Linden Lab will have no liability to you based on its exercise of such right." (Linden Research, Inc., 2009). Linden Lab does not, however, make any mention in the Second Life® TOS of redemption from other sources. Linden Lab also does not state that the Second Life® service is for "entertainment purposes only." And unlike Blizzard, Linden Lab omits any provisions related to gold farming, sale of virtual goods and currency outside of Second Life®, or sale of in-world services outside Second Life®; none of Blizzard's particular prohibitions are echoed in the Second Life® TOS.

The result of the policies expressed in the World of Warcraft EULA and the Second Life® TOS on the respective business operations of Blizzard and Linden Lab is a significant one. Having explicitly banned specific activities in their EULA, Blizzard must be prepared to police their users and enforce their rules to maintain their planned economy. This requires a commitment of resources in the form of development or licensing of software tools to enact enforcement on players in the game – Electronics Arts, Inc., for example, licenses software called PunkBuster from Even Balance, Inc., to "ensure a cheat-free environment for all participants in online games" and requires it for use of Ultima Online (Electronic Arts Inc., 2009) software reporting and analysis to detect trends that might indicate banned activity; and not the least, employees whose job is to log into the game and patrol. As a rough comparison in scale – a very rough comparison – for its 10.9 million World of Warcraft subscribers, Blizzard employs over 2,000 customer service staff, almost all of them Game Masters that police activity in-game, to provide support 24 hours a day, 7 days a week (Activision Blizzard, 2008). This amounts to about 5,450 subscribers for every customer service staff member, as of September 2008. Linden Lab claims 13.2 million Second Life® accounts (Nino, 2008) and employs a total of about 330 people (Linden Research, Inc., 2009), about 40,000 accounts for every employee in any role. Even assuming that not all of the 13.2 million Second Life® accounts claimed by Linden Lab are active, the difference in scale is worth noting. Both Blizzard and Linden Lab provide general technical support; answer questions; and respond to customer disputes and complaints. Blizzard, however, must also expend resources to police their players to detect and eject any offenders that have violated the terms of the World of Warcraft license agreement and managed to achieve some illicit commercial gain, as they did in May of 2006 when they banned more than 30,000 accounts (Reimer, 2006). Figures to precisely quantify the relative costs in this area are not published by either Blizzard or Linden Lab, but it seems reasonable to conclude that the difference in costs to enforce their respective EULA/TOS is material. Blizzard's efforts to stamp out any free market activities related to World of Warcraft are costing them real dollars. Linden Lab believes, by contrast, that its free market is making Linden Lab real dollars in the form of growing interest in the virtual economy and an associated increase in the number of user accounts (Ondrejka, 2005).

Ownership and Intellectual Property

Having set the stage with regard to economic activities in their respective virtual environments, Blizzard and Linden Lab go on to take accordingly different positions on ownership. Blizzard's position is plain:

3. Ownership. All title, ownership rights and intellectual property rights in and to the Game and all copies thereof (including without limitation any titles, computer code, themes, objects, characters, character names, stories, dialog, catch phrases, locations, concepts, artwork, character inventories, structural or landscape designs, animations, sounds, musical compositions and recordings, audio-visual effects, storylines, character likenesses, methods of operation, moral rights, and any related documentation) are owned or licensed by Blizzard. (Blizzard Entertainment, Inc., 2009)

This is a simple and straightforward statement. Blizzard is the originator of all of the content in World of Warcraft and is the owner or licensee of all the content in World of Warcraft. Linden Lab, however, is not the originator of all the content in Second Life®. Consequently, the Second Life® Terms of Service contains more language related to ownership than does the World of Warcraft EULA. For example:

4. You retain copyright and other intellectual property rights with respect to Content you create in Second Life®, to the extent that you have such rights under applicable law. However, you must make certain representations and warranties, and provide certain license rights, forbearances and indemnification, to Linden Lab and to other users of Second Life®. (Linden Research, Inc., 2009)

Linden Lab explicitly clarifies ownership status of all content in Second Life® in another provision by explaining that "users of the service" are responsible for an unknown percentage of content, and that all users must agree to respect the rights of those content owners (Linden Research, Inc., 2009). Linden Lab qualifies this ownership somewhat in other provisions of its TOS by specifying that ownership of user accounts and their related data, regardless of intellectual property rights, are the property of Linden Lab (Linden Research, Inc., 2009). The distinction is subtle, but clear: the intellectual property – for example, the design of a piece of clothing – remains the property of its creator, while the bits that represent the virtual manifestation of the intellectual property are the property of Linden Lab.

The decision by Linden Lab to grant ownership of intellectual property to Residents received some media coverage when it was made in 2003 (Linden Research, Inc., 2003), although this position is not unique, and Linden Lab was not the first virtual world operator to take it (There, Inc., 2003). In terms of the social, economic, and legal implications, the move has been discussed in a number of sources from newspaper articles (Sipress, 2006), to a legal discussion on Law.com (Bringardner, 2007), to student papers on intellectual property law (Gilbert, 2009). Linden Lab's November 14, 2003, announcement regarding intellectual property exempts Linden Lab from responsibility for collecting EU VAT on all but land-related transactions, since license for textures and environmental content owned by Linden Lab is granted by Linden Lab to all Residents via the Second Life® Terms of Service, and all other transactions are conducted between Residents. Linden Lab would similarly not be responsible for any sales and use taxes on, for example, the roughly $100 million in user-to-user transactions that were reported for Q4 2008.

The clarification of ownership in Second Life®'s Terms of Service is critical to Second Life®'s economy. Second Life®'s market economy is built around content created and sold by Residents and is essentially dependent on it (Ondrejka, 2005).

In terms of cost, there is a clear benefit to Linden Lab's business. Part of the reason that Linden Lab employs about 330 people worldwide, while Blizzard employs about 2,700 (Callaham, 2009), is that nearly all of the content available for consumption in Second Life® is produced by Residents, who own it and control it under the Second Life® Terms of Service. All of the content available for consumption in World of Warcraft, however, is produced by Blizzard. Blizzard employs and compensates developers to do the job that Second Life® Residents do "without any expectation of compensation from Linden Lab." (Linden Research, Inc., 2009)

One might wonder whether there is a material business advantage in Linden Lab's free market model for Second Life®. Linden Lab is free from the burden of policing Second Life® Residents for illicit commercial gain; Linden Lab is not required to pay employees to maintain a constant flow of content for Second Life® Residents to consume. As with many things in the real world, the picture is not quite that simple. While Blizzard shoulders burdens that Linden Lab does not, Blizzard has an easily quantifiable source of revenue in that subscription fees are required in order to gain access to World of Warcraft. The 10.9 million players claimed for World of Warcraft are each paying a monthly subscription fee. Linden Lab claims approximately 13.2 million Resident accounts in Second Life®, but most are likely not active; the company reports between 1 and 1.5 million unique visitors to Second Life® for a given 60-day period. In addition, it is unknown how many of the active Resident accounts are subscription accounts, since Linden Lab offers a free service option for Second Life®. The acquisition and long-term retention data for Second Life® and World of Warcraft – for example, of the total visitors to an account registration page, what is the percentage of users that complete the registration process and log in? and for how long do they remain active subscribers? – are not published in any detail.

Enforcement: Rules, Regulations, and Jurisdiction

The restrictions and prohibitions contained within the Second Life® TOS and the World of Warcraft EULA are important within the context of their respective virtual worlds, but when compared to, for example, the body of rules and regulations pertaining to economic activity in the United States, they might as well be non-existent. The 2009 edition of the Internal Revenue Code for example, as of the Second Session of the 110th Congress, is over 3,500 pages and is generally published in three volumes. The relatively minor provisions contained in the Second Life® TOS and the World of Warcraft EULA, coupled with a lack of available real-world recourse for punishment of violations, leaves the market almost entirely free and wide open.

Virtual world operators have plenty of good reasons to keep things simple that have nothing to do with the creation of a free market, and everything to do with their business. Virtual world users are customers, not citizens; they can come and go with a few keystrokes and mouse clicks, and they can choose to pay or not pay. If they like what they see when they come to a virtual world, they will consider paying to stick around. If they continue to like what they see in a virtual world, they may continue to pay. The key word is *may*, because the number of competitors waiting to step in and lure a customer away from World of Warcraft or Second Life® is substantial (K Zero, 2009); it is just as easy for users to try a different virtual world and decide to pay a different operator instead. The practical barrier to exit is almost as low as the barrier to entry. There are no border crossings. There is no need to apply for citizenship, or even a visa. Asynchronous worlds that have no downloadable client, no TOS or EULA, and are free to play through social networks, are especially easy to abandon when something more amusing comes along.

In that context, it is easy to see that virtual world operators will keep things simple partly because rules are plainly not fun. While the repetitive activity known to MMOG players as grinding (Unknown, 2009) won't necessarily keep users from coming back, burdensome and complicated rules and regulations might (Castronova, 2006). Users generally do not view restrictions as entertaining. At best, they cause confusion; at worst, they drive users to simpler, freer, more entertaining environments. Commercial virtual world operators are first and foremost in the business of entertainment, and if engagement in their virtual worlds fails to entertain, users will fail to appear. Even if nothing else changes, revenue will drop as user numbers drop, whether revenue comes from subscriptions or micro-transactions. It is simply detrimental to their business for virtual world operators to make and impose rules and regulations that their users will perceive as burdensome and annoying. Virtual world operators have not yet been observed to put forth advertisements or marketing collateral that promote *burdensome* or *annoying* as forms of fun. They are more than aware that virtual world users can always leave a virtual world for another, or simply return to the real world and perhaps acquire a copy of the U.S. Internal Revenue Code if they are interested in rules and regulations.

Another reason for virtual world operators to limit the constraints they impose on users: if they make rules, they will be called upon to enforce them, and enforcement takes resources and money. This is a direct hit to the bottom line of a virtual world operator. In the case of Blizzard, simple arithmetic suggests that enforcing their prohibition against commercial gain in World of Warcraft is probably costing a significant amount in money and resources. Blizzard's management and board of directors are unlikely to be in favor of spending more money to enforce more rules if they can avoid it *if they can avoid it* being the key phrase, as laws around virtual worlds continue to evolve.

Finally, a somewhat more subtle deterrent to increased regulation by virtual world operators: even if creating and enforcing a complex set of restrictions and regulations were somehow sexy and desirable and easy to market, it puts the virtual world operator in the position of literally laying down the law. In a global environment where governments and tax authorities are already paying new attention to the market economies in and around virtual worlds, a perceived shift from license agreements and terms of service to laws may serve to push the role of the virtual world operator towards government. This is a complicated and uncertain path to tread (Castronova, 2006). If a virtual world operator is perceived as resembling or acting as a government, the hypothetical scenario of the U.S. opening official trade relations with EverQuest II, however unlikely, begins to sound more plausible. A shift in that direction would change the business of virtual worlds forever: imagine virtual world operators reinvented, for instance, as government-sponsored enterprises, like Fannie Mae. Some actions on the part of virtual world operators themselves certainly seem government-like; Linden Lab, for example, banned gambling in Second Life® in 2007 following an FBI investigation into virtual world gambling (Riley, 2007). Linden Lab's vice president of community and support, reminded Second Life® Residents in a blog post under the name Robin Linden that "Resident compliance with real world laws has always been an integral part of our Terms of Service." (Linden [Harper], 2007) Technically this is true in that there are several provisions related to law enforcement in the TOS, although the Second Life® Terms of Service does not explicitly state that real world jurisdictions have blanket authority over activities in Second Life®. In fact, the Second Life® TOS explicitly states that Second Life® "is controlled and operated by Linden Lab from its offices within the State of California, United States of America. Linden Lab makes no representation that any aspect of the Service is appropriate or available for use in jurisdictions outside of the United States" and lays legal responsibility at the feet of their non-U.S. Residents by continuing: "Those who choose to access the Service from other locations are responsible for compliance with applicable local laws." (Linden Research, Inc., 2009) This is a meaningful number: Linden Lab CEO Mark Kingdon has been quoted saying that 60 percent of Second Life® Residents live outside the United States in the real world (Nuttall, 2009). In comparison, There.com, a virtual world service operated by Makena Technology, Inc. ("Makena") that opened its doors to the public in the same year as Second Life®, takes a somewhat different position. Without acknowledging authority by real world law enforcement over the actions of its Members in the virtual world, Makena states that they may terminate its relationship with any customers that violate any law in the real world: "Company may terminate your account and membership upon receiving information involving your violation of any law, regulation or ordinance, and will cooperate with law enforcement agencies on such matters." (Makena Technology, Inc., 2009)

Blizzard makes no statement about the jurisdiction of real world law enforcement over World of Warcraft players except as applied to enforcement of the World of Warcraft End User License Agreement, but this may be the most subservient position of all: in combination with Blizzard's provisions stating its full ownership over all content and data in World of Warcraft, Blizzard could simply be held accountable for activities of players in World of Warcraft that are interpreted as illegal in a real world jurisdiction.

The gray areas become even grayer when one considers the jurisdiction of real world law over virtual property. In November of 2009, officers from the British Central Police e-Crime Unit arrested a man accused of hacking into player accounts to steal virtual identities and virtual property in the popular web-based MMOG, RuneScape (Ahmed, 2009). This may be the first case of its kind in Britain, if not in the world. Theft of avatar identities and virtual possessions is generally prohibited by virtual world operators, but real world law is nearly if not completely nonexistent in this area. If, however, virtual goods have substantial real value – and there is certainly plenty of evidence for it – and the virtual world operator fails to enforce rules against theft of virtual goods, is it logical and reasonable for users to turn to their local law enforcement for redress? Suppose the perpetrator and the victim live in different real world countries? Who has jurisdiction? How can a virtual criminal be brought to justice in the real world? Or is there no justice for criminals in the virtual world?

The relationship and/or resemblance of virtual world operators to government is, in a word, unclear.

The market economies of virtual worlds are potentially unstoppable as profit machines. Virtual world operators obviously have an interest in protecting any aspect of their business that can feed the profit machine, and they have an equal interest in avoiding real world legal regulation that could impact their profit machine (Balkin, 2004). While they may not be concerned about real world arrests of their users, however, they certainly have an interest in not running afoul of real world laws themselves. If it is at all possible for virtual world operators to operate their businesses to combine these interests and keep their profit machine running smoothly, it is undoubtedly to their advantage to find it.

A Virtual Place for My Virtual Stuff: Demand for Virtual Goods

In the real world, much of the economy is devoted to the fulfillment of physical needs: food, shelter, water. Within the boundaries of a virtual world, trade and goods grow out of the pure pursuit of pleasure. Even the need to feed or bathe a MMOG player character is the result of the pursuit of pleasure; the player character is programmed to need food as a gameplay mechanism. Avatars and player characters have no physical needs. They are digital creations spawned upon the whim of a human being in the real world and continue to exist indefinitely as long as their data is stored and the servers are running. As a result, the economies of virtual worlds are not only examples of the purest definition of a market economy; they are a unique illustration of market forces in an environment where no one *needs* to buy or sell anything at all.

Factors that motivate participation in the virtual economy are the same as those that motivate participation in the real world economy. Interestingly, many purchases that serve a practical necessity in the real world are duplicated in the virtual world. In the absence of physical needs – while food and hygiene may be required as a game play mechanism in MMOGs, including World of Warcraft, avatars have no physical need for, say, a toilet or a stove it might be imagined that virtual world users would save their virtual currency for other virtual world purchases. Even a virtual house is not strictly really necessary, except perhaps as storage space; avatars have no need of shelter from freezing cold or driving rain. Avatars never tire of standing, so they have no need of virtual furniture to sit on. Virtual world users buy them regardless. Even when they live in a digital fantasy world where they have absolutely no use for a stove or refrigerator, they still put virtual stoves and refrigerators in their virtual houses. It has been suggested that "digital life has a tendency to replicate social norms, even undesirable ones." (Platoni, 2008) If that is indeed the case, then perhaps it is not surprising that a virtual world user would spend virtual currency on an unnecessary virtual toilet.

Just as in the real world, a great deal of buying behavior does indeed appear to be social in nature. People buy to establish social status; to impress peers or a potential sexual mate; to fulfill a need for self-expression, to display evidence of accomplishment in the form of wealth and/or valuable objects. These motives all exist in the virtual world just as they do in the real world (Martin, 2008): "he who logs out with the most toys wins." (Dibbell, 2006) Because every virtual world has its own culture, the rules for winning in other words, which objects will accomplish the goals of establishing, impressing, fulfilling and displaying, and what methods of acquiring them are acceptable or admirable – are unique to the world and the context of the society within it. For example, in the real world, a beautiful house and a luxury car are attractive symbols of wealth and success. But if an individual were in an environment where, instead of house and car, his social standing and attractiveness were signaled entirely by the color and quality of his socks, he might worry less about the quality of the granite counters in his house or the German engineering of his car, and instead invest his energy in a quest for the perfect delicate lavender shade of angora hosiery. In the virtual world, the worth of a virtual possession can be determined by game play, by rarity, or even by accident (Dibbell, 2006), but the agent in determining worth that originates from all three is social consensus and influences.

Asynchronous virtual worlds like FarmVille or Restaurant City differ from synchronous virtual worlds like Second Life® or World of Warcraft in that social influences are more limited. Users have no contact with large social groups within asynchronous virtual environments; they are unlikely to have contact even with their own friends in asynchronous virtual environments. There are no markets for buying and selling where market forces would determine value, and real world brands that carry real world value have as yet little to no presence in asynchronous worlds. Value is thus largely found in unusual accessories or desirable enhancements to game play, some of which can only be received as gifts from friends, or through real world cash payments to the operator.

Value is also found in freedom from social influences. There are, of course, some forms of consumption that may be freely indulged in the virtual world when they might be suppressed in the real world: participation in the virtual sex trade, for example; or props and decorations to satisfy an interest in fetishism or cosplay. This has been true since the days of MOOs and MUDs (Dibbell, 1993). The virtual world is an appealing outlet for activities that the real world might classify as crimes, vices, or as socially marginal or unacceptable: since users can conceal their identity through a virtual avatar, the virtual world can be viewed as a safe and anonymous place to act out or engage in fantasy, dark or sexual or vindictive or otherwise. Virtual leather gear, virtual sex toys, and virtual weapons are all in ready supply: searches for "dildo" and "gun" in the Second Life® Marketplace return thousands of results. Virtual world users can preserve their real world social reputations and self-perceptions and relegate social and personal experimentation to the virtual world with no real world repercussions (Reed, 2009). In the virtual world, rebellion and fantasy are not only acceptable; MMOG are commonly created with these themes in mind. Some examples are City of Villains, a companion to City of Heroes, developed by Cryptic Studios and published by NCSoft; a game called Criminal Path; an explicit Korean sex MMOG called 3Feel. The user is released from the expectations of the real to freely enjoy his experience without fear of judgment: in the right virtual world, his purchases do not require a plain brown wrapper or stealth by night.

While the rules of virtual value may require a learning curve, it is appealing to play the game, since the risk and investment required for the pursuit of virtual stuff are minor compared to real world risk and investment. Enough virtual currency to acquire a virtual house or virtual angora socks, especially in a MMOG where the currency can be earned through game play, is relatively little in real world dollars; 1000 World of Warcraft gold, for example, can be had for $4 to $6 by performing an internet search for gold sellers. It is more than reasonable to expect that a virtual world user can build or acquire the virtual house of her dreams and fill it with precious virtual possessions for perhaps $50, depending on the virtual world. In an asynchronous world like Zynga's FarmVille, players can farm, earn, and buy without spending any real world money at all, and usually do; less than 3 percent of players across all of Zynga's games pay real money (Miller & Stone, 2009).

Virtual Value

Virtual world users seek valuable possessions in the real world, and they do the same in the virtual world (Martin, 2008). The creation of value, however, is a different process in the virtual world than in the real.

Value is a tricky thing to create from scratch, especially when it is being sculpted from bits of code and graphical assets. Real-world objects that are valuable because of their physical characteristics, for example, cannot translate their value into the virtual world because the real world sensual experience of the physical object cannot be duplicated in the virtual world. Consider a bottle of Chanel perfume, for example, or a mink coat. Delicate fragrances have no meaning in the virtual world; neither does the softness and lushness of mink. Other forms of value attributed to goods are perhaps more translatable, but difficult to establish or guarantee in the virtual world. A virtual Chippendale chair may be as lovely in its own way as its real world counterpart, but a Chippendale chair is also valuable because of its age, condition, and rarity, three attributes that are meaningless in a virtual world where objects do not age or decay and perfect replicas can be conjured from a database in seconds. Finally, there is that marvelous chimera of brand value: the mystical force that makes an aqua blue box with a white satin ribbon from Tiffany so special and guarantees that the contents are lovely, shiny, and expensive; draws a buyer to pay more for the familiar red and white of a Coca-Cola six-pack instead of the store brand cola; and helps to confer upon the legendary Hermès Birkin handbag a market value approximately equivalent to that of a mid-sized American car. Ultimately, however, valuable objects are valuable simply because enough consumers agree that they are valuable, and are willing to pay a price to possess them: a perfect example of market demand. Take Dr. Castronova's example of diamonds, for instance. Because of their unique physical properties, diamonds have a number of industrial applications, but the most valuable diamonds are prized for their beauty. Graphite, less glowing and sparkly than diamond, is much valued in pencil leads, but despite being chemically identical to diamond, graphite is considerably less pretty in a ring, and is unlikely to inspire the same response when presented along with a marriage proposal.

In the virtual world, the virtual world operator has the potential for influence over perceptions of value, and it may exercise that influence, but there is little to no benefit in disrupting value perceptions, if for no other reason that it would upset virtual world users and disrupt their confidence in the economy (Castronova, 2006). Consumer confidence in the virtual world is just as critical a measure of economic health as it is in the virtual world, and both are based on consumer perception: is there faith that the economy will perform with enough predictability to warrant continued spending? The virtual world operator, as the ultimate controlling authority and arbiter in the economic activity of its virtual world, can create unpredictability, intentionally or by accident (Kumar & Remo, 2008). The term "gold sink," describing the insertion of an object or mechanism into the environment of a virtual world with the intent of removing money from the economy, has become so widespread that its definition is included in UrbanDictionary.com (Urban Dictionary, 2009). Virtual world users, especially those in worlds like Second Life® or EVE Online, where user engagement in economic activity is heavily emphasized, have understandable concerns about the attitudes, policies, and plans of virtual world operators (Shang, 2009).

Virtual goods clearly have value, in that millions of consumers have agreed that they have value. And these millions know that the goods are no more than pixels and data; even more, they may have been required to agree that they have no ownership rights over the virtual goods whatsoever. Despite this, the value is there. There has been much written and more said about real world value attached to virtual goods (Siahaan, 2009) (Miller & Stone, 2009) (Dibbell, 2006) (Castronova, 2006) why would one pay real money, money that could be earning interest or dividends or invested in tangible goods, for a bit of art and some code that exists only on a server in a cage in an anonymous air-conditioned colo? Users that have done exactly that may shrug with embarrassment or indifference, or explain the expense with whatever comes to mind. The shift in thinking that results in credit cards being pulled out in front of computer screens all over the world not for a handbag or a sweater that arrives in a package on a truck, but for a tiny rendering of pixels representing a magical sword or a hoverbike, or a virtual bunch of flowers has already happened for millions and will happen for millions more. For the culture, it means a new frontier and a new type of entertainment experience. For tax authorities, it may be a warning. For the business of virtual worlds, the important thing is simply that it happens: over and over and over, to the tune of billions.

Operator Control over Supply and Demand

The power of a virtual world operator to influence supply and demand varies with the nature and structure of its virtual market.

In Second Life®, for example, virtual goods are created, bought and sold by Residents of Second Life®. Linden Lab leases and maintains virtual land for a charge, but does not market its own virtual goods and does not control or limit the supply of virtual goods created by its Residents. As a result, Linden Lab only controls the supply of land.

In There.com, the market is somewhat more complex. Virtual world operator Makena also controls the supply of land and in addition leases pre-constructed housing to its Members. Both Member-created and operator-created virtual goods are bought and sold in the market. Members may only create from templates supplied by Makena, and unlike Second Life® Residents, must submit their creations to be vetted by Makena. Makena publishes guidelines and policies governing the vetting process. When Member-created items are sold in Developer Auctions, a small part of the sale price goes to Makena; the remainder is kept by the seller. Virtual goods created by Makena are sold in Shop Central. Some are designed and created in partnership with corporate brands like Coca-Cola and NBC Universal. All revenue from Shop Central sales goes to Makena.

In World of Warcraft, all virtual goods are created and owned by Blizzard, including any items created or manufactured through game play; players create no original content for the game. The same is true of Zynga's FarmVille.

Among these examples, Linden Lab clearly has limited to no control over supply and demand in the Second Life® market, except for land. All market forces over virtual goods are firmly in the hands of Second Life® Residents, and their ability and willingness to create, sell, and consume those goods. Linden Lab provides tools and support, but if somehow the Residents were to engineer the collapse of the Second Life® economy, Linden Lab would by its own policies be essentially powerless to prevent it.

In contrast, Makena, the operator of There.com, has much stronger influence over supply and demand. In addition to total control over the content of its Shop Central stores, Makena may influence supply of Member-created virtual goods in several different ways. For example, Makena may change its timetable for vetting and approving Member creations. Makena may slow the approval process or halt it altogether. Makena may change the guidelines for Member creations to restrict or prohibit certain classes of creations. Since Members can only create from templates provided by Makena, Makena may plan to release new templates for certain times or to coincide with certain events. Demand can also be influenced; Makena can limit the release of popular or desirable items, or create rare and exceptional goods that cannot be purchased in any of its online stores and can only be awarded by the operator or its agents. In practice, Makena may rarely if at all exercise its power, but the potential is there.

With total control over the creation of virtual goods in their worlds, Blizzard and Zynga would theoretically have the most power over supply and demand in World of Warcraft and FarmVille, respectively, except that World of Warcraft allows players to exchange virtual goods and currency in-game, and gold farming is a thriving, if illicit, activity. As a result, while Blizzard owns and creates all content and virtual goods for World of Warcraft, players have enormous influence over the money supply and can create massive inflation. Because FarmVille allows no exchanges from player to player except for free gifts, Zynga, unlike Blizzard, actually has full power over supply and demand. Zynga may suddenly release new and interesting accessories or enhancements, and just as suddenly take them away; Zynga may introduce new goods that can only be received as gifts from friends in order to encourage players to invite more friends to play. FarmVille currency cannot be used anywhere except in FarmVille – it cannot even be used in other Zynga worlds, like Café World or Roller Coaster Kingdom. FarmVille currency cannot be exchanged between players even within FarmVille.

Running a Virtual World

Attractive though they may be as investments, virtual worlds are not an easy business, and the worlds themselves can be challenging to run. The technologies are relatively new. Outside of the historically common monthly subscription model, revenue models are experimental. The problem of attracting users to a new service is persistent, especially for asynchronous worlds accessed through social networks; since their model is based on a very small percentage of paying customers, they need a large number of customers overall to make money. With large numbers of highly social individuals signing on and spending time, community issues and complaints arise that require dedicated, trained community staff. Even in asynchronous environments, forums must be monitored and moderated. As if all that were not challenging enough, some virtual world technologies must now contend with the rise of mobile devices, the netbook and the unknown territory of cloud computing, which comes with lighter but less powerful user hardware that may complicate certain technological challenges inherent in large volumes of user-created content, particularly 3D content. There is no magic formula for the business of virtual worlds any more than there is for other businesses, especially when the conditions and ingredients are constantly changing. Yet virtual world operators march determinedly forward, searching for the promised land of happy users, steadily increasing revenues, endless content, and satisfied investors.

While MMOG, social games, and services like Second Life® or There.com that describe themselves simply as "virtual worlds" may all be considered virtual or synthetic worlds (Castronova, 2007), they are clearly promoted by their operators as different kinds of online offerings. World of Warcraft, for example, is described on its website as a game and the customers that pay to install and use it are players (Blizzard Entertainment, Inc., 2009). The same is true of the famously economically oriented MMOG EVE Online, with the addition of some bullet points pointing out how EVE Online is different from other MMOG (CCP Games, 2009). Second Life® is described as a 3D virtual world and the people that use it are Residents (Linden Research, Inc., 2009). There.com calls its users Members and describes itself as "an online getaway where you can hang out with your friends and meet new ones--all in a lush 3D environment that's yours to explore!" (Makena Technology, Inc., 2009) None of these virtual world operators markets its service primarily as a virtual marketplace, although virtual economies are given attention by Linden Lab for Second Life® and CCP for EVE Online; in all cases, the primary message to potential customers is clearly *fun*. This makes sense, since the first job of any virtual world operator is to develop a coherent strategy to market its virtual world and attract users. While the brand message may differ, the product being sold is entertainment.

Whether the virtual economy is part of the marketing message of a virtual world operator or not, virtual economies have clearly demonstrated significant value in real dollars. It seems that a clever thing to do from a business standpoint would be to figure out how to make money from the day-to-day operation of a virtual world economy – since one seems to appear whether it is wanted or not (Castronova, 2006) – then create and nourish one to a healthy size, and sit back and watch the revenue roll in. Sadly, as with most things in life, the road to profitability is not as simple as that.

First and foremost, in order for people in a virtual world to spend their virtual currency, there must be something they want to buy. There must be valuable content in the virtual world. Even with a thorough understanding of how content value is created and perceived by virtual world users, virtual world operators must still make a critical and enduring choice about how the content is created.

Some virtual world operators elect to get on the expensive non-stop treadmill of content generation, paying teams of artists and engineers to plan, design, and make content that can be bought and sold by virtual world users. There are many advantages to this, all arising from the fact that the virtual world operator has full control over the content. The content can be tested to eliminate technical problems. It can be reviewed for any possible trademark or copyright violation. It can be made thoroughly inoffensive to any user that might see or interact with it. It can be optimized to require minimal system resources when it is used. If the economy is inflated, gold sinks can be generated. The downside, of course, is the burden of creating it. People to create the content must be hired and managed and directed; they need offices and equipment and software licenses; they expect health and other benefits. And of course, the appetite of virtual world users for content never ends, whether they have the option of buying or selling it or not; one of the draws of all virtual worlds is the possibility of unique virtual experiences that are impossible in the real world. One veteran MMOG developer has estimated that content is as much as 80 percent of the cost of developing a MMOG (Zenke, 2008).

Other virtual world operators choose to take the riskier road and hand over the job of content creation to willing people in their virtual world. Second Life® is a heavily cited example. A MMOG example is EVE Online. Again, there are advantages and disadvantages to user-created content. The most obvious advantage is that the operator is free from the burden of non-stop content generation, allowing the market to scale to a size limited only by the efforts of the users creating the content. To return to the barter example of the user with the virtual sheep and the virtual cheese, an active population of content creators could provide, say, sixteen kinds of sheep and thirty-nine kinds of cheese, giving buyers a dizzying array of choices and making the markets for virtual sheep and virtual cheese far more active and interesting by creating variables in demand: are black sheep more popular than pink sheep? Is runny cheese more popular than holey cheese? With the virtual world operator free to concentrate on content creation tools rather than the content itself, the return on investment in terms of sheer scope is exponentially increased over proprietary content creation. With the proper tools, content creators could not only create an endless stream of content objects; they could create content objects with behavior by scripting or programming any number of diversions: games, activities, puzzles. The operator need never bother creating content at all; all creative resources can be devoted to extending and improving the virtual world experience and to making even more and better tools for content creators, which, it would be hoped, pay off in more and better content for the world.

The downside is the loss of control over the content and its possible effects on the world. Virtual world operators can draft guidelines and rules and require users to agree to them, but operators must then be prepared to review and approve each piece of content for compliance; or be prepared to respond to complaints or even lawsuits related to non-compliance; or possibly both. Quality and artistry may go out the window; in There.com, for example, 3D content submitted by Members is reviewed and approved – and sometimes rejected – by a team of approvers, but a policy established when There.com was launched in 2003 guides approvers to accept all content as long as it adheres to technical and intellectual property restrictions, even if it is poorly made or simply ugly (Bonn, 2003). The content may be broken, or trigger a bug in the world platform, or be deliberately malicious. In 2006, for example, Second Life® was disabled by several well-publicized incidents of "gray goo," self-replicating objects that brought the Second Life® servers to their electronic knees (BBC News, 2006). In response to these incidents, then-CEO Philip Rosedale stated, "In cases where we are able to establish a reasonable equivalance[sp] between that kind of disruption, we have, and we will be, and we will get better at, turning those people in, in general to the FBI here in the US." (Jonas [Avatar Name], 2006) Mr. Rosedale explained his statement by qualifying the "gray goo" incidents as interference in the business of Linden Lab. This statement, however, along with the 2007 statement by Robin Harper of Linden Lab regarding real world law, suggests that Linden Lab is – intentionally or not – relinquishing a measure of control as a virtual world operator by turning to real world authorities to punish virtual world infractions. This may simply be a matter of cost: as previously discussed, policing and enforcement in the virtual world takes resources, just as they do in the real world. The cumulative effect of the statements by Rosedale and Harper, however, may eventually result in legal actions and precedents that have repercussions for all virtual worlds, not just Second Life®.

WHERE TO NOW?

Virtual worlds are – with some exceptions (Moran, 2008) – commercial enterprises, where the ultimate goal of their operators is to make money from whatever entertainment or diversion they provide through their service. The economies of those worlds, especially in MMOG, have not historically been central to the business. Certainly to date, no virtual world operator or entrepreneur has entered the space with the announcement that it was setting out specifically to design and evolve the perfect virtual economy. Perhaps this is the next step.

It is unclear, however, whether such a world could be successfully marketed to the usual MMOG audience purely as a game. In terms of design, user experience and expectations, MMOGs are very different from purely social worlds. Certainly, while creating and nurturing a market economy in a social virtual world is commonplace, the same cannot be said of market economies in MMOG. While game operators and game players clearly recognize the value of a healthy and flourishing economy, the notion of being able to farm currency or to buy (or sell) an advantage in game play offends the notion of fair play at its deepest level. On August 28, 2009, the Chinese game company, Shanda Interactive Entertainment Limited, introduced an updated version of its popular Legend of Mir MMOG. Players from the original game returned to the new version, only to discover changes they did not like: "... if a player has cash, he can purchase equipment to upgrade without having to go through the trouble to combat monsters ..." (EastSouthWestNorth, translated from Chinese, 2009) The players decided to boycott and protest the changes by blockading entry and exit into the game's virtual cities by the thousands.

In order to avoid the kind of retaliation players visited upon Shanda, MMOG operators – whose revenues rely on the satisfaction of players and their willingness to continue playing and paying – still collect revenue through subscription fees, at least in the U.S. (Hyman, 2008). Change is not out of the question. Sony Entertainment Online introduced a new "freemiums" system in its MMOG, Free Realms. Blizzard has allowed for the possibility of introducing micro-transactions to World of Warcraft (Yin-Poole, 2009). As new forms of virtual worlds, however, emerge, revenue models like the free-to-play model, where micro-transactions and other revenue streams support the operator's business, must still succeed in satisfying the desire for fair game play if they want to succeed as a business. Reputation and the goodwill of paying customers are even more important in this age where news and rumors travel through Twitter as fast as packets through fiber optic cable.

Social virtual worlds, where the issue of game play is not a factor, must still deal with fair play in the form of a guarantee for safe and fair trading. A virtual world built entirely around a virtual economy would obviously have this challenge in spades. Technical errors that cause monetary transactions to fail, for example; or misrepresentation in the sale of virtual goods: these are problems that follow users and operators from the real world into the virtual. Wherever emotions are invested as well as currency, and social rules evolve, participants in virtual worlds clearly expect oversight, authority, and punishment from some source. In a world where the economy is the game and the primary activity, the obvious source is the world operator, and yet, for reasons already discussed, the operator has a significant interest in avoiding this role.

Legal considerations for virtual worlds are substantial, and change almost daily. As legal canon struggles to keep up with changes in technology and online behavior, holes in the law gape wide. For example, as Julian Dibbell found, U.S. tax law does not handle income earned through a virtual world (Dibbell, 2006), although this is clearly set to evolve in the foreseeable future (Olson, 2008). While a virtual world designed specifically for the purpose of nourishing a virtual market economy might hold tremendous potential for profit, given the numbers invested in virtual economies to date, the adaptation of governments, law enforcement, and tax authorities to the new paradigm offered by virtual worlds may offset the profit potential with unknown and possibly untenable risk.

The times, they are a-changing, in the virtual world and in the real world. The enormous success of the unique market economies in virtual worlds, a blessing for many and a curse for others – apparently, at least, for the Chinese government – may ultimately cause their reinvention. If the real world cannot devise answers to the difficult questions that have arisen with virtual worlds and their powerful economies, real world rule may simply be forced upon virtual worlds. If the virtual experience becomes little different than the real experience, virtual worlds may not disappear – they have charms other than their economies – but they will likely become something else as yet unknown.

The future form of virtual worlds and future challenges to the business of building and operating them may be unknown, but the potential of virtual economies may readily be declared as limitless. And this may be the ultimate paradigm shift: a blurring or elimination of the boundaries between virtual economies and real economies that brings with it a more general blurring of the boundaries between the virtual and the real. Real world nations establish and manage trade relations with one another; is it really that much of a stretch to imagine a need for real world nations to establish and manage trade relations with a virtual nation? In making games and virtual worlds, virtual world operators are engineering economies that push and pull on the boundaries between the virtual and the real, the digital and the physical. No one ever asks whether newcomers born into a real world economy will be able to participate or will be welcomed to participate; they simply participate, and the economy spins on, ever-changing. Why must virtual economies be any different? Is it really so impossible to picture virtual economic news reported as part of the real world global economic news? Can wealth in a virtual world not be treated the same as portfolio assets manipulated online through a web interface? Could markets and money be the forces that finally bring the long-cherished Metaverse (Stephenson, 1992) dream of a universally shared virtual space into being?

The answers may arrive sooner than anyone can predict.

REFERENCES

Activision Blizzard. (2008, September 15). Investor Presentation. Paris, France: Vivendi.

Ahmed, M. (2009, November 30). *Real-world arrest for man who stole RuneScape virtual characters*. Retrieved November 30, 2009, from Times Online: http://technology.timesonline.co.uk/tol/news/tech_and_web/gadgets_and_gaming/virtual_worlds/article6937026.ece

American Public Media. (2007, July 9). *Online 'gold farming' more than a game*. Retrieved September 3, 2009, from American Public Media: http://marketplace.publicradio.org/shows/2007/07/09/PM200707097.html

Balkin, J. M. (2004). Virtual Liberty: Freedom to Design and Freedom to Play in Virtual Worlds. *Virginia Law Review*, *90*(8), 2043. doi:10.2307/1515641

Biocca, F., & Levy, M. R. (1995). *Communication in the Age of Virtual Reality*. Hillsdale, New Jersey Hove, UK: Lawrence Erlbaum Associates.

Blizzard Entertainment, Inc. (2008, July 29). *Terms of Use Agreement*. Retrieved September 3, 2009, from World of Warcraft: http://www.worldofwarcraft.com/legal/termsofuse.html

Blizzard Entertainment, Inc. (2009, July 29). *End User License Agreement*. Retrieved September 3, 2009, from World of Warcraft: http://www.worldofwarcraft.com/legal/eula.html

Blizzard Entertainment, Inc. (2009, September 3). *World of Warcraft Guide*. Retrieved September 3, 2009, from World of Warcraft: http://www.worldofwarcraft.com/info/basics/guide.html

Bonn, S. (2003, July). personal communication.

Bringardner, J. (2007, February 1). *IP's Brave New World*. Retrieved September 3, 2009, from Law.Com: http://www.law.com/jsp/article.jsp?id=1170237755271

Callaham, J. (2009, May 11). *Blizzard named top game developer in new survey*. Retrieved September 3, 2009, from Big Download: http://news.bigdownload.com/2009/05/11/blizzard-named-top-game-developer-in-new-survey/

Castronova, E. (2001, December). *Virtual Worlds: A First-Hand Account of Market and Society on the Cyberian Frontier.* Retrieved September 3, 2009, from Social Science Research Network: http://ssrn.com/abstract=294828

Castronova, E. (2006). *Synthetic Worlds: The Business and Culture of Online Games* (Paperback ed.). Chicago, IL, USA: University of Chicago Press.

Castronova, E. (2007). *Exodus To The Virtual World* (1st ed.). New York, New York, USA: Palgrave Macmillan.

Cowan, D. (2009, February 25). *NASA Taps Serious Game Devs for Space-Themed MMO.* Retrieved September 3, 2009, from Serious Games Source: http://www.seriousgamessource.com/item.php?story=22468

Dibbell, J. (1993, December 23). *A Rape in Cyberspace.* Retrieved September 3, 2009, from Julian Dibbell: http://www.juliandibbell.com/texts/bungle_vv.html

Dibbell, J. (2006). *Play Money, Or, How I Quit My Day Job and Made Millions Trading Virtual Loot.* New York, New York, USA: Basic Books.

EastSouthWestNorth, translated from Chinese. (2009, August 29). "The Legend" Returns In A Completely Different Format, Several Thousand Netizens Blocked City Gates In Protest. *Chengdu Commercial Daily.*

Eastwick, P. W., & Gardner, W. L. (2009). Is it a game? Evidence for social influence in the virtual world. *Social Influence*, *4*(1), 18–32. doi:10.1080/15534510802254087

Electronic Arts Inc. (2009, September 3). *Ultima Online TOS.* Retrieved September 3, 2009, from Ultima Online: http://www.uo.com/tos_update.html#uotos

European Commission Taxation and Customs Union. (2009, September 3). *VAT on electronic services.* Retrieved September 3, 2009, from European Commission Taxation and Customs Union: http://ec.europa.eu/taxation_customs/taxation/vat/how_vat_works/e-services/index_en.htm

Games, C. C. P. (2009). *Frequently Asked Questions: What is EVE Online?* Retrieved September 3, 2009, from EVE Online: http://www.eveonline.com/faq/faq_01.asp

Gilbert, B. J. (2009, June 2). *The Second Life® of Intellectual Property.* Retrieved September 3, 2009, from Social Science Research Network: http://ssrn.com/abstract=1409091

Hyman, P. (2008, June 5). *MMOG Business Models: Cancel That Subscription!* Retrieved September 3, 2009, from Gamasutra: http://www.gamasutra.com/view/feature/3688/mmog_business_models_cancel_that_.php

Jevons, W. S. (1876). *Money and the Mechanism of Exchange.* New York: D. Appleton and Co.

Johnson, D. R., & Post, D. G. (1996). Law and Borders - The Rise of Law in Cyberspace. *Stanford Law Review*, *48*, 1367. doi:10.2307/1229390

Jonas [Avatar Name], D. (2006, May 16). *Town Hall: Philip Getting Friendly With the Feds.* Retrieved September 3, 2009, from The Alphaville Herald: http://www.secondlifeherald.com/slh/2006/05/town_hall_phili.html

Kincaid, J. (2009, December 1). *Facebook to Roll Out New Privacy Controls To Its 350 Million Users, Kills Regional Networks.* Retrieved December 1, 2009, from TechCrunch: http://www.techcrunch.com/2009/12/01/facebook-privacy-controls/

Kumar, M., & Remo, C. (2008, August 26). *CCP Economist on EVE Online's 'Pure Capitalist' Market.* Retrieved September 3, 2009, from Gamasutra: http://www.gamasutra.com/php-bin/news_index.php?story=19844

Linden [Harper], R. (2007, July 25). *Wagering in Second Life®: New Policy.* Retrieved September 3, 2009, from Second Life® Blogs: Features: https://blogs.secondlife.com/community/features/blog/2007/07/26/wagering-in-second-life-new-policy

Linden Research, Inc. (2003, November 14). *Press Release: Second Life® Residents To Own Digital Creations.* Retrieved September 3, 2009, from Linden Lab: http://lindenlab.com/pressroom/releases/03_11_14

Linden Research, Inc. (2009, September 3). Retrieved September 3, 2009, from Linden Lab: http://lindenlab.com/

Linden Research, Inc. (2009, September 3). *Economic Statistics (Raw Data Files).* Retrieved September 3, 2009, from Second Life®: http://secondlife.com/statistics/economy-data.php

Linden Research, Inc. (2009, January 15). *Second Life® Residents logged nearly 400 million hours in 2008, growing 61% over 2007.* Retrieved September 3, 2009, from Second Life®: https://blogs.secondlife.com/community/features/blog/2009/01/15/second-life-residents-logged-nearly-400-million-hours-in-2008-growing-61-over-2007

Linden Research, Inc. (2009, September 3). *Terms of Service | Second Life®.* Retrieved September 3, 2009, from Second Life®: http://secondlife.com/corporate/tos.php

Linden Research, Inc. (2009, September 3). *Value Added Tax.* Retrieved September 3, 2009, from Second Life®: http://secondlife.com/corporate/vat.php

Linden Research, Inc. (2009, September 3). *What Is Second Life®?* Retrieved September 3, 2009, from Second Life®: http://secondlife.com/whatis/?lang=en-US

Makena Technology, Inc. (2009). *There Member Agreement.* Retrieved September 3, 2009, from There.com: http://www.there.com/tos.html

Makena Technology, Inc. (2009). *What is There?* Retrieved September 3, 2009, from There.com: http://www.prod.there.com/whatIsThere.html

Martin, J. (2008). Consuming Code: Use-Value, Exchange Value, and the Role of Virtual Goods in Second Life®. *Journal of Virtual Worlds Research*, *1*(2).

Miller, C. C., & Stone, B. (2009, November 6). *Virtual Goods Start Bringing Real Paydays.* Retrieved November 23, 2009, from The New York Times: http://www.nytimes.com/2009/11/07/technology/internet/07virtual.html

Ministry of Commerce, The People's Republic of China. (2009, June 29). *China bars use of virtual money for trading in real goods.* Retrieved September 3, 2009, from Ministry of Commerce, The People's Republic of China: http://english.mofcom.gov.cn/aarticle/newsrelease/commonnews/200906/20090606364208.html

Moran, M. (2008, October 13). *Virtual Worlds Are Going Private.* Retrieved September 3, 2009, from Internet Evolution: http://www.internetevolution.com/author.asp?section_id=698&doc_id=164951

News, B. B. C. (2006, November 20). *'Worm' attacks Second Life® world.* Retrieved September 3, 2009, from BBC News: http://news.bbc.co.uk/2/hi/technology/6164806.stm

Nino, T. (2008, April 9). *Second Life® Daily News.* Retrieved September 3, 2009, from Massively: http://www.massively.com/2008/04/09/second-life-daily-news/

Nuttall, C. (2009, January 21). *Second Life® CEO goes virtual shopping.* Retrieved September 3, 2009, from Financial Times Tech Blog: http://blogs.ft.com/techblog/2009/01/second-life-ceo-goes-virtual-goods-shopping/

12 *Of Consumers Have Purchased Virtual Goods.* (2009, July 30). Retrieved September 3, 2009, from Virtual Goods News: http://www.virtualgoodsnews.com/2009/07/12-of-consumers-have-purchased-virtual-goods.html

Olson, N. E. (2008). *Annual Report to Congress Volume 1 (Publication 2104).* United States Department of the Treasury, Internal Revenue Service. Internal Revenue Service.

Ondrejka, C. (2005, September 18). *Aviators, Moguls, Fashionistas and Barons: Economics and Ownership in Second Life®.* Retrieved September 3, 2009, from Social Science Research Network: http://ssrn.com/abstract=614663

Platoni, K. (2008, January/February). *Seeing Is Believing.* Retrieved September 3, 2009, from Stanford Magazine: http://www.stanfordalumni.org/news/magazine/2008/janfeb/features/virtual.html

Plus Eight Star. (2009, April 8). *Virtual Goods in Asia: it's even more than you think!* Retrieved September 3, 2009, from Plus Eight Star: http://www.plus8star.com/2009/04/08/virtual-goods-in-asia-its-even-more-than-you-think-25-times-usa/

ReactionGrid. (2009, September 3). *Economy.* Retrieved September 3, 2009, from ReactionGrid: http://reactiongrid.com/WorldCreation/Economy.aspx

Reed, C. (2009). Why Must You Be Mean to Me? - Crime, Punishment and Online Personality. *Queen Mary School of Law Legal Studies, 2009* (9).

Reimer, J. (2006, June 12). *Blizzard bans 30,000 World of Warcraft accounts.* Retrieved September 3, 2009, from Ars Technica: http://arstechnica.com/old/content/2006/06/7033.ars

Report: Virtual Worlds Growth to Skyrocket. (2009, June 15). Retrieved September 3, 2009, from Virtual Worlds News: http://www.virtualworldsnews.com/2009/06/report-virtual-worlds-growth-to-skyrocket-.html

Riley, D. (2007, July 25). *Second Life® Bans Gambling Following FBI Investigation.* Retrieved September 3, 2009, from TechCrunch: http://www.techcrunch.com/2007/07/25/second-life-bans-gambling-following-fbi-investigation/

Rosenberg, D. (2009, September 14). *Report: Virtual currency No. 1 digital goods purchase.* Retrieved September 14, 2009, from CNET News: http://news.cnet.com/8301-13846_3-10351799-62.html

Seiler, J. (2008, March 17). *What Can Virtual-World Economists Tell Us about Real-World Economies?* Retrieved September 3, 2009, from Scientific American: http://www.scientificamerican.com/article.cfm?id=virtual-world-economists-on-real-economies

Shang, D. (2009, February 24). *Comments, Second Life® Virtual World Expands 44% in Q2.* Retrieved September 3, 2009, from Second Life® Blogs: Features: http://www.scientificamerican.com/article.cfm?id=virtual-world-economists-on-real-economies

Siahaan, A. (2009, November 12). *Indonesian Gamers Pay Big to Play Big.* Retrieved November 23, 2009, from Jakarta Globe: http://thejakartaglobe.com/home/indonesian-gamers-pay-big-to-play-big/341257

Sipress, A. (2006, December 26). *Where Real Money Meets Virtual Reality, The Jury Is Still Out.* Retrieved September 3, 2009, from washingtonpost.com: http://www.washingtonpost.com/wp-dyn/content/article/2006/12/25/AR2006122500635.html

Smith, A. (1994). *The Wealth of Nations* (1994 Modern Library Edition ed.). (E. Cannan, Ed.) New York, New York, USA: Random House.

Stephenson, N. (1992). *Snow Crash.* New York: Bantam Spectra.

Takahashi, D. (2009, April 26). *Games and virtual world fundings reach $936.8 million in 2008.* Retrieved September 3, 2009, from VentureBeat: http://games.venturebeat.com/2009/04/26/second-revision-game-and-virtual-world-fundings-reach-935-million-in-2008/

There, Inc. (2003, March 13). *There, Inc. Developer Addendum to Member Agreement.* Retrieved September 3, 2009, from archive: http://webapps.prod.there.com/developers/developer_agreement.xml

Unknown. (2009, August 25). *Gold farming.* Retrieved September 3, 2009, from Wikipedia: http://en.wikipedia.org/wiki/Gold_farming

Unknown. (2009, September 10). *Grinding (gaming).* Retrieved September 10, 2009, from Wikipedia: http://en.wikipedia.org/wiki/Grinding_(gaming)

Unknown. (2009, September 14). *Market economy.* Retrieved September 14, 2009, from Wikipedia: http://en.wikipedia.org/wiki/Market_economy

Urban Dictionary. (2009). *gold sink.* Retrieved September 3, 2009, from Urban Dictionary: http://www.urbandictionary.com/define.php?term=gold%20sink

Virtual Worlds 2008. (2008, April 4). *Virtual Worlds 2008 - The Evolution of Games and Social Networks: Virtual Worlds Everywhere.* Retrieved November 20, 2009, from Virtual Worlds News: http://www.virtualworldsnews.com/2008/04/virtual-world-3.html

Watson, P. (2005). *Ideas: A History of Thought and Invention, from Fire to Freud.* New York: HarperCollins.

Yin-Poole, W. (2009, March 7). *Blizzard's Tom Chiltn on the future of WoW.* Retrieved September 3, 2009, from Videogamer.com: http://www.videogamer.com/news/blizzards_tom_chilton_on_the_future_of_wow.html?page=4

Zenke, M. (2008, April 2). *IMGDC: BioWare's Waltonn Talks MMO Creation Essentials.* Retrieved September 3, 2009, from Gamasutra: http://www.gamasutra.com/php-bin/news_index.php?story=18089

Zero, K. (2009, September 12). *Growth forecasts for the Virtual Worlds sector.* Retrieved September 14, 2009, from K Zero: http://www.kzero.co.uk/blog/?p=2845

Zynga. (2009, November 23). *Zynga Hits 100 Million Unique Visitors Per Month.* Retrieved November 23, 2009, from Zynga: http://blog.zynga.com/2009/11/zynga-hits-100-million-unique-visitors-per-month.html

Section 2
Human Factors, Legal and Security Issues of Virtual Worlds

Chapter 10
Legal Issues in the Virtual World and E-Commerce

Daniel S. Hoops
Walsh College, USA

ABSTRACT

Cyberspace is such an enormous concept that trying to briefly explain the "rules" for E-Commerce or "cyberlaw" is next to impossible. For an E-Commerce, it is important to understand that there are business-to-business transactions and those involving consumers. In addition to requiring a mastery of many legal specialties, E-Commerce presents legal issues in a virtual environment. Many business practices in a cyberspace are untested in the courts. New and innovative methods of competition, as well as the effects of an international playing field change the playfield constantly. The legalities of this great new frontier pose an impressive and intellectually stimulating challenge. This chapter is a survey and summary of the legal environment in the E-Commerce and the virtual world.

INTRODUCTION TO JURISDICTION IN THE VIRTUAL WORLD

Information sharing, accessibility and efficiency are the true benefits of E-Commerce. The ability to conduct due diligence, analyze a competitive market and make an informed decision in lightening speed is a hallmark of the cyber economy. What happens, however, if there is a problem with a cyber transaction? Where does a party seek redress if they have been wronged?

DOI: 10.4018/978-1-61692-808-7.ch010

Procedural law in the U.S. is an established, yet complicated body of rules that must be followed to determine what will be the proper court to bring a legal action. Once the appropriate judicial system (e.g. state or federal courts) is determined to have jurisdiction, the appropriate venue is then established through another set of well-tested rules of procedure.

How do these questions get answered in cyberspace? If you try to determine where the wrongful act occurred or a party's minimum contacts, could it not be possible that the wrongful conduct or contacts are everywhere AND nowhere? Determining where the defendant resides or conducts business can be complicated if the company does not have a "physical" presence within a particular jurisdiction. This can be problematic when dealing with companies over the Internet (Zippo Manufacturing Company, 1997).

JURISDICTION, VENUE AND CHOICE OF LAWS

The easiest way to navigate the jurisdictional procedure is to answer the following questions: where did the alleged wrongful act occur? Where does the defendant reside or conduct business? Is there another jurisdiction in which the defendant established "minimum contacts" thereby making jurisdiction appropriate there? (International Shoe Company, 1945)

Each dispute must be analyzed using the U.S. Supreme Court's standard that the non-resident defendant must (a) have had some minimum contact with the particular state, and (b) invoking that state's jurisdiction will not offend the "traditional notions of fair play" and "substantial justice".(Ibid; Heliocopteros Nacionales de Columbia, 1984). In other words, did the defendant receive some benefit from the jurisdiction, such as engaging in sales with residents of the particular jurisdiction, advertising within the jurisdiction, having residents of the jurisdiction as members to its website (Helicopteros Nacionales de Columbia).

The fact that a party has its principal place of business and servers located in another jurisdiction does not insulate that party from another state invoking its jurisdictional long-arm statute (Zippo Manufacturing Company; Lakin, 2003; Trintec Industries In, 2005).

Jurisdiction Parties' Consent

One way to avoid being subjected to another state or nation's jurisdiction is through a mandate as to what law will apply should there be a dispute related to the transaction. The "choice of laws" or "choice of venue" provision is a standard term in most contracts. In the event there is a breakdown in an on-line business relationship, next to the parties' signatures, this should be considered one of the more important covenants in any eContract. *Who* will be presiding over the dispute, *where* will the dispute be resolved, and *what* laws will be applied are critical strategies in business.

Language to the following effect should be considered in any agreement between parties in an E-Commerce transaction:

Choice of Law and Venue. This agreement has been entered into in the State of Michigan, United States of America. The validity, interpretation and legal effect of this agreement is governed by the laws of the State of Michigan applicable to contracts entered into and performed entirely within such state (without giving effect to any conflict of laws principles under the laws of the State of Michigan and regardless of the place or places of the actual execution of this agreement or the place or places of the actual performance of this agreement). The Michigan courts (state and federal), only, shall govern jurisdiction over any controversies regarding this agreement, and the parties hereto consent to and irrevocably and unconditionally agree to be subject to the exclusive jurisdiction of said courts located in Wayne County, Michigan, United States (and of the appropriate appellate courts therefrom).

Courts throughout the United States and treaty nations should honor the provisions of a valid and otherwise lawful agreement, including an agreement pre-determining the jurisdiction, venue, choice of laws, if these are terms negotiated between the parties (Hague Conference on Private International Law, 2005).

Alternate Dispute Resolution/ e-Dispute Resolution

An alternative to the traditional method of resolving commercial disputes in the judicial forum is the use of alternative dispute resolution ("ADR"). ADR are informal processes that are intended to resolve conflicts between parties without the necessity of prolonged litigation. The purpose of ADR is to offer aggrieved parties the opportunity to have an informal, impartial decision maker (e.g., an arbitrator or mediator) assist the parties in resolving their conflicts.

Although popular in various commercial settings, especially in resolving customer disputes in the financial services industry, the use of ADR has become very popular in resolving almost all forms of conflict. Mediation and negotiation are simply attempts at settling differences by involving an expert in the field where the parties disagree (such as a securities industry expert or an attorney whose specialty falls in that area).

Arbitration is the more sophisticated, formal and certain of the ADR formats, yet it remains a lot less costly than courtroom litigation. So long as the parties have agreed in advance to arbitrate their claims, courts are reluctant to overturn the decision of an arbitrator and will liberally uphold agreements that require arbitration of claims (Gilmer, 1991). Congress and most of the states have adopted some form of statutory authorization to encourage the arbitration of claims (Federal Arbitration Act, 2000).

In an effort to promote alternate dispute resolution in cyberspace, similar methodologies have come to fruition in the form of eDispute resolution or ADR on-line. Parties may mediate or arbitrate their claims through online chat rooms in which the proceedings may be decided without any in-person interaction between the parties.

Jurisdiction and Judgments - Treaties for Business/E-Commerce

In the event an agreement or dispute arises outside the United States or involves parties from different nations, it is important to be aware of what treaties may apply (Dow Jones, 2002). For most commercial disputes, the primary treaty concerns are (a) what jurisdictions or countries are available for redress, and (b) will the judgment or decision be enforceable in another nation.

The Hague Conference (Hague Conference on Private International law 1971; 2005) is the primary international law that governs the appropriate procedure to be followed in commercial or private legal disputes. For the most part, the Hague Conference on jurisdiction follows closely the U.S. standard for determining jurisdiction, e.g. traditional notions of fair play and substantial justice.

Although there are specific exceptions contained within this Conference, commercial parties can rely on the enforcement of a judgment or ruling entered by a court of a member nation. Essentially, this conference ensures comity between courts of the contracting nations (or nations that have signed this particular treaty under the Hague Conference (Ibid, 1971). Nations must provide this minimal level of confidence for non-resident players in E-Commerce or risk being excluded entirely from cyberspace.

The Hague Conference recently convened a study on adopting a recommendation for choice of law provisions in international contracts. The focus of this "non-binding" recommendation was to advance commercial transactions and arbitration between the parties to international agreements (Ibid, 2005).

Litigation in Cyberspace

If a business or person is aggrieved by a comment posted on an Internet message board, or through the unauthorized disclosure of confidential business information, somebody must react. In general, damage to a business reputation caused by a defamatory remark, or a leaked memorandum can be dire. Imagine the damage that could result if a wrongful act (or comment) is broadcast through the Internet?

How do you respond instantaneously? You should know that between every heartbeat information is being transmitted, forwarded, screenshot, printed, downloaded and scanned throughout the world thousands of times. What if you do not know the identity of the speaker or the source of the leak? How do you stop the information from being spread? What if the source is a hacker from the Philippines? Or Romania? Maybe the rumor was started by a in a chatroom by a competitor in Ohio? Mexico?

The first step, from a non-legal standpoint, is to "stop the bleeding". Somehow a public relations campaign must be commenced. The second step, from a legal standpoint, is to identify the culprit. The question is *how*?

There is a developing body of law, as well as support services, related to the discovery and prosecution of anonymous wrongdoers on the Internet. Commencing a legal action against John Doe or other "unknowns" is not unique to cyberlaw and has been used by companies long before the Internet's debut. By invoking the legal process, companies and individuals are able to (a) seek an injunction against the publication or broadcast trade secrets or other embarrassing information, and (b) obtain the name and identity of an alleged wrongdoer from the on-line host (Columbia Insurance Company 1999). Injunctive relief and the subpoena process can only be used if there is a lawsuit pending in a judicial forum.

All companies should be prepared for the possibility that a disgruntled employee, aggrieved competitor or cyberterrorist decides to act maliciously through cyberspace. The consequences of not being prepared for a cyberattack might be devastating.

PROTECTING INTELLECTUAL PROPERTY IN E-COMMERCE

Intellectual properties are the true essence of E-Commerce. They are inchoate rights or intangible assets whose underlying value is represented not by a touchable object, but by what that asset represents. For example, a trademark protects the integrity of a business logo or slogan. The slogan is the underlying asset, however, the trademark (and its registration) is the property right.

Intangible or intellectual property rights are various depending upon the property right and the underlying asset. They can include formal and registered properties such as trademarks, copyrights and patents, as well as informal or elusive properties such as trade and business secrets, company know-how and goodwill. While intellectual property rights represent something of value, these properties must all be dealt with under a separate set of rules due to the underlying asset's unique qualities. How these properties are infringed and exploited is not the same, as well as the resulting damages.

Registered Intellectual Properties

Copyrights

A copyright is a member of the protected intellectual properties that has qualities that are quite different from patents and trademarks in E-Commerce. For this reason, the U.S. and the international community (Madrid Agreement, 1891). offer broad protection for registration and enforcement of infringement actions.

A common misunderstanding of copyrights is that registration of the property is a requirement for enforcement of an owner's rights. This is not true under U.S. law. Although registration is absolutely recommended for any property that is eligible, protection of the underlying rights does not require registration. Registration simply provides notice to the world that the underlying holder (be it a copyright or trademark) claims ownership of the underlying property. Without registration, proving infringement of the property requires an additional, yet difficult, proceeding to prove that owner has priority rights in the property. Registration of an intellectual property (with the Library of Congress or U.S. Patent and Trademark Office) creates a presumption in favor of the owner that it has a priority right and interest in the underlying property.

Copyright infringements are some of the most litigated intellectual property matters in Cyberspace. With the advancement of digital technologies (and the advent of music sharing websites), there has been more legal wrangling over the rights under copyright than any other intellectual property (A&M Records, 2002). Congress reacted to the developments in digital technology by enacting the Digital Millennium Copyright Act ("DMCA") (17 U.S.C.S §501). In contradiction to the traditional notions of "fair use" of copyrights, e.g. where a person could display a copyrighted work so long as it was not for commercial purposes, the DMCA prohibits the unauthorized use, display or broadcast of any copyrighted works in a digital format due to the fact that the digital technology may allow another to copy, download or otherwise retain the work without compensation to the copyright owner (17 U.S.C.S. §512)[1].

For the hosts of websites, the DMCA provides a safe haven for infringing displays of copyrighted works if the host (a) takes reasonable steps to remove the infringed work, and (b) acts as a "pass-thru" for the materials displayed (17 U.S.C.S §512a)[2].

Prior to the use, display or broadcast of any image, music, video, literary work or similar materials in cyberspace, it is recommended that (a) the source of the materials be determined, and (b) if the owner has not conveyed authorization, select other materials to convey the message. Simple due diligence to determine the works creator will save the embarrassment of infringing upon another's copyright and the financial consequences of an infringement lawsuit.

Trademarks

If a company uses a particular mark to advertise or market its goods and services, protecting this unique mark is absolutely imperative. Why invest time, money and effort into the development of a mark and not obtain the necessary protection of the mark from the later exploitation (or degradation) of the brand? In addition to obtaining U.S. protection in the form of registration of trade and service marks, the Madrid Convention of 1891 offers similar protection on an international level.

Trademarks can be abused in E-Commerce in three ways: a parody of the mark, an unauthorized use of the mark, and a disparagement of the mark. Parodies are usually found in many humorous, often offensive Internet websites. While the intent of the user is usually a folly, the fact remains that the registered owner has not allowed it; hence the parodied use erodes the mark.

Trademark parodies (as well as parody of copyrights) are usually protected under the First Amendment of the U.S. Constitution (LL Bean Inc, 1987; Jordache, 1987; Mutual of Omaha 1987).

Unauthorized use of a mark in a commercial setting often involves someone acting as the registered owner of the mark to exploit their own goods or services as having the same quality as those under which the mark is registered. These uses are clearly subject to an infringement action by the registered owner under theories of likelihood of confusion, fraud and misrepresentation (Avery Dennison coro, 1998).

Domain names have become so closely connected to a company's registered trademark that federal law protects domain names in almost the same manner as a registered trademark (18 U.S.C.S §2252b). Cybersquatting is also considered form of piracy of a trademark owner's mark by registering a web address with the registered owner's mark (15 U.S.C.S. §1125).

Finally, and most relevant to E-Commerce, are the disparagement of the registered mark. Most often found as negative criticism in blogs, comments to blogs or chat room postings, derogatory remarks about the quality of goods or services of the registered owner can have catastrophic consequences. In the event a registered trademark owner is the subject of false commentary, with the intent to mislead the buying public, a defamation action may be appropriate (Barret, 2006).

Patents

Patents are protected under the U.S. and international registration procedures. Anyone seeking to exploit or use a patent-protected process is subject to an infringement action by the owner of the patent. Unauthorized patent uses in E-Commerce usually involve the manufacture and sale of a "protected" process or invention through the Internet. These uses must cease due to the ownership rights a patent holder has in their protected process.

Trade Secrets, Business Methods and Goodwill

Trade secrets are intellectual properties that are not "copyrightable" and fall outside the definition of "patent" for purposes of registration. While these properties may be unique, they have not undergone the expensive process and scrutiny required for a registered patent. Nevertheless, they are valuable assets and the unauthorized exploitation or abuse will cause injury to the owner.

In the event an infringement or "unauthorized use" of their property is asserted, the property owner must seek protection of the courts. However, the owner must prove that there is (a) an actual property right being infringed, (b) the property right belongs to the owner and should be protected, and (c) what the damages are resulting from that unauthorized infringement.

Protecting trade secrets should be of a more paramount concern than protecting a registered patent by the nature of the underlying property (secret v. public) due to the lack of specific intellectual property laws protecting trade secrets.

Non-Disclosure, Covenant not to Compete and Ownership of Intellectual Property

Often a company will discover its proprietary and confidential property has been leaked through employee channels or by other trusted agents. Disgruntled and former employees seeking to feed a grudge can injure or cause great harm to a company within seconds on the Internet (Rush and Pagalia, 2001).

It is absolutely imperative that a company (a) restricts the use of confidential information such as trade secrets, (b) maintains a list of all employees, contractors, agents and other personnel that have access to its intellectual properties, and (c) requires that any person that may come into contact with confidential company secrets sign an agreement setting forth their understanding related to the use, development and disclosure of the company's property. The following may be of assistance in developing an agreement between an employee and company.

Intellectual Property Rights. All copyright, trademark and/or other intellectual property rights of any kind developed during the term and relating to or useful in the Company's business and/or to Employee's duties ("Works") shall be deemed a "work for hire" and shall be and remain the sole and exclusive property of the Company, and Employee shall, to the extent deemed necessary or desirable by the Company, cooperate and assist the Company in perfecting, filing and recording any such rights. To the extent that any Works are not deemed "work for hire", Employee hereby assigns all of the Employee's rights in such Works to the Company and waives any and all moral rights the Employee may have in such Works. Employee's obligations under this Section shall survive the expiration or termination of this Agreement.

Confidentiality. During Employee's employment with the Company, Employee will receive information and training which are proprietary to the Company, including without limitation customer lists, pricing, programming techniques, financial information, sales strategies and methods and promotional programs and techniques. Employee agrees that all such information is the sole and exclusive property of the Company, and that Employee will safeguard all such information and maintain it as secret and confidential and Employee further agrees that Employee will not at any time disclose such information to any third party without the express prior written consent of the General Manager of the Company. Employee's obligations under this Section shall survive the expiration or termination of this Agreement.

In addition to the internal and technical safeguards of company secrets, it is also important to consider a post-disclosure drill. For example, if materials are released on the Internet, is the company prepared to seek immediate relief in a court of equitable jurisdiction? Was the release of the materials a violation of any criminal statutes? Was anyone's private information disclosed? Being prepared in advance will minimize the damage that may result.

International Intellectual Property Rights

Intellectual property rights have historically been given respect and protection throughout the world through the World Intellectual Property Organization ("WIPO") (Berne Convention, 1886; Universal Copyright Convention, 1952; Madrid Agreement, 1891; Patent Cooperation Treaty, 1970). As computer technology advanced, as well as the development of the Internet, worldwide attention was given to guard against piracy of intellectual property owners. In 2002, the WIPO Copyright Treaty was approved to integrate recent developments in digital technology, similar to the DMCA, into a global treaty.

In addition to the treaties executed under the WIPO, the International Intellectual Property Alliance is a private sector consortium representing U.S.-based industries interested in the protection of copyrights throughout the world. This organization has worked on behalf of the U.S. government in seeking global participation in intellectual property treaties. This organization has been at the forefront of criminalizing copyright piracy throughout the world.

COMMERCIAL TRANSACTIONS IN A VIRTUAL WORLD

Understanding the methods of doing business in a virtual world is the key in determining how the legal issues in cyberspace should be resolved. Parties exchange money, goods, services and property amongst themselves, usually in complete anonymity. To comprehend how the law may apply to a commercial transaction in the E-Commerce, a basic understanding of traditional commercial law is required as well as an understanding of the methodologies of E-Commerce.

The first issue that must be addressed is whether a commercial transaction is a business-to-business ("B2B") or business-to-consumer transaction. B2B transactions are purely commercial. The level of sophistication in the subject matter between B2B parties is presumed to be higher than the parties in a business to consumer matter. The law will attempt to level the playing field for consumers based on the fact that they are not experts in whatever industry the business participates. The law, however, can be relaxed when the participants are both businesses who do not need as much protection as someone without their level of expertise. These principals are almost the same as in traditional commercial and consumer protection law.

The next issue is to determine the nexus between the parties to the transaction. Are the participants engaged in a one-on-one transaction? Was it reasonable for one party to rely on the representations of the other party? This "closeness" between the parties is important in determining whether or not detrimental reliance by one party upon the other would be considered reasonable or not. In addition, the law does not place a standard of absolute perfection on anyone, business or consumer, so cyberlaw should be no different.

Finally, it is important to realize that some consumers are simply reckless or motivated by profit when it comes to a dispute with an eBusiness. This is the hallmark of the "Good Samaritan" provision in the Communications Decency Act of 1996 (47 U.S.C.S. § 230). In essence, this provision was enacted to provide (a) personal responsibility for the content posted by individual users of the Internet, and (b) immunity to the hosts of user-generated content when, as a result of the user's own carelessness, he or she suffers some type of injury (Green, 2003, Carafano, 2003; Baetzel, 2003; Ben Ezra, et al, 2000; Zeran, 1997).

Online Contracts

One of the efficiencies in an E-Commerce is this paperless world created by it. Contracts are used in Cyberspace for retail transactions, day-trading, banking, leisure and entertainment. An online agreement can be formed through an electronic signature or notarization, a simple click of a button, and by email correspondence or confirmation between parties.

The Electronic Signatures in Global and National Commerce Act ("E-Sign") (15 U.S.C.S. §7001) and the Uniform Electronic Transactions Act ("UETA") (National Conference of Commissioners) govern the validity of electronic records and signatures related to on-line transactions. Although the federal E-Sign statute has preempted much of the state law governing electronic contracting, it does provide that the UETA will govern transactions in those states that have adopted the UETA. As of this publication, the UETA has been adopted by forty-seven (47) states with New York, Illinois and Washington being the hold-outs. Not all commercial transactions are covered by E-Sign and UETA, including many transactions under the Uniform Commercial Code.[3]

In essence, E-Sign and UETA are legislative attempts to uphold transactions in E-Commerce where traditional contract law fails due to the paperless nature of E-Commerce. For the most part, E-Sign and UETA mandate that a record or signature will not be denied their legal effect or enforceability (a) due to the fact that it is in an electronic form or was formed electronically, (b) if a law requires that the record be in writing, or (c) if a law requires a signature, an electronic signature will be sufficient.

So long as the parties agree to conduct an electronic transaction in the U.S., E-Sign and UETA will be applicable. Agreements entered into by parties through a series of "mouse clicks" on webpages ('click-wrap' agreements) are binding upon both parties (Mudd-Lyman Sales & Service Corp, 2002; Caspi, 1999). A sent email under the UETA is the equivalent of the traditional "mailbox rule".

Presently, the United Nations Commission on International Trade Law has presented a model law regarding electronic signatures for adoption by the member nations to assist E-Commerce.

Validity of the Contract

One of the risks of contracting in E-Commerce is whether or not the party on the other end of a transaction *is* who he, she or it purports to be. If an electronic signature is a satisfactory method of "signing" an agreement, how does a party know that the individual who sent the email-acceptance know that this person is the purported signatory?

Under E-Sign, there is no provision defines *what* is a signature or whether an electronic signature can be attributed to someone. Therefore, any dispute related to an electronic signature must be resolved by reference to the UETA version adopted by the state in which the contract is being interpreted. The problem that can arise, however, is that not every state's version of UETA is identical and what one state may deem an appropriate electronic signature, another state may not.

Age Verification and Capacity

A basic principal under contract law is that an individual must have capacity to be bound by an agreement. Infancy, mental illness and intoxication may be considered factors in determining that an agreement is void due to the contracting party's lack of capacity.

Applying these traditional contract rules to E-Commerce, it is possible to see that the integrity of some agreements could be at risk. Is there really a method for determining that a person executing a contract suffers from dementia? That a minor is the party to a 'click' agreement?

In overturning the Communications Decency Act, the U.S. Supreme Court analyzed the different methods a website could use to verify a user's age. Although a credit card or "adult PIN" may provide some level of verification, the Court found that there was no evidence that any system could adequately screen out juveniles (Reno, 1997; PSINet, 2004). Is it possible now to enforce all contracts in E-Commerce against minors because they cannot be adequately screened? Or will cyberlaw allow minors to vitiate all on-line contracts due to their incapacity to contract as infants? (Foss, 2007) This is part of the direction cyberlaw will nevertheless need to address.

Terms of Use

Most website hosts provide terms and conditions for visitors that use their sites. For sites that use a page link rather than a 'click wrap' agreement, enforcing an agreement that does not require an actual "acceptance" of the terms of use can be problematic. The simple inclusion of an "accept", "submit", "I read" or "ok" button for users to click should be the most elementary function of any website.

Including a choice of law, jurisdiction and venue in a website's terms and conditions can be enforced against a party who has "clicked" or accepted the agreement (Decker, 1999).

Liability Disclaimers, Reservation of Rights and Indemnity

A standard provision in many agreements for the sale of goods is the limitation of liabilities or warranties on the part of the seller. Many such warranties take the form of an "as is" or "final sale" clause within a website's terms and conditions or on-line purchase order. So long as the parties have agreed to the limitation of liability for defects and the agreement term is not considered unconscionable, courts will be reluctant to upset the intent of the contract (M.A. Mortenson Co, Inc, 1999).

Some websites that charge a membership fee for users to access their site for the purpose of on-line dating or social networking may include a waiver of liability as a standard term. These waivers simply provide that the site does not guarantee or verify the statements (such as the age provided by other members) or that users of their site assumed all risk and responsibility for relying on the statements of other users of their website (Doe, 2008).

Another common term used by websites is the owner's right to remove content listed or posted by users, the right to deny a user access, or the right to discontinue the service for any reason. This reservation of rights is a critical liability protection to minimize any potential litigation arising from an alleged copyright infringement or defamatory statement being posted.

In the event a website owner seeks indemnity from another party in a lawsuit, the courts will look to state law to determine if the user of the website explicitly agreed to indemnify the owner for damages under the on-line agreement. If the website owner is savy, the choice of law provision contained within its terms and conditions would most likely include a venue or state with a favorable indemnity law. Indemnity provisions must be conspicuously and clearly stated within the terms of use or purchase order (General Conference of Seventh-Day Adventists, 1995).

Tax Issues in Cyberspace

The threat of a "tax on the Internet" was quickly dispelled in the United States with the enactment of the Internet Tax Freedom Act (the "ITFA") (11 U.S.C.S. §1101). Although the ITFA does not prohibit the taxation of commercial transactions conducted on the Internet, its principal purpose was to provide guidance for the numerous state and local taxing authorities that, conceivably, could tax Internet transactions.[4] The confusion created by the, then-existing, tax regimes for transactions involving the Internet was perceived by many in Congress to have a chilling effect on E-Commerce.

Cyberspace, unfortunately, does not provide a safe-haven from taxes. The difficulty for all taxing authorities is in determining (a) the foundation of a taxable transaction, (b) the characterization and source of any income subject to taxation, and (c) whether intangible goods (such as digital downloads) should be taxed differently than traditional tangible goods. Due to these complex factors and the revenue needs of taxing jurisdictions, it is absolutely imperative for any eBusiness to understand the tax consequences for transactions it conducts with parties in other states and countries.

Congress was not alone in its confusion in *how* or *what* should be taxed in an E-Commerce. Any eBusiness that conducts business on a multinational basis should be certain of the most current tax treaties between those nations involved their business. As diverse as the global nations are culturally, their interpretation and characterization of taxable transactions can be as diverse.[5]

Sales and Use Tax

Sales taxes are generally imposed upon transactions at the point of sale. Use taxes are imposed on the location of the property purchased. This, however, is typically the rule in ordinary commercial transactions involving tangible personal property. The complication in applying sales and use taxes in E-Commerce is due to the character of many eProducts; they are not always tangible property.

Much of the law related to state sales and use taxes developed from mail-order and direct marketing sales companies. Merchants fought the imposition of sales and use taxes by asserting that these taxes violated the due process and commerce clauses of the U.S. Constitution. In resolving the issue, the U.S. Supreme Court determined that an out-of-state merchant must assess or collect a tax on commercial sales transactions, if it has a "substantial nexus" to that state (Scripto, 1960; National Bella Hess, 1967; Quill, 1992). In other words, the state must have jurisdiction over this merchant before it can assess any type of tax under the U.S. Constitution.

This "tax jurisdiction" or nexus is determined by a merchant's physical presence within the state, such as operating a physical store or warehouse, or by enlisting sales representatives within the state. The types of merchant activities that can be considered "presence within a state" may include: (a) renting an office, store or warehouse within the state, (b) hosting trade shows, (c) maintaining a server is in the state, (d), working with a server within the state, (e) keeping inventory or storage, (f), licensing software to individual residents of the state, and (g) hiring or using agents, contractors or related retail outlets within the state (Borders, 2007).

The difficulty with applying sales and use taxes in E-Commerce are a result of the transactions involved; eProducts, such as downloadable music, games, movies, images and software. If the eProducts were merely "view-only" or "listen-only" products, it would appear to be more of a license than an actual use because it is temporary. If the eProduct is purchased from a virtual store, the questions concerning where the tax on that eProduct should be assessed are numerous: where the physical location of the virtual store exists? Where the server of the virtual store is located? Where the physical location of the server holding the eProduct sits? Where the risk of loss occurs?

If a merchant engages in on-line sales transactions of tangible personal property, it should be mindful of the state sales and use taxes applicable in every jurisdiction where sales are conducted. The law continues to develop in the sales and use tax arena. Until these issues are resolved, merchants in E-Commerce should be prepared to collect any such taxes and file a return with the respective jurisdiction (Ibid).

Value-Added Tax ("VAT")

The VAT is a tax applied to the market value or increase in a good at each step of a manufacturing or distribution process. Upon the ultimate sale or disposition of a good, presumably to a consumer, the cost of the good includes the VAT added during each step. Often referred to as a consumption tax, the VAT is very similar to a sales tax in that it is assessed against useable goods.

The VAT is principally used in the European Union and is often believed to be a "fairer" method of taxation. By assessing a tax at each stage of the manufacturing process, it increases the number of taxpayers that, in turn, reduces the number of possible tax evaders.

The same problems that exist with the sales and use taxation for eProducts are also coming to light with the VAT. Until the tax laws are modified to mesh with E-Commerce, it is advisable to treat eProducts as standard tangible goods for purposes of transacting business in those jurisdictions that levy a VAT.

U.S. Income Tax

Under U.S. law, income subject to tax includes any accession to wealth from whatever source derived, unless specifically excluded (26 U.S.C.S §61)[6]. Transactions that involve the sale, exchange or transfer of property can result in gains and losses that may be recognized in calculating gross income (26 U.S.C.S. §1222).

An issue that becomes relevant in E-Commerce is whether or not a transaction involves the sale of an asset or license. The treatment of the transaction can determine whether or not the asset will be taxed as a capital or ordinary asset, whether or not the property may be depreciated as a trade or business asset (26 U.S.C.S. §168)[7], and if the property is even subject to taxation if the asset is used outside the U.S.

Although intangible assets are not eligible for the favorable cost-recovery available to depreciable tangible personal property, an eBusiness may amortize the cost of certain intangibles over a fifteen (15) year period (26 U.S.C.S. §197)[8]. To be eligible for amortization, the business must acquire and hold the intangible assets for their trade or business. The types of intangible assets that may be amortized include goodwill, operating systems, patents, copyrights, formulas, know-how, formats, licenses, covenants not to compete, franchises trademarks and tradenames.

An important consideration for eBusiness relates to the deductions allowable for certain research, development and other experimental expenditures (26 U.S.C.S. §174)[9]. Although amortizing some costs incurred for research and development may be required over a sixty (60) month period, some start-up companies may be eligible for an immediate deduction under U.S. law for costs included software development (Rev. Proc, 1969; Rev. Proc, 1997).

There are numerous circumstances where the U.S. system of taxation has jurisdiction over foreign business and those persons may be subject to U.S. income tax (keep as footnotes).[10] For example, non-U.S. citizens can be subject to taxation for compensation received for personal services performed within the U.S. (26 U.S.C.S. §861a)[11]. If there is a sale of inventory within the U.S. and that inventory had been purchased outside the U.S., any gains, profits or income generated from those transactions may also be subject to taxation (26 U.S.C.S. §862a)[12]. Royalty and rent payments made for property located within the U.S. or for the right to use property within the U.S., such as for patents, copyrights, goodwill, trade secrets and franchises are considered income that is subject to U.S. income tax (26 U.S.C.S. §861a).

To many, the U.S. income tax may appear to be a broad-based levy for purposes of collecting revenue everywhere, including cyberspace. As is evident with the ITFA, U.S. tax laws are also used to create policy and incentives for industry and E-Commerce. Until the concept of cyberspace and E-Commerce is more fully understood, the federal income tax laws will most likely adapt with that understanding.

State Income Taxes

One of the hallmarks of a state's ability to impose an income tax is that the tax must be limited to those persons and properties within the state's jurisdiction (Miller Bros. Co, 1954). The standard in determining whether or not a state can assess an income tax is similar to the nexus standard allowing a state to claim jurisdiction for sales and use taxes. However, a state is limited in imposing income taxes on a business if (a) the only activity of the business is the solicitation of orders by sales representatives, (b) the sales orders are sent out of state for approval, and (c) the sales orders are fulfilled by delivery outside the state (15 U.S.C.S. §381; Wisconsin Department of Revenue, 1992).

For a state to levy an income tax on any interstate business, it must apportion that income tax based in proportion to the amount of benefit the taxpayer achieved by conducting business within that state. The controversy that continues to loom and may be resolved by Congress and the U.S. Supreme Court is how much weight a state may give to the factors it uses to determine apportionment. The apportionment factors are: the percentage of sales achieved, the amount of tangible property located within the state and the company's payroll within the state. By weighing heavily on sales figures, clearly E-Commerce is at a disadvantage.

Customs Duties

Unfortunately for most business, the taxing avarice of government is not limited to the United States. Being mindful of the fact that eBusiness should be more concerned about practical reasons for making business decisions rather than taxation issues, the Organization of Economic Cooperation and Development ("OECD") sought to develop a series of principles for its member countries (keep as footnote). The OECD Model Tax Conference is intended to adopt a series of tax treaties to address the taxation concerns of both government and business.

In its attempt to craft sound tax policy for the global and electronic economies, the OECD has also developed several initiatives to expand the number of member countries.

Protecting Consumers and Privacy

The name "information superhighway" is an appropriate title for Internet considering the amount of information that is gathered, used and processed. There are numerous ways information is collected on-line, including information used to register for a website, information provided by users for purposes of interacting with a website (such as with a social network), information collected through cookies, information through clickstreaming, and information gathered through web beacons or other pixel tags.

Although much of the information gathered may appear to be mundane, understanding an anonymous web browser's trends or likes are a valuable resource for database marketing and advertising purposes. By targeting individuals web browsing habits, user preferences and interests, a better demographic and potential audience is created.

Presently, the U.S. Congress has not approved a statute dealing with the collection and use of generic information from the Internet. California's Online Privacy Protection Act (Cal. Bus.

& Prof. Code §§22,575-22579) mandates that all websites or on-line services that collect identifiable information about users provide a clear statement concerning the information collected and its privacy policy. While this may be a state law, websites must comply with these mandates due to the fact that web access has no borders and California residents would clearly be affected.

Several other states have passed legislation requiring that privacy notices be posted on websites, including two states that deem a misleading statement in an on-line privacy policy shall be deemed a deceptive business practice (Neb. Rev. Stat §87-302a; 18 pa Cons. Stat. §4107).

The Federal Trade Commission ("FTC") has principal authority to enforce the existing privacy statutes as they pertain to deceptive trade practices (15 U.S.C.S. §45a) and identifiable information from the financial services industry (15 U.S.C.S. §6801). The Department Health and Human Services ("HHS") has principal authority to protect private health and medical information that is identifiable (Health Insurance Portability and Accountability Act).

Both the FTC and HHS have approved security rules regulating the storage, disposal and dissemination of any private information. As the risk of identify theft has increased due to relaxed safekeeping of private information, the FTC has made some attempts at enforcing rules directing how companies use private consumer credit information.

CRIMINAL AND SECURITY ISSUES

With the tremendous benefits and efficiencies E-Commerce brings, sadly it brings with it the negative element of cybercrime. There are numerous types of computer crimes ranging from cyberterrorism, corporate espionage, on-line robbery, fraud, piracy and sex crimes. As a result of the increase in and serious consequences of Internet crime, not only were security and privacy concerns increased in the private sector, legislative bodies and law enforcement reacted as well.

All crimes have the following elements: an actor, an action, a victim and a rule that penalizes the actor for the prohibited action. There is no such thing as a "victimless crime". Whether the crime is a person-to-person crime or a cybercrime, these elements are present. The key to cybercrime is trying to identify the actor, the action and the victim because many times the crime appears to be anonymous and victimless due to the nature of cyberspace.

Prosecuting cybercrime requires that law enforcement pursue evidence against the actor through more sophisticated techniques. Yet, surveillance and investigations must comply with the rights prescribed in the U.S. Constitution (especially the 4th Amendment concerning searches and seizures and the 5th Amendment due process of law protections). In addition, a defendant can only be convicted if a trier-of-fact finds that the actor committed the crime beyond all reasonable doubt. Trying to prove a high-tech crime or the extent of the injuries inflicted or the identity of the victims can be extremely difficult and challenging.

Cyber-Terrorism and Corporate Espionage

Whether through a virus or the actions of a hacker, cyber terrorism is simply the act of inflicting as much damage as the cyber terrorist can inflict with a complete and total disregard of the intended targets. The enormous amount of a damage a hacker or virus can cause is incredible. National airports have been shuttered, the U.S. Department of Defense has been hacked, and numerous other major institutions have had their networks infiltrated. These are extremely serious crimes, so the criminal statute is very broad.

The Computer Fraud and Abuse Act (18 U.S.C.S. §1030) is the principal computer crimes law in the U.S. This act criminalizes the actions of a person who "knowingly accesses a computer without authorization" and either "obtains information" or "recklessly causes damage" to the computer or network (18 U.S.C.S. §1030a).

Under the Computer Fraud and Abuse Act, the mere access to an unauthorized computer is a crime, which can include an employee who that has exceeded his or her access privileges. The presumption being that any damage to a computer or network, whether intentionally or negligently, is a serious matter.

The Electronic Communications Privacy Act criminalizes the interception or disclosure of electronic communications without the permission or authority of the owner (18 U.S.C.S. §2510). The original intent of the Electronic Communications Privacy Act was to prevent hackers from obtaining stored "electronic communications" which could include email and trade secrets.

The Economic Espionage Act is a federal statute that provides both criminal and civil penalties for persons that have misappropriated or stolen trade secrets (18 U.S.C.S. §1831). In addition to prosecuting "economic espionage", the Economic Espionage Act may be used against former employees and business competitors for stealing trade secrets (18 U.S.C.S. §1832).

A major misconception about cyber crime is that the crime starts and stops with the initial wrongful act, e.g. the unauthorized access and copying of a file without permission. This is absolutely false. The Economic Espionage Act applies to anyone who transmits, receives or possesses stolen trade secrets (18 U.S.C.S. v1832a). Hence, if a person duplicates, downloads, uploads, alters, destroys, transmits, delivers, sends, mails, communicates or otherwise conveys a trade secret, that person has committed a cybercrime.

Theft, Piracy and Fraud

Pursuant to the Computer Fraud and Access Act, fraud and theft may be alleged if an individual accessed a computer without authorization with the intent to achieve financial gain (18 U.S.C.S. §1030c). One of the requirements of prosecution for theft, piracy or fraud under the Computer Fraud and Access Act is criminal's receipt of something of value for his or her wrongful actions. This would be an essential reason for criminalizing an unauthorized access rather than criminalizing someone who merely viewed information (United States, 1995).

The most financially harmful of all the cyber crimes is the piracy of copyrighted material. Whether the piracy involves music, games, movies, or computer software, the lost revenue to copyright owners is enormous. The U.S. Copyright Act provides that criminal prosecution may be sought if the alleged criminal infringed upon the protected property "for commercial advantage" or "private financial gain" (17 U.S.C.S. §506a).

The criminal fraud statutes criminalize the actions of someone engaged in a misrepresentation or misstatement where the victim believes or relies on for the purpose of receiving the victim's money or property. Most Internet fraud falls within the existing mail fraud and wire fraud statutes because the computer or technology is used as a device to carryout that crime (United States, 1995).

In addition, the transportation of any property, securities or money that is known to have been obtained fraudulently may be prosecuted under the National Stolen Property Act (18 U.S.C.S. §2314). This statute may very well be used as a "catch-all" provision where a computer or network is used as a means to distribute stolen property.

On-Line Predators

One of the real downsides to the Internet is the ease with which many predators now roam. The news is filled daily with law enforcement sting-operations to snare Internet predators and pedophiles. In addition, cyberstalkers have become an issue for many where an actor begins to "stalk" their victim on-line. While many of these crimes appear unique to the Internet, the Internet is merely a new outlet used by these criminals to carry out their same unwanted and criminal advances. With the amount of personal information Internet users upload to social networks, predators have little work to do in identifying potential victims.

With regard to protecting children from content on the Internet and from predators, there are two issues that need to be addressed. The first relates to the use of traditional criminal law to protect children. Prohibiting sexual contact with a minor is still relevant and enforceable against anyone, including Internet pedophiles. Whether the criminal actor has attempted to contact the child, is caught in a sting, or attempts to traffic in pornographic materials with a minor (Child Pornography and Prevention Act), the mere attempt or intent is sufficient to warrant prosecution.

The second issue for legislatures has been to protect minors from accessing particular sites on the Internet for fear that their safety could be jeopardized. There have been two attempts by Congress to pass criminal legislation aimed at protecting children from "on-line predators". Both bites at the apple, however, have been found to be too broad and violated the 1st and 5th Amendments of the U.S. Constitution, most recently in 2008 when the Child On-Line Protection Act (Ibid) was held to be unconstitutional (American Civil Liberties Union, 2008; Reno, 1997).

Under the Communications Decency Act of 1996 (47 U.S.C.S. §230c1), websites that merely host user-generated content are not liable for failing to screen against children from accessing social networks (Doe, 2008). In addition, this law places the burden on the user of the social networks and the content posted by each user being done so at their own risk.

As a result, the use of more traditional criminal law focused at prosecuting the criminal element is the current state of the law. Imposing hefty burdens upon the non-criminal element to safeguard children and restricting the accessibility to the non-criminal element who are also negatively affected by the legislative intent, is not favored by the U.S. courts.

International Crimes

In 2001, the Council of Europe adopted the first international treaty to combat cybercrime. The Convention on Cybercrime provides a series of treaties to combat crimes committed through the Internet and other computer networks that may include copyright infringement, computer-related fraud, child pornography and violations of network security (Convention on Cybercrime, 2001).

REFERENCES

A&M Records v. Napster, 284 F.3d 1091 (9thCir. 2002).

American Civil Liberties Union v. Mukasey, 534 F.3d 181 (3rdCir. 2008).

Avery Dennison Corp. v. Sumpton, 999 F.Supp. 1337 (C.D.Cal. 1998).

Barrett v. Rosenthal, 146 P.3d 510 (Cal. 2006).[13]

Batzel v. Smith, 333 F.3d 1018 (9thCir. 2003)

Ben Ezra, Weinstein, & Co. v. America Online Inc., 206 F.3d 980 (10thCir. 2000)

Borders Online, LLC v. State Board of Equalization, 29 Cal.Rptr.3d 176 (2007)

Cal. Bus. & Prof. Code §§22,575–22,579

Carafano v. Metrosplash.com, Inc., 339 F.3d 1119 (9th Cir. 2003)

Caspi v. Microsoft Network, LLC, 323 N.J. Super 118 (1999).

Child Pornography Prevention Act, 18 U.S.C.S. §2241, et seq.

Columbia Insurance Co. v. Seescandy.com, 185 F.R.D. 573 (N.D. Cal. 1999)[14] (America Online, Inc. v. Anonymous Publicly Traded Co., 542 S.E.2d 377 (Va. 2001)

Berne Convention. (1886). Convention.

ConventionUniversal Copyright (1952).

Convention on Cybercrime, CETS No. 185 (2001 Budapest)

Copyrights: Berne Convention (1886)

Decker v. Circus Circus Hotel, 49 F.Supp.2d 743 (D.N.J. 1999)[15]

Doe v. MySpace, Inc., 528 F.3d 413 (5th Cir. 2008).

Doe v. Sexsearch.com, 551 F.3d 412 (6th Cir. 2008).[16]

Dow Jones & Company Inc. v Gutnick, HCA 56 (2002)[17]

Federal Arbitration Act, 9 USCS §1, et seq.

Foss v. Circuit City Stores, Inc., 477 F.Supp.2d 230 (D.Me. 2007)[18] General Conference of Seventh-Day Adventists v. Aon Reinsurance Agency, Inc., 860 F.Supp. 983 (S.D.N.Y.1994), aff'd 50 F.3d 2 (1995).

Gilmer v. Interstate/Johnson Lane Corp., 500 U.S. 20 (1991).

Green v. America Online (AOL), 318 F.3d 465 (3rd Cir. 2003)

Hague Conference on Private International Law, Convention 16 and Supplementary Protocol 17 (1971)

Hague Conference on Private International Law, Convention 37 (2005).

Health Insurance Portability and Accountability Act, Public Law 104-191

Helicopteros Nacionales de Colombia, S.A. v. Hall, 466 U.S. 408 (1984).[19]

International Shoe Company v. State of Washington, 326 U.S. 310 (1945).

Jordache v. Hogg Wyld, Ltd., 828 F.2d 1482 (10th Cir. 1987)

Lakin v. Prudential Securities, Inc., 348 F.3d 704 (8thCir. 2003)

L.L. Bean Inc. v. Drake Publishers Inc., 811 F.2d 26 (1st Cir.), appeal dismissed, 107 S.Ct. 3254 (1987)

Madrid Agreement (1891).

M.A. Mortenson Co., Inc. v. Timberline Software Corp., 970 P.2d 803 (Wash.App. 1999).

Miller Bros. Co. v. State of Maryland, 347 U.S. 340 (1954).

MuddLyman Sales & Service Corp. v. United Parcel Service, Inc., 236 F.

Mutual of Omaha Insurance Co. v. Novak, 836 F.2d 397 (8th Cir.1987).

National Bellas Hess, Inc. v. Dept. of Revenue of the State of Illinois, 386 U.S. 753 (1967)

National Conference of Commissioners on Uniform State Laws, Revised Uniform Arbitration Act (2000).

Neb.Rev.Stat.§87-302(a)(14); 18 Pa.Cons. Stat.§4107(a)(10).

Patents: Patent Cooperation Treaty (1970).

PSINet, Inc. v. Chapman, 362 F.3d 227 (4th Cir. 2004).

Quill Corp. v. North Dakota, 504 U.S. 298 (1992).

Reno v. American Civil Liberties Union, 521 U.S. 844 (1997) (held that the Communications Decency Act was unconstitutional).

Reno v. American Civil Liberties Union, 521 U.S. 844, 881-882 (1997).

Rev.Proc. 69-21, 1969-2 Cum.Bull. 303;

Rev.Proc. 97-50, 1997-2 Cum.Bull. 525.

Rush, Mark & Paglia, Lucas.(2001). *Preventing, Investigating and Prosecuting Computer Attacks and E-Commerce Crimes: Public or Private Initiatives and Other Federal Reserves*. 18 Computer & Online Industry Litigation Reporter, 16.

Scripto v. Carson, 362 U.S. 207 (1960)

Supp. 2d 907 (N.D. Ill. 2002)

Trademarks: Madrid Agreement (1891).

26U.S.C.S. §174. See, Treas.Reg.§1.174-2(a)(3).

Tres.Reg. §1.861-4(a).

Trintec Industries Inc. v. Pedre Promotional Products Inc., 395 F.3d 1275 (Fed.Cir. 2005).

Truth in Domain Names Act, 18 U.S.C.S. §2252B.

United States. v. Briscoe, 65 F.3d 576 (7thCir. 1995).

United States. v. Czubinski, 106 F.3d 1069 (1stCir. 1997).

11 U.S.C.S. § 1101, et seq.

18 U.S.C.S. §1030, et seq

18 U.S.C.S. §1030(a).

18 U.S.C.S. §1030(c).

15 U.S.C.S. §1125.

26 U.S.C.S. §1222.

26 U.S.C.S. §168.

18 U.S.C.S. §1831.

18 U.S.C.S. §1832

18 U.S.C.S. 1832(a)

26 U.S.C.S. §197.

47 U.S.C.S. §230.

47 U.S.C.S. §230(c)(1).

47 U.S.C.S. §231

18 U.S.C.S. §2314

18 U.S.C.S. §2510.

15 U.S.C.S. §381.

15 U.S.C.S. §45(a)

17 U.S.C.S. §501, et seq.

17 U.S.C.S. §506(a).

17 U.S.C.S. §512.

17 U.S.C.S. §512(a).

26 U.S.C.S. §61

15 U.S.C.S. §6801, et seq.

15 U.S.C.S. §7001, et seq.

26 U.S.C.S. §861(a).

26 U.S.C.S. §862(a).

26 U.S.C.S. §863(b).

Wisconsin Department of Revenue v. William Wrigley, Jr., Co., 505 U.S. 214 (1992).

Zeran v. America Online, Inc., 129 F.3d 327 (4th Cir. 1997).

Zippo Manufacturing Company v. Zippo Dot Com, Inc., 952 Fed.Supp. 1119 (1997).

ENDNOTES

1 Note: this also prohibits the use of copyrighted materials under "fair use" in the academic setting without adequate safeguards used to protect against unauthorized duplication.

2 It should be noted, that a website host should also have a policy for "repeat offenders" of the Digital Millennium Copyright Act. 17 U.S.C.S. §512(i).

3 The Uniform Commercial Code is a model state statute that governs many commercial transactions, including negotiable instruments and the sale of goods.

4 The IFTA created the Advisory Council on Electronic Commerce to make recommendations to Congress and to study all possible taxation issues that may affect E-Commerce, including interstate, intrastate, international

transactions on the Internet and access to the Internet.

5 The Technical Advisory Group on Treaty Characterisation Issues Arising from E-Commerce identified twenty-eight (28) categories of E-Commerce transactions and recommended how these transactions should be uniformly treated under multi-national treaties.

6 Commissioner v. Glenshaw Glass Co., 348 U.S. 426 (1955).
The sale of certain capital assets may result in a reduced tax rate.

7 The cost of tangible personal property used in a trade or business may be recovered over time by the taxpayer.

8 Self-created intangibles (e.g. invented or enhanced by the taxpayer) are not eligible for amortization.

9 Certain expenditures are not deductible, including those for quality control testing; efficiency surveys; management studies; consumer surveys; advertising and promotions; the acquisition of another's patent, model, production or process; or research conducted in connection with literary, historical or similar projects.

10 Note: although the U.S. Internal Revenue Code makes several provisions for taxation of foreign persons, the United States Model Income Tax Convention of September 20, 1996 provides numerous exceptions for residents of countries that are parties to these tax conventions.

11 Where the services are performed is applicable whether or not the recipient of the compensation is a resident of the U.S., where the contract was made with the recipient, or where the payment was made.

12 The U.S. Department of Treasury may allocate income from the sale of certain inventory between U.S. sources and foreign sources.

13 Physicians claimed defendant's negative remarks posted on various on-line newsgroups were defamatory as libel and libel per se

14 In order to receive an injunction or a release of the alleged wrongdoer's names, a party seeking the disclosure (a) must identify the anonymous defendant with sufficient specificity to allow the court to determine that the defendant is a real person or entity that could be sued in federal court, (b) must identify all previous steps taken to locate the elusive defendant; (c) must establish to the court's satisfaction that the plaintiff's suit against the defendant has sufficient merit to withstand a motion to dismiss; and (d) must file a request for discovery with the court, along with a statement of reasons justifying the specific discovery requested, and must identify a limited number of persons or entities from which the plaintiff could take discovery that might lead to identifying information making service of process on the defendant possible.) Also see, In re Subpoena Duces Tecum to America Online, Inc., 52 Va. Cir. 26 (Va. Cir. Ct. 2000), rev'd sub nom.

15 By making hotel reservations through the defendant's website, the plaintiff accepted the terms and conditions in the agreement which included acceptance of the jurisdiction, venue and laws of the State of Nevada

16 So long as the website has not promised that it would independently verify or prevent certain individuals (such as minors) from registering as members, there can be no liability for breach of contract on the part of the website owner if such a promise was not contained within the terms and conditions.

17 (Defamation proceeding commenced by Australian resident for statements published on the Wall Street Journal's website which was accessed in Australia. The court found that the "harm" was caused in Australia

because the plaintiff was an Australian resident).

18 (Plaintiff successfully voided agreement to arbitrate claims due to his infancy at the time he submitted an on-line employment application)

19 IFTA created the Advisory Council on Electronic Commerce to make recommendations to Congress and to study all possible taxation issues that may affect E-Commerce, including interstate, intrastate, international transactions on the Internet and access to the Internet.

Chapter 11
Achieving Realism in 3D Interactive Systems:
Technological Issues

Arman Gukasyan
3DreamTeam LLC, Russia

Nadezhda Ilyina
Vizerra, Russia

Alexander Lavrov
3DreamTeam LLC, Russia

ABSTRACT

Web 2.0 has demonstrated how new technologies can change the structure of the customer-provider relationship. This is evident in the many new business opportunities that have arisen including the growth of 3D environments and virtual worlds. The development of more specialized services and consumer integration creates new marketplaces with new rules of the game. As these new opportunities come to the scene, they will change the face of the world into 3D environments and a multi-agent collaboration. The adoption of virtual worlds depends a great deal on the user experience. The challenges of providing the user with virtual realism is a challenge as many supporting technologies are still in the early development phase. This chapter will discuss several of the issues and tradeoffs involved in developing Real Virtual Worlds.

INTRODUCTION

What is the future of Virtual Worlds from the point of view of technology and content? How can we get the most impact and opportunity from Virtual Worlds? What are those special opportunities Virtual Worlds bring to domains such as tourism and education that depend upon a realistic and accurate user experience in the virtual world?

We are now witnessing the continuing evolution of the technological era as the whole of mankind progresses to era of information. The speed of the transformational growth of technology may be stunning; however it is not a revolution. The past couple of decades have seen several stages

DOI: 10.4018/978-1-61692-808-7.ch011

of this process, and the logical end is the change from a technological to an informational era supported by the use of virtual worlds.

A LITTLE BIT OF HISTORY

We have already progressed through several technological evolution stages. Each stage of development of human-information relations has brought principal changes into the world. Let's take a good look at these stages.

The first stage touched upon the information facilities. All the technologies at that time was aimed to bring the information as close as possible. The Internet allowed the delivery of the information directly to our eye, and search engines appeared to let us obtain the necessary information in the most effective way. At the same time multimedia and animation allowed us to acquire information in the most convenient way.

Tourism and Education have both benefited from this stage. They have allowed the creation of picturesque materials, websites and catalogues. This stage has widened the audience of all companies and resulted in the slight restructuring of activities connected with the information a company wanted to share.

The second stage of technology evolution was more about ways of communication. The unhurried e-mails and faxes yielded to forums, chats and twits. The social networks have increased the speed of distribution of information and made the information flows practically uncontrollable. This stage took much less time a couple of years of social network implementation has brought to life the brand new way of communication. The information became not only picturesque but also personalized and user-generated. From this point on anyone is able to create their own content.

These changes allowed customers to be involved in the process of product development. It allowed them to get timely feedback from all the parties and made customers the active participants of the communication process.

Less obvious, but an important third stage of technology evolution created the opportunity for geo-referencing of the information. This change is a bit limited in usage, but for Tourism it opened a lot of new opportunities.

The fourth stage of technology evolution is the creation of 3D environments which can be updated via Internet. This is the stage are experiencing now; but we haven't worked it out yet.

All these changes prepared us for the next the fifth stage, the revolutionary one. In this stage, information will not be transported to a user anymore, but a user will be placed inside the information space. The virtual worlds era is going to change the relationship between human and information by the creation of informational virtual environments. This will be the synergetic convergence of all the technologies we currently have virtual 3D space, Web 2.0 communication means, geo-referenced information and projected Web 3.0 expertise. The virtual world will become a part of real life and the means of interaction with information. This is what is happening now.

Looking further into the future we can see that the Real Virtuality is coming, where all the five senses will be used for perception of virtual reality. Though it still sounds like science fiction, the equipment and technologies to make it possible are already under development.

COMING OVER TO VIRTUAL WORLDS

What is a Virtual World?

Real Virtuality is somewhere ahead, and to arrive there we need to pass through the Virtual Worlds stage. At this time there is still no universally accepted definition of what a Virtual World is. Here are some of current definitions of virtual world.

1. A **virtual world** is a computer-based simulated environment intended for its users to inhabit and interact via avatars. These

avatars are usually depicted as textual, two-dimensional, or three-dimensional graphical representations, although other forms are possible. Some, but not all, virtual worlds allow for multiple users (Virtual World, (2009a).

2. A **virtual world** is a simulated environment that appears to have the characteristics of some other environment, and in which participants perceive themselves as interactive parts (Virtual World, 2009b).
3. A **virtual world** is a synchronous persistent network of people, represented by avatars, facilitated by computers (Bell, 2007).
4. A **virtual world** is a 3D computer environment in which users are represented on screen as themselves or as made-up **characters and** interact in real time with other users. Massively multiuser online games (MMOGs) and worlds such as Second Life are examples (ZDNet, 2009).

This list could be longer, but we can already see that there is no real understanding of the conditions necessary to make a virtual world. To avoid misunderstanding in further discussion in this chapter, we will define ***virtual world** as a computer-based 3D environment, either inhabited or having the potential for population, that intends a real-time user interaction – with environment or/and with other users.*

Real Virtual Worlds

Real Virtual Worlds are defined as an integration of four factors: 3D view of the world, community, creation, and commerce (3D3C). The more we have of those factors the closer we get to *Real Virtual Worlds* (Sivan 2008).

To illustrate this concept, we have used the following examples of Real Virtual Worlds:

- Second Life (www.secondlife.com) is a virtual world developed by Linden Lab that launched on June 23, 2003 and is accessible via the Internet. A free client application called the Second Life Viewer enables its users, called Residents, to interact with each other through avatars which are graphical representations of themselves. Residents can explore the virtual environment, meet other residents, socialize, participate in individual and group activities, create and trade virtual property and services with one another, or travel throughout the world, which residents refer to as 'the grid' (Second Life, 2009).
- Google Earth (http://earth.google.com) displays satellite images of varying resolution of the Earth's surface, allowing users to visually see things like cities and houses looking perpendicularly down or at an oblique angle, with perspective. The degree of resolution available is based somewhat on the points of interest and popularity, but most land is covered in at least 15 meters of resolution. Google Earth allows users to search for addresses for some countries, enter coordinates, or simply use the mouse to browse the location. Google Earth has the capability to show 3D buildings and structures (such as bridges). These 3D buildings and structures have been build from users' submissions using SketchUp, a 3D modeling program and many buildings and structures from around the world now have detailed 3D models (Google Earth, 2009).
- Vizerra.com (http://vizerra.com/en/) provides a software that allows users to visit famous historical and architectural monuments and see them in high detail. The models are highly-precise. Users can browse the models and landscapes, access the information about the objects, and watch videos. The announced plans of the company include wide educational, entertainment and social opportunities for users.

As this project is being developed by our company, we are able to provide a better insight to the details.

Real Virtual Worlds are often used for the purpose of Tourism and Education. And as soon as we step outside the entertainment sphere towards more serious applications, we face the new requirements related to the value of the content of the virtual worlds.

Authenticity

Virtual Worlds are now used mostly for entertainment, though there are some business and educational applications based on virtual worlds as well. This has resulted because the content for business application takes much more effort to create.

First and foremost the content should be authentic when compared to reality. The Web has faced the authenticity question that led to creation of so-called Web 3.0 concept. "The Semantic Web (or Web 3.0) promises to 'organize the world's information' in a dramatically more logical way than Google can ever achieve with their current engine design. This is especially true from the point of view of machine comprehension as opposed to human comprehension. The Semantic Web requires the use of a declarative ontological language like OWL to produce domain-specific ontologies that machines can use to reason about information and make new conclusions, not simply match keywords" (Fawzi, 2006).

We need to decide how to apply the authenticity concept to the context of virtual worlds as it can be viewed from different perspectives. This concept contains the similarity measure of 3D objects and their real prototypes. The specified degree of abstraction occurs when you are trying to visualize any object: 3D space is used to reproduce only the most significant features of the prototype in terms of current task. This issue comes into particular prominence if we review the examples given below.

Google Earth

Google Earth is one of the most ambitious attempts to virtualize the real world. The Earth, digitized with the help of hi-res satellite pictures, is totally authentic. Many models placed in Google Earth are the recognizable virtual copies of the real objects made by the photo reference, and they appear on the map exactly where they were in the real world. They are highly authentic from this perspective. But detail level is rather low, and that's why the models bearing high resemblance to their prototypes from afar lose the authenticity at close quarters. Thus we can tell that Google Earth is a geographically authentic world but in terms of visualization the authenticity level is rather low. As for inhabitance, currently Google Earth does not have any functions of it.

Second Life

Another large-scale project is Second Life. Its content is socially-authentic as the human social interactions are reproduced in the virtual world. The content does not apply specifically for geographical authenticity or correlation with the real world as the attempt to combine the user freedom with the authentic world design would actually be self-defeating. Visual authenticity is low both due to the users' creativity and technical requirements.

Vizerra.com

The authors developed Vizerra.com to focus on visual and atmospheric authenticity of locations. Such authenticity is achieved by creating the photorealistic content based on real photos and also by provision of real place atmosphere by means of lighting, sound and specific features of a location.

Initially the content was very highly-detailed and used textures taken directly from the photos. Such approach was successful while working with small number of locations (e.g. Tatev monastery (http://vizerra.com/en/locations/tatev). But as the number of locations grew larger, this method had to be abandoned due to hardware limitations. The stored image textures became huge and the models became heavy, so that the image could not be properly rendered and displayed on the average computer of the end user. We have found that the problem of balance between authenticity and technical requirements seems to be the key for Real Virtual Worlds.

To solve this controversy we have developed a special technology that allows us to create the textures which are still highly authentic, but have less demanding technical requirements. The textures creation algorithm is one of the most important know-hows of the company. Thus we have got the utmost visual quality and resemblance to the real object along with high working speed of the rendering and display engine.

The key to the authenticity became the provision of the atmosphere of the real place. The testing of different versions with the help of the users revealed the following: it does not matter to users how accurate single objects are; what matters is the general atmosphere of the location. As a rule, tourists gain in their travels a certain set of emotions connected with landmarks they'd visited, and that's what their memory records for the most part plus a rather small quantity of the brightest details.

Photorealism is also very important as it allows the expression of distance in fictional virtual worlds. The concept of photorealism is quite subjective. People with varying qualification in computer graphics have varying perception of images in terms of photorealism referred to as 'photorealistic levels of perception'. For example, most regular users see the standard 3D renderings as photorealistic while online game users would like to see the higher quality graphics. A computer graphics specialist would look for photorealism in a number of different features, and only the combination of such features would allow him to qualify an image as photorealistic. It is very hard to combine the high-level photorealism with the real time graphics because of its technology demands.

Jim Blinn in his article "The Ancient Chinese Art of Chi-Ting" (Blinn, 1988) stated that computer graphics should be realistic not through the physical means of the real world but through the means which provide the similarity to the real world while being as efficient as possible with demands on computer processing power.

The balance issue between the technological capabilities, freedom of user's actions and authenticity of a virtual world will remain an issue for the foreseeable future. Therefore in the process of creating of the virtual world, key attribute of the location should stay authentic and the other features of minor importance to the general world concept would require less attention and authenticity. It can be predicted, however, that with the growth of overall computer power available to regular users along with the increase in bandwidth of Internet connections, the authenticity of virtual worlds will continue to develop.

Authenticity and Business Application

The authenticity type chosen by virtual world developers define the way the Virtual World can be used.

Google Earth

Google Earth is a valuable application for both Tourist and Educational applications, especially where the geographic data is required. It allows users to dive into the oceans of geo-referenced multimedia data generated all over the world. Routing and location of the POI (Points of Interest), photos and informational layers make this multi user GIS environment highly interesting for both creators and users of content.

Second Life

The specific feature of authenticity makes Second Life valuable to the social aspects of Tourism or Education. Education especially benefits from

Second Life features allowing the virtual simulation of different locations and situations. E.g. there are a lot of projects in Second Life devoted to the social aspects of different countries that allow people to understand each other better.

Vizerra.com

Vizerra.com was initially created with the focus on both Education and Tourism. Educational programs for students interested in culture, architecture and arts can benefit from using edutainment features making people not only look at the World Heritage wonders, but live there. As a Tourist industry tool Vizerra.com holds tremendous potential for promoting, sharing and preserving knowledge of landmarks on a global level. If combined with the technologies of augmented reality of stereo-glasses, visually authentic environments like Vizerra.com can become an exciting pioneer in the development of mutual interaction of reality and virtuality in the next few years.

Content Detalization

Thousands of 3D games created each year throughout the world experience no problems with the content for their fictional worlds. But as soon as you decide to create a Real Virtual World you face a lot of issues and problems. The first issue is the scale of the project. Current state of technologies makes this issue a key one. If you want to reproduce the whole world you have to solve the problem with detail level. Some of the:

Solutions to this problem include the following:

- Google Earth has limited the detail level of the models its engine supports (See Figure 1)
- Second Life created a complicated system of servers, where each server supports its own cluster of territory 256x256 meters in area (Server Architecture, 2009) and also had to limit the level of detail due to the streaming upload provisions. (See Figure 2)
- Vizerra.com creates its highly detailed models in separately uploaded modules (See Figure 3)
- The fantasy worlds like World of Warcraft are not limited by authenticity and use procedure elements instead of unique.

It should be noted that the location size is important for web distribution. The virtual image textures contribute greatly to the location size. But these very textures provide the visual authenticity to the location. What a paradox – how do we make the texture size smaller while trying at the same time not to lose the authenticity?

The authors had to resolve this issue of textures, location and authenticity in their development of vizerra.com. They decided on the following steps:

1. *Get rid of the technical textures.* Use real time lighting methods instead of light maps and we've even got bonus – dynamic light conditions.
2. *Make the textures smaller.* This is a very fast way to reduce the total size of downloaded data. If you reduce the textures by half it will decrease the size of downloaded data fourfold, at the same time passing unnoticed by the regular users. There's a bonus too – users of small-scale systems will be able to download location with small textures and they'll get high system performance.
3. *Optimize the use of textures.* Simple measures like textures multiplication or more efficient use of UV space often come to good without any special technologies. Everything can be solved by quality standards and efficient management of content creation process.
4. *Use procedural textures.* That's rather risky thing to do if you want to create photo realistic authentic textures. Anyway, you should use the scanned photos for it. Reducing the data size when you are focused on vi-

Figure 1. Google Earth

Figure 2. Second Life

Figure 3. Vizerra.com

sual authenticity can be accomplished by constructing the procedural textures from the small bits of photos. As of now we use this method once in a while because we are able to construct the textures with the simpler tools gaining the same result, and procedural surfaces can be reconstructed in a more transparent and quick way.

Content Creation

The other content issue is the method chosen for its creation. There are a lot of technologies which strive to become the unified and open standard for creating the 3D content, but none of them allows non-professionals to create ready to use models for 3D environments. Again we face the balance between the size of the models, system requirements of user hardware and speed/cost of production.

Hand simulation in creation of the mirror worlds clearly is a wasteful and slow process. The problem with the creation of authentic 3D content is attacked in two ways at present: either by the proliferation of content providers along with users' involvement (Google Earth, Second Life) or by automation. Google Earth uploads the scene images from the Digital Globe servers automatically, but nevertheless 3D models are still made by the users manually. Second Life users generate content much quicker because the game itself is a huge marketplace for content creators and consumers. Creators of the content make their profit and because of that, they are interested in creation of high-quality and authentic content. Authenticity is bounded only by system features and Internet connection speed. Like most online games, Second Life requires lightweight content, but that reduces its similarity to the real world.

If you want to encourage users to contribute content creation, it is necessary to place some restrictions on the level of detail and authenticity of your content. Most general users to not have the skills of our professional 3D artists capable of creating a really good authentic model.

Content can also be created using 3D scanning. Laser scanning allows users to create a digital model of all the location as a set of points with 3D coordinates. Laser scanning allows the creation of quite accurate digital 'casts' of the real objects. However, current software cannot yet solve the problem of image recognition with degree of reliability desirable for the users. Therefore laser scanning just makes the task of reproducing the 3D objects in virtual space somewhat easier but does not replace all of the effort required for 3D content creation.

In creating the 3D model for the Pushkin Museum of Fine Arts, the authors had an opportunity to test the 3D scanning method in partnership with Artec Group Company (http://artec-group.com/) for the development of 3D statue models. The low-detailed models for the engine were based on high definition models with a calculation of the difference map between these models. As a result the low-detailed model made for the engine coupled with normal maps provided a image very similar in quality and accuracy to high definition ones. Scanned models had resolution of several millions polygons.

Another fast-growing trend in automated making of 3D objects is photogrammetry - the reconstruction of 3D model based on photos. The primary virtue of this technology is its simplicity. Main task is to provide the high quality automatic reconstruction; currently there are several constantly progressing ways of solving this task. The shortcoming of this technology is its dependence on shooting accuracy and quality of photos and problems with textures' projection on 3D models.

Hence, even with the new technology available, at this time the best way to create good content for Real Virtual Worlds is still to get have them developed manually by artists on the basis of drawings, plans and photos of real objects. The modeling is performed either by users (Second Life, Google Earth) or by project team (Vizerra.

com). The first approach allows the creation of more content of lower quality, the second approach results in less content but of better quality. Though there are some easy-to-use 3D editors for non professional users, to create a good 3D model one should still be a skilled 3D artist.

Currently there are quite a lot of 3D editors available in the computer graphics market intended for users of different qualification and for different application fields. These editors can be divided into 3 basic groups related to their use for creation of the virtual worlds:

1. Commercial tools area available for large scale projects that provide many features beyondfrom modeling and texturing. Three well know vendors inlcude 3Ds Max, Maya, XSI.
2. There are also inexpensive commercial tools like Modo or Cinema4D.
3. Lastly, there are non-commercial tools like SketchUp or Blender. Most of non-professional computer graphics creators generating digital content use this group of tools. SketchUp allows the user to create and distribute simple 3D models. Blender offers much more advanced environment competing with first class products.

USER HARDWARE

Apart from the issues involved in a virtual world creation, there are also concerns about the quality of the user interaction with the virtual world. The mouse, keyboard and regular monitors are not meant to provide a robust interactive interface between users and 3D environments. There have been recent efforts to improve this situation particularly in the area of visualization and additional software functionality.

Visualization

People obtain nearly 80% of information through their eyes. Therefore, the visual part of virtual world is of the utmost importance for the perception of 3D. Many methods are used to enhance the user's immersion into the virtual experience.

The stereo image output is one visual enhancement that is available. This technology forms two separate images – for the left and the right eye respectively (stereopair) – and then each image is assembled separately. Various manufacturers use different methods of stereo imaging including widely known red-green pairs to more complicated and lifelike technologies. Applications that function in real time have a great advantage over the video films as the stereopair for them can be produced without any post-processing demands. When using video films, the shooting process requires the use of special methods and techniques (e.g. 3D photos).

Stereo image can be made through a variety of means. One of most promising current technologies is 3DVision 3D glasses by NVidia (www.nividia.com). This technology uses special software to form the image on a 120 Hz display - 2 superimposed images for the right and left eyes. The 3D glasses filter the signals and user sees 3D images.

Another stereo image technology is offered through the Phillips WoW 3D TV is available which does not require the use of 3D glasses (Stunning 3D Viewing, 2009).

There are also devices that project the 3D image directly on the retina. This technology promises a lot of benefits for improving the user interface between real and virtual world, especially when combined with augmented reality technology. Augmented reality technology allows the user to be deeply immersed inside the virtual world and then projects this world into reality. It involves placing the special marks throughout the real world; then one can see them with the aid of special devices such as video cameras connected to a computer.

Software Features

In order to output any 3D graphics it is necessary to use accelerated libraries of 3D graphics. You cannot have high 3D performance without it. The most well known libraries for the handling of 3D graphics at the time are DirectX and openGl. DirectX is offered by Microsoft Corporation which releases updates to this technology on a regular basis. Historically DirectX has more wide-spread use in computer games area. OpenGl is an open source software that has its roots in science visualization, commercial art and CAD systems where technological transparency, high reliability and cross-platform are of high value,

Interactions with 3D Environment

Users immersed in a virtual world are more than mere spectators; that is why the means of their interaction with the environment are very important. Various devices are used to enhance the user's experience with the virtual reality.

The use of haptic devices can enhance the user experience. These devices use technology to provide the user with a sense of touch in their virtual world. One common haptic device are virtual gloves (http://www.vrealities.com/P5.html). Virtual gloves are a widely used virtual manipulation device that allows users to pinch and grab virtual objects or initiate action. Virtual gloves and VR-headsets are often used in combination to provide an even higher level of an immersive experience. The rapid growth of the virtual worlds is spurring development of this area. One Japanese company NTT Comware (www.ntcomware.com) has recently announced that they have developed a new type of technology Tangible-3D which simulates the feeling of actually grasping objects through the glove sensors.

The depth of penetration into a virtual reality is defined by the number of sensory organs that take part in the perception and control of virtual reality. The creators of a prototype VR-headset from the New York University plan to release a device which would allow the user to receive virtual signals for all five senses[1]. This promising technology could have widespread adoption particularly in the entertainment and educational domains. The main issue facing this new device is the creation of suitable content as the signals for the different receptors must be precisely consistent. If there is a mismatch between the various sense receptors, the user would experience great discomfort because, for example, even slight mismatching of the visual signals for the eyes can result in discomfort such as a headache. When the quantity of channels is increased, this issue becomes more challenging.

CONCLUSION

The next few years will see a period of rapid development of the virtual reality technologies focused on improving the authenticity of the user's experience in virtual worlds. It is quite certain that Real Virtual Worlds authentic to the real world visually, geographically or socially will develop in parallel with these technological innovations. The main issues which the virtual world industry will face in the next few years are:

- Creation of common standard (or several standards) for 3D content it will allow to use one and the same content on different systems;
- Automation of the creation of 3D virtual copies of the real objects to the fullest extent possible;
- Creation of devices allowing to establish the comfortable interaction with the system for as many users as possible.

Moreover, the development of the virtual worlds is interrelated with the continuing evolution of computers and the Internet. It is predicted that increasing immersion in virtual worlds will impact experiences in the real world in a radical way similar to the impact of the computers and mobile communications.

REFERENCES

Anonymous. (2009). Devata.Org. Retrieved on 12/7/09 from http://www.devata.org/2009/08/virtual-or-reality-12-amazing-3d-comparison-photos-at-angkor-wat/

Architecture, S. (2009). Second Life Wiki. Retrieved on 12/7/09 from 'http://wiki.secondlife.com/wiki/Server_architecture

Bell, M. (2007). Definition and Taxonomy of Virtual Worlds. Indiana University. Retrieved on 12/7/09 from http://www.its.bldrdoc.gov/projects/devglossary/_virtual_world.html

Blinn, J. (1988). "The Ancient Chinese Art of Chi-Ting". Jet Propulsion Laboratory, Pasadena, California, Fawzi, Marc. (2006). Wikipedia 3.0: The End of Google? Evolving Trends. Retrieved on 12/7/2009 from 'http://evolvingtrends.wordpress.com/2006/06/26/wikipedia-30-the-end-of-google/

Earth, G. (2009). Wikipedia. Retrieved on 12/8/09 from http://en.wikipedia.org/wiki/Google_Earth

Life, S. (2009). Wikipedia. Retrieved on 12/8/09 from 'http://ru.wikipedia.org/wiki/Second_Life

Sivan, Y. (2008). Real Virtual Worlds SOS *(State of Standards) Q3-2008*. Journal of Virtual Worlds Research. Retrieved on 12/7/09 from http://journals.tdl.org/jvwr/article/view/359/271

Stunning 3D Viewing. (2009). Retrieved on 12/7/09 from http://www.business-sites.philips.com/shared/assets/3dsolutions/downloads/42inchProductLeaflet.pdf

World, V. (2009a). Wikipedia. Retrieved on 12/7/09 from http://en.wikipedia.org/wiki/Virtual_World

World, V. (2009b). Retrieved on 12/7/09 from http://www.its.bldrdoc.gov/projects/devglossary/_virtual_world.html

ZDNet. (2009). *ZDNet Definition for Virtual World.* Retrieved on 12/7/09 from http://www.its.bldrdoc.gov/projects/devglossary/_virtual_world.html

KEY TERMS AND DEFINITIONS

An Avatar (from the Sanskrit word for "descent"): A computer user's representation of himself/herself or alter ego, whether in the form of a three-dimensional model used in computer games, a two-dimensional icon (picture) used on Internet forums and other communities, or a text construct found on early systems such as MUDs.

Authenticity: The quality of being genuine or not corrupted from the original.

Mirror Virtual World (Real Virtual World): A virtual copy of a real location.

Serious Games: Are the games designed for a primary purpose other than pure entertainment.

Virtual World: A computer-based 3D environment, either inhabited or having the potential for population, that supposes a user interaction – with environment or/and with other users (multi-agent systems).

Web 3.0 (Semantic Web): An evolving development of the World Wide Web in which the meaning (semantics) of information and services on the web is defined, making it possible for the web to understand and satisfy the requests of people and machines to use the web content.

Chapter 12
Learning Space in Virtual Environments:
Understanding the Factors Influencing Training Time

M. Kyritsis
Brunel University, UK

S. R. Gulliver
University of Reading, UK

S. Morar
Consultant, UK

ABSTRACT

Learning the spatial layout of an environment is essential in application domains including military and emergency personnel training. Traditionally, whilst learning space from a Virtual Environment (VE), identical training time was used for all users - a one size fits all approach to exposure / training time. This chapter, however, identifies both environmental and individual user differences that influence the training time required to ensure effective virtual environment spatial knowledge acquisition (SKA). We introduce the problem of contradicting literature in the area of SKA, and discuss how the amount of exposure time given to a person during VE training is responsible for the feasibility of SKA. We then show how certain individual user differences, as well as environmental factors, impact on the required exposure time that a particular person needs within a specific VE. Individual factors discussed include: the importance of knowledge and experience; the importance of gender; the importance of aptitude and spatial orientation skills; and the importance of cognitive styles. Environmental factors discussed include: Size, Spatial layout complexity and landmark distribution. Since people are different, a one-size fits all approach to training time does not seem logical. The impact of this research domain is important to VE training in general, however within service and military domains ensuring appropriate spatial training is critical in order to ensure that disorientation does not occur in a life / death scenario.

DOI: 10.4018/978-1-61692-808-7.ch012

INTRODUCTION

The ability to 'learn' the environment before engaging in navigation is an area of interest for a variety of application domains (Egsegian et al., 1993, Foreman et al, 2003). Traditionally spatial training is accomplished by providing users with maps and briefings of an environment. These methods, however, only provide topological (survey) knowledge of the environment, which whilst being more flexible, pays little attention to the details of routes and landmarks (Thorndyke, 1980; Golledge, 1991). Procedural learning has a distinct advantage over survey knowledge, as can be seen in an experiments of Thorndyke and Hayes-Roth (1982) where participants with procedural knowledge of an environment, estimated route distances significantly better than participants who had acquired just survey knowledge. Navigation therefore relies heavily on previously acquired visual information, e.g. the process of re-orientation during navigation in a previously visited environments (Montello, 2005), which relies on previously seen "visual references" in order to adjust bearings during navigation. Maps and other traditional navigational equipment cannot provide the same level of supporting information. VE training, therefore, promises to provide procedural knowledge through exploration, and has caught the attention of a variety of researchers all attempting to discuss whether virtual training is more efficient than training through more traditional methods (Witmer et al., 1995; Goerger et al., 1998; Waller et al., 1998; Foreman et al., 2003).

Learning in virtual environments relies on the ability of users to develop an understanding of space by creating a cognitive map of the environment (Asthmeir et al., 1993; Cobb and d'Cruz, 1994; Silverman and Spiker, 1997; Clark and Wong, 2000; Riva and Gamberini, 2000). Cognitive maps are mental representations of space that people develop in order to acquire an understanding of space, both virtual and real, through either procedural knowledge or survey knowledge (Thorndyke, 1980; Golledge, 1991; Witmer et al., 1995; Goerger et al., 1998). When learning in a procedural manner, cognitive maps are created through the act of navigation (Montello, 2005). Navigation itself is made up of two separate and very distinct processes. The first of these processes is locomotion, which is the movement of a person within an environment. The second process is way-finding, which is the planning of routes that a person undergoes when trying to get to a specific destination (Montello, 2005). It is understood that during self-directed locomotion (where the person is actively moving about in the environment solving problems - such as avoiding obstacles), there is a tendency to acquire more spatial knowledge (Feldman & Acredolo, 1979). Virtual environment training, however, provides self-directed locomotion without the possibility of a dangerous life-threatening situation, making it very suitable for emergency training.

Research concerning spatial knowledge acquisition through VEs, have provided a variety of contradicting results. The findings, although conflicting, appear to be subject to a key influencing factor, 'required exposure time' (Witmer et al., 1996; Darken & Banker, 1998; Waller et al., 1998; Goerger et al., 1998; and Darken and Peterson, 2001). This factor is the exposure time that a user will spend learning the environment in order to achieve spatial knowledge acquisition.

THE IMPACT OF TRAINING TIME

Witmer et al. (1996), Wilson et al. (1996), Waller et al. (1998), and Foreman et al. (2003) all conducted experiments in order to conclude whether spatial knowledge acquisition can be acquired from a VE representation of the real world. These experiments involved a group of participants navigating through virtual space and acquiring spatial knowledge, and then comparing the results to a group that learned the environment through conventional methods such as maps or photographs. These experiments concluded that a VE can be more beneficial than traditional training. However, this is only the case if a long exposure time is given to the users.

Darken and Banker (1998) reported that experts perform better using conventional methods such as maps, while Goerger et al. (1998) reported that all participants had a greater success using conventional methods. Goerger et al. (1998) acknowledge, that with longer exposure times, virtual reality training may in fact be more beneficial, however, this is hard to determine since the exposure times that a user spent in each experiment differed. Waller et al (1998) allowed for two minutes, Darken and Banker allowed for a set 60 minute exposure, and Goerger et al. (1998) allowed for a set 30 minute exposure, yet they referred to this as a short exposure time. It was, therefore unclear how much exposure time is deemed as required, and if in fact various environmental attributes and individual user differences can affect the required exposure time.

In an attempt to clarify this situation, Darken et al. (1999) and Koh et al. (1999) discussed why spatial knowledge acquisition research delivers contradictory results. They both made the argument that individual user differences are an extremely important factor in the development of cognitive maps, and that a one-size-fits all situation may not be possible when determining required exposure time. Darken et al. (1999) also examined how cognitive and biological differences affect a series of cognitive processes, which are critical to navigation. They stated that previous knowledge, aptitude, orientation ability, strategy, perceptual motoric and memorial knowledge, all influenced the navigational skill of the user. According to Koh et al. (1999) and Waller et al. (2001) there is a need to identify these individual differences and to understand how they affect performance when acquiring spatial knowledge. Therefore, this chapter identifies and discusses commonly defined individual differences of users that affect navigation skills, and therefore the exposure time required to acquire spatial knowledge from a VE. Understanding how these individual differences affect navigational skill will help VE trainers understand the required exposure times necessary for a specific user to acquire spatial knowledge from a particular environment. Since people are different, a one-size fits all approach to training time does not seem logical.

The individual differences of users that navigate through an environment is not the only factor that influences the required exposure time. Darken and Peterson (2001) reported that required exposure time is also environment dependent. They explained that some environments provide more cues than others and, therefore, that the exposure time needed alters according to relevant cues (Darken & Peterson, 2001). Darken and Peterson (2001) identified that, regardless of whether the training interface is supported with a map or whether other visual cues are used in combination with the environment, the structure of the environment itself contains factors that support user navigation, which can result in a smaller exposure time requirement. It may seem obvious that the size of an environment impacts the time required to navigate through it, however size is only one of many influencing factors that will be discussed in this chapter.

ENVIRONMENAL FACTORS AFFECTING EXPOSURE TIME

Many of the factors that affect navigational complexity, which apply to the physical world are applicable in the virtual world (Darken & Banker, 1998). Darken and Peterson (2001), broke down an environment into a space made up of building blocks or 'landmarks' that are connected by routes, which are interconnected to form nodes. These interconnected routes and nodes make up the spatial layout of the environment. Environments can be complex in nature and can therefore affect the exposure time required to acquire spatial knowledge (Darken & Peterson, 2001).

Although we have used size as the example, size is only one of the factors that can influence navigation. Research indicates factors include complexity of the spatial layout and landmark information (Darken & Sibert, 1996; Witmer & Sadowski, 1998; Vinson, 1999; and Gouteux & Spelke, 2001). Studies by Goerger et al. (1998) and Gouteux and Spelke (2001), show that spatial layout complexity is an important component of cognitive development. Witmer et al. (1995), Witmer and Sadowski (1998) and Vinson (1999), claim that the number of landmarks and the frequency per square metre, as well as the graphical detail of these landmarks is important.

Research also shows that navigational complexity influences various processes that directly affect navigation. These processes are identified by Stankiewicz and Kalia (2004) as: perception (input of cues and other environmental information at a given time during navigation); accessing the cognitive map (ability of each person to develop a cognitive map of the environment and then apply it to navigation); spatial updating (ability to navigate from different positions in the environment); decision making (logical process to reach a certain goal depending on current position and perception). Moreover, Stankiewicz and Kalia (2004) discuss how various environmental factors such as size influence these processes and make navigation more complex, i.e. how large size burdens perception due to a larger area being processed that requires a more complex cognitive map in spatial memory. Spatial updating takes longer since there are more places and objects to consider, and decision strategy is influenced as more decisions must be made to reach a certain goal (Stankiewicz and Kalia, 2004).

The following sub-sections will discuss critical environmental factors that influence exposure time: size; spatial layout complexity; and landmark potential.

Size

For the scope of this chapter, environmental size refers to the overall raw navigational space available to the user. The differentiation between large-scale and small-scale environments, however is not clearly defined in literature. To Darken and Banker (1998) a large-scaled environment was described as being 1200*700 metres, which we can consider as being large when comparing it to other virtual spaces that represent a house or building, such as the one in Goerger et al. (1998). Obviously, without visual obstructions, size would not be a confounding factor, however in any non-flat featureless environment, as size increases so does the time taken too move (locomote) from one place to another in order to acquire spatial knowledge, which must then be transformed from visual working memory into long-term memory. What may not be so obvious is that navigational strategy is also affected. Butler et al. (1993) demonstrated that distance plays a significant role when navigating. They found that users will most frequently choose to navigate through shorter paths, even if those paths are more complex. Therefore, as size increases so does the amount of exposure time required by a person to acquire spatial knowledge from the environment. The question that seems to arise, however, is how much time is suitable for a specific size.

For a large mountainous region, as used by Darken and Banker (1998), a 60 minute exposure time was considered as being 'short', however to our knowledge no justification for this exposure time was given. For a seven story building, as designed by Goerger et al. (1998), an exposure time of 30 minutes was also considered 'short', however again no justification for this exposure time was given. We have no indication at all, whether navigational complexity increases linearly as size increases when navigating through a virtual environment. If the relationship is not linear, then size becomes more and more critical to consider with respect to exposure time required for SKA.

Spatial Layout Complexity

Spatial layout is the geometrical structure of an environment (Gouteux & Spelke, 2001). When trying to determine what makes a layout more complex, without involving size, spatial layout complexity is the number of objects, such as walls, that obstruct a user's line of sight from reference points, i.e. visible landmarks. This is demonstrated in the work of Kalia and Stankiewicz (2007), who measured the spatial layout complexity in terms of corridors. They found that as the number of corridors in an environment increased, so did its complexity.

In virtual environments the architecture of an environment is important to navigation, as demonstrated by Passini (1984), who discussed how Manhattan's rectangular grid, with visual aids such as numbering of streets and avenues, makes navigation very simple. However, in some cases it is simply not possible to provide architectural simplification (e.g. in a natural mountainous region). Darken and Sibert (1996) explained that environments that do not provide any navigational aids, such as road signs, will be harder to navigate and will ultimately lead to a loss of awareness and disorientation. In an office building, one find signs that point towards different levels and not simply lead to dead ends, however a 'natural environment' has few restrictions and does not follow any architectural laws. In general, complex environments, both natural and man-made, tend to have a lot of visual obstructions to visual references. In mountainous regions, this may be slopes, whilst in a cave or building it may be the walls that obstruct references.

Landmarks

Lynch (1960), Vinson (1999) and Stankiewicz and Kalia (2004) identify that an environment is made up of a variety of landmarks that individuals use to navigate. Stankiewicz and Kalia (2004) broke down the term landmarks into two distinct types: structural landmarks and object landmarks. Structural landmarks are distinct geographical features of an environment that can be used for navigating (e.g. a T-junction), whilst object landmarks are objects in the environment that are independent of the structure (e.g. a statue). In general, landmarks differentiate between different parts of an environment (Weisman, 1981). Although it is rather difficult to understand and predict what landmarks a user will choose when navigating, there are theories. Stankiewicz and Kalia (2004) explained that different landmarks have various benefits for the user with landmark potential defined through the three properties that a landmark may possess.

The first of these properties is persistence, which is whether the landmark is mobile. A parked car is not the best landmark as it has a high chance of moving by the time the user revisits the site. This can cause confusion as users often navigate initially using object landmarks rather than geographic structure (Newman et al., 2007). The second property is whether the landmark is perceptually salient (i.e. visible), and is determined by factors including landmark size and number of obstructions. The third and final property of a landmark is whether or not the landmark is informative. This is important as it informs an individual of their location. Stankiewicz and Kalia (2004) explain that for a landmark to be informative it must be distinctly different from other landmarks, in fact the reason why users have difficulty using landmarks such as statues (Ruddle et al., 1997) is because they cannot easily distinguish between the statues, unless they approach them for a closer inspection. If all three of these factors are satisfied then the landmark can be useful during landmark-based navigational updating, which, as we discussed before, is a process of reorientation that relies on landmarks.

Stankiewicz and Kalia (2004) discovered that participants tend to learn structural landmarks better than object landmarks, and that when spatial knowledge acquisition does occur, the environment structure can be remembered by a user, even as far as a year later after the initial encounter. For example, most people will remember the layout of their first school, but few will remember the location of specific objects.

Vinson (1999) deducted that the landmarks that are frequently available, and visible from various positions in the environment (i.e. paths), are useful in navigation. Frequent landmarks appear to increase navigational performance. For this to apply, however, landmarks must be unique. In natural environments, such as a forest, there is a large amount of non-unique landmarks, such as trees and rocks. These landmarks overpopulate the area, and cannot be used as reference points (which is a very important part of navigational updating), since one tree may not be distinctly different from another. However, man-made structures in a forest environment would stand out as distinct landmarks (Whittaker, 1996). Therefore, it is not just the frequency of landmarks readily available throughout the environment, but also the number of distinct landmarks available that can help a user orientate, decreasing navigational complexity. This information relates to the need for a landmark to be informative, as was suggested by Stankiewicz and Kalia (2004). The assumption is that for a virtual environment, landmark potential can be measured by the number of visible, non-dynamic (not moving) and distinct landmarks available to the environment as a whole, and the frequency of these landmarks per sector (for which a sector may be the maximum view available to the user: a room or a corridor).

INDIVIDUAL DIFFERENCES IMPACTING USER NAVIGATION

Individual differences have been considered for many years in Visuospatial research, which considers a very broad spectrum of research of understanding concerning images, space and spatial knowledge acquisition (Hegarty and Waller, 2005). This chapter considers the key individual user differences: gender, experience / knowledge, orientation skill, age, and cognitive styles. As suggested by Darken et al. (1999), each of these human attributes influence the navigational skills of the user when they navigate in a novel environment.

Gender Issues in Navigation

There is evidence that gender plays a significant role in acquiring spatial knowledge from a VE. Waller et al. (1998) showed that females were particularly disorientated in a virtual maze, since they reported large bearing errors when drawing a retrospective maze map. Although women's ability is more constrained when learning spatial characteristics of a virtual environment, their difficulty when navigating in the maze may be constrained by strategy rather than ability. Both Sandstrome et al. (1998) and Moffat et al. (1998) have provided explanations as to why male users navigate better in a maze. One of the deficiencies of a maze is that it relies heavily on geometrical navigation, rather than the use of landmark cues. Sandstrome et al. (1998) concluded that women rely heavily on the use of object landmarks for navigation, where men seem to use both structural landmarks and object landmarks.

The difficulty that women may face when navigating through an environment with limited landmarks, suggests that the required exposure time required by women to acquire the spatial information is increased when environments lack well placed object landmarks. Accordingly, women have problems navigating environments that are complex by nature (such as a maze), however this does not mean that for other types of environments their navigation skills will suffer, or that if given enough exposure time their knowledge of the environment will not equal that of the men. This theory is backed by Vila et al. (2002), who indicate that as exposure time in the environment increases, the navigational differences between the genders decreases.

Knowledge and Experience of Environment and IT System

Knowledge concerning the system, whether it is a desktop computer that allows for mouse and keyboard input, or if it an immersive device, can have a limiting effect due to an overload of mental tasks. This overload is described by Booth et al. (2000) and is explained to be a limitation to attention due to unfamiliar controls and interfaces. According to Booth et al (2000) this occurs mainly because there is an attention dividing of tasks, which are required to navigate and perceive the information seen on the screen. More effort is required to understand and interact with the interface, therefore not enough attention is given to creating cognitive maps of the environment. In compensation, a longer exposure time is required.

More effort is also required if an environment is novel (i.e. if the user has never navigated through this type of architectural structure). In HCI, the difference during navigation between experts VS novices is critical for interface design (Dix et al., 1993; Eberts, 1994). Kuipers (1975), Brewer (2000) and Mania et al. (2005) explain how experience with a certain type of environment gives rise to certain structures in human knowledge memory. These structures are called schemas and are formed in human memory due to past experiences (Pelagatti et. al. 2009). Schemas consist of perceptual information and language comprehension, and are invoked when interacting with new information. The required exposure time to learn an environment depends on memory performance, which is in turn influenced by Schemas, which are affected by the consistency of items in the environment, i.e. whether an item is likely to exist in such an environment (Brewer and Nakamura, 1984). Another theory is called the inconsistent effect and argues that inconsistent items positively influence memory (Lampinen et al., 2001). It is clear that schemas are highly relevant to landmark information and that a person with strong past experiences navigating through a certain type of environment will be more able to recognize key landmarks, and therefore create a cognitive map faster than a similar person with no experience navigating within such an environment.

Knowledge of the environment was considered to be a variable in the experiment of Darken and Banker (1998), who only selected experienced mountaineers for their experiment. Darken and Banker (1998) reported, however, that the advanced mountaineers did not benefit from the 60 minute exposure time in the VE, yet did benefit from using a map. Interestingly, they did not, to the best of our knowledge, test user orientation skills. Instead, Darken and Banker (1998) used participants that have a large experience with navigating through real wilderness using cues and maps. This does not mean, however, that these participants were experienced with the VE system, or had a high aptitude and orientation skill.

Aptitude and Spatial Orientation Skills

The most discussed individual user difference, in the area of spatial knowledge acquisition, is orientation skill. Most experiments testing for spatial knowledge acquisition attempt to keep orientation skill consistent amongst participants (Witmer et al., 1996; Goerger et al., 1998; and Waller et al., 1998). It is obvious that research considers spatial orientation skills as being a very influential attribute during a variety of areas involving human-computer interaction, such as browsing and other visual tasks (Gomez et al., 1986; Vicente et al., 1987; Stanney & Salvendy, 1995). There is strong evidence that individuals have different orientation abilities, which are simply biological in nature (Smith & Millner, 1981; Maguire et al., 1996; Maguire et al., 1999; Maguire et al., 2000). Research points to the hippocampus area, which is placed in the centre of the brain, as being responsible for providing spatial memory. To measure spatial and spatial orientation, various spatial visualisation and orientation tests that can determine a person's orientation skill, such as the Guilford-Zimmerman orientation survey (Guilford & Zimmerman, 1948). Other tests exist (such as spatial memory, and spatial scanning tests), but spatial orientation tests are thought to be more successful in determining a user's ability to acquire spatial knowledge (Waller, 2001).

Although the orientation skill of a user is often thought to be the most critical individual difference, there is actually no proof that it has the most impact on the required exposure time. Additional research is required to more fully investigate how orientation skill impacts spatial knowledge acquisition.

Age Differences in Navigation

Age plays an important role in navigation due to an overall change in sensory abilities, as well as various knowledge and cognitive skills, which are developed through life (Cohen & Scheupfer, 1980; Mathews, 1992; Wilkniss et al., 1997; Pine et al., 2002). Hasher and Zacks (1979) suggest that spatial ability is an automatic process that does not demand cognitive abilities, and therefore should not be affected by age. According to Cohen and Scheupfer (1980), pre-adolescents navigate through a novel environment just as well as adults if the knowledge being acquired is through procedural means (i.e. direct exploration). Problem occur however when transferring survey knowledge to procedural knowledge, since the ability to navigate through the environment using abstract mental representations is only developed in later stages of adolescence (Mathews, 1992). Cohen and Scheupfer (1980) theorized that pre-adolescents are burdened when navigating through a novel environment using survey knowledge and abstract mental information (i.e. from a map). Pine et al. (2002) found that when navigating freely through a virtual city, adolescents reached as many goals and learned the environment as quickly as adults. Pine et al. (2002), however, also found that when asked to recall information, such as label points of interest on a map, adults significantly exceeded adolescents. Adults, therefore, have a better ability of transferring procedural to survey knowledge.

As an adult reaches old age they suffer from various issues surrounding both their sensory and orientation skills. Salthouse et al. (1990) argues that as people get older, they find it increasingly hard to process new information, whilst trying to retrieve information from memory. According to Kirasic (2000), navigation becomes increasingly difficult as age increases due to declines in perceptual, cognitive and motor abilities. It seems that disorientation in spatial navigation becomes more and more frequent when a person exceeds the age of seventy, even if there is no sign of mental deterioration (Hunt and Waller, 1999). Research suggests that in terms of learning navigational space, older people find it increasingly hard to retrace routes and learn maps (Wilkniss et al., 1997), orientate with respect to other environmental objects (Aubrey & Dobbs, 1990), as well as make distance and direction judgments (Kirasic, 2000). One of the most difficult problems that older people face is the attention divide (Darroch et al., 2005). Because of this, the ability to acquire spatial knowledge through a virtual medium could be beneficial to older ages, since it would help them learn novel environments without the risk of facing physical tiredness.

Cognitive Styles

The concept of people adopting different strategies in order to solve problems and make decisions was first presented by Allport (1937) who presented cognitive styles as a person's preferred way of perceiving, remembering, thinking and problem solving. Since then research has looked into cognitive styles, and has referred to them as persistent strategies adapted by individuals when faced with problem solving tasks (Robertson, 1985). In more detail, cognitive styles affect perceiving, remembering, organizing, processing, thinking and problem solving (Liu & Ginther, 1999).

Many different learning strategies are consistently adopted by a user in order to solve a problem. Messick (1976) identified as many as 19 different cognitive styles, and Smith (1984) identified 17. Schmeck (1988) grouped them using two distinctly different, but general, learning styles. The first is a more holist learning style, which is referred to as field-dependent and seems to emerge from activity in the right hemisphere of the brain. The second is a more analytical learning style that is referred to as field-independent and seems to emerge from activity in the left hemisphere of the brain.

Field-dependent people are more passive when learning (Witkin et al.,1977), and prefer to learn information by focusing on the information as a whole - rather than breaking it down. Field-independent users are more active when learning new information and prefer to acquire information in a serial fashion by breaking it down (Pask, 1979). Goodenough (1976) and Witkin et al. (1977) stated that field-independent people sample more relevant cues to solve a problem, whilst field-dependent people sample more irrelevant cues to the current problem. In terms of landmarks, which are considered cues for navigation, field-independent users will benefit more from informative landmarks. This is also seen in research concerning 'hypermedia navigation' (Chen & Macredie, 2001), which indicates that field-dependent users were more efficient when they had to take a more holistic strategy, and navigate using a map of the overall system. In this research field-independent users benefited more from an analytical strategy, which included a depth-search of the entire system (Ford and Chen, 2001).

RELATIONSHIP BETWEEN ENVIRONMENTAL AND INDIVIDUAL DIFFERENCES

Since people are different, a one-size fits all approach to training time does not seem logical. By summarizing all we have discussed so far, and by closely examining the research presented in the previous sections, we show that certain individual user differences 'react' more strongly with specific environmental factors. The reaction between these properties critically influences the overall navigational complexity of the environment and therefore the required exposure time. Figure 1 illustrates the various interactions between the individual user differences and environmental factors, as discussed in this chapter. Figure 1 was developed by the authors in order to accommodate for the significance of various individual user differences during navigation when particular environmental properties are present. The top layer represents the environmental factors, the middle layer represents the individual user differences, and the bottom layer represents the cognitive categorization that these individual user differences belong to, as discussed by Darken et al. (1999). By closely examining Figure 1 we see that most individual user differences impact on all types of environments. The only exception seems to be gender and cognitive styles. This diagram is extracted from supporting literature and is therefore hypothetical in nature.

SUMMARY AND REVIEW OF BUSINESS IMPLICATIONS

This chapter presents a variety of literature suggesting that spatial knowledge acquisition through VE navigation is feasible, but is influenced by the exposure time given to a user to learn the environment. It was deducted through a comparison of previous studies, that individual cognitive and biological differences impact on the navigational skill of the user, and lead to higher exposure time requirements for spatial knowledge acquisition. These individual user differences affect various skills such as knowledge, aptitude, ability and strategy and have been identified as gender, age, orientation skills, knowledge / experience and cognitive styles. However, individual differences are not the only properties that affect exposure time requirements. Various structural factors of an environment render the environment more or less environmentally complex, and therefore influence the exposure time needed to acquire spatial knowledge as well (Darken and Peterson, 2001). These environmental factors are: size, spatial complexity, and landmark potential.

From a business perspective the fact that i) VEs can be used acquiring spatial knowledge, and ii) that a one-size exposure duration is in appropriate, has significant implications. Much spatial knowledge training relates to real world space that is either under-development or potentially unsafe. In such cases on-site training of service, emergency and support staff is impossible, yet the result of badly trained staff has safety implication in the case of an emergency or security breach. Imagine, in the case of a fire at a major sporting event (e.g. World cup or the Olympic Games), the international implications of emergency staff not knowing the layout of a stadium. What legal and political implications exist for government if it can be shown that the military had not provided soldiers with either appropriate training techniques (i.e. VEs) or VE exposure duration that later led to death. In such cases, learning using maps and briefings is restricted because of the individual user differences of the demographic groups involved. Training each and every member of staff in real-world space cannot practically be achieved, however the implication of badly trained staff has significant legal, political and ethic implications. What is the solution?

Considerable research suggests that individual user differences impact exposure time for all types of environments, with two exceptions (i.e. gender and cognitive styles): gender is a critical factor only when navigation in low-landmark maze-like environments (see Figure 1); cognitive style impacts spatial knowledge acquisition with field-independent users acquiring spatial knowledge faster from complex environments, and field-dependent users having the advantage in large environments. Orientation skill and environmental knowledge impacts duration time in all environments, yet these individual differences are not easily trained and require significant periods

Figure 1. The stages of the information-processing model affected by environmental factors and individual user differences

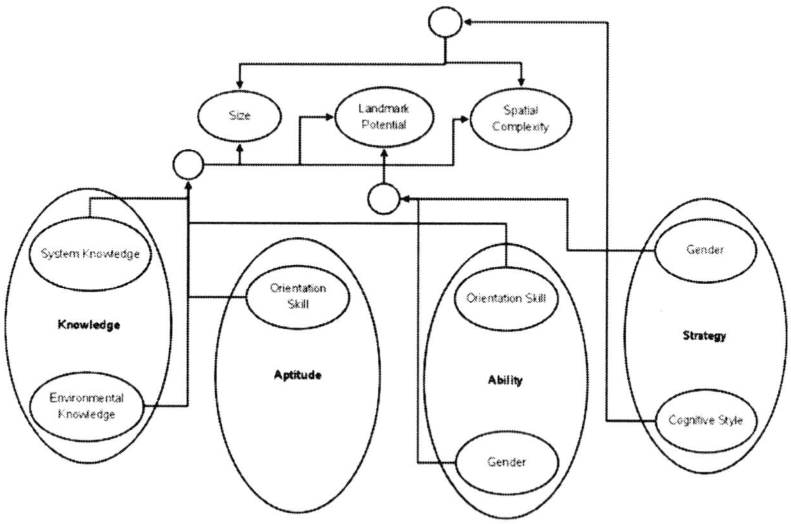

of prolonged training (i.e. possibly years) before any noticeable improvement can be measured.

Since significant periods of prolonged training is not possible to increase natural ability of service or military staff, relevant compensation (i.e. additional training within the specific space in question) must be given to cancel out low natural ability. As exposure of untrained staff to dangerous environments is not appropriate, use of spatial training within a VE is a good option for removing many of these safety concerns. Currently, however, there is no research, to the best of our knowledge that is able to quantify the impact of individual differences on exposure duration. Additional research is needed to facilitate VE designers in their understanding of how learning spatial knowledge for a VE impact different users, and what can be done with cue placement to maximize information acquisition, and limit frustration and disorientation. VE mapping, modeling and use in spatial training is of growing importance. It offers significant potential in the effective training of staff, yet a one-size fits all approach cannot be use justified. Only once individual use differences are quantified, can anyone effectively provide spatial training that is appropriate to the specific user.

REFERENCES

Allport, G. W. (1937). *Personality: A psychological interpretation.* New York: Holt & Co.

Asthmeir P. Feiger W. & Muller S. (1993), Virtual design: a generic VR system for

Astur, R. S., Ortiz, M. L., & Sutherland, R. J. (1998). A characterization of performance by men and women in a virtual Morris water task: A large and reliable sex difference. *Behavioural Brain Research, 93*(12), 185–190. doi:10.1016/S0166-4328(98)00019-9

Aubrey, J. B., & Dobbs, A. R. (1990). Age and sex differences in the mental realignment of maps. *Experimental Aging Research, 16*(3), 133–139. doi:10.1080/07340669008251540

Booth K. Fisher B. Page S. Ware C. & Widen S. (2000). Wayfinding in a virtual environment. *Graphics Interface.*

Brewer, W. F. (2000). Bartlett's concept of the schema and its impact on theories of knowledge representation in contemporary cognitive psychology. In Saito (Ed.), Bartlett, culture and cognition, 69-89, Psychology Press.

Brewer, W. F., & Nakamura, G. V. (1984). The nature and functions of schemas. *Handbook of social cognition,* 1, 119160.

Butler, D. L., Acquino, A. L., Hissong, A. A., & Scott, P. A. (1993). Wayfinding by Newcomers in a Complex Building. *Human Factors, 35*(1), 159173.

Chen, S. Y., & Macredie, R. D. (2001). Cognitive styles and hypermedia navigation: Development of a learning model. *Journal of the American Society for Information Science and Technology, 53*(1), 315. doi:10.1002/1532-2890(2000)9999:9999<::AID-ASI1074>3.0.CO;2-2

Clark, S. A., & Wong, B. L. W. (2000). QTVR Support for Teaching Operative Procedures in Dentistry. People and Computer XIV. Usability or Else! *Proceedings of HCL 2000,* London.

Cobb S.U.G. & D'Cruz, M. D. (1994) First UK national survey on industrial application of virtual reality. *VR News,* 3.

Cohen, R., & Schuepfer, T. (1980). The representation of landmarks and routes. *Child Development, 51,* 1065–1071. doi:10.2307/1129545

Darken, R. P., Allard, T., & Achille, L. B. (1999). Spatial Orientation and Wayfinding in Large Scale Virtual Spaces II. *Presence (Cambridge, Mass.), 8*(6).

Darken, R. P., & Banker, W. P. (1998). Navigating in Natural Environments: A Virtual Environment Training Transfer Study. *Proceedings of VRAIS, 98*, 12–19.

Darken, R. P., & Peterson, B. (2001). Spatial Orientation, Wayfinding, and Representation. In Stanney, K. (Ed.), *Handbook of Virtual Environment Technology*. Stanney.

Darken, R. P., & Sibert, J. L. (1996). Wayfinding strategies and behaviours in large virtual worlds. *Proceedings of ACM CHI96*, 142-149.

Darroch, I. Goodman J. Brewster S. & Gray P. (2005) The Effect of Age and Font Size on Reading Text on Handheld Computers. *Proceedings of IFIP INTERACT05: Human-Computer Interaction,* pp. 253-266.

Dix, A. Finlay J. Abowd G. & Beale R. (1993). *Human computer interaction*. New York: Prentice Hall.

Doyle, S., Dodge, M., & Smith, A. (1998). The potential of web - based mapping and virtual reality technologies for modeling urban environments. *Computers, Environment and Urban Systems*, *22*(2), 137–155. doi:10.1016/S0198-9715(98)00014-3

Eberts, R. E. (1994). *User interface design*. Englewood Cliffs, NJ: Prentice Hall.

Egsegian, R., Pittman, K., Farmer, K., & Zobel, R. (1993). Practical applications of virtual reality to firefighter training. In *Proceedings of the 1993 Simulations Multiconference on the International Emergency Management and Engineering Conference* (pp. 155–160). San Diego, CA: Society of Computer Simulation

Feldman, A., & Acredolo, L. P. (1979). The effect of active versus passive exploration on memory for spatial location in children. *Child Development*, *50*, 698–704. doi:10.2307/1128935

Ford, N., & Chen, S. Y. (2001). Matching/mismatching revisited: An empirical study of learning and teaching styles. *British Journal of Educational Technology*, *32*(1), 5–22. doi:10.1111/1467-8535.00173

Foreman, N., Stanton, D., Wilson, P., & Duffy, H. (2003). Spatial Knowledge of a Real School Environment Acquired From Virtual or Physical Models by Able Bodied Children and Children With Physical Disabilities. *Journal of Experimental Psychology*, *9*(2), 67–74.

Gallistel, C. R. (1990). *The organisation of learning*. Cambridge M.A: The MIT Press.

Goerger, S. Darken R. Boyd M. Gagnon T. Liles S. Sullivan J. & Lawson J.P (1998).Spatial Knowledge Acquisition from Maps and Virtual Environments in Complex Architectural Spaces. Proceedings of the 16th Applied Behavioral Sciences Symposium, 2223, April, U.S. Air Force Academy. Colorado Springs, 610.

Golledge, R. G., Dougherty, V., & Bell, S. (1995). Acquiring Spatial Knowledge: Survey versus Route Based Knowledge. *Unfamiliar Environments Reginald Annals of the Association of American Geographers*, *85*(1), 13158.

Gomez, L. M. Egan D.E. & Bowers C. (1986). Learning to use a text editor: Some learner characteristics that predict success. *HumanComputer Interaction*, 2, 1–23.

Goodenough, D. (1976). The role of individual differences in field dependence as a factor in learning and memory. *Psychological Bulletin*, *83*, 675–694. doi:10.1037/0033-2909.83.4.675

Gouteux, S., & Spelke, E. (2001). Children's use of geometry and landmarks to reorient in an open space. *Cognition*, *81*, 119–148. doi:10.1016/S0010-0277(01)00128-7

Guilford, J. P., & Zimmerman, W. S. (1948). The Guilford Zimmerman Aptitude Survey. *The Journal of Applied Psychology*, *32*, 24–34. doi:10.1037/h0063610

Hasher, L., & Zacks, R. T. (1979). Automatic and effortful processes in memory. *Journal of Experimental Psychology*, *108*, 356–388.

Hegarty, M., & Waller, D. (2004). A dissociation between mental rotation and perspective-taking spatial abilities. *Intelligence*, *32*, 175–191. doi:10.1016/j.intell.2003.12.001

Howes, A. Jones D. Payne S. & Ruddle R. (1999). Navigating Discontinuous Virtual Worlds. *Workshop on Spatial cognition in real and virtual environments at the Max Planck Institute*, Tuebingen.

Hunt, E. & Waller, D. (1999). Orientation and wayfinding: A review. *ONR Technical Report.*

industrial applications. *Computer Graphics*, *17*, 671–677.

Kirasic, K. C. (2000). Age differences in adults' spatial abilities, learning environmental layout, and wayfinding behavior. *Spatial Cognition and Computation*, *2*, 117–134. doi:10.1023/A:1011445624332

Koh, G., Wiegand, T. E., Garnett, R., Durlach, N., & Cunningham, B. S. (1999). Use of Virtual Environments for Acquiring Configurational Knowledge about Specific RealWorld Spaces. *Preliminary Experiment*, *8*(6), 632–656.

Kuipers, B. J. (1975). A frame for frames: Representing knowledge for recognition. In Bobrow, D. G., & Collins, A. (Eds.), *Representation and understanding: Studies in cognitive science*. New York: Academic Press.

Lampinen, J., Copeland, S., & Neuschatz, J. (2001). Recollections of things schematic: rooms schemas revisited. *Cognition*, *27*, 1211–1222.

Liu, Y., & Ginther, D. (1999). Cognitive Styles and Distance Education. *Online Journal of Distance Learning Administration*, *2*(3).

Lynch, K. (1960). *The Image of the city*. The MIT press.

Maguire, E. A. (1999). Burgess N. & O'Keefe J. (1999) Human spatial navigation: cognitive maps, sexual dimorphism, and neural substrates. *Current Opinion in Neurobiology*, *9*, 171–177. doi:10.1016/S0959-4388(99)80023-3

Maguire, E. A. Gadian D.G. Johnsrude I.S. Good C.D. Ashburner J. Frackowiak R.S.J. & Frith C.D. (2000). Navigation related structural change in the hippocampi of taxi drivers. *Proceedings of the national academy of science* (USA), 97(8)

Maguire, E. A., Frackowiak, R. S. J., & Frith, C. D. (1996). Recalling Routes around London: Activation of the Right Hippocampus in Taxi Drivers. *The Journal of Neuroscience*, *17*(18), 7103–7110.

Mania K. Robinson A. & Brandt K.R. (2005). The effect of memory schemas on object recognition in virtual environments. *Presence: Teleoperators and Virtual Environments archive, 14*(5), 606 – 615

Mathews, M. H. (1992). *Making Sense of Place: Children's Understanding of Large Scale Environments*. Hertfordshire, England: Harvester Wheatsheaf.

Messick, S. (1976). *Individuality in learning*. San Francisco: Jossey-Bass.

Moffat, S. D., Hampson, E., & Hatzipantelis, M. (1998). Navigation in a "virtual" maze: sex differences and correlation with psychometric measures of spatial ability in humans. *Evolution and Human Behavior*, *19*, 73–78. doi:10.1016/S1090-5138(97)00104-9

Montello, D. R. (2005) Navigation. In P. Shah & A. Miyake (Eds.), The Cambridge Handbook of Visuospatial Thinking. Cambridge University Press, 257-294.

Newman, E. L., Caplan, J. B., Kirschen, P., Korolev, I. O., Sekuler, R., & Kahana, M. J. (2007). Learning your way around town: How virtual taxicab drivers learn to use both layout and landmark information. *Cognition*, *104*, 231–253. doi:10.1016/j.cognition.2006.05.013

Pask, G. (1979). *Final report of S.S.R.C. Research programme HR 2708*. Richmond (Surrey): System Research Ltd.

Passini, R. (1984). *Wayfinding in Architecture*. New York: Van Nostrand Reinhold Company Inc.

Pelagatti, G., Negri, M., Belussi, A., & Migliorini, S. (2009). From the conceptual design of spatial constraints to their implementation in real systems. In *Proceedings of the 17th ACM SIGSPATIAL international Conference on Advances in Geographic information Systems (Seattle, Washington, November 04 - 06, 2009)*. (GIS '09. ACM, pp 448-451)New York, NY.

Pine, D. S., Grun, J., Maguire, E. A., Burgess, N., Zarahn, E., & Koda, V. (2002). Neurodevelopmental Aspects of Spatial Navigation: A Virtual Reality fMRI Study. *NeuroImage*, *15*, 396–406. doi:10.1006/nimg.2001.0988

Riva, G., & Gambrini, L. (2000). Virtual reality in telemedicine. *Telemedicine Journal*, *6*, 327–340. doi:10.1089/153056200750040183

Robertson, I. T. (1985). Human information processing strategies and style. *Behaviour & Information Technology*, *4*(1), 19–29. doi:10.1080/01449298508901784

Rose, F. D., Attree, E. A., Brooks, B. M., Parslow, D. M., & Penn, P. R. (2000). Training in virtual environments: transfer to real world tasks and equivalence to real task training Authors. *Ergonomics*, *43*(4), 494–511. doi:10.1080/001401300184378

Rose, F. D., & Foreman, N. P. (1999). Virtual reality. *The Psychologist*, *12*, 551–554.

Ruddle, R. A., Payne, S. J., & Jones, D. M. (1997). Navigating buildings in "desktop" virtual environments: Experimental investigations using extended navigational experience. *Journal of Experimental Psychology. Applied*, *3*, 143–159. doi:10.1037/1076-898X.3.2.143

Salthouse, T., Donald, K., & Saults, S. (1990). Age, Self Assessed Health Status and Cognition. *Journal of Gerontology*, *45*(4), 156–160.

Salthouse T.A. (1992). Why do adult age differences increase with task complexity?, 28, 905–918.

Sandstrome, N. J., Kaufman, J., & Huettel, S. A. (1998). Males and females use different distal cues in a virtual environment navigation task. *Brain Research. Cognitive Brain Research*, *6*, 351–360. doi:10.1016/S0926-6410(98)00002-0

Schmeck, R. R. (1988). *Learning strategies and learning styles*. Plenum Press.

Silverman, D. R., & Spiker, V. A. (1997), Ancient wisdom—future technology. *Proceedings of the Human Factor and Ergonomics Society, 41st Annual Meeting*. Albuquerque, New Mexico.

Smith, M. L., & Milner, B. (1981). The role of the right hippocampus in the recall of spatial location. *Neuropsychologia*, *19*, 781–793. doi:10.1016/0028-3932(81)90090-7

Smith, R. M. (1984). *Learning how to learn*. Milton Keynes: Open University.

Stankiewicz, B. J., & Kalia, A. (2004). Acquisition and Retention of Structural versus Object Landmark Knowledge When Navigating through a Large Scale Space. *Journal of Experimental Psychology. Human Perception and Performance*, *33*(2), 378–390. doi:10.1037/0096-1523.33.2.378

Stanney, K. M., Mourant, R. R., & Kennedy, R. S. (1998). Human Factors Issues in Virtual Environments: A Review of the Literature. *Presence (Cambridge, Mass.)*, *7*(4), 327–351. doi:10.1162/105474698565767

Stanney, K. M., & Salvendy, G. (1995). Information visualization; assisting low spatial individuals with information access tasks through the use of visual mediators. *Ergonomics*, *38*(6), 1184–1198. doi:10.1080/00140139508925181

Thorndyke, P. (1980). *Performance models for spatial and locational cognition (R2676ONR)*. Washington, D.C.: The Rand Corporation.

Thorndyke, P., & Hayes-Roth, B. (1982). Differences in spatial knowledge acquired from maps and navigation. *Cognitive Psychology*, *14*, 560–589. doi:10.1016/0010-0285(82)90019-6

Vicente, K. J., Hayes, B. C., & Williges, R. C. (1987). Assaying and isolating individual differences in searching a hierarchical file system. *Human Factors*, *29*(3), 349–359.

Vila, J. Beccue B. Anandikar S. (2002). The Gender Factor in Virtual Reality Navigation and Wayfinding. *Proceedings of the 36th Hawaii International Conference on System Sciences (HICSS'03).*

Vinson, N. G. (1999) Design Guidelines for Landmarks to Support Navigation in Virtual Environments. *Proceedings of CHI '99*, Pittsburgh, PA.

Waller, D., Hunt, E., & Knapp, D. (1998). The transfer of spatial knowledge in virtual environment training. *Presence (Cambridge, Mass.)*, *7*, 129–143. doi:10.1162/105474698565631

Waller, D., Knapp, D., & Hunt, E. (2001). Spatial Representations of Virtual Mazes: The Role of Visual Fidelity and Individual Differences. *Human Factors. The Journal of the Human Factors and Ergonomics Society*, *43*(1), 147–158. doi:10.1518/001872001775992561

Weisman, J. (1981). Evaluating achitectural legibility: Way-finding in the built environment. *Environment and Behavior*, *13*, 189–204. doi:10.1177/0013916581132004

Whitaker, L. A. (1996). Getting around in the natural world. *Ergonomics in Design*, *4*, 3, 11–15.

Wilkniss, S. M., Jones, M., Korel, D., Gold, P., & Manning, C. (1997). Agerelated differences in an ecologically based study of route learning. *Psychology and Aging*, *12*(2), 372–375. doi:10.1037/0882-7974.12.2.372

Wilson, P. N., Foreman, N., & Tlauka, M. (1997). Transfer of spatial information from a virtual to a real environment. *Human Factors*, *39*(4), 526–531. doi:10.1518/001872097778667988

Witkin, H. A., Moore, C. A., Goodenough, D. R., & Cox, P. W. (1977). Fielddependent and field independent cognitive styles and their educational implications. *Review of Educational Research*, *47*, 1–64.

Witmer B.G. Bailey J.H. & Knerr B.W. (1995), Training Dismounted Soldiers in Virtual Environments: Route Learning and Transfer. U.S. Army Research Institute for the Behavioral and Social Sciences

Witmer, B. G., Bailey, J. H., Knerr, B. W., & Parsons, K. C. (1996). Virtual spaces and real world places: transfer of route knowledge. *International Journal of Human-Computer Studies*, *45*(4), 413–428. doi:10.1006/ijhc.1996.0060

Witmer, B. G., & Sadowski, W. J. (1998). Nonvisually guided locomotion to a previously viewed target in real and virtual environments. (Special Section: Virtual environments: Models, Methodology, and Empirical Studies). *Human Factors*, *40*, 478–485. doi:10.1518/001872098779591340

Chapter 13
Opening the Content Pipeline for OpenSim-Based Virtual Worlds

Shenlei E. Winkler
Fashion Research Institute, Inc, USA

ABSTRACT

Open-Simulator (Open-Sim) refers to a three dimensional application environment that can be used to develop virtual worlds similar to those that exist in Second Life®. Open-Sim is considered open source software, i.e., software that is developed by a community of volunteers and is available for use by the public free of charge (Open Simulator, 2009). Although participants in virtual worlds are generally considered by law to be the owner of any Intellectual Property (IP) they create, content creators and owners of OpenSim-based virtual worlds struggle with issues surrounding licensing, content delivery, and usage in these immersive spaces. The Fashion Research Institute (FRI) is specifically exploring these issues in a case study involving the licensing its Shengri La virtual world creations to external users. This case study is the basis of ongoing legal research by FRI's legal steering committee of attorneys from the American Bar Association's Virtual Worlds and Online Gaming committee who are working on a pro bono (volunteer) basis. This chapter presents the result of the ongoing case study. It offers a practitioner's view of issues related to licensing and distribution of content in virtual worlds.

INTRODUCTION

The coming diaspora of content creators from closed grids such as Second Life® to other open source, open grids run on the OpenSim platform offer both exciting opportunities as well as dangerous pitfalls for the unprepared. Opening new marketplaces to content creators has the ability to add appreciably to the global marketplace, with virtual goods accounting for $2.6 billion in sales in 2008 (Virtual Goods News, 2009), with that number expected to increase exponentially in the near future.

Participants in virtual worlds consider the content they create to be their own Intellectual Property (IP). However, these content creators

DOI: 10.4018/978-1-61692-808-7.ch013

with several issues involving the licensing, content delivery, and usage of their creations. "The intersection of intellectual property laws and the virtual world raises a panoply of issues and concerns…" (Kane & Duranske, 2008, p. 12). The Fashion Research Institute (FRI) is currently involved in a case study designed to explore the issues involved in the licensing of content created for its *Shengri La* virtual world. This case study is the result of collaboration among FRI's legal steering committee of attorneys from the American Bar Association's Virtual Worlds and Online Gaming committee who are working on a *pro bono* (volunteer) basis.

Content creation for these OpenSim-based grids requires an appreciable amount of time and dedication by content creators. The current technology is limited and much of the time is spend re-developing the same content for each virtual area or grid where they wish their content to be available. Although OpenSim Archive Resource (OAR) files do enable some content creators to develop content once, and move it around as OAR files, most content creators lack the knowledge to perform this function.

It is anticipated that upcoming technology advances will enable these content creators to readily move their content around and make it more widely and readily available. Before content creators will accept these new technology solutions and make their content available to commercial grid operators, legal considerations governing the licensing of their content need to be addressed. These include the functional legal definition of terms which are generally accepted by the legal community; the development of content quality standards against which content may be assessed and qualified; the deployment of development frameworks to help ensure that content creators can issue certificates of originality and produce documentation to prove authenticity of their content; and finally, the standardization of contractual agreements between content creators and users, content creators and grid operators, and grid operators and users.

The following chapter focuses on these considerations in the context of an existing case study involving the content developers at Fashion Research Institute (FRI) and engineers at Intel® Labs. In this case study, large-scale, complex virtual builds and creations are developed on both FRI and Intel hardware. The content is continually moved back and forth between the hardware servers of the two companies. The existing agreement between FRI and Intel defines the use of this content for research, and serves as a test bed to help determine additional licensing issues related to content development, content curation, and management needs.

BACKGROUND

"There is widespread potential for copyright infringement in virtual worlds and, indeed, there is widespread infringement of copyrights" (Ibid, p. 13). Licensing content into virtual worlds is often compared to the settling of the American 'Wild West' with content developers claiming new space and pitting themselves against content thieves and other risks. There is also confusion within the content developer community about how the terms of service (TOS) and end user licensing agreement (EULA) of a given virtual world impacts their intellectual property ownership and protection of their rights. Many content producers, who develop virtual goods for sale and use in these immersive spaces are understandably leery of exposing themselves to the risk of loss of their intellectual property when moving into a new virtual world where the TOS and EULA may be even less well understood. With the advent of low barrier-to-entry worlds such as Second Life® and OpenSim, licensing considerations for managing a recognized brand and protecting brand extension become even more pressing.

CONTENT LICENSING AND DISTRIBUTION

Fashion Research Institute is working with a selected group of attorneys to explore how licensing is best addressed in a metaverse of OpenSim-based virtual worlds. Using a specific FRI case study with Intel Labs as an exemplar, this chapter will examine licensing considerations for content producers who wish to extend their content into the very wildest of all the new immersive space frontiers, OpenSim.

OpenSim (http://www.opensimulator.org) is an open source, virtual world platform which originated in 2007. The source code is developed and maintained by a loosely organized group of developers. The platform uses client viewers in common with another popular virtual world, Second Life®. The backend functionality of OpenSim is much broader than Second Life®, and enables users and operators of OpenSim-based virtual worlds to have access to a much wider array of functionality into backend systems such as enterprise resource planning, business intelligence, and other database driven applications.

This capability has expanded the use of virtual worlds within private enterprise environments. In a private enterprise environment, the owners and operators of the private virtual worlds have control over all content once it is placed in the virtual environment. However, owners and operators do not have any control over what sort of content gets uploaded to their region, although they can remove content when needed. In order to protect against unwanted content being loaded into their virtual environment, enterprises use firewalls as a common security measure to guard against inappropriate access to the internal virtual worlds. Firewalls use a combination of software and hardware functionality to limit the information transmitted to and from a private network. However, as with any sort of private network, the primary security hole with content behind a private enterprise firewall is the enterprise's own employees, who can copy and restore content onto other virtual worlds. Firewalls will not stop content theft by insiders. Insider security threats are considered more common than external security breaches by hackers (McCue, 2008). This is a substantial security vulnerability and one which cannot be readily managed by currently available technological solutions.

A lack of control over internal virtual world content means that content creators must trust the virtual world operator to abide by whatever agreement is in place regarding the dispensation of their content. It also means that there is a dangerous chasm into which a content creator can fall, in which unscrupulous virtual word operators force a change of the creator and ownership tags on content instantiated into these OpenSim-based worlds. In this situation, content developers who have not kept careful records through time-stamped files and other forms of documentation could find themselves in a situation where they may attempt legal recourse but lack documentation to prove their claims of infringement.

There are several aspects of OpenSim-based worlds and Second Life®® regions which should be considered by any entity which plans to use these immersive spaces. Any content (text, images, 3-D models, and so on) which can be viewed by the user using a viewer is not currently protected by digital rights management technology. The process of 'viewing' a scene composed of images, models, text, and/or code downloads the images and models onto the user's hard drive, where it is stored in cache. Practically speaking, each user is able to obtain a copy of anything they have virtually seen, or 'viewed' using their viewer. This content is now stored on their hard drive until such time as they 'dump their cache' or clear out old images and model information.

That fact that users are able to maintain their own copy of developed content is what underpins much of the content theft that occurs in virtual worlds and is the ultimate conundrum to licensing content into these virtual worlds. OpenSim virtual world operators want their users to see the content, but there is no easy or cost effective way to block users from acquiring and retaining copies of that content on their hard drive. It is assumed that most users of virtual worlds have no intention to use this copied content for nefarious purposes, either because of socio-cultural conditioning against stealing or because they lack the technological know-how. Others users, however, are not bound by similar moral or ethical codes, and do have the technological wherewithal to steal this content and 'launder' it to resell on other virtual worlds under their own name. This poses the question as to how rightful owners of the content can be protected if there is no easy or effectual technology solution. It becomes a pressing matter for the existing legal channels to provide that protection for content in OpenSim-based virtual worlds.

In the United States and in most other developed countries, copyright, patent, and similar intellectual property (IP) laws are well-established and understood by the legal communities in these respective countries. While IP laws do vary from country to country, there is general agreement that protecting creators' rights to their creations help to ensure that these creators continue to invent and create, which in turn helps support the economy of these countries. Legal channels already exist that protect content creators of all classes. As Duranske (2008, p. 12)) states, "While intellectual property rights in virtual creations are somewhat controversial, they share a common basis with other IP rights, including copyright, trademark, patent, and trade secret law, which are more firmly grounded in established law". What is missing, however, are legal definitions which can be used to create contracts which will withstand scrutiny in the event of a legal challenge; an understanding of the content creators about how they need to protect their own work; and standards for both this sort of content and for legal agreements that govern engagements between content creators and virtual world operators.

In this case study, FRI made an agreement with Intel Labs to provide content for OpenSim-based virtual areas or regions referred to as *Science Sim* (http://www.sciencesim.com) as part of a year-long research arrangement. In developing this agreement, several licensing issues emerged and were able to be resolved using existing laws and language. Because the nature of the agreement was to conduct research, there was both an explicit and implicit understanding between the parties as to the extent of agreement for the sharing of content. Both sides agreed to use great care in moving content back and forth between FRI content creators and Intel Labs' hosted regions. But both sides also acknowledged that there was no technological way to protect the individual FRI content creator from theft by users of these regions. It is important to note that the agreement in this case study involved research and should not be considered a typical legal agreement that might be executed between a typical content creator and a commercial OpenSim-based virtual world.

In order to maintain strict control over the developed content, FRI has established several practices. The development of content provided to the *ScienceSim* regions is scrupulously tracked: with originating concepts logged and filed with intermediate files and resources maintained. Original digital formats, such as Photoshop files showing the full layer set for images, are versioned and maintained, enabling the content creators to issue a *certificate of originality* and to substantiate it in the event of a legal challenge. Unfortunately, current virtual world content standards have not evolved enough to offer a standard format for providing certificates of originality. This is an area which will require further attention in the future in order that all stakeholders in the licensing process are protected.

In order to protect the IP of their content, content creators must be able to issue a *certificate of originality* for their content to entities which license it. Content Creators must be able to assure the licensing entity that it is not receiving 'laundered' content or exposing itself to legal repercussions if it hosts unauthorized content. The concept of a certificate of originality has been in existence in software companies and used by many of the multinational business organizations for many years, and it is an accepted standard form among these entities (Fitzgerald, 2003). Applying the concept to the more tenuous realm of content creation is something which is understandable both by the legal complex and by enterprise entities.

Fashion Research Institute (FRI) has defined a series of requirements for content creators working them to help license their content. These requirements have evolved from the agreements that FRI has made with Intel Labs to provide content into *ScienceSim*. It is critical that FRI and other content creators protect themselves and any downstream licensors from legal challenges around ownership of the content. FRI created a framework within which content creators are required to work and document their work as described earlier. FRI also provides standards against which content is judged in order to issue a certificate of originality. Tracking content back to its moment of instantiation provides a degree of protection against future claims against creator, licensor, licensee, and law-abiding users. While nuisance claims may arise, they can be easily defended against with the use of this documentation. Tracking content also provides the content creator with date-stamped original files which may be admissible as evidence in the event that the content creator's work is infringed and they seek legal recourse. The ability to use these tracked files as evident is germane because it enables all stakeholders to be guaranteed of protection which already exists in extant legal channels.

An area which requires further exploration and input from the legal, technology, and content development communities, is to create a definition of terms that will be commonly used in the virtual world space, and which are properly aligned with existing legal definitions. These definitions will enable all virtual world stakeholders to develop licensing agreements and contracts to safely move content between content creators and OpenSim-based grid operators without concern for IP ownership issues.

In addition to aligning technology and content development terms to legal definitions, existing terms of service (TOS) and end user licensing agreements (EULA) must also be evaluated in terms virtual content creation in order to protect all stakeholders. Currently, most OpenSim-based worlds have relatively loose EULA and TOS agreements which primarily address users' rights and privileges with regards to the actual user experience (Duraske).

However, minimal attention has been addressed to content considerations in the event that a user identifies content which has clearly been laundered or in violation of another entity's trademark, patent, or copyright. This is a fairly common occurrence in virtual worlds and immersive spaces where users can create their own content. Either from ignorance or intent, a user locates and introduces content which is clearly infringing on existing intellectual property. One example evident by a visit to a virtual world was the use of a Monopoly® board observed in an OpenSim-based region. The game of Monopoly is owned by Hasbro® (http://www.hasbro.com/monopoly/en_US/), and it is highly unlikely that Hasbro would allow its intellectual property to be used casually by a user who is probably not paying the licensing fee to use this artwork and who may not know (or care) that the presence of this artwork could be legally actionable. The OpenSim-based region operator may not even be aware that this artwork is present on their grid, but the operator could be held liable in the event that Hasbro, the real owner of this intellectual property, opted to pursue legal recourse. Although the operator might argue that they cannot know the details or provenance of every last image or 3D model introduced into their space, it is unlikely that this argument would prove to be a very successful defense. The Monopoly board is but one example, however many other examples are easily seen in a visit to a virtual world such as Second Life®. These are examples of infringement which occur and are unreported simply because the user base currently has no ability to report; does not understand how to report; or does not care to report infringements.

While the Digital Millennium Copyright Act (DMCA) contains provisions (Safe Harbour) to protect the unsuspecting web hosting service from claims of infringement by original copyright owners (Duranske). There is a question as to what happens when the entity which is hosting the virtual world is also the entity which employs the infringer, and consequently benefits from infringement. Does the DMCA automatically extend to virtual world content which is placed on a commercial grid operator's facilities? If so, who is liable for this infringement? Is the content launderer liable for instantiating the laundered content into the virtual world or, the commercial grid operator for allowing laundered content onto their grid, or both parties?

As OpenSim-based worlds mature, these sorts of considerations will require more formal legal attention. The current generation of client viewers (the software used to access these virtual worlds) do not incorporate any digital rights management, so it falls into the purview of the legal community to help define not only the terms used to discuss these worlds and their content, but also the behaviors which are permitted within the worlds and by the actual creators and operators. Only through establishing an appropriate legal structure can the content pipeline into these virtual worlds be protected to enable the development of a 3-D Internet and the formation of a web of federated virtual worlds.

TOWARDS A WORKING LEXICOGRAPHY

A thorough discussion of standardized legal agreements is beyond the scope of this chapter, however we will offer working definitions of key terms that would benefit both OpenSim-based grid operator and content creator for OpenSim-based worlds. The definitions are not technical definitions and do not correspond to the architecture or implementation of the underlying OpenSim code., Given the fluid nature of the OpenSim codebase, it is important that these terms are not linked to actual implementation details in the code, in order to prevent the definitions from becoming obsolete as the code itself changes.

The first terms to be defined are *Grid Operator, Content Creator, Grid,* and *Asset*, as these define the relationships of any contract written to provide content between the actual makers and the consumers.

- The *Content Creator* is the original creator of any sort of data, or content, intended for a virtual world. While this entity may be referred to as a *content developer*; the two terms are slightly different because a developer may take original concepts created by the content creator and further develop them into actual saleable products, as for example the development of landscaping products, which may use images created by a *Content Creator* combined with primitive units created by the Developer or by another Content Creator. Any individual or entity which engages in creating images, animations, sounds, scripts/code, models, apparel, builds, regions, RAW files and any other asset used in a virtual world scene is a *Content Creator*. *Content Developers* will be unable to issue a certificate of originality unless the Content Creator(s) with whom she works can do so.
- A *Grid Operator* is an entity which engages in the business of creating a grid of virtual world regions; provides the hardware, hosting and system administration. Linden Lab is currently the most well-known grid operator, with tens of thousands of regions in the Second Life® grid. *Grid Operators*

range from individual user creating private 'walled gardens' for their own purposes to commercial entities running larger grids composed of thousands of regions. For the purposes of developing a licensing contract, a Grid Operator must be able to provide appropriate documentation that it is a legally organized entity. Such documentation may include a Dun & Bradstreet number or an Employee Identification Number.

- An *Asset* is defined as anything included in the virtual world to create visual immersion for an avatar-represented user. *Assets* can include the scripting code that makes the virtual content interactive, images ('textures'), 3-D models composed of various meshes or in an OpenSim-based world, primitive units, sounds, animations, and all other objects, scripts or files introduced to a specific virtual world instance. *Assets* also include the images and data required to create the virtual world (sky, water, clouds, earth, etc.).
- The usage of the term *Grid* here is specific to Second Life® and OpenSim-based virtual worlds. It refers to a collection of regions which form a discrete virtual world which may or may not be accessible from other such collections of virtual worlds. OpenSim-based virtual worlds have the ability to be hypergrid enabled, which allows users to travel from grid to grid easily. As of August 2009, users' assets were confined to their home grid or region, but this is expected to be addressed before the end of 2009.

Agreements made between *Grid Operators* and *Content Creators* or *Developers* need to address certain considerations, including existing agreements that the Grid Operator has developed and with which the grid users are expected to comply. These existing agreements are called the *Terms of Service* (TOS) and the End User Licensing Agreements EULA.

- A *Terms of Service Agreement (TOS)* is an agreement made between a provider of software and a user of that software, which can govern everything from accessibility, the use of the software, software availability, intellectual property developed on the software platform, expected user behavior while using the software, and other related matters. The critical functional difference to users between EULAs and TOSs are that a TOS agreement governs the software and the user's interaction with it, while the EULA governs the assets and content and the user's expected interaction and behavior towards and with those aspects.
- *End User Licensing Agreement (EULA)* is a legal agreement presented to users before entering any particular OpenSim-based virtual world. The precise time of presentment of the agreement (e.g., at time of sign-up or at time of initial log-in) varies by grid; the terms may also vary but they all cover how the user may engage with the specific virtual world and how they may use content found in that world.

Both of these agreements must be reviewed and considered when establishing a contract between a Grid Operator and Content Creator. Existing contracts impact how the terms of content licensing agreements are defined. Specific existing terms contained within these agreements may prohibit some content creators from licensing content to a given Grid Operator.

Similarly, a Grid Operator will want to be assured that any content it is licensing will be original content. A Content Creator must be able to provide a *Certificate of Originality (CoO)*, which is a document that attests that all work provided by a Content Creator is original, and that all development documentation has been maintained and can be produced in the event of a legal challenge. The current state of content creation does not customarily require CoOs, but as enterprise users seek content for propagation into their OpenSim-based virtual worlds these users will insist that such documentation be provided. The ability of a Content Creator to provide such documentation will yield the additional benefit of providing some degree of protection to the Content Creator because they will have kept the mandatory records which substantiate their claims to originality. Such records may include time-stamped versioned files; files which include layers of development (for example, Photoshop files); and versions and revisions of files as well as email or formal documented approvals of custom work.

Content Creators have their own lexicography, as well, which covers the process of creation.

- For example, a *Build* is anything created by a user of a particular OpenSim-based virtual world, which is instantiated into an OpenSim-based region. This can include simple individual primitive-based objects to more complex collections of objects that have been textured and scripted to create an entire region. Builds may be created using both in-world tools, in which case they exist within the region file from their original instantiation, which provides superior tracking and reporting abilities along with the capacity to track creator intent for the object and creator tags. Builds may also be created using off-line tools such as Photoshop, Illustrator, Maya 3DS Max, and other related software tools.
- Builds may be developed from a *Primitive Unit or 'Prim'*, which is a simple mesh object created by the in-world content development tools included in both Second Life® and OpenSim. Prims are the basis of much of the content creation which occurs in virtual worlds and are themselves largely simple platonic solids with a default basic texture applied to them by the server software at the point that a user creates them. These objects may be linked together to create larger or more complex objects, and may be textured with images, scripted, as well as have various other parameters adjusted in order to create an array of products which range from art to apparel. Primitives may be created by either an avatar-represented user or by software running either within the world or externally on other servers.
- Some Builds are created to become *Virtua,* which are virtual goods intended for the retail virtual good market in various immersive spaces. This chapter focuses on OpenSim-based virtual worlds, but virtua appears and is sold in a wide array of other virtual worlds ranging from World of Warcraft to Second Life®.
- Builds are the basis of *Scenes*, which are a set of assets within a region which is being presented to a user at any given moment. A scene may change rapidly depending upon the whether or not the user is moving, and the direction in which the avatar user is facing.
- A *Region* is a critical part of Second Life® and OpenSim-based virtual worlds. A Region is a volume unit within a virtual world. Second Life® and OpenSim-based virtual worlds currently define the working region as being a square area of 256 meters by 256 meters, with the height of the volume being essentially unlimited, although the functional limitation is closer to 4,000 meters. A recent development in the OpenSim code has enabled "Megaregions" which are single large regions composed of up to 9 regular regions. A region of space can hold assets of different types, including avatars, scripts, primitive objects, and images, before latency overwhelms the

viewer and the user experience degrades to the point where the region is no longer usable by the avatar user. The practical limit on the numbers of these assets for OpenSim-based virtual worlds varies according to the kind of hardware being used to host the region and the amount of bandwidth available to the user. More powerful hardware can handle larger numbers of assets and avatar users than less powerful hardware. The precise mix and balance of types of assets will also vary according to hardware and to type. Improvements to the software will push the limits further. Licensing contracts may need to consider how many regions are included in the license for purposes of the pricing of assets.

- Regions are where the critical *User Experience* occurs. User Experience is defined as all aspects of a virtual world presented to an avatar-represented individual in that world. This includes latency of movement; clarity of images and textures; and ability of the user to participate and engage with other users and with the world into which they are logged-in. While the region conditions,e quantity and quality of the assets in the region help define the User Experience, it is also based on factors over which neither the Grid Operator nor the Content Creator have any control. For example, the specific hardware and software configuration of a given user may simply not be powerful enough to display a Region and its Assets with any degree of acuity, which will lead to a degraded User Experience. A given User may not have sufficient bandwidth in order to have a good User Experience. Poorly created, un-optimized Assets may also contribute to a degraded User Experience. User Experience is enhanced when the user experiences good content (however tangentially) and to that end, it is critical to be able to offer quality licensed content.

There are additional terms which relate to the technology of OpenSim-based virtual worlds. The working definitions provided for these terms are not tied to any particular implementation of the technology. These terms include *Client, Server*, and *Viewer*.

- A *Client* can be the connection of an avatar-represented user into the virtual world, or it can mean the viewer used to see the virtual world. *Client*, when used by the administrators managing the OpenSim-based virtual world, means a user connection into the OpenSim software. Client, when used by users means the viewer itself, which is software which enables the user to log-in to the OpenSim-based virtual world server. For the purpose of writing contracts, Client should be regarded as the Viewer.
- *Viewers* are software that enables an avatar-represented user to log into an immersive space such as Second Life® or an OpenSim-based virtual world by connecting to a Second Life® or OpenSim server. Viewer code is distinct from server code. There are many viewers available to users, each with its own pros and cons. Some of the viewers make it easier for users to 'copy' content, for example the Meerkat viewer, which has a built-in capability to copy content. Some viewer creators have attempted a modicum of DRM protection by building in a requirement that users not copy anything that hasn't been clearly tagged for copying or which they themselves have not made as the original creator. These are considered are weak DRM measures and can be readily hacked. Individual users have preferred viewers, and while each viewer has its own strength and weakness, it is impossible to mandate

that users only use a particular viewer unless the virtual world requires it. For example with *RealExtend*, an OpenSim-based virtual world has a proprietary viewer which its users are required to use.

In developing licensing contracts, it should be generally assumed that most of these OpenSim-based virtual worlds will not have a proprietary viewer or that these viewers will provide any sort of DRM. Language written into the contracts should accordingly address those facts.

- An important term to understand is *Server*, which is the software running the simulation of the OpenSim or Second Life®-based world. OpenSim-based virtual worlds often have separate servers for different components of the software, such as an asset server, and a hosting server which interconnect to deliver the user experience of the virtual world. As distributed content delivery mechanisms are further developed, asset servers will be more widely separated from the virtual world servers. In this instance, Assets residing on the asset Server are handled by a different entity than the Grid Operator or Content Creator. As a result, contracts written to enable content licensing between Grid Operators and Content Creators using distributed content delivery will need to reflect that there may be a tertiary party involved. This also adds an additional term, the Content Distributor.
- The *Content Distributor* acts as a content aggregator and clearinghouse for Content Creators, providing technology services in the form of distributed content delivery; legal services in the form of standardized agreements; quality assurance and control for the Grid Operator; policing of content to help address issues of infringement; royalty collection and disbursement; and v-Commerce solutions for Content Creators and Grid Operators. As new OpenSim-based virtual worlds emerge, the importance of an established Content Distributor will increase to Content Creators, Grid Operators, and Users, all of whom will have a need for the services provided by this entity.

These terms, defined as part of this case study are only an initial starting point. As OpenSim-based virtual worlds continue to develop, new terms and definitions will develop alongside them. The terms defined here are not analogous to the technical definitions used by developers. They should be considered functional definitions intended to provide a framework for discussion for use in standardized contracts. These terms will also help to establish common agreement grid operators, the content developers, and to a lesser extent, the end content consumer. There is no doubt that further enhancements will occur to these working definitions until they enter into practice as generally accepted terminology and are used to develop standardized licensing contracts.

FUTURE RESEARCH DIRECTIONS

As an increasing number of enterprise users enter virtual worlds such as OpenSim-based worlds, there will be increased pressure on both content creators and grid operators to provide high quality content, and to ensure that the content provided does not infringe on existing IP rights. The establishment of clearly understood standards which can be used to support both certificates of originality and as guidelines to develop legally binding contracts is clearly required. The evolution virtual worlds standards is already begun (Sivan, 2009).

FRI maintains that more focus should be placed on defining specific terminology for use in standardized agreements, so that the rights of both content creators and grid operators are protected. New content delivery mechanisms will present tremendous growth opportunities along with considerable legal concerns if legal terms related to content creation are not defined in. Similarly, grid operators must be protected against claims of copyright infringement by original copyright owners, in the event that one or more of their users infringe and bring laundered content onto their grid. Methods of establishing complicity between grid operators and users must be defined, in order to allow original copyright owners recourse against infringers.

Additionally, a clear definition of how aspects of virtual world content are copyrighted is needed. The state of the art with OpenSim-based worlds has enabled a number of delivery mechanisms for content between OpenSim-based worlds. These include Inventory Archive Resource (IAR) files and, OpenSim Archive Resource (OAR) files. Soon distributed asset services will also enable content delivery from one grid to another. This creates an array of questions which will require both legal and technological answers to help ensure that all virtual world stakeholders are protected and can engage in business in an environment which is legally circumscribed.

Because OpenSim as a platform is so new, many new topics, concerns and considerations can be expected to arise. The most pressing ones are content quality standards, definition of legal terms, and standardized legal agreements. Once these standards become established, there will undoubtedly develop an array of additional topics which will require focused attention. These topics may include including ownership of performances; how regions are actually licensed; for what purpose the content will be used; and how these questions should be best addressed.

Additionally, current terms of service agreements do not address future concerns about content developers' ability to extract their content from a given region or grid. This is an area which will become increasingly critical, especially as content creators who began their careers in closed grids such as Second Life® wish to extract their content and take it elsewhere.

CONCLUSION

The coming diaspora of content creators from closed grids such as Second Life® to the open source environments run on the OpenSim platform offer both exciting opportunities and dangerous pitfalls for the unprepared. Opening new marketplaces to content creators has the ability to add appreciably to the global marketplace, accounting for $2.6 billion in sales in 2008 (Virtual Goods News, 2009). Addressing the legal considerations of content licensing; developing and enforcing standards for content creation; and defining standardized contracts will help open this new area of business while protecting all stakeholders in the value chain. Virtual worlds are already a reality, but their widespread adoption will be hindered until legal guidelines can be created to protect those whose creative vision gives form and live to the units that will form the backbone of this next technological wave.

Creating a working lexicography for the use of the legal practice in developing standardized agreements is critical to the continued evolution of these OpenSim-based virtual worlds. Talented content creators, justifiably leery of exposing their intellectual property to an unregulated environment, will be afforded the protection of existing legal channels, but only if a bridge between this new space and existing legal terms and contracts can be built. The foundation of that bridge is a functional, generally accepted lexicography of key terms, the usage of which can be generally agreed to by legal and lay practitioners negotiating appropriate content licensing agreements.

REFERENCES

Fitzgerald, S. (2003). Managing Your Intellectual Property. *FindLaw.* Retrieved on 12/3/09 from http://library.findlaw.com/2003/May/5/132714.html

Kane, S., & Duranske, B. (2008). Virtual Worlds. Real World Issues. Retrieved on 12/3/09 from http://www.abanet.org/intelprop/magazine/LandslideSep08_Kane.pdf

McCue, A. (2008). Beware the insider security threat. CIO Jury Articles. Retrieved on 12/3/09 from http://www.silicon.com/ciojury/0,3800003161,39188671,00.htm

Monopoly. Retrieved from http://www.hasbro.com/monopoly/en_US/ (Hasbro, © 2008)

OpenSim. Retrieved from http://www.opensimulator.org. (OpenSimulator, © 2007)

ScienceSim. Retrieved from http://www.sciencesim.com.

Second Life®®. Retrieved from http://secondlife.com/corporate/tos.php. (Linden Lab®, © 2008)

Simulator, O. (2009). Main Page. Retrieved on 12/3/09 from http://opensimulator.org/wiki/Main_Page

Sivan, Y. (2009). Overview: State of Virtual World Standards in 2009. *Virtual Worlds Research.* Retrieved on 12/1/09 from https://journals.tdl.org/jvwr/article/view/671/539

Takashi, D. (2009). Virtual Good Saees to Reach $1 Billion in 2009 As Social Games Pay Off Big. Retrieved on 12/3/09 from http://games.venturebeat.com/2009/10/14/virtual-goods-sales-to-hit-1-billion-in-2009-as-social-games-pay-off-big/

Virtual Goods News. (2009). Report: Virtual Worlds Growth to Skyrocket. Retrieved on 12/14/09 from http://www.virtualworldsnews.com/2009/06/report-virtual-worlds-growth-to-skyrocket-.html

ADDITIONAL READING

Balkin, J., & Noveck, B. (2006). *The State of Play: Law, Games, and Virtual Worlds (Ex Machina: Law, Technology, and Society).* New York: New York University Press.

Bartle, R. (2004). *Designing Virtual Worlds.* Indianapolis: New Riders.

Bethke, E., & Hoffman, E. (2008). *Settlers of the New Virtual Worlds.* Long Beach: Philomath Press.

Castronova, E. (2008). *Exodus to the Virtual World: How Online Fun is Changing Reality.* New York: Palgrave MacMillan.

Duranske, B. (2008). *Virtual Law: Navigating the Legal Landscape of Virtual Worlds.* Chicago: ABA Publishing.

Lamoureux, E. L., Baron, S. L., & Stewart, C. (2009). *Intellectual Property Law and Interactive Media: Free for a Fee (Digital Formations).* New York: Peter Lang Publishing. Law http://www.law.com.

Nuara, L. T., Kiwi, T. C., & Brown, P. (2008). *Information Technology Law Institute 2008: New Directions: Social Networks, Blogs, Privacy, Mash-Ups, Virtual Worlds and OpenSource.* Virtual Goods News http://www.virtualgoodsnews.com.

Virtual Worlds News. Retrieved from http://www.virtualworldsnews.com.

Winkler, S. E. (2009). *Designing Dreams: The Art & Business of Avatar Apparel Design & Development.* New York: Fashion Research Foundation.

Winkler, S. E. (2009). *Shengri La Spirit: A Designer's Perspective of the Making of OpenSim.* New York: Fashion Research Foundation.

KEY TERMS AND DEFINITIONS

Content: Digital assets which are created by individuals or teams and used to develop virtual worlds.

Creator Intent: The intention of the creator towards his asset, whether it be allowed to be broadly and freely distributed under any of the many licensing schemes, or if they wish a given asset to be copied but not transferrable to others. Intent can allow copying, transferrable, and modifications to the original asset; currently both Second Life® and OpenSim-based worlds only allow the creator to mark these three intents, which fails to allow for a content creator's intent of their asset for transfer between Second Life® and OpenSim-based worlds.

Creator: Tag: To the user in the virtual world, it is the name of the individual who created any discreet bit of content, which can be examined by any user by looking at the property screen of that content. This is the original creator and should not be changed.

Digital Millennium Copyright Act of 1998 (DMCA): The best working definition for the DMCA can be found at the Wikipedia, at http://en.wikipedia.org/wiki/Digital_Millennium_Copyright_Act.

Digital Rights Management (DRM): Usually a technology solution that prohibits illegal or not allowed copying of digital assets.

Inventory Archive Resource (IAR): A new file format unique to OpenSim-based virtual worlds, invented by a core OpenSim developer to assist in moving user's inventory between grids. This can be compared to a user's suitcase. It is a very new file format and has not been extensively tested.

OpenSim Archive Resource (OAR): A new file format unique to OpenSim-based virtual worlds, invented by a core OpenSim developer to assist in moving entire regions full of content from grid to grid. Care must be taken in restoring OARs onto new regions, or the content creator and owner tags are changed, removing the original information. **OpenSimulator (OpenSim):** Open source virtual world platform which uses a viewer in common with Second Life®. For more information, please visit http://www.opensimulator.org.

Owner Tag: The person who currently owns a given asset. This tag is fluid and can change depending on who currently possesses that asset. Second Life®: Closed source virtual world platform developed and owned by Linden Lab, which uses a viewer in common with OpenSim. For more information, please visit http://www.secondlife.com.

User: Individual who has a registered account and an avatar representation on any given virtual world. Users may or may not verify their real life identity.

Chapter 14
Security and Privacy Concerns of Virtual Worlds

Greg Gogolin
Ferris State University, USA

ABSTRACT

This chapter looks at security and privacy concerns of virtual worlds by investigating the use and capabilities of current and emerging technologies such as gaming, blogging, podcasting, virtual meetings, and virtual worlds. Security and privacy concerns will be investigated in the context of exploits and IT-related security risks, access management and confidentiality, reputation and product risk management, resource management, financial considerations and accountability, and safety. Several technologies and personal practices are reviewed, as well as ways to mitigate or eliminate their associated risks. The core principles of information security -confidentiality, integrity, and availability - provide an overall framework for the chapter.

INTRODUCTION

Digitally created worlds are changing the face of E-Commerce and extending the use of Internet technologies to create a more immersive experience for customers. With the challenges in things such as identity theft, fraud and virtual stalking, businesses will not be able to fully leverage Virtual Worlds if they fail to address security and privacy concerns.

This chapter will investigate the use and capabilities of current and emerging technologies such as gaming, blogs, podcasting, virtual meetings and virtual worlds in the context of their productive utility and security risks presented. Security and privacy concerns will be investigated in the following areas:

1. Exploits and IT-Related Security Risks
2. Access Management and Confidentiality
3. Reputation and Product Risk Management
4. Resource Management

DOI: 10.4018/978-1-61692-808-7.ch014

5. Financial Considerations and Accountability
6. Safety

The chapter will conclude with a summary and a look at emerging trends and future direction in security and privacy of virtual worlds and E-Commerce.

BACKGROUND

In the late 1990's, E-Commerce was hyped as a way for small start-up companies to compete on a level playing field with established corporate behemoths. The demise of brick and mortar stores was widely predicted and common sense business practices were thought of as outdated. The "Internet Bubble" burst by 2001 and most realized the error in forgetting the basics. Companies learned a lot about the Internet, E-Commerce and their business during the Bubble, but an area that lagged the Bubble in terms of attention and focus was that of security. Ten years later, hacking, identity theft, privacy and similar information security issues have become central to the business model.

Social networking through the use of Internet sites such as Facebook, MySpace, Twitter and LinkedIn became among the most popular uses of the Internet as the first decade of the new millennium drew to a close, with Facebook #2, MySpace #12, Twitter #14 and LinkedIn #39 in Alexa's rankings of the top 500 global Internet sites (Alexa.com, 2009). Online gaming and virtual world technology have become mainstream, aided by the advancement of home gaming systems gaining Internet technology. This has led to massively multiplayer online role-playing games (MMORPG), which can entail literally tens of thousands of players participating in an online gaming experience in a virtual world.

Virtual worlds like Second Life®, There.com, and more business-focused offerings are on the brink of becoming valuable work tools. Major companies and public-sector organizations such as BP, IBM, Intel, and the US Army are investing heavily in virtual world technologies. (Driver & Jackson, 2008). In fact, Driver and Jackson predict that by 2013 the 3-D Internet will be as important for work as the Web is today. This view was supported in an article in CIO magazine (Lynch, 2008) that projected enterprise versions of online virtual worlds like Second Life® would be just as important to business as the Web is today. This may be a stretch because the same research organization (Forrester Research) recently reported that "only 11% of enterprises have adopted virtual worlds to augment their work." (Rutherford, 2009).

From the point of view of most business leaders, the utility of virtual worlds in business is not apparent. Keitt (2009) attributes this to virtual world vendors not doing a particularly good job articulating their value. Instead, the central message of virtual world providers is that they allow for groupings that can be augmented or reduced on the fly while also allowing users to consider information from multiple applications simultaneously. King (2008) reports that companies such as IBM, Sun, Xerox, Cisco and Unilever are using 3D technology and virtual worlds in this very manner for things like strategy sessions, employee meetings, mixers, and recruiting. While the use of virtual worlds for functions such as E-commerce shows much promise, security and privacy are critical success factors. The purpose of this chapter is to investigate many of the issues that are part of the security and privacy equation for success.

ISSUES, CONTROVERSIES, PROBLEMS

The security and privacy concerns associated with virtual worlds and E-commerce are immense and multi-faceted. This is an environment where people and organizations are asked to trust that which may not be real or easily verified. Because this is a rapidly evolving situation and set of circumstances that in many cases break precedent, the societal norms, laws, ethics and values struggle to adapt.

The core principles of information security are widely accepted as confidentiality, integrity, and availability. Confidentiality means access to information is only provided to those with proper authorization. Integrity means that data is accurate, and that updates are not made by unauthorized agents and that authorized agents cannot make unauthorized updates. Assuring that authorized agents have timely and uninterrupted access to information is known as availability. Together these three principles are known as the CIA Triad. This model is a well known security policy commonly espoused by such leading information security organizations such as the International Information Systems Security Consortium, also known as ISC2. In order to investigate virtual world security and privacy concerns, the CIA Triad provides a context for evaluating the six areas that will be covered in this chapter. Once again, the six areas are:

1. Exploits and IT-Related Security Risks
2. Access Management and Confidentiality
3. Reputation and Product Risk Management
4. Resource Management
5. Financial Considerations and Accountability – org crime, law enforcement
6. Safety – including psychological

The six categories will be applied sequentially to the broad topic of security and privacy concerns of virtual worlds.

Exploits and IT-Related Security Risks

An exploit is a software, hardware, virtual, or social engineering feat that takes advantage of a vulnerability to compromise security. Exploits may be manifested in any combination of hardware, software, virtual or social mechanisms. Exploits can be created inadvertently due to lack of vigilance or with the intention of mischief. Organizations often use risk management strategies to reduce, mitigate or eliminate potential exploits, but with the interconnected and dynamic environment that defines virtual worlds, exploits will continue to exist. This forces strategic thinking and proactive mechanisms in order to thrive in such an environment.

Consequences of exploits can manifest themselves in many ways including destroyed or altered content, compromising a server or host and subjecting it to remote control, leaking information, reducing the capacity of resources, and assuming identity. In order to more fully understand exploits and IT-related security risk, we should clarify the context of the environments we are dealing with. For the purposes of this chapter, virtual worlds will include Web 2.0 technologies such as wikis, blogs, virtual communities, on-line gaming, social networking sites, interactive content and video sharing sites.

One approach to minimize risk is isolating things within a shared environment so that if one area is compromised, other areas will still be secure. This is the promise of virtualization software such as VMware, Parallels and Virtual PC. Hardware manufacturers are starting to add input/output memory management units (IOMMUs) to their products. IOMMUs allow virtualized environments to directly access a slice of device memory for their needs while keeping other parts of the memory secure from snooping. In addition, other software-only approaches mimic IOMMUs' mapping techniques. (Jackson, 2008).

Another approach to reducing IT related security risks and exploits while maintaining the CIA Triad is to diligently patch and test software and vendor updates. Note that proper testing includes regression testing techniques. While this won't necessarily resolve zero day exposures, it will provide relief from ongoing threats. Certainly antivirus, spyware and firewall technologies are ways to further reduce the exposure footprint.

Security exploits in virtual worlds can take different forms than typical operating system exploits, which are often at the mercy of a vendor patch cycle. Sometimes these exploits are multifaceted. For example, it is possible to exploit a player to steal Linden dollars, and then cash them out for real US dollars. All the victim has to do is have video enabled and enter a piece of land owned by the attacker. (Independent Security Evaluators, 2009).

Virtual world interactions such as voice, texting, chat room, blog, podcast, and video – as well as their supporting technologies - are additional sources of potential risk. Since companies are using virtual world technologies for things like meetings and strategy sessions, an understated problem is the ability of someone in attendance making a copy of the conversation and material and distributing it outside the organization. In many ways organizations have more to fear from their employees than from people that are outside the organization. When the employee is masquerading as a unicorn or maybe a wooden horse from Troy tracking them down may be nearly impossible.

New exploits are introduced or discovered on an almost daily basis. If an exploit is discovered, as much information as possible should be captured including things like operating system with service pack level, graphics card and other hardware, installed and running software, and connectivity and access constraints. Digital forensics investigators find considerable value in preserving the contents of main memory (RAM) to assist in tracking down the exploit cause and implications. A copy of the environment is often made for forensic analysis and to attempt to recreate the exploit.

Access Management and Confidentiality

In a virtual world, a person is often represented as an avatar. The avatar can be some sort of image of oneself, an image of someone else, or it can be something like a narwhal. At some point the decision often has to be made whether to trust the avatar or not, particularly if commerce is involved. Because identity authentication is difficult, productive corporate use of virtual world technology can currently best be realized in an environment where access management and confidentiality can reliably be assured. That place primarily exists in an area internal to the corporation and within its firewall system. To use another technology as a metaphor an Intranet type of approach.

Confidentiality is ensuring that private information is kept private. Maintaining confidentiality is of paramount concern in a virtual world because disclosure of a seemingly minor detail can expose the real identity of someone. If someone is participating in a virtual community, they may be exploring things through role playing or other manner that they would never consider in a real world setting. Disclosure of their identity could range from embarrassing to extremely damaging. The use of a power-leveling service (paying someone to move a character up a level) is one potential exploit. Virtual worlds could also be used for simulation in a corporate setting. In this scenario also, breaching confidentiality can have a far reaching impact.

Threats to privacy can also lead to extremely embarrassing situations if private information about personal financial challenges is made public. This very situation occurred in 2009 when HSBC exposed sensitive data about customers going through bankruptcy proceedings (McMillan, 2009). Similarly, Facebook Inc. concluded internally that its company value was $3.7 billion, not the $15 billion implied in a 2007 investment made by Microsoft when Facebook agreed to sell a 1.6 percent stake to the software maker for $240 million (Liedtke, 2009). This illustrates some of the issues that arise from filing legal documents online, and you can bet it strained the Facebook Microsoft relationship when these details became public.

One of the most important action steps to minimize the risk of a breach in confidentiality from a technical perspective is to work toward encryption at the data storage and data transmission points with a sufficiently complex encryption scheme. An end-to-end scheme will make data difficult to interpret in the event of a breach.

Reputation and Product Risk Management

One of the fundamental considerations of risk management is to balance risk with its potential implications on revenue. If a risk exposure has the potential to dramatically impact revenue, it needs a lot more planning and management than an exposure that has limited or no impact.

Effective use of computer technology can be the great equalizer when small organizations go up against larger organizations. It is also provides a means to communicate with a large audience, whether the message is accurate or not. The credibility of the message often relies on the source. It is common for someone to masquerade as someone else. That is why it is critical for organizations to register not only Internet domains for their companies and product lines, but they also register misspellings, derivatives and derogatory terms that may be associated with their company or products something this author refers to as derivative and derogatory slander. WalmartSucks.com is an example of a domain that other companies have learned from. When a company registers these domains they are safely parked and can't be used by those attempting to provide a negative face or message. A similar technique can be applied to technologies such as blogs, Twitter, LinkedIn, Facebook, MySpace and other popular media. After all, if a Twitter feed comes from an account named Newsweek, the average person is likely to think it is legitimate. Individuals can also utilize the practice of registering accounts and domains so that their reputation isn't compromised.

Reputation and Product risk management can also have an ethical component. If the investment is in a virtual world, users can introduce things that can be lethal. For example, Second Life® allows age-based role-playing that can take on various forms. It can be as innocuous as people acting out a family dynamic, or as potentially troubling as two adults engaging in sexual role playing, with one of the avatars made to look like a child. Even so, legal experts said such virtual behavior between adults isn't likely to break the law, since there are no real children involved. (Terdiman, 2006). That can be of little consequence, because if an undesired activity occurs, the damage to a reputation may be unrecoverable. It can be even more insidious if the person involved in the activity is masquerading as someone else.

Blogs and podcasts are ways to quickly disseminate information to a wide audience. Information presented in this manner is often viewed as reliable and accurate when in fact the integrity of the source has not been verified. Misinformation can be spread at an alarming rate, and once the cat is out of the bag on the Internet, retracting or correcting the information is nearly impossible. Search engines typically have limited integrity checks built in to their hashes, so accurate information may be overshadowed by inaccurate information. Private information and reputations can suffer from a seemingly harmless post. A correction/clarification capability on a website and other media points can provide some relief.

Resource Management

Resource management could be an entire book by itself. In this chapter, we'll just focus on people. From a personal perspective, people can waste considerable time in a virtual world with no apparent benefit and dramatic loss of productivity. The seductive nature of virtual worlds can be subtle at first, but then grow into something Castronova (2005) describes as toxic immersion. Simply stated, toxic immersion is losing people to a space that, by any standard of human worth, dignity, and well-being, is not good for them. So rather than an exploit focused on financial resources, exploits can have mental and human resource targets. If an individual, corporation or culture becomes too engrossed in a toxic immersion activity, long term viability is doubtful as productivity will diminish or cease.

It is often stated that Google keeps coming out with multiple products in an effort to keep Microsoft off balance and unsure of the real target market. This could make Microsoft's decisions on strategic resource allocation more difficult. New technologies often need a framework to be developed in order for them to be appropriately evaluated or viable. This applies to organizations that are considering a virtual component to their business. IT planners will need to be alert and cautious to the sweet candy effect of virtualization so that they don't needlessly waste resources. Without strategic guidance advised in research, there could be unintended consequences such as silos, dysfunctional operations, fragmented management, and poor procurement processes. (Weiss, 2009). These are many of the same issues that virtual worlds were thought to solve. In fact, they may just change their color, which leads us into the next aspect of our evaluation.

Resource management includes training and education of the workforce. Making people aware of safe practices that include strong password policies and aspects related to the CIA Triad are among the most important security and privacy practices that an organization can implement. Procedures for handling employees that leave an organization are also important so that exposure or proliferation of trade secrets does not occur. Many proactive organizations are conducting forensic analysis of the computers and digital devices used by employees that leave the organization to determine if behavior detrimental to the organization has occurred. For example, forensic analysis can determine recent file activity including what files were accessed or deleted, as well as if external storage devices were connected to a device.

Financial Considerations and Accountability

Financial considerations generally revolve around how to maximize profits, whether from an individual's perspective or an organizational decision on virtual world involvement. Where money flows there is a natural attraction of those looking to compete for or receive the money. The real-world value of transactions in virtual communities is rising steadily, and is likely to continue growing. One estimate places the value of commerce in Second Life® at $265,000 a day, and it is estimated that average turnover is rising by up to 15 per cent a month. If these trends continue, Second Life's overall gross domestic product could be close to $700m in 2007. (Foley, 2006).

Credit cards have limits to their usefulness in virtual worlds. No confirmation of identity feature with a bank is required to complete a transaction, and the average person does not accept credit cards. Real money can change hands in a variety of ways including commercial payment systems such as PayPal®, mobile payment systems such as Paymo®, and monetized software providers such as fatfoogoo®. Each of these methods has unique advantages, but a key piece is that the account holder does not have to provide financial information. PayPal is a fast way to send money abroad, Paymo allows paying over a cell phone via text messaging, while fatfoogoo provides financial interaction and in-game economies. Mobile payment systems, contactless payment systems, and micropayment systems are but a few more of the multitude of ways to handle virtual financial considerations. The speed at which accounts can be brought up and down and the inherent challenges to ensure trustworthiness make fraud management a real concern.

Some virtual worlds are creating their own currency exchanges, which opens the door for several questionable practices including conversion between real money and virtual currency, tax implications, and international exchanges. Additional issues include the virtual world being dissolved, change in terms of service, laws, and rapid changes in technology can make investments vaporize. Second Life® changed their terms of service and people lost their investments. Accountability needs to be maintained at all levels, including those who host the virtual world, or else there is no long term future for commerce in virtual worlds.

The way money can be made and spent in virtual worlds can be skill based and fair play. However, while games like World of Warcraft have concentrated on fantasy challenges, Second Life® and Entropia have created worlds much like our own, where virtual property magnates, clothes designers and prostitutes offering virtual sex make hundreds of thousands of real US dollars a year (Foley, 2006). Facebook has a type of currency in its FarmVille application as do many gaming sites, so the implications are complex.

If this sounds like the territory of organized crime, it may be. When a gaming account is compromised, generally the series of events that follows is that the account assets are converted to virtual currency, and then the virtual currency is exchanged for real money. The potential for viruses or virtual illnesses to propagate this scenario is very real and extremely attractive to organized crime. In fact, organized crime organizations host their own virtual worlds. The challenges faced by law enforcement, including trained staff, budget, and jurisdiction, make investigation and prosecution of this type of activity nearly impossible.

Safety

The virtual world workspace is not what it seems, and the people (or avatars) may not be either. One person may have multiple avatars that have different levels of authority and capability. They may be used to gang up on someone to influence them or give the impression that 'everyone' is doing something. For the individual, this means exercising vigilance. For the corporation, this means anticipating safety concerns and planning for them.

Psychological safety is one of the more far reaching concerns. Bullying can have a lasting impact and can lead to suicide in extreme cases. But another type of psychological safety involves terrorism. Virtual worlds are used for recruitment, training and simulation of terrorist activities. What may seem like a harmless game over time may evolve into a terrorist obsession particularly when youth or the psychologically fragile are the recruitment targets. A corporation may find out after the fact that they were a terrorist tool, and the implications can be grim.

Certainly a discussion about safety would not be complete without reference to safe practices such as protecting your identity, personal information and financial information. Parents need to be aware of the potential for child exploitation and stalking. Safety steps include not giving instant messaging (IM) or contact information to someone that isn't known in the real world. Children need to inform an adult if someone asks to meet them, and adults need to take similar safety steps such as having the meeting in a public place and letting others know of the meeting.

Bulletin board sites and those that allow posting are areas where the potential for bullying and predation, profanity, and potential leakage of identifiable information is high. The volume of activity at these sites can be such that it isn't practical for moderators to review all activity. Moderation software is a development that is targeted at this problem by making the job more efficient. Profiles can be created to track online safety violations and some tools can provide information that may help track drug movement and use. This can be very useful in a corporate setting when the organization doesn't want situations to spiral out of control. Safety can be taken a step further by simply making reporting of inappropriate behavior simple.

Other virtual world technologies that can have a dramatic impact on safety and privacy are the geolocation and near field communications. Both of these technologies have the potential to generate limitless new applications. Geolocation provides the geographic location of a device and is common in cell phone technology. The unsuspecting can be participating in virtual world situation and potentially be geographically exposed, something this author refers to as geolocation jumping. There are currently available cell phone exploits that permit a third party to remotely listen to phone calls between two other unsuspecting parties. These exploits also provide the ability to remotely enable the microphone on a cell phone and listen to conversation between individuals that don't even have their cell phone is in use.

Near field communication is a short range high frequency wireless communication technology that enables exchange of information between devices that are within 10 cm of proximity. NFC utilize are currently directed for use in mobile devices such as phones. The device can be used for applications such as contactless card and function as a credit card, ticket, or passive radio frequency tag. Even a US Passport has radio frequency capabilities. The unsuspecting can have their identifying information scanned by someone who comes in close proximity with a reader. Powering off devices when not in use, employing Faraday capable shields, or even wrapping devices and passports in aluminum foil, are protective measures that can be easily followed.

Solutions and Recommendations

Security and privacy concerns in a virtual world are complex, and as such require a multifaceted approach. Educating those involved in virtual worlds is the best approach to overcoming security and privacy concerns. Education is not just for the user it includes organizations, regulators, law enforcement and governments and it should have a strong ethics component. It won't be easy, and it certainly is an ongoing process. Common fraud prevention practices should be put into place, and they should extend to the IT staff. Traditional approaches to information security apply in virtual worlds and should be followed: robust passwords that remain secret, malware and virus awareness, being careful with financial transactions, and not frequenting seedy locations. Famous athletes often make headlines for their late night escapades at bars. The bottom line is that if they weren't at a location where trouble lurks in the first place, their problems wouldn't have had the opportunity to get started. Gogolin's security principle applies: Practice proactive prevention, not reactive response.

Additional security steps beyond what is covered in this chapter may be necessary, and one should realize that the same technologies that are used to compromise security and privacy can be leveraged to protect it. Wikis and blogs are examples of ways to share concerns as well as expertise and solutions. Keeping in close contact with information security and financial monitoring services, as well as keeping up to date on software maintenance and patches are frequently cited techniques.

Social networking is currently one of the main functions of virtual worlds, but it can also be a seductive poison. Sites like Facebook and LinkedIn often contain enough information to allow successful phishing attacks, identity theft, and fraud. People should be vigilant when using these types of tools and should not put things like addresses, birth date or email addresses in a publicly viewable area. If an email address is publicly viewable, it should be an alternate address – not a primary address that may also be tied to bank accounts and other personal activities.

A person's IP address may become as sacred as a social security number in the not too distant future. Use of firewalls, proxy servers, and anonymizing tools can provide a level of security. They can also be leveraged to mask activities, so they are popular with those with dark intent. Fortunately, many providers of these technologies will turn over their logs for law enforcement purposes.

Security and privacy in virtual communities is as much the responsibility of the provider as it is of the participant. Breaches to the provider's infrastructure in many ways are easier to exploit from the inside than the outside. In virtual communities where monetary transactions take place, proper logging of activities in an auditable format as well as adequate testing and quality assurance is necessary to reduce potential risk. Auditing of activities and transactions should have some form of validation to detect fraud and make implementing exploits more difficult. For example, financial transactions should have externally validated dynamic and transparent constraints and procedures that are outside of the security rights and capabilities of a potential exploit implementer. Vendors don't have to reinvent the wheel and can look to employ standardized approaches that are utilized by others rather than proprietary solutions. For example, transactions, logging, and auditing can be functions of middleware tied to databases that can be utilized by the industry. Table 1 contains a summary of many of the security and privacy considerations that have been reviewed, as well as potential action steps.

Laws and regulations need to keep pace with the developments of virtual worlds. They need to be constructed in a way that is agile and adaptable to a rapidly changing environment rather than the current reactionary approach that can lag the issue by several years. Simply changing the location of a virtual server from one state or country to another should not be a way to stay ahead of the law. Cross jurisdictional approaches with interagency cooperation are key to making virtual worlds viable.

Table 1. Summary of security and privacy considerations

Consideration	Action Step
Isolate things within shared environment	Utilize techniques such as virtualization software
Noncurrent resources	Apply patches, bug fixes, test environment
Virtual dollars stolen and converted	Carry small balances, safeguard accounts
Cloning virtual meetings	Log activities of participants, particularly in corporate environment
Identity authentication	Limit use of technologies where authentication cannot be assured
Disclosure of private information or identity	Utilize encryption, aliasing, and limit disclosure
Data theft	End-to-end encryption, access control
Derogatory and derivative slander	Register domains and their derivatives with ICANN and all popular social media. Monitor social media
Unethical or innocuous activity	Monitor social media, ethics education, choose where to frequent
Propagated misinformation	Correction/clarification capability on website and in social media. Monitor.
Productivity loss and toxic immersion	Education, job rotation, utilization of productivity metrics
Oblivious or naive security and privacy behavior	Training and education including ethics and safe practices
Misuse or theft of virtual currency	Maintain small balances, employ safe and secure practices
Organized crime	Realize that it is prolific in a virtual environment, employ safe and secure practices
Child exploitation, stalking	Education, employ safe and secure practices, limit the online activities and capabilities of children, report violations to law enforcement
Inappropriate comments and information posted on bulletin boards	Employ moderation software, allow for easy reporting/flagging by participants
Geolocation jumping	Turn off or disable capability when not using GIS.
Near field communications hijacking	Turn off devices when not in use; utilize Faraday bags or aluminum foil.

FUTURE RESEARCH DIRECTIONS

It is clear that law enforcement is ill-equipped to operate in a virtual environment. Things can be very difficult to track, and in some situations the victim is virtual, which makes prosecution difficult. By current standards, there has to be an actual victim (not virtual) for there to be a crime. In the case where there is an actual victim, it can be nearly impossible to distinguish between reality and fantasy. This can be further complicated by the cross-jurisdictional nature of electronic crime.

Regulation suffers from a similar approach of the caboose driving the train. Technologies and exploits are contrived and implemented so fast that regulation is consistently years behind the issues. Unless regulation and law enforcement can become current, widespread adoption for virtual world technology in E-Commerce will continue to suffer. New ways to handle financial considerations that instill confidence and accountability are other areas that would be ideal research opportunities.

CONCLUSION

In the not so distant past computer and information security was an afterthought that was not taken seriously. Those days are truly in the rear view mirror and will never return. In fact, the pace of change and the implications to security and privacy will make future developments even more dramatic. We will look back at today and wonder why we thought the challenges were prodigious.

Virtual worlds and online communities can be an enjoyable and productive environment when approached with eyes wide open. When approached with eyes wide shut it can be a brutal, regrettable and painful existence. The vast majority of virtual world participants have good intentions and participate for enjoyment and convenience. However, vigilance is as important in a virtual world as it is on an intercity street.

REFERENCES

Alexa.com. (December, 2009). *Alexa Top 500 Global Internet Sites*. Retrieved on the world wide web December 3, 2009. http://www.alexa.com/topsites/global;0

Castronova, E. (2005). *Synthetic Worlds: the business and culture of online games*. Chicago: University of Chicago Press.

Driver, E., & Jackson, P. (January 7, 2008). *Getting Real Work Done in Virual Worlds*. Forrester Research. www.forrester.com/rb/research.

Foley, S. (December 31, 2006). *Game on: criminals set sights on virtual realities*. The Independent. http://www.independent.co.uk/news/business/news/game-on-criminals-set-sights-on-virtual-realities-430265.html

Independent Security Evaluators. (2009). *Exploiting Second Life*.

Jackson, J. (2008). *Securing the virtual world*. Government Computer News. Retrieved on the world wide web November 5, 2009. http://gcn.com/Articles/2008/07/25/Securing-the-virtual-world.aspx?Page=1

Keitt, T. (July 28, 2009). *The Real Value of Virtual Worlds*. Forrester Research. www.forrester.com/rb/research.

King, R. (May 2, 2008). *The (Virtual) Global Office*. Business Week. http://www.businessweek.com/technology/content/may2008/tc2008052_842516.htm

Liedke, M. (February 11, 2009). Facebook appraisal pegs company's value at #3.7B. Associated Press. Retrieved on the world wide web December 5, 2009. http://www.sfgate.com/cgi-bin/article.cgi?f=/n/a/2009/02/10/state/n230703S73.DTL

Lynch, C. (January 9, 2008). *This is Not a Game: Virtual Worlds Coming to Your Business, Forrester Predicts*. Retrieved on the world wide web August 2, 2009. http://www.cio.com/article/170850/This_Is_Not_a_Game_Virtual_Worlds_Coming_to_Your_Business_Forrester_Predicts

McMillan, R. (December 4, 2009). *HSBC exposed sensitive bankruptcy data*. Computerworld. Retrieved on the world wide web December 5, 2009. http://www.computerworld.com/s/article/9141834/HSBC_exposed_sensitive_bankruptcy_data?taxonomyId=17

Retrieved on the World Wide Web November 5, 2009. http://securityevaluators.com/content/case-studies/sl/

Rutherford, M. (November 4, 2009). *The Promise and Perils of Virtual Worlds (Part 2)*. Maxping. Retrieved on the world wide web November 5, 2009. http://maxping.org/business/real-life/the-promise-and-perils-of-virtual-worlds-%28part-2%29.aspx

Terdiman, D. (April 12, 2006). *Phony kids, virtual sex*. Cnet News. Retrieved on the world wide web November 5, 2009. http://news.cnet.com/Phony-kids,-virtual-sex/2100-1043_3-6060132.html

Weiss, G. (February 11, 2009) *The Great Virtualization Dilemma of the Next Decade: What You Need to Know*. Gartner Group. GartnerGroup.com/technology/research/reports..

ADDITIONAL READING

Access Control and Security Systems http://www.securitysolutions.com

ACM http://www.acm.org

Audit, E. D. P. Control and Security http://www.auerbach-publications.com/ejournals/pro

Benefl. T.http://www.benefitmag.com

Boannews. http://www.boannews.com

Cipher. http://www.ieee-security.org/cipher.html

Computer Fraud and Security http://www.compseconline.com

Computer Law and Security Report http://www.compseconline.com

Computer World http://computerworld.com

Crypto-Gram http://www.counterpane.com/crypto-gram.html

Digital ID World http://www.digitalidworld.com

Disaster Recovery Journal http://www.drj.com

duct_info/product_detail.asp?id=146

Edge http://www.itbusiness.ca/it/client/en/edge/home.asp

Evidencia Digital Magazine http://www.guiatecnico.com.br/evidenciadigital

Federal Computer Week http://www.fcw.com

Federal Times http://www.federaltimes.com

FrontLine Quarterly Newsletter http://www.gocsi.com/awareness/front.jhtml

Government Computer News http://www.gcn.com

Government Security http://govtsecurity.com

Government Security News http://www.gsn-magazine.com

Government Technology http://www.govtech.net

Homeland Defense Journal http://www.homeland-defensejournal.com

ICT Security http://www.tecnaeditrice.com/

IEEE Computer Society http://www.computer.org/

Information Security Bulletin http://www.chi-publishing.com

Information Security http://www.infosecuritymag.com

Information Security Today http://www.infosectoday.com

Information Storage and Security Journal http://www.sys-con.com/issj

InformationSecurity http://www.itsec.ru

InfoSecurity Professional http://www.isc2.org/infosecurity_magazine/default.aspx

Infosecurity Today Online http://www.infosecurity-magazine.com

(IN)SECURE Magazine http://www.insecuremag.com

Intelligent Enterprise http://www.intelligententerprise.com

Internet Security Review http://www.isr.net

Internet World http://www.internetworld.com

ISACA Journal http://www.isaca.org

(ISC)2 Journal http://www.isc2.org/journal

ITworld.com http://www.itworld.com

Journal of Cryptology http://www.iacr.org/jofc/jofc.html

Journal of Information. Law & Technology http://elj.warwick.ac.uk/jilt

Journal of Information Technology http://www.palgrave-journals.com/jit

Les Nouvelles.net http://www.lesnouvelles.net/index.html

LinuxSecurity.com http://www.linuxsecurity.com

Magazine Scitum http://www.magazcitum.com.mx/

National Defense http://www.nationaldefensemagazine.org

Net Report: Storage, Networking, Security http://www.netreport.ro

Network Security http://www.compseconline.com/publications/prodnet.htm

Privacy and Security Law Report http://www.bna.com/products/corplaw/pvln.htm

Privacy Journal http://www.privacyjournal.net

SC Magazine http://www.scmagazine.com

Search Security http://www.searchsecurity.de

Secure Enterprise http://www.securitypipeline.com/se

SecureID News http://www.secureidnews.com

Security Lab http://www.securitylab.ru

Security News Portal http://www.securitynews-portal.com

Security Port Newsletters http://www.security-port.com/security-newsletters.htm

SecurityInfoWatch.com http://www.securityinfowatch.com

SecurityManager.de http://www.securitymanager.de

SIAM Journal on Computing http://www.siam.org/journals/sicomp.php

SiC-Seguridad en Inform·tica y Comunicaciones http://www.revistasic.com

Technology in Government http://www.itbusiness.ca/it/client/en/techgovernment/home.asp

TechWeb: The Business Technology Network http://www.techweb.com

The Information Security Journal http://www.kes.info

The Journal of Computer Security http://www.csl.sri.com/programs/security/jcs

TopLine Quarterly Newsletter http://www.gocsi.com/awareness/topline.jhtml

Virus Bulletin http://www.virusbtn.com

ZATAZ Magazine http://www.zataz.com

KEY TERMS AND DEFINITIONS

Asset: A desirable trait or something of value.

Availability: Assuring that authorized agents have timely and uninterrupted access to information.

CIA Triad: Information security principle defined as Confidentiality, Integrity and Availability.

Confidentiality: Access to information is only provided to those with proper authorization.

Derivative Slander: Utilizing a misspelling, alteration or play on a name for the purposes of confusion, misconception or attempted gain by association.

Derogatory Slander: Utilizing a misspelling, alteration or play on a name for the purposes of lessening the merit or reputation of a person, organization or thing.

Exploit: A software, hardware, virtual, or social engineering feat that takes advantage of a vulnerability to compromise security.

Geolocation: Provides the geographic location of a device and is common in cell phone technology.

Geolocation Jumping: Acquiring someone's geographic location by obtaining their coordinates from their device in an unsuspecting manner.

Gogolin's Security Principle: Practice proactive prevention, not reactive response.

Integrity: Data is accurate, and updates are not made by unauthorized agents – and that authorized agents cannot make unauthorized updates.

MMORPG: Massively multiplayer online role-playing game played on the Internet that features at least one persistent world.

Near Field Communication: A short range high frequency wireless communication technology that enables exchange of information between devices that are within 10 cm of proximity.

Power-Leveling Services: Pay a person or company to move a character up a level (level up) on the player's behalf.

Productive Utility: Something providing measurable benefit.

Risk: The likelihood that a specific threat will manifest itself.

Threat: An indication or warning of a potentially undesirable outcome.

Toxic Immersion: Losing people to a space that, by any standard of human worth, dignity, and well-being, is not good for them.

Vulnerability: A security flaw caused by an absence or weakness of a countermeasure or safeguard.

Chapter 15
The Role of Standards for E-Commerce in Virtual Worlds

Joerg H. Kloss
Consultant, Germany

ABSTRACT

This chapter discusses the topic of standards for Virtual Worlds with emphasis on their usability as a stable and reliable basis for long-term investments into 3D-E-Commerce. The text explains why standards are important for the success of Virtual Worlds as well as the business in these shared online 3D environments, and what the relevant criteria are to decide for the right technology and/or provider. Although sometimes in the shadow of popular proprietary platforms there are already many different candidates for a Virtual World standard, currently in different states of development. By choosing a 3D platform, E-Commerce providers will decide about their business potential and at the same time strengthen one or another standard in the current technical competition phase. So it is important to get an overview about the current approaches, their advantages and disadvantages as well as the tendencies for the future developments. In this chapter the reader will be sensitized for the issues of standardization, compatibility and interoperability of Virtual Worlds for successful E-Commerce applications. An overview about the current approaches supports the orientation and decision for the different technologies. Some concrete XML-based code examples realized in the international ISO standard for interactive 3D-Graphics X3D demonstrates the practical deployment of highly compatible concepts. An outlook to the further integration of interactive 3D graphics into the Next Generation Web respectively the 3D Internet completes the overview.

DOI: 10.4018/978-1-61692-808-7.ch015

INTRODUCTION

Although many companies have left the flagship Second Life®, the potential for Virtual Worlds (VW) is still forecasted as one of the most driving technologies and applications also in economically challenging times. While Gartner Research prognosticated 80% of active Internet users in VW's by 2011 [Gartner, 2007] and 70% of corporate organizations with their own VW's by 2012 [Gartner, 2008], Forrester Research expected the 3D-Internet by 2013 [Forrester, 2008]. And even during a serious global recession, VW's seem to be an appropriate way for cost savings in travel, training and collaboration for companies.

Today's VW's are not at all in a consolidation phase, yet. On the contrary, the number of VW's is currently exploding according to the figures of e.g. KZERO Research [Kzero, 2009] or the Association of VW's [AVW, 2009]. Hundreds of VW's are classified into different categories over various levels, like Game, Social and Business worlds with subcategories like MMORPG's, branded, mirror, teen or intra worlds. Also the number of users and hours of usage in VW's increases, and new technologies are supporting the trend to dissolve the boundaries between the real and virtual world with mobile and ubiquitous devices, localization and augmented reality approaches as well as life logging of objects and users.

Most of these different platforms, technologies and channels are offering an enormous potential for applying E-Commerce approaches to VW's. On the other hand, the large number of different technical platforms and proprietary approaches seems to be also one of the major hurdles for a broader breakthrough of VW's in today's business. While it is already hard for the user to decide for one of the many existing VW's, it is even harder for the provider to choose and invest into the 'right' VW platform to offer its E-Commerce service. How many of the target customers can be reached via this platform, what existing services and 3D models can be imported or need to be rebuild with in-world tools, are the customers able to teleport virtual goods to other VW platforms, how stable and secure is the platform and how long will the operator exist etc.?

So far, these questions have to be answered with lots of uncertainty, even if the provider decides to operate his own proprietary VW platform. To make the right decision for the own VW engagement is essential for the success of the intended E-Commerce solution. With always limited budgets an investor could theoretically try to be on as much as possible platforms, but probably just with moderate success and attractiveness due to limited resources per engagement. So it is a business critical decision to bet on the right horse also in VW's. Building new 3D models per platform with proprietary in-world tools, loosing assets by teleporting between different VW's and being dependent on commercial and political decisions of single platform operators increases both, the expenses and the frustration of the E-Commerce providers as well as the many private consumers.

BACKGROUND

To simplify the questions and to overcome the current main challenges of missing interoperability between VW's, compatibility of 3D assets and teleporting of avatars, standards are required for VW's. Identified as one of the major challenges in the community, different standardization approaches are currently under development. Not all of them are intended to become recognized as an official standard, but by providing a generic 3D interface to one or more of the dominant web browsers they have the potential to become a de facto standard. Also the feature sets differ tremendously between the various approaches. While one covers the whole spectrum of a fully featured VW including multi-user functionality, persistent asset management and in-world tools, the others just provide a standardized interface for 3D graphics. Furthermore, also the latter could differ in the level of abstraction they provide to handle 3D graphics operations.

The more features are included and the higher the abstraction level, the faster and easier a VW could be set up, but also the functionalities become more determined, and individual E-Commerce solutions become harder or even impossible to implement. So it will be probably impossible to develop one single standard that covers all of the heterogeneous requirements at once. On the other hand, also combinations of different approaches could be possible, e.g. by using a standardized 3D data exchange format between different fully featured VW platforms. At this early time of the evolving VW market most approaches are somehow monolithic, and driven by interests of new market players, manufacturers, investors, and their short-term rate of return. The walkover of one de facto standard is not always the best but sometimes the fastest solution, while establishing an industry standard normally takes much longer, tending to a more reliable long-term perspective.

3D INTERNET APPROACHES

As stated out before the spectrum of possible 3D-Internet and/or standardization approaches is broad. Moreover, it develops further during the time, so the following overview could just deliver a snapshot of the current dynamic situation, but shows at least the main tendencies. The listed systems represent typical examples of the main directions and differences of the approaches, and provide good starting points for the selection of a potential E-Commerce platform.

Stand Alone Server Platform with OpenSimulator

In the style of the proprietary architecture of the popular VW Second Life® the Open Source server "OpenSIM" [OpenSimulator, 2009] provides the most fully featured platform (under BSD license) for operating complex VW's. Consumers can use the Second Life® stand-alone client for access, and are provided with a growing number of features similar to the commercial platform. Although proprietary in its architecture, OpenGrids based on OpenSIM are expected to be compatible with each other, and to offer some very basic teleportation functionality [VWN, 2008] via the so called Hypergrid, but still by loosing almost all of the assets from one world to another. As communication protocol the Second Life® Open Grid Protocol [SL, 2008] is used. Like with the original platform the 3D objects are modeled with in-world tools, and behavior to 3D objects is given by using more and more features of the Linden Scripting Language (LSL). The server software is still in its infancy (alpha version) and focused on the integration of basic features. OpenSIM is not mainly intended to become an official standard for VW's, but to be an open platform for different VW providers.

Plug-in 3D API with Google O3D

To enrich the Web with 3D graphics Google released and furthermore develops "O3D" [Google, 2009a]. Realized as a proprietary browser plug-in for standard web browsers on Windows, Macintosh and Linux platforms, 3D content can be displayed directly in the browser window after downloading and installing the O3D plug-in. O3D extends JavaScript by providing a high-level API for 3D graphics based on the systems low-level graphics libraries, like OpenGL or Direct3D. To develop 3D applications with O3D some deeper knowledge about 3D graphics and advanced scripting in JavaScript is required from the Web designer. This is especially true if behaviors of 3D objects have to be developed in JavaScript in a non-declarative way that is interpreted at runtime. As an API for 3D graphics O3D focus on the graphics functions, and additional features needed in the context of VW's have to be implemented in pure JavaScript. Google provides a sample Collada converter [Google, 2009b], and suggests to export 3D models from common modeling tools to standard Collada files that can be imported to O3D.

Integrated 3D Interface with Khronos WebGL

In response to a proposal from Mozilla, the Khronos Group has initiated the development of an open, royalty-free standard for bringing accelerated 3D graphics to the Web [Khronos, 2009a]. Also this approach uses JavaScript for developing 3D graphics, but it does not require a separate plug-in for the Web browser. By binding JavaScript directly to the standard graphics library OpenGL ES 2.0 (Open Graphics Library for Embedded Systems), which is available on most computer systems, Web developers can access low-level graphics functions to build 3D applications from scratch, running directly within the Web browser. It is assumed that the runtime performance of JavaScript increases further, so that the low-level graphics access is not decelerated by the scripting language. Manufacturers of popular Web browsers are intending to implement support for WebGL, and a first public release of the standard is expected for the first half of 2010 [Khronos, 2009b]. While the consumption of 3D on the Web could become easier with WebGL, the low-level graphics work of Web designers surely also becomes more challenging, especially by adding further VW functionalities in pure JavaScript.

Streamed 3D Multimedia with MPEG-4

Although better known for its audio and video compression features, the multimedia standard MPEG-4 also incorporates 3D graphics components [Kuehhirt, 2007]. As an international established standard according to ISO/IEC 14496 the object orientated version also includes concepts for interaction with 2D and 3D graphics components within binary media streams. The binary scene description format BIFS (Binary Format for Scenes) respectively its XML variant XMT-A (eXtensible MPEG-4 Textual Format), defined under ISO/IEC 14496-11, are integrating components of the 3D standard X3D in the MPEG-4 scene graph [ISO, 2005]. Besides the fact that the 3D subset is still not well-known in public also very few MPEG-4 players implement and support it yet, like e.g. the player "BS Contact MPEG-4" from Bitmanagement [Bitmanagement, 2009]. This could change rapidly when the functionality of streaming interactive 3D content becomes more important also for VW's in the future.

3D Data Exchange with Collada

Also managed by the Khronos Group the 3D format Collada (Collaborative Design Activity) was originally defined as cost and time saving data exchange format for 3D content interchange between different 3D development tools used within the game production process [Arnaud, 2006]. To jump between the different tools back and forth without losing any of the tool specific 3D assets, a common 3D data framework was defined as a more or less universal XML-based schema that could be easily adapted furthermore to new concepts in the evolving field of 3D graphics. This schema not only encodes basic 3D elements but also advanced concepts like e.g. animation, physics as well as kinematics [Khronos, 2009c]. Although supported by most of the 3D tools currently used to build professional high-end 3D content, Collada is neither designed nor suitable as a runtime format for 3D real-time graphics. It works perfect as intermediate format between 3D developments tools, but to be used within VW's it should transformed into dedicated formats like O3D or X3D.

ISO Standard for Interactive 3D Worlds with X3D

The international standard X3D according to ISO/IEC 19775 is available already today, designed and maintained by the international Web3D consortium [Web3D, 2009a], with origins in the VRML standard, widely used within different application fields and professional 3D tools since many years [Kloss, 1998]. With its basis on the Internet standard XML, the declarative scene description language and open data format X3D is fully compatible to the other Web standards of the World Wide Web Consortium (W3C), and therefore integrates seamlessly also into Web 2.0, Semantic Web as well as 3D Internet approaches. Thus VW's build with X3D are not only interoperable with each other, but also with other current and future XML-based Web applications. Many X3D viewers are currently available as stand-alone and/or as plug-in for almost all web browsers. Besides a complete set of 3D basic elements X3D also defines advanced components for animation, interaction as well as distributed multi-user worlds. By optionally integrating JavaScript, or programming the specified external application interface (EAI/SAI) with Java,.NET or any other programming language X3D offers nearly unlimited possibilities for setting up all kinds of interactive 3D online applications [Kloss, 2010].

Most of the other approaches described before are still far away from international accepted standards, currently in an early development phase, and therefore offer only a weak basis for decisions about long-term investments into E-Commerce solutions for VW's. Furthermore, some of them have a limited focus on just elementary 3D graphics features, and exclude additional concepts that are important to VW's as well. Because of that the further discussion is based on the advanced and established concepts of the international ISO standard X3D.

EXAMPLES IN X3D

In order to demonstrate how easy basic VW concepts can be realized in X3D, and what advantages the 3D standard implicates some example code snippets are provided and explained in the following. Of course, this chapter cannot deliver a complete introduction into world building with X3D. To learn how to develop VW's with X3D there are at least two standard books available, one in English [Brutzman, 2007] and one in German [Kloss, 2010] language.

One of the main advantages of X3D is the smooth integration into existing Web environments. The idea for X3D respectively its ancestor VRML (Virtual Reality Modeling Language) was born already 1994 on the first W3C conference with the inventor of the World Wide Web, Tim Berners-Lee. Since then the evolution of the two key languages of the Web, HTML and VRML was closely linked with each other. When HTML became XHTML, also VRML became X3D, linked together now even more closely by the common basis of XML. But also before, the two worlds of 2D Web pages and 3D worlds have been already integrated quite well just by embedding the X3D world (.x3d) in the HTML document with the HTML tag <embed> or <object> with or without frames, as shown in the following HTML code.

```
<!DOCTYPE HTML PUBLIC "-//W3C//DTD
HTML 4.01    Transitional//EN">
<html>
<head>
  <title>Embed X3D within HTML</ti-
tle>
  <meta name="author" content="My
Self">
</head>
<body>
  <center>
    <h2>HTML and X3D</h2>
    <embed src="Email3D.x3d"
height="300" width="500">
```

```
    <p><b>Go for it</b><p>
</body>
</html>
```

The other way round it is also quite straightforward to integrate other applications into X3D worlds. The X3D specification [Web3D, 2009b] defines a so called "node" with the term "Anchor" that allows calling another application via the field "url" by its specific URI schema. By clicking the 3D box within the following X3D scene, the local email client is called, and the email address of the receiver as well as the subject text is inserted automatically. By that you can send emails from within the 3D world without implementing a dedicated 3D email client. This also works for text and audio chats as well as for videoconferencing from within an X3D world just by calling and integrating other Web applications. The following code shows the complete X3D file for calling an email client by clicking a 3D box.

```
<?xml version='1.0'
encoding='UTF-8'?>
<!DOCTYPE X3D PUBLIC "ISO//Web3D//DTD
X3D 3.2//EN">
<X3D profile='Interchange' ver-
sion='3.2'>
<head>
  <meta name='filename'
content='Email3D.x3d'/>
</head>
<Scene>
  <Transform DEF="mailbox" transla-
tion="1 2 0">
    <Anchor url="mailto:me@x3d.
edu?subject=Hello3D!"
    description="Please click the box
to send an Email!">
      <Shape>
        <Box size="2 3 2"/>
      </Shape>
    </Anchor>
  </Transform>
</Scene>
</X3D>
```

While comparing the HTML file with the X3D file it becomes obvious how similar and straightforward the two Web languages are. To run the two example codes, and embed the X3D file into the HTML file, just enter them separately into a text editor, save them with the extensions. html and.x3d, and call the HTML file. If an X3D plug-in is installed, the Web browser will show the HTML text including the X3D world.

Another example demonstrates, how powerful the X3D scene description language is, and how easily important features of VW's can be realized. If different X3D files respectively 3D environments shall be connected to one single big VW or Hypergrid, the X3D node "Inline" can be used in one central X3D file to load in and integrate all other X3D files into one, as shown in the following X3D code.

```
<?xml version='1.0'
encoding='UTF-8'?>
<!DOCTYPE X3D PUBLIC "ISO//Web3D//DTD
X3D 3.2//EN">
<X3D profile='Interchange' ver-
sion='3.2'>
<head>
  <meta name='filename'
content='Central.x3d'/>
</head>
<Scene>
  <Transform translation="0 0 -100">
    <Inline url="North.x3d"
load="true">
  </Transform>
  <Transform translation="100 0 0">
    <Inline url="East.x3d"
load="true">
  </Transform>
  <Transform translation="0 0 100">
    <Inline url="South.x3d"
load="true">
```

```
  </Transform>
  <Transform translation="-100 0 0">
    <Inline url="West.x3d"
load="true">
  </Transform>
</Scene>
</X3D>
```

When loading the file Central.x3d into the X3D viewer respectively browser, all other X3D files (North, East, South, and West) are also loaded immediately, and positioned accordingly to one common 3D world. This makes sense if a static 3D scene is composed of many complex 3D objects which are difficult to model in one single X3D file, or if they are collected from public 3D libraries somewhere in the Internet. But if a user shall be able to move through an endless Hypergrid of connected 3D worlds, the single X3D files must be loaded and unloaded dynamically, depending on the movements of the user. This can be realized in X3D by applying different interactivity components, namely sensors to measure the changing user position, and events that are routed to the Inline nodes and their field "load" to change its value. If the user moves for example from the central grid towards the north grid, the load field of North receives a true value that forces the Inline node to load and integrate the file North.x3d. At the same time the user removes himself from the South, so the south grid can be unloaded by sending the load field of South a false value.

FUTURE DEVELOPMENT DIRECTIONS

Although X3D fulfils already many of the features required by demanding VW worlds on the most reliable basis of an international ISO standard, there is no idleness in the further development and extension of the scope of services. Interactive 3D graphics and VW is a highly emerging market that will develop much further in the near future, driven by new challenges from the games, mobile, and many other entertainment and business industries. Also the global working groups of the Web3D consortium will continue to work to hold X3D on the cutting-edge.

As identified in the comparison of the different 3D-Internet approaches, the trend towards seamless integration of 2D and 3D content on the Web is obvious. The easier 3D can be used, and the less the cross-media break, the higher the user acceptance and finally the success of E-Commerce with and within VW's. X3D is already highly integrated into the Web and its many different applications, as demonstrated above. And the integration is proceeding further by benefiting from the common XML basis of the main Web languages. Therefore X3D code can already be integrated right into XHTML code by defining and using the so called namespaces of the XML derivates, as shown in the following code example that mixes XHMTL and X3D code.

```
<?xml version="1.0" encoding="utf-8"
?>
<!DOCTYPE html PUBLIC "-//W3C//DTD
XHTML 1.0 Strict//EN"
  "http://www.w3.org/TR/xhtml1/DTD/
xhtml1-strict.dtd">
<html xmlns="http://www.w3.org/1999/
xhtml">
<head>
  <title>XHTML with X3D</title>
</head>
<!-- Filename: Mixed.xhtml -->
<body>
  <h1>Combination of namespaces</h1>
  <p>XHTML code followed by X3D
code...</p>
  <x3d:x3d xmlns:x3d="http://www.
web3d.org/specifications/     x3d-
3.0.xsd">
    <x3d:Scene>
      <x3d:Shape><x3d:Box x3d:size="2
```

```
2 2" /></x3d:Shape>
    </x3d:Scene>
  </x3d:x3d>
  <p>... and back to XHTML code.</p>
</body>
</html>
```

The successor of the current version XHTML 1.0 is called HTML5, and is currently under development by the W3C as working draft [W3C, 2009]. The new HTML will restructure the former concepts and will strengthen the role of the DOM (Document Object Model) as the central representation of a Web document. X3D finds favour as the standard declarative 3D description format for embedding 3D imagery into the new HTML version. So efforts are currently undertaken to couple the X3D scene graph with the DOM tree, and to source out as much as possible redundant tasks from the X3D system to the central Web browser. The better that works, the bigger the chance that X3D will be fully integrated within all upcoming HTML5 browsers, with no further need of plug-ins.

CONCLUSION

As described in the former paragraphs, to choose the 'right' VW platform for a successful E-Commerce solution is not an easy decision. The field of VW's is very dynamic and many different system approaches are currently competing for their breakthrough. Many of them are still in a very early stage of development, and a stable, reliable and broad basis is not yet conceivable. Some approaches are quite generic but low-level, others are fully featured but proprietary. The international ISO standard X3D stands out of this group of current approaches to some extent, due to its long history, broad usage in many different application fields, powerful scope of services, flexibility and conceptual openness, ease of use, compatibility and interoperability as well as reliability and independency. The sometimes confusing VW market with an ever increasing number of different approaches and new worlds is not a reason to wait and watch, it is an invitation to join a whole new market with all its usual risks, chances and challenges.

REFERENCES

W3C, (2009) retrieved 3. December 2009, from http://www.w3.org/TR/html5/

Arnaud, R., & Barnes, M. C. (2006) *Collada - Sailing the gulf of 3D digital content creation.* Wellesley, MA: A K Peters, Ltd.

AVW Association of Virtual Worlds. (2009) retrieved 29. November 2009, from http://www.associationofvirtualworlds.com/publication/the-blue-book/

Bitmanagement, (2009) retrieved 3. December 2009, from http://www.bitmanagement.com/en/products/interactive-3d-clients/bs-contact-mpeg-4

Brutzman, D., & Daly, L. (2007) *X3D - Extensible 3D graphics for web authors*. Morgan Kaufmann Publishers, Elsevier Inc, 2007

Forrester,(2008) retrieved 29. November 2009, from http://www.forrester.com/Research/Document/Excerpt/0,7211,43450,00.html

Gartner, (2008) retrieved 29. November 2009, from http://www.gartner.com/it/page.jsp?id=670507

Gartner,(2007) retrieved 29. November 2009, from http://www.gartner.com/it/page.jsp?id=503861

Google. (2009a) retrieved 3. December 2009, from http://code.google.com/apis/o3d/

Google. (2009b) retrieved 3. December 2009, from http://code.google.com/apis/o3d/docs/artdesignerguide.html

ISO. (2005) retrieved 3. December 2009, from http://www.iso.org/iso/iso_catalogue/catalogue_tc/catalogue_detail.htm?csnumber=38560

Khronos, (2009a) retrieved 3. December 2009, from http://www.khronos.org/news/press/releases/khronos-launches-initiative-for-free-standard-for-accelerated-3d-on-web/

Khronos, (2009b) retrieved 3. December 2009, from http://www.khronos.org/news/press/releases/khronos-webgl-initiative-hardware-accelerated-3d-graphics-internet/

Khronos, (2009c) retrieved 3. December 2009, from http://www.khronos.org/collada/

Kloss, J. H. (2010). *X3D - Programmierung interaktiver 3D-Anwendungen für das Internet*. Munich: Addison-Wesley Verlag.

Kloss, J. H., Rockwell, R., Szabo, K., & Duchrow, M. (1998). *VRML97 - Der neue Standard fuer interaktive 3D-Welten im World Wide Web*. Munich: Addison Wesley Longman Verlag GmbH.

Kuehhirt, U., & Rittermann, M. (2007). *Interaktive audiovisuelle Medien*. Munich: Carl Hanser Verlag.

Kzero, (2009) retrieved 29. November 2009, from http://www.kzero.co.uk/radar.php

OpenSimulator. (2009) retrieved 1. December 2009, from http://opensimulator.org/wiki/Main_Page

SL Second Life® Open Grid Protocol, (2008) retrieved 1. December 2009, from http://wiki.secondlife.com/wiki/SLGOGP_Draft_1

VWN Virtual Worlds News. (2008) retrieved 1. December 2009, from http://www.virtualworldsnews.com/2008/07/ibm-and-linden.html

Web3D Consortium, (2009a) retrieved 3. December 2009, from http://www.web3d.org/

Web3D Consortium, (2009b) retrieved 3. December 2009, from http://www.web3d.org/x3d/specifications/

Section 3

The Future of Virtual Worlds and E-Commerce

Chapter 16
Culture-Sensitive Virtual E-Commerce Design with Reference to Female Consumers in Saudi Arabia

Khulood Rambo
University of Reading, UK

Kecheng Liu
University of Reading, UK

ABSTRACT

Virtual E-Commerce can deliver product information that is similar to the information obtained from direct product examination. Both, interactivity and customer involvement can enhance the entertainment value of the online shopping experience. However, if virtual E-Commerce aims to become a truly global platform for collaboration, then it is vital to keep in mind that consumers' behaviour is bound by their cultures. This chapter study the factors that demonstrate the positive effect of designers on people's lives; virtual E-Commerce can contribute to world peace, economic growth is driven by female consumers, and Saudi female e-consumers reluctance to adopt E-Commerce compared to Saudi male e-consumers in spite of the facts that they are both the most financial and shopping savvy in the world. This chapter provides a semiotic diagnosis of the six socio-cultural dimensions that should be considered in the design of virtual E-Commerce targeting the Saudi Arabian female market.

INTRODUCTION

Electronic commerce (E-Commerce) has attracted an increasing research activities in recent years, different perspectives of E-Commerce have been examined to effectively utilize this online retailing for commercial purposes (Sait, Al-Tawil, & Hussien, 2004) (Jamal & Ahmed, 2007). Some researchers argue that the development of E-Commerce has been constrained by the inability of online consumers to feel, touch, and sample products through web-interfaces, as they are able to do in traditional shopping store (Jiang & Benbasat, 2004). Virtual E-Commerce can deliver product information that is similar to the informa-

DOI: 10.4018/978-1-61692-808-7.ch016

tion obtained from direct product examination. In addition, the interactivity and customer involvement created by virtual E-Commerce can enhance the entertainment value of the online shopping experience (Kim & Forsythe, 2008).

Although virtual E-Commerce phenomenon is growing rapidly; it is primarily based on western knowledge, traditions, backgrounds, culturally bound ontologies and epistemologies. There is little if any attention paid to other cultures (Mohd Yusof & Zakaria, 2007). However, consumers' behaviour is bound by their cultures (Hofstede G., 1998). Cultural issues can affect all aspects of product design and localisation. For example, local currencies, accounting preferences, and formats of local addresses, contact details such as names and phone numbers needs to be appropriate to the target market[1] (Lommel & Ray, 2007). Cultural factors can play a significant role in accepting and rejecting a product by a specific market. It can make the difference between a product that works and is successful in a market, versus one that is frustrating for or even rejected by customers.

One possibility is particularly enticing is the potential of virtual worlds to contribute to world peace. A propensity to engage in trade appears to be a human universal, a social instinct evolved in part to reduce the chances of violent conflict among the trading parties. From an international trade perspective, this can lead to two main benefits: a reduction in the likelihood that individuals from different nations will be willing engage one another in violent conflict; and possibly, better and cheaper products and services (Kock, 2008).

It is important for business owners, market researchers, web designers, human factors specialists to be aware that marketing to women is currently the most effective business growth strategy. Women are the most financially attractive target audience and therefore marketing to them will accelerate higher shareholder value (Roberts & Cunningham, 2008; Ellwood & Shekar, 2008). It is necessary to acknowledge that women are the real boss when it comes to buying; starting from buying the weekly grocery shopping to buying cars, furniture, and even more. Also we need to understand that women are different from men in many psychological and behavioural ways that affect their relationship with brands (Ellwood & Shekar, 2008).

In spite that Saudi Arabia is becoming the largest retail market in the Arabian peninsula (Sohail, 2008) and it is an emerging market for the majority of the global retailers (Thomas, 2008), E-Commerce, as a concept, is not very clear in the minds of the respondents. For them, it is a next generation phenomenon, not even one-fifth of the people have ever tried visiting E-Commerce website or bought anything online. Their reasons for not adopting online shopping were: the complexity of online shopping process as in viewing products, selecting desired items, placing orders, and making payments. Also some respondents are not keen to use credit cards to make online payments (for religious reasons). Others consider it unsafe to buy on the internet and give out their personal information. Besides, majority think there might be concerns regarding the after sales services if they buy goods online (Commision, 2008). Moreover, there is a perceptible significant difference between the numbers of males and females with positive responses towards adopting E-Commerce. Studies to investigate the factors that act as obstacles to Saudi female consumers' adoption of E-Commerce have not been carried out yet (Sait, Al-Tawil, & Hussien, 2004) (Sait S., Al-Tawil, Sanaullah, & Faheemuddin, 2007) (Rambo, Liu, & Nakata, 2009).

Various approaches exist to enable researchers to understand the way people from different cultures perceive, understand, and respond to IT applications. Semiotics is a discipline that makes sense of the hidden messages produced by a culture (Nadin & Zakia, Creating Effective Advertising Using Semiotics, 1994). In other words, semiotics identifies the way an individual interpreter of a sign understands that sign. In principle, the interpreter integrates his/her background knowledge in the new semiosis, i.e., s/he refers to her/his personal encyclopaedia in interpreting the sign. Based on human differences, the background knowledge of each interpreter is different, sometimes even within the same culture. Therefore, it is essential to get to the semiotic identification of the user of the sign in order to achieve effective interaction design. We need to know how much the user knows then we will know how the user will understand the interface. If designers are able to know what users know then only designers will be able to know how users will interact with their designs.

Organisational semiotics (OS) is an organisation-centred analysis and design tool kit. It is based on the idea of information field. An information field is a set of shared social norms that express knowledge about desirable, acceptable, and exemplary behaviour in a community. An organisation is such a community in which the information field enables people to behave in an organised fashion. The shared social norms in an information field can be seen as generating forces that make the members of the community tend to behave or think in a certain way. Organisations, especially bureaucratic organisations, can be described in terms of cultural and legal norms that regulate people's behaviour (Stamper R. K., Organisational Semiotics: Informatics without the computer?, 2001) (Stamper R. K., Information in business and administrative systems, 1973) (Gazendam, Jorna, & Liu, 2004).

This chapter intends to benefit from organisational semiotics (OS) discipline to achieve its three aims. (1) To provide a diagnosis of the six semiotic dimensions that can encode the flexibility for social interactions and representations of virtual E-Commerce design in a way that is sensitive Saudi Arabian female consumers. (2) To demonstrate the positive impact of designers on the improvement of Saudi female consumers life styles. (3) To offer advice on how other researchers can use ritual observation to inform and inspire their virtual world designs.

The rest of the chapter is organized as follows: The next section (Background) will summarize the broad definitions and discussions on virtual E-Commerce, culture-sensitive interaction design, online female consumers, and the culture of Saudi Arabian females. The third section (An Organisational Semiotics Approach to Culture-Sensitive Virtual E-Commerce Design) will present some socio-cultural issues and controversies about Saudi females and discuss their influence on virtual E-Commerce design as well as a (Semiotic Diagnosis) of the six semiotic dimensions involved in identifying the main socio-cultural virtual E-Commerce design requirements. The fifth section (Future Research Direction) will present the next steps in validating the proposed model to solve the culture-sensitive interaction design problem and points out some areas for future work. Finally, the sixth section (Conclusion) will discusses the findings, limitations, and implications of the chapter.

BACKGROUND

This section provides broad definitions and discussions of the main topics of the chapter. Firstly, virtual E-Commerce: the main aspects of the phenomenon. Secondly, culture sensitive interaction design: a brief retrospective of the topic is discussed and why is it important in virtual E-Commerce. Thirdly, online female consumers: a basic explanation of the need to shift marketing strategies to female consumers. And lastly: Saudi Arabian female culture: brief explanation of the main aspects of the social system in Saudi Arabia and the Saudi female culture..

VIRTUAL E-COMMERCE

Virtual worlds, where thousands of people can interact simultaneously within the same three-dimensional environment, represent a frontier in social computing with critical implications for business, education, social sciences, and our society at large (Messinger, et al., 2009). These worlds are socially enriched by allowing users to choose 3D avatars to represent themselves and their life styles. They are able to construct buildings, houses, families, children, pets, trees, and even roller coasters. All these 3D objects are rendered in real-time (Yee, Bailenson, Urbanek, Chang, & Merget, 2007) (Mohd Yusof & Zakaria, 2007) (Messinger, et al., 2009).

Unlike traditional in-store shopping, where shopping information is conveyed to consumers through multiple channels, including the store environment, displays of products, product trials, and service. Business to consumer (B2C) electronic commerce (E-Commerce) depends solely on Web interfaces to both communicate such information and manage customer relationships (Jiang & Benbasat, 2004). Some researchers argue that this limitation could be partly alleviated by providing consumers with virtual product experience(VPE), to enable potential customers to experience products virtually (Jiang & Benbasat, 2004). Visualisation technologies are implemented in virtual E-Commerce (such as Virtual Try-on) to provide better pre-purchase information similar to that obtained in trying on clothing to reduce poor online clothing choices and the expenses associated with returns (Kim & Forsythe, 2008).

Online clothing sales are growing rapidly and are now greater than online sales for computer hardware. Nevertheless, returns for clothing bought online are twice as high (%14) as for other products bought online, resulting in increased coast of restocking and reselling the merchandise. Because shoppers will not easily abandon the habit of trying on clothes, it is important that online clothing retailers more effectively use product The rapid growth of high-speed internet access (now in 50% of U.S. households) has made it possible for online shoppers to download product images quickly. Product visualisation technologies such as Virtual Try-on may reduce the risk and increase the entertainment value associated with purchasing clothing online, thereby bridging the gap between online and offline clothes-shopping experiences (Kim & Forsythe, 2008).

Researchers have conducted several studies to examine the effect of virtual product experience (VPE) on consumer learning. They have found that consumers provided with a VPE environment pay closer attention to product attributes and are actively engaged in evaluating products (Jiang & Benbasat, 2004) have compared subjects' reported product knowledge with three-dimensional versus two-dimensional product presentations. The results of these studies indicate that an interactive three-dimensional presentation results in greater product knowledge (Jiang & Benbasat, 2004).

It is still difficult to predict the impact that virtual worlds will have on individuals, groups, and the society as a whole in the future (Kock, 2008). However, these environments may prove to be successful because of the increasingly rich social contexts based on spatial cognition (Shneiderman & Plaisant, 2010). However, researchers found that our social interactions in online virtual environments, such as second life, are governed by the same social norms as social interactions in the physical world. This finding has significant implications for using virtual worlds to study human social interaction (Yee, Bailenson, Urbanek, Chang, & Merget, 2007).

CULTURE SENTIVE INTERACTION DESIGN

The word *culture* (from the Latin 'colo,-ere', meaning 'to cultivate',' to inhabit' or 'to honour') has been defined and used in many ways throughout different contexts. More than 156 different definitions for culture can be identified (Kroeber & Kluckhohn, 1952) (Kooijmans & Rauterberg, 2007). One of the most popular definitions of culture in the field of anthropology is suggested by the British anthropologist Edward Taylor in the nineteenth century. Taylor defines culture as "the complex whole which includes knowledge, belief, art, morals, law, custom, and any other capabilities and habits acquired by man as a member of society". Another more recent definition by Downs "a mental map which guides us in our relations to our surroundings and to other people" (Ferraro, 2001).

Despite the web's great success as a technology and the significant amount of computing infrastructure on which it is built, it remains as an entity, surprisingly unstudied. There are still technical and social challenges that must be overcome to model the web as a whole, keep it growing, and understand it's continues social impact in different cultures (Hendler, Shadbolt, Hall, Berners-Lee, & Weitzner, 2008). Many studies carried out shows that users show resistance to, and reject products in western metaphors in favour of products localised according to their cultural traditions (Jamal & Ahmed, 2007) (Russo & Boor, 1993) (Zahedi, Van Pelt, & Song, 2001).

There is no denying that culture influences human interaction, acceptance, and adoption of a product. All learned behaviour consisting of thoughts, feelings, attitudes, and actions are obtained by culture. The challenge is to study different cultures, understand their variability, needs, and expectations, and formalize it as requirements to design products which aim to improve user's experience from different cultures (de Galdo & Nielson, 1996). Users who were raised learning to read Arabic, Chinese, or Japanese will scan the screen differently from users who were raised learning to read English or French. Users from reflective or traditional cultures may prefer interfaces with stable displays from which they select a single item, while users from action-oriented or novelty-based cultures may prefer animated screens and multiple clicks (Shneiderman & Plaisant, 2010).

Consumers' behaviour is bound by their culture (Hofstede G., 1998). In B2C E-Commerce applications it is very important to take cultural aspects into consideration when designing an E-Commerce website. It is expected that when websites are tailored to suite the target market's culture, users will adopt these applications more easily and intuitively which will have better online experience. Selected photos and images that represent the target market represent an easy way to enhance the vendors' trustworthiness (Aldiri, Hobbs, & Qahwaji, 2008).

More and more is being learned about computer users from different cultures, but designers are still struggling to establish guidelines for designing for multiple languages and cultures. The growth of worldwide computer market (many U.S. companies have more than half of their sales in overseas markets) means that designers must prepare for internationalisation (del Galdo & Nielson, International User Interfaces, 1996) (Neilson, 1998) (Shneiderman & Plaisant, 2010).

Designers were often excused from cultural and linguistic slips, never the less, in this era of globalisation there is a great shift now towards reaching beyond borders (Aykin, Chavan, Dray, & Prabu, 2007). The current highly competitive atmosphere means that more effective localisation may produce a strong advantage to develop effective designs, companies run usability studies with users from different countries, cultures, and language communities (Shneiderman & Plaisant, 2010).

To date, it has been common to 'localise' such a product by looking at the dominant cultural characteristics of the culture where the product is being exported for use. Indeed it is equally important to look at the culture (where the product is being exported for use) not just as it is supposed to be but also as it is. The difference between 'cultural ideal' and 'cultural practice' does indeed provide some rich opportunity areas for value added design solutions (Chavan, 2007). Therefore understanding the way indigenous people live their lives is vital to provide successful design solutions for international users a cross-culture (del Galdo, et al., 1996). For example, global businesses have been focusing only on issues to do with local preferences of the target market.i.e. language translation, currency, date and time format, and other areas of cultural adaptation include colours, images, signs, symbols, shapes...etc. Taking for granted that these changes would be enough to gain the target market's acceptance and approval of these applications (de Galdo & Nielson, 1996) (Jagne, Guven, & Atakan, 2006). However, an in-depth understanding of the target market's perceptual, evaluative, cognitive, and behavioural processes is essential to guarantee the acceptance of the target market.

The way culture is currently being integrated into interaction design requires considerable improvements. Using the approach taken by some leading cultural anthropologists and international business consultants like Hofstede (Hofstede & Hofstede, 2005), Trompenaars (Trompenaars, 1993), Hall (Hall E. T., The Silent Language, 1956), Victor (de Galdo & Nielson, 1996), and Hannerz (Hannerz, 1992) in developing *cultural models*. A cultural model compares the similarities and differences of two or more cultures by using *international variables* (Hoft, 1995). International variables are categories that organise *cultural data*. Cultural data can reflect national cultures, corporate cultures, the cultural diversity of groups of users, international markets, and so on as is appropriate for international user interface (de Galdo & Nielson, 1996).

Other researchers argue that these models are not used effectively by the user interface design community. One of the issues that are a major concern for cross cultural developers is the validity of these cultural models that are derived from other disciplines. Specially that these cultural models were developed in the past for different purposes, i.e. business arena and target audience. The difficulty is that these characteristics are descriptive and not prescriptive, they cannot be used deductively. It would be quite wrong to take the characterisation of Hofstede and others, and from these attempts to deduce how a particular cultural group would respond to particular technology. Also the link between for instance, Hofstede theories and web usability is unproven and that guidelines such as Marcus (Marcus, 2001) need rigorous testing and much further validation. The cultural models seem to describe cultures more than to be followed as guidelines for cross-cultural web design (Smith A., Dunckley, French, Minocha, & Chang, 2004) (Fitzgerald W., 2004) (Jagne, Guven, & Atakan, 2006) (Hall P., 2001).

New approaches to culture centred design encourage designers to set aside from Hofstede and other simple descriptive cultural frameworks and engage with the culture directly (de Galdo & Nielson, 1996) (Hall P., 2001). This approach alerts designers to be careful from stereotyping their markets by using existing cultural models. Researchers argue that this approach will provide better understanding of indigenous users from different cultures (Jagne, Guven, & Atakan, 2006).

ONLINE FEMALE CONSUEMRS

"The hand that clicks the mouse, rules the web" (Feather, 2001). Studies show that there are more women than men online in the United States and Europe (Feather, 2001) (DiVita, 2003) (Ellwood & Shekar, 2008). Women now are capable of balancing the world in the palm of thier hands (DiVita, 2003) (Ellwood & Shekar, 2008). Women also are primarily responsible for most family matters (such as healthcare, shopping, making appointments and scheduling). They are leading their families, and societies at large, into the "*Web Lifestyle*". Women are simply more-inclined than men to use the Internet to accomplish necessary and important personal and family-related tasks; to get things done as part of their demanding lifestyle. The implications for society are that the Web Lifestyle has gone main stream. For business and marketing, this means that the way to reach consumers is through the multimedia Internet, *not* through traditional media (Feather, 2001) (DiVita, 2003).

The rising influence of the female consumer is dramatic in every sector; by 2025, it is estimated that women will account for 60% of the UK's personal wealth (Roberts & Cunningham, 2008). By 2010, women are expected to control $12 trillion, or 60% of America's wealth. (Business Week & Gallup, 2004). Statistics show that in 2001, women overtook men online.In 2002 during christmas shopping season, 63% of Americans shopped online. researchers are claiming that more than half of them were women. In 2003, 45% of Internet surfers are men – 55% are women." (DiVita, 2003). Women are believed to account for nearly 60% of new car purchases and 89% of new bank accounts. In the UK, nearly two thirds of computer purchases are said to be made by women, and more than 40% in the automative sector. More over women make 63% of online shopping customers and 80% of purchase decisoins in house hold categories (Feather, 2001) (DiVita, 2003) (Ellwood & Shekar, 2008) (Roberts & Cunningham, 2008).

Women's primary characteristics illustrates how powerful these arguments are: women are more perceptive and have higher empathy for others, more interested in creating long-lasting relationships, better communicators than men, more engaged with managing their self esteem, they invest more energy into nurturing and sharing their emotions, and they are better able to analyse complex messages and build the bigger picture (DiVita, 2003) (Ellwood & Shekar, 2008) (Roberts & Cunningham, 2008). "*Women don't buy brands they join them*" (Popcorn & Marigold). The wider context of female consumption habits as: marketing to women is a shift from male values to female values: from competition to collaboration, from rational towards emotional and intuitive, from focused activity to understanding the wider context (Wendy & Gordon, 2004) (DiVita, 2003) (Ellwood & Shekar, 2008) (Roberts & Cunningham, 2008).

It is important to understand the strategy of marketing to the one group of shoppers comprised of your mother, wife, sister, daughter, mother-in-law, girl friend and all her friends- a group of interesting individuals who go online looking for you, every day. Marketing to women is not about painting products pink or adding frilly patterns to the packaging; it is rather a new approach in the marketing and web design discipline (Ellwood & Shekar, 2008). Marketing to women covers a spectrum of attitudes and behaviours that demonstrate an increasing emphasis on feminine traits over masculine ones. However, design affects all purchasing decisions. Poor design sends people clicking to a competitor. The goal is a positive consumer experience, not flashy colours and loud music that distract visitors from their purpose which is to buy something (Feather, 2001) (DiVita, 2003) (Aldiri, Hobbs, & Qahwaji, 2008).

What is the secret of online success? The secret of online success is selling to the right market. A market composed of eager shoppers, people who have money to spend and who are passionate on spending their money on shopping.a market composed of women. In this this new era of shopping where the marketplace is connected by the mobile medium of the internet, women are the consumerws who are sold on the convenience of shopping online. Online success for business owners is attainable if and only if they focus their marketing on women because we are the big spender online (Feather, 2001) (DiVita, 2003) (Ellwood & Shekar, 2008) (Roberts & Cunningham, 2008).

SAUDI ARABIAN FEMALE'S CULTURE

Saudi Arabia is an Islamic country, governed by Islamic Sharia law (Ahmed, 2008). Sharia literally means "The Way" and refers to the body of Islamic law codified by the Quran (Holy Book) and prophetic teachings and traditions (Esposito & Mogahed, 2007). Islam acts as a primary force in determining the social norms, patterns of behaviour, values, traditions, obligations, and practices (Almunajjed, 1997) (Al-Saggaf, 2004). While

Islamic law is derived from various theological schools of jurisprudence interpreting Divine Law; these scholarly interpretations vary depending on the local customs and social traditions of a specific social reality and does not necessarily apply to other Islamic regions. For instance, some of the restrictions on Saudi female are mainly imposed by scholarly interpretations (Almunajjed, 1997) (Esposito & Mogahed, 2007). The right to hold leadership positions at cabinet and national council levels can be cited as an example. This being said; it is necessary to mention that on 14th. February.2009 Saudi Arabia has named a woman as a deputy minister of girls education. The most senior role ever held by a female in the country (Jazeera, 2009) (Rambo, Liu, & Nakata, 2009).

The Law in Saudi Arabia does not permit women to mix with unrelated men. Gender segregation is a general rule that touches on virtually every aspect of public and social life. Education, banking, access to public transportation and job opportunities are still rooted in strongly held traditional values that do not permit the mixing of the sexes. Almost all public places have areas that are restricted to women. Restaurants have special family dining rooms for women. There are shopping centres exclusively for women, and certain boutiques in Jeddah have a closed door with 'for Ladies only' written on it. Busses are divided into two sections to create a separate seating area for women. Banks have women only branches (Almunajjed, 1997; Al-Saggaf, 2004; Rambo, Liu, & Nakata, 2009).

There is a strong sense in the Arabian society of what is public and what is private. Women (in Saudi Arabia), belong to the private world (Lipsky, 1952) (Almunajjed, 1997). In this segregated world the male-female dichotomy is linked to a public-private world where females are associated with the concept of indoors and males with the outdoors. Public space is a male space. It is the area of business and political activity. Mosques are also in the public domain. Thus, economic, political and religious activities are associated with the male. Private space is associated with females' family members and intimate relationships (Deaver, 1979; Almunajjed, 1997). The private domain may be seen as a kind of retreat, a sanctuary where women belong to the private domain. To protect this sanctuary of the private space is the duty of all males. This is accomplished architecturally through externally opaque surfaces, tightly controlled access areas, and internal courtyards to provide outside space.' (Deaver, 1979; Almunajjed, 1997; Ahmed, 2008).

Houses in Saudi Arabia include a distinct area where women entertain each other away from men. When there is a female social gathering in a Saudi house, the male family members are informed a head of time so they'll know they are not suppose to go to the part of the house where the female gathering is taking place. The same applies to weddings and parties which are considered the most entertaining social events in the Saudi society. There are usually two separate halls one for males and the other for females to celebrate wedding parties. Saudi female usually spend great time and effort planning for their wedding parties including the delegates as this is the most amusing opportunities for Saudi females to look at each other and talk about their display, beauty, jewellery, and their extravagant attires (Almunajjed, 1997) (Ahmed, 2008).

The practice of segregation and confining women to their own company is an institutional mechanism designed to regulate women's behaviour. Restrictions placed on women's mobility reflect the particular importance given by the society to the concept of 'family honour', as the honour of a woman's male guardian (husband, father, brother, or even son) is tied to her illicit social conduct with unrelated men. Both Saudi female's chastity and fidelity are both of vital importance to the pride and honour of the family. This is why precautions such as segregation and seclusion are taken by the male members to safeguard the purity of their women from any illicit conduct. The Arabian sensitivity towards this issue resulted in the whole society being structured in such a way as to keep 'a woman within strictly defined limits that make it difficult if not impossible for her to conduct such a demeanour (Mackey, 2003) (Ahmed, 2008).

Separation of the sexes is therefore maintained physically, socially, and psychologically. Segregation is psychologically and socially processed into gender. A system of rules, mores, norms, and beliefs deemed to be appropriate to each sex are expressed in the values, customs, and laws pertaining to the education and working systems to the country. As a result of these physical, psychological and social processes, a host of cultural prescriptions and expectation arise which constitute a reality of unimaginable power to guide, shape, and control that is to 'genderise' behaviour. So taken for granted the walls of the world that surround each individual, which they are rarely noticed and even more rarely breathed. Once such a separating two-world pattern of work and space allocation has been established, it tends to perpetuate itself (Bernard, 1987).

As a result, Saudi women appear in public veiled in an abaya (a thin flowing black robe that covers the entire length of the body, from head to feet); the reason Saudi Arabia became known as the land of invisible women (Ahmed, 2008). The veil is a symbol for the seclusion of women. Modest attires form an important part of good manners of Muslims. Wearing hijab is required when appearing in public areas. Hijab is the Arabic word that means veil, it is derived from the verb 'hajaba', to conceal or render invisible by using the shield (Almunajjed, 1997) (Al-Saggaf, 2004) (Ahmed, 2008).

In spite of the fact that the Islamic Law advice women to cover themselves modestly, the practices of veiling (covering the heads or faces by a piece of thin material (Dictionaries, 2009)) and seclusion were adapted by the Arabs from previous civilisations mainly by the upper classes as a sign of status and prestige (Levy, 1957; Hatem, Fall 1985; Lerner, 1987). Although wearing hijab is compulsive rule that applies to all women in Saudi Arabia. There are major critical debates among the Saudi society. For most women, veils have moral, religious, and cultural connotations. While some women strongly believe that Islam is the reason for wearing a veil, others argue that it is more of a traditional value only or if it is a religious value then it should not be forced, instead, it should be optional (Almunajjed, 1997).

A Semiotic Analysis to Culture-Sensitive Virtual E-Commerce Design: With Reference to Female Consumers in Saudi Arabia

This section presents the main focus of the chapter. Firstly, it will present the socio-cultural factors that are believed to influence the Saudi online female consumers. Secondly, it will briefly introduce the OS discipline and implement the semiotic framework on the socio-cultural factors to provide a semiotic analysis of the six dimensions that are- according to the author- the main socio-cultural dimensions to be considered when designing culture-sensitive interaction solution.

The Socio-Cultural Factors Influencing Saudi Arabian Female Market

It is important to mention that when it comes to buying, Saudi female consumer is as equal as any female consumer in the world; she is the boss when it comes to buying, especially when she is financially independent. None the less, most of financial dependent women are still the boss when it comes to buying.

In Saudi Arabia, shopping in brick and mortar (physical) stores is the most popular if not the only females' leisure activity where they can hang out with friends while shopping or after work or during holidays (Abdul-Muhmin & Umar, 2007). It is not a solitary action but a shared and sociable experience. Being together, female consumers can obtain advice from others; or just use the activity as an opportunity for social interaction (Qiu, Jiang, & Benbasat, 2006). The Saudi shopping malls are among the finest in the world with their glittering and appealing displays of goods from all around the world. The latest fashion from Rome, Paris, London and New York arrive in Saudi Arabia faster than they do to most other major cities in the world. But for their entire western style glitz, the malls also reflect the Saudi culture which mandates women to be covered to make sure that the sexes remain largely segregated. Nevertheless, there are many Gucci, Channel and Armani clad women under the shrouding abayas (Rambo, Liu, & Nakata, 2009).

Saudi females are the most financially savvy in the world. The times article scatters some very interesting factors about Saudi women; a 2007 Barclays wealth survey found that Saudi women are the most financially savvy in the world in terms of investing, retirement, and estate planning; the Middle East Economic Digest estimates that gulf woman control around $246 billion, projected to hit $385 billion by 2011; Women own about a third of brokerage accounts and 40% of family-firms in Saudi Arabia (On Sugar, 2008; Rambo, Liu, & Nakata, 2009).

In addition to the fact that Saudi female consumers are required to be fully covered by wearing modest attires in shops and public places, they are encouraged to be escorted by a male guardian or a mature female such as a mother, aunt, or an elder female relative or friend to ensure that younger females remain safe and protected. Also females in Saudi Arabia do not drive cars. Instead, they either get to shops via their male guardian's car, or their private drivers, or via public transportation which is less common practice among the Saudi females (Ahmed, 2008; Rambo, Liu, & Nakata, 2009).

Another cultural aspect of the physical (traditional) stores in the Saudi shops is the sales people. Sales people in Saudi shops are male foreign guest workers, even those selling women clothing and cosmetics. That is the reason for not having fitting rooms in females clothing shops. Instead, women have to put down a deposit and take garments to the ladies to try them on (Almunajjed, 1997) (Ahmed, 2008).

Moreover, four of the five Islamic formal prayers become due in different times during the shops opening hours in Saudi Arabia. In each prayer time, people are required to answer the call for prayers and shops get closed. Each closing time is around 30 minutes, in which shopping activities stops, and all customers are required to vacate the shops. Male customers and shop keepers are called to pray in mosques; while females either remain waiting outside the shops or darting to pray in discrete areas set aside for ladies' prayer (Ahmed, 2008; Rambo, Liu, & Nakata, 2009).

Also religious Islamic police are found around the shops to ensure that both consumers and sales people are behaving according to the shopping cultural norms. i.e. shops get closed during prayer times, men including customers and shopkeepers answer the call for prayers, women are properly veiled in public areas, and strange men and women are kept segregated and not mingling with one another (Ahmed, 2008; Rambo, Liu, & Nakata, 2009).

Although brick and mortar shopping is the only leisure activity for Saudi females; yet there are some pros and cons on the practice of female shopping in Saudi Arabia. E-Commerce B2C applications or online shopping provides an ideal alternative to Saudi females considering their shopping cultural norms. On the other hand, Designers can make a difference in the way people live their lives. They are solutions seekers and innovators. It is their core to provide design solutions to meet the needs, expectations, and variations of their customers, or create a great intuitive product that brings the most revenue (Aykin, Chavan, Dray, & Prabu, 2007). in order to persuade Saudi females to use the ideal alternative (online shopping) more effort would be required to tailor these applications in a way that can both sustain the pros and overcome the cons of brick-and-mortar shopping for female consumers in Saudi Arabia.

Virtual E-Commerce could be the key to produce some kind of collaborative and interactive online shopping where the Saudi female can share the enjoyment and sociability of hanging out with friends and family or even male guardians while shopping. It will take good design of virtual E-Commerce interfaces (pure, constrained, or enhanced) and more research on finding the payoffs beyond the entertaining features that appeal to first-time users. However, success will come to designers who provide compelling content, relevant features, appropriate entertainment, and novel social-media structure support. By studying Saudi females' performance and measuring their satisfaction, those designers will be able to polish their designs and refine guidelines for others to follow (Shneiderman & Plaisant, 2010).

Before discussing any culture-sensitive virtual E-Commerce design requirements, it is essential to become aware the Saudi female readiness to use virtual E-Commerce i.e. hardware availability, software availability, internet adoption...etc

The Internet was introduced in Saudi Arabia between 1998-1999 after a long period of discussion and consultations with the Saudi authorities. It was finally agreed that a tailored version would be made available to the public. To enable this tailoring a huge filter system was set up in conjunction with an American company. The reason for having such a filter system was that the Saudi authorities had serious concerns about the arrival of undesirable materials to homes of the Saudi society via computer screens (Al-Saggaf, 2004) (Sait, Al-Tawil, & Hussien, 2004).However, studies show that the Saudi society remains reluctant to adopt E-Commerce business to consumer transactions (Sait, Al-Tawil, & Hussien, 2004; Alfuraih, 2008; Commision, 2008; Thomas, 2008). In spite the fact that the country is becoming the largest retail market in the Arabian Peninsula (Sohail, 2008). Furthermore, the numbers of positive male respondents towards E-Commerce overshadows the numbers of female respondents. No studies in the literature so far were found to investigate the reasons causing this enormous difference between males and females.

According to a recent report released by the Communications and Information Technology Commission in Saudi Arabia; only 43% respondents mostly younger ones claim to be aware of E-Commerce. However, among these claimants, the understanding of the term is found to be quite varied with regards to mode of payment. 28% feel that E-Commerce means 'display of items for sale on website that can be ordered and cash paid on delivery', while 26% know that the items displayed on ecommerce site can be bought online using a regular credit card. 21% even mention that in ecommerce, items are displayed for sale on website, which can be bought by personally visiting the shop. Another 16% think that the items can be seen online and an internet credit card has to be used for that. The proportion of people across the board claiming that they are aware of E-Commerce concept increased to 56% when they were prompted with the definition of E-Commerce, that is, 'E-Commerce is a concept which helps you buying and selling of goods and services on the internet (Commision, 2008).

Also 83% respondents have never ever visited an E-Commerce site. Even the 17% people who do visit E-Commerce site, do not do so more than 3 out of the 10 times that they log on to internet. The behaviour with regards to E-Commerce usage in Saudi is uniform with respect to provinces, gender and age. Only 6% people have ever bought or sold anything on the internet - mainly, airlines tickets and hotel bookings. This not so favourable behaviour towards the use of E-Commerce in Saudi is either because people don't consider it safe to buy through internet 29% or they don't need to buy through internet since everything they need is available otherwise 27%. About 15% of the people also overtly express dislike towards the idea of buying through internet. Others mention things like, difficulty in reaching these goods, buying through internet being very expensive, it is being a complex method, lack of quality and no after sales service.

About two-third believe that 'shopping online is something for the next generation' and that there are concerns on after sale service when we buy something on internet (Commision, 2008).

However, computer ownership among individuals in Saudi Arabia currently stands at 68% for 15-60 age group, and about 73% for 15-25 age groups. 2 out of 5 households in Saudi Arabia own a computer desktop. Little less than half the households own a laptop. Also Internet is the prime reason for using computers in Saudi Arabia 48%. The Internet connectivity stands at 44% use dial up connection and 47% use Broadband/DSL. Almost all computer users use Internet at least once a week. Only 5% use it less frequently and these are mainly women: whereas the majority (60%) use it every day. Windows XP is the most widely used operating system in Saudi Arabia. With about 64% respondents using Window XP Home and 23% using Windows XP Professional in their PC. However, Windows XP Home is the favourite across zones, age groups and socio-economic classes (Commision, 2008).

According to Linden Lab Official system requirements to download and use second life; Internet connection should be either cable or DSL as minimum requirements. Also the operating system minimum requirement is either windows XP or Vista to run second life. This means only users who have DSL connection are able to download and use virtual E-Commerce applications where as users that are using the dial up connection will not be able to do so because second life is not compatible with dial-up internet, satellite internet, and some wireless internet services (Official, 2009).

In terms of language preferences, Arabic is widely used than any other language; 12% use English, 18% have both languages in their systems, and the remaining percentage uses Arabic only (Commision, 2008). It is vital to note that 65% of the nationals are less than 14, which indicate that the entire generation is both internets savvy and relatively able to communicate in English. As a result, online retail in the GCC[2] countries is soon expected to match the penetration levels in the US and Europe (Thomas, 2008). This being said, it is necessary to provide an Arabised version of virtual E-Commerce applications.

Age and academic discipline are also found as of the major factors influencing Saudi female perception of Internet adoption. It was found that female academics that are specialised in medicine, technology, science, business and linguistics are more eager to use Internet than female academics that are specialised in Arabic language, humanities, and religious studies. The study also annotates other technical factors hindering the Saudi female academics from using the internet such as: the filtration of some websites; filtration sometimes blocks some useful information. The lack of Arabised websites is another factor. Lack of content varieties in the available Arabised websites is a third factor. Also the lack of sufficient and affordable facilities for female training and the lack of female IT specialists and ladies only IT shops that can provide assistance and technical support to female users in a gender-segregated society can be a major factor. In addition to the English language barrier, accessibility, and usability issues (Al-Kahtani, Ryan, & Jefferson, 2006) which should be tailored and localised to local preferences.

Semiotics Diagnosis

The challenge is what strategies one should adopt when designing products and interfaces for use in other countries or other cultures (Chavan, 2007).In this era of globalisation, it is increasingly important to create a tool kit of methods that bridge the gap between the notions of '*culture*' and '*technology*'. A set of methods that helps designers to understand the target market's culture and the social norms that govern their behaviour may help to bridge this gap.

Organisational semiotics is a branch of semiotics that deals with all kinds of semiotic aspects in organisations like behaviour of people, behaviour of departments, and behaviour of information systems. It analyse organisations based on the use of all kinds of signs, texts, sign-based artefacts as communication medium. These texts, signs, and documents are studied in their relation to their author, their reader, the world they represent, and other texts (Liu, 2000)(Gazendam, et al., 2004).

It provides approaches, frameworks, and methods to both analyse and design organisations. It views organisations as information systems while technology is only a tool that facilitates the automation of some of the social norms within the organisation. It believes that information systems exist since the existence of humanity, long before the invention of technology. It claims that for us to be able to design and develop successful information systems we need to first thoroughly understand the social reality of the problem owners, their communication, interactions, and patterns of behaviour. Then and only then we can design and develop successful technology. It believes that we should model and map the social reality of organisations in our information systems. Therefore, organisational semiotics view organisation as a community of people who share knowledge of desirable behaviour, and participate in the social construction of this knowledge (Stamper, 1973) (Stamper, 2001).

This chapter propose an organisational semiotics approach to design culture-sensitive virtual E-Commerce with reference to the Saudi female market. The semiotic framework was selected as an analytical tool to diagnose the problem. The six layers establishing the framework will form the six main cultural dimensions that designers should encounter when designing culture-sensitive virtual E-Commerce applications. Once analysts and designers are able to comprehensively identify components (set of norms) for each of these six dimensions, they will be able to provide sufficient culturally tailored design solutions.

This framework was recommended by FRISCO (Faulkenberg, et al., 1998) as a philosophical foundation for information systems work. Properties of signs are divided into six layers where each focuses on a different set of norms. It will diagnose the problem situation from two major perspectives; IT platform and the Human Information Functions.

However, some researchers argue that International variables can focus on both objective and subjective cultural differences. Objective cultural differences include easy to reach variables; political and economic contexts, text directionality in writing systems, and time, date, name, and addresses format. While subjective cultural differences are the value systems, behavioural systems, and intellectual systems of one or more cultural grouping of users. Attitudes towards authority, technology, and concepts of time and space can also be cited as examples of subjective cultural differences (Hoft, 1995).

Firstly, the ***IT platform perspective*** this perspective provides an analysis of the objective cultural differences of the problem owner, meaning that in this level analyst and designers are able to identify the easy to reach variables of a specific group or culture. The IT platform level is divided to three layers:

The Physical world layer in this layer the concern is about the physical representation of a sign. Signs can be viewed as signals, traces, physical distinctions, hardware...etc. In the context of capturing physical cultural differences; designers need to become aware of the penetration levels of the physical (Hardware) equipments among a specific group or culture. This will help the designer to suggest the most suitable design solutions to the current penetration levels of hardware use among members of a certain culture.

For example, most of the countries in the developing world are constrained by economic impediments. This will eventually affect their access to computer machines. For instance, Most of the low-income population in South Africa have do not own a computer, yet the number of people with mobile handsets is far much higher than number of people with bank accounts. Therefore, many banking institutions have taken this opportunity to initiate mobile banking (m-banking) therefore designers are (Chong, et al., 2008).

In the context of designing virtual E-Commerce to female consumers in Saudi Arabia, as mentioned earlier, PC ownership in Saudi is considerably higher among the younger age group with about 73% of the 15-25 years segment owning any of the personal computing devices. With regards to the type of personal computer used, Saudi is predominantly a desktop market, with almost nine out of every ten PC owners owning a desktop. Laptops do have good penetration and are owned by close to half the PC owner population (46%) (Commision, 2008).

The Empiric layer in this layer the concern is about information that can be viewed as stream of signals which must be transported from one location to another, regardless of what this information mean. In the context of capturing empiric cultural differences, designers need to become aware of the telecommunication infrastructure penetration levels i.e. internet connectivity, bandwidth (rate of data transfer), download time...etc among the members of the target culture. All this information will help designers to make judgement about the most suitable design solution to this specific culture. For example, if the problem owners has dial up connection only, then designers need to suggest design solutions that does not require high speed or contain huge downloadable content in addition to software availability.

In the context of designing virtual E-Commerce to female consumers in Saudi Arabia, as mentioned above, both, the dial up as well as the DSL/Broadband connections are equally popular among internet users. Among the 95% of people who are aware of what type of internet connection they are using, 44% claim to be using Dial up connection and 47% use DSL/Broadband. However, it is interesting to see that the proportion of dial-up connection users as compared to the broadband is more among the fifty-five years plus users (Commision, 2008). Also the operating system that is mostly used among the Saudi population is windows XP. From the information provided in this level designers will become aware that the telecommunication infrastructure in Saudi Arabia is suitable for the minimum requirement of using virtual worlds.

The Syntactic layer in this layer the concern is about the rules that compose complex structures from simple ones, language, writing direction, logic, mathematical expression, or a sentence can be composed of some basic parts according to the rules. In the context of capturing the syntactic cultural differences, designers need to know the language of the users, characters, numerals, special characters, and diacriticals, left-to-right versus right-to-left versus vertical input and reading, date and time formats, numeric and currency formats, weights and measures, telephone number and addresses formats, names and titles (Mr., Ms., Mme., M., Dr.), social security, national identification, and passport numbers formats, capitalisation and punctuation, sorting sequences, pluralisation, grammar, and spelling. The list is long and yet incomplete (Shneiderman & Plaisant, 2010). This information will help designers to set their designs quite confidently to suite cultural syntactic structure of the target users.

In the context of designing virtual E-Commerce to female consumers in Saudi Arabia, as mentioned earlier, Arabic is the official language in Saudi Arabia, type of writing system is abjad, words are written in horizontal lines from right to left, there are 28 letters in Arabic, numerals (eastern Arabic numerals) are written from left to right; the digits on the highest value goes on the left and the digits on the lowest value goes on the right,, the official calendar used in Saudi Arabia is the Islamic (*Hijrah*) calendar. This calendar has twelve lunar months, the beginnings and endings of which are determined by the sighting of the crescent moon (Huda, 2009). The date format in Saudi Arabia is (dd/mm/yyyy). The Saudi standard time zone is UTC/GMT +3 hours. The currency is the Saudi

Riyal (SAR). Some of the Saudi females prefer to use their male guardian names as in C/O (care of) or to be called as the mother of (first child's name, son or daughter, mainly son) rather than using their first names (Rambo, Liu, & Nakata, 2009).

Secondly, the ***Human Information Function perspective*** this perspective provides an analysis of the subjective cultural differences of the problem owners, meaning that in this level analyst and designers are able to identify the cultural differences that refer to a person's perspective opinion, particular feelings, beliefs, and desires. These differences present unsubstantiated personal opinions, in contrast to knowledge and fact-based beliefs. Since organisational semiotics adopts a radical subjectivist paradigm (Liu K., 2000), it is quite suitable to be implemented in capturing such subjective cultural differences.

On this note, It is important to recap the following; studies show that participants of virtual worlds behave according to the same social rules in physical worlds even though the mode of movement and navigation is entirely different (i.e. using keyboard and mouse as opposed to bodies and legs) (Yee, Bailenson, Urbanek, Chang, & Merget, 2007). This means it is possible to study social interaction in virtual world. Hence, the local knowledge of the participants in virtual worlds cannot be overstated. We need to capture the local social norms governing people's behaviour of each culture. Then these social norms should be formalised as cultural design requirements. This perspective will produce thorough design solutions considering different dimensions of local preferences. Hence, the percentage of approval, acceptance, and adoption of target market would be highly increased. *The Human Information Function* level is divided to three layers:

The Semantic layer in this layer the concern is about meaning, in other words, how meanings are constituted, maintained, and used in our communications with other people. Our approach to meaning treats it as a relationship between signs and human behaviour, which helps us interpret changes to what people value and perceive as changes at the semantic layer (Liu K., 2000) (Stamper, Liu, Hafkamp, & Ades, 2000).

In the context of culture-sensitive interaction design ***The semantic layer*** would represent the same components of ***cultural markers*** (Badre, 2001; Fitzgerald W., 2004) also known as ***cultural attractors*** (Smith A., Dunckley, French, Minocha, & Chang, 2004) which are defined as the interface design components, features, and elements that can be changed to match the preference of local culture such as: colours, colour combinations, banner adverts, trust signs that represents values or heroes of a specific culture, use of metaphors to represent any cultural rituals, language cues, navigation controls. On the other hand it is also necessary for designers to know the markers that offense this user group to avoid using them. This approach is based on understanding the intended meaning and cultural messages that the interface elements convey. Some researchers argue that this approach is the most promising approach in analysing and designing culture-sensitive websites (Fitzgerald W., 2004; Smith A., Dunckley, French, Minocha, & Chang, 2004).

In the context of designing virtual E-Commerce for Saudi female, an avatar is an interactive, social representation of a user. It comes in different dimensions, and- like people- they view the world from different perspectives. It can be based on a real person's appearance or look nothing like them. Usually avatars are a mix of the real and the imagined. They represent an internet user. Users can choose avatars that resemble themselves, but often they choose bizarre characters or fantasy images with desirable characteristics such as unusual strength or beauty. Avatars allow people to interact with a computer system (such as a video game), and/or with other people (such as in online chat environment) (Mohd Yusof & Zakaria, 2007) (Meadows, 2008) (Messinger, et al., 2009) (Shneiderman & Plaisant, 2010).

Since no man ever looks at the world with pristine eyes. S/he sees it edited by a definite set of customs, institutions, social norms and ways of thinking. Even in her/his philosophical probing s/he cannot go behind these stereotypes; her/his very concepts of the true and the false will still have reference to her/his particular traditional customs (Benedict, 1985). For example, it is of great significant to enable Saudi female consumers to customise her avatar in the virtual worlds as she would present herself in the real world. Many participants would prefer to have their avatars veiled in hijab and abayas as they do in the real worlds. None the less, Saudi female consumers would have the choice not to do so. Also the representation of goods and garments should be customised according to the Saudi female preference and needs. For example, in online clothing sales it is important to display the type of clothes that suites the Saudi female consumers in terms of culture and moral believes. Another example, would be to know the times of special religious festivities.i.e. Ramadan month, Eid Al-Fitr, Eid Al-Adha, Hajj...etc

In the Pragmatic layer the concern is about intentions, signs which are used to get things done need to be accompanied by some sign of intention. If we were able to express our own meanings and understand other's meaning, our signs are then well enough organised to express our intention. Problems at this level include negotiation across cultural boundaries, conducting commercial relationships in the context of changing laws, more sophisticated relationships with customers and suppliers, and data interchange (Liu K., 2000) (Stamper, Liu, Hafkamp, & Ades, 2000).

In the context of culture- sensitive interaction design, ***the pragmatic layer*** is presented in the attitudes, intentional behaviour, and actions of the target users. Designers need to know the target users' intentions, as differences in experience, values, and expectations can create difficulties in understanding. Designers need to understand the target users' intentions and provide design solutions that triggers users to interact with and take an action. Keeping in mind that intention of designers and users can have different influence on the design.

In the context of virtual E-Commerce design for Saudi female consumer, as mentioned earlier in general, Saudi women live their lives with the feeling that they belong to the private segment of the Saudi society, they lives is completely segregated from men, they cover themselves in a veil or hijab when appear in public, they do not feeling comfortable when interacting with men, they don't feel comfortable even when they need mention their full names whenever they have to provide full details about themselves. In public areas- physically or virtually- they prefer to be anonymous. This factor will have a significant reflect on three areas: the names of the avatars, the payment details when placing orders, and on the title and first name format. For example, name format should have the option that enable female consumer not to fill in her first name. As mentioned previously, in the Saudi culture some female don't prefer to use their first name. Their preference is to use their last name, their male guardian name, or their children name as in the 'mother of (son's name)'.

Electronic payment methods are also good examples that demonstrate the necessity to consider local intentional behaviours. Payment methods must account for local payment preferences. It is wrong to assume that credit cards payment method is the universal payment method across-cultures. These issues vary by country or region (Sait, Al-Tawil, & Hussien, 2004) (Alfuraih, 2008) (Thomas, 2008). It is important to point out that the Islamic prohibition of financial interest in Saudi Arabia has caused long debate about the acceptability of owning and using credit cards. While studies show that credit card penetration in the country is relatively low; it also shows that Saudi females are more likely than males to own the cards (Alfuraih, 2008; Thomas, 2008; Abdul-Muhmin & Umar, 2007). Nevertheless, in the process of designing E-Commerce applications, it is worth providing other payment options such as;

cash payments on goods delivery, cheques, bank transfers, postal orders, and paying via debit cards.

The Social World layer in this layer the social value of information is rooted. Signs and norms have no value if they don't produce some kind of *social change*. This level involves signs that change a person's beliefs, values, and action in a social world which are presented in the commitments, contracts, and social agreements in the real world (Liu, 2000) (Stamper, et al., 2000).

In the context of culture-sensitive interaction design, the main purpose of this research is presented in this layer. Designers need to have answers to these questions: What is the social (cultural) value of this system (product)? How can designers change their target users' lives or improve their life styles while acknowledging their beliefs, values, and culture? How can designers persuade their target market to adopt a technology or a product that should improve their experiences while maintaining their target markets customs and traditions? How can designers provide modern digital solutions to their target market that can improve their lives but does not challenge their social norms?

In the context of designing virtual E-Commerce for Saudi female consumers: What is the social value of virtual E-Commerce to Saudi female e-consumers? How can designers change the Saudi female understanding and perception about E-Commerce? How can designers encourage Saudi female consumers to participate in virtual E-Commerce? How can designers convince Saudi female consumers that virtual E-Commerce improves their physical shopping experience? How can designers turn the socio-cultural barriers that Saudi women face in the real world to opportunities where she can have better experience, better lifestyles, and the chance to connect with the world with a click of a mouse? It is also important to encounter other stakeholders who have the authority to influence or change Saudi female consumers' decision. For example, Saudi female decision to purchase online can be influenced by her male guardian; therefore, it is necessary to consider the male guardian role and responsibility while designing virtual E-Commerce applications. Another example in the same context, Internet in Saudi Arabia is filtered by KACST to stop any unsuitable contents from passing to the Saudi population; therefore, we need to consider the content filtration while designing applications targeting the Saudi female consumers market.

We have just discussed the six cultural dimensions that represent the main differences that designers should encounter when designing culture application. These six cultural dimensions are obtained from the six properties of signs from the semiotic framework (Faulkenberg, et al., 1998). (Fig.1)Some researchers argue that culture-sensitive interaction designers can produce effective localised designs by analysing only one or two of the dimensions discussed earlier (Marcus, 2001; Fitzgerald W., 2004; Badre, 2001).while we believe that the analysis of the six dimensions together is essential when designing culture sensitive application.

A suggestion that can improve communication among people in different cultures in virtual E-Commerce, is to enable some kind of language translation mechanism that enable international participants to communicate with each other, meeting one another, without the need to speak each other's languages, this mechanism should enable people to communicate successfully regardless of the language that they speak. Enabling international participants to successfully communicate with one another crossing the language barriers will bring a fruitful collaboration among all participants. Consumers are able to purchase products from any virtual shop in the world even if they don't speak the same language and business owners on the other hand would be able to display and sell their products to worldwide consumers. Participants will be introduced to one another's cultures, listen to other cultures music, and learn one another's dance moves. Virtual worlds will then truly resemble the world as a global village.

Virtual E-Commerce represents a frontier of opportunities for both business owners and consumers; everyone can live in peace with one another. Since it is difficult if not impossible to separate ourselves from others, virtual E-Commerce can provide the dream land where we can manifest the way life can be upon this planet. In this land, people can live among one another in a variety of personalities, cultures, values, and believes. There would also be a wide range of interpretations, expressions, representations, interaction, and communication protocols among the people who live on this land. People can also implement among their local communities a variety of social, legal, political and financial systems, variety of religions, and all and every kind of orientations. A world that enable people to find their true strengths within their differences, to come together with their differences not agreeing with one another but understanding that their differences create the bases from which they all create and that in this creation of this world, it will neither oppress nor discriminate others.

FUTURE RESEARCH DIRECTIONS

The chapter provide a semiotic diagnosis of culture-sensitive virtual E-Commerce design targeting female consumers in Saudi Arabia. This research proposes a model based on organisational semiotics to capture, analyse and design culture-sensitive interaction applications in the context of Saudi female consumers' design requirement of E-Commerce applications: a Semeiotic diagnosis using the semiotic framework is the first phase in the model. The next phase will be ontological modelling to the social reality of the problem domain. This phase will provide a semantic analysis to the meaning of E-Commerce from the Saudi society perspective or in other words it will model the way Saudi female consumers perceive it to be. After that, the social norms that have been captured in the previous phases will be formalised as design

Figure 1. Semiotic framework (Faulkenberg, et al., 1998): semiotic analysis of the six cultural dimensions influencing culture-sensitive virtual E-Commerce design targeting female consumers in Saudi Arabia

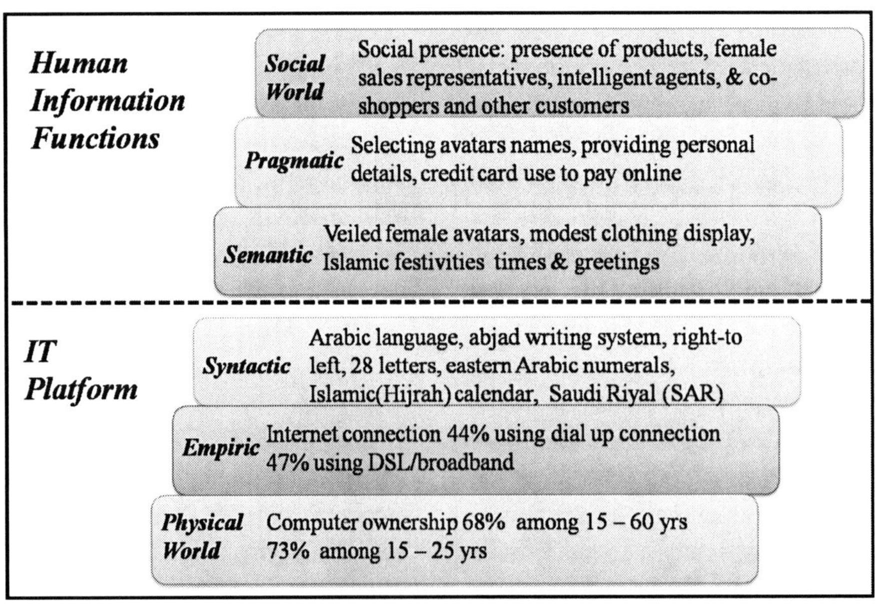

patterns and guidelines to E-Commerce targeting female consumers in Saudi Arabia. And a design prototype will be produced in the following phase based on the socio-cultural norms obtained from the previous process. Then an evaluation to the design by the female consumers will take place.

CONCLUSION

The chapter mainly suggest a solution to improve online multicultural and multilingual communication. It semiotically analyse the different cultural dimensions that designers should analyse when designing culture-sensitive interaction design. It also introduce the organisational semiotics discipline in the context of culture sensitive interaction design, it analyse the socio-cultural factors influencing the design of virtual E-Commerce applications targeting female consumers in Saudi Arabia.

Women are primarily responsible for most family matters (such as healthcare, shopping, making appointments and scheduling). Women are simply more-inclined than men to use the Internet to accomplish necessary and important personal and family-related tasks; to get things done as part of their demanding lifestyle. The implications for society are that the Web Lifestyle has gone main stream. Especially those women who live developing regions where they can shift their disadvantaged circumstances to opportunities for success in all levels of education, health, employability, business, investment, and simply a way to connect with the globe. For business and marketing, this means that the way to reach consumers is through the multimedia Internet, *not* through traditional media (Feather, 2001) (DiVita, 2003).

The findings in this chapter are based on both existing literature and observation of the author. Real data will be collected from Saudi female participants to validate findings and be examined on the next phases of this research.

REFERENCES

Abdul-Muhmin, A., & Umar, Y. (2007). *Credit card ownerdhip and usage behaviour in Saudi Arabia: The impact of demographics and attitudes toward debt.* Journal of Financial Services Mrketing: Palgrave macmillan.

Ahmed, Q. (2008). *The Land of Invisible Women: A female Doctor's Journey in the Saudi Kingdom.* Naperville, Illinois: Sourcebooks.

Al-Kahtani, N., Ryan, J., & Jefferson, T. (2006). *How Saudi female faculty perceive internet technology usage and potential.* Amsterdam: IOS Press, Information Knowledge System Management.

Al-Saggaf, Y. (2004). The Effect of Online Community on Offline Community in Saudi Arabia. *16* (2).

Aldiri, K., Hobbs, D., & Qahwaji, R. (2008). *The Human Face of E-Business: Engendering Consumer Initial Trust Through the Use of Images of Sales Personnel on E-Commerce Web Sites. International Journal of E-Business Research.* Hershey, PA: IGI Publishing.

Alfuraih, S. (2008). *E-Commerce and E-Commerce Fraud in Saudi Arabia: A case Study.* IEEE Computer Society.

Almunajjed, M. (1997). Women. In *Saudi Arabia Today.* London: Palgrave.

Aykin, N., Chavan, A. L., Dray, S. M., & Prabu, G. (2007). *Panel Discussion: Global Innovative Design for Social Change. Usability and Internationalisation. HCI and Culture. 4559.* Heidelberg: Springer Berlin.

Badre, A. (2001). *The Effects of Cross Cultural Interface Design Orientation on World Wide Web User Performance.* Georgia: Georgia Institute of Technology.

Benedict, R. (1985). *Patterns Of Culture*. London: George Routledge & Sons LTD.

Commision, C. a. (2008). *Communication and Information Technology Commision*. Retrieved April 9th, 2009, from Internet Usage in the Kingdom of Saudi Arabia: Individuals: www.citc.gov.sa de Galdo, E., & Nielson, J. (1996). *International User Interfaces*. New York: John Wiley & Sons.

Deaver, S. (1979). *World of Women: Anthropological Studies of Women in the Societies of the World. Praeger Publishers Inc*. The Contemporary Saudi Women. In E. Bourguignon.

del Galdo, E. (2001). Internationalisation then and now. Designing for global markets. Third International Workshop on Internationalisation of Prodcuts and Systems.

Dictionaries, C. (2009). *Cambrdige|Dictionaries Online*. (Cambridge University Press) Retrieved May 07, 2009, from Cambridge Advanced Learner's Dictionary: http://dictionary.cambridge.org/

DiVita, Y. (2003). *Dickless Marketing: Smart Marketing to Women Online*. 1stBooks.

Ellwood, I., & Shekar, S. (2008). *Wonder Woman: Marketing Secrets for the Trillion-Dollar Customer*. London: Palgrave Macmillan.

Esposito, J., & Mogahed, D. (2007). *Who Speakes for Islam? what a billion muslims really think*. New York: Gallup Press.

Faulkenberg, E., Hesse, W., Lindgren, P., Nilsson, B., Oei, J., & Rolland, C. (1998). *A Framework of Information System Concepts*. FRISCO.

Feather, F. (2001). *Future Consumer.Com: The Webolution of shopping to 2010*. Oxford: Capstone Publishing Ltd.

Ferraro, G. (2001). *Cultural Anthropology: An Applied Perspective*. Wadsworth, thomson learning.

Fitzgerald, W. (2004). *Models for cross-cultural communications for cross-cultural website design*. Canada: National Research Council Canada.

Gazendam, H. W., Jorna, R. J., & Liu, K. (2004). An organisational semiotic view on interculturality and globalisation. *IASS 2004 Conference*. IASS 2004 Conference.

Hall, E. T. (1959,1981). *The Silent Language*. New York: Doubleday.

Hall, P. (2001). *The Cross Cultural web* (Vols. 109 - 113). Bukinghamshire: 3rd International Workshop on Internationalisation of Products and Systems.

Hannerz, U. (1992). *Cultural Complexity; Studies in the Social Organisation of Meaning*. New York: Columbia University Press.

Hatem, M. (Fall 1985). *Conservative Patriarchal Modernization in the Arabian Gulf States* (Vol. 11). Washington DC: Contemporary Marxism.

Hendler, J., Shadbolt, N., Hall, W., Berners-Lee, T., & Weitzner, D. (2008). *Web Science: An Interdisciplinary Approach to Understanding the Web* (*Vol. 51*). Communications of the ACM.

Hofstede, G. (1998). *Masculinity and Femininity: The Taboo Dimension of National Cultures*. London: Sage Publications.

Hofstede, G., & Hofstede, G. J. (2005). *Cultures and Organisations: software of the mind*. New York: McGraw-Hill.

Hoft, N. (1995). *International Technical Communication: How to Export Information about High Technology*. New York: John Wiley & Sons.

Huda. (2009). *The Islamic Calendar: The Originis of the Hijra Calnder Used by Muslims*. Retrieved December 18, 2009, from About.COM:Islam: http://islam.about.com/cs/calendar/a/hijrah_calendar.htm

Huizingh, E. K. (2000). The content and the design of website: An empirical study. *37* (3 (123-134)).

Jagne, J., Guven, A. S., & Atakan, S. (2006). *Cross-cultural interface design strategy*. Springer-Verlag.

Jamal, A., & Ahmed, A. (2007). Socio-cultural Factors Influencing Consumer Adoption of Online Transactions. *Eighth World Congres on the Managment of eBusieness (WCMeB 2007)*. IEEE Computer Society.

Jazeera, A. (2009, February 14th). *Al Jazeera News*. (AlJazeera.NET) Retrieved March 3rd, 2009, from Middle East News: http://english.aljazeera.net/news/middleeast/2009/02/200921411274294629.html

Jiang, Z., & Benbasat, I. (2004). *Virtual Product Experience: Effects of Visual and Functional Control of Prodcuts on Perceived Diagnosticity and Flow in Electronic Shopping* (*Vol. 21*, p. 3). Jounral of Management Information Systems.

Kim, J., & Forsythe, S. (2008). *Adoption of Virtual Try-On Technology for Online Apparel Shopping*. Journal of Interactive Marketing, V22/2: Wiley Interscience.

Kock, N. (2008). E-Collaboration and E-Commerce. In *Virtual Worlds: The potential of Second life and World of Warcraft. International Journal of e-collaboration*. Hershey, PA: IGI Global.

Kooijmans, T., & Rauterberg, M. (2007). *Cultural Computing and the Self Concept: Towards Unconscious Metamorphosis*. Amsterdam: IFIP.

Kroeber, A., & Kluckhohn, C. (1952). *Culture: A critical review of concepts and definitions*. Cambridge, Massachusetts: Peabody Museum.

Lerner, G. (1987). *The Creation of Patriarchy (Women and History)*. Oxford, UK: Oxford University Press.

Levy, R. (1957). *The Social Structure of Islam*. New York: Cambridge University Press.

Lipsky, G. (1952). *Its people, its society, its culture*. Saudi Arabia: HRAF Press.

Liu, K. (2000). Semiotics. In *Information Systems Engineering*. Cambridge, UK: Cambridge University Press.

Lommel, A., & Ray, R. (2007). *The Globalisation Industry Primer: An Introduction to preparing you business and products for success in international markets*. Switzerland: The Localisation Industry Standards Association.

Mackey, S. (2003). *The Saudis: Inside The Desert Kingdom*. New York: W.W.Norton and Company Ltd.

Marcus, A. (2001). *Aaron Marcos*.

Meadows, M. S. (2008). *I, AVATAR: The Culture and Consequences of Having a Second Life*. Berkeley: New Riders.

Messinger, P., Stroulia, E., Lyons, K., Bone, M., Niu, R., & Smirnov, K. (2009). *Virtual worlds - past, present, and future: New directions in social computing* (*Vol. 47*). ScienceDirect.

Mohd Yusof, S. A., & Zakaria, N. (2007). Islamic perspective: virtual worlds as a western - centric technology. *38* (4).

Nadin, M., & Zakia, R. (1994). *Creating Effective Advertising Using Semiotics* (Vols. 0-913069-46-9). New York: The Consultant Press, LTD.

Neilson, J. (1998). *Useit.com*. Retrieved 05 07, 2009, from The Web Usage Paradox: Why do people use something this bad?: http://www.useit.com/alertbox/980809.html

Official, L. L. (2009, October 22). *Linden Lab Official: System Requirements*. Retrieved December 15, 2009, from System Requirements: http://secondlife.com/support/system-requirements/

On Sugar. (2008, August 8th). Retrieved March 3rd, 2009, from Your Two Cents: Could Female-Only Banks Be Benificial?: http://www.savvy-sugar.com/1851766.

Qiu, L., Jiang, Z., & Benbasat, I. (2006). *Real Experience in a Virtual Store: Designing for Presence in Online Shopping.* Pacific Asia Conference on Information Systems (PACIS 2006).

Rambo, K., Liu, K., & Nakata, K. (2009). *The Socio-Cultural Factors Influencing Online Female Consumers in Saudi Arabia* (Vol. International Conference on Computational Science and Engineering). Vancouver, IEEE International Conference on Social Computing: IEEE Computer Society.

Roberts, P., & Cunningham, J. (2008). *Feminisation of Brands*. Haymarket Business Publications Ltd.

Russo, P., & Boor, S. (1993). How fluent is your interface? Designing for international users. *The Conference on Human Factors in Computing Systems. 342-347.* Boston: Addison Wesley Longman Publishing.

Sait, S., Al-Tawil, K., Sanaullah, S., & Faheemuddin, M. (2007). *Impact of Internet Usage in Saudi Arabia: A Social Perspective.* International Journal of Information Technology and Web Engineering.

Sait, S. M., Al-Tawil, K. M., & Hussien, S. A. (2004). *E-Commerce in Saudi Arabia: Adoption and Perspectives* (Vol. 12). Dahran: AJIS.

Shneiderman, B., & Plaisant, C. (2010). *Designing the User Interface: Strategies for effective Human-Computer Interaction.* Boston: Addison Wisley (Pearson).

Smith, A., Dunckley, L., French, T., Minocha, S., & Chang, Y. (2004). *A proccess model for developing usable cross-cultural websites (Vol. Interacting with Computers 16).* London: Elsevier.

Sohail, S. (2008). Shopping Behavior and Evaluation of Store Features: Perspectives from a Food Market in the Arabian Peninsula. *Journal of International Food & Agribusiness Marketing*, *20*(3). doi:.doi:10.1080/08974430802157580

Stamper, R. (1997). Organisation as a software: a new quality benchmark. *Quality in Software Engineering.* Delhi: IFIP WG8.1 Working Conference.

Stamper, R. (2000). *Exploring the Semantics of COmmunication Acts. LAP Workshop*. Achen.

Stamper, R., Liu, K., Hafkamp, M., & Ades, Y. (2000). *Understanding the Roles of Signs and Norms in Organisations: A semiotic appoach to information system design.* 12-27: Journal of Behaviour & Information Technology.

Stamper, R. K. (1973). *Information in business and administrative systems*. New York: Wiley.

Thomas, K. (2008). Changing attiudes to online trading. *MEED: Middle East Economic Digest*, *52*(32), 40–41.

Trompenaars, F. (1993). *Riding the waves of culture: Understanding Cultural Diversity in Business*. London: Nicholas Brealy.

Yee, N., Bailenson, J., Urbanek, M., Chang, F., & Merget, D. (2007). *The Unbearable Likness of Being Digital: The Persistence of Nonverbal Social Norms in Online Virtual Environments. Mary Ann Liebert, Inc.* Cyber Psychology & Behaviour.

Zahedi, F., Van Pelt, W., & Song, J. (2001). A conceptual Framework for internstional webdesign. *83-103* (44).

ENDNOTES

1 LISA: Localisation Industry Standard Association: is an organisation that provides a forum in which organisations can exchange information on globalisation best practices, strategies, standards, and business issues.

2 Politically, the Arabian Peninsula consists of Saudi Arabia, Kuwait, Bahrain, Qatar, the United Arab Emirates, the Sultanate of Oman, and the Republic of Yemen. Together, these countries (excluding the Republic of Yemen) constitute the Gulf Cooperation Council (GCC).

Chapter 17
The Future of Virtual Worlds in E-Commerce

William G. Burns III
Andromeda Media Group, USA

ABSTRACT

The future of the evolving, collaborative communications structure will be impacted to an enormous and ever increasing degree by the merging of e-commerce and virtual worlds. Such media outlets will bring new and innovative methods by which to interact with clients and customers, as well as business to business. As these technologies continue to evolve, bringing higher definition, realism, and the power to manipulate potential customer experiences, increasing numbers of people will come to the realization that virtual worlds and similar environments are an essential part of an online communications experience. Evidence of this paradigm shift can be noted in the multitudes of brand names which also inhabit these virtual environments through countless offerings and marketing campaigns.

"Entrepreneurship does not just guide the process of having an idea and then building a business. A true entrepreneur has to predict the future."- Dustin Curtis, The Science of Entrepreneurship

INTRODUCTION

Street lights grasp at the darkness of the city as the advertisements flicker in and out of focus to the passing patrons. Above, a floating sentinel scans each passer-by with mechanical precision, displaying each person's identification via holographic display to those who care to see. Some women, some men, various ages and demographics light up the display, as well as various species.

Further along the dimly lit street, digital screens scroll through social media displays from various accounts, showing an information stream unending. Elsewhere, a crowd enjoys the nightlife at a popular club floating in the sky, miles above the mainland. Clouds wisp past the balcony enticing those who dare to take flight with drinks in hand. Like some fantastic dream, these patrons

DOI: 10.4018/978-1-61692-808-7.ch017

do not fall to a gruesome death, but instead glide carelessly across the air. A message displays on a H.U.D. from a friend asking to join at the current location, and within an instant, another person materializes nearby.

This is the future of electronic commerce and virtual environments. It takes place in a space which blends fantasy and reality, comprising a hybrid reality of streaming information, targeted marketing, and the ability to sell to anyone, anywhere, at any time. It is the culmination of digital evolution, the ideas of many brought to existence through pure imagination and executed in real time. This information stream will be ubiquitous and come from countless sources, including sources from businesses wishing to reach a demographic target within an ever shortening time frame. In a world of accelerated progress and shorter spans between paradigm shifts, how will businesses manage the information overload that will be part of everyday life going forward?

In the future there will be no compulsion for a business to submit manually the same information to many places. Instead, information will increasingly be integrated into what can best be described as a "many to many" approach of real time communication. This form of publication will evolve from today's traditional "one to many" approach as an RSS feed would solicit response from whatever media form it is embedded in (Web, Mobile, Virtual World), regardless of where such feeds are displayed digitally and physically. Details and examples of this type of many to many networking are prevalent today in infancy as the proliferation of high-end brand names continually creates virtual environment offerings to extend marketing reach and offer a tailored environment to potential clients within a high technology setting.

Technology is continuing to improve by leaps and bounds, as too is the rate of this improvement. Thus, it is safe to say that the abilities of virtual environments will also improve at an ever increasing rate, being directly based on the enhanced technologies which were present prior to current offerings and soon to reach into a realm of hyper realism. Businesses can no longer afford to be passive with their approaches to e-commerce and virtual worlds, nor can businesses be passive in regards to social media. While it would be assumed that these types of technologies would require separate tactics, the future of these technologies will exhibit a seamless merger whereby the data and services of one sector will be readily and easily available to other services and technologies through cross integration.

The rate of data proliferation is consistently increasing by orders of magnitude over smaller lengths of time. Instead of 'more of the same', the new challenge becomes how to integrate this vast and continually growing storehouse of information into trending knowledge to aid businesses when, how, and where it is required.

If any business is going to be successful going forward, that business must embrace constructive ways to avoid metaphor shear. Consumers will have a shorter window of opportunity to interact with any one business, so businesses must endeavor to capture interest not by shouting louder than any other, since consumers will increasingly tune this deafening noise out, as possibilities explode outwards. Instead, a business will thrive in the future by utilizing smarter and more targeted approaches. In this chapter, specific examples will be explained in order to clarify the fine line between passive and aggressive marketing tactics and how each affect the consumer in a positive or negative manner.

In a world of information overload, businesses must strive to strike a balance between e-commerce efforts and the consumer demographic target. Businesses will not only have to be smarter and faster, but will have to act responsibly in order to avoid over saturation of any particular method.

BACKGROUND

Somewhere in the world today, an Internet user is logging into a social media outlet account or virtual environment. With a few basic credentials, and by the soft glow of a flat screen, this user will wield enormous power from a simple home computer, or even from a mobile device connected through data streams such as Wi-Fi or more advanced technologies. From this central outlet, one can post updates, participate in promotional offerings, share various forms of media, and converse with friends. When participating in a virtual environment, this user will literally alter the world around them, wielding enormous powers of creation.

In the future, the social communications platforms will no longer be confined within a walled garden, but instead will proliferate through various forms of communication and media at the press of a single key. What begins as a simple status update on a social media network, proliferates across the world to mobile phones and devices, as well as other social media networks and services. It will be passed along by others, replied to, indexed by major search engines, and even displayed in a virtual environment where anyone may see those words and thoughts, and even reply. In the future, social media and virtual environments will empower users with what can only be described as the keystroke heard around the world.

With the proliferation of Web 2.0 technologies such as social media (Facebook, Myspace, Twitter) as well as instant information syndication methods and virtual worlds technologies, the traditional market model whereby information propagates from prospective major outlets who hold strong controls on the market, are rendered obsolete. In a world where any business can interface equally with any consumer and vice-versa, it is no longer possible to utilize a static approach to reach the masses. Thus, it comes to light that businesses can no longer expect to reach the targeted demographics by merely participating within each community separately, nor can businesses hold the power to dictate a controlled message to the intended audience. Instead, businesses must find methods by which to propagate the message clearly and concisely through a single means of dynamic distribution, whilst the message itself reaches the many networks involved regardless of the permutations which said message will undergo in the process. In the future, electronic commerce and affiliated marketing must evolve to embrace the ubiquity and transparency that will become a social environment.

It must also be understood that bigger does not always mean better when it comes to the industry of virtual environments and social media marketing. Brand and corporate demographic reach are not empowered further by the brick and mortar paradigm, but instead, businesses must strive to reinvent brand identity on a smaller scale to reach highly targeted audiences. As such, methods of distribution will evolve to reach a targeted and precise audience in a fashion of one point of distribution to many outlets, with a virtual world environment being but one of many conduits for the message through syndication methods. With this distribution evolution, businesses will also find that the audience is not simply passive but provides real time feedback, offering an unprecedented communications channel unlike anything ever seen before.

This real time communications channel also requires that the old processes evolve to acknowledge and embrace the understanding that control over the entire distribution channel for products and services must be partially relinquished. In turn, this will be the hardest step for any business entity in the coming years to adapt to, often finding it hard to relinquish even partial control in return for a higher and more targeted demographic reach. Often times the efforts will seem to evolve into an entirely new entity, as the client and demographic target proliferate the message and content in manners which the originator would never have foreseen. So too, the highly collaborative nature in this field provides for near instantaneous feedback and permutation from the target demographic in the form of comments, positive and negative response, as well as various evolutions of the original message in media forms as well as "copy-cat" offerings unforeseen by the originating entity.

In terms of massive multi-user virtual environments, there exists a mentality by which the very participants of the respective systems are encouraged to not only be consumers but also producers of content. In this manner, a business solution must be offered which does not violate current accepted practice, or attempt to redefine existing conduits of practice for the participants. Instead, it must be noted that in order to be successful in the virtual worlds demographic, one must utilize existing tools made available to the intended consumer while offering a product or service which is both better than consumer created versions while adhering to pricing standards as defined by the virtual environment which said product or service exists within. In short, such practices concerning business within a virtual environment adhere to one of the bullet points made clear in 1991 by Chip Morningstar and F. Randall Farmer when both collaboratively wrote the essay Lessons Learned from Lucasfilm's Habitat. In this groundbreaking essay it was stated simply to "Work within the system."

While relinquishing complete or even partial control over the intended message or product may seem as though it should be avoided, businesses must take caution not to revert to previous brick and mortar approaches, as such thinking has little to no positive effect in this collaborative environment structure. In short, the best way to avoid a negative backlash is to adhere to the retailer saying "The customer is always right!", exponentially so in the 21st century as the lines of communication are held by multitudes, and spread at the speed of fiber optic.

WELCOME TO THE MERITOCRACY

Logging into the virtual environment, users began to notice that the frequency of system updates began to increase, eventually culminating into passive updates streaming behind the scenes. Dynamically updating the protocols and software did away with cumbersome batch updates and awkward installations from the past. Rightly so, it was noted, because the near constant updates would have made it completely impossible to utilize the technologies in any other manner, and each time the users logged into their accounts, the virtual environment greeted them with more to offer and ever higher fidelity.

Technology is continuing to improve by leaps and bounds, and shows no signs of slowing down within a lifetime. Thus, so too will the abilities and technologies which make up virtual worlds environments continue to evolve at an ever increasing pace. Businesses can no longer afford to utilize standardized approaches to e-commerce and virtual worlds, nor can a business treat social media outlets as individual strategies. The future of e-commerce and these technologies will require a different frame of mind, a proactive mindset, in order to think ahead in relation to new technologies and how such can be used as part of the marketing arsenal. In the coming years, the continuing paradigm shifts will revolutionize the way business is done in the 21st century and usher in an age of accelerating returns as the time to enact a campaign shortens by astounding rates. Within the next five to ten years, it will become apparent that years of research and months of careful planning to act on a trend will only leave a business with multimillion dollar failures in the public eye.

Instead, research and planning in relation to virtual worlds environment projects must outline a manner by which to create a dynamically evolving approach, whereby a virtual environment would continually be updated and revised, offer a selection of high quality free content, while also incorporating dynamically updating informational content such as social media integration within the environment. Planning a dynamic approach to virtual environments, one must also take into consideration the frequency of events held at said virtual location, as the more activity which is perceived to exist at the virtual location, the more activity it will attract.

Unlike the past twenty years, a virtual environment represents a living and breathing community in real time, versus prior static approaches to marketing and demographic targeting whereby simply constructing a polished and professional website was enough to continue a presence online. In the same manner as the world wide web before it, the virtual environment exists with abundant automation solutions, but one must balance automation with live and dedicated persons to interact with consumers and businesses as if the virtual location were a real location. To do otherwise today and in the future will only serve to fracture the hard earned trust and interest of the consumer.

As the global digital community evolves with ever increasing capacity, what will drive the mentality of the participants is innovation and collaboration, as it does today. Keeping in mind the general law of accelerating returns (Kurzweil, 2001), progress will continually accelerate, with new breakthroughs and paradigms in what seem like shorter periods of time. In the 21st century alone, technology will not experience 100 years of progress (at today's rate). Instead, innovation will see an explosion of accelerated progress in terms of 20,000 years of progress (at today's rate). While accelerating returns have an effect on all manner of society and technology, when the subset for virtual worlds environments and collaborative media are extrapolated, the growth and innovation follows the same aspects as the entirety of the curve.

In relation to the understanding of electronic commerce, social media and virtual environments as a whole, this rapidly increasing explosion of information, extrapolation and return will drastically reduce the reaction times and windows of opportunity to act upon incoming trends. Businesses, in turn, will soon find that the once forgiving attitudes of the general demographic will instead be more fickle in attention span and opportunity for adoption of branding.

Long term evaluation of case studies and trends will no longer be possible, or of the current technologies in place. Waiting for a case study to be published which states that there is a viable demographic to reach will instead be an exercise in futility, unless such information takes a dynamic approach instead of a static approach. In the time it takes to analyze and mobilize efforts in a concerted manner based on static reports, the trend will have passed in favor of yet another. What is more disconcerting about this future is that these shifts will happen with increasing frequency, and with less time passing between occurrences, ultimately overlapping and merging into an ubiquitous stream of information and media.

What, then, of the future of electronic commerce and the virtual environment? Many questions should be raised concerning these extrapolations and predictions, but most importantly one should ask if the future of electronic commerce requires the ability to see the future itself and make predictions. While trend forecasting often is an integral part of a marketing strategy today, there will soon come a time when trend forecasting becomes a mandatory part of business ventures and no longer an option. Unlike the prior century, where the pace of technological achievement moved at a slow enough speed to afford the time for prolonged research and decision making, businesses must instead learn to analyze the future paradigms and put into place strategies which will act upon trends which are forthcoming. In this manner, the future of e-commerce, social media and virtual environments will adhere to the idea of "staying ahead of the curve".

In order to properly understand the nature of accelerated returns, it must first be outlined in a broader sense from the beginning. In relation to this, there is no better explanation of this concept than from the man who is credited with its inception, R. Kurzweil, PhD, with the writing of The Law Of Accelerating Returns:

The first technological steps-sharp edges, fire, the wheel--took tens of thousands of years. For people living in this era, there was little noticeable technological change in even a thousand years. By 1000 A.D., progress was much faster and a paradigm shift required only a century or two. In the nineteenth century, we saw more technological change than in the nine centuries preceding it. Then in the first twenty years of the twentieth century, we saw more advancement than in all of the nineteenth century. Now, paradigm shifts occur in only a few years time. The World Wide Web did not exist in anything like its present form just a few years ago; it didn't exist at all a decade ago. The paradigm shift rate (i.e., the overall rate of technical progress) is currently doubling (approximately) every decade; that is, paradigm shift times are halving every decade (and the rate of acceleration is itself growing exponentially). So, the technological progress in the twenty-first century will be equivalent to what would require (in the linear view) on the order of 200 centuries. In contrast, the twentieth century saw only about 25 years of progress (again at today's rate of progress) since we have been speeding up to current rates. So the twenty-first century will see almost a thousand times greater technological change than its predecessor. (KurzweilAI.net March 7, 2001.)

As time moves forward, the rate of technological achievement increases in shorter periods of time, following an exponential curve in advancement. In terms of computer hardware, the paradigm of Moore's Law only describes the shrinking of integrated circuitry and doubling of computational power on a predictable time line, but also creates a profound parallel when extended to related technological advancements. Computing capacity doubles, size reduces, and costs remain the same. Therefore, with ever increasing computing power in the hands of the consumer, society can only expect rapid development of virtual environments with ever increasing levels of detail and fidelity. When coupled with The Law of Accelerating Returns, not only will consumers be empowered with drastically increased computing capacity, but such will occur over drastically decreasing amounts of time.

The extrapolation of Moore's Law, put forward by R. Kurzweil as The Law of Accelerating Returns, shows that not only will Moore's Law progress into a new paradigm, but it will do so in each phase with exponential speed of return. This also applies to how the culture within that time frame will respond and work with data in various forms. Where once the general population experienced media in a passive manner (newspapers, television, radio, early internet), the exponential aspects of The Law of Accelerating Returns will be taking place in a more noticeable manner through increasingly non-passive means (Video-On-Demand, RSS, Blogging, Social Media, Virtual Environments, Mirror Worlds, and Augmented Reality).

This, in turn, will give way to an increasingly complex and connected means of communications and community, as the Web 2.0 paradigm merges with, and creates, a new standard of global interconnectivity and 'always online' state through a high fidelity virtual environment or series of competing environments. These new breeds of virtual environments will benefit from the accelerated return of technological innovation in that such will have access to a dynamically superior means of communications and realism in what will seem like shorter periods of time between releases.

As a result, businesses can no longer rest on laurels in hopes that a product or service will sustain the business model indefinitely. In retrospect, businesses should instead be looking ahead of the curve and planning accordingly prior to the arrival of such technologies and paradigm shifts if the goal is to capitalize on these trends effectively and in a timely manner.

An excellent example of a relevant paradigm shift can be expressed through the recent demographics for Facebook (as of January 2010) whereby it was shown that there was an explosive 922% growth in the 55+ demographic (up from 513% in July 2009), while in the same time frame the college demographic usage dropped by 55%, (down further from a 20% loss in July 2009). (P. Corbett, istrategy labs, January 2010). As this trend suggests, Facebook has become over saturated with higher aged demographics at the expense of the original demographic intention. Another point illustrated by this information is that after the initial build up of the high school and college aged demographics, business aspects began to infiltrate these social circles in order to commercialize on an already existing trend. When it was realized that there existed a huge potential in this area, others began to apply targeted marketing in increasing numbers, even to the point where entire seminars were and are being held with attendees of corporate culture evangelizing social media outlets to reach targeted demographics. Through the over saturation of a particular method by corporate means, the intended outcome of the approach has seen negative outcomes and backlash in the forms of major privacy concerns and participant uneasiness, (Corbett, 2010).

In response to the unprecedented corporate influx of such spaces (representing the higher age brackets), the precise demographic for which the corporate influences wished to reach began to have a negative reaction, and the social spaces which were the private haven of the younger demographic increasingly became less appealing on what will soon be seen as an accelerating pace between paradigm shifts. Prior to the initial surge of popularity for Facebook, a very similar order of events happened in regards to the social media service Myspace, whereby the same pattern of events unfolded. When it began, Myspace attracted high school and college demographics. As the service began to attract further involvement from corporate interests, the service began to degrade in appeal to the original demographics. When Myspace was purchased, and a large number of corporate interests flooded into the service for marketing and advertising to the original demographics, those demographics began to leave for greener pastures to Facebook.

With Facebook, the course of events are repeating as the floodgates of corporate involvement are opened and the companies which originally utilized MySpace to market to that demographic jump ship and praise Facebook as the next big thing. The original demographics for Facebook were (as originally seen with Myspace) high school and college aged, but with a 922% increase in users aged 55 and older, which can be easily understood to include businesses and corporate aspects, the original demographics are beginning to slip just as they originally did with MySpace under the same circumstances. Using trend forecasting, it can be said that Facebook will inevitably fall prey to the same fate as MySpace, and for the same mitigating circumstances. Corporate saturation of any service inherently breaks a tolerance for metaphor shear, thus angering the users and driving them elsewhere.

One question concerning this chapter's focus on social media would be to ask exactly how the trends for social media services relate to virtual worlds environments. While virtual environments are more complex and subscribe to herd mentality, social media services and virtual environments share much of the same trending and therefore create an excellent dynamic case study prior to utilization of virtual environments for business purposes. Since a business aspect of virtual environments does not enjoy the immediate benefit of a captive audience, one must think dynamically and creatively in order to create a presence which will ensure not only repeat audiences but also higher return on investment.

METAPHOR SHEAR AND MARKETING

Anyone who uses a word processor for very long inevitably has the experience of putting hours of work into a long document and then losing it because the computer crashes or the power goes out. Until the moment that it disappears from the screen, the document seems every bit as solid and real as if it had been typed out in ink on paper. But in the next moment, without warning, it is completely and irretrievably gone, as if it had never existed. The user is left with a feeling of disorientation (to say nothing of annoyance) stemming from a kind of metaphor shear--you realize that you've been living and thinking inside of a metaphor that is essentially bogus. - In The Beginning Was The Command Line, Neal Stephenson

Metaphor shear, as defined by Neal Stephenson, speaks mostly of the metaphor layers which make it possible to relate to the working environment which a participant is utilizing for the current task at hand. While the explanation put forth here is one of extremes (by which all of the layers have suddenly, and without warning, disappeared), there are other forms of metaphor shear which must be taken into account when dealing with virtual environments.

When creating a virtual environment, one must take into account the totality of the environment that is being created, whereby the ultimate goal is to subject the audience to a form of total immersion through sensory illusion. When this illusion, or metaphor layer, is in place, the participating audience will become immersed in the imaginary world with an intent and focus which excludes physical life. To the participant, the imagination becomes real. It is no wonder that when this illusion is broken, known as metaphor shear, that the immersed audience often becomes irate and prone to backlash against the very tactics which were responsible for breaking the metaphor illusion. A simple example of this in practice would be the implementation of banner advertising on a website, whereby the banners are a distraction to the focus of the individual, but can also extend to the subtle irritations and interruptions which can build up mentally as though it were a single shear.

A more severe form of metaphor shear can be induced through the implementation of pop-up or full page interstitial advertising on a website, whereby the focus and metaphor is quickly and violently disrupted for the individual, thus creating a feeling of anger and retribution against such tactics in use by which were responsible for the metaphor shear. In this context, the retribution and anger over the intrusiveness of advertising on websites has led to the creation of a digital counterstrike known as AdBlock Plus (for the Mozilla Firefox web browser). According to statistics compiled by adblockplus.org (the originator of this service), there are well over three million current users of the service and rising, a number so large that a form of disdain has developed among many web service providers who have built services around the revenues generated by such advertising. No longer able to generate the amount of traffic to advertisers, this form of revenue generation is quickly dwindling as a result, with no end in sight.

In regards to the proliferation of such advertisement blocking services as AdBlock Plus, web developers have instead decided to lash out against the people who utilize this software and thus deprive said users of services unless the users disable the advertisement blocking component while on the website. While the intention of this maneuver by website developers was to effectively force the audience to forgo methods of advertisement blocking in favor of the content which the site was offering, much to the chagrin of the site developer community, the audience by and large chose the ability to continue blocking the advertisements as a method by which to effectively control the continued metaphor experience, bypassing the content provider in favor of others with similar content but being less demanding of the audience's browsing preferences.

In the context of a virtual environment, the rules of engagement follow heavily on the aforementioned insights and developments of the worldwide community. By and large, the tactics are forced to evolve into a more passive role with interaction and assimilation as the ultimate goal. Arbitrary inclusions are no longer tolerated by these digital demographics, nor are the shotgun tactics with which the industry has become accustomed to. It can no longer be put forth as a marketing option to blanket many forms of communication and demographics with generic messages in hopes for a percentage of return. Instead, one should closely relate to the media form that is chosen as the conduit, whereby interaction, sincerity, and community driven focus are essential.

In this modern age and going forward, marketing strategies which have proven most successful are the ones which have targeted a narrow demographic, utilized viral marketing strategies to reach a specific demographic, and have relied on the power of social media interaction in spreading the message. Examples of this new strategy include such marketing efforts as "Where In The Hell Is Matt?" sponsored by Stride Gum (http://www.wherethehellismatt.com), whereby a video blog of an individual simply dancing at different locations around the world gained massive popularity and through the nature of viral marketing, has spread worldwide with millions of views. Also of note, is the branding and marketing strategy concerning the Old Spice brand (http://www.oldspice.com) in which "The Old Spice Guy" transcended mere commercials and went further into a Youtube campaign, answering questions from Twitter via Youtube responses. This marketing strategy targeted a specific demographic and relied on the nature of social media interaction in order to reach a wide audience with a limited budget. In these cases, it can be seen that embracing the nature of collaborative and social media has given an exponential return on investment while remaining within the layer of metaphor and being non-intrusive as a form of advertising. In contrast, the fine line of metaphor shear is noted to have one of two outcomes dependent on whether the tactics involved utilize passive or direct marketing. When an entity chooses direct marketing, be it within social media or a virtual environment structure, and ignores the fundamental rule of working within the system, the marketing strategy is perceived as a metaphor shear to the integration of the digital illusion, much like a disruptive interstitial. When an entity instead chooses a passive manner of integrated marketing, and works within the system, the results are often far superior and exhibit a polar opposite reaction to the negative backlash of metaphor shear.

The goal of marketers interested in creating successful viral marketing programs is to identify individuals with high Social Networking Potential (SNP) and create Viral Messages that appeal to this segment of the population and have a high probability of being passed along. Keeping in mind the process of viral marketing, applications within a virtual world environment adhere to the same principles set forth by which promotional efforts are based on a digital word of mouth campaign as well as remains within the metaphor layer which it is presented. Since the efforts of future campaigns will rely on trend forecasting in order to fully realize the potential of the chosen outlet in conjunction with the understanding of the Law of Accelerating Returns, it is clear that the future of e-commerce in relation to virtual environments must adhere to a strict guideline of passive and highly integrated means if such strategies are to remain fruitful in a time of increasingly narrowing windows of opportunity.

Another recent case of metaphor shear in terms of business practice and marketing has been illustrated with the fiasco concerning the Amazon Kindle e-book reader and the electronic books 1984 by George Orwell and Animal Farm (Pogue, 2009). Due to the licensing agreements, or lack thereof, an electronic version of these books was made available through the third party distribution channels whereby the books in question were purchased and downloaded for usage by a large number of clients. The issue at hand concerning this was that the person who had made these electronic books available did not secure the rights to distribute these works, and thus the works were mass distributed in violation of copyright.

The solution from Amazon.com at that time was one which was cause for alarm, and many parallels with the themes of the books in question, in that Amazon.com chose to simply delete the books from the Kindle devices of the users who had paid for and downloaded said copies, after which Amazon.com reimbursed those users for the purchase price of those electronic books within the accounts in mention. Due to the nature of these actions, and how Amazon.com handled the error of not properly processing the submission of the books prior to releasing those books for active sale to customers worldwide, the end result was that millions of customers awoke that morning and found that a product which was paid for was suddenly, and without warning, missing from the device.

In relation to the idea of metaphor shear, the aftermath of these actions caused a whirlwind of negative feedback for the Amazon.com service and resulted in much criticism over the lack of foresight to have been prepared for such an inevitability within a third party submission service. In the end, it was the users whom were left with the feeling of metaphor shear and the implications of whether the materials which were purchased were truly safe from the control of a third party. In context, the scenario is akin to whether after a book is purchased via a bookstore in real life if the owner of said bookstore has any right to enter an individual's home and remove that book from the person's library while leaving the purchase price on the kitchen table with an apology note. It is this metaphorical transition, as well as the rapid intolerance of unexpected metaphor shear, which is causing the most damage in the reputations of retailers around the world in the digital age.

SOLUTIONS AND RECOMMENDATIONS

Sometimes experiments fail, forcing you to step back and reevaluate your hypothesis. Or change your business slightly. The most successful businesses start with theories for the future, especially in rapidly evolving fields like the technology industry, and they're not afraid to rapidly iterate when they find the company isn't working. - Dustin Curtis, The Science of Entrepreneurship

When considering the importance of virtual environments in relation to electronic commerce, one must understand that in the future, the solutions will not be as defined as available today. Ubiquitous integration of a myriad of media forms will continually blur the previously well defined lines of each, creating what can only be described today as a future whereby no single service, technology or approach can truly be considered separate from another. Social media campaigns will integrate into a virtual environment, while virtual environments will be streamed to various venues through Internet, mobile and currently unpredictable methods of communication. Updates to social media will abound from the virtual world spaces and propagate to social media sites, syndication, and even back to other virtual spaces. The happenings of a virtual event would be talked about through various syndication methods (RSS, Twitter, Facebook) whereby such syndication will further propagate to regular Internet users via feeds on websites as well as mobile updates. In turn, the users who receive and view these syndicated updates will respond from various locations worldwide, from countless devices and connections, to provide a real-time communications stream.

Information is Ubiquitous, Cross Integration is Mandatory

When faced with this realization, it would not be prudent to suggest that a single solution is appropriate when dealing with virtual worlds technologies. Instead, only general guidelines can be put forth in order to foster a better understanding of the future and how best to deal with what will soon be an overwhelming amount of communications and asynchronous information streams. To this point, it must be mentioned that due to the evolving and collaborative nature of communications and of virtual environments, a company wishing to include personal branding and marketing of a product or service within a virtual environment must adhere to the socially accepted channels of integration in order to avoid metaphor shear at all costs.

In the case of SecondLife, currently the most influential and popular virtual environment system, there already exists a conduit of market integration which is utilized by a majority of the virtual citizens. This service is the chosen online marketplace for services, real estate and product transactions. Businesses wishing to rapidly propagate services or products should keep in mind the cardinal rule of working within the system, and within the SecondLife platform, one should release virtual goods and services through the systems already in place.

Another consideration when dealing with virtual environments is to make certain that the virtual version of the product which is being made available is of the highest quality within the virtual marketplace. Since the integrated marketplace is built specifically to encourage any of the virtual environment users to create products and services for sale, a business entity is competing with what can be seen as hundreds or thousands of unauthorized or copy-cat versions of a brand. As of this writing, a cursory search for the term "Coca-Cola" returned thirty-eight pages of products which directly or indirectly incorporate the Coca-Cola brand. There are ten items per page, and with thirty-eight pages, a grand total of three-hundred and eighty unauthorized products exist. This count does not include the hundreds or thousands more products which are unlisted but still for sale at the vendor locations of the currently listed items, so it is safe to surmise that what is listed is merely a fraction of the total in question.

Enforcing Unauthorized Brand Proliferation is Futile in most Cases

The Streisand effect is a primarily online phenomenon in which an attempt to censor or remove a piece of information has the unintended consequence of causing the information to be publicized widely and to a greater extent than would have occurred if no censorship had been attempted. It is named after American entertainer Barbra Streisand, following a 2003 incident in which her attempts to suppress photographs of her residence inadvertently generated further publicity. As early as 1993, John Gilmore observed that "the Net treats censorship as damage and routes around it." Examples of such attempts include censoring a photograph, a number, a file, or a website (for example via a cease-and-desist letter). Instead of being suppressed, the information receives extensive publicity, often being widely mirrored across the Internet or distributed on file-sharing networks. - Streisand effect, 2010

While companies such as Coca-Cola do not appear to be pursuing unauthorized brand usage in the virtual world, it may be more relevant to state that there is such a high number of recurring offenses, and high probability of incurring the Streisand effect, that the company has decided that it is not worth the effort to try and keep up. If giants in the industry such as Coca-Cola are not putting in widespread efforts to curb unauthorized brand usage in virtual environments, then the question becomes how to successfully promote and sell a brand in a virtual environment when the very users in question are capable of copying brands and merchandise?

While it is true that such places as SecondLife are working on various methods by which to safeguard intellectual properties on behalf of brand owners, the overall process is a series of "cat and mouse" maneuvers and should not be taken as an infallible method of protection. To this point, it can be said that one should not attempt to curb existing violations of branding usage within these communities. Instead, the effort is best applied to working within the system, while doing something which only the business which owns the brand can accomplish better than the unauthorized brands.

Build a Better Product or Service and Release it in the Virtual World for Free

Much of the point of electronic commerce within virtual worlds environments is to sell a product or service, but that is not to say that the services and products being sold must be directly related to the initial purchase of virtual items. Virtual items hold an ability to do something which a real world product cannot easily accomplish, whereby the virtual item can contain scripted elements which can give virtual owners the ability to purchase said item for real, while the virtual version remains free. In this manner, the initial costs for the virtual product creation are offset through the vast proliferation of intelligent and dynamic promotion contained within each item. An example of this tactic can be explained from the viewpoint of a popular brand such as RayBan Sunglasses.

If the company wished to create a virtual world promotion and presence for the purpose of electronic commerce and marketing, utilizing the prior mentioned tactic of creating branded and dynamically integrated virtual products would accomplish both goals. Creating official RayBan brand virtual sunglasses and related products, each with scripting for various features and of course the ability to purchase the real life counterpart via the online RayBan store, the brand (in combination with high quality design and implementation) would be better than any other currently on offer within the marketplace system. Giving such high quality virtual items away for free would directly undermine copy-cat and unauthorized vendors which rely heavily on the revenue brought in from the branding on the unauthorized products sold. In turn, the officially branded items in conjunction with the lowest possible selling point (free) which contain a method by which owners of said virtual items could click through to order a real life version would be the best solution for all issues involved while not creating metaphor shear or negative backlash.

Another example of this strategy includes the value added model with delayed return on investment. Through offering a service or item in the virtual environment at little or no cost, a business would be deferring revenue to a connected source affiliated with the originating free item in question. In relation to services, a company may offer for free, seminars or events in the virtual environment while making available for purchase additional materials from said event including audio and video recordings as well as electronic books, case studies, and related media. In this manner, the events and seminars would be free to all who wish to attend, but related materials would be for sale in order to offset costs and generate a revenue stream from the existing demographics which have attended the event and wish to follow through with further materials.

Virtual Products are Perceived the Same as Physical Products

While real life products or services may have a tangibility, a virtual product or service retains the perception of being every bit as real as the attributed counterpart in real life (assuming such exists). When selling products or services in a virtual environment, it is essential to understand that some products and services exist purely as virtual items alone, and therefore cannot subscribe to the prior recommendation of creating high quality products to release for no cost, (unless for purely marketing related purposes)

In this manner, solutions for intellectual property protection should be actively sought and implemented if the goal is to generate revenue purely from virtual product sales. Due to the uncommonly complicated nature of adequately protecting virtual intellectual property, it is only recommended to offer high quality items at no cost if the intention is to promote an outside source of revenue or promote further sales via a virtual location. Possible solutions for high level intellectual property protection have been discussed aside from upcoming policy and system changes to be made via Linden Lab. Whether or not streaming script or server-side solutions for authorization are implemented in order to drastically deter or eliminate intellectual property and virtual items theft is a matter of free market forces, but remain a topic of high interest for any entity wishing to indulge in electronic commerce within a virtual environment.

Use Automation Sparingly

While there exists a plethora of automation options in a virtual environment such as SecondLife, one must take care as to the actual usage of these methods in conjunction with an overall appearance. If a business has a real life office, it is encouraged practice to have a virtual office as well within a three dimensional environment such as SecondLife only if said business can be easily translated to the virtual environment in a useful or interesting manner.

While automation tools and tactics should be utilized, one should keep in mind that much like a real life office there are business hours. Within this context, a real life office should offer live staff to assist clients, and so too should a virtual location in the way of knowledgeable and helpful staff availability within the virtual environment. While not available for the entire twenty-four hours, live staff should be available virtually for at least reasonably acceptable time periods during business hours.

During the times which a real life office would be closed, automation options should be utilized or hiring of purely virtual staff to attend the virtual location and continue where the real life staff are not available. In this manner, one will find that the exchange rate for dollar to virtual currencies such as L$ (linden) are far from an equal ratio, and as of this writing one dollar is equivalent to L$267 (LindeX Market Data, Aug 10th 2010). The average expected pay for virtual work is also much lower than real life expectations due to the unevenly balanced virtual currency. As a result, L$700 per hour (about $2.70) is often sufficient and greatly appreciated from virtual employees. While this may seem a very low rate of compensation, often times establishments in the virtual environment will instead offer only the ability to be compensated solely through received tips, leaving virtual staff compensation to a luck of the draw scenario.

Pay Virtual Employees Well

Because virtual environments will continue to increase in relevance in the future, so too will the balance between virtual environment work and virtual payment begin to normalize. As a result, it is simply good practice today to compensate virtual environment workers in a manner which does not reflect the current norms, but instead much closer to a real life rate for the same types of work. In the case of SecondLife, while the common compensation today for virtual positions is a paltry L$700 per hour or less ($2.70), it is a wise decision to offer much higher in terms of compensation to virtual employees and as close to a real world working wage as possible converted to the virtual world currency.

By example, current rates for virtual positions are around L$700 per hour or less, but as compensation one should instead break this trend and offer as much as L$2,000 per hour ($7.72). In this manner, a business entity would create loyalty from virtual employees as well as a desire to do whatever it takes in order to retain the position held. Treating virtual employees as expendable is currently the industry standard, but due to the ever increasing importance of virtual environments, this attitude will not be sustained much longer. Therefore it is advised to act on a forthcoming trend in advance and instead pay virtual employees as close to real world compensations as possible.

Localization Restriction in a Global Environment does not Work

One of the many aspects to remember when dealing with electronic commerce and virtual environments is that the nature of a virtual environment is global and perceived without borders. Due to this mentality, it would be seen as a shortfall or level of incompetence if a business entity were to implement a structure which makes the assumption of specific locality at the exclusion of others. Since a virtual environment is a dynamic arena, one must take care to incorporate dynamic streams of information and availability within the virtual space.

For instance, it would not be prudent to incorporate a virtual space which sells a product or service to a regional locale while not being available to others. In example, one could imagine the inability of a product to be delivered to clients outside of a single country, or a service only offered to a small city in the world. The nature of virtual environments is global and the avatars which inhabit such environments are blind to borders or regional restrictions. So too must the entrepreneur of virtual environments remain keen to these nuances of digital culture and communities if one is to succeed.

As far as localization as a restriction, one should avoid this scenario. What should not be avoided is localization as a benefit to international clientèle. Showing that one is completely understanding of the global network which it exists is crucial to success in the virtual environment. In this example, one should remember to include language options when designing signage, offer internationalization of social media integration and make a best effort to converse with possible clients in a native language.

Use of Dynamic Currency is a Must

Services and products offered within the confines of a virtual world environment should adhere to the ability to offer said product or service for a fee which matches as many local currencies as possible. This is to say that a single static currency is unlikely to garner sales, due to the prior rule concerning localization as a restriction. In this case, a dynamic currency should be used when selling products or services within the global virtual environment structure, or purely billed via the internally accepted virtual currency standard. In respect to SecondLife, the L$ (Linden Dollar) is a dynamic currency within the virtual environment since it translates to worldwide currencies when withdrawn to the individual user's bank account or Paypal.

Allow Liberal Avatar Representation of Staff and Clients

In a virtual environment, the line between fantasy and reality is blurred and often times indistinguishable when dealing with what is real and what is solely in the realm of imagination. It is not uncommon to do business with an anthropomorphic animal at the same virtual table as a human looking avatar, nor is it uncommon that a gender be misrepresented via the avatar versus the actual inhabitant of said form. In so much as recommendations concerning avatar dress code, the general acceptable practice incorporates this understanding and does not force inhabitants or employees to adopt a real world representation. When dealing with acceptable avatar representation, one must understand that only the most broad of terms should apply, with no restriction on the implied species or gender of said participant.

That being said, rules of conduct and general acceptability for representation still do apply in the context of appropriate attire or adult themed representation restrictions. Therefore, it is prudent that one should keep in mind the broader acceptability practices while remaining lenient with cross species and cross gender representations. Doing so will ensure that a company taking part in a virtual environment does not intentionally create an atmosphere of implied social hostility in an already liberal social space.

In the same aspect, it is not uncommon to find that serious business and personal interests often are represented within an avatar entity. Combat role-play or other personal interests are abundant within the confines of a virtual environment, and are found alongside serious business interest displays. While the first inclination of a serious business is to revoke such involvements on behalf of staff, it is highly advisable to allow continued involvement during personal time as long as such involvement does not interfere with business practice. Just as it can be said that personal time is not the domain of company time in the real-world, so it holds true in the virtual environment.

Concerning avatar representations, liberal yet tasteful representation should be considered the benchmark ideal. However, it is in poor taste and contributing to metaphor shear if a business entity should create a requirement to either change a liberal (yet socially acceptable) avatar or require that the person behind the avatar create a separate account and avatar for the sole purpose of business. The latter request would be the same as requesting a new hire to undergo plastic surgery in order to better appeal to the workplace, as well as gives a clear indication that the business entity neither understands the environment they work within nor has any respect for the avatar persona by which the person in question utilizes as their in-world representation, while drastically increasing the probability of invoking the Streisand effect in terms of attempted censorship.

Use Trend Forecasting and Dynamic Case Studies

Before engaging in any particular virtual environment or strategy, first build a trend forecast from existing case studies and chart projections for the next five years. If the projections do not live up to the requirement of a long term engagement, or accurate projections cannot be created due to a method being too new, re-evaluate company involvement. By doing this, a company will stay ahead of the curve and be able to act on incoming trends in advance.

While such advice seems to contradict the compass of this chapter by recommending long-term research prior to utilization, it must be noted that a dynamic approach is much different than a static approach. By extrapolating trends from existing research on a particular virtual environment or strategy, one may gauge an accurate expectation for the growth and impression of a particular system in advance, as well as garner an understanding concerning how best to integrate an electronic commerce solution within said virtual environment. In short, the recommendation is not to perform long-term case studies and research, but instead extrapolate and predict trends for the next two to five years based on currently existing materials and research. If the trend is sufficient to sustain a presence and continued involvement for a company, then it is recommended to move swiftly before such opportunity is lost to the next paradigm shift.

Serious as a LOLCAT

There is a reason why pictures of cats with badly spelled sayings, a twenty minute rock opera about milk, a single man dancing in different places around the world, and a reality bending ladies man in a bath towel garner more results and ROI than traditional advertising. This is also the same reason why business in virtual environments succeed or fail. Doing business in the arena of social media and virtual environments requires a business to be spontaneous and often times outright nonsensical. Such is also the case for the prime foundations of the asynchronous communications of the future, in that perception of human nature versus a faceless entity will be the deciding factor. Community, sincerity, and a more personal relationship with consumers are the future. The community aspects are not restricted to a single method or walled garden, and as such, what is done in one media form will spread across various networks and possibly back to the originating source. Because of this future, one should establish a high level of interconnectivity and ubiquitous information collaboration up front while learning to embrace the community in ways which do not always reflect a mantra of "strictly business".

FURTHER RESEARCH DIRECTIONS

Due to the ever changing nature of virtual environments and electronic commerce techniques, future directions of research will continuously adapt and change to oncoming paradigm shifts. With dynamic trends and forecasting, one cannot be certain as to which trend or expected paradigm to follow with complete certainty. As such, further research directions concerning electronic commerce and virtual environments should adhere only to guidelines and the flexibility to work with many courses of experimentation in order to facilitate winning strategies and ongoing progress.

As recommended in this chapter, current trends and forecasts should be examined in order to garner a baseline by which to begin future directions of forecasts and research today, keeping in mind that acceleration of trends will be forthcoming in the near future. By analyzing the current trends and research from leading companies such as Kzero.co.uk one may be able to properly begin creating a dynamic approach suitable for staying ahead of subsequent paradigm shifts, and in many cases even predicting them.

CONCLUSION

Technological progress for the 21st century will be astounding, and the progress that will be seen as a result will become an ubiquitous stream of services, products and information, interconnected in real time. Concerning virtual environments and electronic commerce, one should keep in mind that the future happens to be one of sincerity and direct customer and client interaction.

Keeping this in mind, the strategies and general suggestions outlined in this chapter will not offer a "magic bullet" approach to virtual environments and electronic commerce. Instead, what is offered in this chapter are guidelines to follow when constructing a marketing strategy utilizing this form of real-time media. As a result, it is highly recommended that the additional readings be incorporated into a total encompassing understanding of the nature of virtual environments prior to attempting an enactment of a strategy going forward.

REFERENCES

Corbett, P. (2010, January 4). Facebook Demographics and Statistics Report 2010 – 145% Growth in 1 Year istrategy labs. Retrieved August 10, 2010, from istrategy labs Web site: [REMOVED HYPERLINK FIELD]http://www.istrategylabs.com/2010/01/facebook-demographics-and-statistics-report-2010-145-growth-in-1-year/

Curtis, D. (2009, February 15). The science of entrepreneurship. (7), Retrieved from http://dustincurtis.com/the_science_of_entrepreneurship.html

Effect, S. (2010, August 10). In *Wikipedia, the free encyclopedia*. Retrieved August 13, 2010, from http://en.wikipedia.org/wiki/Streisand_effect

Kurzweil, R. (2001, March 7). Kurzweilai.net. Retrieved September 2, 2009, from Kurzweilai.net Web site: http://www.kurzweilai.net/articles/art0134.html

Pogue, D. (2009, July 17). Some ebooks are more equal than others- pogue's posts blog-nytimes.com. Retrieved September 2, 2009, from The new york times Web site: http://pogue.blogs.nytimes.com/2009/07/17/some-e-books-are-more-equal-than-others/

ADDITIONAL READING

Abramowicz, M. (2007, Summer). The politics of prediction. *Innovations: Technology, Governance, Globalization*, *2*(3), 89–96. doi:10.1162/itgg.2007.2.3.89

Benedikt, M. (1991). *Cyberspace: first steps*. MA: The MIT Press.

Bray, D. A., & Konsynksi, B. R. (2006). *Virtual worlds, virtual economies, virtual institutions* [working paper series]. Retrieved from http://www2.gsu.edu/~wwwets/instructionalsupport/secondlife/Virtual_Worlds_Virtual_Economies.pdf

Bustos, L. (2007, September). 110 ways retailers are using social media marketing. retrieved from http://www.getelastic.com/social-media-examples/

"Cyberspace: First Steps", Chip Morningstar, F. Randall Farmer, 1991

Dibble, J. (2006). *Play money: or how I lost my day job and struck it rich in virtual loot farming*. New York, NY: Basic Books.

Jorden, L. (2009).intel saves budget and goes green with virtual world conference: rivers run red's immersive workspaces in secondlife. LindenLab.

Lakhani, K. R., & Panetta, J. A. (2007, Summer). The principles of distributed innovation. *Innovations: Technology, Governance, Globalization*, *2*(3), 97–112. doi:10.1162/itgg.2007.2.3.97

Malaby, T. M. (2007, Summer). Contriving constraints (the gameness of Second Life® and persistence of scarcity). *Innovations: Technology, Governance, Globalization*, *2*(3), 62–67. doi:10.1162/itgg.2007.2.3.62

Mitham, N. (2008). *7 point plan for marketing in virtual worlds*. Kzero Research.

Mitham, N. (2008). the 5 rules of virtual brand management. Kzero Research.

Mitham, N. (2008). *The luxury brands case study*. Kzero Research.

Mitham, N. (2008). *The travel and tourism case study*. Kzero Research.

Mitham, N. (2008). *The definitive guide to brands in virtual worlds*. Kzero Research.

Mitham, N. (2009). *The automobile case study*. Kzero Research.

Ondrejka, C. (2007, Summer). Collapsing geography (second life, innovation, and the future of national power.). *Innovations: Technology, Governance, Globalization*, *2*(3), 27–54. doi:10.1162/itgg.2007.2.3.27

7Point Plan For Marketing in Virtual Worlds, Kzero Research, http://www.kzero.co.uk, 2008

Spence, J. (2008). Demographics of Virtual Worlds. *Journal of Virtual Worlds Research, 1*(2). Retrieved from http://www.docstoc.com/docs/6528905/Demographics-of-Virtual-Worlds.

Stephenson, N. (1992). *Snow crash*. New York, NY: Bantam Dell.

Stephenson, N. (1999). *In the beginning was the command line*. New York, NY: Harper Collins.

"The 5 Rules of Virtual Brand Management", Kzero Research, http://www.kzero.co.uk, 2008

The Definitive Guide to Brands in Virtual Worlds. Kzero, http://www.kzero.co.uk, 2008

"The Law of Accelerating Returns", Ray Kurzweil, *KurzweilAI.net March7,2001* Kurzweil, R (2001, March 7). Kurzweilai.net. from Kurzweilai.net Web site: http://www.kurzweilai.net/articles/art0134.html

The Science of Entrepreneurship, Dustin Curtis (February 15, 2009) http://dustincurtis.com/the_science_of_entrepreneurship.html

"The Singularity is Near", Raymond Kurzweil, March 09, 2006

VirtualWorlds,RealMoney: Security and Privacy in Massively-Multiplayer Online Games and Social and Corporate Virtual Worlds, EINSA, November 2008, multiple contributors

KEY TERMS AND DEFINITIONS

Augmented Reality (AR): is a term for a live direct or indirect view of a physical real-world environment whose elements are merged with or augmented by virtual computer-generated imagery creating a mixed reality.

Avatar: A representation of an electronic participant in a digital space.

Blog: (a contraction of the term "web log") is a type of website, usually maintained by an individual with regular entries of commentary, descriptions of events, or other material such as graphics or video. Entries are commonly displayed in reverse-chronological order. "Blog" can also be used as a verb, meaning to maintain or add content to a blog.

Herd Mentality: Herd mentality describes how people are influenced by their peers to adopt certain behaviors, follow trends, and/or purchase items. Examples of the herd mentality include the early adopters of high technology products such as cell phones and iPods, as well as stock market trends, fashions in apparel, cars, home décor, etc.

Law of Accelerating Returns: As time moves forward: the rate of technological achievement increases over shorter periods of time, following an exponential curve. In short, the time required to advance technologically decreases exponentially over time, accelerating progress and returns.

Metadata: Commonly known as "data about data" it is the data describing context, content and structure of records and their management through time.

Metaphor Shear: originally defined by Neal Stephenson, speaks mostly of the metaphor layers which make it possible to relate to the working environment which a participant is utilizing for the current task at hand. While the explanation put forth here is one of extremes (by which all of the layers have suddenly and without warning disappeared) this idea also extends to the abrupt interruption of a single layer of metaphor which the participant has become immersed in.

Mirror World: Mirror worlds are virtual worlds that replicate the physical world in a virtual environment using a complex system of analytical data recorded by geographic information systems (GIS). Satellite imagery and aerial and ground photography are captured, analyzed and digitally modeled to create an accurate map of the earth in a mirror world (i.e. the virtual globe software Google Earth). 3D modeling of mirror worlds is restricted to the mapping of the actual physical space to be represented. A mirror world is a one-to-one digital model of its counterpart in the physical world.

Moore's Law: describes a long-term trend in the history of computing hardware. Since the invention of the integrated circuit in 1958, the number of transistors that can be placed inexpensively on an integrated circuit has increased exponentially, doubling approximately every two years.

Paradigm Shift: A complete change in thinking or belief systems that allows the creation of a new condition previously thought impossible or unacceptable.

RSS: (most commonly translated as "Really Simple Syndication" but sometimes "Rich Site Summary") is a family of web feed formats used to publish frequently updated works—such as blog entries, news headlines, audio, and video—in a standardized format. An RSS document (which is called a "feed", "web feed", or "channel") includes full or summarized text, plus metadata such as publishing dates and authorship.

Twitter: (Twitter.com) A micro-blogging service allowing participants to post short status updates in real time from various outlets to an online space.

Viral Marketing: The buzzwords viral marketing and viral advertising refer to marketing techniques that use pre-existing social networks to produce increases in brand awareness or to achieve other marketing objectives (such as product sales) through self-replicating viral processes, analogous to the spread of pathological and computer viruses.

Virtual Environment: is a technology which allows a user to interact with a computer simulated environment, whether that environment is a simulation of the real world or an imaginary world, or a hybrid of the two (see also Augmented Reality).

Chapter 18
Virtual Worlds:
Good Enough Substitute?

Charles P. Schultz
Research in Motion, USA

ABSTRACT

Christensen (2002) describes that new technologies and solutions replace established goods and services as a result of being "good enough" replacements. That is, the value of functions provided by a new solution outweighs any further incremental improvements to the entrenched product. The new value could be in terms of size, convenience, cost or other dimensions pertinent to many consumers. These attributes might be traded off for capacity or performance or other factors which are deemed less important than the new benefits. Virtual worlds are providing new value in many areas of commerce, business, health and recreation. They are not a fad. They are part of an ongoing change. Virtual worlds are in an opportunistic position to supplant many existing solutions and may be only one or two breakthroughs away from displacing more.

INTRODUCTION

This chapter examines the many aspects of virtual worlds and the solutions they offer in light of Christensen's concept of good enough replacements. A number of solutions currently provided by virtual worlds will be described and evaluated in their present state in comparison to real world equivalents. Dimensions such as cost, usability and functionality are all subject to an initial analysis, followed by thoughts on what paths could be taken for virtual world solutions to evolve further and provide more advantages. As Peter Drucker says in his book "Managing in the Next Society"

How do you turn transition to an advantage? By looking at every change, looking out every window, and asking "Could this be an opportunity? Is the new thing a genuine change or simply a fad?" And the difference is very simple: A change is something people do and a fad is something people talk about. (Drucker, 2002, p. 47)

DOI: 10.4018/978-1-61692-808-7.ch018

Throughout this chapter, the following questions will be addressed:

- Where are we on a trajectory from local stores to online goods and services with a richer virtual shopping experience?
- What enabling technologies are required to drive a significant shift to virtual goods?
- What role can shopping and informational portals play in virtual world commerce?
- What types of virtual goods are currently being purchased and for what purpose?
- What goods and services are likely to become part of the next wave of virtual purchases and ownership?

FROM LOCAL STORES TO ONLINE GOODS

Traditional Retailers

Online retailers continue to have success and growth in the current economy, with sales projected to rise 11% to $156 billion in 2009, and accounting for 7% of overall retail revenue (Legatt, 2009). In case you thought Amazon is just a book purchasing site, they also have significant business in sales of music, food, electronics, household supplies, cosmetics and many other types of products. In 2004, electronics sales overtook their book sales (Ouchi, 2004) and their profit from electronics sales doubled in 2008 ("Amazon Profit Doubles," 2008). Online-only discounts, ease of pay, and inexpensive or free shipping also minimize the disadvantages and create an online incentive.

Amazon's online shopping experience has also been able to accomplish their success due to a number of explicit advantages over brick and mortar shopping. First, many sites provide shoppers with "social" features such as peer reviews of products, search capabilities, and recommendations for similar or related items. Amazon.com provides personal lists you can maintain on their site such as a Wish List, Shopping List and Wedding Registry. They also have a number of programs to inject human beings into the shopping and discovery process. The Amazon Vine™ program is an invitation-only program that identifies respected reviewers based on their review history. Amazon also indicates Top Customer Reviewers based on how quickly they review items once they become available and how popular those items become. The degree to which "real people" are obviously involved in the shopping experience through recommendations and lists and so on does much to remove the inhuman aspects of shopping online.

3D Worlds

Recently, virtual shopping has developed into an experience that can be successfully integrated into an interactive 3D virtual world. For example, many people are familiar with the acquisition and purchasing of clothing imbued with special powers for their online avatars in game worlds such as Final Fantasy Online and World of Warcraft. But did you know the casual online world of Zwinky.com claims to have sold a total 46 million virtual clothing items, and was expecting an estimated $1.5 billion dollars in real cash to be spent on such items in 2008 (Shropshire, 2008)? As part of a further blending of the virtual and real, Zwinky's "Zbucks" currency is also available through pre-paid cards at Target and 7-11, who also host virtual cash for other popular online worlds such as Habbo Hotel and Kaneva ("Zwinky Adds Pre-Paid," 2008).

While all your virtual world clothing purchases fit, you can't take it with you as the saying goes. Or can you? In 2008, Gaia Online™ began selling real world clothing items through their storefront web page ("Pullover Gnome Sweatshirt," 2009). By entering a code you receive with the real world item, an identical virtual item will be sent to your online avatar to wear in the virtual world.

To further enhance your real-world appearance, Shiseido and Sega have teamed up to provide a virtual cosmetic "try before you buy" experience on the Nintendo DS. Using a picture of the user's face, the effects of different cosmetics and colors are applied to your image. There is currently no direct way to purchase the items you selected for your makeover, but the expectation is that once you have found a satisfactory combination, you can purchase the specific items online or at a local store. (Sim, 2009)

So where is this all heading? Besides currency and clothes, in a seven month period in 2008, Gaia Online™ inhabitants spent their hard-earned gold to purchase a total of 700,000 Scion virtual cars. A positive experience with the online version of the car could (and should) very well lead to real world sales. It should at least be a factor in getting more people to head to the dealer and check out the real thing. Car manufacturers and dealers should take more steps to leverage this tech-savvy demographic by offering special packages and incentives, such as satellite radio and MP3 player docking. These customers would also appreciate an upgrade to their virtual vehicle subsequent to their real world purchase.

Creative and ambitious marketers and decision-makers in other industries would do well to offer their own virtual simulations and services to generate new real world customers.

VIRTUAL OWNERSHIP

As consumers are spending more and more money on a wider variety of virtual world goods and services ("Virtual Goods," 2009), we should consider if ownership of virtual goods is as good, or even better in some respects, than real-world (physical, tangible) ownership. In both cases, it's important to be able to:

- Prove ownership
- Access or use the item when needed
- Be able to exchange the item for other goods or currency
- Transport the item for use wherever the owner is
- Use the item in a way that fulfills a purpose

Virtual Goods

Virtual goods have the potential to overcome many negative aspects of real world ownership. Space is required to store real world items, energy may be needed to power a real world item for use and real world items, purchases and transactions may be subject to taxes and/or fees. Virtual items, on the other hand, require no physical storage, do not consume energy and are not bound by physical limitations. Virtual items also provide the owner the potential to inventory, organize and tag for easy discovery. Ever had to look for an article you remember reading in a magazine you subscribe to? You have to remember something about the article's title and maybe which issue of the magazine it's in. And where did you put that magazine anyway – or did you throw it out already? Finding a virtual item that can be tagged, such as a photo in Flickr or a song in your digital library, is much easier.

Unfortunately, there are presently some negative aspects to virtual ownership. Ownership and portability may be restricted to a user's identity and relationship within a specific virtual world. For example, clothing and gold earned playing World of Warcraft cannot be transferred or utilized in Second Life®. Also, the person must have two identities effectively translating to multiple jobs or careers in order to customize and enjoy their time in each world, and may have to pay subscription fees for each world.

At the present, there are no guarantees of the persistence or consistency of virtual items, and no means to insure them against damages, loss or theft. If a user loses an item due to a wiped database, a software glitch, or their own neglect (e.g. through a trade or leaving the item unattended), they may have no recourse to recover the item and will have to decide between purchasing the item again if such an item is still available or going without.

Virtual Banking

Virtual world banks have the potential to return much higher interest rates to depositors, such as the SL Bank in Second Life® which was able to sustain a 24%-30% return to depositors for a period of time (Sidel, 2008). However, as idyllic our present views are of virtual worlds, they are still subject to unfortunate circumstances or intentionally bad acts. The banking system in Second Life® went through a rough six months between 2007 and 2008. First, there was the collapse of Ginko Financial, the largest bank in Second Life® at the time, in August of 2007. L$200M was lost, which had a value of US$750,000 at that time. (L$ refers to Linden Dollars which are the native currency of Second Life®.) Then, in November of 2007, a number of L&L Bank and Trust ATMs were hacked. Depositors lost an estimated L$3.2M (Hynes, 2007). Finally, at the beginning of 2008, Second Life® chose to close down 12 unchartered banks, causing depositors to rush to withdraw their funds (Sidel, 2008).

Continued episodes like these have some calling for more oversight and controls ("Bank Failure," 2007) and will erode trust in the financial systems of Second Life®, and the financial systems of virtual worlds in general. Virtual worlds striving to retain consumer trust and wanting to become more mainstream can expect to fall under regulatory scrutiny and practices that parallel real world controls. These practices and controls need to be carefully balanced so that the virtual worlds can retain their advantages, such as the ability to operate efficiently enough to offer higher interest rates than real world banks, and continue to encourage investors and depositor activity.

Figure 1. Second Life® Banking Crisis Timeline, 2007-2008

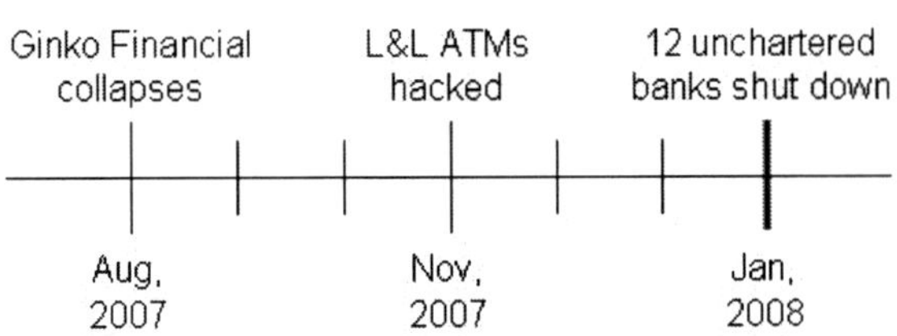

Taxation of Virtual Assets and Transactions

Virtual worlds must resist forces that will attempt to impose real world penalties, causing their advantages to erode. Second Life® has been compelled to collect a Value Added Tax (VAT) from users who inhabit European Union countries in real life ("Value Added Tax," 2009). While transactions conducted strictly within Second Life® are not taxed, transactions that cross the boundary with our real world which are subject to VAT include

- Premium account registration
- Purchases from the Land Store
- Land use fees
- Private Region fees
- Land auctions
- LindeX transaction fees

These measures could motivate residents to employ new or established forms of tax avoidance, such as employing a non-EU resident acting as an agent to purchase land without the obligation to pay the VAT and then sell or transfer ownership, which is a transaction that would not be subject to the VAT. One can imagine a virtual real estate broker setting up office in Second Life® to perform such a service.

Another matter related to taxes and virtual real estate is the concept of private countries. The May-June 2009 issue of The Futurist magazine reported on artificial islands that are being constructed in the real world and sold to individuals who wish to establish their own country. This gives the owner self-rule and potential access to advantageous programs and resources not available to mere individuals or corporations, such as the ability to avoid income, sales and corporate taxes. (Frey, 2009) It's not hard to imagine a resourceful person or consortium setting up a virtual country for similar purposes.

Discussions of virtual taxation in the U.S. have alternated between imposing a system similar to our real world laws (Terdiman, 2006) and a hands-off approach to taxation until virtual money is converted into a real world form, which then becomes subject to existing rules and regulations ("Congressman: No Tax," 2006). For the moment, virtual world participants from the United States can take advantage of growing wealth in virtual worlds without paying any taxes while the assets remain in the virtual world. This certainly provides an incentive to invest within virtual worlds and grow wealth more rapidly without annual obligations such as a real estate tax.

HEALTHCARE AND VIRTUAL WORLDS

Diagnosis and Treatment

What does "virtualization" of healthcare mean for society? Some virtualization benefits are reduced consumption of resources due to less travel to doctors and diagnostic facilities, lower cost to establish and maintain a virtual facility versus a "real" one, and access to a greater range of medical services by and providers, independent of distance, nationality or access to transportation. Doctors, nurses and technicians can all benefit from more opportunities to practice in virtual situations more frequently than they can in the real world, and at a lower cost.

Virtual worlds also provide a more natural conduit for creating, storing and accessing electronic medical records. Patients with chronic diseases are, to a large extent, managed by data. That is, one or more key measurements let doctors know if the patient is properly managing their disease and if prescribed medications or treatments are having the desired positive effects on the disease. Furthermore, search engines and social "tagging" can make virtualized health records easy to be recorded, shared, analyzed and discovered by family members, physicians, researchers or anyone else granted access by the record owner.

A health-centric virtual world called WellWorld was demonstrated at the 2005 Games For Health conference and the Children With Diabetes 2005 Friends for Life Conference. WellWorld was designed to bring data collected by Motorola's MOTOHEALTH™ system into a game world where positive results, such as blood glucose level within an optimum range, would be translated into points or other rewards to be used by the player. WellWorld also showed how branded locations and information portals could be used by player-patients to get help on using new devices, order supplies or access instructional videos related to their condition and medications. The game was designed to provide feedback, information and motivation for young people with chronic diseases to feel more in control and confident about managing their health. Peer support would also play a positive role in the multiplayer setting which would foster communication and cooperation (Bogost, 2005). Although WellWorld was never completed and deployed for its intended use, it would be a step in the right direction for current health solution providers to pick up where it left off, in order to validate and refine the initial concept and its basic principles. Ease of integration with multiple health information collection and reporting systems would advance the cause of such an approach. Whether the WellWorld concept is best implemented as a stand-alone solution or embedded within existing 3D game or non-game worlds intended for different demographics such as Second Life®, Whyville, or City of Heroes should also be explored.

Training and Simulation

Medical training programs are springing up in virtual reality, and they may bring big changes to the way health-care professionals learn their craft. (Lafsky, 2009).

Surgery and emergency response simulations provide much needed practice that is practical and applicable to real-life situations, at much less cost and difficulty in setting up these scenarios in a real world setting. Equipment, vehicles and actors performing as victims are all for free. Cities do not need to be disrupted and any city real or imaginary can be modeled sufficiently for an effective simulation. This also produces a "green" solution as no fuel is consumed by emergency vehicles, no medical waste is created and no actual hazardous agents are released into the atmosphere. Hazmat suits costing $4,000-$10,000 which may have to be disposed of after a single use can be spared and kept ready for real world use ("Protective Clothing," 2009). Even the fuel that would be consumed by the participants flying and driving to the scene of a real world exercise is saved by this approach.

Virtualized Patients

From the patient perspective, virtual health worlds bring social support to the user, which have been shown to impact compliance. The virtuality of the experience allows peers, professionals, coaches and family to become part of the support network. The user does not have to feel they are alone with their particular problem. A suitably equipped world can remove the fear of the unknown by supplying information that gives the user knowledge and potentially mastery over their disease or disability.

The real person behind the virtual avatar is less physically constrained than in the real world. People who cannot easily travel due to real-world obligations can explore virtual worlds without the hassle or expense of air travel, rental cars and hotels. Virtual world inhabitants who have real world physical or mental disorders are on equal footing with other virtual world inhabitants and have equal access to locations, products and services. Patients can attend counseling or therapy sessions without having to endure the stress and discomfort of leaving home.

VIRTUAL WORLD SUBSTITUTES IN TIMES OF THREAT OR DISASTER

As a society we are too familiar with actual and threatened events that affect social patterns as they relate to commerce and finances. Natural disasters and company shutdowns can have local affects, while acts of terrorism, perceived or real pandemics (avian flu, swine flu, etc.) and recessionary periods threaten real-world wealth and commerce.

Virtual Travel

As described in (Brahmbhatt, 2005), a pandemic outbreak could have indirect effects such as a fall in tourism due to fear of disease or imposed travel restrictions, and reduced use of transportation, hotels and restaurants. Periods of regional or global terrorism would have a similar impact. While real world locales could suffer from the outbreak of disease or economic downturns, virtual worlds can act as substitutes for many of the experiences that people would otherwise be deprived of.

Second Life® hosts virtual facsimiles of popular real world vacation spots such as Dublin and Venice. As three-dimensional re-creations, avatars can walk through the streets and buidings, getting as close as they want, and viewing details from any angle. Virtual worlds don't just have the capacity to faithfully replicate a location, but also to provide replicas of locations at different points in history, and at a much lower cost than attempting such a feat in the real world. Some popular historical spots in Second Life® are Paris, 1900 complete with the Notre Dame cathedral, and a replica of Deadwood, South Dakota as it was in 1876 ("Deadwood 1876," 2008).

Back in 2006, Starwood Hotels began creating a unique hotel design in Second Life® that would not only contribute to the user's simulation of a "real" vacation, but also provide valuable feedback about how people move through and make use of the hotel's innovative design. However, they pulled out the following year (Jana, 2006). Crowne Plaza has been more successful, with a conferencing center added to the hotel proper, and a web page for booking rooms available on their online website.

Virtual Work

As the workplace has changed and as decentralized information workers demand tools to allow them to work together, companies have to rethink their collaboration, training, and knowledge management schemes.(Keitt, T., Dewing, H., Daley, E., 2008)

A disruption of work due to absent employees could affect production of goods and services. Having a "safe haven" virtual world in place as a contingency for workers to continue to meet and work together free of the threat of violence or disease could alleviate this.

Corporate events, training and meetings can continue uninterrupted thanks to solutions available from Second Life®, Qwaq and Forterra Systems. Virtual events can be held at less than 5% of the cost of the real world equivalent and have been utilized by large companies like IBM as well as individual conference organizers (Morrison, 2009). Attendees may even receive virtual swag like t-shirts and backpacks to add to the realism.

Virtual conferencing solutions provide on-demand, secure environments to meet the needs of a range of virtual workspace requirements, such as:

- Virtual offices and participant Avatars
- VOIP and text communications
- Access to slides, videos and documents
- Interactive virtual whiteboards and sticky notes
- Audio and video recording of sessions

If meeting and working in the virtual sounds appealing to you, you can get Manpower to help with interview skills and placement. Their presence in Second Life® is consistent with the goal of "translating changing work trends into practical programs designed to prepare people for work in new environments" Virtual jobs offer opportunities for demographics that require flexibility, and the nature of virtual worlds allows many people with real-world handicaps to compete on equal terms with other virtual job seekers. Blurring the line between realities, virtual world training has also led to applicants getting a real world job. (King, 2009).

Virtual Education

Educational institutions from grade school through graduate school could see their operations suspended during serious outbreaks. Having virtual world replicas or equivalents would allow students to stay on schedule with their education goals. A number of accredited educational institutions already have online classes and facilities, so these could continue uninterrupted.

Even young children can flourish in a virtual education setting, as they are being raised with access to computers at a young age and have shown the ability to utilize electronic learning tools, even becoming expert helpers within their classroom (Hutinger, 2006). A number of accredited virtual K-12 school programs, such as the Plano Home School Academy and the Virginia Virtual Academy are available on the internet. However, "virtual" grade school offerings are electronic versions of home school programs and do not employ virtual worlds at this time. Still, under conditions where restricted travel and communion with other is undesirable, this is a satisfactory replacement for the traditional school complex.

San Jose State University, The Australian Radio Film and TV School and Edinburgh University are examples of schools of higher learning that have virtual facilities for individual academic programs ("Second Life®: Universities," 2009), but so far no school has gone "all in" to provide their full range of classes and degrees in a 3D virtual world setting. Virtual corporate and professional training has taken a more comprehensive approach. IBM is one of many companies who provide conferences and technical sessions. Conversely, Second Life® has itself become the subject of many degree and certificate programs, including an Information Technology Certification program at the University of Florida. ("IT Training Committee," 2009).

In a 2007 Training Media Review article (Hall & Nguyen, 2007), Chuck Hamilton of IBM's Center for Advanced Learning shared the important capabilities of virtual worlds like Second Life® which contribute to an effective virtual training environment:

- Sense of self: Ability to create an avatar to look the way you want to look
- Death of distance: Ability to bring together people from across the globe
- Power of presence, space, and co-creation: Ability to collaborate and interact socially
- Pervasiveness of practice: Ability to learn in a safe environment by practicing
- Enrichment of experience: Ability to create diverse experiences, e.g., battlefield simulations, building molecules together, walking through a rain forest

Shopping for Real World Goods

Most commerce could continue virtually uninterrupted if consumers could have access to a richer online experience where shoppers can interact directly with virtual copies of products rather than have to rely on flat pictures, or catalogs that could fail to reach the consumer's home if postal deliveries are also disrupted as a result of an outbreak. Some attempts, such as car dealerships in Second Life® seem to fall short because the quality of the representation is still not good enough to convey the experience of the product without being able to experience the visceral elements of the car, such as sounds, vibrations, smells, how the seat and the steering wheel feel, and the overall "vibe" you get from being in and moving with the car in real life. Brand awareness is the best that virtual car dealers can hope to achieve with the present technologies.

The Shiseido beauty application described earlier in this chapter also provides a good substitute during times when going to busy public places and being physically handled could pose a health risk. An extended period of restrictions could motivate more "try before you buy" virtualizations.

Virtual Worship

Virtual Worship is a reality in Second Life®, which hosts churches, synagogues and mosques.Just as radio evangelism reached a new audience in the 1920's in the United States, and later "Televangelism" reached a growing number of households that were being equipped with televisions in the 1950's, virtual world worship is a new frontier which doesn't make sense to many people at the moment, but has a unique demographic that will embrace the media and, as a result, hear the message.

Online places of worship can be filled with avatars who fly, dress up as animals, squat atop the piano, skateboard their way into the service, and who generally don't follow the real world behavior norms of churches, synagogues, temples and mosques. Real world practitioners who enter a virtual church may need some time to get used to fellow worshippers, but traditionalists will appreciate the familiar experiences one would find in a in a church, including bible study groups, group prayers, communion, live sermons delivered with slides and audio, and live worship music. There is even an ongoing debate about whether Holy Communion is legitimate if delivered in a virtual world (Madron, 2009).

Virtual worship sites also have the luxury of being able to dispense a free electronic Bible or other holy book to your inventory with a single click, at no cost. In Second Life®, donations to qualifying churches are even tax deductible. While a local or regional emergency situation could discourage worshippers from traveling and attending a physical location to gather on Saturday or Sunday, virtual houses of worship could swell, serving as a "good enough" substitute for many people.

Virtual Entertainment

Music and video events in a virtual world can take on proportions and forms beyond what is physically possible at a real world venue. Internet broadcaster DBC Radio TV describes themselves as "an interactive cross media company, discovering new talents and trends in the world of digital network, in music, art, culture, ideas and knowledge" ("DBC radio," 2009). Links to Second Life® and pictures from Second Life® events are featured on their homepage, as well as a text chat window exposed simultaneously to interactions from users on the web and those occupying Second Life®. At their Second Life® location they provide live events streaming music from real world artists and DJs. Virtual music events facilitate personal interactions and allow participants to gather safely in groups without the worries of exposure to health risks.

INTERACTIONS, SIMULATIONS AND SUBSTITUTES?

This section provides an assessment of major categories of virtual world experiences in terms of the ability of present technologies and virtual word deployments to provide interaction, simulations and/or act as a substitute for the real world equivalent. Table 1 at the end of this section summarizes the results, revealing opportunities for the future where a particular capability is not yet met.

An *interaction* indicates that the avatar's actions can influence its surroundings (elements in the virtual world). For example, touching a kiosk can cause an information page to appear or put a digital product manual into the avatar's inventory. In this case the item is not consumed, but there may or may not be a virtual cost for performing the function. The virtual world elements may be based on a real world equivalent, e.g. Notre Dame Cathedral or a National Institutes of Health office. Alternatively, they may be fashioned after something that is entirely imagined or cannot be achieved with present technology, such as a crystal tree or a floating video screen.

A *simulation* provides a virtual environment, tools and behaviors that reflect real world characteristics to the greatest extent possible. The fidelity of the simulation and results relies heavily on how accurate the technology can immerse participants in the experience and software can model real world results in response to virtual stimuli. Virtual world simulations generally cost less that real world activities, do not consume real world resources (which could be prohibitively scarce, expensive, and/or dangerous), and do not produce waste as a by-product. Some simulations may be beyond what is achievable by our available resources and technology – such as simulating a trip to Saturn on a flying surfboard.

Being a *substitute* means the virtual world provides a service or function that is available in the real world, but with some advantage such as eliminating the need for physical travel or being accessible at all hours of the day. The services provided by the substitute should be good enough that users are willing to pay for the substitute, but they will expect a lower cost than the real world equivalent. A substitute should also provide output that manifests in the real world such as receiving a degree from a virtual campus, hearing music played in a virtual disco on your real world megawatt sound system, or a feeling of relaxation after visiting a virtual spa.

Travel

Virtual World travel can be *interactive*, as there are many examples of sites that are not only recreated at a visual level, but also provide basic user actions such as being able to receive a virtual guidebook for the locale, or picking a virtual apple from a tree. As far as being able to *simulate* the real world experience, there are many faithful reproductions and some are intentionally targeted to faithfully reflect the site at a time in the past - something the user can no longer do in real life. Virtual worlds can provide the ability to navigate around the location in ways that would be difficult or impossible to do in real life, such as flying over buildings or up into the dome of a cathedral to get a unique view. For many cyber-travelers, virtual worlds may fall short of providing a complete substitute, by virtue of being unable at the time to provide

- Tactile feedback when objects are touched
- Smells in the air from flowers or animals or local restaurants, or
- How the weather feels damp, dry, hot, cold, windy, etc.

These qualities are not important for providing a substitute for many other experiences, but are a big part of what the person remembers and requires as being distinct to their travels (Burton-Hill, 2008).

Healthcare

There are many instances of interactions with virtual healthcare facilities, but none that actually treat the physical human controlling the avatar. Treatment services are available on a fee basis over the internet, but these are not delivered through a virtual world environment. This could be because strict medical regulations and scrutiny may be required once the virtual world plays a role in administering medical advice or treatment. The cost of malpractice insurance and other liability safeguards could be prohibitive to sustaining profitable virtual world health services.

Forterra Systems' OLIVE™ platform is an example of a "good enough" substitute and supplement for real-world medical training. It is a sophisticated tool for providing virtualized environments in which to train users in collaborative medical procedures and emergency response. Its benefits include reduced medical errors through improved communication and team skills, and expanded training opportunities available to a broad range of care-givers. Prominent users include the US Army and the National Institutes of Health. ("Forterra Awarded CPP," 2008).

Workplace

Examples above show that workers are able to interact with one another in virtual worlds or meeting rooms via voice and video. They can also interact with elements in the virtual meeting room designed for collaborative functions such as whiteboards.

A *simulation* of a workplace is a whole other matter. In such a case, the purpose would be to create a simulation of people and or machines which are described or defined by various operating parameters, and then seeing which combinations yield drastic (best and worst) results. This reminds me of a time when I tried to use The SIMS™ game to program the personality traits of different co-workers and then put them in a house to see how they would get along learning which would be friends, which would fight, which would miss their ride to work, etc. General purpose virtual worlds are not currently suited for this, though there may be proprietary corporate tools which attempt to achieve those purposes.

Virtual workplace substitution is already alive and well, driven by the cost and logistic savings over real world gatherings.

Education

As described earlier, corporate and university institution involvement in virtual worlds ranges from providing classroom interactions through voice and information to providing professional certifications and university degrees. Second Life® has been used to provide a research environment suitable for students earn a Master's Degree (Adams, 2008), replacing brick-and-mortar classrooms and real-world experiments with virtual world environments and participants.

There are many sites on the internet providing "virtual libraries" but they tend to be merely web sites. San Jose State University describes a comprehensive set of goals achieved by their presence and interactivity in Second Life®, such as simulating interviews and interacting with groups and communities (SLIS Second Life® Wiki, 2009):

- Groups and Events - begin support groups and hold community events
- Interfaces and Web Connectivity - connect database and applications to the 3D setting
- Professional Services Role-play - practice interacting with clients and interviewing them
- Commerce and Creativity - build and sell interesting objects
- Personal Discovery and Identity - create a new persona and practice in business settings
- Marketing and Outreach - create a new branch and promote your current services

Worship

Virtual places of worship can provide multiple interaction opportunities between participants through text messaging, gesturing and voice communications during church services, prayer time, mid-week study meetings and after-service conversations on the lawn. Users can also interact with some elements in the environment such as lighting a candle or receiving a virtual holy book with the click of a mouse.

To simulate the experience of a real world church, preachers stand behind a pulpit on a stage fashioned after the style one would expect in the real world (although this is not a necessity), and use virtual overhead screens to show announcements, hymn lyrics and bible quotes during the service.

A virtual place of worship can provide the same range of experiences that it does in real life, to the extent that there are many church members in Second Life® who do not have a real-world church they attend. Some real world clergy recognize virtual worlds as new mission fields (Hill, 2007), furthering the notion that virtual churches are sufficient substitutes for many worshippers.

Entertainment

Virtual entertainment venues appear in all shapes and sizes, from hotels and restaurants to discos and concert events. Virtual hotels and restaurants have not fared well as substitutes for the real-world experience due to their reliance on first-person physical interaction with the environment, such as sleeping overnight on a hotel bed, or physically smelling and eating food prepared at a five-star restaurant. However, the ability to create visually compelling and accurate models in the virtual world do allow designers to try out designs and get simulation feedback on aesthetics as avatars flow through the space and interact with it wherever possible (Hartman, 2007). The feedback from virtual users can have a positive impact on what users experience in the real-world venue.

Virtual events are not only staffed by "amateurs" but have drawn the attention of well known artists and other serious artists looking to make a name and grow their fan base ("Whyville," 2006).

Attending virtual entertainment events proves to be an acceptable substitute for many people who enjoy concerts and the club scene.

SUBSTITUTES FOR VIRTUAL WORLDS

Just as virtual worlds can provide a low-cost alternative to many real world experiences, new technologies have emerged with their own benefits and weaknesses to provide lower cost substitutes for traditional virtual world implementations and interfaces.

Mobile Access

Mobile devices are poised to provide an alternative to virtual world software that consumes lots of memory and CPU cycles on your computing platform (PC, tablet, smartphone, etc.). A modern smartphone, pad, tablet or handheld game device could become a "window" to a virtual world without hosting any of the world's software locally. The storage and CPU consumption would be indistinguishable from a browser or desktop app. The ability to provide a rich virtual environment is a function of the remote hosting machine rather than your own device, so you can retain your hardware and still be able to experience the advanced graphics and performance of the evolving virtual worlds you participate in. This approach should also provide an advantage and incentive for virtual world developers who would not have to consider users' hardware limitations, OS, and other technical variations that add cost and time to the development and maintenance of virtual worlds.

Cloud Hosting

Cloud computing services also fit the bill as virtual world hosts. Virtual Worlds "in the cloud" can update and evolve as they like without excluding users based on technology and without having to "dumb down" the capabilities of the world in order to retain their user base. The other limiting technology that needs to be addressed is to provide consistently higher data speeds to residences, schools, and other populated locales. Emerging wireless 4G networks and increased build-out of higher speed cable data services would be essential to realizing ubiquitous wired and wireless access to cloud-based virtual worlds.

Social Networks

While Virtual Worlds are currently positioned to substitute for services and experiences versus the "real" world, social networks are also growing in participation and rising up as a competitor for virtual activity by providing services and

Figure 2. Summary of virtual experience capabilities

EXPERIENCE	CAPABILITY		
	Interact	Simulate	Substitute
Shopping	●	●	◘
Travel	●	●	◘
Healthcare	●	●	◘
Workplace	●	○	●
Education	●	◘	●
Worship	●	○	●
Entertainment	●	○	●

● = fully sufficient capability
◘ = partially sufficient capability
○ = insufficient capability

experiences that are "good enough" substitutes for those available in virtual worlds. The top 25 social networks had over 226 million unique visits in January, 2009 (Kazeniac, 2009) which is 39% the size of the 579 million virtual world accounts measured in the second quarter of 2009 ("Virtual Worlds Popularity," 2009). While not an apples-to-apples comparison, this shows that social networks are on the same scale as 3D worlds in terms of population and participation.

Many social networks serve as a type of 2D virtual world where users have a persona that may or may not reflect their real-world goals and behaviors, but they lack the virtual world capabilities of having a 3D avatar and the ability to navigate and interact within a 3D space. On his TerraNova blog, Bruce Damer suggests that achieving the biggest footprint with the lowest barrier to entry could be accomplished by incorporating "small worlds" into social virtual world platforms (Damer, 2008).

This is exactly what Facebook, which now ranks as the largest single social network, has accomplished, by becoming a very large 2D gaming platform with over 44 million users subscribing to a variety of games provided by Zynga (Takahashi, 2009) and other interactive game publishers. Monetary transactions in these 2D games generally take the form of paying US dollars to receive a gamed-specific currency which is then used to pay for virtual goods that users exchange for items that give them an advantage in the game, or provide a unique item or pet for their avatar. Facebook also has a microtransaction gift shop where you can pay real money to send music, virtual gifts, e-cards, virtual sports memorabilia and even "real" gifts to other Facebook users.

Game-based transactions are significant in these social networks, contributing to consulting firm Piper Jaffray's projection that total US revenues from virtual goods will reach $621 million in 2009, a huge increase of 134% over revenues in 2008 ("Virtual Goods," 2009). Double-digit increases are projected to continue through 2013, according to their "Pay to Play" report, when US virtual goods revenues will reach nearly $2.5 billion. A logical strategy would be to bring the essential services of 3D worlds to social network users rather than attempt – at a cost – to tear them away to a totally separate environment to benefit from those services.

CONCLUSION

Virtual worlds are becoming more and more a part of people's lives, either through their explicit participation or through the effects these worlds are having on society as a whole. The sophistication of many virtual world implementations and solutions is already suited to provide a "good enough" substitute for many equivalent real world experiences. Utilizing the virtual world instead of the real world may be the result of a user's preference, borne out of necessity due to work or social circumstances, or simply to reap the unique advantages that the virtual experience has to offer. Despite this, analysis of the present state of virtual solutions versus more ideal solutions reveals some opportunities for incremental improvements and radical innovations.

New innovation, investment and development will go to where the money flows. If non-gaming 3D worlds (e.g. Second Life®) are unable to increasingly monetize their goods and services, they could lose the critical mass of paid transactions necessary to sustain development and maintenance of the machines and software that keep those worlds running. High-speed mobile access and cloud hosting can drive the growth of virtual world participation by decreasing the cost and increasing the accessibility of virtual worlds.

The future of virtual worlds could be a peaceful coexistence of social 2D worlds and fully interactive 3D worlds, a future where 2D and 3D worlds move towards each other to provide a balanced blend of capabilities versus cost, or a future where one approach wins while the other is left to provide niche solutions for the rest of the market.

REFERENCES

Adams, A. (2008). *Graduate Student Earns Degree in Second Life® Virtual World.* Retrieved November 29, 2009, from http://www.prlog.org/10106569-graduate-student-earns-degree-in-second-life-virtual-world.html

Amazon profit doubles on sales of electronics. (2008). Retrieved September 5, 2009, from http://retailnu.wordpress.com/2008/07/26/amazon-profit-doubles-on-sales-of-electronics/

Bank Failure in Second Life® Leads to Calls for Regulation. (2007). Retrieved September 13, 2009, from http://www.wired.com/gaming/virtualworlds/news/2007/08/virtual_bank

Bogost, I. (2005). *Event Wrap Up: Games for Health 2005.* Retrieved September 15, 2009, from http://www.gamasutra.com/view/feature/2413/event_wrap_up_games_for_health_.php

Brahmbhatt, M. (2005). *Avian and Human Pandemic Influenza – Economic and Social Impacts.* Retrieved September 5, 2009, from http://www.who.int/mediacentre/events/2005/World_Bank_Milan_Brahmbhattv2.pdf

Burton-Hill, C. (2008). 'I wanted to walk, smell and touch the landscape'. Retrieved November 29, 2009, from http://www.guardian.co.uk/travel/2008/nov/23/safari-south-africa

Christensen, C. (2002). *The Innovator's Dilemma.* New York, New York: HarperCollins Publishers.

Congressman: No Tax on MMO Transactions. (2006). *GamePolitics.* Retrieved September 13, 2009, from http://www.gamepolitics.com/2006/10/20/congressman-no-tax-on-mmo-transactions

Damer, B. (2008). Virtually Eternal: A Positive Pathway to a Healthy and Sustainable Virtual Worlds Industry. *Terra Nova.* Retrieved December 1, 2009, from http://terranova.blogs.com/terra_nova/2008/07/virtually-etern.html.

DBC radio tv live broadcast streaming Second Life®. (2009). Retrieved November 30, 2009, from http://www.dbc-radio.net/

Deadwood 1876. (2008). Retrieved September 13, 2009 from Second Life® Wikia Web site: http://secondlife.wikia.com/wiki/Deadwood_1876

Drucker, P. (2002). *Managing in the Next Society.* New York, New York: St. Martin's Press.

Forterra Awarded CPP by US Army. (2008). Retrieved September 15, 2009, from http://news.filefront.com/forterra-awarded-cpp-by-us-army/

Frey, T. (2009, May-June). Own Your Own Island Nation. *The Futurist, 43*(3), 30.

Gross, S. (2007). Take a virtual vacation: Travel in Second Life®. *USATODAY.com.* Retrieved December 1, 2009, from http://www.usatoday.com/tech/gaming/2007-05-11-virtual-vacation_N.htm

Hall, T., & Nguyen, F. (2007). IBM@Play on Second Life®. Retrieved September 14, 2009, from Training Media Review Web site: http://www.tmreview.com/Review.asp?ID=1581

Hartman, D. (2007). *Virtual Hotel Tours.* Retrieved November 30, 2009, from http://www.travelandleisure.com/articles/virtual-hospitality/1

Hill, K. (2007). *Jesuits Push Everlasting Life on Second Life®.* Retrieved November 29, 2009, from http://www.linuxinsider.com/story/58578.html?wlc=1259542452

Hutinger, P. (2006). *Preschool Classroom Computer Experts.* Retrieved September 13, 2009, from http://www.wiu.edu/thecenter/articles/exp.html

Hynes, A. (2007). *The Latest Second Life® Banking Crisis*. Retrieved September 13, 2009, from http://www.orient-lodge.com/node/2614

IT Training Committee – UF Information Technology Certification. (2009). Retrieved December 1, 2009, from http://it-train.ufl.edu/challenge/courses.asp?ID=666

Jana, R. (2006). *Starwood Hotels Explore Second Life® First*. Retrieved September 13, 2009, from BusinessWeek Web site: http://www.businessweek.com/innovate/content/aug2006/id20060823_925270.htm

Kazeniac, A. (2009). *Social Networks: Facebook Takes Over Top Spot, Twitter Climbs*. Retrieved November 30, 2009, from http://blog.compete.com/2009/02/09/facebook-myspace-twitter-social-network/

Keitt, T., Dewing, H., & Daley, E. (2008). *Will Unified Communications Make Virtual Worlds Relevant to Business?* Retrieved September 15, 2009, from http://www.forrester.com/Research/Document/Excerpt/0,7211,47262,00.html

King, R. (2009). *Power of Collaboration: Manpower's First Anniversary in Second Life®*. Retrieved December 1, 2009, from http://files.shareholder.com/downloads/MAN/230983917x0x215173/e64509d2-5734-4bf3-a6fd-fec3592fea6c/DIP_Manpower_July2008.pdf

Lafsky, M. (2009). Can Training in Second Life® Teach Doctors to Save Real Lives? *Discover*. Retrieved on September 9, 2009, from http://discovermagazine.com/2009/jul-aug/15-can-medical-students-learn-to-save-real-lives-in-second-life

Legatt, H. (2009). *Forrester: Growth forecast for 2009 online retail sales*. Retrieved September 5, 2009, from BizReport Web site: http://www.bizreport.com/2009/01/forrester_growth_forecast_for_2009_online_retail_sales.html

Madron, T. (2009). *Can we provide Holy Communion over the Web?* Retrieved September 15, 2009, from http://www.ewcnet.com/communion//holycommunion.htm

Morrison, S. (2009). Corp meetings, training reinvigorate Second Life®. Retrieved September 14, 2009, from Total Telecom Web site: http://www.totaltele.com/view.aspx?ID=448199

Ouchi, M. (2004). *Electronic gear outsells books on Amazon.com*. Retrieved September 12, 2009 from The Seattle Times Web site: http://seattletimes.nwsource.com/html/businesstechnology/2002105349_amazon01.html

Pasteur, E. (2007). Crowne Plaza – a Hotel With a Difference. Retrieved September 13, 2009, from Second Life® Insider Web site: http://www.secondlifeinsider.com/2007/07/03/crowne-plaza-a-hotel-with-a-difference/

Protective Clothing – Hazmat Gear. (2009). Retrieved September 15, 2009, from http://www.sccfd.org/clothing_hazmat.html

Pullover Gnome Sweatshirt. (2009). Retrieved September 12, 2009, from http://www.gaiastore.com/servlet/the-265/Pullover-Gnome-Sweatshirt/Detail

Second Life®: Universities and Private Islands. (2009). Retrieved December 1, 2009, from http://www.simteach.com/wiki/index.php?title=Second_Life:_Universities_and_Private_Islands

Shropshire, C. (2008). *Avatar Shopping*. Retrieved September 12, 2009 from Houston Chronicle Web site: http://www.chron.com/disp/story.mpl/chronicle/5868468.html

Sidel, R. (2008). Cheer Up, Ben: Your Economy Isn't As Bad as This One. Retrieved September 13, 2009, from http://online.wsj.com/article/SB120104351064608025.html?mod=hpp_us_inside_today

Sim, M. (2009). Virtual "Try Before You Buy". Retrieved September 12, 2009, from http://www.coolbusinessideas.com/archives/virtual_try_before_you_buy.html

SLIS Second Life® Wiki. (2009). Retrieved November 29, 2009, from http://slisweb.sjsu.edu/sl/index.php/Main_Page

Takahashi, D. (2009). Zynga becomes No. 1 in number of online gamers. Retrieved November 30, 2009, from http://games.venturebeat.com/2009/07/31/zynga-becomes-no-1-in-numbers-of-online-gamers/

Terdiman, D. (2006). IRS taxation of virtual game assets inevitable. *CNET News*. Retrieved September 13, 2009, from http://news.cnet.com/IRS-taxation-of-online-game-virtual-assets-inevitable/2100-1043_3-6140298.html

Value Added Tax. (2009). Retrieved September 12, 2009 from Second Life® Web site: http://secondlife.com/corporate/vat.php

Virtual Goods Mean Real Dollars. (2009). Retrieved September 12, 2009, from eMarketer Web site: http://www.emarketer.com/Article.aspx?R=1007226

Virtual Worlds Popularity Spikes. (2009). Retrieved November 30, 2009, from http://www.virtualworldsnews.com/2009/07/virtual-world-popularity-spikes.html

Whyville Launches First Virtual Concert Tour With Tween Popstar Stacie Orrico. (2006). Retrieved November 30, 2009 from http://findarticles.com/p/articles/mi_pwwi/is_200612/ai_n16885882/

Zwinky Adds Pre-Paid ZBucks Cards in Target. (2008). Retrieved September 12, 2009, from Virtual World News Web site: http://www.virtualworldsnews.com/2008/01/zwinky-adds-pre.html

ADDITIONAL READING

An Analytical Look at the Currency of Second Life®. (2008). Retrieved September 5, 2009, from http://www.associatedcontent.com/article/763399/an_analytical_look_at_the_currency.html

Avatar Services Now Available for your Mobile Phone. (2008). Retrieved September 15, 2009, from http://www.handcellphone.com/archives/avatar-services-now-available-for-your-mobile-phone

Beard, L., Wilson, K., Morra, D., & Keelan, J. (2009). A Survey of Health-Related Activities on Second Life®. Retrieved on September 8, 2009, from http://www.jmir.org/2009/2/e17

Castronova, E. (2005). *Synthetic Worlds*. Chicago, Illinois: The University of Chicago Press.

Children with Diabetes – Focus Groups. (2005). Retrieved September 15, 2009, from https://www.childrenwithdiabetes.com/activities/orlando2005/focusgroups.htm

Christensen, C., Anthony, S., & Roth, E. (2004). Healing the 800-Pound Gorilla. In *Seeing What's Next*. Boston Massachusetts: Harvard Business School Publishing.

Cisco Live in Second Life®. (2008). Retrieved September 14, 2009, from http://blogs.cisco.com/virtualworlds/comments/cisco_live_in_second_life/

Coleman, D., & Levine, S. (2008). Collaboration 2.0, Chapter 6, Collaboration 2.5. *HappyAbout.info*.

CrossWorlds Xchange. (2009). Retrieved September 5, 2009, from http://www.crossworldsxchange.com/

Crowne Plaza's Second Life® Meeting Room Reservation. (2007). Retrieved September 13, 2009, from http://www.secondlife.crowneplaza.com/

Digital Beauty Services. (2009). Retrieved September 12, 2009, from http://www.trendcentral.com/Webapps/App/SnapShots/Article.aspx?ArticleId=7513

Dykeman, M. (2008). MMORPG Gamers and Social Media Junkies More Alike Than You'd Think. Mashable. Retrieved August 21, 2009, from http://mashable.com/2008/09/05/gamers-and-social-media-users/

Economy of Second Life®. Wikipedia. Retrieved September 5, 2009, from http://en.wikipedia.org/wiki/Economy_of_Second_Life

Ge, J. (2006). Chinese Gold Farmers Preview. *YouTube*. Retrieved August 22, 2009, from http://www.youtube.com/watch?v=ho5Yxe6UVv4

Good, O. (2008). Inmate Sues Warcraft for Eleventeen Zillion Gold. *Kotaku*. Retrieved August 21, 2009, from http://kotaku.com/5079755/inmate-sues-warcraft-for-eleventeen-zillion-gold

Good, O. (2009). Scientists Analyzing Entire Server Logs from Everquest 2. *Kotaku*. Retrieved August 21, 2009, from http://kotaku.com/5157952/scientists-analyzing-entire-server-logs-from-everquest-2

Greene, M. (2008). Virtual Worlds for Fun and Research. *Kotaku*. Retrieved August 21, 2009, from http://kotaku.com/5029517/virtual-worlds-for-fun-and-research

Gustafson, D., Shaw, B., Isham, A., Dillon, D., & Spartz, J. (2008). Exploring the Potential of the Web-based Virtual World of Second Life® to Improve Substance Abuse Treatment Outcomes. Retrieved September 8, 2009 from http://www.rwjf.org/pr/product.jsp?id=34428

Heying, J. (2009). Lindens vs. Dollars, debate continues. *Lavender Life*. Retrieved September 5, 2009, from http://lavendercorp.blogspot.com/2009/05/lindens-vs-dollars-debate-continues.html

Hughes, G. (2008). San Jose State sets up campus in Second Life®. *Yahoo! Tech*. Retrieved September 8, 2009, from http://tech.yahoo.com/blog/hughes/27994

Insurance for Virtual World Businesses. (2008). Retrieved September 7, 2009, from http://www.3dinternetlaw.com/Blog/files/4ec387e5734aeb7d4025ce8e9077b4f6-5.html

1900IV. Notre Dame. (2007). Retrieved from Chey's Second Life® Web site: http://cheyennepal.blogspot.com/2007/06/paris-1900-iv-notre-dame.html

Joly, K. (2007). A Second Life® for Higher Education? *University Business*. Retrieved September 8, 2009, from http://www.universitybusiness.com/viewarticle.aspx?articleid=797

Linde, X. ™ Market Data. (2009). Retrieved September 5, 2009, from http://secondlife.com/statistics/economy-market.php

Maestri, N. (2007). Retail chains venture into virtual worlds. *Reuters*. Retrieved August 23, 2009, from http://www.reuters.com/article/newsOne/idUSN1025860620070112

MOTOHEALTH™ Overview. (2009). Retrieved September 15, 2009, from http://www.motorola.com/content.jsp?globalObjectId=5509-8703

Nexon Sells Cards in 7-11. (2007). *Virtual World News*. Retrieved on September 5, 2009, from http://www.virtualworldsnews.com/2007/11/nexon-sells-car.html

Null, C. (2009). Virtual campus draws virtually no students. *Yahoo! Tech*. Retrieved on September 8, 2009, from http://tech.yahoo.com/blog/null/88899

Opens New, I. B. M. 3D Virtual Healthcare Island on Second Life®. (2008). Retrieved on September 5, 2009, from http://www-03.ibm.com/press/us/en/pressrelease/23580.wss

Parloff, R. (2007). Virtual Worlds, Real Litigation. *Fortune*. Retrieved August 21, 2009, from http://features.blogs.fortune.cnn.com/category/virtual-worlds/

Qwaq Forums Virtual World Collaboration Solutions. (2009). Retrieved September 15, 2009, from http://www.qwaq.com/solutions/index.php

Schultz, C. (2007). Gen G. *Vconomics*. Retrieved August 22, 2009, from http://vconomics.blogspot.com/2007_07_01_archive.html

Schultz, C. (2007). Looks Good on Paper. Vconomics. Retrieved August 22, 2009, from http://vconomics.blogspot.com/2007_05_01_archive.html

Schultz, C. (2007). The Perfect Gift for Father's Day. *Vconomics*. Retrieved August 22, 2009 from http://vconomics.blogspot.com/2007_06_01_archive.html

Schultz, C. (2008). Right Here In My Backyard. *Vconomics*. Retrieved August 22, 2009 from http://vconomics.blogspot.com/2008_04_01_archive.html

Second Life, B. ® (2007). Retrieved September 13, 2009, from BusinessWeek Web site: http://www.businessweek.com/magazine/content/07_24/b4038417.htm

Second Life® Gospel. (2009). Retrieved September 15, 2009, from http://www.internetevangelismday.com/secondlife-evangelism.php

Shukula, A. (2008). Beyond Facebook Gifts: Virtual Currencies 101. *Mashable*. Retrieved August 21, 2009, from http://mashable.com/2008/12/18/virtual-currency/

SJSU's School of Library and Information Science Second Life® Portal. (2009). Retrieved September 13, 2009, from http://slisweb.sjsu.edu/sl/index.php/Main_Page

Social Effects of H5N1. (2009). Retrieved September 5, 2009, from Wikipedia Web site: http://en.wikipedia.org/wiki/Social_effects_of_H5N1

Sydell, L. (2008). In Tough Economic Times, Video Games Console. *NPR*. Retrieved August 21, 2009, from http://www.npr.org/templates/story/story.php?storyId=94884967&ft=1&f=1006

Systems, F. – 3D Virtual Training and Collaboration Software. (2009). Retrieved September 15, 2009, from http://www.hospitalmanagement.net/contractors/courses/forterra-systems/

Terdiman, D. (2005). Virtual gaming's elusive exchange rates. *ZDNet News*. Retrieved on September 5, 2009, from http://news.zdnet.com/2100-1040_22-144073.html

The Linden Dollar Game. (2007). *Capitalism 2.0*. Retrieved September 5, 2009, from http://randolfe.typepad.com/randolfe/2007/02/intersecting_tr.html

The Role of Streaming Media in the Future of Virtual Events. (2009). Retrieved November 30, 2009, from http://www.stream57.com/news/s57virtualedge20090611.html

Using Second Life® as a Business Tool. (2007). Retrieved September 14, 2009, from http://www.informationweek.com/blog/main/archives/2007/04/using_second_li_2.html

Villacampa, A. The Economics of World of Warcraft. Retrieved September 5. 2009 from http://www.lewrockwell.com/orig7/villacampa1.html

Virginia Virtual Academy. (2009). Retrieved September 13, 2009, from http://www.k12.com/vava/

Virtual Worlds - Better Experience and Less Costly Than Conference Calls. (2009). Retrieved September 8, 2009, from http://it.toolbox.com/vendors/forterra-systems-virtual-world-software/news/virtual-worlds-better-experience-and-less-costly-than-conference-calls-373

Wade, L. (2009). Social support can be a lifeline during health crisis. *CNN.com*. Retrieved August 23, 2009, from http://www.cnn.com/2009/HEALTH/06/15/social.support.benefit/index.html

Weinberger, D. (2007). Everything Is Miscellaneous, Chapter 5, The Laws of the Jungle. *Henry Holt and Company, LLC*.

What is Amazon Vine™? Retrieved September 5, 2009, from http://www.amazon.com/gp/vine/help\

WoW Gold Inflation. (2006). Retrieved September 5, 2009 from http://tobolds.blogspot.com/2006/02/wow-gold-inflation.html

Zero Worldswide, K. (2009). Retrieved November 30, 2009, from http://www.kzero.co.uk/blog/

Compilation of References

(Ed.). (2009). *Making the Virtual World Learning Experience Better. ELearning Future*. Retrieved on 12/1/09 from http://www.elearningfuture.com/making-the-virtual-world-learning-experience-better/

A&M Records v. Napster, 284 F.3d 1091 (9thCir. 2002).

Aarseth, E. J. (1997). *Cybertext: Perspectives on Ergodic Literature*. Baltimore, MD: John Hopkins University Press.

Abdul-Muhmin, A., & Umar, Y. (2007). *Credit card ownerdhip and usage behaviour in Saudi Arabia: The impact of demographics and attitudes toward debt.* Journal of Financial Services Mrketing: Palgrave macmillan.

Abrams, S., & Grun, S. (2008). Mundanes at the Gate… and Perverts Within: Managing Internal and External Threats to Communities Online. In Adams, T. L., & Smith, S. A. (Eds.), *Electronic Tribes*. Austin, TX: University of Texas Press.

Active Worlds. (2008). *Active Worlds*. Retrieved June 8, 2008, from http://www.activeworlds.com/

Activision Blizzard. (2008, September 15). Investor Presentation. Paris, France: Vivendi.

Adams, A. (2008). *Graduate Student Earns Degree in Second Life® Virtual World*. Retrieved November 29, 2009, from http://www.prlog.org/10106569-graduate-student-earns-degree-in-second-life-virtual-world.html

Ågerfalk, P. J., & Fitzgerald, B. (2008). Outsourcing to an unknown workforce: exploring opensourcing as a global sourcing strategy. *Management Information Systems Quarterly*, *32*(2), 385–409.

Ahmed, Q. (2008). *The Land of Invisible Women: A female Doctor's Journey in the Saudi Kingdom*. Naperville, Illinois: Sourcebooks.

Ahmed, M. (2009, November 30). *Real-world arrest for man who stole RuneScape virtual characters*. Retrieved November 30, 2009, from Times Online: http://technology.timesonline.co.uk/tol/news/tech_and_web/gadgets_and_gaming/virtual_worlds/article6937026.ece

Air Education and Training Command. (2008), *AETC White Paper*. Retrieved on 11/29/09 from http://www.aetc.af.mil/library/whitepaper.asp

Air Education and Training Command. (2008), AETC White Paper. Retrieved on 11/29/09 from http://www.aetc.af.mil/library/whitepaper.asp

AirSpace Smithsonian. (2009), Wild New Yonder. *The Daily Planet*. Retrieved on 11/29/09 from http://blogs.airspacemag.com/daily-planet/2009/08/17/wild-new-yonder/

Aitoro, J. (2007). *Uncle Sam Get a (Second) Life*. Channel Web. Retrieved on 11/30/09 from http://www.crn.com/government/199400068;jsessionid=2X20YIPJOUFODQE1GHRSKH4ATMY32JVN

Ajzen, I., & Fishbein, M. (1980). *Understanding attitudes and predicting social behavior*. Upper Saddle River, NJ: Prentice Hall.

Aldiri, K., Hobbs, D., & Qahwaji, R. (2008). *The Human Face of E-Business: Engendering Consumer Initial Trust Through the Use of Images of Sales Personnel on E-Commerce Web Sites. International Journal of E-Business Research*. Hershey, PA: IGI Publishing.

Alexa.com. (December, 2009). *Alexa Top 500 Global Internet Sites*. Retrieved on the world wide web December 3, 2009. http://www.alexa.com/topsites/global;0

Alexander, R. (2003). *Massively Multiplayer Game Development*. Hingham, MA: Charles River Media, Inc.

Alfuraih, S. (2008). *E-Commerce and E-Commerce Fraud in Saudi Arabia: A case Study*. IEEE Computer Society.

Al-Kahtani, N., Ryan, J., & Jefferson, T. (2006). *How Saudi female faculty perceive internet technology usage and potential*. Amsterdam: IOS Press, Information Knowledge System Management.

Allport, G. W. (1937). *Personality: A psychological interpretation*. New York: Holt & Co.

Almunajjed, M. (1997). Women. In *Saudi Arabia Today*. London: Palgrave.

Al-Saggaf, Y. (2004). The Effect of Online Community on Offline Community in Saudi Arabia. *16* (2).

Alves, T. R., & Roque, L. (2007) Because Players Pay: The Business Model Influence on MMOG Design. *Proceedings of DiGRA 2007: Situated Play*, September, Tokyo, Japan, (pp. 658-663).

Amazon (2009). *mturk*. Retrieved September 21, 2009, from https://www.mturk.com/mturk/welcome

Amazon profit doubles on sales of electronics. (2008). Retrieved September 5, 2009, from http://retailnu.wordpress.com/2008/07/26/amazon-profit-doubles-on-sales-of-electronics/

American Business Media. (2009, July 21). *Business-to-Business Magazines Continue to Decline*. Retrieved August 23, 2009, from American Business Media: http://www.americanbusinessmedia.com/abm/NewsBot.asp?MODE=VIEW&ID=2093

American Civil Liberties Union v. Mukasey, 534 F.3d 181 (3rdCir. 2008).

American Public Media. (2007, July 9). *Online 'gold farming' more than a game*. Retrieved September 3, 2009, from American Public Media: http://marketplace.publicradio.org/shows/2007/07/09/PM200707097.html

Anderson, J., Ashraf, N., Douther, C., & Jack, M. (2001). Presence and Usability in Shared Space Virtual Conferencing. *Cyberpsychology & Behavior*, *4*(2), 287–305. doi:10.1089/109493101300117965

Anon. (2002). Online Gaming Industry Reports, *Datamonitor*, Retrieved September 10, 2009, from www.datamonitor.com.

Anon. (2005). A model economy. *Economist*, January 22, p. 73

Anon. (2009). *About QuakeCon*, Retrieved September 14, 2009, from http://web.archive.org/web/20000816025343/www.quakecon.org/about.html

Anon. (2009). Second Life® transactions reach $1B. *GamingIndustry*, Retrieved September 23, 2009, from http://www.gamedaily.com/articles/news/second-life-transactions-reach-1-billion/

Anonymous. (2009). Devata.Org. Retrieved on 12/7/09 from http://www.devata.org/2009/08/virtual-or-reality-12-amazing-3d-comparison-photos-at-angkor-wat/

Apperley, T. H. (2006). Genre and game studies: Toward a critical approach to video game genres. *Simulation & Gaming*, *37*(1), 6–23. doi:10.1177/1046878105282278

Applications, N. (n.d.). *Market Share by Net Applications*. Retrieved August 25, 2009, from Market Share: http://marketshare.hitslink.com/browser-market-share.aspx?qprid=1

Architecture, S. (2009). Second Life Wiki. Retrieved on 12/7/09 from [1]http://wiki.secondlife.com/wiki/Server_architecture

Arnaud, R., & Barnes, M. C. (2006) *Collada - Sailing the gulf of 3D digital content creation*.Wellesley, MA: A K Peters, Ltd.

Ash, K. (2009). Characteristics of 'Highly Qualified' Online Teachers. *Digital Directions*. Retrieved on 12/8/09 from http://www.edweek.org/dd/article/2009/06/17/04characteristics

Ashforth, B., & Mael, F. (1989). Social Identity Theory and the Organization. *Academy of Management Review*, *14*(1), 20–30. doi:10.2307/258189

Asthmeir P. Feiger W. & Muller S. (1993), Virtual design: a generic VR system for

Astur, R. S., Ortiz, M. L., & Sutherland, R. J. (1998). A characterization of performance by men and women in a virtual Morris water task: A large and reliable sex difference. *Behavioural Brain Research*, *93*(12), 185–190. doi:10.1016/S0166-4328(98)00019-9

Atkins, G. (2003). *More than a Game: the Computer Game as a Fictional Form*. Manchester, UK: Manchester University Press.

Aubrey, J. B., & Dobbs, A. R. (1990). Age and sex differences in the mental realignment of maps. *Experimental Aging Research*, *16*(3), 133–139. doi:10.1080/07340669008251540

Avatar. (2008). In *Wikipedia, The Free Encyclopedia*. Retrieved June 6, 2008, from http://en.wikipedia.org/w/index.php?title=Avatar&oldid=216339962

Avery Dennison Corp. v. Sumpton, 999 F.Supp. 1337 (C.D.Cal. 1998).

AVW Association of Virtual Worlds. (2009) retrieved 29. November 2009, from http://www.associationofvirtualworlds.com/publication/the-blue-book/

AWEDU. (2009). *Self Guided Tour*. Retrieved on 12/12/09 from http://edu.activeworlds.com/tour/worlds.html

Aykin, N., Chavan, A. L., Dray, S. M., & Prabu, G. (2007). *Panel Discussion: Global Innovative Design for Social Change. Usability and Internationalisation. HCI and Culture. 4559*. Heidelberg: Springer Berlin.

Badre, A. (2001). *The Effects of Cross Cultural Interface Design Orientation on World Wide Web User Performance*. Georgia: Georgia Institute of Technology.

Bain, Ben. (2008). Taking Intelligence Analysis to the Virtual World. Federal Computer Week. Retrieved on 11/28/09 from http://fcw.com/Articles/2008/09/04/Taking-intelligence-analysis-to-the-virtual-world.aspx

Baker, C. (2008). *Hatters Island*. Retrieved on 12/8/09 from http://hattersisland.blogspot.com/

Balfour, B. (2009). Top 3 Reasons People Buy Virtual Goods. *Viximo, Virtual Goods Made Easy Web Site*. Retrieved August 16, 2009, from http://blog.viximo.com/corporate/2009/07/15/top-3-reasons-people-buy-virtual-goods/

Balkin, J. M. (2004). Virtual Liberty: Freedom to Design and Freedom to Play in Virtual Worlds. *Virginia Law Review*, *90*(8), 2043. doi:10.2307/1515641

Bank Failure in Second Life® Leads to Calls for Regulation. (2007). Retrieved September 13, 2009, from http://www.wired.com/gaming/virtualworlds/news/2007/08/virtual_bank

Barnard, J. (2007). Homeland Security Goes Virtual with Training. First Coast News. Retrieved on 11/30/09 from http://www.firstcoastnews.com/news/topstories/news-article.aspx?storyid=81724

Barnes, J. (2005). The New Action Heroes. *U.S. News and World Report*. Retrieved on 11/28/09 from http://www.usnews.com/usnews/news/articles/051121/21heroes.htm

Barrett v. Rosenthal, 146 P.3d 510 (Cal. 2006).[13]

Bartle, R. (2003). *Designing Virtual Worlds*. New Riders Games.

Bartle, A. R. (2004). *Designing Virtual Worlds*. Berkeley, CA: New Riders Publishing.

Barton, M. (2008). *Dungeons and desktops: the history of computer role-playing games*. Wellesley: A K Peters

Batzel v. Smith, 333 F.3d 1018 (9thCir. 2003)

Baumann, J. (1993). Military Applications of Virtual Reality. *The Encyclopedia of Virtual Environments*. Retrieved on 11/28/09 from http://www.hitl.washington.edu/scivw/EVE/II.G.Military.html

Bedau, M. A. (2003). Artificial life: organization, adaptation and complexity from the bottom up. *Trends in Cognitive Sciences*, *7*(11), 505–512. doi:10.1016/j.tics.2003.09.012

Bedford, C. (1998). LAN Parties: It's a Scene Baby! *Looneygames*, Retrieved September 14, 2009, from http://www.loonygames.com/content/1.8/feat/index2.php

Beer, S. (2007). *Second Life® a Security Risk for Business: Gartner*. ITWire. Retrieved on 11/30/09 from http://www.itwire.com/content/view/13912/53/

Bell, M. (2008). Toward a Definition of Virtual Worlds. *Journal of Virtual Worlds Research, 1*(1).

Bell, M. (2007). Definition and Taxonomy of Virtual Worlds. Indiana University. Retrieved on 12/7/09 from http://www.its.bldrdoc.gov/projects/devglossary/_virtual_world.html

Ben Ezra, Weinstein, & Co. v. America Online Inc., 206 F.3d 980 (10thCir. 2000)

Benedict, R. (1985). *Patterns Of Culture*. London: George Routledge & Sons LTD.

Benford, S., Bowers, J., Fahlén, L. E., Greenhalgh, C., & Snowdon, D. (1995). User embodiment in collaborative virtual environments. *CHI '95: Proceedings of the SIGCHI conference on Human factors in computing systems*, 242-249.

Benkler, Y. (2006). *The wealth of networks: How social production transforms markets and freedom*. New Haven: Yale University Press.

Ben-Zeev, A. (2004). *Love Online: emotions on the internet*. Cambridge, UK: Cambridge University Press. doi:10.1017/CBO9780511489785

Berne Convention. (1886). Convention.

Berthon, P., Pitt, L., Cyr, D., & Campbell, C. (2008). E-readiness and trust: macro and micro dualities for e-commerce in a global environment. *International Marketing Review, 25*(6), 700–714. doi:10.1108/02651330810915592

Betterverse.org. (2009). Flood of new government tenders for virtual world projects from DHS, US Army, Canada, and NATO. Retrieved on 11/27/09 from http://www.betterverse.org/2009/09/flood-of-new-government-tenders-for-virtual-world-projects-from-dhs-us-army-canada-and-nato.html

Bickmore, T., & Cassell, J. (2001). Relational agents: a model and implementation of building user trust. *CHI '01: Proceedings of the SIGCHI conference on Human factors in computing systems*, 396-403.

Bigelow, L. (2009). How Your Brand Can Click With a Tough Audience. *WeeWorld Web Site*. Retrieved August 16, 2009, from http://www.weeworld.com/about/news_item.aspx?home=yes&NewsID=281

Bimber, O., & Raskar, R. (2005). *Spatial augmented reality: Merging real and virtual worlds*. Wellesley, MA: AK Peters.

Biocca, F., & Levy, M. R. (1995). *Communication in the Age of Virtual Reality*. Hillsdale, New Jersey Hove, UK: Lawrence Erlbaum Associates.

Bitmanagement, (2009) retrieved 3. December 2009, from http://www.bitmanagement.com/en/products/interactive-3d-clients/bs-contact-mpeg-4

Blanchard, A., & Markus, M. (2004). The Experienced 'Sense' of a Virtual Community: Characteristics and Processes. *The Data Base for Advances in Information Systems, 35*(1), 65–79.

Blau, P. M. (1964). *Exchange and power in social life*. New York: John Wiley & Sons.

Blazer, C. (2006). The Five Indicia of Virtual Property. *Pierce Law Review, 5*, 137.

Blinn, J. (1988). "The Ancient Chinese Art of Chi-Ting". Jet Propulsion Laboratory, Pasadena, California, Fawzi, Marc. (2006). Wikipedia 3.0: The End of Google? Evolving Trends. Retrieved on 12/7/2009 from [1]http://evolvingtrends.wordpress.com/2006/06/26/wikipedia-30-the-end-of-google/

Blizzard Entertainment, Inc. (2008, July 29). *Terms of Use Agreement.* Retrieved September 3, 2009, from World of Warcraft: http://www.worldofwarcraft.com/legal/termsofuse.html

Blizzard Entertainment, Inc. (2009, July 29). *End User License Agreement.* Retrieved September 3, 2009, from World of Warcraft: http://www.worldofwarcraft.com/legal/eula.html

Blizzard Entertainment, Inc. (2009, September 3). *World of Warcraft Guide.* Retrieved September 3, 2009, from World of Warcraft: http://www.worldofwarcraft.com/info/basics/guide.html

Bloomfield (Ed.) (2007). *Metanomics.* Retrieved 17:49, June 8, 2008, from http://www.dryesha.com/2007/12/video-of-3d3c-metaverse-metanomics-talk.html and http://www.metanomics.net/

Boellstorff, T. (2008). *Coming of Age in Second Life: An Anthropologist Explores the Virtually Human.* Princeton, NJ: Princeton University Press.

Bogost, I. (2005). *Event Wrap Up: Games for Health 2005.* Retrieved September 15, 2009, from http://www.gamasutra.com/view/feature/2413/event_wrap_up_games_for_health_.php

Bonn, S. (2003, July). personal communication.

Book, B. (2004). In Moving Beyond the Game: Social Virtual Worlds. Paper presented on the panel The Culture of Play at the conference *State of Play 2: Reloaded.* New York Law School, October 28-30.

Booth K. Fisher B. Page S. Ware C. & Widen S. (2000). Wayfinding in a virtual environment. *Graphics Interface.*

Borders Online, LLC v. State Board of Equalization, 29 Cal.Rptr.3d 176 (2007)

Brahmbhatt, M. (2005). *Avian and Human Pandemic Influenza – Economic and Social Impacts.* Retrieved September 5, 2009, from http://www.who.int/mediacentre/events/2005/World_Bank_Milan_Brahmbhattv2.pdf

Brainyquote (2009). *Brainyquote.* Retrieved 14:52, December 05, 2009, from http://www.brainyquote.com/quotes/keywords/commerce.html

Brewer, W. F. (2000). Bartlett's concept of the schema and its impact on theories of knowledge representation in contemporary cognitive psychology. In Saito (Ed.), Bartlett, culture and cognition, 69-89, Psychology Press.

Brewer, W. F., & Nakamura, G. V. (1984). The nature and functions of schemas. *Handbook of social cognition,* 1, 119160.

Brightman, J. (2008). Video Games Explode: Global Revenues Now on Par with Box Office, *Game Daily*, retrieved September 21, 2009, from http://www.gamedaily.com/articles/news/video-games-explode-global-revenues-now-on-par-with-box-office/?biz=1

Bringardner, J. (2007, February 1). *IP's Brave New World.* Retrieved September 3, 2009, from Law.Com: http://www.law.com/jsp/article.jsp?id=1170237755271

Brown, A. (2009). *A Second Look at Second Life: Virtual Worlds and Education.* East Carolina University.

Brown, A., & Green, T. (2009). Issues and Trends in Instructional Technology: Wb 2.0, Second Life® and STEM Share the Spotlight. In Orey, McClendon, V.J. & Branch, R.M. (Eds.) Educational Media and Technology Yearbook, 34, 7-23.

Brutzman, D., & Daly, L. (2007) *X3D - Extensible 3D graphics for web authors.* Morgan Kaufmann Publishers, Elsevier Inc, 2007

Bumgardner, J. (2009, Retrieved in January 2009). The Palace history web: http://www.jbum.com/history/index.html.

Burdea, G. C., & Coiffet, P. (2003). *Virtual reality technology.* Hoboken, NJ: John Wiley & Sons.

Burr, V. (1995). *An introduction to social constructionism.* London: Routledge. doi:10.4324/9780203299968

Butler, D. L., Acquino, A. L., Hissong, A. A., & Scott, P. A. (1993). Wayfinding by Newcomers in a Complex Building. *Human Factors, 35*(1), 159173.

Caillois, R. (1957). *Les jeux et les hommes.* Gallimard.

Cal. Bus. & Prof. Code §§22,575–22,579

Callaham, J. (2009, May 11). *Blizzard named top game developer in new survey.* Retrieved September 3, 2009, from Big Download: http://news.bigdownload.com/2009/05/11/blizzard-named-top-game-developer-in-new-survey/

Camp, B. T. (2007). The Play's the Thing: A Theory of Taxing Virtual Worlds. *The Hastings Law Journal, 59*, 1.

Carafano v. Metrosplash.com, Inc., 339 F.3d 1119 (9th Cir. 2003)

Carlson, N. (2009, January 8). *Time To Stop Laughing: Selling Virtual Goods, Zynga Profits On Revenues Close To $50 Million.* Retrieved August 23, 2009, from www.businessinsider.com: http://www.businessinsider.com/2009/1/time-to-stop-laughing-selling-virutal-goods-zynga-profits-on-50-million-revenues

Carolis, B., Carofiglio, V., Bilvi, M., & Pelachaud, C. (2002). APML: A markup language for believable behavior generation. *Embodied conversational agents - let's specify and evaluate them! held in conjunction with AAMAS02.*

Casanueva, J. S. (2000). *Presence and co-presence in collaborative virtual environments.* University of Cape Town, Department of Computer Science.

Cashmore, P. (2006, May 30). *Second Life® + Web 2.0 = Virtual World Mashups!* Retrieved August 23, 2009, from mashable.com: http://mashable.com/2006/05/30/second-life-web-20-virtual-world-mashups/

Caspi v. Microsoft Network, LLC, 323 N.J. Super 118 (1999).

Cassell, J., Pelachaud, C., Badler, N., Steedman, M., Achorn, B., Becket, T., et al. (1994). Animated conversation: rule-based generation of facial expression, gesture & spoken intonation for multiple conversational agents. *SIGGRAPH '94: Proceedings of the 21st annual conference on Computer graphics and interactive techniques*, 413-420.

Castronova, E. (2006). *Synthetic Worlds: The Business and Culture of Online Games*. University Of Chicago Press.

Castronova, E. (2005). *Synthetic worlds: The business and culture of online game*. Chicago: University of Chicago Press.

Castronova, E. (2005). *Synthetic Worlds: The Business and Culture of Online Games*. Chicago: University of Chicago Press.

Castronova, E., Williams, D., Shen, C., Ratan, R., Xiong, L., Huang, Y., & Keegan, G. (2009). As real as real? Macroeconomic behavior in a large-scale virtual world. *New Media & Society, 11*(5), 685–707. doi:10.1177/1461444809105346

Castronova, E. (2007). *Exodus To The Virtual World* (1st ed.). New York, New York, USA: Palgrave Macmillan.

Castronova, E. (2005). *Synthetic Worlds: the business and culture of online games*. Chicago: University of Chicago Press.

Castronova, E. (2001, December). *Virtual Worlds: A First-Hand Account of Market and Society on the Cyberian Frontier.* Retrieved September 3, 2009, from Social Science Research Network: http://ssrn.com/abstract=294828

Castronova, E. (2006). *Synthetic Worlds: The Business and Culture of Online Games* (Paperback ed.). Chicago, IL, USA: University of Chicago Press.

Cavanaugh, Cathy. (2008). Real Learning Happens in Virtual Schools. Threshold. 10; Fall 2008.

Centers for Disease Control and Prevention. (2009). *Social Media at CDC.* Retrieved on 12.8.09 from http://www.cdc.gov/SocialMedia/Tools/VirtualWorlds.html

Chalf, P., & Rosenau, D. (2003). *Intelligence, Police and Counterterrorism: Assessing Post-911 Initiatives*. Rand Corporation. Retrieved on 11/30/09 from http://www.rand.org/nsrd/terrpanel/additional/intelinputv2.pdf

Chen, S. Y., & Macredie, R. D. (2001). Cognitive styles and hypermedia navigation: Development of a learning model. *Journal of the American Society for Information Science and Technology, 53*(1), 315. doi:10.1002/1532-2890(2000)9999:9999<::AID-ASI1074>3.0.CO;2-2

Cheng, L., Farnham, S., & Stone, L. (2002). Lessons Learned: Building and Deploying Shared Virtual Environments. *The Social Life of Avatars: Presence and Interaction in Shared Virtual Environments and Scientific Visualisation,* pp. 90-111.

Child Pornography Prevention Act, 18 U.S.C.S. §2241, et seq.

Clark Vance, D. (2008). Like a Neighbourhood of Sisters: Can Culture be Formed Electronically. In *Adams, T.L. & Smith, S.A. (2008). Electronic Tribes*. Austin, TX: University of Texas Press.

Clark, S. A., & Wong, B. L. W. (2000). QTVR Support for Teaching Operative Procedures in Dentistry. People and Computer XIV. Usability or Else! *Proceedings of HCL 2000*, London.

Claro, M. (2007). Video games and education, Retrieved September 14, 2009, from www.oecd.org/dataoecd/14/60/39548100.pdf

Clubpenguin (2008). *Clubpenguin.* Retrieved 17:49, June 8, 2008, from http://corporate.disney.go.com/news/corporate/2007/2007_0801_clubpenguin.html and http://venturebeat.com/2007/08/01/disney-buys-club-penguin-in-700-million-deal/

Cobb S.U.G. & D'Cruz, M. D. (1994) First UK national survey on industrial application of virtual reality. *VR News,* 3.

Coe, J. M. (2003, October 1). *The New B-to-B Fundamentals.* Retrieved August 23, 2009, from Target Online: http://www.targetmarketingmag.com/article/the-new-b-to-b-fundamentals-1-907-words-27824_1.html

Cohen, R., & Schuepfer, T. (1980). The representation of landmarks and routes. *Child Development*, *51*, 1065–1071. doi:10.2307/1129545

Cole, V. 2006). Wharton Dean: Virtual Worlds are the Future of MBA Education. Retrieved on 12/8/09 from http://www.joystiq.com/2006/03/16/wharton-dean-virtual-worlds-are-the-future

Coleman, J. S. (1988). Social capital in the creation of human capital. *American Journal of Sociology*, *94*, 95–120. doi:10.1086/228943

Collins, S. (2008). *Virtual Worlds in Education.* EDUCAUSE Evolving Technologies Committee.

Columbia Insurance Co. v. Seescandy.com, 185 F.R.D. 573 (N.D. Cal. 1999)[14] (America Online, Inc. v. Anonymous Publicly Traded Co., 542 S.E.2d 377 (Va. 2001)

Commision, C. a. (2008). *Communication and Information Technology Commision.* Retrieved April 9th, 2009, from Internet Usage in the Kingdom of Saudi Arabia: Individuals: www.citc.gov.sa de Galdo, E., & Nielson, J. (1996). *International User Interfaces.* New York: John Wiley & Sons.

Connect, K. (2009). About. Retrieved on 12/11/09 from http://www.kidzconnect.org/about

Consortium, M. (retrieved in January 2009.). MPEGV, 2009: http://www.chiariglione.org/mpeg/working documents.htm#MPEGV

ConventionUniversal Copyright (1952).

Convention on Cybercrime, CETS No. 185 (2001 Budapest)

Conway, D. (2008). *ODNI Asks: Which MMOG Make You a Spy? Zero Intelligence Agents*. Retrieved on 11/28/09 from http://www.drewconway.com/zia/?p=197

Copyrights: Berne Convention (1886)

Corbett, P. (2010, January 4). Facebook Demographics and Statistics Report 2010 – 145% Growth in 1 Year istrategy labs. Retrieved August 10, 2010, from istrategy labs Web site: [REMOVED HYPERLINK FIELD]http://www.istrategylabs.com/2010/01/facebook-demographics-and-statistics-report-2010-145-growth-in-1-year/

Corps of Discovery. (2003). *The Seven Army Values.* Retrieved on 11.28.09 from http://www.history.army.mil/lc/the%20mission/the_seven_army_values.htm

Cova, B., Kozinets, R. V., & Shankar, A. (2007). *Consumer Tribes*. Oxford: Butterworth-Heinemann.

Cowan, D. (2009, February 25). *NASA Taps Serious Game Devs for Space-Themed MMO.* Retrieved September 3, 2009, from Serious Games Source: http://www.seriousgamessource.com/item.php?story=22468

CP-MI.org. (2009). Welcome. Retrieved on 11/29/09 from http://www.cp-mi.org/14701.html

Curtis, D. (2009, February 15). The science of entrepreneurship. (7), Retrieved from http://dustincurtis.com/the_science_of_entrepreneurship.html

D. Sánchez-Guzmán, César Mora, R. García-Salcedo. (2009). Intelligent Agents: A Physics Education Opportunity in Latin-America. Lat. Am. J. Phys. Educ. Vol. 3, No. 2, May 2009.

Damer, B. (1997). *Avatars! Exploring and Building Virtual Worlds on the Internet*. Berkeley, CA: Peachpit Press.

Darken, R. P., Allard, T., & Achille, L. B. (1999). Spatial Orientation and Wayfinding in Large Scale Virtual Spaces II. *Presence (Cambridge, Mass.)*, *8*(6).

Darken, R. P., & Banker, W. P. (1998). Navigating in Natural Environments: A Virtual Environment Training Transfer Study. *Proceedings of VRAIS*, *98*, 12–19.

Darken, R. P., & Peterson, B. (2001). Spatial Orientation, Wayfinding, and Representation. In Stanney, K. (Ed.), *Handbook of Virtual Environment Technology*. Stanney.

Darken, R. P., & Sibert, J. L. (1996). Wayfinding strategies and behaviours in large virtual worlds. *Proceedings of ACM CHI96*, 142-149.

Darroch, I. Goodman J. Brewster S. & Gray P. (2005) The Effect of Age and Font Size on Reading Text on Handheld Computers. *Proceedings of IFIP INTERACT05: Human-Computer Interaction,* pp. 253-266.

Davis, A., Murphy, J., Owens, D., Kazanchi, D., & Zigurs, I. (2009). Avatars, People, and Virtual Worlds: Foundations for Research in Metaverses. *Journal of the Association for Information Systems*, *10*(20), 90–117.

Davis, F. D. (1989). Perceived usefulness, perceived ease of use, and user acceptance of information technology. *Management Information Systems Quarterly*, *13*(3), 319–339. doi:10.2307/249008

Davis, F. D. (1993). User acceptance of information technology: system characteristics, user perceptions and behavioral impacts. *International Journal of Man-Machine Studies*, *38*(3), 475–487. doi:10.1006/imms.1993.1022

Davis, F. D., Bagozzi, R. P., & Warshaw, P. R. (1989). User acceptance of computer technology: a comparison of two theoretical models. *Management Science*, *35*(8), 982–1003. doi:10.1287/mnsc.35.8.982

Deaux, K., Reid, A., Mizraha, K., & Ethier, K. A. (1995). Parameters of Social Identity. *Journal of Personality and Social Psychology*, *68*(2), 280–291. doi:10.1037/0022-3514.68.2.280

Deaver, S. (1979). *World of Women: Anthropological Studies of Women in the Societies of the World. Praeger Publishers Inc.* The Contemporary Saudi Women. In E. Bourguignon.

Decker v. Circus Circus Hotel, 49 F.Supp.2d 743 (D.N.J. 1999)[15]

Dejwakh, V. (2008). *Virtual Worlds and Web 3.0: Examined, Compared, Analyzed.* In-Stat.

Dejwakh, V. (2008). Virtual Worlds and Web 3.0 Examined, Compared, Analyzed. *Instat,* IN0804326CM. Retrieved August 16, 2009, from http://www.instat.com/abstract.asp?id=212&SKU=IN0804326CM

del Galdo, E. (2001). Internationalisation then and now. Designing for global markets. Third International Workshop on Internationalisation of Prodcuts and Systems.

Dell Considering Virtual Goods System on Official Forums. (2009, January 9). Retrieved from Virtual Goods News: http://www.virtualgoodsnews.com/2009/01/dell-considering-virtual-goods-system-on-official-forums.html

Dell, K. (2007). Second Life's Real World Problems. *Time Magazine Web Site*. Retrieved August 16, 2009, from http://www.time.com/time/magazine/article/0,9171,1651500,00.html

Derryberry, A. (2008). *Serious Games: Online Games for Learning*. Retrieved on 11/28/09 from http://www.adobe.com/resources/elearning/pdfs/serious_games_wp.pdf

Dibbell, J. (2006). *Play money: or, How I quit my day job and made millions trading virtual loot.* New York: Basic Books.

Dibbell, J. (2006). *Play Money, Or, How I Quit My Day Job and Made Millions Trading Virtual Loot*. New York, New York, USA: Basic Books.

Dibbell, J. (1993). *A Rape in Cyberspace*, Retrieved September 10, 2009, from http://www.juliandibbell.com/texts/bungle.html.

Dibbell, J. (1993, December 23). *A Rape in Cyberspace.* Retrieved September 3, 2009, from Julian Dibbell: http://www.juliandibbell.com/texts/bungle_vv.html

Dickey, M. (2003). 3D Virtual worlds: An Emerging Technology for Tradition and Distance Leerning. Ohio Learning Network Conference 2003. Retrieved on 12/8/09 from http://www.oln.org/conferences/OLN2003/papers/Dickey3DVirtualWorlds.pdf

Dictionaries, C. (2009). *Cambrdige|Dictionaries Online*. (Cambridge University Press) Retrieved May 07, 2009, from Cambridge Advanced Learner's Dictionary: http://dictionary.cambridge.org/

DiPaola, S., & Collins, D. (2002). A 3D Virtual Environment for Social Telepresence. *in Proc. Western Computer Graphics Symp.*

Direct Marketing Association. (2008-2009). *The Power of Direct Marketing.* New York: Direct Marketing Association.

DiVita, Y. (2003). *Dickless Marketing: Smart Marketing to Women Online.* 1stBooks.

Dix, A. Finlay J. Abowd G. & Beale R. (1993). *Human computer interaction*. New York: Prentice Hall.

Doe v. MySpace, Inc., 528 F.3d 413 (5thCir. 2008).

Doe v. Sexsearch.com, 551 F.3d 412 (6thCir. 2008).[16]

Dow Jones & Company Inc. v Gutnick, HCA 56 (2002)[17]

Doyle, S., Dodge, M., & Smith, A. (1998). The potential of web - based mapping and virtual reality technologies for modeling urban environments. *Computers, Environment and Urban Systems*, *22*(2), 137–155. doi:10.1016/S0198-9715(98)00014-3

Driver, E., & Driver, S. (2009). ThinkBalm Immersive Internet Business Value Study, Q2 2009. *Immersive Internet Analyst Report Series, Issue #2*. Retrieved August 16, 2009, from http://www.thinkbalm.com/2009/05/26/thinkbalm-publishes-business-value-study/

Driver, E., & Jackson, P. (January 7, 2008). *Getting Real Work Done in Virual Worlds*. Forrester Research. www.forrester.com/rb/research.

Earth, G. (2009). Wikipedia. Retrieved on 12/8/09 from http://en.wikipedia.org/wiki/Google_Earth

EastSouthWestNorth, translated from Chinese. (2009, August 29). "The Legend" Returns In A Completely Different Format, Several Thousand Netizens Blocked City Gates In Protest. *Chengdu Commercial Daily.*

Eastwick, P. W., & Gardner, W. L. (2009). Is it a game? Evidence for social influence in the virtual world. *Social Influence*, *4*(1), 18–32. doi:10.1080/15534510802254087

Eberts, R. E. (1994). *User interface design*. Englewood Cliffs, NJ: Prentice Hall.

Educational, S. L. (2009). *Simteach*. Retrieved in August, 2009, from http://www.simteach.com/wiki/index.php?title=Top_20_Educational_Locations_in_Second_Life

Effect, S. (2010, August 10). In *Wikipedia, the free encyclopedia*. Retrieved August 13, 2010, from http://en.wikipedia.org/wiki/Streisand_effect

Egges, A., & Magnenat-Thalmann, N. (2005). Emotional Communicative Body Animation for Multiple Characters. In *Proc. First International Workshop on Crowd Simulation (V-Crowds '05)*, 31-40.

Egsegian, R., Pittman, K., Farmer, K., & Zobel, R. (1993). Practical applications of virtual reality to firefighter training. In *Proceedings of the 1993 Simulations Multiconference on the International Emergency Management and Engineering Conference* (pp. 155–160). San Diego, CA: Society of Computer Simulation

Eiffel. (2009). *European Future Internet Portal*. Retrieved in January 2009, from http://www.future-internet.eu/

Electronic Arts Inc. (2009, September 3). *Ultima Online TOS*. Retrieved September 3, 2009, from Ultima Online: http://www.uo.com/tos_update.html#uotos

Ellison, D. M. (2007). Social network sites: Definition, history, and scholarship. *Journal of Computer-Mediated Communication*, *13*(1), 11.

Ellwood, I., & Shekar, S. (2008). *Wonder Woman: Marketing Secrets for the Trillion-Dollar Customer*. London: Palgrave Macmillan.

Encyclopedia.com. (2009). United States: Worldwide Military Spending on Virtual Training totaled $7.9bn in 2008. Retrieved on 11/27/09 from HTTP://WWW.ENCYCLOPEDIA.COM/DOC/1G1-206025778.HTML

E-Spaces. (2009). *CyberTown first prototype*. Retrieved in January, 2009, from http://www.e-spaces.com/lbw/portfolio/projects/port_cybertown.htm.

Esposito, J., & Mogahed, D. (2007). *Who Speakes for Islam? what a billion muslims really think*. New York: Gallup Press.

European Commission Taxation and Customs Union. (2009, September 3). *VAT on electronic services*. Retrieved September 3, 2009, from European Commission Taxation and Customs Union: http://ec.europa.eu/taxation_customs/taxation/vat/how_vat_works/e-services/index_en.htm

Exchange, P. R. (2009). Front Page. Retrieved on 12/1/09 from http://pacificrimx.wordpress.com/2009/10/

Farber, D. (2007, August 1). *The Future of Virtual Worlds*. Retrieved August 29, 2009, from blogs.zdnet.com: http://blogs.zdnet.com/BTL/?p=5825

Farhoomand, A., & Lovelock, P. (2001). *Global E-Commerce*. Singapore: Prentice Hall.

Faulkenberg, E., Hesse, W., Lindgren, P., Nilsson, B., Oei, J., & Rolland, C. (1998). *A Framework of Information System Concepts*. FRISCO.

Fawcett, B. (Ed.). (2006). *The battle for Azeroth: Adventure, alliance and addiction: insights into the World of Warcraft*. Dallas, TX: BenBella Books, Inc.: Distributed by Independent Publishers Group.

Feather, F. (2001). *Future Consumer.Com: The Webolution of shopping to 2010*. Oxford: Capstone Publishing Ltd.

FedBizOpps. (2008a). *MyBase, 3D On-Line Training Environment Software*. Retrieved on 11/27/09 from https://www.fbo.gov/index?s=opportunity&mode=form&id=807445bf1dab0abd47b4829a72a8691c&tab=core&_cview=0

FedBizOpps.gov. (2008b). *MyBase (Prototype) 3D Virtual Learning Environment*. Solicitation Number: FA3002-08-RFI001. Retrieved on 11/29/09 from https://www.fbo.gov/index?s=opportunity&mode=form&tab=core&id=5dfd2502b6ebd48d2493bdf78c807899&_cview=0

FedBizOps. Gov. (2009). *This RFI seeks input on virtual world technologies and web based training systems*. Retrieved on 11/29/09 from https://www.fbo.gov/index?s=opportunity&mode=form&tab=core&id=e2ccbe350033dd333f17f9458695b8e3&_cview=1&cck=1&au=&ck=

Federal Arbitration Act, 9 USCS §1, et seq.

Federal, V. W. C. (2009). Challenge. Retrieved on 11/28/09 from http://fvwc.army.mil/FVWC-Main.html

Feldman, A., & Acredolo, L. P. (1979). The effect of active versus passive exploration on memory for spatial location in children. *Child Development*, *50*, 698–704. doi:10.2307/1128935

Ferraro, G. (2001). *Cultural Anthropology: An Applied Perspective*. Wadsworth, thomson learning.

Fitzgerald, W. (2004). *Models for cross-cultural communications for cross-cultural website design*. Canada: National Research Council Canada.

Fitzgerald, S. (2003). Managing Your Intellectual Property. *FindLaw*. Retrieved on 12/3/09 from http://library.findlaw.com/2003/May/5/132714.html

Fleming, L., & Waguespack, D. M. (2007). Brokerage, Boundary Spanning, and Leadership in Open Innovation Communities. *Organization Science*, *18*(2), 165–180. doi:10.1287/orsc.1060.0242

Foley, S. (December 31, 2006). *Game on: criminals set sights on virtual realities.* The Independent. http://www.independent.co.uk/news/business/news/game-on-criminals-set-sights-on-virtual-realities-430265.html

Ford, N., & Chen, S. Y. (2001). Matching/mismatching revisited: An empirical study of learning and teaching styles. *British Journal of Educational Technology*, *32*(1), 5–22. doi:10.1111/1467-8535.00173

Foreman, N., Stanton, D., Wilson, P., & Duffy, H. (2003). Spatial Knowledge of a Real School Environment Acquired From Virtual or Physical Models by Able Bodied Children and Children With Physical Disabilities. *Journal of Experimental Psychology*, *9*(2), 67–74.

Forman, R. W. (2000, November). Creating Convergence, *Scientific American*.

Forrester,(2008) retrieved 29. November 2009, from http://www.forrester.com/Research/Document/Excerpt/0,7211,43450,00.html

Foss v. Circuit City Stores, Inc., 477 F.Supp.2d 230 (D.Me. 2007)[18] General Conference of Seventh-Day Adventists v. Aon Reinsurance Agency, Inc., 860 F.Supp. 983 (S.D.N.Y.1994), aff'd 50 F.3d 2 (1995).

Friedman, T. (1999). Civilization and its discontents: Simulation, Subjectivity and Space. In Smith, G. M. (Ed.), *On a Silver Platter* (p. 137). New York: New York University Press.

Frontier, E. (2009, January 20). U.S. [Sunnyvale, CA: Efficient Frontier]. *Search Engine Performance Report, Q4*, 2008.

Fur Culture. (2008). *Fur Culture*. Retrieved June 8, 2008, from http://furry.wikia.com

Gallistel, C. R. (1990). *The organisation of learning*. Cambridge M.A: The MIT Press.

Games, C. C. P. (2009). *Frequently Asked Questions: What is EVE Online?* Retrieved September 3, 2009, from EVE Online: http://www.eveonline.com/faq/faq_01.asp

Gartner (2007). Gartner Says 80 Percent of Active Internet Users Will Have A "Second Life" in the Virtual World by the End of 2011. *Gartner Newsroom*. Retrieved August 16, 2009, from http://www.gartner.com/it/page.jsp?id=503861

Gartner (2008). Gartner Says 90 Percent of Corporate Virtual World Projects Fail Within 18 Months. *Gartner Newsroom*. Retrieved August 16, 2009, from http://www.gartner.com/it/page.jsp?id=670507

Gartner, (2008) retrieved 29. November 2009, from http://www.gartner.com/it/page.jsp?id=670507

Gartner,(2007) retrieved 29. November 2009, from http://www.gartner.com/it/page.jsp?id=503861

Gartner. (2007). Gartner Says 80 Percent of Active Internet Users Will Have A "Second Life" in the Virtual World by the End of 2011. Retrieved on 12/13/09 from http://www.gartner.com/it/page.jsp?id=503861

Garvey, C. (1990). *Play*. Boston: Harvard University Press.

Gary. (2009). The Virtual Worlds Hype cycle for 2009. Retrieved on 12/8/09 from http://222.muvedesign.com/the-virtual-worlds-hype-cycle-for-2009

Gazendam, H. W., Jorna, R. J., & Liu, K. (2004). An organisational semiotic view on interculturality and globalisation. *IASS 2004 Conference*. IASS 2004 Conference.

Gebhard, P. (2005). ALMA: a layered model of affect. *AAMAS '05: Proceedings of the fourth international joint conference on Autonomous agents and multiagent systems*, 29-36.

Gelernter, D. (1992). *Mirror Worlds: or the Day Software Puts the Universe in a Shoebox...How It Will Happen and What It Will Mean*. New York: Oxford University Press.

Gilbert, B. J. (2009, June 2). *The Second Life® of Intellectual Property.* Retrieved September 3, 2009, from Social Science Research Network: http://ssrn.com/abstract=1409091

Gilmer v. Interstate/Johnson Lane Corp., 500 U.S. 20 (1991).

Globalfirepower. (2008). United States of America Military Strength. Retrieved on 11/27/09 from http://www.globalfirepower.com/country-military-strength-detail.asp?country_id=United-States-of-America

Godin, S. (2008). *Tribes*. London: Piatkus.

Goerger, S. Darken R. Boyd M. Gagnon T. Liles S. Sullivan J. & Lawson J.P (1998).Spatial Knowledge Acquisition from Maps and Virtual Environments in Complex Architectural Spaces. Proceedings of the 16th Applied Behavioral Sciences Symposium, 2223, April, U.S. Air Force Academy. Colorado Springs, 610.

Golembiewski, R. T., & McConkie, M. (1975). The centrality of interpersonal trust in group processes. In Cooper, G. L. (Ed.), *Theories of Group Processes* (pp. 131–185). London: John Wiley.

Golledge, R. G., Dougherty, V., & Bell, S. (1995). Acquiring Spatial Knowledge: Survey versus Route Based Knowledge. *Unfamiliar Environments ReginaldAnnals of the Association of American Geographers*, *85*(1), 13158.

Gomez, L. M. Egan D.E. & Bowers C. (1986). Learning to use a text editor: Some learner characteristics that predict success. *HumanComputer Interaction*, 2, 1–23.

Goncalves, L., Kallmann, M., & Thalmann, D. (2001). Programming Behaviors with Local Perception and Smart Objects: An Approach to Solve Autonomous Agent Tasks. *SIGGRAPH 2001*.

González, F. A. L. (2005). *Nuevas Técnicas para la Animación del Comportamiento de Agentes Virtuales Autónomos*. (Phd Thesis). Departamento de Matemática Aplicada y Ciencias de la Computación de la Universidad de Cantabria.

Goodenough, D. (1976). The role of individual differences in field dependence as a factor in learning and memory. *Psychological Bulletin*, *83*, 675–694. doi:10.1037/0033-2909.83.4.675

Google. (2009a) retrieved 3. December 2009, from http://code.google.com/apis/o3d/

Google. (2009b) retrieved 3. December 2009, from http://code.google.com/apis/o3d/docs/artdesignerguide.html

Gos. (2008, April 13). In *Wikipedia, The Free Encyclopedia*. Retrieved June 6, 2008, from http://en.wikipedia.org/w/index.php?title=Gur&oldid=205242560

Gouteux, S., & Spelke, E. (2001). Children's use of geometry and landmarks to reorient in an open space. *Cognition*, *81*, 119–148. doi:10.1016/S0010-0277(01)00128-7

Grassian, E., & Trueman, R. (2007). Stumbling, Bumbling, Teleporting and Flying...Librarian Avatars in Second Life®. *RSR. Reference Services Review*, *35*(1), 84–89. doi:10.1108/00907320710729373

Green, J., & Hannon, C. (2007). *Their Space: Education for a digital generation*. London: Demos.

Green v. America Online (AOL), 318 F.3d 465 (3rd Cir. 2003)

Grimes, S., & Feenberg, A. (2009). Rationalizing Play: A Critical Theory of Digital Gaming. *The Information Society*, *25*(2), 105–118. doi:10.1080/01972240802701643

Grönroos, C. (2008). Service Logic Revisited: Who Creates Value? And Who Co-creates? *European Business Review*, *20*(4), 298–314. doi:10.1108/09555340810886585

Guilford, J. P., & Zimmerman, W. S. (1948). The Guilford Zimmerman Aptitude Survey. *The Journal of Applied Psychology*, *32*, 24–34. doi:10.1037/h0063610

Gurley, B. (2009, March 2). *How to Monetize a Social Network: MySpace and Facebook Should Follow TenCent*. Retrieved August 29, 2009, from AbovetheCrowd.com: http://abovethecrowd.com/2009/how-to-monetize-a-social-network-myspace-and-facebook-should-follow-tencent/

Hagel, J., & Armstrong, A. G. (1996). The real value of on-line communities. *Harvard Business Review*, *74*(3), 134–141.

Hagel, J. * Armstrong, A.G. (1997). *Net gain: Expanding markets through virtual communities*. Boston: Harvard Business School Press.

Hague Conference on Private International Law, Convention 16 and Supplementary Protocol 17 (1971)

Hague Conference on Private International Law, Convention 37 (2005).

Hall, E. T. (1959,1981). *The Silent Language*. New York: Doubleday.

Hall, P. (2001). *The Cross Cultural web* (Vols. 109 - 113). Bukinghamshire: 3rd International Workshop on Internationalisation of Products and Systems.

Hannerz, U. (1992). *Cultural Complexity; Studies in the Social Organisation of Meaning*. New York: Columbia University Press.

Hansen, S. (2008). Virtual Worlds: Synopsis of User Interfaces and Accessibility Initiatives. In *Proc. of 14th Australasian World Wide Web Conference, AusWeb*.

Harasim, L. (1989). On-line education: A new domain. In Mason, R., & Kaye, A. (Eds.), *Mindweave: Communication, Computers and Distance Education* (pp. 50–62). Oxford, UK: Pergamon Press.

Harris, C. (2008). Government Consortium to Investigate Virtual World Best Practices. *Digital Communities*. Retrieved on 11/30/09 from http://www.govtech.com/dc/articles/420596

Harrison McKnight, D., & Chervany, N. L. (2002). What Trust Means in E-Commerce Customer Relationships: An Interdisciplinary Conceptual Typology. *International Journal of Electronic Commerce*, *6*(2), 35–59.

Harrison, D. (2009a). Engaging Students in Virtual learning. Campus Technology. Retrieved on 12/8/09 from http://campustechnology.com/Articles/2009/04/22/Engaging-students-in-virtual-learning

Harrison, D. (2009b). Real-Life Teaching in a Virtual World. Campus Technology. Retrieved on 12/8/09 from http://campustechnology.com/articles/2009/02/12/Real-Life-Teaching-in-a-virtual-world

Hasher, L., & Zacks, R. T. (1979). Automatic and effortful processes in memory. *Journal of Experimental Psychology*, *108*, 356–388.

Hatem, M. (Fall 1985). *Conservative Patriarchal Modernization in the Arabian Gulf States* (Vol. 11). Washington DC: Contemporary Marxism.

Health Insurance Portability and Accountability Act, Public Law 104-191

Hegarty, M., & Waller, D. (2004). A dissociation between mental rotation and perspective-taking spatial abilities. *Intelligence*, *32*, 175–191. doi:10.1016/j.intell.2003.12.001

Helicopteros Nacionales de Colombia, S.A. v. Hall, 466 U.S. 408 (1984).[19]

Hemphill, T. A. (2006). A Taxonomy of closed and open source software industry business models. *International Journal of Innovation and Technology Management*, *3*(1), 61–82. doi:10.1142/S0219877006000661

Hendler, J., Shadbolt, N., Hall, W., Berners-Lee, T., & Weitzner, D. (2008). *Web Science: An Interdisciplinary Approach to Understanding the Web* (*Vol. 51*). Communications of the ACM.

Hine, C. (2000). *Virtual Ethnography*. Thousand Oaks, CA: Sage Publications.

Hoffman, D. L. (2008). *Generating Customer Insights from the "Social Web": Are Marketers Ready to Give Up Control? Direct Marketing Educational Foundation Research Summit*. Las Vegas: Direct Marketing Educational Foundation.

Hofstede, G. (1998). *Masculinity and Femininity: The Taboo Dimension of National Cultures*. London: Sage Publications.

Hofstede, G., & Hofstede, G. J. (2005). *Cultures and Organisations: software of the mind*. New York: McGraw-Hill.

Hoft, N. (1995). *International Technical Communication: How to Export Information about High Technology*. New York: John Wiley & Sons.

Holsapple, C. W., & Sasidharan, S. (2005). The dynamics of trust in B2C e-commerce: a research model and agenda. *Information Systems and e-Business Management*, 3, pp. 377–403.

Homeland Security NTARC News. (2009). Second Life® Raises Awareness with Disaster Zone Project. *National Terror Alert*. Retrieved on 11/29/09 from http://www.nationalterroralert.com/updates/2009/10/26/second-life-raises-awareness-with-disaster-zone-project/

Hongpaisanwiwat, C., & Lewis, M. (2003). *Attentional Effect of Animated Character*. INTERACT.

Horrigan, J. (2009, June 17). *Home Broadband Adoption 2009*. Retrieved August 23, 2009, from www.pewinternet.org: http://www.pewinternet.org/Reports/2009/10-Home-Broadband-Adoption-2009.aspx

Howard, J. (2008). *Quests: Design, Theory and History in Games and Narratives*. Wellesley: A.K. Peters.

Howes, A. Jones D. Payne S. & Ruddle R. (1999). Navigating Discontinuous Virtual Worlds. *Workshop on Spatial cognition in real and virtual environments at the Max Planck Institute*, Tuebingen.

Howgego, T. (2009). *Map of World of Warcraft online communities*, Retrieved September 18, 2009, from http://timhowgego.com/map-of-world-of-warcraft-online-communities.html

Huda. (2009). *The Islamic Calendar: The Originis of the Hijra Calnder Used by Muslims*. Retrieved December 18, 2009, from About.COM:Islam: http://islam.about.com/cs/calendar/a/hijrah_calendar.htm

Huizingh, E. K. (2000). The content and the design of website: An empirical study. *37* (3 (123-134)).

Hunt, E. & Waller, D. (1999). Orientation and wayfinding: A review. *ONR Technical Report*.

Hunter, V. (1997). *Business-to-Business Marketing: Creating a Community of Customers*. Lincolnwood, IL: NTC Business Books.

Hyman, P. (2008, June 5). *MMOG Business Models: Cancel That Subscription!* Retrieved September 3, 2009, from Gamasutra: http://www.gamasutra.com/view/feature/3688/mmog_business_models_cancel_that_.php

IARPA. (2009). *Reynard Proposer's Day Conference*. Retrieved on 11/28/09 from http://conference.brtrc.com/reynard/Overview.aspx

IBM. (2009). IBM Business Center. Retrieved on 12/13/09 from http://www.ibm.com/3dworlds/businesscenter/us/en/

IMVU. (2008). *IMVU*. Retrieved 17:49, June 8, 2008, from http://imvu.anshechung.com/index.php

Inc., W. (2009). Worlds Inc. Retrieved in January 2009, from http://www.worlds.com/

Independent Security Evaluators. (2009). *Exploiting Second Life*.

industrial applications. *Computer Graphics*, *17*, 671–677.

Inflection Point. (2009). *In Wikipedia, The Free Encyclopedia*. Retrieved 07:03, September 1, 2009, from http://en.wikipedia.org/w/index.php?title=Inflection_point&oldid=311230495

In-Q-Tel. (2009). *Forterra Systems*. Retrieved on 12/8/09 from http://www.iqt.org/technology-portfolio/forterra_systems.html.

International Shoe Company v. State of Washington, 326 U.S. 310 (1945).

ISO. (2005) retrieved 3. December 2009, from http://www.iso.org/iso/iso_catalogue/catalogue_tc/catalogue_detail.htm?csnumber=38560

Jackson, J. (2008). *Securing the virtual world*. Government Computer News. Retrieved on the world wide web November 5, 2009. http://gcn.com/Articles/2008/07/25/Securing-the-virtual-world.aspx?Page=1

Jackson, J. (2009). Navy Creates a Virtual World to Test Submarine Design. *Government Computer News*. Retrieved on 11/28/09 from http://www.gcn.com/Articles/2009/08/24/Data-visualization-sidebar-2-Navy-sub.aspx

Jackson, L., & Gauntlett, D. (2009). University of Westminister. Retreieved on 12/13/09 from http://www.childreninvirtualworlds.org.uk/pdfs/Gauntlett_and_Jackson_May_2008.pdf

Jagne, J., Guven, A. S., & Atakan, S. (2006). *Cross-cultural interface design strategy*. Springer-Verlag.

Jamal, A., & Ahmed, A. (2007). Socio-cultural Factors Influencing Consumer Adoption of Online Transactions. *Eighth World Congres on the Managment of eBusieness (WCMeB 2007).* IEEE Computer Society.

Jarok (1998). Guide to Roleplaying, *Tharsis Gate: Imaginary Realities*, Retrieved September 12, 2009, from http://www.tharsis-gate.org/articles/imaginary/GUIDET~1.HTM.

Jazeera, A. (2009, February 14th). *Al Jazeera News*. (Al-Jazeera.NET) Retrieved March 3rd, 2009, from Middle East News: http://english.aljazeera.net/news/middleeast/2009/02/200921411274294629.html

Jean, G. (2006). Game Branches Out into Real Combat Training. *National Defense NDIA Business and Technology Magazine*. Retrieved on 11/28/09 from http://www.nationaldefensemagazine.org/archive/2006/February/Pages/games_brance3042.aspx

Jevons, W. S. (1876). *Money and the Mechanism of Exchange*. New York: D. Appleton and Co.

Jiang, Z., & Benbasat, I. (2004). *Virtual Product Experience: Effects of Visual and Functional Control of Prodcuts on Perceived Diagnosticity and Flow in Electronic Shopping* (*Vol. 21*, p. 3). Jounral of Management Information Systems.

Johnson, D. R., & Post, D. G. (1996). Law and Borders - The Rise of Law in Cyberspace. *Stanford Law Review*, *48*, 1367. doi:10.2307/1229390

Johnson, M. (2009). A Second Life® Virtual Clinic for Medical Student Training. Retrieved on 12/13/09 from http://www.slideshare.net/magistra12/a-second-life-virtual-clinic-for-medical-student-training-presentation

Jonas [Avatar Name], D. (2006, May 16). *Town Hall: Philip Getting Friendly With the Feds*. Retrieved September 3, 2009, from The Alphaville Herald: http://www.secondlifeherald.com/slh/2006/05/town_hall_phili.html

Jones, S. K. (2006). *Creative Strategy in Direct and Interactive Marketing*. Chicago: RACOM Books.

Jones, S. K. (2009). *Business-to-Business Internet Marketing* (5th Edition ed.). New York: Maximum Press.

Jordache v. Hogg Wyld, Ltd., 828 F.2d 1482 (10th Cir. 1987)

Jordan, B. (2009). Island Getaways for Vets a 'Click' Away. Military.com. Retrieved on 12/1/09 from http://www.military.com/news/article/island-gataways-for-vets-a-click-away.html

Joslin, C., Giacomo, T. D., & Magnenat-Thalmann, N. (2004). Collaborative Virtual Environments, from Birth to Standardization. *IEEE Communications Magazine. Special Issue on Networked Virtual Environments*, *42*(4), 65–74.

Juul, J. (2005). *Half-Real: Video Games between Real Rules and Fictional Worlds*. Cambridge, MA: MIT Press.

Kametsu, A. (2007). Virtual worlds moving towards the 'multiverse' era, *Nomura Research Institute Papers*, October 1, 122

Kane, S., & Duranske, B. (2008). Virtual Worlds. Real World Issues. Retrieved on 12/3/09 from http://www.abanet.org/intelprop/magazine/LandslideSep08_Kane.pdf

Kardaras, D., & Karakostas, B. (2007). Virtual Communities in Banking Customer Retention. In *Dasgupta, S. Encyclopedia of Virtual Communities and Technologies*. Hershey, PA: Idea Group Reference.

Kasap, Z., & Magnenat-Thalmann, N. (2007). Intelligent virtual humans with autonomy and personality: State of the Art. *Intelligent Decision Technologies*, *1*(1-2), 3–15.

Keegan, V. (2009). Virtual Worlds are Getting a Second Life. *Guardian.co.uk,* 1. Retrieved August 16, 2009, from http://www.guardian.co.uk/technology/2009/jul/29/virtual-worlds

Keitt, T. (July 28, 2009). *The Real Value of Virtual Worlds*. Forrester Research. www.forrester.com/rb/research.

Kelly, R.V. (2004). *Massively Mutiplayer Online Role-Playing Games: The People, the Addiction and the Playing Experienc*e. Jefferson: McFarland & Co.

Kennedy, B. (2002). Uncle Same Wants You (To Play this Game). New York Times. Retrieved on 11/28/09 from http://www.nytimes.com/2002/07/11/technology/uncle-sam-wants-you-to-play-this-game.html?sec=&spon=&&scp=1&sq=wardynski&st=cse

Khronos, (2009a) retrieved 3. December 2009, from http://www.khronos.org/news/press/releases/khronos-launches-initiative-for-free-standard-for-accelerated-3d-on-web/

Khronos, (2009b) retrieved 3. December 2009, from http://www.khronos.org/news/press/releases/khronos-webgl-initiative-hardware-accelerated-3d-graphics-internet/

Khronos, (2009c) retrieved 3. December 2009, from http://www.khronos.org/collada/

Kids, G. (2009). The Power of Virtual Civics Education. Retrieved on 12/11/09 from http://www.holymeatballs.org/2009/12/sl_the_power_of_virtual_civics.html#more

Kim, Y. (2004). *Pedagogical agents as learning companions: the effects of agent affect and gender on student learning, interest, self-efficacy, and agent persona*. Department of Educational Psychology and Learning Systems.

Kim, J. W., Choi, J., Qualls, W., & Han, K. (2008). It takes a marketplace community to raise brand commitment: the role of online communities. *Journal of Marketing Management*, *24*(3-4), 409–431. doi:10.1362/026725708X306167

Kim, J., & Forsythe, S. (2008). *Adoption of Virtual Try-On Technology for Online Apparel Shopping*. Journal of Interactive Marketing, V22/2: Wiley Interscience.

Kincaid, J. (2009, December 1). *Facebook to Roll Out New Privacy Controls To Its 350 Million Users, Kills Regional Networks*. Retrieved December 1, 2009, from TechCrunch: http://www.techcrunch.com/2009/12/01/facebook-privacy-controls/

King, D., Delfabbro, P., & Griffiths, M. (2009 in press). Video game structural characteristics: A new psychological taxonomy. *International Journal of Mental Health and Addiction*.

King, R. (May 2, 2008). *The (Virtual) Global Office*. Business Week. http://www.businessweek.com/technology/content/may2008/tc2008052_842516.htm

King, W. (2009). Virtual Battle Space 2 Army Gaming system Debuts. Retrieved on 11/29/09 from http://www.army.mil/-news/2009/02/26/17502-virtual-battle-space-2-army-gaming-system-debuts/

Kirasic, K. C. (2000). Age differences in adults' spatial abilities, learning environmental layout, and wayfinding behavior. *Spatial Cognition and Computation*, *2*, 117–134. doi:10.1023/A:1011445624332

Klastrup, L. (2003). A Poetics of Virtual Worlds. *Proceedings of the Fifth International Digital Arts and Culture Conference, RMIT*.

Kloss, J. H. (2010). *X3D - Programmierung interaktiver 3D-Anwendungen für das Internet*. Munich: Addison-Wesley Verlag.

Kloss, J. H., Rockwell, R., Szabo, K., & Duchrow, M. (1998). *VRML97 - Der neue Standard fuer interaktive 3D-Welten im World Wide Web.* Munich: Addison Wesley Longman Verlag GmbH.

Kock, N. (2008). E-Collaboration and E-Commerce. In *Virtual Worlds: The potential of Second life and World of Warcraft. International Journal of e-collaboration*. Hershey, PA: IGI Global.

Koda, T., & Maes, P. (1996). Agents with faces: the effect of personification. In *Proc. of the IEEE International Workshop on Robot and Human Communication*, 189-194.

Koh, G., Wiegand, T. E., Garnett, R., Durlach, N., & Cunningham, B. S. (1999). Use of Virtual Environments for Acquiring Configurational Knowledge about Specific RealWorld Spaces. *Preliminary Experiment*, *8*(6), 632–656.

Kooijmans, T., & Rauterberg, M. (2007). *Cultural Computing and the Self Concept: Towards Unconscious Metamorphosis*. Amsterdam: IFIP.

Koster, R. (2009). *Online World Timeline*. Retrieved in January 2009, from http://www.raphkoster.com/gaming/mudtimeline.shtml

Kozinets, R. (1999). E-Tribalised Marketing?: The Strategic Implications of Virtual Communities of Consumption. *The Journal of Consumer Research*, *29*(3), 20–38.

Kramer, R. (1999). Trust and distrust in organizations: Emerging perspectives, enduring questions. *Annual Review of Psychology*, *50*, 569–598. doi:10.1146/annurev.psych.50.1.569

Kroeber, A., & Kluckhohn, C. (1952). *Culture: A critical review of concepts and definitions*. Cambridge, Massachusetts: Peabody Museum.

Kuehhirt, U., & Rittermann, M. (2007). *Interaktive audiovisuelle Medien*. Munich: Carl Hanser Verlag.

Kuipers, B. J. (1975). A frame for frames: Representing knowledge for recognition. In Bobrow, D. G., & Collins, A. (Eds.), *Representation and understanding: Studies in cognitive science*. New York: Academic Press.

Kumar, M., & Remo, C. (2008, August 26). *CCP Economist on EVE Online's 'Pure Capitalist' Market*. Retrieved September 3, 2009, from Gamasutra: http://www.gamasutra.com/php-bin/news_index.php?story=19844

Kurzweil, R. (2001, March 7). Kurzweilai.net. Retrieved September 2, 2009, from Kurzweilai.net Web site: http://www.kurzweilai.net/articles/art0134.html

Kzero, (2009) retrieved 29. November 2009, from http://www.kzero.co.uk/radar.php

L.L. Bean Inc. v. Drake Publishers Inc., 811 F.2d 26 (1st Cir.), appeal dismissed, 107 S.Ct. 3254 (1987)

Lab, L. (2009). How Meeting In Second Life® Transformed IBM's Technology Elite Into Virtual World Believers. *Second Life® Grid Web Site*. Retrieved August 16, 2009, from http://secondlifegrid.net.s3.amazonaws.com/docs/Second_Life_Case_IBM_EN.pdf

Lakin v. Prudential Securities, Inc., 348 F.3d 704 (8thCir. 2003)

Lamont, I. (2009). Second Life® Enterprise to bring security, enterprise apps to virtual meetings. The Industry Standard. Retrieved on 12/1/09 from http://www.thestandard.com/news/2009/11/05/second-life-enterprise-bring-security-enterprise-apps-world-activities.

Lampinen, J., Copeland, S., & Neuschatz, J. (2001). Recollections of things schematic: rooms schemas revisited. *Cognition*, *27*, 1211–1222.

Laurent, A. (2008). DSHS Joins the Virtual World. Next. Gov. Retrieved on 11/30/09 from http://www.nextgov.com/nextgov/ng_20080514_8611.php

Lawrence, E., Lawrence, J., Newton, S., Dann, S., Corbitt, B., & Thanasankit, T. (2003). *Internet Commerce: Digital Models for Business* (3rd ed.). Milton: John Wiley & Sons.

Leadbeater, C. (2009). *We-Think*. London: Profile Books.

Lefebvre, R. C. (2009, February). *Demographics of Social Network Users*. Retrieved August 29, 2009, from http://socialmarketing.blogs.com/r_craiig_lefebvres_social//2009/02/demographics-of-social-network-users.html

Lehdonvirta, V. (2009). Virtual item sales as a revenue model: identifying attributes that drive purchase decisions. *Electronic Commerce Research*, *9*(1/2), 97–113. doi:10.1007/s10660-009-9028-2

Lerner, G. (1987). *The Creation of Patriarchy (Women and History)*. Oxford, UK: Oxford University Press.

Level design. (2008). In *Wikipedia, The Free Encyclopedia*. Retrieved June 9, 2008, from http://en.wikipedia.org/w/index.php?title=Level_design&oldid=209252053

Levy, R. (1957). *The Social Structure of Islam*. New York: Cambridge University Press.

Li, C., & Bernoff, J. (2008). *Groundswell: Winning in a World Transformed by Social Technologies*. Boston: Harvard Business Press.

Li, C., & Bernoff, J. (2008). *Groundswell - Winning in a World Transformed by Social Technologies*. Boston, Massachusetts: Harvard Business School Publishing.

Liedke, M. (February 11, 2009). Facebook appraisal pegs company's value at #3.7B. Associated Press. Retrieved on the world wide web December 5, 2009. http://www.sfgate.com/cgi-bin/article.cgi?f=/n/a/2009/02/10/state/n230703S73.DTL

Life, S. (2009). Wikipedia. Retrieved on 12/8/09 from [1]http://ru.wikipedia.org/wiki/Second_Life

Life, S. (2009a). *Second Life® Architecture*. Retrieved in January 2009, from http://wiki.secondlife.com/wiki/Structural_Design_Overview

Life, S. (2009b). *Second Life®*. Retrieved in January 2009, from http://www.secondlife.com

Life, S. ® (2009b). *Military Lands. Second Life® Wiki*. Retrieved on 12/1/09 from http://wiki.secondlife.com/wiki/Military_Lands

Life, S. ®. (2009a). Resident: Maccus McCullough. Retrieved on 11/28/09 from http://world.secondlife.com/resident/f365f959-24e9-46cc-a2ed-43208a4fbf7b

Linden [Harper], R. (2007, July 25). *Wagering in Second Life®: New Policy*. Retrieved September 3, 2009, from Second Life® Blogs: Features: https://blogs.secondlife.com/community/features/blog/2007/07/26/wagering-in-second-life-new-policy

Linden Research, Inc. (2003, November 14). *Press Release: Second Life® Residents To Own Digital Creations*. Retrieved September 3, 2009, from Linden Lab: http://lindenlab.com/pressroom/releases/03_11_14

Linden Research, Inc. (2009, January 15). *Second Life® Residents logged nearly 400 million hours in 2008, growing 61% over 2007*. Retrieved September 3, 2009, from Second Life®: https://blogs.secondlife.com/community/features/blog/2009/01/15/second-life-residents-logged-nearly-400-million-hours-in-2008-growing-61-over-2007

Linden Research, Inc. (2009, September 3). *Economic Statistics (Raw Data Files)*. Retrieved September 3, 2009, from Second Life®: http://secondlife.com/statistics/economy-data.php

Linden Research, Inc. (2009, September 3). Retrieved September 3, 2009, from Linden Lab: http://lindenlab.com/

Linden Research, Inc. (2009, September 3). *Terms of Service | Second Life®*. Retrieved September 3, 2009, from Second Life®: http://secondlife.com/corporate/tos.php

Linden Research, Inc. (2009, September 3). *Value Added Tax*. Retrieved September 3, 2009, from Second Life®: http://secondlife.com/corporate/vat.php

Linden Research, Inc. (2009, September 3). *What Is Second Life®?* Retrieved September 3, 2009, from Second Life®: http://secondlife.com/whatis/?lang=en-US

Linden, T. (2009). The Second Life® Economy - First Quarter 2009 in Detail. *Second Life® Web Site*. Retrieved August 16, 2009, from https://blogs.secondlife.com/community/features/blog/2009/04/16/the-second-life-economy--first-quarter-2009-in-detail

Lipsky, G. (1952). *Its people, its society, its culture*. Saudi Arabia: HRAF Press.

Liu, Y., & Ginther, D. (1999). Cognitive Styles and Distance Education. *Online Journal of Distance Learning Administration*, *2*(3).

Liu, K. (2000). Semiotics. In *Information Systems Engineering*. Cambridge, UK: Cambridge University Press.

Lommel, A., & Ray, R. (2007). *The Globalisation Industry Primer: An Introduction to preparing you business and products for success in international markets*. Switzerland: The Localisation Industry Standards Association.

Lowood, H. (2005). Real-Time Performance: Machinima and Games Studies. *International Digital Media and Arts Journal*, *2*(1), 10–17.

Lowood, H. (2006). High Performance Play: The Making of Machinima. *Journal of Media Practice*, *7*(1), 25–42. doi:10.1386/jmpr.7.1.25/1

Lusch, R. F., & Vargo, S. L. (2006). Service-dominant logic: reactions, reflections and refinements. *Marketing Theory*, *6*(3), 281–288. doi:10.1177/1470593106066781

Lynch, D. C., & Rose, M. T. (Eds.). (1993). *Internet System Handbook*. Reading, MA: Addison-Wesley.

Lynch, K. (1960). *The Image of the city*. The MIT press.

Lynch, C. (January 9, 2008). *This is Not a Game: Virtual Worlds Coming to Your Business, Forrester Predicts*. Retrieved on the world wide web August 2, 2009. http://www.cio.com/article/170850/This_Is_Not_a_Game_Virtual_Worlds_Coming_to_Your_Business_Forrester_Predicts

M.A. Mortenson Co., Inc. v. Timberline Software Corp., 970 P.2d 803 (Wash.App. 1999).

Mack, D.J. (2008). iTax: An analysis of the laws and policies behind the taxation of property transactions in a virtual world, *Administrative Law Review*, Summer, 60, 3

Mackey, S. (2003). *The Saudis: Inside The Desert Kingdom*. New York: W.W.Norton and Company Ltd.

Maes, P., Darrell, T., Blumberg, B., & Pentland, A. (1995). The ALIVE system: full-body interaction with autonomous agents. In *Proceedings of Computer Animation '95*. 11-18, 209.

Maguire, E. A. (1999). Burgess N. & O'Keefe J. (1999) Human spatial navigation: cognitive maps, sexual dimorphism, and neural substrates. *Current Opinion in Neurobiology*, *9*, 171–177. doi:10.1016/S0959-4388(99)80023-3

Maguire, E. A., Frackowiak, R. S. J., & Frith, C. D. (1996). Recalling Routes around London: Activation of the Right Hippocampus in Taxi Drivers. *The Journal of Neuroscience*, *17*(18), 7103–7110.

Maguire, E. A. Gadian D.G. Johnsrude I.S. Good C.D. Ashburner J. Frackowiak R.S.J. & Frith C.D. (2000). Navigation related structural change in the hippocampi of taxi drivers. *Proceedings of the national academy of science* (USA), 97(8)

Makena Technology, Inc. (2009). *There Member Agreement*. Retrieved September 3, 2009, from There.com: http://www.there.com/tos.html

Makena Technology, Inc. (2009). *What is There?* Retrieved September 3, 2009, from There.com: http://www.prod.there.com/whatIsThere.html

Mania K. Robinson A. & Brandt K.R. (2005). The effect of memory schemas on object recognition in virtual environments. *Presence: Teleoperators and Virtual Environments archive, 14*(5), 606 – 615

Marcus, A. (2001). *Aaron Marcos*.

Martin, J. (2008). Consuming Code: Use-Value, Exchange Value, and the Role of Virtual Goods in Second Life®. *Journal of Virtual Worlds Research*, *1*(2).

Matheson, K. (2008). Army Experience Center offers simulations at Mall. USA Today. Retrieved on 11/28/09 from http://www.usatoday.com/news/military/2008-08-30-army-experience-center_N.htm?csp=34

Mathews, M. H. (1992). *Making Sense of Place: Children's Understanding of Large Scale Environments*. Hertfordshire, England: Harvester Wheatsheaf.

McCue, A. (2008). Beware the insider security threat. CIO Jury Articles. Retrieved on 12/3/09 from http://www.silicon.com/ciojury/0,3800003161,39188671,00.htm

McCullough, A. (2009), Wii Combat Game Features Marines. Marine Times. Retrieved on 11/28/09 from http://www.marinecorpstimes.com/news/2009/10/marine_wii_101809w/

McGuire, C. (2009). Online Degrees versus Traditional Degrees. Retrieved on 12/8/09 from http://ezinarticles.com/?online-degrees-versus-traditional-degrees

McMillan, R. (December 4, 2009). *HSBC exposed sensitive bankruptcy data*. Computerworld. Retrieved on the world wide web December 5, 2009. http://www.computerworld.com/s/article/9141834/HSBC_exposed_sensitive_bankruptcy_data?taxonomyId=17

Meadows, M. S. (2008). *I, AVATAR: The Culture and Consequences of Having a Second Life*. Berkeley: New Riders.

Mehrabian, A. (1968). Communication without words. *Psychology Today*, *2*(4), 53–56.

Meska, B. (2007). *Virtual Doctors: Medical Training in Second Life*. Retrieved on 12/13/09 from http://juniordr.com/world/index.php/20071219160/Life/Virtual-doctors-medical-training-in-Second-Life.html

Messick, S. (1976). *Individuality in learning*. San Francisco: Jossey-Bass.

Messinger, P., Stroulia, E., Lyons, K., Bone, M., Niu, R., & Smirnov, K. (2009). *Virtual worlds - past, present, and future: New directions in social computing* (*Vol. 47*). ScienceDirect.

Metaverse, U. (2009). *Metaverse U 1.0*. Retrieved August 16, 2009, from http://metaverse.stanford.edu/metaverse-u-1-0-archive/conference-videos/conference-videos

Microsystems, S. (2009). MPK20: Sun's Virtual Workplace. Retrieved on 12/12/09 from http://research.sun.com/projects/mc/mpk20.html

Military.com. (2008). Magazine focuses on Army Gaming. Retrieved on 11/28/09 from http://www.military.com/entertainment/games/game-news/magazine-focuses-on-army-gaming

Miller Bros. Co. v. State of Maryland, 347 U.S. 340 (1954).

Miller, C. C., & Stone, B. (2009, November 6). *Virtual Goods Start Bringing Real Paydays*. Retrieved November 23, 2009, from The New York Times: http://www.nytimes.com/2009/11/07/technology/internet/07virtual.html

Ministry of Commerce, The People's Republic of China. (2009, June 29). *China bars use of virtual money for trading in real goods*. Retrieved September 3, 2009, from Ministry of Commerce, The People's Republic of China: http://english.mofcom.gov.cn/aarticle/newsrelease/commonnews/200906/20090606364208.html

Moffat, S. D., Hampson, E., & Hatzipantelis, M. (1998). Navigation in a "virtual" maze: sex differences and correlation with psychometric measures of spatial ability in humans. *Evolution and Human Behavior*, *19*, 73–78. doi:10.1016/S1090-5138(97)00104-9

Mohd Yusof, S. A., & Zakaria, N. (2007). Islamic perspective: virtual worlds as a western - centric technology. *38* (4).

Mokitown. (2009). *Mokitown*. Retrieved in January 2009, from http://www.mokitown.com/mokitown_prehome/home_en.jsp.

Monopoly. Retrieved from http://www.hasbro.com/monopoly/en_US/ (Hasbro, © 2008)

Montagu, E. (1955). *The Man Who Never Was*. Penguin Books.

Montello, D. R. (2005) Navigation. In P. Shah & A. Miyake (Eds.), The Cambridge Handbook of Visuospatial Thinking. Cambridge University Press, 257-294.

Morales, J. T. P. M. R. M. (2008). *Inteligencia Artificial: Técnicas, métodos y aplicaciones*. New York: McGraw-Hill.

Moran, M. (2008, October 13). *Virtual Worlds Are Going Private*. Retrieved September 3, 2009, from Internet Evolution: http://www.internetevolution.com/author.asp?section_id=698&doc_id=164951

Morgan, R. M., & Hunt, S. D. (1994). The commitment-trust theory of relationship marketing. *Journal of Marketing*, *58*(3), 20–38. doi:10.2307/1252308

Morgenstern, J. (2007, February 18). *Gift gifts on Facebook!* Retrieved August 23, 2009, from www.facebook.com: http://blog.facebook.com/blog.php?post=2234372130

Morningstar, C., & Farmer, F. R. (1991). The lessons of Lucasfilm's habitat. 273-302.

Morningstar, C., & Farmer, F. R. (1991). The Lessons of Lucasfilm's Habitat. In Benedikt (Ed.), *Cyberspace: First Steps*. Cambridge, MA: MIT Press. (also Retrieved June 9, 200 from http://www.fudco.com/chip/lessons.html

Mountjoy, B. (2008). When Virtual Meets Reality: WoW, Second Life® May Become Targets of Terrorists, CIA. Firefox News. Retrieved on 11/29/09 from http://firefox.org/news/articles/1580/1/When-Virtual-Meets-Reality-WoW-Second-Life-May-Become-Targets-of-Terrorists-CIA/Page1.html

Moya, L. J., & Tolk, A. (2007). *Towards a taxonomy of agents and multi-agent systems.* Paper presented at the SpringSim '07: Proceedings of the 2007 spring simulation multiconference.

MuddLyman Sales & Service Corp. v. United Parcel Service, Inc., 236 F.

Mulligan, J. (1999). History of Online Games, *Tharsis Gate: Imaginary Realities*, Retrieved September 14, 2009, from http://www.tharsis-gate.org/articles/imaginary/HISTOR~1.HTM

Musseum, D. C. (2009). Maze War 30th anniversary. Retrieved in January 2009, from http://www.digibarn.com/history/04-VCF7-MazeWar/index.html.

Mutual of Omaha Insurance Co. v. Novak, 836 F.2d 397 (8thCir.1987).

Nadin, M., & Zakia, R. (1994). *Creating Effective Advertising Using Semiotics* (Vols. 0-913069-46-9). New York: The Consultant Press, LTD.

National Aeronautics and Space Administration. (2009). CoLab Virtual Overview. Retrieved on 12/8/09 from http://colab.arc.nasa.gov/virtual

National Bellas Hess, Inc. v. Dept. of Revenue of the State of Illinois, 386 U.S. 753 (1967)

National Conference of Commissioners on Uniform State Laws, Revised Uniform Arbitration Act (2000).

National Oceanic and Atmospheric Administration. (2009). NOAA Virtual World. Retrieved on 12/8/09 from http://www.esrl.noaa.gov/outreach/#sl

National Priorities Project. (2007a). Spending on Military Recruiting. Retrieved on 11/27/09 from http://www.nationalpriorities.org/charts/Spending-on-Military-Recruiting-2.html

National Priorities Project. (2007b). *Military Recruiting 2007: Army Misses Benchmarks by Greater Margin.* Retrieved on 11/30/09 from http://www.nationalpriorities.org/militaryrecruiting2007

Naughton, L. (2008). Magic, Myth and Mayhem: Tribalization in the Digital Age. In *Adams, T.L. & Smith, S.A. (2008). Electronic Tribes.* Austin, TX: University of Texas Press.

Neb.Rev.Stat.§87-302(a)(14); 18 Pa.Cons.Stat.§4107(a)(10).

Neilson, J. (1998). *Useit.com.* Retrieved 05 07, 2009, from The Web Usage Paradox: Why do people use something this bad?: http://www.useit.com/alertbox/980809.html

Newman, J. (2004). *Videogames.* London: Routledge.

Newman, E. L., Caplan, J. B., Kirschen, P., Korolev, I. O., Sekuler, R., & Kahana, M. J. (2007). Learning your way around town: How virtual taxicab drivers learn to use both layout and landmark information. *Cognition, 104,* 231–253. doi:10.1016/j.cognition.2006.05.013

News, B. B. C. (2006). 'Worm" Attack Second Life® World. BBC News. Retrieved on 11/30/09 from http://news.bbc.co.uk/2/hi/technology/6164806.stm

News, B. B. C. (2006, November 20). *'Worm' attacks Second Life® world.* Retrieved September 3, 2009, from BBC News: http://news.bbc.co.uk/2/hi/technology/6164806.stm

NextMed. (2009). *MMVR18.* Retrieved on 12/13/09 from http://www.nextmed.com/index.html

Ng, B. D., & Wiemer-Hastings, P. (2005). Addiction to the Internet and Online Gaming. *Cyberpsychology & Behavior, 8*(2), 110–113. doi:10.1089/cpb.2005.8.110

Nino, T. (2008, April 9). *Second Life® Daily News.* Retrieved September 3, 2009, from Massively: http://www.massively.com/2008/04/09/second-life-daily-news/

NMC. (2009). *Second Life® Virtual Early High School Program at East Carolina University.* Retrieved on 12/11/09 from http://222.nmc.org/spotlight/member/7320

Noane, E. (2008). One Avatar, Many Worlds: Companies want to let users carry their avatar identities online. *MIT Technology Review*, Retrieved September 25, 2009, from http://www.technologyreview.com/web/20529/page1/

Nuttall, C. (2008). Second Life's maiden voyage across the metaverse, *Financial Times*, Retrieved July, 8, 2008, from http://blogs.ft.com/techblog/2008/07/second-lifes-maiden-voyage-across-the-metaverse/

Nuttall, C. (2009, January 21). *Second Life® CEO goes virtual shopping.* Retrieved September 3, 2009, from Financial Times Tech Blog: http://blogs.ft.com/techblog/2009/01/second-life-ceo-goes-virtual-goods-shopping/

Nwana, H. S. (1996). Software Agents: An Overview. *The Knowledge Engineering Review*, *11*(3), 205–244. doi:10.1017/S026988890000789X

O'Harrow, J. Robert. (2008). Spies Battleground Turns Virtual. The Washington Post. Retrieved on 11/29/09 from http://www.washingtonpost.com/wp-dyn/content/article/2008/02/05/AR2008020503144.html?wpisrc=newsletter&wpisrc=newsletter&wpisrc=newsletter

O'Neil, M. (2009). *Cyber Chiefs: Autonomy and Authority in Online Tribes*. London: Pluto Press.

Of Consumers Have Purchased Virtual Goods. (2009, July 30). Retrieved September 3, 2009, from Virtual Goods News: http://www.virtualgoodsnews.com/2009/07/12-of-consumers-have-purchased-virtual-goods.html

Official, L. L. (2009, October 22). *Linden Lab Official: System Requirements*. Retrieved December 15, 2009, from System Requirements: http://secondlife.com/support/system-requirements/

Olson, N. E. (2008). *Annual Report to Congress Volume 1 (Publication 2104).* United States Department of the Treasury, Internal Revenue Service. Internal Revenue Service.

On Sugar. (2008, August 8th). Retrieved March 3rd, 2009, from Your Two Cents: Could Female-Only Banks Be Benificial?: http://www.savvysugar.com/1851766.

Ondrejka, C. (2005, September 18). *Aviators, Moguls, Fashionistas and Barons: Economics and Ownership in Second Life®.* Retrieved September 3, 2009, from Social Science Research Network: http://ssrn.com/abstract=614663

O'Neill, N. (2009, July 16). *Zynga Expands The Gap, Surpassing 60 Million Monthly Active Users.* Retrieved August 23, 2009, from All Facebook: http://www.allfacebook.com/2009/07/zynga-expands-the-gap-surpassing-60-million-monthly-active-users/

OpenSim. Retrieved from http://www.opensimulator.org. (OpenSimulator, © 2007)

OpenSimulator. (2009) retrieved 1. December 2009, from http://opensimulator.org/wiki/Main_Page

O'Reilly, T. (2005, September 30). *What Is Web 2.0: Design Patterns and Business Models for the Next Generation of Software.* Retrieved August 23, 2009, from Oreilly: http://oreilly.com/web2/archive/what-is-web-20.htm

Ortiz, A. (2008). *Avatars for emotional interaction.* University of the Basque Country.

Papagiannidis, S., Bourlakis, M., & Li, F. (2008). Making real money in virtual worlds: MMORPGs and emerging business opportunities, challenges and ethical implications in metaverses. *Technological Forecasting and Social Change*, *75*, 610–622. doi:10.1016/j.techfore.2007.04.007

Pargman, D., & Jakobsson, P. (2006). The Magic is Gone: A Critical Examination of the Gaming Situation." In *Proceedings of Mediaterra: Gaming Realities*, October 4-8, Athens.

Parsons, M. (2007, October 26). *The Future of Virtual Worlds: The Passionate Fans of Online Worlds Such as Second Life® are Looking Forward to a Bright and Intriguing Future.* Retrieved August 29, 2009, from technology.timesoneline.co.uk: http://www.islamonline.net/servlet/Satellite?c=Article_C&cid=1248078566632&pagename=Zone-English-HealthScience%2FHSELayout

Pask, G. (1979). *Final report of S.S.R.C. Research programme HR 2708*. Richmond (Surrey): System Research Ltd.

Passini, R. (1984). *Wayfinding in Architecture*. New York: Van Nostrand Reinhold Company Inc.

Patents: Patent Cooperation Treaty (1970).

Pechar, E. (2008). *Virtual Worlds and Education.* Office of Policy Analysis and Research. Georgia Tech Research Institute.

Pelagatti, G., Negri, M., Belussi, A., & Migliorini, S. (2009). From the conceptual design of spatial constraints to their implementation in real systems. In *Proceedings of the 17th ACM SIGSPATIAL international Conference on Advances in Geographic information Systems (Seattle, Washington, November 04 - 06, 2009).* (GIS '09. ACM, pp 448-451)New York, NY.

Perry, D. (2009). How video games can sweep in the cash. *Business Week*, Retrieved September 22, 2009, from http://images.businessweek.com/ss/08/08/0815_make_money_from_games/1.htm

Pine, D. S., Grun, J., Maguire, E. A., Burgess, N., Zarahn, E., & Koda, V. (2002). Neurodevelopmental Aspects of Spatial Navigation: A Virtual Reality fMRI Study. *NeuroImage*, *15*, 396–406. doi:10.1006/nimg.2001.0988

Platoni, K. (2008, January/February). *Seeing Is Believing.* Retrieved September 3, 2009, from Stanford Magazine: http://www.stanfordalumni.org/news/magazine/2008/janfeb/features/virtual.html

Plus Eight Star. (2009, April 8). *Virtual Goods in Asia: it's even more than you think!* Retrieved September 3, 2009, from Plus Eight Star: http://www.plus8star.com/2009/04/08/virtual-goods-in-asia-its-even-more-than-you-think-25-times-usa/

Pogue, D. (2009, July 17). Some ebooks are more equal than others- pogue's posts blog-nytimes.com. Retrieved September 2, 2009, from The new york times Web site: http://pogue.blogs.nytimes.com/2009/07/17/some-e-books-are-more-equal-than-others/

Polsson, K. (2009). *Chronology of Video Game Systems*, Retrieved September 20, 2009, from http://www.islandnet.com/~kpolsson/vidgame/vid2007.htm

Power Level. (2008). Retrieved June 8, 2008, from http://www.power-level.net/

Prahalad, C. K., & Ramaswamy, V. (2003). The new frontier of experience innovation. *MIT Sloan Management Review*, *44*(4), 12–18.

Prendinger, H., Ma, C., Yingzi, J., Nakasone, A., & Ishizuka, M. (2005). Understanding the effect of life-like interface agents through users' eye movements. *ICMI '05: Proceedings of the 7th international conference on Multimodal interfaces*, 108-115.

Prensky, M. (2002). Digital Natives. Digital Immigrants. Learners Together. Retrieved on 11/30/09 from http://www.learnerstogether.net/digital-natives-digital-immigrants/53

PSINet, Inc. v. Chapman, 362 F.3d 227 (4^{th}Cir. 2004).

Qiu, L., Jiang, Z., & Benbasat, I. (2006). *Real Experience in a Virtual Store: Designing for Presence in Online Shopping.* Pacific Asia Conference on Information Systems (PACIS 2006).

Quill Corp. v. North Dakota, 504 U.S. 298 (1992).

Rambo, K., Liu, K., & Nakata, K. (2009). *The Socio-Cultural Factors Influencing Online Female Consumers in Saudi Arabia* (Vol. International Conference on Computational Science and Engineering). Vancouver, IEEE International Conference on Social Computing: IEEE Computer Society.

Rayport, J. F., & Sviokla, J. J. (1994). Managing in the market-space. *Harvard Business Review*, *72*(6), 141–150.

ReactionGrid. (2009, September 3). *Economy.* Retrieved September 3, 2009, from ReactionGrid: http://reactiongrid.com/WorldCreation/Economy.aspx

Reed, C. (2009). Why Must You Be Mean to Me? - Crime, Punishment and Online Personality. *Queen Mary School of Law Legal Studies, 2009* (9).

Reimer, J. (2006, June 12). *Blizzard bans 30,000 World of Warcraft accounts.* Retrieved September 3, 2009, from Ars Technica: http://arstechnica.com/old/content/2006/06/7033.ars

Reno v. American Civil Liberties Union, 521 U.S. 844 (1997) (held that the Communications Decency Act was unconstitutional).

Reno v. American Civil Liberties Union, 521 U.S. 844, 881-882 (1997).

Report: Virtual Worlds Growth to Skyrocket. (2009, June 15). Retrieved September 3, 2009, from Virtual Worlds News: http://www.virtualworldsnews.com/2009/06/report-virtual-worlds-growth-to-skyrocket-.html

Retrieved on the World Wide Web November 5, 2009. http://securityevaluators.com/content/case-studies/sl/

Reuters, E. (reporter) (2007). *Second Life.* Retrieved June 8, 2008, from http://secondlife.reuters.com/stories/2007/03/27/amsterdam-sold-for-us50000/

Rev.Proc. 69-21, 1969-2 Cum.Bull. 303;

Rev.Proc. 97-50, 1997-2 Cum.Bull. 525.

Rheingold, H. (1993). *The Virtual Community: Homesteading in the Electronic Frontier.* New York: Harper Collins.

Rheingold, H. (2000). *The virtual community: Homesteading on the electronic frontier.* Cambridge, MA: MIT Press (Earlier version of this book appeared in 1993, and 1994).

Rice, R. E. (1992). Contexts of research on organizational computer-mediated communication: a recursive review. In Lea, M. (Ed.), *Contexts of computer-mediated communication* (pp. 113–144). New York: Harvester Wheatsheaf.

Richeson, R. (2008). AETC opens virtual doors to MyBase. U.S. Air Force. Retrieved on 11/29/09 from http://www.af.mil/news/story.asp?id=123126243

Ridings, C. M. (2006). Virtual communities and social capital theory. In *Dasgupta, S. Encyclopedia of Virtual Communities and Technologies*. Hershey, PA: Idea Group Reference.

Riley, D. (2007, July 25). *Second Life® Bans Gambling Following FBI Investigation.* Retrieved September 3, 2009, from TechCrunch: http://www.techcrunch.com/2007/07/25/second-life-bans-gambling-following-fbi-investigation/

Riva, G., & Gambrini, L. (2000). Virtual reality in telemedicine. *Telemedicine Journal*, *6*, 327–340. doi:10.1089/153056200750040183

Roadmap, M. (2009). *Metaverse Roadmap Web Site.* Retrieved August 16, 2009, from http://www.metaverseroadmap.org/

Roberts, P., & Cunningham, J. (2008). *Feminisation of Brands*. Haymarket Business Publications Ltd.

Robertson, G. G., Card, S. K., & MacKinlay, J. D. (1993). Nonimmersive Virtual Reality. *Computer*, *26*(2), 81–83. doi:10.1109/2.192002

Robertson, I. T. (1985). Human information processing strategies and style. *Behaviour & Information Technology*, *4*(1), 19–29. doi:10.1080/01449298508901784

Rose, F. D., Attree, E. A., Brooks, B. M., Parslow, D. M., & Penn, P. R. (2000). Training in virtual environments: transfer to real world tasks and equivalence to real task training Authors. *Ergonomics*, *43*(4), 494–511. doi:10.1080/001401300184378

Rose, F. D., & Foreman, N. P. (1999). Virtual reality. *The Psychologist*, *12*, 551–554.

Rosenberg, D. (2009, September 14). *Report: Virtual currency No. 1 digital goods purchase.* Retrieved September 14, 2009, from CNET News: http://news.cnet.com/8301-13846_3-10351799-62.html

Ruddle, R. A., Payne, S. J., & Jones, D. M. (1997). Navigating buildings in "desktop" virtual environments: Experimental investigations using extended navigational experience. *Journal of Experimental Psychology. Applied*, *3*, 143–159. doi:10.1037/1076-898X.3.2.143

Rufer-Bach, K. (2009). *The Second Life® Grid - The Official Guide to Communication, Collaboration, and Community Engagement.* Indianapolis, Indiana: Wiley.

Rush, Mark & Paglia, Lucas.(2001). *Preventing, Investigating and Prosecuting Computer Attacks and E-Commerce Crimes: Public or Private Initiatives and Other Federal Reserves.* 18 Computer & Online Industry Litigation Reporter, 16.

Russo, P., & Boor, S. (1993). How fluent is your interface? Designing for international users. *The Conference on Human Factors in Computing Systems. 342-347.* Boston: Addison Wesley Longman Publishing.

Rutherford, M. (November 4, 2009). *The Promise and Perils of Virtual Worlds (Part 2).* Maxping. Retrieved on the world wide web November 5, 2009. http://maxping.org/business/real-life/the-promise-and-perils-of-virtual-worlds-%28part-2%29.aspx

Ryan, R. M., Rigby, C., & Przybylski, A. (2006). The Motivational Pull of Video Games: A Self-Determination Theory Approach. *Motivation and Emotion*, *30*(4), 347–363. doi:10.1007/s11031-006-9051-8

Rymaszewski, M., Au, W. J., Wallace, M., Winters, C., Ondrejka, C., & Batsone-Cunningham, B. (2007). *Second Life: the official guide*. New Jersey: Wiley Publishing.

Sait, S. M., Al-Tawil, K. M., & Hussien, S. A. (2004). *E-Commerce in Saudi Arabia: Adoption and Perspectives* (Vol. 12). Dahran: AJIS.

Sait, S., Al-Tawil, K., Sanaullah, S., & Faheemuddin, M. (2007). *Impact of Internet Usage in Saudi Arabia: A Social Perspective.* International Journal of Information Technology and Web Engineering.

Salen, K., & Zimmerman, E. (2004). *Rules of Play: Game Design Fundamentals*. Cambridge, MA: MIT Press.

Salthouse, T., Donald, K., & Saults, S. (1990). Age, Self Assessed Health Status and Cognition. *Journal of Gerontology*, *45*(4), 156–160.

Salthouse T.A. (1992). Why do adult age differences increase with task complexity?, 28, 905–918.

Sanchez, J. (2009). A social history of virtual worlds. *Library Technology Reports*, *45*(2), 9–12.

Sandstrome, N. J., Kaufman, J., & Huettel, S. A. (1998). Males and females use different distal cues in a virtual environment navigation task. *Brain Research. Cognitive Brain Research*, *6*, 351–360. doi:10.1016/S0926-6410(98)00002-0

Sawhney, M., & Prandelli, E. (2000). Communities of Creation: Managing Distributed Innovation in Turbulent Markets. *California Management Review*, *42*(4), 24–54.

Schmeck, R. R. (1988). *Learning strategies and learning styles*. Plenum Press.

Schock. (2008). Strengths and Challenges of Medication Education in Virtual Worlds. Retrieved on 12/13/09 from http://www.shockmd.com/2008/10/25/strengths-and-challenges-of-medical-education-in-virtual-worlds/

Schrader, P., & McCreery, M. (2008). The acquisition of skill and expertise in massively multiplayer online games. *Educational Technology Research and Development*, *56*(5/6), 557–574. doi:10.1007/s11423-007-9055-4

Schrock, K. (2007). Lighthouse Learning Island. Retrieved on 12/11/09 from http://kathyschrock.net/blog/2007/06/lighthouse-learning-island.html

Schroeder, R. (2008). Defining Virtual Worlds and Virtual Environments. *Journal of Virtual Worlds Research*, *1*(1).

Schroeder, R. (2002). Copresence and Interaction in Virtual Environments: An Overview of the Range of Issues. In *Proceedings of the 5th Annual International Workshop: Presence*, 274-295.

ScienceSim. Retrieved from http://www.sciencesim.com.

Scripto v. Carson, 362 U.S. 207 (1960)

Second Life® Blogs. (2006). *Urgent Security Announcement. Second Life®.* Retrieved on 11/30/09 from https://blogs.secondlife.com/community/features/blog/2006/09/08/urgent-security-announcement

Second Life® Grid. (2009). *Virtual Environment Enable New Models of Learning*. Retrieved on 12/11/09 from http://secondlifegrid.net/slfe/educaton-use-virtual-world

Second Life® in Education. (2009). *Virtual World Resources*. Retrieved on 12/8/09 from http://sleducation.wikispaces.com/virtualworlds

Second Life®®. Retrieved from http://secondlife.com/corporate/tos.php. (Linden Lab®, © 2008)

Security, H. (2008). *Director, Federal Law Enforcement Training Center: Connie L. Patrick.* Retrieved on 11/20/09 from http://www.dhs.gov/xabout/structure/biography_0125.shtm

Seiler, J. (2008, March 17). *What Can Virtual-World Economists Tell Us about Real-World Economies?* Retrieved September 3, 2009, from Scientific American: http://www.scientificamerican.com/article.cfm?id=virtual-world-economists-on-real-economies

Sensorama. (2008, February 26). In *Wikipedia, The Free Encyclopedia*. Retrieved June 6, 2008, from http://en.wikipedia.org/w/index.php?title=Sensorama&oldid=194083017

Seto, T.P. (2008). *When is a Game Only a Game?: The Taxation of Virtual Worlds* (August, 12 2008). Loyola-LA Legal Studies Paper No. 2008-24

Shan, L. M., Sutanto, J., Kankanhalli, A., & Tan, B. C. Y. (2007). Virtual community models in relation to e-business models. In *Dasgupta, S. Encyclopedia of Virtual Communities and Technologies*. Hershey, PA: Idea Group Reference.

Shang, D. (2009, February 24). *Comments, Second Life® Virtual World Expands 44% in Q2.* Retrieved September 3, 2009, from Second Life® Blogs: Features: http://www.scientificamerican.com/article.cfm?id=virtual-world-economists-on-real-economies

Shaughnessy, L. (2008). *CIA, FBI push 'Facebook for Spies'*. CNN. Retrieved on 11/28/09 from http://www.cnn.com/2008/TECH/ptech/09/05/facebook.spies/index.html

Sherr, I. (2008). Virtual Campuses: The Education of the Future? Retrieved on 12/8/09 from http://www.mg.co.za/article/2008-06-06-virtual-campuses-the-education-of-the-future

Sherson, G. (1999). Intelligent Agents: An Education System For The Year 2003. Victoria University of Wellington. Retrieved on 12/14/09 from http://www.shersonmedia.com/grant/cv/items/papers/Intelligent_Agents_Education_2003.pdf

Shneiderman, B., & Plaisant, C. (2010). *Designing the User Interface: Strategies for effective Human-Computer Interaction.* Boston: Addison Wisley (Pearson).

Siahaan, A. (2009, November 12). *Indonesian Gamers Pay Big to Play Big*. Retrieved November 23, 2009, from Jakarta Globe: http://thejakartaglobe.com/home/indonesian-gamers-pay-big-to-play-big/341257

Silverman, D. R., & Spiker, V. A. (1997), Ancient wisdom—future technology. *Proceedings of the Human Factor and Ergonomics Society, 41st Annual Meeting.* Albuquerque, New Mexico.

Simulator, O. (2009). Main Page. Retrieved on 12/3/09 from http://opensimulator.org/wiki/Main_Page

Sipress, A. (2006, December 26). *Where Real Money Meets Virtual Reality, The Jury Is Still Out.* Retrieved September 3, 2009, from washingtonpost.com: http://www.washingtonpost.com/wp-dyn/content/article/2006/12/25/AR2006122500635.html

Sivan, Y. (2008). 3D3C real virtual worlds defined: The immense potential of merging 3D, community, creation, and commerce. *Journal of Virtual Worlds Research, 1*(1).

Sivan, Y. (2008). The 3D3C Metaverse: A new medium is born. In Samuel-Asran, T., & Caspi, D. (Eds.), *New Media and Innovative Technology* (pp. 133–159). Beer-Sheva, Israel: Ben-Gurion University Press.

Sivan, Y. (2008). Real Virtual Worlds SOS *(State of Standards) Q3-2008.* Journal of Virtual Worlds Research. Retrieved on 12/7/09 from http://journals.tdl.org/jvwr/article/view/359/271

Sivan, Y. (2009). Identity 3D3C: Confronting the Security and Privacy Challenges in virtual Worlds. *Cutter IT journal, 22*(4), 35-42.

Sivan, Y. (2009). Overview: State of Virtual World Standards in 2009. *Virtual Worlds Research.* Retrieved on 12/1/09 from https://journals.tdl.org/jvwr/article/view/671/539

Sivan, Y. (2009). Overview: State of Virtual World Standards in 2009. *Virtual Worlds Research.* Retrieved on 12/1/09 from https://journals.tdl.org/jvwr/article/view/671/539

SL Second Life® Open Grid Protocol, (2008) retrieved 1. December 2009, from http://wiki.secondlife.com/wiki/SLGOGP_Draft_1

Slater, M., Steed, A., McCarthy, J., & Maringelli, F. (1998). The influence of body movement on subjective presence in virtual environments. *Human Factors*, *40*(3), 469–477. doi:10.1518/001872098779591368

Slater, M., & Usoh, M. (1994). Body centered interaction in immersive virtual environments. *Artificial life and virtual reality*, 125-148.

Slater, M., Usoh, M., Benford, S., Snowdon, D., Brown, C., Rodden, T., et al. (1996). Distributed Extensible Virtual Reality Laboratory (DEVRL). *Virtual Environments and Scientific Visualisation*, 137-148.

Smart, J., Cascio, J., & Paffendorf, J. (2007). *Metaverse Roadmap: Pathways to the 3D Web*. Retrieved September 19, 2009, from http://www.metaverseroadmap.org.

Smith, M. L., & Milner, B. (1981). The role of the right hippocampus in the recall of spatial location. *Neuropsychologia*, *19*, 781–793. doi:10.1016/0028-3932(81)90090-7

Smith, A., Dunckley, L., French, T., Minocha, S., & Chang, Y. (2004). *A proccess model for developing usable cross-cultural websites (Vol. Interacting with Computers 16)*. London: Elsevier.

Smith, A. (1994). *The Wealth of Nations* (1994 Modern Library Edition ed.). (E. Cannan, Ed.) New York, New York, USA: Random House.

Smith, G. (2009, June 15). Why marketers will approach the semantic Web with different language and tools. *AdWeek*.

Smith, R. M. (1984). *Learning how to learn*. Milton Keynes: Open University.

Snow Crash. (2007). *In Wikipedia, The Free Encyclopedia*. Retrieved February 23, 2007, from http://en.wikipedia.org/w/index.php?title=Snow_Crash&oldid=108444297

Snowdon, D., & Jaa-Aro, K. (1996). Body-Centred Configuration in Collaborative Virtual Environments. In *Proceedings of the 2nd FIVE International Conference*, 48-54.

Sohail, S. (2008). Shopping Behavior and Evaluation of Store Features: Perspectives from a Food Market in the Arabian Peninsula. *Journal of International Food & Agribusiness Marketing*, *20*(3). doi:. doi:10.1080/08974430802157580

Sok Huhh, J. (2006). Some Facts on MapleStory, *GameStudy.org*, Retrieved September 12, 2009, from http://www.gamestudy.org/eblog/?p=32

Spence, J. (2008). Demographics of Virtual Worlds. *Journal of Virtual Worlds Research*, *1*(2).

st Century Schools. (2009). The Purpose of Education - Critical Pedagogy for the Democratic Society. Retrieved on 11/14/09 from http://www.21stcenturyschools.com/Purpose_of_Education.htm

Stamper, R. (2000). *Exploring the Semantics of COmmunication Acts. LAP Workshop*. Achen.

Stamper, R. K. (1973). *Information in business and administrative systems*. New York: Wiley.

Stamper, R. (1997). Organisation as a software: a new quality benchmark. *Quality in Software Engineering*. Delhi: IFIP WG8.1 Working Conference.

Stamper, R., Liu, K., Hafkamp, M., & Ades, Y. (2000). *Understanding the Roles of Signs and Norms in Organisations: A semiotic appoach to information system design.* 12-27: Journal of Behaviour & Information Technology.

Stankiewicz, B. J., & Kalia, A. (2004). Acquisition and Retention of Structural versus Object Landmark Knowledge When Navigating through a Large Scale Space. *Journal of Experimental Psychology. Human Perception and Performance*, *33*(2), 378–390. doi:10.1037/0096-1523.33.2.378

Stanney, K. M., Mourant, R. R., & Kennedy, R. S. (1998). Human Factors Issues in Virtual Environments: A Review of the Literature. *Presence (Cambridge, Mass.)*, *7*(4), 327–351. doi:10.1162/105474698565767

Stanney, K. M., & Salvendy, G. (1995). Information visualization; assisting low spatial individuals with information access tasks through the use of visual mediators. *Ergonomics*, *38*(6), 1184–1198. doi:10.1080/00140139508925181

State of Play Conference (2007). *New York Law School / State of Play Conference*. Retrieved August 16, 2009, from http://www.nyls.edu/centers/harlan_scholar_centers/institute_for_information_law_and_policy/events?lightwindow_url=%2Findex.php%3FcID%3D1721

Stephen, T. (2008). *'Grand Theft Auto IV' posts record first-week sales*. Retrieved June 8, 2008 from http://www.mtv.com/news/articles/1586971/20080507/id_0.jhtml

Stephenson, N. (1992). *Snow Crash*. New York: Bantam Books.

Stephenson, N. (1992). *Snow Crash*. New York: Bantam Spectra.

Straaten, P. V. D. (2000). *Interaction Affecting the Sense of Presence in Virtual Reality*. Research Task Final Report, Delft University of Technology, Faculty of Information Technology and Systems.

Strauss, J., El-Ansary, A., & Frost, R. (2003). *E-Marketing* (3rd ed.). Upper Saddle River, New Jersey: Prentice Hall.

Stunning 3D Viewing. (2009). Retrieved on 12/7/09 from http://www.business-sites.philips.com/shared/assets/3dsolutions/downloads/42inchProductLeaflet.pdf

Suffern Middle School. (2009). Barriers, Fences and Conflicts. Retrieved on 12/11/09 from http://ramapoislands.edublogs.org/

Supp. 2d 907 (N.D. Ill. 2002)

Susan Vega Second Life® Show (2006). *The making of.* Retrieved June 8, 2008, from http://www.youtube.com/watch?v=bQL8_HB1HtQ

Sutanonpaiboon, J., & Abuhamdieh, A. (2008). Factors Influencing Trust in Online Consumer-to-Consumer (C2C) Transactions. *Journal of Internet Commerce*, *7*(2), 203–219. doi:10.1080/15332860802067706

Takahashi, D. (2009, April 26). *Games and virtual world fundings reach $936.8 million in 2008*. Retrieved September 3, 2009, from VentureBeat: http://games.venturebeat.com/2009/04/26/second-revision-game-and-virtual-world-fundings-reach-935-million-in-2008/

Takashi, D. (2009). Virtual Good Saees to Reach $1 Billion in 2009 As Social Games Pay Off Big. Retrieved on 12/3/09 from http://games.venturebeat.com/2009/10/14/virtual-goods-sales-to-hit-1-billion-in-2009-as-social-games-pay-off-big/

Takashi, P. (2008). Why do we spend so much on National Security? *The Huffington Post*. Retrieved on 11/27/09 from http://www.huffingtonpost.com/patrick-takahashi/why-do-we-spend-so-much-o_b_116535.html

Tampere, U. o. (2009). *Review of Virtual Communities*. Retrieved in January 2009, from http://www.cs.uta.fi/~kjr/ACHCI/tang.html.

Taylor, T. L. (2006). *Play between worlds: Exploring online game culture*. Cambridge, MA: MIT Press.

Taylor, T. L. (2005). *Play between Worlds: Exploring Online Game Culture*. Cambridge, MA: MIT Press.

Team Orlando. (2009a). *Team Orlando Capabilities*. Retrieved on 11/29/09 from http://www.teamorlando.org/capabilities/index.shtml

Team Orlando. (2009b). News. Retrieved on 11/29/09 from http://www.teamorlando.org/news/2009/05-21-09.shtml

Terdiman, D. (2007). *Tech Titans Seek Virtual World Interoperability*. CNet News. Retrieved on 12/109 from http://news.cnet.com/Tech-titans-seek-virtual-world-interoperability/2100-1043_3-6213148.html

Terdiman, D. (April 12, 2006). *Phony kids, virtual sex*. Cnet News. Retrieved on the world wide web November 5, 2009. http://news.cnet.com/Phony-kids,-virtual-sex/2100-1043_3-6060132.html

Testa, B. M. (2008). *Much More than a Game. Defense Systems*. Retrieved on 11/28/09 from http://defensesystems.com/articles/2008/05/much-more-than-a-game.aspx

The Sims. (2008). In *Wikipedia, The Free Encyclopedia.* Retrieved June 7, 2008, from http://en.wikipedia.org/w/index.php?title=The_Sims&oldid=217644539

There, Inc. (2003, March 13). *There, Inc. Developer Addendum to Member Agreement.* Retrieved September 3, 2009, from archive: http://webapps.prod.there.com/developers/developer_agreement.xml

Thomas, K. (2008). Changing attiudes to online trading. *MEED: Middle East Economic Digest, 52*(32), 40–41.

Thomas. (2009). Virtual Worlds Offer Meaningful Educational Opportunities for Children. Open Education. Retrieved on 2/8/09 from http://www.openeducation.net/2008/06/29-virtual-worlds-offer-meanngful-educational-opportunities-for-children

Thorndyke, P. (1980). *Performance models for spatial and locational cognition (R2676ONR).* Washington, D.C.: The Rand Corporation.

Thorndyke, P., & Hayes-Roth, B. (1982). Differences in spatial knowledge acquired from maps and navigation. *Cognitive Psychology, 14*, 560–589. doi:10.1016/0010-0285(82)90019-6

TJ Keitt, E. D. (2009). *The Real Value of Virtual Worlds: A Guide for Hooking Business Customers and Partners With This New Technology.* Forrester Research.

Toffler, A. (1980). *The Third Wave.* New York: William Collins Sons and Co. Ltd.

Toles, J. (2008). The Virtual Classroom: An Enhancement or Replacement to Traditional Education. Georgia State University. Retrieved on 12/8/09 from http://digitalarchive.gsu.edu/univ_lib_ura/3

Top Social Networks Re-Rank. (2009, January). Retrieved August 29, 2009, from Compete.com: http://www.compete.com

Top Ten Search Engines - Top 10 SEs. (n.d.). Retrieved August 25, 2009, from SEO Consultants: http://www.seoconsultants.com/search-engines/

Trademarks: Madrid Agreement (1891).

Tres.Reg. §1.861-4(a).

Trewin, S. M., Laff, M. R., Cavender, A., & Hanson, V. L. (2008). Accessibility in Virtual Worlds. *CHI '08 extended abstracts on Human factors in computing systems.*

Trewin, S., Hanson, V. L., Laff, M., & Cavender, A. (2008). PowerUp: an accessible virtual world. *ASSETS*, 177-184.

Trintec Industries Inc. v. Pedre Promotional Products Inc., 395 F.3d 1275 (Fed.Cir. 2005).

Trompenaars, F. (1993). *Riding the waves of culture: Understanding Cultural Diversity in Business.* London: Nicholas Brealy.

Truth in Domain Names Act, 18 U.S.C.S. §2252B.

uMind. (2009).Simulation Based Training. Retrieved on 12/14/09 from http://www.umindsoft.com/En/simulations.html

United States General Accounting Office. (2002). MILITARY PERSONNEL: Active Duty Benefits Reflect Changing Demographics, but Opportunities Exist to Improve. Report to the Subcommittee on Armed Services, US Senate. Retrieved on 11/30/09 from http://www.gao.gov/new.items/d02935.pdf

United States. v. Briscoe, 65 F.3d 576 (7th Cir. 1995).

United States. v. Czubinski, 106 F.3d 1069 (1st Cir. 1997).

Unknown. (2009, August 25). *Gold farming.* Retrieved September 3, 2009, from Wikipedia: http://en.wikipedia.org/wiki/Gold_farming

Unknown. (2009, September 10). *Grinding (gaming).* Retrieved September 10, 2009, from Wikipedia: http://en.wikipedia.org/wiki/Grinding_(gaming)

Unknown. (2009, September 14). *Market economy.* Retrieved September 14, 2009, from Wikipedia: http://en.wikipedia.org/wiki/Market_economy

Urban Dictionary. (2009). *goldsink.* Retrieved September 3, 2009, from Urban Dictionary: http://www.urbandictionary.com/define.php?term=gold%20sink

Valente, A. (2009). *Trade Shows -- Going Virtual.* Retrieved August 25, 2009, from http://www.fitcommerce.com: http://www.fitcommerce.com/Blueprint/Page.aspx?pageld=517&portalld=2&tabindex=5

Vanegas, K. (2007). Second Life® Virtual World. The Washington Post. Retrieved on 12/11/09 from http://blog.washingtonpost.com/hs/mckinley/2007/05/second_life_virtual_world.html

Vargo, S. L., & Lusch, R. F. (2008). Service-dominant Logic: Continuing the Evolution. *Journal of the Academy of Marketing Science*, *36*, 1–10. doi:10.1007/s11747-007-0069-6

Vicente, K. J., Hayes, B. C., & Williges, R. C. (1987). Assaying and isolating individual differences in searching a hierarchical file system. *Human Factors*, *29*(3), 349–359.

Vila, J. Beccue B. Anandikar S. (2002). The Gender Factor in Virtual Reality Navigation and Wayfinding. *Proceedings of the 36th Hawaii International Conference on System Sciences (HICSS'03).*

Vilhjalmsson, H. H. (1997). *Autonomous Communicative Behaviours in Avatars*. Media Laboratory, Massachusetts Institute of Technology.

Vinson, N. G. (1999) Design Guidelines for Landmarks to Support Navigation in Virtual Environments. *Proceedings of CHI '99*, Pittsburgh, PA.

Virtual Goods News. (2009). Report: Virtual Worlds Growth to Skyrocket. Retrieved on 12/14/09 from http://www.virtualworldsnews.com/2009/06/report-virtual-worlds-growth-to-skyrocket-.html

Virtual World News. (2008a). Air Force Unveils Potential Plans for MyBase Virtual World. *Virtual World News*. Retrieved on 11/29/09 from http://www.virtualworldsnews.com/2008/02/air-force-unvei.html

Virtual World News. (2008b). *Homeland Security Building Virtual Classroom for a Virtual World.* Retrieved on 11/29/09 from http://www.virtualworldsnews.com/2008/05/homeland-securi.html

Virtual World News. (2009). Quickstat – Mafia Wars Hits 4 Million Users Milestone. *Virtual World News Web Site.* Retrieved August 16, 2009, from http://www.virtualworldsnews.com/2009/07/quickstat-mafia-wars-hits-4m-user-milestone.html

Virtual Worlds 2008. (2008, April 4). *Virtual Worlds 2008 - The Evolution of Games and Social Networks: Virtual Worlds Everywhere.* Retrieved November 20, 2009, from Virtual Worlds News: http://www.virtualworldsnews.com/2008/04/virtual-world-3.html

Virtualeconomies (2007). *Virtualeconomies.* Retrieved June 8, 2008, from http://www.virtualeconomies.net/2007/01/23/50-of-wow-users-bought-crusade-in-first-24-hours/

von Hippel, E., & von Krogh, G. (2003). Open source software and the "private-collective" model: Issues for organization science. *Organization Science*, *14*(2), 209–223. doi:10.1287/orsc.14.2.209.14992

VWN Virtual Worlds News. (2008) retrieved 1. December 2009, from http://www.virtualworldsnews.com/2008/07/ibm-and-linden.html

W3C, (2009) retrieved 3. December 2009, from http://www.w3.org/TR/html5/

Wagner, A. (2009). 12% Of Americans Bought Virtual Goods In Past 12 Months: Survey. *Frank N. Magid Associates, Inc. Web Site.* Retrieved August 16, 2009, from http://www.magid.com/company_info/news_article.asp?articleID=3199

Waller, D., Hunt, E., & Knapp, D. (1998). The transfer of spatial knowledge in virtual environment training. *Presence (Cambridge, Mass.)*, *7*, 129–143. doi:10.1162/105474698565631

Waller, D., Knapp, D., & Hunt, E. (2001). Spatial Representations of Virtual Mazes: The Role of Visual Fidelity and Individual Differences. *Human Factors. The Journal of the Human Factors and Ergonomics Society*, *43*(1), 147–158. doi:10.1518/001872001775992561

Waters, J. (2009). A 'Second Life' for Educators. The Journal. Retrieved on 12/11/09 from http://thejournal.com/Articles/2009/01/01/A-Second-Life-For-Educators

Watson, P. (2005). *Ideas: A History of Thought and Invention, from Fire to Freud*. New York: HarperCollins.

Web3D Consortium, (2009a) retrieved 3. December 2009, from http://www.web3d.org/

Web3D Consortium, (2009b) retrieved 3. December 2009, from http://www.web3d.org/x3d/specifications/

Weisman, J. (1981). Evaluating achitectural legibility: Way-finding in the built environment. *Environment and Behavior*, *13*, 189–204. doi:10.1177/0013916581132004

Weiss, G. (February 11, 2009) *The Great Virtualization Dilemma of the Next Decade: What You Need to Know*. Gartner Group. GartnerGroup.com/technology/research/reports..

Whitaker, L. A. (1996). Getting around in the natural world. *Ergonomics in Design*, *4*, 3, 11–15.

White, K. (2009). Benefits of Higher Education. Retrieved on 12/9/09 from http://www.streetdirectory.com/travel_guide/14429/education/benefits_of_online_education.html

Whyville. (2009). *Whyville*. Retrieved in January 2009, from http://www.whyville.net/smmk/nice

Wilkniss, S. M., Jones, M., Korel, D., Gold, P., & Manning, C. (1997). Agerelated differences in an ecologically based study of route learning. *Psychology and Aging*, *12*(2), 372–375. doi:10.1037/0882-7974.12.2.372

Williams, R. L., & Cothrell, J. (2000). Four Smart Ways to Run Online Communities. *Sloan Management Review*, *41*(4), 81–91.

Wilostar3D. (2009). Overview. Retrieved on 12/12/09 from http://www.wilostar3d.com/overview.htm

Wilson, P. N., Foreman, N., & Tlauka, M. (1997). Transfer of spatial information from a virtual to a real environment. *Human Factors*, *39*(4), 526–531. doi:10.1518/001872097778667988

Wilson, N. (2009). Virtual Worlds for Business. Clever Zebra. Retrieved 12/13/09 from http://cleverzebra.com/book

Wisconsin Department of Revenue v. William Wrigley, Jr., Co., 505 U.S. 214 (1992).

Wise, J. (2008). Surviving on the USS Trayer, the Navy's Disaster Simulator. *Popular Mechanics*. Retrieved on 11/29/09 from http://www.popularmechanics.com/technology/military_law/4288185.html

Witkin, H. A., Moore, C. A., Goodenough, D. R., & Cox, P. W. (1977). Fielddependent and field independent cognitive styles and their educational implications. *Review of Educational Research*, *47*, 1–64.

Witmer, B. G., Bailey, J. H., Knerr, B. W., & Parsons, K. C. (1996). Virtual spaces and real world places: transfer of route knowledge. *International Journal of Human-Computer Studies*, *45*(4), 413–428. doi:10.1006/ijhc.1996.0060

Witmer, B. G., & Sadowski, W. J. (1998). Nonvisually guided locomotion to a previously viewed target in real and virtual environments. (Special Section: Virtual environments: Models, Methodology, and Empirical Studies). *Human Factors*, *40*, 478–485. doi:10.1518/001872098779591340

Witmer B.G. Bailey J.H. & Knerr B.W. (1995), Training Dismounted Soldiers in Virtual Environments: Route Learning and Transfer. U.S. Army Research Institute for the Behavioral and Social Sciences

Wolf, M. (Ed.). (2001). *The Medium of the Video Game*. Austin, TX: University of Texas Press.

World, V. (2009a). Wikipedia. Retrieved on 12/7/09 from http://en.wikipedia.org/wiki/Virtual_World

World, V. (2009b). Retrieved on 12/7/09 from http://www.its.bldrdoc.gov/projects/devglossary/_virtual_world.html

Worlds, A. (2009). Participants. Retrieved on 12/12/09 from http://www.activeworlds.com/edu/awedu_participants.asp

Wyld, D. (2008). *Government in 3D: How Public Leaders can Draw on Virtual Worlds*. IBM Center for the Business of Government.

Wyld, D. (2008). *Government in 3D: How Public Leaders Can Draw on Virtual Worlds*. IBM Center for The Business of Government.

Yahia, M. (2009, July 21). *The Future of Virtual Worlds: At the Crossroads Between Real and Sci-Fi.* Retrieved August 29, 2009, from islamonline.net: http://www.islamonline.net/servlet/Satellite?c=Article _C&cid=1248078566632&pagename=Zone-English-HealthScience%2FHSELayout

Yee, N., Bailenson, J., Urbanek, M., Chang, F., & Merget, D. (2007). *The Unbearable Likness of Being Digital: The Persistence of Nonverbal Social Norms in Online Virtual Environments. Mary Ann Liebert, Inc.* Cyber Psychology & Behaviour.

Yellowlees, P. (2009). Virtual Reality Meets Health Education. Information Age Health. Retrieved on 12/13/09 from http://informationagehealth.blogspot.com/2009/09/virtual-reality-medical-education-in.html

Yin-Poole, W. (2009, March 7). *Blizzard's Tom Chiltn on the future of WoW.* Retrieved September 3, 2009, from Videogamer.com: http://www.videogamer.com/news/blizzards_tom_chilton_on_the_future_of_wow.html?page=4

Zahedi, F., Van Pelt, W., & Song, J. (2001). A conceptual Framework for internstional webdesign. *83-103* (44).

ZDNet. (2009). *ZDNet Definition for Virtual World.* Retrieved on 12/7/09 from http://www.its.bldrdoc.gov/projects/devglossary/_virtual_world.html

Zenke, M. (2008, April 2). *IMGDC: BioWare's Waltonn Talks MMO Creation Essentials.* Retrieved September 3, 2009, from Gamasutra: http://www.gamasutra.com/php-bin/news_index.php?story=18089

Zeran v. America Online, Inc., 129 F.3d 327 (4th Cir. 1997).

Zero, K. (2009, September 12). *Growth forecasts for the Virtual Worlds sector.* Retrieved September 14, 2009, from K Zero: http://www.kzero.co.uk/blog/?p=2845

Zillman, D., Byrant, J., & Sapolsky, N. (1989). Enjoyment from Sports Spectatorship. In Goldstein, J. (Ed.), *Sports, Games and Play* (pp. 241–278). Hillsdale: Laurence Erlbaum.

Zippo Manufacturing Company v. Zippo Dot Com, Inc., 952 Fed.Supp. 1119 (1997).

Zynga. (2009, November 23). *Zynga Hits 100 Million Unique Visitors Per Month.* Retrieved November 23, 2009, from Zynga: http://blog.zynga.com/2009/11/zynga-hits-100-million-unique-visitors-per-month.html

About the Contributors

Barbara L. Ciaramitaro, Ph.D., is a professor at Ferris State University in the United States. Before joining the academic world, Dr. Ciaramitaro worked for over 20 years in various industries in managing all aspects of Information Technology. She is considered a respected author, teacher, and speaker on Web 2.0 technologies and information security. Dr. Ciaramitaro is an avid virtual world enthusiast constantly exploring the many avenues in which virtual worlds are becoming integrated with our daily lives. Dr. Ciaramitaro holds a Ph.D. from Nova Southeastern University with a graduate certificate in Information Security, a M.S. from Central Michigan University and a B.A. in Psychology from Wayne State University.

* * *

Paul Blowers is Director of IT Enterprise Architecture and Chief Architect for Kelly Services. Kelly is a world leader in workforce management services and human resources solutions. Paul joined Kelly in 2007 and has more than 14 years of global Information Technology experience in systems architecture and large, complex systems integration delivery. Previously, he worked at Accenture and has traveled internationally working on IT systems initiatives around the world. He holds a bachelor's degree in Mathematics and Psychology from Kalamazoo College. Paul lives in Royal Oak, Michigan with his wife and two cats. With a "real world" little boy on the way, he finds less and less time to spend in Virtual Worlds.

William G. Burns III is the CEO and Project Manager for Andromeda Media Group, and former CTO for VR5 Online. He is the recipient of multiple awards for virtual environment excellence, an executive consultant for multiple corporate interests, and has worked closely with the gaming and virtual environment industries since the mid-1990s. A member of the Association of Virtual Worlds, contributor to the Metaverse Roadmap, and cited in various industry research publications, William is an unsung hero in today's virtual environment innovation. His disciplines extend across a wide range of subjects while focusing on the core of virtual environments, strategy, and architecture. In the course of his career, William has worked for small businesses, celebrities, Fortune 500 companies, and research initiatives bringing his unique understanding and dynamic trend forecasting abilities to the table, with often brilliant results. Since the early 1990's, William has been a driving force for the virtual environment industry with contributing research and designs for multiple projects, consulting and collaborating with members of the video game industry as well as various marketing companies and technology innovators. His leadership and insight have created a level of excellence in virtual environments which continue to set the bar of future projects for countless virtual environment users worldwide. Often called the "Steve Jobs of Virtual Environments" by some industry experts, William continues today as an accurate compass of the virtual environment industry for the future. For further information or inquiries, he may be reached via email via darianknight@gmail.com , via Twitter feed at http://www.twitter.com/darianknight, or directly within Second Life under the name Aeonix Aeon.

Maria del Puy Carretero studied Computer Science at the University of the Basque Country UPV (2004). She was an intern during the summer of 2002 at Telenor S.L. and carried out her final year project at Vicomtech (July 2003-february2004). Since October 2004 she has worked as a Scientific Collaborator at Vicomtech, within the area of 3D Animation, Interactive Virtual Environments and HCI. She is currently pursuing her doctoral studies and has research interests in Interaction with Virtual Characters on mobile devices and the Internet.

Alex Garcia-Alonso studied Mechanical Engineering at the University of Navarre (1980) and obtained his Ph. D. (1990). He has collaborated in six books, two video, thirteen papers in journals, four invited conferences, thirty five communications, directed six Ph. D., collaborations with four research institutions (CEIT, EUVE, LABEIN and Vicomtech). He has imparted invited lectures in five universities, worked or directed many I+D for the industry such as Mechanical Dynamics Inc., Aerospatiale, Alenia, CASA or the European Space Agency. He has collaborated with more than thirty companies.

Greg Gogolin spent almost 20 years in IT before becoming a professor at Ferris State University in 1999. He has worked as a programmer, database administrator, systems analyst and project manager at small and multi-national corporations. Dr. Gogolin actively consults and is a licensed Private Investigator specializing in digital forensics cases. He has degrees in Arts, Computer Information Systems, Applied Biology, Computer Information Systems Management, and Administration, with his doctorate from Michigan State University. He holds CISSP, EnCE and PMP certifications, and is particularly thankful to have the opportunity to teach some of the brightest students in the world in the Bachelor of Science in Information Security & Intelligence and Master of Science in Information Systems Management programs at Ferris State University.

Arman Gukasyan is Chief Executive Officer of 3DreamTeam LLC. He is leader of the team and the source of inspiration for the whole project, making the things work and move on. His excellent communication and presentation skills and strategic vision make the company grow worldwide. He has international experience and all-round education in Marketing and Law.

S. R. Gulliver received a BEng. (Hons) degree in Microelectronics, an MSc. degree (Distributed Information Systems) and a PhD in 1999, 2001, and 2004 respectively. Gulliver worked within the Human Factors Integration Defence Technology Centre (HFI DTC), before getting a job as a lecturer at Brunel University (2005-2008). Now, as a lecturer within the Informatics Research Centre (IRC) within Henley Business School (Reading University), his research interests relate to the broad topic of pervasive Informatics, and primarily relates to human factors, perceptual and information acquisition aspects of computer and multimedia systems. Dr Gulliver currently supervises research relating to content including: VR information acquisition, dynamic schene description, attention analysis, context-aware analysis, intelligent building and security systems, display adaptation and content personalisation of multimedia perception.

Tracy Harwood is a Senior Research Fellow at the Institute of Creative Technologies, De Montfort University, Leicester, UK. She has previously held the position of Principal Lecturer in Marketing and senior management posts in medical supplies, commodity trading and publishing industries. She was awarded a National Teacher Fellowship in 2004. She gained her PhD in 2003 in buyer-supplier negotiations from De Montfort University. Current research interests are in relationship marketing within the context of digital culture, virtual communities, particularly focusing on identity, co-creation and participation, social networking and impact upon business model evolution. She is also interested in machinima, the making of original films using 3D computer games engines in real time, and its socio-cultural and relational implications, having directed the First European Machinima Festival in 2007 at the IOCT. Most recently, she has project managed the university's investment in Phoenix Square digital media centre, which opened to the public in Autumn 2009.

Daniel Hoops is an Assistant Professor, Business Law and Taxation Department, at Walsh College. In addition, Mr. Hoops has been a practicing attorney since 1995. His areas of expertise include estate and business planning and taxation. Mr. Hoops is a graduate of the University of Michigan (BMA, Trumpet Performance – 1991), the Michigan State University-Detroit College of Law (JD, cum laude – 1994) and the University of Miami Graduate School of Law (Master of Laws, Estate Planning – 1995). Daniel Hoops is a frequent lecturer on estate planning topics nationally and is a co-author of several legal publications, including Planning for Estates and Administration in Michigan (WestGroup), Family Estate Planning Guide (WestGroup), How To Build A Successful Estate Practice (WestGroup), Bringing and Defending a Will Contest in Michigan (MSU-DCL Law Review, 1997) and Connecting the Dots: Tyree Guyton's Heidelberg Project (Wayne State University Press, 2008). In addition to his law practice, Daniel Hoops is a board member of the internationally recognized Heidelberg Project, Detroit, Michigan. (www.heidleberg.org)

Lee Hwang is an experienced senior producer whose background in virtual worlds began in 2000 at There, Inc. As one of the original producers and designers for There.com, she was responsible for the features and systems that made up the social architecture of that virtual world, including Groups, Events, and Forcefield. In 2003, Lee designed a feature called PortaZones, inspired by Wile E. Coyote's® Acme Portable Hole, which later became the foundation for a new and unique model for virtual land use. In 2006, Lee produced the launch of Virtual Laguna Beach for Makena Technologies and MTV Networks Music Group, a project which won a National Academy of Television Arts & Sciences Technology & Engineering Emmy Award for Outstanding Achievement in Advanced Media Technology for Creation of Nontraditional Programs or Platforms, four months after its launch. Lee also produced the launch of CC Metro for Makena Technologies and The Coca-Cola Company in 2007 and led the management of Coca-Cola's line of virtual branded products to an average of nearly double their original value. Nadezhda Ilyina is Business Development Officer of Vizerra.com project. After 3 years experience in 3D GIS systems she became one of those who started Vizerra to life. Nadezhda's passion for travel and history and her vision of future gave basis to many interesting projects and ideas.

Jim Jones has worked in the information security field for the past 15 years with government, commercial, and research organizations. During this time he has led multiple security projects, directed a security operations center, led a digital forensics team, and served as the principle investigator for research projects with DARPA, DHS, and AFRL. Professor Jones actively consults in the areas of digital forensics, information security, and intelligence analysis. Dr. Jones holds a B.S. in Industrialand Systems Engineering from Georgia Tech, a M.S. in Mathematical Sciences from Clemson University, and a Ph.D. in Computational Sciences and Informatics from George Mason University. Dr. Jones is a Principal Scientist with Science Applications International Corporation and a professor at Ferris State University.

Susan K. Jones is a Professor of Marketing at Ferris State University and the owner of Susan K. Jones & Associates, a consulting firm focused on direct and interactive marketing and advertising. Professor Jones joined Ferris State in 1990 and started SKJ & Associates in 1980. Her teaching and research specialties include direct marketing, advertising and e-commerce marketing. She has authored, co-authored or edited nearly 30 books on marketing, collectibles and time management, including Creative Strategy in Direct and Interactive Marketing, Business-to-Business Internet Marketing, The IMC Handbook: Readings and Cases in Integrated Marketing Communications, and Marketing Convergence. Professor Jones holds a Master's Degree in Advertising from Northwestern University, where she was inducted into the Hall of Achievement of the Medill School of Journalism. Other awards she has earned include: an Alumni Service Award from Northwestern University; the Charles Downs Award (lifetime achievement) from the Chicago Association of Direct Marketing; the Robert Clarke Award (educator of the year) from the Direct Marketing Educational Foundation; and the Andi Emerson Award for contributions to the direct marketing creative community from the John Caples International Awards. Professor Jones lives in Grand Rapids, Michigan with her husband, William T. Jones. The Joneses have two grown sons.

Rita J. King is the CEO and Creative Director of Dancing Ink Productions, a company that works globally with various companies, think-tanks, universities and not-for-profits toward a new global culture and economy in the Imagination Age. She is a Senior Fellow at two think-tanks: The Carnegie Council for Ethics in International Affairs and the Center for the Study of the Presidency and Congress. She is Innovator-in-Residence at IBM's Analytics Virtual Centerin support of Smarter Planet. Her photographs, essays, journalistic work and art have been widely published and exhibited internationally.

Joerg H. Kloss is one of the early pioneers of interactive 3D graphics on the Internet. He started to build Virtual Worlds already years ago, hold lectures on symposia, and published articles and books about the 3D standards VRML and X3D. He holds a Master's degree in Computational Linguistics, Psychology and Economics, and currently works as a telecommunications professional and consultant in Germany.

Markos Kyritsis graduated in 2002 and was awarded a BSc (Hons) in Computer Science. He then undertook a part-time PhD in Brunel University, which focused on Virtual Reality Training. He successfully completed his PhD in 2009. Although he spent most of his time working as a developer for a variety of I.T. companies, mostly developing 3D and 2D games, he has a list of publications that mainly focus on the area of Spatial Knowledge Acquisition. His research interests include: Virtual Reality information acquisition and training, interaction on small hand-held devices, and gaming (especially 3D games).

Alexander Lavrov is Chief Technology Officer at 3DreamTeam LLC. He is Fellow of the ACM, IEEE, IGDA, AIAS and Eurographics. Also he is senior lecturer at Moscow State University of Culture and Arts. Previously he was technical director in science films studio, advertising studios and instructor in computer graphics school.

Kecheng Lui is the director of the Informatics Research Centre at the University of Reading. His current responsibilities include but not limited to being the director of informatics programmes, the deputy director for sustainable built environments (TSBE), the programme director of MSc Applied Informatics, MSc Informatics by Research, MSc Informatics (delivered in Beijing), and PhD supervision with more than 10 completions and on-going projects in various subject fields: semiotic methods for organisational analysis, modelling business processes with norms, adaptive information systems architecture, business intelligence for decision support, context-aware modelling for collaborative work, requirements articulation and web service composition, service integration using pragmatic web, intelligent pervasive spaces for living and working, semantic processing of imagery and sensory data in healthcare, agent technology for smart homes, performance assessment for intelligent and green buildings, interoperable services in e-government systems, and dynamic agility of inter-organisational value chains.

Sonali Morar received an BSc (Hons) in Information Systems and a PhD in 1998 and 2002, respectively. She worked as a lecturer at Brunel University for five years, during which time she published work relating to Virtual Environments, Human Factors, User Experience, and Mobile Displays. Despite continued association with Brunel University, Sonali has since moved professionally into industry where she has worked on usability projects in the UK and internationally. Her usability projects have been within various sectors including wireless, healthcare, energy, online finance and travel. Currently, she works as a User Experience consultant in the US.

Amalia Orriz studied Computer Engineering in the University of Deusto ESIDE (2000). In 2001 she studied a master in Virtual Reality in the University of Deusto ESIDE. She has been the head of the Edutainment and inclusion department in Vicomtech until 2009. This department has been hardly involved in the Virtual World research field. She has published in several national and international congresses related with computer graphic and finished her PhD thesis in the Computer Engineering Faculty of the Basque Country University.

David Oyarzun studied Computer Science in the University of the Basque Country (2002). From October 2002 to April 2003 he gave coaching about Artificial Intelligence. At present time he is working in Vicomtech as project manager in the 3D Animation, Interactive Virtual Environments and HCI department and he is a PhD candidate in the area of avatar animation and interaction in virtual environments in the University of the Basque Country. He has several publications in international conferences and journals, and coordinates a Spanish research working group on Virtual Worlds composed by about 40 members including companies, universities and research centres.

Khulood Rambo is holding MSc degree in information systems management from the University of Greenwich (2007). Currently she is pursuing her PhD degree in informatics at the Informatics Research Centre in the University of Reading. Her current research aims to understand the influence of culture on both technology adoption and technology design, to bridge the gap between the notions of 'culture' and 'technology'. More specifically she is capturing the socio- cultural norms and requirements influencing the adoption of e-commerce by online female consumers in Saudi Arabia. More importantly, she is aiming to formalise these norms to Interface design guidelines and patterns using methods from the socio-technical analytical approach organisational semiotics. The areas of research that she is interested in include human computer interaction, semiotics, organisational studies, cultural studies, psychology, sociology, philosophy, and information and communication technologies.

Charles P Schultz is currently a Software Architect at Research in Motion, leading the development of enterprise social networking applications for BlackBerry smartphones. In his career, Charles has made contributions to the fields of software engineering, software quality, personal robotics, education, telemedicine and gaming. His numerous publication and presentation credits include the Florida Instructional Computing Conference, IEEE Latin America Test Workshop, Games for Health, and the Wireless Enterprise Symposium. Charles' book Game Testing All In One was published in 2005 and he currently serves as a Board Member of the South Florida Chapter of the International Game Developers Association (IGDA). He has 16 US Patents issued and is accredited as a Certified Software Quality Engineer, Six Sigma Green Belt, and Frisbee Master.

Yesha Sivan is a senior lecturer at the Department of Software Engineering at the Shenkar College of Engineering and Design. He is also the founder of Metaverse Labs (MVL) - a leading think tank focusing on connecting virtual and real worlds. Dr. Sivan professional experience includes developing and deploying innovative solutions for corporate, hi-tech, government, and defense environments (see for example: the Harvard 9-Keys for Knowledge Infrastructure). He published numerous papers in the areas of Strategy and IT, knowledge, 3D3C virtual worlds, and standards. Dr. Sivan received his doctorate from Harvard University. His avatar is Dera Kit, and his blog is http://www.dryesha.com. He has taught EMBA, MBA, engineering and design in the areas of strategic value of IT, the emergence of virtual worlds, and software development in virtual worlds.

Shenlei Winker is the Founder and CEO of the Fashion Research Insituted loced in New York City. She is a 30 year veteran of the fashion industry. Her work spans both couture and mass market design and development for the real life apparel industry. Winkler has also enjoyed success in Second Life, where she has designed fashion since 2005, with three popular brands including Prim & Proper (one of the top Second Life earners in 2006), Flash & Trash, and Debutante. Her educational background includes three design degrees, including two from the prestigious Fashion Institute of Technology. Ms. Winkler has been instrumental in developing large-scale creative installations in OpenSim-based worlds, most notably Shengri La Spirit. Winkler may often be found in the Fashion Research Institute Shengri La regions in Second Life, where her seminal orientation program for immersive spaces may be experienced.

Index

Symbols

A

D

E

F

G

H

I

R

S

W

X

Y

Z

LaVergne, TN USA
07 October 2010
199852LV00005B/3/P

9 781616 928087